SIX PLAYS
BY CONTEMPORARIES OF
SHAKESPEARE

SIX PLAYS
BY CONTEMPORARIES OF
SHAKESPEARE

EDITED

WITH AN INTRODUCTION BY

C. B. WHEELER

OXFORD UNIVERSITY PRESS

LONDON   OXFORD   NEW YORK

1971

Oxford University Press

LONDON OXFORD NEW YORK

GLASGOW TORONTO MELBOURNE WELLINGTON

CAPE TOWN SALISBURY IBADAN NAIROBI DAR ES SALAAM LUSAKA ADDIS ABABA

BOMBAY CALCUTTA MADRAS KARACHI LAHORE DACCA

KUALA LUMPUR SINGAPORE HONG KONG TOKYO

ISBN 0 19 281107 X

First published in The World's Classics, 1915

First issued as an Oxford University Press paperback
by Oxford University Press, London, 1971

PRINTED LITHOGRAPHICALLY IN GREAT BRITAIN
AT THE UNIVERSITY PRESS, OXFORD
BY VIVIAN RIDLER
PRINTER TO THE UNIVERSITY

CONTENTS

INTRODUCTION

SUN-WORSHIPPERS are not necessarily unmindful of the stars ; indeed the two cults went hand in hand with the ancients, for though the greater light ruled the day, they felt no less the need of the lesser lights to rule the night. But among the English-speaking races of the world the pre-eminent glory of Shakespeare has been too often allowed to eclipse the splendour of his contemporaries, whose names may indeed be familiar to students of literature, but whose works are as little read as the Talmud or the Koran. A hundred years ago this was not so much the case, as the numerous Collections of Old Plays by Dodsley and others will prove, and it is in the hope that the modern novel-reading public will be attracted to the rich mine of the Elizabethan and Jacobean dramatists that this selection of six plays by Shakespeare's contemporaries has been made.

The work of selection has been no easy one ; with such an *embarras de choix* the duty of rejection became increasingly painful, for each omission was not merely lacerating the editorial sense of justice—a matter of small moment to the public—but was certain to rouse a reasonable regret in the minds of those who knew the value of what was discarded.

But though no fitting apology can be made for

my sins of omission, it is a less hopeless task to explain why I have selected the six plays which are here given.

The Shoemaker's Holiday has been chosen mainly for the sake of Simon Eyre, surely the breeziest character that has ever set foot on the stage, Falstaff not excepted. Indeed the fat knight, however amusing we may find him, was, as he himself admits, 'little better than one of the wicked', whereas the Shoemaker, while always 'as merry as a pie', is a model to all industrious apprentices and a paragon of civic virtue. His cheerfulness and his inexhaustible energy, backed by his determination that every one else shall be as cheerful and energetic as himself, his tyranny over his household, tempered by timely submission when there was mutiny in the air, the wealth and originality of his opprobrious epithets, to be paralleled only by those of Mr. Chucks the Boatswain in *Peter Simple*—all these make up a character irresistibly ludicrous, one whose portrait will be hung unforgettably in the reader's mind.

The pity and horror of *The White Devil* would demand its inclusion in any selection of tragedies. A reprint of the play might well take for a motto,

> There's so much good in the worst of us,
> And so much bad in the best of us,
> That it ill becomes the first of us
> To fling a stone at the rest of us.

The virtuous Duke of Florence and his brother the

Cardinal win little sympathy from the reader in their denunciations of Vittoria as murderess and adulteress ; while the most rigid upholder of the Ten Commandments cannot but be touched by the nobility of her attitude at her trial and in the last tragic scene, her passionate plea for justice in face of the abuse and brow-beating of her judges. Indeed, if the fatuity of a husband might ever be deemed justification for his wife's connivance in his murder—which is perhaps an extreme plea—it would be so in the case of the wretched Camillo. And yet with all her proud spirit Vittoria had her moments of weakness, of regrets for her crimes, and of longings for a cleaner life ; a Devil, perhaps, and ' yet a woman too ', one who in happier fortunes would have been the mother of heroes.

The Knight of the Burning Pestle has been chosen, not so much for the scenes in which Ralph is seen ' riding abroad, redressing human wrongs '— for, *pace* Cervantes and his admirers, parodies of knight errantry savour somewhat of blasphemy— as for the wholly delightful characters of the Citizen and his Wife as members of the audience. Their insistence on the appearance of a particular actor and their comparative indifference to the play, their entire disregard of the plot and repeated demands for the introduction of some wholly unconnected ' turn ', their marked preference for hackneyed themes and situations—all these bring them curiously near to the playgoers of London to-day. The character of the Wife, whose simplicity exceeds even that of her husband, and whose sympathies are invariably on the wrong side, is one of the most humorous pieces of satire ever put on the stage ; while her general kindliness and the genuine goodness of her heart, her childlike reliance on her husband, who was ' the frowningest little thing when he was angry ', and the simple and natural affection of this quaint couple for each other and for Ralph, make up as pretty a picture of a happy family as one could wish to see.

Philaster owes its inclusion mainly to the figure which first won popularity for it on its appearance, that of Bellario, one of the first of the Elizabethan heroines driven by love to disguise herself as a page, and worthy to find a place beside Shakespeare's Viola. The play also affords an apt illustration of the fact that a virtuous politician, like Voltaire's *bon père de famille*, is ' *capable de tout* ' ; there is indeed nothing like the wickedness of a truly good man when he has persuaded himself to commit some infamy for a good end. That this should be regarded as excusable is one of the puzzles of human nature ; but it certainly is so, and therefore Dion in the play, after blasting the reputation of an innocent woman for a political end, after causing untold misery and almost bringing about two murders, is freely pardoned on the preposterous ground that he ' meant well '. The evils of jealousy have been depicted in many plays, from *Othello* downwards, but perhaps the depths of frenzied imbecility to which a jealous lover will go have never been more clearly depicted than in *Philaster*, where the hero is transformed at once from an apparently reasonable being to a homicidal maniac upon evidence which even a modern journalist would scout.

The Duchess of Malfi is necessarily included in any selection of tragedies. If the aim of tragedy is indeed to purge man's soul by fear and pity, Webster may be said to have reached the pinnacle of art in some of the scenes of this play. For sheer horror it is unsurpassed in the English language, and deserves to be ranked with *Oedipus Tyrannus* of Sophocles. As Lamb says, with reference to one scene, ' To move a horror skilfully, to touch a soul to the quick, to lay upon fear as much as it can bear, to wean and weary a life till it is ready to drop, and then step in with mortal instruments to take its last forfeit ; this only a Webster can do.'—*Spec. of Eng. Dram. Poets.* The faults of the play will be manifest to the least critical reader, but they will not dwell in his mind when he has followed the Duchess through her long-drawn agony and watched swift-winged Nemesis swooping upon her murderers.

A New Way to Pay Old Debts has been chosen not merely for its general interest of plot and character, or the admirably painted figure of the scoundrelly Sir Giles Overreach (supposed to be taken from the notorious Sir Giles Mompesson), but for the curiously modern atmosphere which hangs about it. We seem to have left behind the gloom and the strength, whether tragic or comic, of the Elizabethans and to be mixing with people fashioned far more like ourselves. Indeed, barring a few obsolete or unusual expressions, the work might almost be a product of some early Victorian. This is not meant as disparagement, for the play fully deserves inclusion in the present selection as a bright and entertaining comedy, touched here and there with tragic possibilities, as every play must be if it is to resemble life, and ending with poetic justice appropriately meted out to the sheep and the goats, as a comedy audience love to have it. The moral of the play—a perfectly sound one—is that, however well ' Esse quam Videri ' may serve as a motto for a noble family, the direct opposite is the principle which pays in practical life : a man is judged to be or to possess what he appears to be or to possess. Many an adventurer has lived comfortably on his reputation for wealth ; indeed, the whole of modern commerce and finance is based on credit, and Massinger's play affords a good illustration of the value of credit in social life. For, in man's dealings with his fellows, to him that is thought to have shall be given, and from him that is thought not to have every attempt will be made to take away that which he hath.

C. B. W.

1915

THE SHOEMAKER'S HOLIDAY

Thomas Dekker

(?1570– ?1641)

THE earliest extant edition of *The Shoemaker's Holiday* is the quarto of 1600, though from Henslowe's Diary it appears that an edition was published in the previous year. No copy of this, however, is known to exist. Four more quarto editions appeared in 1610, 1618, 1631, and 1657, of which the last certainly and possibly the last but one were subsequent to Dekker's death. Each of them appears to have been printed from its immediate predecessor, and, while correcting some of its errors, to have introduced fresh ones of its own.

For more than two hundred years no fresh edition appeared, but in 1862 Mr. Fritsche brought out an edition at Thorn, taking his text from a copy of the 1618 edition at Dantzig. He first divided the play into scenes, of which he made twenty in all; he also added several stage directions, and suggested a good many conjectural readings, some of which have been accepted by subsequent editors. The play next appeared in Dekker's *Dramatic Works* published in four volumes by Pearson in 1873, the anonymous editor of which would seem to have possessed neither the industry nor the knowledge necessary for his great task.

This was certainly not the case with his successors, Drs. Warnke and Proescholdt, who brought out an admirable edition of the play at Halle in 1886, collating all the early texts and completing Fritsche's arrangement of the play by grouping his Scenes into Acts; they also added a number of useful notes on the many obscure words and references that occur in the play. Their text was adopted by Mr. Ernest Rhys in his volume of Dekker's Plays in the Mermaid Series (1887), and has been mainly followed in the present edition, such deviations as I have made being generally in the way of a more conservative following of the earliest quarto.

THE SHOMAKERS

Holiday.

OR

The Gentle Craft.

With the humorous life of Simon
Eyre, shoomaker, and Lord Maior
of London.

As it was acted before the Queenes most excellent Ma-
iestie on New-yeares day at night last, by the right
honourable the Earle of Notingham, Lord high Ad-
mirall of England, his seruants.

Printed by Valentine Sims dwelling at the foote of Adling
hill, neere Bainards Castle, at the signe of the White
Swanne, and are there to be sold.

1 6 0 0.

THE FIRST THREE-MAN'S SONG

O the month of May, the merry month of May,
    So frolick, so gay, and so green, so green, so
       green !
O, and then did I unto my true love say :
    ' Sweet Peg, thou shalt be my summer's queen !

' Now the nightingale, the pretty nightingale,
    The sweetest singer in all the forest's choir,
Entreats thee, sweet Peggy, to hear thy true love's
       tale ;
    Lo, yonder she sitteth, her breast against a brier.

' But O, I spy the cuckoo, the cuckoo, the cuckoo ;
    See where she sitteth : come away, my joy ; 10
Come away, I prithee : I do not like the cuckoo
    Should sing where my Peggy and I kiss and toy.'

O the month of May, the merry month of May,
    So frolick, so gay, and so green, so green, so
       green !
And then did I unto my true love say :
    ' Sweet Peg, thou shalt be my summer's queen ! '

THE SECOND THREE-MAN'S SONG

This is to be sung at the latter end.

Cold 's the wind, and wet 's the rain,
    Saint Hugh be our good speed :
Ill is the weather that bringeth no gain,
    Nor helps good hearts in need.

Trowl [1] the bowl, the jolly nut-brown bowl,
    And here, kind mate, to thee :
Let 's sing a dirge for Saint Hugh's soul,
    And down it merrily.

Down a down heydown a down,
        [Close with the tenor boy.]
    Hey derry derry, down a down ! 10
Ho, well done ; to me let come !
    Ring compass [2], gentle joy.

Trowl the bowl, the nut-brown bowl,
    And here, kind mate, to thee : &c.
      [Repeat as often as there be men to drink; and
          at last when all have drunk, this verse:

Cold 's the wind, and wet 's the rain,
    Saint Hugh be our good speed :
Ill is the weather that bringeth no gain,
    Nor helps good hearts in need.

---

[1] Send round.   [2] (?) Come full circle.

THE PROLOGUE

As wretches in a storm (expecting day),
With trembling hands and eyes cast up to heaven,
Make prayers the anchor of their conquered hopes,
So we, dear goddess, wonder of all eyes,
Your meanest vassals, through mistrust and fear
To sink into the bottom of disgrace
By our imperfect pastimes, prostrate thus
On bended knees, our sails of hope do strike,
Dreading the bitter storms of your dislike.
Since then, unhappy men, our hap is such,   10
That to ourselves ourselves no help can bring,
But needs must perish, if your saint-like ears
(Locking the temple where all mercy sits)
Refuse the tribute of our begging tongues :
Oh grant, bright mirror of true chastity,
From those life-breathing stars, your sun-like eyes,
One gracious smile : for your celestial breath
Must send us life, or sentence us to death.

DRAMATIS PERSONAE.[1]

THE KING.
THE EARL OF CORNWALL.
SIR HUGH LACY, Earl of Lincoln.
ROWLAND LACY, otherwise HANS, } His Nephews.
ASKEW,
SIR ROGER OTELEY,[2] Lord Mayor of London.
MASTER HAMMON,
MASTER WARNER, } Citizens of London.
MASTER SCOTT,
SIMON EYRE, the Shoemaker.
ROGER, commonly called
    HODGE,
FIRK,   } EYRE'S Journeymen.
RALPH,
LOVELL, a Courtier.
DODGER, Servant to the EARL OF LINCOLN.
A DUTCH SKIPPER.
A BOY.
Courtiers, Attendants, Officers, Soldiers, Hunters, Shoe-
    makers, Apprentices, Servants.

ROSE, Daughter of SIR ROGER.
SYBIL, her Maid.
MARGERY, Wife of SIMON EYRE.
JANE, Wife of RALPH.

SCENE.—London and Old Ford.

[1] Added by Fritsche (1862).
[2] Spelt also Otley and Otly in the quartos.

THE SHOEMAKER'S HOLIDAY

ACT THE FIRST

SCENE I.—A Street in London.

Enter the LORD MAYOR and the EARL OF LINCOLN.

LINCOLN.   My lord mayor, you have sundry times
Feasted myself and many courtiers more :
Seldom or never can we be so kind
To make requital of your courtesy.
But leaving this, I hear my cousin Lacy
Is much affected to your daughter Rose.
   LORD MAYOR.   True, my good lord, and she loves
     him so well
That I mislike her boldness in the chase.
   LINCOLN.   Why, my lord mayor, think you it
     then a shame,
To join a Lacy with an Oteley's name ?   10
   LORD MAYOR.   Too mean is my poor girl for his
     high birth ;
Poor citizens must not with courtiers wed,
Who will in silks and gay apparel spend
More in one year than I am worth, by far :
Therefore your honour need not doubt my girl.
   LINCOLN.   Take heed, my lord, advise you what
     you do !
A verier unthrift lives not in the world,
Than is my cousin ; for I'll tell you what :
'Tis now almost a year since he requested
To travel countries for experience ;   20
I furnished him with coin, bills of exchange,
Letters of credit, men to wait on him,
Solicited my friends in Italy
Well to respect him.   But to see the end :
Scant had he journeyed through half Germany,
But all his coin was spent, his men cast off,

His bills embezzled,[1] and my jolly coz,
Ashamed to show his bankrupt presence here,
Became a shoemaker in Wittenberg,
A goodly science for a gentleman   30
Of such descent ! Now judge the rest by this :
Suppose your daughter have a thousand pound,
He did consume me more in one half year ;
And make him heir to all the wealth you have,
One twelvemonth's rioting will waste it all.
Then seek, my lord, some honest citizen
To wed your daughter to.
    LORD MAYOR.   I thank your lordship.
[Aside] Well, fox, I understand your subtilty.—
As for your nephew, let your lordship's eye
But watch his actions, and you need not fear,
For I have sent my daughter far enough.   41
And yet your cousin Rowland might do well,
Now he hath learned an occupation ;
And yet I scorn to call him son-in-law.
    LINCOLN.   Ay, but I have a better trade for him :
I thank his grace, he hath appointed him
Chief colonel of all those companies
Mustered in London and the shires about,
To serve his highness in those wars of France.
See where he comes !—

Enter LOVELL, LACY, and ASKEW.

               Lovell, what news with you ?
    LOVELL.   My Lord of Lincoln, 'tis his highness'
    will,   51
That presently your cousin ship for France
With all his powers ; he would not for a million,
But they should land at Dieppe within four days.
    LINCOLN.   Go certify his grace, it shall be done.
                          [Exit LOVELL.
Now, cousin Lacy, in what forwardness
Are all your companies ?
    LACY.   All well prepared.

[1] Squandered.

The men of Hertfordshire lie at Mile-end,
Suffolk and Essex train in Tothill-fields,
The Londoners and those of Middlesex,   60
All gallantly prepared in Finsbury,
With frolic spirits long for their parting hour.
 LORD MAYOR.   They have their imprest,[1] coats,
  and furniture ; [2]
And, if it please your cousin Lacy come
To the Guildhall, he shall receive his pay ;
And twenty pounds besides my brethren
Will freely give him, to approve our loves
We bear unto my lord, your uncle here.
 LACY.   I thank your honour.
 LINCOLN. Thanks, my good lord mayor.
 LORD MAYOR.   At the Guildhall we will expect
  your coming.   [Exit.
 LINCOLN.   To approve your loves to me ?   No
  subtilty !   71
Nephew, that twenty pound he doth bestow
For joy to rid you from his daughter Rose.
But, cousins both, now here are none but friends,
I would not have you cast an amorous eye
Upon so mean a project as the love
Of a gay, wanton, painted citizen.
I know, this churl even in the height of scorn
Doth hate the mixture of his blood with thine.
I pray thee, do thou so ! Remember, coz,   80
What honourable fortunes wait on thee :
Increase the king's love, which so brightly shines,
And gilds thy hopes. I have no heir but thee,—
And yet not thee, if with a wayward spirit
Thou start from the true bias of my love.
 LACY.   My lord, I will for honour, not desire
Of land or livings, or to be your heir,
So guide my actions in pursuit of France,
As shall add glory to the Lacys' name.
 LINCOLN.   Coz, for those words here's thirty
  Portuguese [3],   90

---

[1] Advance of pay.   [2] Weapons.
[3] A gold coin, varying in value from £3 5s. to £4 10s.

And, nephew Askew, there's a few for you.
Fair Honour, in her loftiest eminence,
Stays in France for you, till you fetch her thence.
Then, nephews, clap swift wings on your designs :
Begone, begone, make haste to the Guildhall ;
There presently I'll meet you.   Do not stay :
Where honour beckons, shame attends delay.
                                        [Exit.

ASKEW.   How gladly would your uncle have you
    gone !
LACY.   True, coz, but I'll o'erreach his policies.
I have some serious business for three days,   100
Which nothing but my presence can dispatch.
You, therefore, cousin, with the companies,
Shall haste to Dover ; there I'll meet with you :
Or, if I stay past my prefixèd time,
Away for France ; we'll meet in Normandy.
The twenty pounds my lord mayor gives to me
You shall receive, and these ten Portuguese,
Part of mine uncle's thirty.   Gentle coz,
Have care to our great charge ; I know, your
    wisdom
Hath tried itself in higher consequence.   110
ASKEW.   Coz, all myself am yours : yet have
    this care,
To lodge in London with all secrecy ;
Our uncle Lincoln hath, besides his own,
Many a jealous eye, that in your face
Stares only to watch means for your disgrace.
LACY.   Stay, cousin, who be these ?

Enter SIMON EYRE, MARGERY his wife, HODGE, FIRK, JANE,
        and RALPH with a piece.[1]

EYRE.   Leave whining, leave whining ! Away
with this whimpering, this puling, these blubbering
tears, and these wet eyes ! I'll get thy husband
discharged, I warrant thee, sweet Jane ; go to !
HODGE.   Master, here be the captains.   121

------

[1] i.e. a piece of work ; here a pair of shoes.

EYRE.   Peace, Hodge ; husht, ye knave, husht !

FIRK.   Here be the cavaliers and the colonels, master.   124

EYRE.   Peace, Firk ; peace, my fine Firk ! Stand by with your pishery-pashery,[1] away ! I am a man of the best presence ; I'll speak to them, an they were Popes.—Gentlemen, captains, colonels, commanders ! Brave men, brave leaders, may it please you to give me audience. I am Simon Eyre, the mad shoemaker of Tower Street ; this wench with the mealy mouth that will never tire is my wife, I can tell you ; here 's Hodge, my man and my foreman ; here 's Firk, my fine firking [2] journeyman, and this is blubbered Jane. All we come to be suitors for this honest Ralph. Keep him at home, and as I am a true shoemaker and a gentleman of the Gentle Craft,[3] buy spurs yourselves, and I'll find ye boots these seven years.   140

MARGERY.   Seven years, husband ?

EYRE.   Peace, midriff, peace ! I know what I do. Peace !

FIRK.   Truly, master cormorant, you shall do God good service to let Ralph and his wife stay together. She 's a young new-married woman ; if you take her husband away from her a night, you undo her ; she may beg in the daytime ; for he 's as good a workman at a prick and an awl, as any is in our trade.   150

JANE.   O let him stay, else I shall be undone.

FIRK.   Ay, truly, she shall be laid at one side like a pair of old shoes else, and be occupied [4] for no use.

LACY.   Truly, my friends, it lies not in my power :

---

[1] Chatter.   [2] Frisking.

[3] cf. Greene, *George-a-Greene* (1592), ' You shall be no more called Shoemakers, but you and yours to the world's end shall be called the trade of the Gentle Craft.'

[4] cf. *2 Henry IV*, II. iv. 160.

The Londoners are pressed, paid, and set forth
By the lord mayor ; I cannot change a man.

HODGE. Why, then you were as good be a
corporal as a colonel, if you cannot discharge one
good fellow ; and I tell you true, I think you do
more than you can answer, to press a man within
a year and a day of his marriage.   162

EYRE. Well said, melancholy Hodge ; gramercy,
my fine foreman.

MARGERY. Truly, gentlemen, it were ill done
for such as you, to stand so stiffly against a poor
young wife ; considering her case, she is new-
married, but let that pass : I pray, deal not
roughly with her ; her husband is a young man,
and but newly entered, but let that pass.   170

EYRE. Away with your pishery-pashery, your
pols and your edipols ! [1] Peace, midriff ; silence,
Cicely Bumtrinket ! Let your head speak.

FIRK. Yea, and the horns too, master.   174

EYRE. Too soon, my fine Firk, too soon !
Peace, scoundrels ! See you this man ? Captains,
you will not release him ? Well, let him go ; he's
a proper shot ; let him vanish ! Peace, Jane, dry
up thy tears, they'll make his powder dankish.
Take him, brave men ; Hector of Troy was an
hackney [2] to him, Hercules and Termagant [3]
scoundrels, Prince Arthur's Round-table—by the
Lord of Ludgate—ne'er fed such a tall, such a
dapper swordsman ; by the life of Pharaoh, a
brave, resolute swordsman ! Peace, Jane ! I say
no more, mad knaves.   186

FIRK. See, see, Hodge, how my master raves
in commendation of Ralph !

HODGE. Ralph, th' art a gull, by this hand, an
thou goest not.   190

---

[1] Various forms of asseveration.
[2] i.e. a common drudge.
[3] An imaginary deity whom the Mohammedans were
supposed to worship ; represented in mystery plays as
a violent, overbearing personage.

ASKEW.   I am glad, good Master Eyre, it is my
   hap
To meet so resolute a soldier.
Trust me, for your report and love to him,
A common slight regard shall not respect him.
   LACY.   Is thy name Ralph ?
   RALPH.   Yes, sir.
   LACY.   Give me thy hand ;
Thou shalt not want, as I am a gentleman.
Woman, be patient ; God, no doubt, will send
Thy husband safe again ; but he must go,
His country's quarrel says it shall be so.   199
   HODGE.   Th' art a gull, by my stirrup, if thou
dost not go.   I will not have thee strike thy gimlet
into these weak vessels ;   prick thine enemies,
Ralph.

Enter DODGER.

   DODGER.   My lord, your uncle on the Tower-hill
Stays with the lord mayor and the aldermen,
And doth request you with all speed you may,
To hasten thither.
   ASKEW.   Cousin, come let 's go.[1]
   LACY.   Dodger, run you before, tell them **we**
   come.—   [Exit DODGER.
This Dodger is mine uncle's parasite.
The arrant'st varlet that e'er breathed on **earth** ;
He sets more discord in a noble house   211
By one day's broaching of his pickthank tales,[2]
Than can be salved again in twenty years,
And he, I fear, shall go with us to France,
To pry into our actions.
   ASKEW.   Therefore, coz,
It shall behove you to be circumspect.
   LACY.   Fear not, good cousin.—Ralph, hie **to**
   your colours.
   RALPH.   I must, because there is no remedy ;
But, gentle master and my loving dame,

[1] Cousin, let 's go. 1600.
[2] Tales told to curry favour.

As you have always been a friend to me,   220
So in my absence think upon my wife.

JANE.   Alas, my Ralph.

MARGERY.   She cannot speak for weeping.

EYRE.   Peace, you cracked groats,[1] you mustard tokens,[2] disquiet not the brave soldier. Go thy ways, Ralph !

JANE.   Ay, ay, you bid him go ; what shall I do When he is gone ?

FIRK.   Why, be doing with me or my fellow Hodge ; be not idle.   229

EYRE.   Let me see thy hand, Jane. This fine hand, this white hand, these pretty fingers must spin, must card, must work ; work, you bombast-cotton-candle-quean ;[3] work for your living, with a pox to you.—Hold thee, Ralph, here's five sixpences for thee ; fight for the honour of the Gentle Craft, for the gentlemen shoemakers, the courageous cordwainers, the flower of St. Martin's, the mad knaves of Bedlam, Fleet Street, Tower Street and Whitechapel ; crack me the crowns of the French knaves ; a pox on them, crack them ; fight, by the Lord of Ludgate ; fight, my fine boy !

FIRK.   Here, Ralph, here's three twopences : two carry into France, the third shall wash our souls at parting, for sorrow is dry. For my sake, firk the *Basa mon cues*.[4]   245

HODGE.   Ralph, I am heavy at parting ; but here's a shilling for thee. God send thee to cram thy slops with French crowns, and thy enemies' bellies with bullets.

RALPH.   I thank you, master, and I thank you all.   250

Now, gentle wife, my loving lovely Jane,
Rich men, at parting, give their wives rich gifts,

---

[1] Worthless coins.
[2] Coupons given to purchasers of mustard.
[3] Bombast is another name for cotton ; a cotton candle is one with a cotton wick.
[4] Thrash the Mounseers.

I'd set mine old debts against my new driblets,
And the hare's foot against the goose giblets,[1] 50
For if ever I sigh, when sleep I should take,
Pray God I may lose my maidenhead when I wake.

ROSE. Will my love leave me then, and go to
France ?

SYBIL. I know not that, but I am sure I see
him stalk before the soldiers. By my troth, he is
a proper man ; but he is proper that proper doth.
Let him go snick up,[2] young mistress.

ROSE. Get thee to London; and learn perfectly,
Whether my Lacy go to France, or no.
Do this, and I will give thee for thy pains 60
My cambric apron and my Romish gloves,
My purple stockings and a stomacher.
Say, wilt thou do this, Sybil, for my sake ?

SYBIL. Will I, quoth a ? At whose suit ? By
my troth, yes I'll go. A cambric apron, gloves,
a pair of purple stockings, and a stomacher ! I'll
sweat in purple, mistress, for you ; I'll take
anything that comes a God's name. O rich !
a cambric apron ! Faith, then have at ' up tails
all '.[3] I'll go jiggy-joggy to London, and be here
in a trice, young mistress. [Exit. 71

ROSE. Do so, good Sybil. Meantime wretched I
Will sit and sigh for his lost company. [Exit.

SCENE II.—A Street in London.

Enter ROWLAND LACY, like a Dutch Shoemaker.

LACY. How many shapes have gods and kings
devised,
Thereby to compass their desired loves !
It is no shame for Rowland Lacy, then,
To clothe his cunning with the Gentle Craft,
That, thus disguised, I may unknown possess

---

[1] A proverbial phrase for setting one thing off against
another ; cf. Dekker's *Westward Ho*, v. iv.
[2] Go and be hanged ! [3] i.e. Start with alacrity.

The only happy presence of my Rose.
For her have I forsook my charge in France,
Incurred the king's displeasure, and stirred up
Rough hatred in mine uncle Lincoln's breast.
O love, how powerful art thou, that canst change
High birth to baseness, and a noble mind　　　　11
To the mean semblance of a shoemaker !
But thus it must be. For her cruel father,
Hating the single union of our souls,
Hath secretly conveyed my Rose from London,
To bar me of her presence ; but I trust,
Fortune and this disguise will further me
Once more to view her beauty, gain her sight.
Here in Tower Street with Eyre the shoemaker
Mean I a while to work ; I know the trade,　　　20
I learnt it when I was in Wittenberg.
Then cheer thy hoping spirits, be not dismayed,
Thou canst not want : do Fortune what she can,
The Gentle Craft is living for a man.　　　　[Exit.

SCENE III.—An open Yard before EYRE's House.

Enter EYRE, making himself ready.

EYRE. Where be these boys, these girls, these
drabs, these scoundrels ? They wallow in the fat
brewis [1] of my bounty, and lick up the crumbs of
my table, yet will not rise to see my walks cleansed.
Come out, you powder-beef [2] queans ! What, Nan !
what, Madge Mumble-crust ! Come out, you fat
midriff-swag-belly-whores, and sweep me these
kennels that the noisome stench offend not the
noses of my neighbours. What, Firk, I say ;
what, Hodge ! Open my shop-windows ! What,
Firk, I say !　　　　11

Enter FIRK.

FIRK. O master, is 't you that speak bandog [3]
and Bedlam this morning ? I was in a dream, and

---

[1] Bread soaked in broth.　　　[2] Salt beef.
[3] A dog kept tied up.

mused what madman was got into the street so early; have you drunk this morning that your throat is so clear?

EYRE. Ah, well said, Firk; well said, Firk. To work, my fine knave, to work! Wash thy face, and thou 'lt be more blest. 19

FIRK. Let them wash my face that will eat it. Good master, send for a souse-wife,[1] if you will have my face cleaner.

Enter HODGE.

EYRE. Away, sloven! avaunt, scoundrel!— Good-morrow, Hodge; good-morrow, my fine foreman.

HODGE. O master, good-morrow; y' are an early stirrer. Here 's a fair morning.—Good-morrow, Firk, I could have slept this hour. Here 's a brave day towards. 29

EYRE. Oh, haste to work, my fine foreman, haste to work.

FIRK. Master, I am dry as dust to hear my fellow Roger talk of fair weather; let us pray for good leather, and let clowns and ploughboys and those that work in the fields pray for brave days. We work in a dry shop; what care I if it rain?

Enter MARGERY.

EYRE. How now, Dame Margery, can you see to rise? Trip and go, call up the drabs, your maids. 39

MARGERY. See to rise? I hope 'tis time enough, 'tis early enough for any woman to be seen abroad. I marvel how many wives in Tower Street are up so soon. Gods me, 'tis not noon,— here 's a yawling![2]

EYRE. Peace, Margery, peace! Where's Cicely Bumtrinket, your maid? She has a privy fault, she f—ts in her sleep. Call the quean up; if my

---

[1] Woman who pickled pigs' faces. [2] Bawling.

men want shoe-thread, I'll swinge her in[1] a
stirrup.

FIRK. Yet, that's but a dry beating; here's
still a sign of drought.   51

Enter LACY, as HANS, singing.

HANS.   Der was een bore van Gelderland
               Frolick sie byen;
           He was als dronck he cold nyet stand,
               Upsolce sie byen.
           Tap eens de canneken,
           Drincke, schone mannekin.[2]

FIRK. Master, for my life, yonder's a brother
of the Gentle Craft; if he bear not Saint Hugh's
bones,[3] I'll forfeit my bones; he's some uplandish[4]
workman: hire him, good master, that I may
learn some gibble-gabble; 'twill make us work the
faster.   63

EYRE. Peace, Firk! A hard world! Let him
pass, let him vanish; we have journeymen enow.
Peace, my fine Firk!

MARGERY. [Sarcastically] Nay, nay, y' are best
follow your man's counsel; you shall see what
will come on't: we have not men enow, but we
must entertain every butter-box;[5] but let that
pass.   71

---

[1] i.e. with. Cf. *Philaster* IV. ii. ' He shall shoot in a stone-
bow for me.'
    [2]   There was a boor from Gelderland,
          Jolly they be;
    He was so drunk he could not stand,
          Half-seas-over (?) they be:
    Tap once the cannikin,
    Drink, pretty mannikin!
[3] Hugh, a prince of Britain, learnt the Gentle Craft in his
travels and worked for a year as an apprentice; falling in
love with a Christian damsel, he adopted her faith and was
martyred under Diocletian. His brother shoemakers took
his bones from the gibbet and made them into tools for
their trade.
[4] Country.   [5] A contemptuous term for a Dutchman.

HODGE. Dame, 'fore God, if my master follow your counsel, he'll consume little beef. He shall [1] be glad of men, an he can catch them.

FIRK. Ay, that he shall.

HODGE. 'Fore God, a proper man, and I warrant, a fine workman. Master, farewell ; dame, adieu ; if such a man as he cannot find work, Hodge is not for you. [Offers to go.

EYRE. Stay, my fine Hodge. 80

FIRK. Faith, an your foreman go, dame, you must take a journey to seek a new journeyman ; if Roger remove, Firk follows. If Saint Hugh's bones shall not be set a-work, I may prick mine awl in the walls, and go play. Fare ye well, master ; good-bye, dame.

EYRE. Tarry, my fine Hodge, my brisk foreman ! Stay, Firk !—Peace, pudding-broth ! By the Lord of Ludgate, I love my men as my life. Peace, you gallimafry ! [2]—Hodge, if he want work, I'll hire him. One of you to him ; stay,—he comes to us. 92

HANS. Goeden dach, meester, ende u vro oak.[3]

FIRK. Nails, if I should speak after him without drinking, I should choke. And you, friend Oake, are you of the Gentle Craft ?

HANS. Yaw, yaw, ik bin den skomawker.[4]

FIRK. Den skomaker, quoth a ! And hark you, skomaker, have you all your tools, a good rubbing-pin, a good stopper, a good dresser, your four sorts of awls, and your two balls of wax, your paring knife, your hand- and thumb-leathers, and good St. Hugh's bones to smooth up your work ? 103

HANS. Yaw, yaw ; be niet vorveard. Ik hab all de dingen voour mack skooes groot and cleane.[5]

FIRK. Ha, ha ! Good master, hire him ; he'll

---

[1] Ought to.   [2] A dish of different hashed meats.
[3] Good day, master, and you, mistress, too.
[4] Yes, yes, I am a shoemaker.
[5] Yes, yes ; be not afraid. I have everything, to make shoes big and little.

make me laugh so that I shall work more in mirth
than I can in earnest.

EYRE.   Hear ye, friend, have ye any skill in the
mystery of cordwainers ?   110

HANS.   Ik weet niet wat yow seg ; ich verstaw
you niet.[1]

FIRK.   Why, thus, man :   [Imitating by gesture a
shoemaker at work.]   Ich verste u niet, quoth a.

HANS.   Yaw, yaw, yaw ; ick can dat wel doen.[2]

FIRK.   Yaw, yaw ! He speaks yawing like a
jackdaw that gapes to be fed with cheese-curds.
Oh, he'll give a villanous pull at a can of double-
beer ; but Hodge and I have the vantage, we must
drink first, because we are the eldest journeymen.

EYRE.   What is thy name ?   121

HANS.   Hans—Hans Meulter.

EYRE.   Give my thy hand ; th' art welcome.—
Hodge, entertain him ; Firk, bid him welcome ;
come, Hans.   Run, wife, bid your maids, your
trullibubs,[3] make ready my fine men's breakfasts.
To him, Hodge !

HODGE.   Hans, th' art welcome ; use thyself
friendly, for we are good fellows ; if not, thou
shalt be fought with, wert thou bigger than a
giant.   131

FIRK.   Yea, and drunk with, wert thou Gargan-
tua.   My master keeps no cowards, I tell thee.—
Ho, boy, bring him an heel-block, here's a new
journeyman.

Enter Boy.

HANS.   O, ich wersto you ; ich moet een halve
dossen cans betaelen ; here, boy, nempt dis
skilling, tap eens freelicke.[4]   [Exit Boy.

EYRE.   Quick, snipper-snapper, away ! Firk,

---

[1] I know not what you say ; I understand you not.
[2] Yes, yes, yes ; I can do that well.
[3] A cant term for anything very trifling.—*Nares.*
[4] O, I understand you ; I must pay for a half-dozen cans ;
here, boy, take this shilling, tap once freely.

scour thy throat, thou shalt wash it with Castilian liquor.   141

Enter Boy.

Come, my last of the fives,[1] give me a can. Have to thee, Hans ; here, Hodge ; here, Firk ; drink, you mad Greeks, and work like true Trojans, and pray for Simon Eyre, the shoemaker.—Here, Hans, and th' art welcome.

FIRK. Lo, dame, you would have lost a good fellow that will teach us to laugh. This beer came hopping in well.

MARGERY. Simon, it is almost seven.   150

EYRE. Is 't so, Dame Clapper-dudgeon ?[2] Is 't seven a clock, and my men's breakfast not ready ? Trip and go, you soused conger, away ! Come, you mad hyperboreans ; follow me, Hodge ; follow me, Hans ; come after, my fine Firk ; to work, to work a while, and then to breakfast !   [Exit.

FIRK. Soft ! Yaw, yaw, good Hans, though my master have no more wit but to call you afore me, I am not so foolish to go behind you, I being the elder journeyman.   [Exeunt. 160

SCENE IV.—A Field near Old Ford.

Holloaing within. Enter Master WARNER and Master HAMMON, attired as Hunters.

HAMMON.   Cousin, beat every brake, the game 's not far,
This way with wingèd feet he fled from death,
Whilst the pursuing hounds, scenting his steps,
Find out his highway to destruction.
Besides, the miller's boy told me even now,
He saw him take soil,[3] and he holloaed him,
Affirming him to have been so embost[4]
That long he could not hold.

WARNER.   If it be so,
'Tis best we trace these meadows by Old Ford.

---

[1] A small size of last.   [2] Cant term for a beggar.—*Nares.*
[3] Take to the water.   [4] Exhausted.

A noise of Hunters within.   Enter a Boy.

HAMMON.   How now, boy ?   Where 's the deer ?
    speak, saw'st thou him ?   11

BOY.   O yea ; I saw him leap through a hedge,
and then over a ditch, then at my lord mayor's
pale.   Over he skipped me, and in he went me,
and ' holla ' the hunters cried, and ' there, boy ;
there, boy ! ' But there he is, 'a mine honesty.

HAMMON.   Boy, God amercy.   Cousin, let 's
    away ;
I hope we shall find better sport to-day.   [Exeunt.

SCENE V.—Another part of the Field.

Hunting within.   Enter ROSE and SYBIL.

ROSE.   Why, Sybil, wilt thou prove a forester ?

SYBIL.   Upon some, no [1] ; forester, go by ; no,
faith, mistress.   The deer came running into the
barn through the orchard and over the pale ;
I wot well, I looked as pale as a new cheese to
see him.   But whip, says goodman Pin-close, up
with his flail, and our Nick with a prong, and
down he fell, and they upon him, and I upon
them.   By my troth, we had such sport ; and in
the end we ended him ; his throat we cut, flayed
him, unhorned him, and my lord mayor shall eat
of him anon, when he comes.   [Horns sound within.

ROSE.   Hark, hark, the hunters come ; y' are
    best take heed,   13
They'll have a saying to you for this deed.

Enter Master HAMMON, Master WARNER, Huntsmen, and Boy.

HAMMON.   God save you, fair ladies.

SYBIL.   Ladies !   O gross ! [2]

WARNER.   Came not a buck this way ?

ROSE.   No, but two does.

---

[1] No indeed ; formed apparently on the analogy of, upon
my word, upon my soul, &c. Cf. upon some, ay, *inf*.
[2] Stupid.

HAMMON. And which way went they ? Faith,
we'll hunt at those.

SYBIL. At those ? upon some, no : when, can
you tell ?   18

WARNER. Upon some, ay.

SYBIL.   Good Lord !

WARNER.   Wounds ! Then farewell !

HAMMON. Boy, which way went he ?

BOY.   This way, sir, he ran.

HAMMON. This way he ran indeed, fair Mistress
Rose ;

Our game was lately in your orchard seen.

WARNER. Can you advise, which way he took
his flight ?

SYBIL. Follow your nose ; his horns will guide
you right.

WARNER. Th' art a mad wench.

SYBIL.   O, rich !

ROSE.   Trust me, not I.

It is not like that the wild forest-deer

Would come so near to places of resort ;

You are deceived, he fled some other way.

WARNER. Which way, my sugar-candy, can you
shew ?

SYBIL. Come up, good honeysops, upon some,
no.   30

ROSE. Why do you stay, and not pursue your
game ?

SYBIL. I'll hold my life, their hunting-nags be
lame.

HAMMON. A deer more dear is found within this
place.

ROSE. But not the deer, sir, which you had in
chase.

HAMMON. I chased the deer, but this dear
chaseth me.

ROSE. The strangest hunting that ever I see.

But where 's your park ?   [She offers to go away.

HAMMON. [My park ?] 'Tis here : O stay !

ROSE. Impale me [in 't], and then I will not stray.

WARNER. They wrangle, wench ; we are more
kind than they.

SYBIL. What kind of hart is that dear heart,
you seek ?   40

WARNER. A hart, dear heart.

SYBIL.   Who ever saw the like ?

ROSE. To lose your heart, is 't possible you can ?

HAMMON. My heart is lost.

ROSE.   Alack, good gentleman !

HAMMON. This poor lost heart would I wish
you might find.

ROSE. You, by such luck, might prove your
hart a hind.

HAMMON. Why, Luck had horns, so have I
heard some say.

ROSE. Now, God, an 't be his will, send Luck
into your way.

Enter the LORD MAYOR and Servants.

LORD MAYOR. What, Master Hammon ? Welcome to Old Ford !

SYBIL. Gods pittikins, hands off, sir ! Here's
my lord.

LORD MAYOR. I hear you had ill luck, and lost
your game.   50

HAMMON. Tis true, my lord.

LORD MAYOR.   I am sorry for the same.
What gentleman is this ?

HAMMON.   My brother-in-law.

LORD MAYOR. Y' are welcome both; sith For-
tune offers you
Into my hands, you shall not part from hence,
Until you have refreshed your wearied limbs.—
Go, Sybil, cover the board !—You shall be guest
To no good cheer, but even a hunter's feast.

HAMMON. I thank your lordship.—Cousin, on
my life,
For our lost venison I shall find a wife.   [Exeunt.

LORD MAYOR. In, gentlemen ; I'll not be
absent long.—   60

This Hammon is a proper gentleman,
A citizen by birth, fairly allied ;
How fit an husband were he for my girl !
Well, I will in, and do the best I can,
To match my daughter to this gentleman.   [Exit.

ACT THE THIRD

Scene I.—A Room in Eyre's House.

Enter Hans, Skipper, Hodge, and Firk.

SKIPPER. Ick sal yow wat seggen, Hans ; dis
skip, dat comen from Candy, is al vol, by Got's
sacrament, van sugar, civet, almonds, cambrick,
end alle dingen, towsand towsand ding. Nempt it,
Hans, nempt it vor v meester. Daer be de bils
van laden. Your meester Simon Eyre sal hae good
copen. Wat seggen yow, Hans ? [1]

FIRK. Wat seggen de reggen, de copen slopen—
laugh, Hodge, laugh !   9

HANS. Mine liever broder Firk, bringt Meester
Eyre tot det signe vn Swannekin ; daer sal yow
finde dis skipper end me. Wat seggen yow, broder
Firk ? Doot it, Hodge.[2] Come, skipper.

[Exeunt Hans and Skipper.

FIRK. Bring him, quoth you ? Here's no
knavery, to bring my master to buy a ship worth
the lading of two or three hundred thousand
pounds. Alas, that's nothing ; a trifle, a bauble,
Hodge.   18

HODGE. The truth is, Firk, that the merchant

[1] I'll tell you what, Hans ; this ship that comes from
Candia, is all full, by God's sacrament, of sugar, civet,
almonds, cambric, and all things, a thousand, thousand
things. Take it, Hans, take it for your master. There are
the bills of lading. Your master, Simon Eyre, shall have
a good bargain. What say you, Hans ?

[2] My dear brother Firk, bring Master Eyre to the sign of
the Swan ; there shall you find this skipper and me. What
say you, brother Firk ? Do it, Hodge.

owner of the ship dares not shew his head, and therefore this skipper that deals for him, for the love he bears to Hans, offers my master Eyre a bargain in the commodities. He shall have a reasonable day of payment; he may sell the wares by that time, and be an huge gainer himself.

FIRK. Yea, but can my fellow Hans lend my master twenty porpentines as an earnest penny?

HODGE. Portegues,[1] thou wouldst say; here they be, Firk; hark, they jingle in my pocket like St. Mary Overy's bells.[2]   30

Enter EYRE and MARGERY.

FIRK. Mum, here comes my dame and my master. She'll scold, on my life, for loitering this Monday; but all's one, let them all say what they can, Monday's our holiday.

MARGERY. You sing, Sir Sauce, but I beshrew your heart,
I fear, for this your singing we shall smart.

FIRK. Smart for me, dame; why, dame, why?

HODGE. Master, I hope you'll not suffer my dame to take down your journeymen.   39

FIRK. If she take me down, I'll take her up; yea, and take her down too, a button-hole lower.

EYRE. Peace, Firk; not I, Hodge; by the life of Pharaoh, by the Lord of Ludgate, by this beard, every hair whereof I value at a king's ransom, she shall not meddle with you.—Peace, you bombast-cotton-candle-quean; away, queen of clubs; quarrel not with me and my men, with me and my fine Firk; I'll firk you, if you do.

MARGERY. Yea, yea, man, you may use me as you please; but let that pass.   50

EYRE. Let it pass, let it vanish away; peace! Am I not Simon Eyre? Are not these my brave men, brave shoemakers, all gentlemen of the

[1] i.e. Portuguese, see note on p. 9.
[2] i.e. St. Mary of the Bank-side; now incorporated in St. Saviour's, Southwark.

Gentle Craft ?   Prince am I none, yet am I nobly
born,[1] as being the sole son of a shoemaker.   Away,
rubbish !   vanish, melt ;   melt like kitchen-stuff.

MARGERY.   Yea, yea, 'tis well ;   I must be called
rubbish, kitchen-stuff, for a sort [2] of knaves.   53

FIRK.   Nay, dame, you shall not weep and wail
in woe for me.   Master, I'll stay no longer ;   here's
an inventory of my shop-tools.   Adieu, master ;
Hodge, farewell.

HODGE.   Nay, stay, Firk ;   thou shalt not go
alone.

MARGERY.   I pray, let them go ;   there be more
maids than Mawkin, more men than Hodge, and
more fools than Firk.

FIRK.   Fools ?   Nails !   if I tarry now, I would
my guts might be turned to shoe-thread.   69

HODGE.   And if I stay, I pray God I may be
turned to a Turk, and set in Finsbury [3] for boys to
shoot at.—Come, Firk.

EYRE.   Stay, my fine knaves, you arms of my
trade, you pillars of my profession.   What, shall
a tittle-tattle's words make you forsake Simon
Eyre ?—Avaunt, kitchen-stuff !   Rip, you brown-
bread Tannikin ; [4] out of my sight !   Move me not !
Have not I ta'en you from selling tripes in Eastcheap, and set you in my shop, and made you
hail-fellow with Simon Eyre, the shoemaker ?   And
now do you deal thus with my journeymen ?
Look, you powder-beef-quean, on the face of
Hodge, here's a face for a lord.   83

FIRK.   And here's a face for any lady in Christendom.

EYRE.   Rip, you chitterling, avaunt !   Boy, bid
the tapster of the Boar's Head fill me a dozen cans
of beer for my journeymen.

---

[1] This, a favourite saying of Eyre's, sounds like a quotation
from a contemporary dramatist.   [2] Set.
[3] A famous practising ground for archery.
[4] A diminutive of Ann, applied specially to German or
Dutch girls.

FIRK.   A dozen, cans ? O brave! Hodge, now
I'll stay.   90
EYRE.   [Aside to the Boy].   An the knave fills any
more than two, he pays for them. [Exit Boy. Aloud.]
A dozen cans of beer for my journeymen. [Re-enter
Boy.] Here, you mad Mesopotamians, wash your
livers with this liquor. Where be the odd ten ?
[Aside] No more, Madge, no more.—Well said. Drink
and to work !—What work dost thou, Hodge ?
what work ?
HODGE.   I am a-making a pair of shoes for my
lord mayor's daughter, Mistress Rose.   100
FIRK.   And I a pair of shoes for Sybil, my lord's
maid. I deal with her.
EYRE.   Sybil ? Fie, defile not thy fine work-
manly fingers with the feet of kitchen-stuff and
basting-ladles. Ladies of the court, fine ladies,
my lads, commit their feet to our apparelling ; put
gross work to Hans. Yark [1] and seam, yark and
seam !
FIRK.   For yarking and seaming let me alone,
an I come to 't.   110
HODGE.   Well, master, all this is from the bias.[2]
Do you remember the ship my fellow Hans told
you of ? The skipper and he are both drinking at
the Swan. Here be the Portigues to give earnest.
If you go through with it, you cannot choose but
be a lord at least.
FIRK.   Nay, dame, if my master prove not a
lord, and you a lady, hang me.
MARGERY.   Yea, like enough, if you may loiter
and tipple thus.   120
FIRK.   Tipple, dame ? No, we have been bargain-
ing with Skellum Skanderbag : [3] can you Dutch

---

[1] Thrust, sc. the awl through the leather.
[2] Off the point.
[3] German : Schelm, a scoundrel. Skanderbag, or Scander
Beg (i.e. Iskander Bey), a Turkish name for George Castriota,
the Albanian hero, who freed his country from the Turks
(1443–67)

spreaken for a ship of silk Cyprus, laden with
sugar-candy?[1]

Enter the Boy with a velvet coat and an Alderman's gown.
EYRE puts them on.

EYRE. Peace, Firk; silence, Tittle-tattle!
Hodge, I'll go through with it. Here's a seal-
ring, and I have sent for a guarded gown[2] and
a damask cassock. See where it comes; look here,
Maggy; help me, Firk; apparel me, Hodge; silk
and satin, you mad Philistines, silk and satin. 130

FIRK. Ha, ha, my master will be as proud as a
dog in a doublet, all in beaten[3] damask and velvet.

EYRE. Softly, Firk, for rearing of the nap, and
wearing threadbare my garments. How dost thou
like me, Firk? How do I look, my fine Hodge?

HODGE. Why, now you look like yourself,
master. I warrant you, there's few in the city,
but will give you the wall, and come upon you
with the right worshipful. 139

FIRK. Nails, my master looks like a threadbare
cloak new turned and dressed. Lord, Lord, to
see what good raiment doth! Dame, dame, are
you not enamoured?

EYRE. How say'st thou, Maggy, am I not
brisk? Am I not fine?

MARGERY. Fine? By my troth, sweetheart, very
fine! By my troth, I never liked thee so well in my
life, sweetheart; but let that pass. I warrant, there
be many women in the city have not such handsome
husbands, but only for their apparel; but let that
pass too. 151

Re-enter HANS and Skipper.

HANS. Godden day, mester. Dis be de skipper
dat heb de skip van marchandice; de commodity
ben good; nempt it, master, nempt it.[4]

---

[1] He means to say a ship from Cyprus and Candia (Crete)
laden with silk and sugar.—*Warnke and Proescholdt.*

[2] A gown with guards or facings. [3] Embroidered.

[4] Good day, master. This is the skipper that has the ship of
merchandise; the commodity is good; take it, master, take it.

EYRE. Godamercy, Hans ; welcome, skipper.
Where lies this ship of merchandise ?

SKIPPER. De skip ben in revere ; dor be van
Sugar, cyvet, almonds, cambrick, and a towsand
towsand tings, gotz sacrament ; nempt it, mester :
ye sal heb good copen.[1]   160

FIRK. To him, master ! O sweet master ! O
sweet wares ! Prunes, almonds, sugar-candy,
carrot-roots, turnips, O brave fatting meat ! Let
not a man buy a nutmeg but yourself.

EYRE. Peace, Firk ! Come, skipper, I'll go
aboard with you.—Hans, have you made him
drink ?   167

SKIPPER. Yaw, yaw, ic heb veale gedrunck.[2]

EYRE. Come, Hans, follow me. Skipper, thou
shalt have my countenance in the city.   [Exeunt.

FIRK. Yaw, heb veale gedrunck, quoth a. They
may well be called butter-boxes, when they drink
fat veal and thick beer too. But come, dame, I
hope you'll chide us no more.

MARGERY. No, faith, Firk ; no, perdy, Hodge.
I do feel honour creep upon me, and which is
more, a certain rising in my flesh ; but let that
pass.   178

FIRK. Rising in your flesh do you feel, say you ?
Ay, you may be with child, but why should not
my master feel a rising in his flesh, having a gown
and a gold ring on ? But you are such a shrew,
you'll soon pull him down.

MARGERY. Ha, ha ! prithee, peace ! Thou
mak'st my worship laugh ; but let that pass. Come,
I'll go in ; Hodge, prithee, go before me ; Firk,
follow me.

FIRK. Firk doth follow : Hodge, pass out in
state   [Exeunt. 189

---

[1] The ship is in the river; there are sugar, civet, almonds,
cambric, and a thousand thousand things, God's sacrament !
take it, master ; you shall have a good bargain.

[2] Yes, yes, I have drunk well.

SCENE II.—London: a Room in LINCOLN's House.

Enter the EARL OF LINCOLN and DODGER.

LINCOLN. How now, good Dodger, what's the
news in France ?

DODGER. My lord, upon the eighteenth day of
May
The French and English were prepared to fight ;
Each side with eager fury gave the sign
Of a most hot encounter. Five long hours
Both armies fought together ; at the length
The lot of victory fell on our sides.
Twelve thousand of the Frenchmen that day died,
Four thousand English, and no man of name
But Captain Hyam and young Ardington,   10
Two gallant gentlemen, I knew them well.

LINCOLN. But Dodger, prithee, tell me, in this
fight
How did my cousin Lacy bear himself ?

DODGER. My lord, your cousin Lacy was not
there.

LINCOLN. Not there ?

DODGER.   No, my good lord.

LINCOLN.   Sure, thou mistakest.
I saw him shipped, and a thousand eyes beside
Were witnesses of the farewells which he gave,
When I, with weeping eyes, bid him adieu.
Dodger, take heed.

DODGER.   My lord, I am advised,
That what I spake is true : to prove it so,   20
His cousin Askew, that supplied his place,
Sent me for him from France, that secretly
He might convey himself thither.[1]

LINCOLN.   Is't even so ?
Dares he so carelessly venture his life
Upon the indignation of a king ?
Has he despised my love, and spurned those
favours

---

[1] 'hither' in all the quartos.

Which I with prodigal hand poured on his head ?
He shall repent his rashness with his soul ;
Since of my love he makes no estimate,
I'll make him wish he had not known my hate. 30
Thou hast no other news ?

DODGER.   None else, my lord.

LINCOLN. None worse I know thou hast.—
   Procure the king
To crown his giddy brows with ample honours,
Send him chief colonel, and all my hope
Thus to be dashed ! But 'tis in vain to grieve,
One evil cannot a worse [one] [1] relieve.
Upon my life, I have found out his plot ;
That old dog, Love, that fawned upon him so,
Love to that puling girl, his fair-cheeked Rose,
The lord mayor's daughter, hath distracted him, 40
And in the fire of that love's lunacy
Hath he burnt up himself, consumed his credit.
Lost the king's love, yea, and I fear, his life,
Only to get a wanton to his wife,
Dodger, it is so.

DODGER.   I fear so, my good lord.

LINCOLN. It is so—nay, sure it cannot be ! [2]
I am at my wits' end. Dodger !

DODGER.   Yea, my lord.

LINCOLN. Thou art acquainted with my ne-
   phew's haunts ;
Spend this gold for thy pains ; go seek him out ;
Watch at my lord mayor's—there if he live, 50
Dodger, thou shalt be sure to meet with him.
Prithee, be diligent.—Lacy, thy name
Lived once in honour, now ['tis] dead in shame.—
Be circumspect.   [Exit.

DODGER.   I warrant you, my lord.   [Exit.

---

[1] Fritsche's conjecture; W. and Pr. suggest 'more worse',
and cite *Lear* II. ii. 155.
[2] In this line the pause takes the time of a beat.

Scene III.—London : a Room in the Lord Mayor's House.

Enter the Lord Mayor *and Master* Scott.

lord mayor.   Good Master Scott, I have been
 bold with you,
To be a witness to a wedding-knot
Betwixt young Master Hammon and my daughter.
O, stand aside ; see where the lovers come.

Enter Master Hammon *and* Rose.

rose.   Can it be possible you love me so ?
No, no, within those eyeballs I espy
Apparent likelihoods of flattery.
Pray now, let go my hand.
hammon.   Sweet Mistress Rose,
Misconstrue not my words, nor misconceive
Of my affection, whose devoted soul   10
Swears that I love thee dearer than my heart.
rose.   As dear as your own heart ? I judge it
 right ;
Men love their hearts best when th' are out of sight.
hammon.   I love you, by this hand.
rose.   Yet hands off now !
If flesh be frail, how weak and frail 's your vow !
hammon.   Then by my life I swear.
rose.   Then do not brawl ;
One quarrel loseth wife and life and all.
Is not your meaning thus ?
hammon.   In faith, you jest.
rose.   Love loves to sport ; therefore leave love,
 y' are best.   19
lord mayor.   What ? square they, Master Scott ?
scott.   Sir, never doubt,
Lovers are quickly in, and quickly out.
hammon.   Sweet Rose, be not so strange in
 fancying me.
Nay, never turn aside, shun not my sight :
I am not grown so fond, to fond [1] my love
On any that shall quit it with disdain ;

    [1] Another spelling of 'found'.

If you will love me, so—if not, farewell.

LORD MAYOR. Why, how now, lovers, are you
    both agreed ?

HAMMON. Yes, faith, my lord.

LORD MAYOR. 'Tis well, give me your hand.

Give me yours, daughter.—How now, both pull
    back ?

What means this, girl ?

ROSE.   I mean to live a maid.

HAMMON. [Aside.] But not to die one ; pause,
    ere that be said.   31

LORD MAYOR. Will you still cross me, still be
    obstinate ?

HAMMON. Nay, chide her not, my lord, for
    doing well ;

If she can live an happy virgin's life,

'Tis far more blessed than to be a wife.

ROSE. Say, sir, I cannot : I have made a vow,

Whoever be my husband, 'tis not you.

LORD MAYOR. Your tongue is quick ; but
    Master Hammon, know,

I bade you welcome to another end.

HAMMON. What, would you have me pule and
    pine and pray,   40

    With ' lovely lady ', ' mistress of my heart ',

' Pardon your servant ', and the rhymer play,

    Railing on Cupid and his tyrant's-dart ;

Or shall I undertake some martial spoil,

Wearing your glove at tourney and at tilt,

And tell how many gallants I unhorsed—

Sweet, will this pleasure you ?

ROSE.   Yea, when wilt begin ?

What, love rhymes, man ? Fie on that deadly sin !

LORD MAYOR. If you will have her, I'll make
    her agree.

HAMMON. Enforced love is worse than hate to me.

[Aside.] There is a wench keeps shop in the Old
    Change,   51

To her will I ; it is not wealth I seek,

I have enough, and will prefer her love

Before the world.—[Aloud.]   My good lord mayor,
  adieu.
Old love for me, I have no luck with new.   [Exit.
  LORD MAYOR.   Now, mammet,[1] you have well
    behaved yourself,
But you shall curse your coyness if I live.—
Who's within there ? See you convey your mistress
Straight to th' Old Ford ! I'll keep you straight
  enough.
Fore God, I would have sworn the puling girl 60
Would willingly accept of [2] Hammon's love ;
But banish him, my thoughts !—Go, minion, in !
                                          [Exit ROSE.
Now tell me, Master Scott, would you have thought
That Master Simon Eyre, the shoemaker,
Had been of wealth to buy such merchandise ?
  SCOTT.   'Twas well, my lord, your honour and
    myself
Grew partners with him ; for your bills of lading
Shew that Eyre's gains in one commodity
Rise at the least to full three thousand pound
Besides like gain in other merchandise. 70
  LORD MAYOR.   Well, he shall spend some of his
    thousands now,
For I have sent for him to the Guildhall.

Enter EYRE.

See, where he comes. Good morrow, Master Eyre.
  EYRE.   Poor Simon Eyre, my lord, your shoe-
    maker.
  LORD MAYOR.   Well, well, it likes yourself to
    term you so.

Enter DODGER.

Now, Master Dodger, what's the news with you ?
  DODGER.   I'd gladly speak in private to your
    honour.

[1] Doll, puppet.
[2] Fritsche's conjecture for ' accepted Hammon's ' of the
quartos.

LORD MAYOR. You shall, you shall.—Master
　Eyre and Master Scott,
I have some business with this gentleman ;
I pray, let me entreat you to walk before　　　　80
To the Guildhall ; I'll follow presently.
Master Eyre, I hope ere noon to call you sheriff.
　　EYRE. I would not care, my lord, if you might
call me King of Spain.—Come, Master Scott.
　　　　　　　　　　[Exeunt EYRE and SCOTT.
　　LORD MAYOR. Now, Master Dodger, what's the
news you bring ?
　　DODGER. The Earl of Lincoln by me greets
　　your lordship,
And earnestly requests you, if you can,
Inform him, where his nephew Lacy keeps.
　　LORD MAYOR. Is not his nephew Lacy now in
　　France ?
　　DODGER. No, I assure your lordship, but dis-
　　guised　　　　　　　　　　　　　　　90
Lurks here in London.
　　LORD MAYOR.　　　　London ? is 't even so ?
It may be ; but upon my faith and soul,
I know not where he lives, or whether he lives :
So tell my Lord of Lincoln.—Lurks in London ?
Well, Master Dodger, you perhaps may start him ;
Be but the means to rid him into France,
I'll give you a dozen angels for your pains :
So much I love his honour, hate his nephew.
And, prithee, so inform thy lord from me.
　　DODGER. I take my leave.　　[Exit DODGER.
　　LORD MAYOR. Farewell, good Master Dodger.
Lacy in London ? I dare pawn my life,　　　101
My daughter knows thereof, and for that cause
Denied young Master Hammon in his love.
Well, I am glad I sent her to Old Ford.
Gods Lord, 'tis late ; to Guildhall I must hie ;
I know my brethren stay my company.　　[Exit.

SCENE IV.—London : a Room in EYRE's House.

Enter FIRK, MARGERY, HANS, and HODGE.

MARGERY. Thou goest too fast for me, Roger.
O, Firk !

FIRK. Ay, forsooth.

MARGERY. I pray thee, run—do you hear ?—
run to Guildhall, and learn if my husband, Master
Eyre, will take that worshipful vocation of Master
Sheriff upon him. Hie thee, good Firk.

FIRK. Take it ? Well, I go ; an he should
not take it, Firk swears to forswear him. Yes,
forsooth, I go to Guildhall.   10

MARGERY. Nay, when ? thou art too com-
pendious and tedious.

FIRK. O rare, your excellence is full of eloquence. [Aside.] How like a new cart-wheel my dame
speaks, and she looks like an old musty ale-bottle
going to scalding.

MARGERY. Nay, when ? thou wilt make me
melancholy.   18

FIRK. God forbid your worship should fall into
that humour ;—I run.   [Exit.

MARGERY. Let me see now, Roger and Hans.

HODGE. Ay, forsooth, dame—mistress I should
say, but the old term so sticks to the roof of my
mouth, I can hardly lick it off.

MARGERY. Even what thou wilt, good Roger ;
dame is a fair name for any honest Christian ; but
let that pass. How dost thou, Hans ?

HANS. Mee tanck you, vro.[1]   28

MARGERY. Well, Hans and Roger, you see, God
hath blest your master, and, perdy, if ever he
comes to be Master Sheriff of London—as we are
all mortal—you shall see, I will have some odd
thing or other in a corner for you : I will not be
your back-friend ;[2] but let that pass. Hans, pray
thee, tie my shoe.

---

[1] I thank you, mistress.   [2] False friend.

HANS. Yaw, ic sal, vro.[1]

MARGERY. Roger, thou know'st the length of my foot ; as it is none of the biggest, so I thank God, it is handsome enough ; prithee, let me have a pair of shoes made, cork, good Roger, wooden heel too. 41

HODGE. You shall.

MARGERY. Art thou acquainted with never a farthingale-maker, nor a French hood-maker ? I must enlarge my bum, ha, ha ! How shall I look in a hood, I wonder ! Perdy, oddly, I think.

HODGE. [Aside.] As a cat out of a pillory.—Very well, I warrant you, mistress.

MARGERY. Indeed, all flesh is grass ; and, Roger, canst thou tell where I may buy a good hair ? 51

HODGE. Yes, forsooth, at the poulterer's in Gracious Street.[2]

MARGERY. Thou art an ungracious wag ; perdy, I mean a false hair for my periwig.

HODGE. Why, mistress, the next time I cut my beard, you shall have the shavings of it ; but they are all true hairs.

MARGERY. It is very hot, I must get me a fan or else a mask. 60

HODGE. [Aside.] So you had need, to hide your wicked face.

MARGERY. Fie, upon it, how costly this world's calling is ; perdy, but that it is one of the wonderful works of God, I would not deal with it. Is not Firk come yet ? Hans, be not so sad, let it pass and vanish, as my husband's worship says.[3]

HANS. Ick bin vrolicke, lot see yow soo.[3]

HODGE. Mistress, will you drink a pipe of tobacco ? 70

---

[1] Yes, I will, mistress.

[2] A corruption of Grass-church (now Gracechurch) Street, called after St. Bennet's, known as the Grass Church from 'the Herbe market there kept '.—*Stow*, p. 214 (1603).

[3] I am merry ; let 's see you so.

MARGERY. Oh, fie upon it, Roger, perdy!
These filthy tobacco-pipes are the most idle
slavering baubles that ever I felt. Out upon it!
God bless us, men look not like men that use
them.

Enter RALPH, being lame.

HODGE. What, fellow Ralph? Mistress, look
here, Jane's husband! Why, how now, lame?
Hans, make much of him, he's a brother of our
trade, a good workman, and a tall soldier.

HANS. You be welcome, broder.   80

MARGERY. Perdy, I knew him not. How dost
thou, good Ralph? I am glad to see thee well.

RALPH. I would [to] God you saw me, dame, as
    well
As when I went from London into France.

MARGERY. Trust me, I am sorry, Ralph, to see
thee impotent. Lord, how the wars have made
him sunburnt! The left leg is not well; 'twas
a fair gift of God the infirmity took not hold a
little higher, considering thou camest from France;
but let that pass.   90

RALPH. I am glad to see you well, and I rejoice
To hear that God hath blest my master so
Since my departure.

MARGERY. Yea, truly, Ralph, I thank my
Maker; but let that pass.

HODGE. And, sirrah Ralph, what news, what
    news in France?

RALPH. Tell me, good Roger, first, what news
    in England?
How does my Jane? When didst thou see my
    wife?
Where lives my poor heart? She'll be poor indeed,
Now I want limbs to get whereon to feed.   100

HODGE. Limbs? Hast thou not hands, man?
Thou shalt never see a shoemaker want bread,
though he have but three fingers on a hand.

RALPH. Yet all this while I hear not of my Jane.

MARGERY. O Ralph, your wife,—perdy, we know not what's become of her. She was here a while, and because she was married, grew more stately than became her ; I checked her, and so forth ; away she flung, never returned, nor said bye nor bah ; [1] and, Ralph, you know, ' ka me, ka thee.' [2] And so, as I tell ye— Roger, is not Firk come yet ?   112

HODGE. No, forsooth.

MARGERY. And so, indeed, we heard not of her, but I hear she lives in London ; but let that pass. If she had wanted, she might have opened her case to me or my husband, or to any of my men ; I am sure, there's not any of them, perdy, but would have done her good to his power. Hans, look if Firk be come.   120

HANS. Yaw, ik sal, vro.   [Exit HANS.

MARGERY. And so, as I said—but, Ralph, why dost thou weep ? Thou knowest that naked we came out of our mother's womb, and naked we must return ; and, therefore, thank God for all things.

HODGE. No, faith, Jane is a stranger here ; but, Ralph, pull up a good heart, I know thou hast one. Thy wife, man, is in London ; one told me, he saw her awhile ago very brave and neat ; we'll ferret her out, an London hold her.   131

MARGERY. Alas, poor soul, he's overcome with sorrow ; he does but as I do, weep for the loss of any good thing. But, Ralph, get thee in, call for some meat and drink, thou shalt find me worshipful towards thee.

RALPH. I thank you, dame ; since I want limbs and lands,   137
I'll trust to God, my good friends, and my hands.[3]
                                        [Exit.

---

[1] A farewell, courteous or insulting.

[2] Serve me, and I'll serve thee.

[3] ' I'll to God, my good friends, and to these my hands,' 1600, 1610. ' I'll trust to God, my good friends, and to my hands,' the three other quartos.

Enter HANS *and* FIRK *running.*

FIRK. Run, good Hans ! O Hodge, O mistress !
Hodge, heave up thine ears ; mistress, smug up [1]
your looks ; on with your best apparel ; my master
is chosen, my master is called, nay, condemned by
the cry of the country to be sheriff of the city
for this famous year now to come. And time now
being, a great many men in black gowns were
asked for their voices and their hands, and my
master had all their fists about his ears presently,
and they cried ' Ay, ay, ay, ay ',—and so I came
away—

    Wherefore without all other grieve   150
    I do salute you, Mistress Shrieve.[2]

HANS. Yaw, my mester is de groot man, de
shrieve.

HODGE. Did not I tell you, mistress ? Now
I may boldly say : Good-morrow to your worship.

MARGERY. Good-morrow, good Roger. I thank
you, my good people all.—Firk, hold up thy hand :
here 's a threepenny piece for thy tidings.

FIRK. 'Tis but three-half-pence, I think. Yes,
'tis three-pence, I smell the rose.[3]   160

HODGE. But, mistress, be ruled by me, and do
not speak so pulingly.

FIRK. 'Tis her worship speaks so, and not she.
No, faith, mistress, speak me in the old key :
' To it, Firk ', ' there, good Firk ', ' ply your
business, Hodge ', ' Hodge, with a full mouth ',
' I'll fill your bellies with good cheer, till they
cry twang '.

Enter EYRE *wearing a gold chain.*

HANS. See, myn liever broder, heer compt my
meester.   170

---

[1] Smarten up.   [2] Sheriff.
[3] Firk seems to have confused the coins : from 1561 silver
threepences and three-half-pences were issued with a rose
at the back of the Queen's head ; the groat (4*d.*) and the
half-groat had no rose.—Hawkins, *Silver Coins of England.*

MARGERY. Welcome home, Master Shrieve;
I pray God continue you in health and wealth.

EYRE. See here, my Maggy, a chain, a gold
chain for Simon Eyre. I shall make thee a lady;
here's a French hood for thee; on with it, on with
it! dress thy brows with this flap of a shoulder
of mutton,[1] to make thee look lovely. Where be
my fine men? Roger, I'll make over my shop and
tools to thee; Firk, thou shalt be the foreman;
Hans, thou shalt have an hundred for twenty.[2]
Be as mad knaves as your master Sim Eyre hath
been, and you shall live to be Sheriffs of London.—
How dost thou like me, Margery? Prince am I none,
yet am I princely born. Firk, Hodge, and Hans!

ALL THREE. Ay, forsooth, what says your
worship, Master[3] Sheriff? 186

EYRE. Worship and honour, you Babylonian
knaves, for the Gentle Craft. But I forgot myself;
I am bidden by my lord mayor to dinner to Old
Ford; he's gone before, I must after. Come,
Madge, on with your trinkets! Now, my true
Trojans, my fine Firk, my dapper Hodge, my
honest Hans, some device, some odd crotchets,
some morris, or such like, for the honour of the
gentlemen shoemakers. Meet me at Old Ford,
you know my mind. Come, Madge, away. Shut
up the shop, knaves, and make holiday. [Exeunt.

FIRK. O rare! O brave! Come, Hodge;
follow me, Hans; 198
We'll be with them for a morris-dance. [Exeunt.

SCENE V.—A Room at Old Ford.

Enter the LORD MAYOR, ROSE, EYRE, MARGERY in a French
hood, SYBIL, and other Servants.

LORD MAYOR. Trust me, you are as welcome to
Old Ford
As I myself.

---

[1] A hood. [2] i.e. For the twenty Portuguese previously lent.
[3] 'Mistris' in the four earliest quartos.

MARGERY. Truly, I thank your lordship.

LORD MAYOR. Would our bad cheer were worth the thanks you give.

EYRE. Good cheer, my lord mayor, fine cheer ! A fine house, fine walls, all fine and neat.

LORD MAYOR. Now, by my troth, I'll tell thee, Master Eyre,
It does me good, and all my brethren,
That such a madcap fellow as thyself
Is entered into our society. 9

MARGERY. Ay, but, my lord, he must learn now to put on gravity.

EYRE. Peace, Maggy, a fig for gravity ! When I go to Guildhall in my scarlet gown, I'll look as demurely as a saint, and speak as gravely as a justice of peace ; but now I am here at Old Ford, at my good lord mayor's house, let it go by, vanish, Maggy, I'll be merry ; away with flip-flap, these fooleries, these gulleries. What, honey ? Prince am I none, yet am I princely born. What says my lord mayor ? 20

LORD MAYOR. Ha, ha, ha ! I had rather than a thousand pound,
I had an heart but half so light as yours.

EYRE. Why, what should I do, my lord ? A pound of care pays not a dram of debt. Hum, let's be merry, whiles we are young ; old age, sack and sugar will steal upon us, ere we be aware.

LORD MAYOR. It's well done ; Mistress Eyre, pray, give good counsel
To my daughter.

MARGERY. I hope, Mistress Rose will have the grace to take nothing that's bad. 30

LORD MAYOR. Pray God she do ; for i' faith, Mistress Eyre,
I would bestow upon that peevish girl
A thousand marks more than I mean to give her
Upon condition she'd be ruled by me.
The ape still crosseth me. There came of late
A proper gentleman of fair revenues,

Whom gladly I would call [a] son-in-law :
But my fine cockney would have none of him.
You'll prove a coxcomb for it, ere you die :
A courtier, or no man must please your eye.   40

EYRE. Be ruled, sweet Rose : th' art ripe for a
man. Marry not with a boy that has no more
hair on his face than thou hast on thy cheeks.
A courtier ? wash,[1] go by ! stand not upon
pishery-pashery : those silken fellows are but
painted images, outsides, outsides, Rose ; their
inner linings are torn. No, my fine mouse, marry
me with a gentleman grocer like my lord mayor,
your father ; a grocer is a sweet trade : plums,
plums. Had I a son or daughter should marry out
of the generation and blood of the shoemakers, he
should pack ; what, the Gentle Trade is a living
for a man through Europe, through the world.
              [A noise within of a tabor and a pipe.

LORD MAYOR. What noise is this ?   54

EYRE. O my lord mayor, a crew of good fellows
that for love to your honour are come hither with
a morris-dance. Come in, my Mesopotamians,
cheerily.

Enter HODGE, HANS, RALPH, FIRK, and other Shoemakers, in
    a morris ; after a little dancing the LORD MAYOR speaks.

LORD MAYOR. Master Eyre, are all these shoe-
    makers ?   59

EYRE. All cordwainers, my good lord mayor.

ROSE. [Aside.] How like my Lacy looks yond'
    shoemaker !

HANS. [Aside.] O that I durst but speak unto my
    love !

LORD MAYOR. Sybil, go fetch some wine to
    make these drink.
You are all welcome.

ALL.   We thank your lordship.
              [ROSE takes a cup of wine and goes to HANS.

        [1] Nonsense.

ROSE. For his sake whose fair shape thou
    represent'st,
Good friend, I drink to thee.

HANS. Ic bedancke, good frister.[1]

MARGERY. I see, Mistress Rose, you do not
want judgment ; you have drunk to the properest
man I keep.   70

FIRK. Here be some have done their parts to
be as proper as he.

LORD MAYOR. Well, urgent business calls me
    back to London :
Good fellows, first go in and taste our cheer ;
And to make merry as you homeward go,
Spend these two angels in beer at Stratford-Bow.

EYRE. To these two, my mad lads, Sim Eyre adds
another ; then cheerily, Firk ; tickle it, Hans, and
all for the honour of shoemakers. [All go dancing out.

LORD MAYOR. Come, Master Eyre, let's have
    your company.   [Exeunt.

ROSE.   Sybil, what shall I do ?

SYBIL.   Why, what's the matter ?

ROSE. That Hans the shoemaker is my love
    Lacy,   82
Disguised in that attire to find me out.
How should I find the means to speak with him ?

SYBIL. What, mistress, never fear ; I dare
venture my maidenhead to nothing, and that's
great odds, that Hans the Dutchman, when we
come to London, shall not only see and speak with
you, but in spite of all your father's policies [2] steal
you away and marry you. Will not this please
you ?   91

ROSE. Do this, and ever be assured of my love.

SYBIL. Away, then, and follow your father to
London, lest your absence cause him to suspect
something :
    To-morrow, if my counsel be obeyed,
    I'll bind you prentice to the Gentle Trade.
                                        [Exeunt.

---

[1] I thank you, good maid.   [2] Devices.

ACT THE FOURTH

Scene I.—A Street in London.

JANE in a Seamster's shop, working. Enter Master
HAMMON, muffled; he stands aloof.

HAMMON. Yonder's the shop, and there my
    fair love sits.
She's fair and lovely, but she is not mine.
O, would she were ! Thrice have I courted her,
Thrice hath my hand been moistened with her
    hand,
Whilst my poor famished eyes do feed on that
Which made them famish. I am infortunate :
I still love one, yet nobody loves me.
I muse, in other men what women see,
That I so want ! Fine Mistress Rose was coy,
And this too curious ![1] Oh, no, she is chaste,   10
And for she thinks me wanton, she denies
To cheer my cold heart with her sunny eyes.
How prettily she works, oh pretty hand !
Oh happy work ! It doth me good to stand
Unseen to see her. Thus I oft have stood
In frosty evenings, a light burning by her,
Enduring biting cold, only to eye her.
One only look hath seemed as rich to me
As a king's crown ; such is love's lunacy.
Muffled I'll pass along, and by that try   20
Whether she know me.
JANE.   Sir, what is't you buy ?
What is't you lack, sir, calico, or lawn,
Fine cambric shirts, or bands, what will you buy ?
HAMMON. [Aside.] That which thou wilt not sell.
    Faith, yet I'll try :
How do you sell this handkercher ?
JANE.   Good cheap.
HAMMON. And how these ruffs ?
JANE.   Cheap too.

[1] Fastidious.

HAMMON. And how this band?

JANE. Cheap too.

HAMMON. All cheap; how sell you then this hand?

JANE. My hands are not to be sold.

HAMMON. To be given then! Nay, faith, I come to buy.

JANE. But none knows when.

HAMMON. Good sweet, leave work a little while; let's play. 30

JANE. I cannot live by keeping holiday.

HAMMON. I'll pay you for the time which shall be lost.

JANE. With me you shall not be at so much cost.

HAMMON. Look, how you wound this cloth, so you wound me.

JANE. It may be so.

HAMMON. 'Tis so.

JANE. What remedy?

HAMMON. Nay, faith, you are too coy.

JANE. Let go my hand.

HAMMON. I will do any task at your command; I would let go this beauty, were I not In mind to disobey you by a power That controls kings: I love you!

JANE. So, now part.

HAMMON. With hands I may, but never with my heart. 41 In faith, I love you.

JANE. I believe you do.

HAMMON. Shall a true love in me breed hate in you?

JANE. I hate you not.

HAMMON. Then you must love?

JANE. I do. What are you better now? I love not you.

HAMMON. All this, I hope, is but a woman's fray, That means: come to me, when she cries: away!

In earnest, mistress,[1] I do not jest,
A true chaste love hath entered in my breast.
I love you dearly, as I love my life,   50
I love you as a husband loves a wife ;
That, and no other love, my love requires.
Thy wealth, I know, is little ; my desires
Thirst not for gold. Sweet, beauteous Jane, what's
    mine
Shall, if thou make myself thine, all be thine.
Say, judge, what is thy sentence, life or death ?
Mercy or cruelty lies in thy breath.

    JANE.   Good sir, I do believe you love me well ;
For 'tis a silly conquest, silly pride
For one like you—I mean a gentleman—   60
To boast that by his love-tricks he hath brought
Such and such women to his amorous lure ;
I think you do not so, yet many do,
And make it even a very trade to woo.
I could be coy, as many women be,
Feed you with sunshine smiles and wanton looks,
But I detest witchcraft ; say that I
Do constantly believe you, constant have——

    HAMMON.   Why dost thou not believe me ?

    JANE.   I believe you ;
But yet, good sir, because I will not grieve you
With hopes to taste fruit which will never fall,
In simple truth this is the sum of all :   72
My husband lives, at least, I hope he lives.
Pressed was he to these bitter wars in France ;
Bitter they are to me by wanting him.
I have but one heart, and that heart's his due.
How can I then bestow the same on you ?
Whilst he lives, his I live, be it ne'er so poor,
And rather be his wife than a king's whore.

    HAMMON.   Chaste and dear woman, I will not
    abuse thee,   80
Although it cost my life, if thou refuse me.
Thy husband, pressed for France, what was his
    name ?

                [1] A trisyllable.

JANE.   Ralph Damport.

HAMMON.   Damport ?—Here's a letter sent
From France to me, from a dear friend of mine,
A gentleman of place ; here he doth write
Their names that have been slain in every fight.

JANE.   I hope death's scroll contains not my
love's name.

HAMMON.   Cannot you read ?

JANE.   I can.

HAMMON.   Peruse the same.
To my remembrance such a name I read   89
Amongst the rest. See here.

JANE.   Ay me, he's dead !
He's dead ! if this be true, my dear heart's slain !

HAMMON.   Have patience, dear love.

JANE.   Hence, hence !

HAMMON.   Nay, sweet Jane,
Make not poor sorrow proud with these rich tears.
I mourn thy husband's death, because thou
mourn'st.

JANE.   That bill is forged ; 'tis signed by forgery.

HAMMON.   I'll bring thee letters sent besides to
many,
Carrying the like report : Jane, 'tis too true.
Come, weep not : mourning, though it rise from
love,
Helps not the mournèd, yet hurts them that mourn.

JANE.   For God's sake, leave me.

HAMMON.   Whither dost thou turn ?
Forget the dead, love them that are alive ;   101
His love is faded, try how mine will thrive.

JANE.   'Tis now no time for me to think on love.

HAMMON.   'Tis now best time for you to think
on love,
Because your love lives not.

JANE.   Though he be dead,
My love to him shall not be buried ;
For God's sake, leave me to myself alone.

HAMMON.   'Twould kill my soul, to leave thee
drowned in moan.

Answer me to my suit, and I am gone ;
Say to me yea or no.   No.
> JANE.
> HAMMON.   Then farewell !   110
One farewell will not serve, I come again ;
Come, dry these wet cheeks ; tell me, faith, sweet
> Jane,
Yea or no, once more.
> JANE.   Once more I say, no ;
Once more be gone, I pray ; else will I go.
> HAMMON.   Nay, then I will grow rude, by this
> white hand,
Until you change that cold ' no ' ; here I'll stand
Till by your hard heart——
> JANE.   Nay, for God's love, peace !
My sorrows by your presence more increase.
Not that you thus are present, but all grief
Desires to be alone ; therefore in brief   120
Thus much I say, and saying bid adieu :
If ever I wed man, it shall be you.
> HAMMON.   O blessed voice ! Dear Jane, I'll urge
> no more,
Thy breath hath made me rich.
> JANE.   Death makes me poor.
[Exeunt.

SCENE II.—London : a Street before HODGE's Shop.

HODGE, at his shop-board, RALPH, FIRK, HANS, and
a Boy at work.

ALL.   Hey, down a down, derry.

HODGE.   Well said, my hearts ; ply your work
to-day, we loitered yesterday ; to it pell-mell, that
we may live to be lord mayors, or aldermen at least.

FIRK.   Hey, down a down, derry.

HODGE.   Well said, i' faith ! How say'st thou,
Hans, doth not Firk tickle it ?

HANS.   Yaw, mester.

FIRK.   Not so neither, my organ-pipe squeaks
this morning for want of liquoring. Hey, down
a down, derry !   11

HANS.   Forward, Firk, tow best un jolly yongster.
Hort, ay, mester, ic bid yo, cut me un pair vampres
vor Mester Jeffre's boots.[1]

HODGE.   Thou shalt, Hans.

FIRK.   Master !

HODGE.   How now, boy ?

FIRK.   Pray, now you are in the cutting vein,
cut me out a pair of counterfeits, or else my work
will not pass current ; hey, down a down !   20

HODGE.   Tell me, sirs, are my cousin Mistress
Priscilla's shoes done ?

FIRK.   Your cousin ? No, master ; one of your
aunts,[2] hang her ; let them alone.

RALPH.   I am in hand with them ; she gave
charge that none but I should do them for her.

FIRK.   Thou do for her ? then 'twill be a lame
doing, and that she loves not. Ralph, thou
might'st have sent her to me, in faith, I would
have yearked and firked your Priscilla. Hey,
down a down, derry. This gear will not hold.

HODGE.   How say'st thou, Firk, were we not
merry at Old Ford ?   33

FIRK.   How, merry ? why, our buttocks went
jiggy-joggy like a quagmire. Well, Sir Roger
Oatmeal, if I thought all meal of that nature,
I would eat nothing but bagpuddings.

RALPH.   Of all good fortunes my fellow Hans
had the best.

FIRK.   'Tis true, because Mistress Rose drank
to him.   41

HODGE.   Well, well, work apace. They say,
seven of the aldermen be dead, or very sick.

FIRK.   I care not, I'll be none.

RALPH.   No, nor I ; but then my Master Eyre
will come quickly to be lord mayor.

[1] Forward, Firk, thou art a jolly youngster. Hark, ay,
master, I bid you, cut me a pair of vamps for Master Jeffrey's
boots. 'Vamps,' upper leathers of a shoe.

[2] A cant term for a prostitute or procuress.

C

Enter SYBIL.

FIRK.   Whoop, yonder comes Sybil.

HODGE.   Sybil, welcome, i' faith ; and how dost thou, mad wench ?

FIRK.   Syb-whore, welcome to London.   50

SYBIL.   Godamercy, sweet Firk ; good lord, Hodge, what a delicious shop you have got ! You tickle it, i' faith.

RALPH.   Godamercy, Sybil, for our good cheer at Old Ford.

SYBIL.   That you shall have, Ralph.

FIRK.   Nay, by the mass, we had tickling cheer, Sybil ; and how the plague dost thou and Mistress Rose and my lord mayor ? I put the women in first.   60

SYBIL.   Well, Godamercy ; but God's me, I forget myself, where 's Hans the Fleming ?

FIRK.   Hark, butter-box, now you must yelp out some spreken.

HANS.   Wat begaie you ? Vat vod you, Frister ?[1]

SYBIL.   Marry, you must come to my young mistress, to pull on her shoes you made last.

HANS.   Vare ben your egle fro, vare ben your mistris ?[2]

SYBIL.   Marry, here at our London house in Cornhill.   71

FIRK.   Will nobody serve her turn but Hans ?

SYBIL.   No, sir. Come, Hans, I stand upon needles.

HODGE.   Why then, Sybil, take heed of pricking.

SYBIL.   For that let me alone. I have a trick in my budget. Come, Hans.

HANS.   Yaw, yaw, ic sall meete yo gane.[3]

[Exit HANS and SYBIL.

HODGE.   Go, Hans, make haste again. Come, who lacks work ?   80

[1] What do you want ? what would you, girl ?
[2] Where is your noble lady, where is your mistress ?
[3] Yes, yes, I will go with you.

FIRK. I, master, for I lack my breakfast; 'tis munching-time and past.

HODGE. Is't so? why, then leave work, Ralph. To breakfast! Boy, look to the tools. Come, Ralph; come, Firk. [Exeunt.

Enter a Serving-man.

SERVING-MAN. Let me see now, the sign of the Last in Tower Street. Mass, yonder's the house. What, haw! Who's within?

Enter RALPH.

RALPH. Who calls there? What want you, sir? 90

SERVING-MAN. Marry, I would have a pair of shoes made for a gentlewoman against to-morrow morning. What, can you do them?

RALPH. Yes, sir, you shall have them. But what length's her foot?

SERVING-MAN. Why, you must make them in all parts like this shoe; but, at any hand, fail not to do them, for the gentlewoman is to be married very early in the morning.

RALPH. How? by this shoe must it be made? by this? Are you sure, sir, by this? 101

SERVING-MAN. How, by this? Am I sure, by this? Art thou in thy wits? I tell thee, I must have a pair of shoes, dost thou mark me? a pair of shoes, two shoes, made by this very shoe, this same shoe, against to-morrow morning by four a clock. Dost understand me? Canst thou do't?

RALPH. Yes, sir, yes—ay, ay!—I can do't. By this shoe, you say? I should know this shoe. Yes, sir, yes, by this shoe, I can do't. Four a clock, well. Whither shall I bring them? 111

SERVING-MAN. To the sign of the Golden Ball in Watling Street; enquire for one Master Hammon, a gentleman, my master.

RALPH. Yea, sir; by this shoe, you say?

SERVING-MAN. I say, Master Hammon at the

Golden Ball; he's the bridegroom, and those shoes
are for his bride.   118

RALPH.   They shall be done by this shoe; well,
well, Master Hammon at the Golden Shoe—I
would say, the Golden Ball; very well, very well.
But I pray you, sir, where must Master Hammon
be married?

SERVING-MAN.   At Saint Faith's Church, under
Paul's.[1] But what's that to thee? Prithee, dispatch those shoes, and so farewell.   [Exit.

RALPH.   By this shoe, said he. How am I
   amazed
At this strange accident! Upon my life,
This was the very shoe I gave my wife,   129
When I was pressed for France; since when, alas!
I never could hear of her: 'tis the same,
And Hammon's bride no other but my Jane.

Enter FIRK.

FIRK.   'Snails, Ralph, thou hast lost thy part of
three pots, a countryman of mine gave me to
breakfast.

RALPH.   I care not; I have found a better thing.

FIRK.   A thing? away! Is it a man's thing, or
a woman's thing?

RALPH.   Firk, dost thou know this shoe?

FIRK.   No, by my troth; neither doth that
know me! I have no acquaintance with it, 'tis
a mere stranger to me.   142

RALPH.   Why, then I do; this shoe, I durst be
   sworn,
Once covered the instep of my Jane.
This is her size, her breadth, thus trod my love;
These true-love knots I pricked; I hold my life,
By this old shoe I shall find out my wife.

FIRK.   Ha, ha! Old shoe, that wert new! How

---

[1] 'At the west end of this Jesus chapel, under the choir
of Paul's, also was a parish church of St. Faith, commonly
called St. Faith under Paul's.'—*Stow*, p. 331 (1603).

a murrain came this ague-fit of foolishness upon
thee ?   150

RALPH.   Thus, Firk : even now here came a
    serving-man ;
By this shoe would he have a new pair made
Against to-morrow morning for his mistress,
That 's to be married to a gentleman.
And why may not this be my sweet [1] Jane ?

FIRK.   And why may'st not thou be my sweet
ass ? Ha, ha !

RALPH.   Well, laugh and spare not ! But the
    truth is this :
Against to-morrow morning I'll provide
A lusty crew of honest shoemakers,   160
To watch the going of the bride to church.
If she prove Jane, I'll take her in despite
From Hammon and the devil, were he by.
If it be not my Jane, what remedy ?
Hereof I am sure, I shall live till I die,
Although I never with a woman lie.   [Exit.

FIRK.   Thou lie with a woman, to build nothing
but Cripple-gates ! Well, God sends fools fortune,
and it may be, he may light upon his matrimony
by such a device ; for wedding and hanging goes
by destiny.   [Exit.

SCENE III—London : a Room in the LORD MAYOR'S
House in Cornhill.

Enter HANS and ROSE, arm in arm.

HANS.   How happy am I by embracing thee !
Oh, I did fear such cross mishaps did reign,
That I should never see my Rose again.

ROSE.   Sweet Lacy, since fair opportunity
Offers herself to further our escape,
Let not too over-fond esteem of me
Hinder that happy hour. Invent the means,
And Rose will follow thee through all the world.

HANS.   Oh, how I surfeit with excess of joy,

---

[1] A disyllable, as in *Hamlet*, I. iii. 8.

Made happy by thy rich perfection !　　　10
But since thou pay'st sweet interest to my hopes,
Redoubling love on love, let me once more
Like to a bold-faced debtor crave of thee,
This night to steal abroad, and at Eyre's house,
Who now by death of certain aldermen
Is mayor of London, and my master once,
Meet thou thy Lacy, where in spite of change,
Your father's anger, and mine uncle's hate,
Our happy nuptials will we consummate.　　　19

Enter SYBIL.

SYBIL.　Oh God, what will you do, mistress ?
Shift for yourself, your father is at hand ! He's
coming, he's coming ! Master Lacy, hide yourself in
my mistress ! For God's sake, shift for yourselves !

HANS.　Your father come, sweet Rose—what shall
I do ?
Where shall I hide me ?　How shall I escape ?

ROSE.　A man, and want wit in extremity ?
Come, come, be Hans still, play the shoemaker,
Pull on my shoe.

Enter the LORD MAYOR.

HANS.　　　Mass, and that's well remembered.

SYBIL.　Here comes your father.

HANS.　Forware, metresse, 'tis un good skow, it
sal vel dute, or ye sal neit betallen.[1]　　　31

ROSE.　Oh God, it pincheth me ; what will you
do ?

HANS.　[Aside.] Your father's presence pincheth,
not the shoe.

LORD MAYOR.　Well done ; fit my daughter well,
and she shall please thee well.

HANS.　Yaw, yaw, ick weit dat well ; forware,
'tis un good skoo, 'tis gimait van neits leither ; se
euer, mine here.[2]

---

[1] In truth, mistress, 'tis a good shoe, it shall do well, or
you shall not pay.

[2] Yes, yes, I know that well ; in truth, 'tis a good shoe,
'tis made of neat's leather ; only look, sir !

Enter a Prentice.

LORD MAYOR. I do believe it.—What's the news
with you ?

PRENTICE. Please you, the Earl of Lincoln at
the gate   40
Is newly 'lighted, and would speak with you.

LORD MAYOR. The Earl of Lincoln come to
speak with me ?
Well, well, I know his errand. Daughter Rose,
Send hence your shoemaker, dispatch, have done !
Syb, make things handsome ! Sir boy, follow me.

[Exit.

HANS. Mine uncle come ! Oh, what may this
portend ?
Sweet Rose, this of our love threatens an end.

ROSE. Be not dismayed at this ; whate'er befall,
Rose is thine own. To witness I speak truth,
Where thou appoint'st the place, I'll meet with
thee.   50
I will not fix a day to follow thee,
But presently steal hence. Do not reply :
Love which gave strength to bear my father's hate,
Shall now add wings to further our escape.

[Exeunt.

SCENE IV.—Another Room in the same House.

Enter the LORD MAYOR and the EARL OF LINCOLN.

LORD MAYOR. Believe me, on my credit, I speak
truth :
Since first your nephew Lacy went to France,
I have not seen him. It seemed strange to me,
When Dodger told me that he stayed behind,
Neglecting the high charge the king imposed.

LINCOLN. Trust me, Sir Roger Oteley, I did
think
Your counsel had given head to this attempt,
Drawn to it by the love he bears your child.
Here I did hope to find him in your house ;
But now I see mine error, and confess,   10

My judgment wronged you by conceiving so.
   LORD MAYOR. Lodge in my house, say you?
     Trust me, my lord,
I love your nephew Lacy too too dearly,
So much to wrong his honour; and he hath done so,
That first gave him advice to stay from France.
To witness I speak truth, I let you know,
How careful I have been to keep my daughter
Free from all conference or speech of him;
Not that I scorn your nephew, but in love
I bear your honour, lest your noble blood   20
Should by my mean worth be dishonoured.
   LINCOLN. [Aside.] How far the churl's tongue
    wanders from his heart!
—Well, well, Sir Roger Oteley, I believe you,
With more than many thanks for the kind love
So much you seem to bear me. But, my lord,
Let me request your help to seek my nephew,
Whom if I find, I'll straight embark for France.
So shall your Rose be free, my thoughts at rest,
And much care die which now lies in my breast.

Enter SYBIL.

   SYBIL. Oh Lord! Help, for God's sake! my
mistress; oh, my young mistress!   31
   LORD MAYOR. Where is thy mistress? What's
    become of her?
   SYBIL. She's gone, she's fled!
   LORD MAYOR.   Gone! Whither is she fled?
   SYBIL. I know not, forsooth; she's fled out of
doors with Hans the shoemaker; I saw them scud,
scud, scud, apace, apace!
   LORD MAYOR. Which way? What, John!
    Where be my men? Which way?
   SYBIL. I know not, an it please your worship.
   LORD MAYOR. Fled with a shoemaker? Can
this be true?
   SYBIL. Oh Lord, sir, as true as God's in
Heaven.   41

LINCOLN. [Aside.] Her love turned shoemaker? I
am glad of this.

LORD MAYOR. A Fleming butter-box, a shoe-
maker !
Will she forget her birth, requite my care
With such ingratitude ? Scorned she young
Hammon
To love a honnikin,[1] a needy knave ?
Well, let her fly, I'll not fly after her,
Let her starve, if she will ; she's none of mine.

LINCOLN. Be not so cruel, sir.

Enter FIRK with shoes.

SYBIL. [Aside.] I am glad, she's 'scaped.

LORD MAYOR. I'll not account of her as of my
child.   50
Was there no better object for her eyes
But a foul drunken lubber, swill-belly,
A shoemaker ? That's brave !

FIRK. Yea, forsooth ; 'tis a very brave shoe,
and as fit as a pudding.

LORD MAYOR. How now, what knave is this?
From whence comest thou ?

FIRK. No knave, sir. I am Firk the shoemaker,
lusty Roger's chief lusty journeyman, and I come
hither to take up the pretty leg of sweet Mistress
Rose, and thus hoping your worship is in as good
health, as I was at the making hereof, I bid you
farewell, yours, Firk.   62

LORD MAYOR. Stay, stay, Sir Knave !

LINCOLN. Come hither, shoemaker !

FIRK. 'Tis happy the knave is put before the
shoemaker, or else I would not have vouchsafed to
come back to you. I am moved, for I stir.

LORD MAYOR. My lord, this villain calls us
knaves by craft.

FIRK. Then 'tis by the Gentle Craft, and to
call one knave gently, is no harm. Sit your worship

---

[1] A term of abuse, not given in *N.E.D.*

merry! [Aside to SYBIL.] Syb, your young mistress—
I'll so bob them, now my Master Eyre is lord
mayor of London.   72
 LORD MAYOR. Tell me, sirrah, whose man are
you ?
 FIRK. I am glad to see your worship so merry.
I have no maw to this gear, no stomach as yet to
a red petticoat.   [Pointing to SYBIL.
 LINCOLN. He means not, sir, to woo you to his
  maid,
But only doth demand whose man you are.
 FIRK. I sing now to the tune of Rogero. Roger,
my fellow, is now my master.   81
 LINCOLN. Sirrah, know'st thou one Hans, a
  shoemaker ?
 FIRK. Hans, shoemaker ? Oh yes, stay, yes,
I have him. I tell you what, I speak it in secret :
Mistress Rose and he are by this time—no, not
so, but shortly are to come over one another with
' Can you dance the shaking of the sheets ? ' It
is that Hans—[Aside.] I'll so gull these ·diggers ! [1]
 LORD MAYOR. Know'st thou, then, where he is ?
 FIRK. Yes, forsooth ; yea, marry !   90
 LINCOLN. Canst [2] thou, in sadness ?
 FIRK. No, forsooth ; no marry !
 LORD MAYOR. Tell me, good honest fellow,
  where he is,
And thou shalt see what I'll bestow of thee.
 FIRK. Honest fellow ? No, sir ; not so, sir ;
my profession is the Gentle Craft ; I care not for
seeing, I love feeling ; let me feel it here ; aurium
tenus, ten pieces of gold ; genuum tenus, ten pieces
of silver ; and then Firk is your man—[Aside] in
a new pair of stretchers.[3]   100
 LORD MAYOR. Here is an angel, part of thy
  reward,
Which I will give thee ; tell me where he is.
 FIRK. No point ! [4] Shall I betray my brother ?

---

[1] i.e. Diggers for information. [2] Knowest.
[3] Lies.   [4] Not a bit !

no ! Shall I prove Judas to Hans ? no ! Shall I cry treason to my corporation ? no, I shall be firked and yerked then. But give me your angel ; your angel shall tell you.

LINCOLN. Do so, good fellow ; 'tis no hurt to thee.

FIRK. Send simpering Syb away. 109

LORD MAYOR. Huswife, get you in. [Exit SYBIL.

FIRK. Pitchers have ears, and maids have wide mouths ; but for Hauns-prauns, upon my word, to-morrow morning he and young Mistress Rose go to this gear, they shall be married together, by this rush, or else turn Firk to a firkin of butter, to tan leather withal.

LORD MAYOR. But art thou sure of this ?

FIRK. Am I sure that Paul's steeple is a handful higher than London Stone.[1] or that the Pissing-Conduit [2] leaks nothing but pure Mother Bunch ? [3] Am I sure I am lusty Firk ? God's nails, do you think I am so base to gull you ? 123

LINCOLN. Where are they married ? Dost thou know the church ?

FIRK. I never go to church, but I know the name of it ; it is a swearing church—stay a while, 'tis—Ay, by the mass, no, no,—tis—Ay, by my troth, no, nor that ; 'tis—Ay, by my faith, that, that, 'tis, Ay, by my Faith's Church under Paul's Cross. There they shall be knit like a pair of stockings in matrimony ; there they'll be inconie.[4]

LINCOLN. Upon my life, my nephew Lacy walks In the disguise of this Dutch shoemaker. 132

FIRK. Yes, forsooth.

[1] A stone now cased in the wall of St. Swithin's Church, Cannon Street, which marked the centre from which the old Roman-roads radiated.

[2] A small conduit erected about 1500 near the Stocks Market where the Mansion House now stands.—*Stow*, pp. 17, 184 (1603).

[3] Here evidently used for water—why is not apparent.

[4] A cant word of unknown origin and meaning ; perhaps 'fine, dainty '

LINCOLN. Doth he not, honest fellow ?

FIRK. No, forsooth ; I think Hans is nobody but Hans, no spirit.

LORD MAYOR. My mind misgives me now, 'tis so, indeed.

LINCOLN. My cousin speaks the language, knows the trade.

LORD MAYOR. Let me request your company, my lord ;
Your honourable presence may, no doubt,   140
Refrain their headstrong rashness, when myself
Going alone perchance may be o'erborne.
Shall I request this favour ?

LINCOLN.   This, or what else.

FIRK. Then you must rise betimes, for they mean to fall to their ' hey-pass and repass ',[1] ' pindy-pandy, which hand will you have,' [2] very early.

LORD MAYOR. My care shall every way equal their haste.
This night accept your lodging in my house,
The earlier shall we stir, and at Saint Faith's
Prevent this giddy hare-brained nuptial.   150
This traffic of hot love shall yield cold gains :
They ban our loves, and we'll forbid their banns.[3]
                                                     [Exit.

LINCOLN. At Saint Faith's Church thou say'st ?

FIRK. Yes, by my [4] troth.

LINCOLN. Be secret, on thy life.   [Exit.

FIRK. Yes, when I kiss your wife ! Ha, ha, here's no craft in the Gentle Craft. I came hither of purpose with shoes to Sir Roger's worship, whilst Rose, his daughter, be cony-catched by Hans. Soft now ; these two gulls will be at Saint Faith's Church to-morrow morning, to take Master Bridegroom and Mistress Bride napping, and they,

---

[1] A juggler's formula.
[2] A term used in a children's game, a small object being hidden in one of two closed hands.
[3] Spelt ' baines ' in the quartos.
[4] ' Their ' in the quartos.

in the meantime, shall chop up the matter at the
Savoy. But the best sport is, Sir Roger Oteley
will find my fellow lame Ralph's wife going to
marry a gentleman, and then he'll stop her instead
of his daughter. Oh, brave! there will be fine
tickling sport. Soft now, what have I to do? Oh,
I know; now a mess of shoemakers meet at the
Woolsack in Ivy Lane, to cozen my gentleman of
lame Ralph's wife, that's true.   171

    Alack, alack!
    Girls, hold out tack! [1]
    For now smocks for this jumbling
    Shall go to wrack.   [Exit.

ACT THE FIFTH

SCENE I.—A Room in EYRE's House.

Enter EYRE, MARGERY, HANS, and ROSE.

EYRE. This is the morning, then, say,[2] my
oully, my honest Hans, is it not?

HANS. This is the morning that must make us
two happy or miserable; therefore, if you——

EYRE. Away with these ifs and ans, Hans, and
these et caeteras! By mine honour, Rowland Lacy,
none but the king shall wrong thee. Come, fear
nothing, am not I Sim Eyre? Is not Sim Eyre
lord mayor of London? Fear nothing, Rose: let
them all say what they can; dainty, come thou to
me—laughest thou?   11

MARGERY. Good my lord, stand her friend in
what thing you may.

EYRE. Why, my sweet Lady Madgy, think you
Simon Eyre can forget his fine Dutch journeyman?
No, vah! Fie, I scorn it, it shall never be cast in
my teeth, that I was unthankful. Lady Madgy,
thou had'st never covered thy Saracen's head with
this French flap, nor loaden thy bum with this

---

[1] (?) Stand at bay.   [2] 'stay' in the quartos.

farthingale ('tis trash, trumpery, vanity) ; Simon
Eyre had never walked in a red petticoat, nor
wore a chain of gold, but for my fine journeyman's
Portigues.—And shall I leave him ? No ! Prince
am I none, yet bear a princely mind.   24

HANS. My lord, 'tis time for us to part from hence.

EYRE. Lady Madgy, Lady Madgy, take two or
three of my pie-crust-eaters, my buff-jerkin varlets,
that do walk in black gowns at Simon Eyre's
heels ; take them, good Lady Madgy ; trip and
go, my brown queen of periwigs, with my delicate
Rose and my jolly Rowland to the Savoy ; see
them linked, countenance the marriage ; and when
it is done, cling, cling together, you Hamborow
turtle-doves. I'll bear you out, come to Simon
Eyre ; come, dwell with me, Hans, thou shalt eat
minced-pies and marchpane.¹ Rose, away, cricket ;
trip and go, my Lady Madgy, to the Savoy ; Hans,
wed, and to bed ; kiss, and away ! Go, vanish !

MARGERY. Farewell, my lord.   39

ROSE. Make haste, sweet love.

MARGERY.   She'd fain the deed were done.

HANS. Come, my sweet Rose ; faster than deer
        we'll run.   [Exeunt all but EYRE.

EYRE. Go, vanish, vanish ! Avaunt, I say !
By the Lord of Ludgate, it 's a mad life to be
a lord mayor ; it 's a stirring life, a fine life, a
velvet life, a careful life. Well, Simon Eyre, yet
set a good face on it, in the honour of Saint Hugh.
Soft, the king this day comes to dine with me, to
see my new buildings ; his majesty is welcome, he
shall have good cheer, delicate cheer, princely
cheer. This day, my fellow prentices of London
come to dine with me too ; they shall have fine
cheer, gentlemanlike cheer. I promised the mad
Cappadocians, when we all served at the Conduit
together,² that if ever I came to be mayor of

¹ Marzipan.
² One of the duties of apprentices was to fetch water for
the household from the conduits.

London, I would feast them all, and I'll do 't, I'll
do 't, by the life of Pharaoh ; by this beard, Sim
Eyre will be no flincher.   Besides, I have procured
that upon every Shrove Tuesday, at the sound of
the pancake bell,[1] my fine dapper Assyrian lads
shall clap up their shop windows, and away.   This
is the day, and this day they shall do 't, they shall
do 't.   62

Boys, that day are you free, let masters care,
And prentices shall pray for Simon Eyre.

                                                            [Exit.

SCENE II.—A Street near St. Faith's Church.

Enter HODGE, FIRK, RALPH, and five or six Shoemakers,
  all with cudgels or such weapons.

HODGE.   Come, Ralph ; stand to it, Firk.   My
masters, as we are the brave bloods of the shoemakers, heirs apparent to Saint Hugh, and perpetual benefactors to all good fellows, thou shalt
have no wrong ; were Hammon a king of spades,
he should not delve in thy close without thy
sufferance.   But tell me, Ralph, art thou sure 'tis
thy wife ?   8

RALPH.   Am I sure this is Firk ?   This morning,
when I stroked[2] on her shoes, I looked upon her,
and she upon me, and sighed, asked me if ever I
knew one Ralph.   Yes, said I.   For his sake, said
she—tears standing in her eyes—and for thou art
somewhat like him, spend this piece of gold.   I
took it ; my lame leg and my travel beyond sea
made me unknown.   All is one for that : I know
she 's mine.   17

FIRK.   Did she give thee this gold ?   O glorious
glittering gold !   She 's thine own, 'tis thy wife,
and she loves thee ; for I'll stand to 't, there 's no
woman will give gold to any man, but she thinks
better of him, than she thinks of them she gives

---

[1] Rung about 11 a.m. originally to call people to confession,
later as a sign that the holiday had begun.
[2] Fitted.

silver to. And for Hammon, neither Hammon nor hangman shall wrong thee in London. Is not our old master Eyre, lord mayor ? Speak, my hearts.

ALL. Yes, and Hammon shall know it to his cost.

Enter HAMMON, *his Serving-man,* JANE, *and others.*

HODGE. Peace, my bullies ; yonder they come.

RALPH. Stand to 't, my hearts. Firk, let me speak first.   30

HODGE. No, Ralph, let me.—Hammon, whither away so early ?

HAMMON. Unmannerly, rude slave, what 's that to thee ?

FIRK. To him, sir ? Yes, sir, and to me, and others. Good-morrow, Jane, how dost thou ? Good Lord, how the world is changed with you ! God be thanked !

HAMMON. Villains, hands off ! How dare you touch my love ?

ALL THE SHOEMAKERS. Villains ? Down with them ! Cry clubs for prentices !   40

HODGE. Hold, my hearts ! Touch her, Hammon ? Yea, and more than that : we'll carry her away with us. My masters and gentlemen, never draw your bird-spits ; shoemakers are steel to the back, men every inch of them, all spirit.

THOSE OF HAMMON'S SIDE. Well, and what of all this ?

HODGE. I'll show you.—Jane, dost thou know this man ? 'Tis Ralph, I can tell thee ; nay, 'tis he in faith, though he be lamed by the wars. Yet look not strange, but run to him, fold him about the neck and kiss him.   52

JANE. Lives then my husband ? Oh God, let me go,
Let me embrace my Ralph.

HAMMON.   What means my Jane ?

JANE. Nay, what meant you, to tell me, he was slain ?

HAMMON. [O] pardon me, dear love, for being
  misled.
[To RALPH.] 'Twas rumoured here in London, thou
  wert dead.
FIRK. Thou seest he lives. Lass, go, pack home
with him. Now, Master Hammon, where's your
mistress, your wife ?   60
SERVING-MAN. 'Swounds, master, fight for her !
Will you thus lose her ?
SHOEMAKERS. Down with that creature ! Clubs !
Down with him !
HODGE. Hold, hold !
HAMMON. Hold, fool ! Sirs, he shall do no wrong.
Will my Jane leave me thus, and break her faith ?
FIRK. Yea, sir ! She must, sir ! She shall, sir !
What then ? Mend it !
HODGE. Hark, fellow Ralph, follow my counsel :
set the wench in the midst, and let her choose her
man, and let her be his woman.   71
JANE. Whom should I choose ? Whom should
  my thoughts affect
But him whom Heaven hath made to be my love ?
Thou art my husband, and these humble weeds
Make thee more beautiful than all his wealth.
Therefore, I will but put off his attire,
Returning it into the owner's hand,
And after ever be thy constant wife.
HODGE. Not a rag, Jane ! The law 's on our side ;
he that sows in another man's ground, forfeits his
harvest. Get thee home, Ralph ; follow him, Jane ;
he shall not have so much as a busk-point from thee.
FIRK. Stand to that, Ralph ; the appurtenances
are thine own. Hammon, look not at her !   84
SERVING-MAN. O, 'swounds, no !
FIRK. Blue coat, be quiet, we'll give you a new
livery else , we'll make Shrove Tuesday Saint
George's Day [1] for you. Look not, Hammon,

---

[1] On which day a festival attended by blue-coats, or
serving-men, was held at St. Paul's. See Nares, *Glossary*,
s.v. George, St.

leer not ! I'll firk you ! For thy head now, [not]
one glance, one sheep's eye, anything, at her !
Touch not a rag, lest I and my brethren beat you
to clouts.   92

SERVING-MAN. Come, Master Hammon, there's
no striving here.

HAMMON. Good fellows, hear me speak ; and,
honest Ralph,
Whom I have injured most by loving Jane,
Mark what I offer thee : here in fair gold
Is twenty pound, I'll give it for thy Jane ;
If this content thee not, thou shalt have more.

HODGE. Sell not thy wife, Ralph ; make her
not a whore.

HAMMON. Say, wilt thou freely cease thy claim
in her,   100
And let her be my wife ?

ALL THE SHOEMAKERS.   No, do not, Ralph.

RALPH. Sirrah Hammon, Hammon, dost thou
think a shoemaker is so base to be a bawd to
his own wife for commodity ? Take thy gold,
choke with it ! Were I not lame, I would make
thee eat thy words.

FIRK. A shoemaker sell his flesh and blood ?
Oh, indignity !

HODGE. Sirrah, take up your pelf, and be
packing.

HAMMON. I will not touch one penny, but in lieu
Of that great wrong I offerèd thy Jane,   111
To Jane and thee I give that twenty pound.
Since I have failed of her, during my life,
I vow, no woman else shall be my wife.
Farewell, good fellows of the Gentle Trade :
Your morning mirth my mourning day hath made.
                                              [Exit.

FIRK. [To the Serving-man.] Touch the gold,
creature, if you dare ! Y 'are best be trudging.
Here, Jane, take thou it. Now let's home, my hearts.

HODGE. Stay ! Who comes here ? Jane, on
again with thy mask !   121

Enter the EARL OF LINCOLN, the LORD MAYOR, and
Servants.

LINCOLN. Yonder's the lying varlet mocked us so.

LORD MAYOR. Come hither, sirrah !

FIRK. I, sir ? I am sirrah ? You mean me, do
you not ?

LINCOLN. Where is my nephew married ?

FIRK. Is he married ? God give him joy, I am
glad of it. They have a fair day, and the sign is in
a good planet, Mars in Venus.

LORD MAYOR. Villain, thou toldst me that my
daughter Rose   130
This morning should be married at Saint Faith's ;
We have watched there these three hours at the least,
Yet see we no such thing.

FIRK. Truly, I am sorry for 't ; a bride's a
pretty thing.

HODGE. Come to the purpose. Yonder's the
bride and bridegroom you look for, I hope. Though
you be lords, you are not to bar by your authority
men from women, are you ?   139

LORD MAYOR. See, see, my daughter's masked.

LINCOLN.   True, and my nephew,
To hide his guilt, [now] counterfeits him lame.

FIRK. Yea, truly ; God help the poor couple,
they are lame and blind.

LORD MAYOR. I'll ease her blindness.

LINCOLN.   I'll his lameness cure.

FIRK. [Aside to the Shoemakers.] Lie down, sirs,
and laugh ! My fellow Ralph is taken for Rowland
Lacy, and Jane for Mistress Damask Rose. This
is all my knavery.

LORD MAYOR. What, have I found you, minion ?

LINCOLN.   O base wretch !
Nay, hide thy face, the horror of thy guilt   150
Can hardly be washed off. Where are thy powers ?
What battles have you made ? O yes, I see,
Thou fought'st with Shame, and Shame hath con-
quered thee.

This lameness will not serve.

LORD MAYOR.   Unmask yourself.

LINCOLN. Lead home your daughter.

LORD MAYOR.   Take your nephew hence.

RALPH. Hence ! 'Swounds, what mean you ?
Are you mad ? I hope you cannot enforce my wife
from me. Where 's Hammon ?

LORD MAYOR. Your wife ?

LINCOLN. What Hammon ?   160

RALPH. Yea, my wife ; and, therefore, the
proudest of you that lays hands on her first, I'll
lay my crutch 'cross his pate.

FIRK. To him, lame Ralph ! Here 's brave
sport !

RALPH. Rose call you her ? Why, her name is
Jane. Look here else ; do you know her now ?

                              [Unmasking JANE.

LINCOLN. Is this your daughter ?

LORD MAYOR.   No, nor this your nephew.
My Lord of Lincoln, we are both abused
By this base, crafty varlet.   170

FIRK. Yea, forsooth, no varlet ; forsooth, no
base; forsooth, I am but mean ; no crafty neither,
but of the Gentle Craft.

LORD MAYOR. Where is my daughter Rose ?
Where is my child ?

LINCOLN. Where is my nephew Lacy married ?

FIRK. Why, here is good laced mutton,[1] as I
promised you.

LINCOLN. Villain, I'll have thee punished for
this wrong.

FIRK. Punish the journeyman villain, but not
the journeyman shoemaker.   180

Enter DODGER.

DODGER. My lord, I come to bring unwelcome
news.
Your nephew Lacy and your daughter Rose

---

[1] To lace a joint was to make incisions down the sides.

Early this morning wedded at the Savoy,
None being present but the lady mayoress.
Besides, I learnt among the officers,
The lord mayor vows to stand in their defence
'Gainst any that shall seek to cross the match.

LINCOLN. Dares Eyre the shoemaker uphold the
    deed ?

FIRK. Yes, sir, shoemakers dare stand in a
woman's quarrel, I warrant you, as deep as
another, and deeper too.   191

DODGER. Besides, his grace to-day dines with
    the mayor ;
Who on his knees humbly intends to fall
And beg a pardon for your nephew's fault.

LINCOLN. But I'll prevent him ! Come, Sir
    Roger Oteley ;
The king will do us justice in this cause.
Howe'er their hands have made them man and wife,
I will disjoin the match, or lose my life.   [Exeunt.

FIRK. Adieu, Monsieur Dodger ! Farewell,
fools ! Ha, ha ! Oh, if they had stayed, I would
have so lambed [1] them with flouts ! O heart, my
codpiece-point is ready to fly in pieces every
time I think upon Mistress Rose ; but let that pass,
as my lady mayoress says.   204

HODGE. This matter is answered. Come, Ralph ;
home with thy wife. Come, my fine shoemakers,
let 's to our master's, the new lord mayor, and there
swagger this Shrove Tuesday. I'll promise you
wine enough, for Madge keeps the cellar.

ALL. O rare ! Madge is a good wench.

FIRK. And I'll promise you meat enough, for
simp'ring Susan keeps the larder. I'll lead you to
victuals, my brave soldiers ; follow your captain.
O brave ! Hark, hark !   [Bell rings.

ALL. The pancake-bell rings, the pancake-bell !
Trilill, my hearts !   216

FIRK. O brave ! O sweet bell ! O delicate
pancakes ! Open the doors, my hearts, and shut
                    [1] Whipped.

up the windows ! keep in the house, let out the
pancakes ! Oh, rare, my hearts ! Let's march
together for the honour of Saint Hugh to the
great new hall [1] in Gracious Street-corner, which
our master, the new lord mayor, hath built.

RALPH.   O the crew of good fellows that will
dine at my lord mayor's cost to-day !   225

HODGE.   By the Lord, my lord mayor is a most
brave man. How shall prentices be bound to pray
for him and the honour of the gentlemen shoemakers !
Let's feed and be fat with my lord's bounty.

FIRK.   O musical bell, still ! O Hodge, O my
brethren ! There's cheer for the heavens : venison-
pasties walk up and down piping hot, like sergeants;
beef and brewis [2] comes marching in dry-fats, [3]
fritters and pancakes come trowling in in wheel-
barrows ; hens and oranges hopping in porters'-
baskets, collops and eggs in scuttles, and tarts
and custards come quavering in in malt-shovels.

Enter more Prentices.

ALL.   Whoop, look here, look here !

HODGE.   How now, mad lads, whither away so
fast ?   240

FIRST PRENTICE.   Whither ? Why, to the great
new hall, know you not why ? The lord mayor
hath bidden all the prentices in London to breakfast this morning.

ALL.   Oh, brave shoemaker, oh, brave lord of
incomprehensible good fellowship ! Whoo ! Hark
you ! The pancake-bell rings.   [Cast up caps.

FIRK.   Nay, more, my hearts ! Every Shrove
Tuesday is our year of jubilee ; and when the
pancake-bell rings, we are as free as my lord
mayor ; we may shut up our shops, and make
holiday. I'll have it called Saint Hugh's Holiday.

---

[1] 'Simon Eyre, Draper, Mayor 1446, builded the Leaden
hall for a common garner of corn to the use of this City.'—
Stow. Maitland gives the date as 1419.

[2] See note on p. 18.   [3] Barrels.

ALL. Agreed, agreed ! Saint Hugh's Holiday.

HODGE. And this shall continue for ever. 254

ALL. Oh, brave ! Come, come, my hearts ! Away, away !

FIRK. O eternal credit to us of the Gentle Craft ! March fair, my hearts ! Oh, rare ! [Exeunt.

SCENE III.—A Street in London.

Enter the KING and his Train over the stage.

KING. Is our lord mayor of London such a gallant ?

NOBLEMAN. One of the merriest madcaps in your land.

Your grace will think, when you behold the man,
He 's rather a wild ruffian than a mayor.
Yet thus much I'll ensure your majesty.
In all his actions that concern his state,
He is as serious, provident, and wise,
As full of gravity amongst the grave,
As any mayor hath been these many years.

KING. I am with child,[1] till I behold this huff-cap.[2] 10

But all my doubt is, when we come in presence,
His madness will be dashed clean out of countenance.

NOBLEMAN. It may be so, my liege.

KING. Which to prevent
Let some one give him notice, 'tis our pleasure
That he put on his wonted merriment.
Set forward !

ALL. On afore ! [Exeunt.

SCENE IV.—A Great Hall.

Enter EYRE, HODGE, FIRK, RALPH, and other Shoemakers, all with napkins on their shoulders.

EYRE. Come, my fine Hodge, my jolly gentlemen shoemakers ; soft, where be these cannibals,

---

[1] i.e. In suspense. [2] Swaggerer.

these varlets, my officers ? Let them all walk and
wait upon my brethren ; for my meaning is, that
none but shoemakers, none but the livery of my
company shall in their satin hoods wait upon the
trencher of my sovereign.

FIRK.   O my lord, it will be rare !   8

EYRE.   No more, Firk ; come, lively ! Let your
fellow prentices want no cheer ; let wine be
plentiful as beer, and beer as water. Hang these
penny-pinching fathers, that cram wealth in
innocent lambskins. Rip, knaves, avaunt ! Look
to my guests !

HODGE.   My lord, we are at our wits' end for
room ; those hundred tables will not feast the
fourth part of them.   17

EYRE.   Then cover me those hundred tables
again, and again, till all my jolly prentices be
feasted. Avoid, Hodge ! Run, Ralph ! Frisk
about, my nimble Firk ! Carouse me fathom-
healths to the honour of the shoemakers. Do they
drink lively, Hodge ? Do they tickle it, Firk ?

FIRK.   Tickle it ? Some of them have taken
their liquor standing so long that they can stand
no longer ; but for meat, they would eat it, an
they had it.   27

EYRE.   Want they meat ? Where 's this swag-
belly, this greasy kitchenstuff cook ? Call the
varlet to me ! Want meat ? Firk, Hodge, lame
Ralph, run, my tall men, beleaguer the shambles,
beggar all Eastcheap, serve me whole oxen in
chargers, and let sheep whine upon the tables like
pigs for want of good fellows to eat them. Want
meat ? Vanish, Firk ! Avaunt, Hodge !

HODGE.   Your lordship mistakes my man Firk ;
he means, their bellies want meat, not the boards ;
for they have drunk so much, they can eat nothing.

Enter HANS, ROSE, and MARGERY.

MARGERY.   Where is my lord ?

EYRE.   How now, Lady Madgy ?   40

MARGERY. The king's most excellent majesty is new come ; he sends me for thy honour ; one of his most worshipful peers bade me tell thou must be merry, and so forth ; but let that pass.

EYRE. Is my sovereign come ? Vanish, my tall shoemakers, my nimble brethren ; look to my guests, the prentices. Yet stay a little ! How now, Hans ? How looks my little Rose ?

HANS. Let me request you to remember me. I know, your honour easily may obtain   50 Free pardon of the king for me and Rose, And reconcile me to my uncle's grace.

EYRE. Have done, my good Hans, my honest journeyman ; look cheerily ! I'll fall upon both my knees, till they be as hard as horn, but I'll get thy pardon.

MARGERY. Good my lord, have a care what you speak to his grace.   55

EYRE. Away, you Islington whitepot ! [1] hence, you hopperarse ! you barley-pudding, full of maggots ! you broiled carbonado ! [2] avaunt, avaunt, avoid, Mephistophilus ! Shall Sim Eyre learn to speak of you, Lady Madgy ? Vanish, Mother Miniver-cap ; [3] vanish, go, trip and go ; meddle with your partlets [4] and your pishery-pashery, your flewes [5] and your whirligigs ; go, rub, out of mine alley ! Sim Eyre knows how to speak to a Pope, to Sultan Soliman, to Tambur-laine, [6] an he were here, and shall I melt, shall I droop before my sovereign ? No, come, my Lady Madgy ! Follow me, Hans ! About your business, my frolic free-booters ! Firk, frisk about,

[1] ' A dish, made of milk, eggs, and sugar, baked in a pot.'—
Webster.

[2] A piece of meat scored across for broiling.

[3] Fur-cap.

[4] Bands or collars.

[5] Properly the chaps of a hound ; here perhaps the flaps of a hood.

[6] Dekker is thinking, no doubt, of Kyd's *Soliman and Perseda* (1599) and Marlowe's *Tamburlaine* (1590).

and about, and about, for the honour of mad
Simon Eyre, lord mayor of London.   74

FIRK.   Hey, for the honour of the shoemakers.
                                          [Exeunt.

SCENE V.—An Open Yard before the Hall.

A long flourish, or two.   Enter the KING, Nobles, EYRE,
    MARGERY, LACY, ROSE.   LACY and ROSE kneel.

KING.   Well, Lacy, though the fact was very foul
Of your revolting from our kingly love
And your own duty, yet we pardon you.
Rise both, and, Mistress Lacy, thank my lord
    mayor
For your young bridegroom here.   5
EYRE.   So, my dear liege, Sim Eyre and my
brethren, the gentlemen shoemakers, shall set your
sweet majesty's image cheek by jowl by Saint
Hugh for this honour you have done poor Simon
Eyre.   I beseech your grace, pardon my rude
behaviour ; I am a handicraftsman, yet my heart
is without craft ; I would be sorry at my soul,
that my boldness should offend my king.
KING.   Nay, I pray thee, good lord mayor, be
    even as merry   14
As if thou wert among thy shoemakers ;
It does me good to see thee in this humour.
EYRE.   Say'st thou me so, my sweet Dioclesian ?
Then, humph ! Prince am I none, yet am I princely
born.   By the Lord of Ludgate, my liege, I'll be
as merry as a pie.[1]   20
KING.   Tell me, in faith, mad Eyre, how old
    thou art.
EYRE.   My liege, a very boy, a stripling, a
younker ; you see not a white hair on my head,
not a grey in this beard.   Every hair, I assure thy
majesty, that sticks in this beard, Sim Eyre values
at the King of Babylon's ransom, Tamar Cham's[2]

---

[1] Magpie.
[2] Tamerlane (Tamburlaine), Cham, or Khan, of Tartary.

beard was a rubbing brush to 't : yet I'll shave it off, and stuff tennis-balls with it, to please my bully king.

KING. But all this while I do not know your age. 30

EYRE. My liege, I am six and fifty year old, yet I can cry humph ! with a sound heart for the honour of Saint Hugh. Mark this old wench, my king : I danced the shaking of the sheets with her six and thirty years ago, and yet I hope to get two or three young lord mayors, ere I die. I am lusty still, Sim Eyre still. Care and cold lodging brings white hairs. My sweet Majesty, let care vanish, cast it upon thy nobles, it will make thee look always young like Apollo, and cry humph ! Prince am I none, yet am I princely born.

KING. Ha, ha ! 42
Say, Cornwall, didst thou ever see his like ?

CORNWALL. Not I, my lord.

Enter the EARL OF LINCOLN and the LORD MAYOR.

KING. Lincoln, what news with you ?

LINCOLN. My gracious lord, have care unto yourself,
For there are traitors here.

ALL. Traitors ? Where ? Who ?

EYRE. Traitors in my house ? God forbid ! Where be my officers ? I'll spend my soul, ere my king feel harm.

KING. Where is the traitor, Lincoln ?

LINCOLN. Here he stands.

KING. Cornwall, lay hold on Lacy !—Lincoln, speak, 51
What canst thou lay unto thy nephew's charge ?

LINCOLN. This, my dear liege : your Grace, to do me honour,
Heaped on the head of this degenerous boy
Desertless favours ; you made choice of him,
To be commander over powers in France.
But he——

KING. Good Lincoln, prithee, pause a while !
Even in thine eyes I read what thou wouldst speak.
I know how Lacy did neglect our love,
Ran himself deeply, in the highest degree,   60
Into vile treason——

LINCOLN.   Is he not a traitor ?

KING. Lincoln, he was ; now have we pardoned
  him.
'Twas not a base want of true valour's fire,
That held him out of France, but love's desire.

LINCOLN. I will not bear his shame upon my
  back.

KING. Nor shalt thou, Lincoln ; I forgive you
  both.

LINCOLN. Then, good my liege, forbid the boy
  to wed
One whose mean birth will much disgrace his bed.

KING. Are they not married ?

LINCOLN.   No, my liege.

BOTH.   We are.

KING. Shall I divorce them then ? O be it far,
That any hand on earth should dare untie   71
The sacred knot, knit by God's majesty ;
I would not for my crown disjoin their hands,
That are conjoined in holy nuptial bands.
How say'st thou, Lacy, wouldst thou lose thy Rose ?

LACY. Not for all India's[1] wealth, my sovereign.

KING. But Rose, I am sure, her Lacy would
  forgo ?

ROSE. If Rose were asked that question, she'd
  say no.

KING. You hear them, Lincoln ?

LINCOLN.   Yea, my liege, I do.

KING. Yet canst thou find i' th' heart to part
  these two ?   80
Who seeks, besides you, to divorce these lovers ?

LORD MAYOR. I do, my gracious lord, I am her
  father.

KING. Sir Roger Oteley, our last mayor, I think ?

[1] ' Indians ' in all the quartos.

NOBLEMAN. The same, my liege.

KING. Would you offend Love's laws ?
Well, you shall have your wills. You sue to me,
To prohibit the match. Soft, let me see—
You both are married, Lacy, art thou not ?

LACY. I am, dread sovereign.

KING. Then, upon thy life,
I charge thee not to call this woman wife.

LORD MAYOR. I thank your grace.

ROSE. O my most gracious lord !

[Kneels.

KING. Nay, Rose, never woo me ; I tell you
true,   91
Although as yet I am a bachelor,
Yet I believe, I shall not marry you.

ROSE. Can you divide the body from the soul,
Yet make the body live ?

KING. Yea, so profound ?
I cannot, Rose, but you I must divide.
This fair maid, bridegroom,[1] cannot be your bride.
Are you pleased, Lincoln ? Oteley, are you
pleased ?

BOTH. Yes, my lord.

KING. Then must my heart be eased ;
For, credit me, my conscience lives in pain,   100
Till these whom I divorced, be joined again.
Lacy, give me thy hand ; Rose, lend me thine !
Be what you would be ! Kiss now ! So, that's
fine.
At night, lovers, to bed !—Now, let me see,
Which of you all mislikes this harmony.

LORD MAYOR. Will you then take from me my
child perforce ?

KING. Why, tell me, Oteley : shines not Lacy's
name
As bright in the world's eye as the gay beams
Of any citizen ?

LINCOLN. Yea, but, my gracious lord,
I do mislike the match far more than he ;   110

---

[1] 'Fair maid, this bridegroom,' in all the quartos.

Her blood is too too base.

KING.   ·   Lincoln, no more.
Dost thou not know that love respects no blood,
Cares not for difference of birth or state ?
The maid is young, well born, fair, virtuous,
A worthy bride for any gentleman.
Besides, your nephew for her sake did stoop
To bare necessity, and, as I hear,
Forgetting honours and all courtly pleasures,
To gain her love, became a shoemaker.
As for the honour which he lost in France,   120
Thus I redeem it : Lacy, kneel thee down !—
Arise, Sir Rowland Lacy ! Tell me now,
Tell me in earnest, Oteley, canst thou chide,
Seeing thy Rose a lady and a bride ?

> LORD MAYOR. I am content with what your
> grace hath done.

> LINCOLN. And I, my liege, since there's no
> remedy.

> KING. Come on, then, all shake hands : I'll
> have you friends ;

Where [1] there is much love, all discord ends.
What says my mad lord mayor to all this love ?

> EYRE. O my liege, this honour you have done
> to my fine journeyman here, Rowland Lacy, and
> all these favours which you have shown to me this
> day in my poor house, will make Simon Eyre live
> longer by one dozen of warm summers more than
> he should.

> KING. Nay, my mad lord mayor, that shall be
> thy name,   137

If any grace of mine can length thy life,
One honour more I'll do thee : that new building,
Which at thy cost in Cornhill is erected,
Shall take a name from us ; we'll have it called
The Leadenhall,[2] because in digging it
You found the lead that covereth the same.

---

[1] A disyllable.
[2] Stow says there was a building on the site with this
name at least as early as 1362.

EYRE.   I thank your majesty.

MARGERY.   God bless your grace !

KING.   Lincoln, a word with you !

Enter HODGE, FIRK, RALPH, *and more Shoemakers.*

EYRE.   How now, my mad knaves ?   Peace,
speak softly, yonder is the king.

KING.   With the old troop which there we keep
in pay,
We will incorporate a new supply.
Before one summer more pass o'er my head,
France shall repent England was injured.   150
What are all those ?

LACY.   All shoemakers, my liege,
Sometime [1] my fellows ; in their companies
I lived as merry as an emperor.

KING.   My mad lord mayor, are all these shoemakers ?

EYRE.   All shoemakers, my liege ; all gentlemen
of the Gentle Craft, true Trojans, courageous
cordwainers ; they all kneel to the shrine of holy
Saint Hugh.   158

ALL THE SHOEMAKERS.   God save your majesty !

KING.   Mad Simon, would they anything with us ?

EYRE.   Mum, mad knaves ! Not a word ! I'll
do 't ; I warrant you.—They are all beggars, my
liege ; all for themselves, and I for them all, on
both my knees do entreat, that for the honour of
poor Simon Eyre and the good of his brethren,
these mad knaves, your grace would vouchsafe
some privilege to my new Leadenhall, that it
may be lawful for us to buy and sell leather there
two days a week.

KING.   Mad Sim, I grant your suit, you shall
have patent   170
To hold two market-days in Leadenhall,
Mondays and Fridays, those shall be the times.
Will this content you ?

ALL.   Jesus bless your grace !

EYRE.   In the name of these my poor brethren

------

[1] ' Sometimes ' in the quartos.

shoemakers, I most humbly thank your grace. But
before I rise, seeing you are in the giving vein and
we in the begging, grant Sim Eyre one boon more.

KING. What is it, my lord mayor ?

EYRE. Vouchsafe to taste of a poor banquet
that stands sweetly waiting for your sweet presence.

KING. I shall undo thee, Eyre, only with feasts ;
Already have I been too troublesome ;　　　　　182
Say, have I not ?

EYRE. O my dear king,[1] Sim Eyre was taken
unawares upon a day of shroving, which I promised
long ago to the prentices of London.

For, an 't please your highness, in time past,
I bare the water-tankard, and my coat
Sits not a whit the worse upon my back ;
And then, upon a morning, some mad boys,
It was Shrove Tuesday, even as 'tis now,　　　191
Gave me my breakfast, and I swore then by the
stopple of my tankard, if ever I came to be lord
mayor of London, I would feast all the prentices.
This day, my liege, I did it, and the slaves had an
hundred tables five times covered ; they are gone
home and vanished ;

Yet add more honour to the Gentle Trade,
Taste of Eyre's banquet, Simon 's happy made.

KING. Eyre, I will taste of thy banquet, and
will say,　　　　　　　　　　　　　　　　200
I have not met more pleasure on a day.
Friends of the Gentle Craft, thanks to you all,
Thanks, my kind lady mayoress, for our cheer.—
Come, lords, a while let 's revel it at home !
When all our sports and banquetings are done,
Wars must right wrongs which Frenchmen have
　　begun.　　　　　　　　　　　　　[Exeunt.

---

[1] Probably all this speech was originally in verse ; there
are many differences of reading in the quartos.

THE WHITE DEVIL
OR
VITTORIA COROMBONA

John Webster
(?1580–1625)

The White Devil was probably produced in 1608, or at
the latest in the following year. It was first printed in
1612 in quarto; the extant copies of this edition are
by no means identical, several readings being quoted
from it by Dyce which are not to be found in either
of the British Museum copies. This being the only
edition which Webster can have seen, I have followed
it wherever it was possible to do so. A second quarto
appeared in 1631, which corrected some of the obvious
errors of the first, and two later quartos were issued in
1665 and 1672. The former of these divides the play
into Acts, and the latter divides the Acts into Scenes,
the division, however, being one which did not commend
itself to subsequent editors. Dyce's edition of Webster's
Works appeared in 1830, with a second edition in 1857;
both text and notes bear witness to his admirable judgement and scholarship. Dyce's text was adopted by
Mr. J. A. Symons in his Mermaid edition of Webster
(1888), where the Act and Scene divisions, which Dyce
had omitted, and the localities which he had indicated
only in footnotes, were inserted in the text. Professor
M. W. Sampson of Indiana University issued a careful
edition of the play in 1904 based on the text of the first
quarto, the variations in the other quartos being noted.
He made some valuable suggestions on the difficult
question of line arrangement, some of which I have
adopted.

D

THE
WHITE DIVEL,

OR,

The Tragedy of *Paulo Giordano*
Vrsini, Duke of *Brachiano*,

With

The Life and Death of Vittoria
Corombona the famous
Venetian Curtizan.

Acted by the Queenes Maiesties Seruants.

Written by IOHN WEBSTER.

Non inferiora secutus.

LONDON,
Printed by *N.O.* for *Thomas Archer,* and are to be sold
at his Shop in Popes head Pallace, neere the
Royall Exchange. 1612.

DRAMATIS PERSONAE

MONTICELSO, a Cardinal, afterwards Pope.
FRANCISCO DE MEDICIS, Duke of Florence.
BRACHIANO,[1] otherwise Paulo Giordano Ursini, Duke of
    Brachiano, Husband of Isabella.
GIOVANNI, his Son by Isabella.
COUNT LODOVICO.
CAMILLO, Husband of Vittoria.
FLAMINEO, Brother of Vittoria, Secretary to Brachiano.
MARCELLO, Brother of Vittoria, Attendant on Francisco de
    Medicis.
HORTENSIO, an Officer of Brachiano.
ANTONELLI, } Friends of Count Lodovico.
GASPARO, }
A Young Lord.
*GUIDANTONIO, an Attendant on Isabella.
DOCTOR JULIO.
Conjurer.
Lawyer.
*JAQUES, a Moor, Servant to Giovanni.
*CHRISTOPHERO, an Attendant on Doctor Julio.
Ambassadors, Physicians, Officers, Attendants, &c.

ISABELLA, Sister of Francisco de Medicis, Wife of Brachiano.
VITTORIA COROMBONA, married first to Camillo, afterwards
    to Brachiano.
CORNELIA, Mother of Vittoria, Flamineo, and Marcello.
ZANCHE, a Moor, Waiting-woman to Vittoria.
Matron of the House of Convertites.

* Mutae personae.

SCENE.—Rome, afterwards Padua.

[1] To secure the right pronunciation Webster changed the
spelling from Bracciano.

THE WHITE DEVIL

OR

VITTORIA COROMBONA

ACT THE FIRST

SCENE I.—A Street in Rome.

Enter COUNT LODOVICO, ANTONELLI, and GASPARO.

LODOVICO.   Banished ?

ANTONELLI.   It grieved me much to hear
the sentence.

LODOVICO.   Ha, ha ! O Democritus, thy gods
That govern the whole world—courtly reward
And punishment !   Fortune 's a right whore :
If she give aught, she deals it in small parcels,
That she may take away all at one swoop.
This 'tis to have great enemies :—God quit [1] them !
Your wolf no longer seems to be a wolf
Than when she 's hungry.

GASPARO.   You term those enemies
Are men of princely rank.

LODOVICO.   O, I pray for them. 10
The violent thunder is adored by those
Are pashed [2] in pieces by it.

ANTONELLI.   Come, my lord,
You are justly doomed : look but a little back
Into your former life ; you have in three years
Ruined the noblest earldom.

GASPARO.   Your followers
Have swallowed you like mummia [3] and, being sick
With such unnatural and horrid physic,
Vomit you up i' the kennel.

ANTONELLI.   All the damnable degrees

---

[1] Requite.   [2] Smashed.
[3] A drug prepared from a mummy.

Of drinkings have you staggered through : one
   citizen
Is lord of two fair manors called you master   20
Only for caviare.[1]
   GASPARO.   Those noblemen
Which were invited to your prodigal feasts
(Wherein the phoenix scarce could scape your
   throats)
Laugh at your misery ; as fore-deeming you
An idle meteor, which, drawn forth the earth,
Would be soon lost i' the air ;—
   ANTONELLI.   Jest upon you,
And say you were begotten in an earthquake,
You have ruined such fair lordships.
   LODOVICO.   Very good.
This well goes with two buckets : I must tend
The pouring out of either.
   GASPARO.   Worse than these ;   30
You have acted certain murders here in Rome,
Bloody and full of horror.
   LODOVICO.   'Las,—they were flea-bitings.
Why took they not my head, then ?
   GASPARO.   Oh, my lord,
The law doth sometimes mediate, thinks it good
Not ever to steep violent sins in blood :
This gentle penance may both end your crimes,
And in the example better these bad times.
   LODOVICO. So ; but I wonder, then, some great
   men scape
This banishment : there's Paulo Giordano Ursini,
The Duke of Brachiano, now lives in Rome,   40
And by close panderism seeks to prostitute
The honour of Vittoria Corombona ;
Vittoria, she that might have got my pardon
For one kiss to the duke.
   ANTONELLI.   Have a full man within you.
We see that trees bear no such pleasant fruit
There where they grew first as where they are new
   set :

[1] i.e. he had sold his estates to purchase dainties.

Perfumes, the more they are chafed, the more they render
Their pleasing scents ; and so affliction
Expresseth virtue fully, whether true
Or else adulterate.

LODOVICO.   Leave your painted comforts :
I'll make Italian cut-works [1] in their guts,   51
If ever I return.

GASPARO.   O, sir !

LODOVICO.   I am patient.
I have seen some ready to be executed
Give pleasant looks and money, and grown familiar
With the knave hangman : so do I, I thank them,
And would account them nobly merciful,
Would they dispatch me quickly.

ANTONELLI.   Fare you well :
We shall find time, I doubt not, to repeal
Your banishment.

LODOVICO.   I am ever bound to you :
This is the world's alms ; pray, make use of it.
Great men sell sheep thus to be cut in pieces,   61
When first they have shorn them bare and sold
their fleeces.   [Exeunt.

SCENE II.—A Room in CAMILLO's House.

Sennet.[2] Enter BRACHIANO, CAMILLO, FLAMINEO,
VITTORIA COROMBONA, and Attendants.

BRACHIANO. Your best of rest !

VITTORIA.   Unto my lord the duke
The best of welcome !—More lights ! attend the
duke.   [Exeunt CAMILLO and VITTORIA.

BRACHIANO. Flamineo,—

FLAMINEO.   My lord ?

BRACHIANO.   Quite lost, Flamineo !

FLAMINEO. Pursue your noble wishes, I am
prompt

[1] Open-work, or embroidery.
[2] A set of notes on a trumpet as a signal for a ceremonial
entry.

As lightning to your service. O, my lord,
[Whispers.] The fair Vittoria, my happy sister,
Shall give you present audience.—Gentlemen,
Let the caroche [1] go on ; and 'tis his pleasure
You put out all your torches, and depart.   9
                              [Exeunt Attendants.

BRACHIANO.   Are we so happy ?
FLAMINEO.   Can't be otherwise ?
Observed you not to-night, my honoured lord,
Which way soe'er you went, she threw her eyes ?
I have dealt already with her chambermaid,
Zanche the Moor ; and she is wondrous proud
To be the agent for so high a spirit.

BRACHIANO.   We are happy above thought,
     because 'bove merit.   16

FLAMINEO.   'Bove merit !—we may now talk
freely—'bove merit ! What is't you doubt ? her
coyness ? that's but the superficies of lust most
women have : yet why should ladies blush to hear
that named which they do not fear to handle ?
Oh, they are politic : they know our desire is
increased by the difficulty of enjoying ; where a
satiety is a blunt, weary, and drowsy passion. If
the buttery-hatch at court stood continually open,
there would be nothing so passionate crowding, nor
hot suit after the beverage.   27

BRACHIANO.   Oh, but her jealous husband !

FLAMINEO.   Hang him ! a gilder that hath his
brains perished with quicksilver is not more cold
in the liver : the great barriers [2] moulted not more
feathers than he hath shed hairs, by the confession
of his doctor : an Irish gamester that will play
himself naked, and then wage all downward [3] at
hazard, is not more venturous : so unable to please
a woman, that, like a Dutch doublet, all his back
is shrunk into his breeches.   37

[1] Coach.   [2] i.e. at a tournament.
[3] From Ric. Stanyhurst's ' Description of Ireland ' in
Holinshed we gather that they staked their locks of hair
and their finger and toe nails.

Shrowd you within this closet, good my lord :
Some trick now must be thought on to divide
My brother-in-law from his fair bedfellow.　　40
　　BRACHIANO.　Oh, should she fail to come !
　　FLAMINEO.　I must not have your lordship thus
unwisely amorous.　I myself have loved a lady,
and pursued her with a great deal of under-age
protestation, whom some three or four gallants
that have enjoyed would with all their hearts have
been glad to have been rid of.　'Tis just like a
summer birdcage in a garden ; the birds that are
without despair to get in, and the birds that are
within despair, and are in a consumption, for fear
they shall never get out.　Away, away, my lord !
　　　　　　　　　　　　　　　[Exit BRACHIANO.
See, here he comes.　This fellow by his apparel
Some men would judge a politician ;　　53
But call his wit in question— you shall find it
Merely an ass in 's foot-cloth.[1]

Re-enter CAMILLO.[2]

　　　　　　　　　How now, brother ?
What, travelling to bed to your kind wife ?
　　CAMILLO.　I assure you, brother, no ; my
　　　　voyage lies
More northerly, in a far colder clime :
I do not well remember, I protest,
When I last lay with her.
　　FLAMINEO.　Strange you should lose your count.
　　CAMILLO.　We never lay together, but ere
　　　　morning　　61
There grew a flaw [3] between us.

[1] An ornamental cloth laid on a horse's back and reaching
to his feet on either side.
[2] It is hardly possible to mark with any certainty the
stage-business of this play.　Though Brachiano, who has
just withdrawn into a ' closet ', appears again when Flamineo
calls him (p. 99), it would seem that the audience were to
imagine that a change of scene took place here to another
apartment, as Flamineo says (p. 96) :　' Sister, my lord
attends you in the banqueting-house '.—*Dyce*.　　[3] Squall.

FLAMINEO.   'T had been your part
To have made up that flaw.
   CAMILLO.   True, but she loathes
I should be seen in 't.
   FLAMINEO.   Why, sir, what's the matter ?
   CAMILLO. The duke, your master, visits me,
   I thank him ;
And I perceive how, like an earnest bowler,
He very passionately leans that way
He should have his bowl run.
   FLAMINEO.   I hope you do not think—
   CAMILLO. That noblemen bowl booty ? [1] faith,
   his cheek
Hath a most excellent bias ; it would fain   70
Jump with my mistress.[2]
   FLAMINEO.   Will you be an ass,
Despite your Aristotle ? or a cuckold,
Contrary to your Ephemerides,
Which shows you under what a smiling planet
You were first swaddled ?
   CAMILLO.   Pew-wew, sir, tell not me
Of planets nor of Ephemerides :
A man may be made cuckold in the day-time,
When the stars' eyes are out.
   FLAMINEO.   Sir, God b' wi' you ;
I do commit you to your pitiful pillow
Stuffed with horn-shavings.
   CAMILLO.   Brother.—
   FLAMINEO.   God refuse me !
Might I advise you now, your only course   81
Were to lock up your wife ;—
   CAMILLO.   'Twere very good.
   FLAMINEO. Bar her the sight of revels ;—
   CAMILLO.   Excellent.
   FLAMINEO. Let her not go to church, but like
   a hound

  [1] Properly, to play badly in order to encourage a pigeon
to stake more.
  [2] A play on the word, which also means the jack at
bowls.

In lyam [1] at your heels ;—

   CAMILLO.   'Twere for her honour.

   FLAMINEO.   And so you should be certain in one fortnight
Despite her chastity or innocence,
To be cuckolded, which yet is in suspense :
This is my counsel, and I ask no fee for 't.

   CAMILLO.   Come, you know not where my nightcap wrings me.   90

   FLAMINEO.   Wear it o' the old fashion ; let your large ears come through, it will be more easy : —nay, I will be bitter. Bar your wife of her entertainment ? Women are more willing and more gloriously chaste when they are least restrained of their liberty. It seems you would be a fine capricious mathematically jealous coxcomb ; take the height of your own horns with a Jacob's staff [2] afore they are up. These politic inclosures for paltry mutton make more rebellion in the flesh than all the provocative electuaries [3] doctors have uttered [4] since last jubilee.   102

   CAMILLO.   This doth not physic me.

   FLAMINEO.   It seems you are jealous : I'll show you the error of it by a familiar example. I have seen a pair of spectacles fashioned with such perspective art, that, lay down but one twelve pence o' the board, 'twill appear as if there were twenty ; now, should you wear a pair of these spectacles, and see your wife tying her shoe, you would imagine twenty hands were taking up of your wife's clothes, and this would put you into a horrible causeless fury.   113

   CAMILLO.   The fault there, sir, is not in the eyesight.

   FLAMINEO.   True ; but they that have the yellow jaundice think all objects they look on to

---

[1] Or 'lyme', a leash. The quartos have 'leon'. Dyce made the correction.

[2] An instrument for taking altitudes.

[3] Medicinal pastes.   [4] Offered for sale.

be yellow. Jealousy is worser ; her fits present to
a man, like so many bubbles in a basin of water,
twenty several crabbed faces ; many times makes
his own shadow his cuckold-maker. See, she comes.

Re-enter VITTORIA.

What reason have you to be jealous of[1] this
creature ? what an ignorant ass or flattering knave
might he be counted, that should write sonnets to
her eyes, or call her brow the snow of Ida or
ivory of Corinth, or compare her hair to the
blackbird's bill,[2] when 'tis liker the blackbird's
feather ! This is all ; be wise, I will make you
friends ; and you shall go to bed together. Marry,
look you, it shall not be your seeking ; do you
stand upon that by any means : walk you aloof ;
I would not have you seen in 't. [CAMILLO retires.]
Sister (my lord attends you in the banqueting-
house) ; your husband is wondrous discontented.

    VITTORIA. I did nothing to displease him : I
carved to him at supper-time.   136
    FLAMINEO. (You need not have carved him, in
faith ; they say he is a capon already. I must now
seemingly fall out with you.) Shall a gentleman
so well descended as Camillo,—(a lousy slave, that
within this twenty years rode with the black
guard[3] in the duke's carriage, 'mongst spits and
dripping-pans)—   143
    CAMILLO. Now he begins to tickle her.
    FLAMINEO. An excellent scholar,—(one that
hath a head filled with calves' brains without any
sage in them),—come crouching in the hams to
you for a night's lodging ?—(that hath an itch in 's
hams, which like the fire at the glass-house hath
not gone out this seven years.)—Is he not a courtly
gentleman ?—(when he wears white satin, one
would take him by his black muzzle to be no

_____
[1] i.e. about.   [2] Which is yellow.
[3] The lowest menials who rode in the vehicles which
carried the pots and pans.

other creature than a maggot.) —You are a goodly
foil, I confess, well set out—(but covered with a
false stone, yon counterfeit diamond.)

CAMILLO. He will make her know what is in
me.

FLAMINEO. (Come, my lord attends you ; thou
shalt go to bed to my lord)—

CAMILLO. Now he comes to 't. 160

FLAMINEO. (With a relish as curious as a
vintner going to taste new wine.)—[To CAMILLO.]
I am opening your case hard.

CAMILLO. A virtuous brother, o' my credit !

FLAMINEO. He will give thee a ring with a
philosopher's stone in it.

CAMILLO. Indeed, I am studying alchymy.

FLAMINEO. Thou shalt lie in a bed stuffed with
turtles' feathers ; swoon in perfumed linen, like
the fellow was smothered in roses. So perfect shall
be thy happiness, that, as men at sea think land
and trees and ships go that way they go, so both
heaven and earth shall seem to go your voyage.
(Shalt meet him ; 'tis fixed with nails of diamonds
to inevitable necessity.) 175

VITTORIA. How shall 's rid him hence ?

FLAMINEO. I will put the brees [1] in 's tail—set
him gadding presently.—[To CAMILLO.] I have
almost wrought her to it, I find her coming : [2]
but, might I advise you now, for this night I
would not lie with her ; I would cross her humour
to make her more humble. 182

CAMILLO. Shall I, shall I ?

FLAMINEO. It will show in you a supremacy of
judgement.

CAMILLO. True, and a mind differing from the
tumultuary opinion ; for, *quae negata, grata.*

FLAMINEO. Right : you are the adamant [3] shall
draw her to you, though you keep distance off.

CAMILLO. A philosophical reason. 190

[1] Gadflies.   [2] Favourably disposed.   [3] Magnet.

FLAMINEO. Walk by her o' the nobleman's fashion, and tell her you will lie with her at the end of the progress.[1]

CAMILLO. [Coming forward.] Vittoria, I cannot be induced, or, as a man would say, incited——

VITTORIA. To do what, sir?

CAMILLO. To lie with you to-night. Your silk-worm useth to fast every third day, and the next following spins the better. To-morrow at night I am for you.   200

VITTORIA. You'll spin a fair thread, trust to 't.

FLAMINEO. [Aside to CAMILLO.] But, do you hear, I shall have you steal to her chamber about mid-night.

CAMILLO. Do you think so? why, look you, brother, because you shall not think I'll gull you, take the key, lock me into the chamber, and say you shall be sure of me.

FLAMINEO. In troth, I will; I'll be your jailer once. But have you ne'er a false door?   210

CAMILLO. A pox on 't, as I am a Christian! Tell me to-morrow how scurvily she takes my unkind parting.

FLAMINEO. I will.

CAMILLO. Didst thou not mark [2] the jest of the silkworm? Good-night: in faith, I will use this trick often.

FLAMINEO. Do, do, do. [Exit CAMILLO; and FLA-MINEO locks the door on him.] So now you are safe.— Ha, ha, ha! thou entanglest thyself in thine own work like a silkworm.[3] Come, sister; darkness hides your blush. Women are like curst [4] dogs: civility keeps them tied all daytime, but they are let loose at midnight; then they do most good, or most mischief.—My lord, my lord!   225

---

[1] Royal journey.
[2] So the last quarto; the three others have 'make'; query 'take'.
[3] The 1672 quarto begins Scene iii after this.
[4] Bad-tempered.

Re-enter BRACHIANO. ZANCHE brings out a carpet, spreads
    it, and lays on it two fair cushions.

BRACHIANO. Give credit, I could wish time
    would stand still,
And never end this interview, this hour :
But all delight doth itself soon'st devour.

       Enter CORNELIA behind, listening.

Let me into your bosom, happy lady,
Pour out, instead of eloquence, my vows :   230
Loose me not, madam ; for, if you forgo me,
I am lost eternally.
    VITTORIA.   Sir, in the way of pity,
I wish you heart-whole.
    BRACHIANO.   You are a sweet physician.
    VITTORIA. Sure, sir, a loathèd cruelty in ladies
Is as to doctors many funerals ;
It takes away their credit.
    BRACHIANO.   Excellent creature !
We call the cruel fair : what name for you
That are so merciful ?   [Embraces her.
    ZANCHE.   See, now they close.
    FLAMINEO. Most happy union !
    ·CORNELIA. My fears are fall'n upon me :
    O, my heart !   240
My son the pander ! now I find our house
Sinking to ruin. Earthquakes leave behind,
Where they have tyrannized, iron, or lead, or
    stone ;
But, woe to ruin, violent lust leaves none !
    BRACHIANO. What value is this jewel ?
    VITTORIA.   'Tis the ornament
Of a weak fortune.
    BRACHIANO. In sooth, I'll have it ; nay, I will
    but change
My jewel for your jewel.
    FLAMINEO.   Excellent !
His jewel for her jewel :—well put in, duke.
    BRACHIANO. Nay, let me see you wear it.

VITTORIA. Here, sir ?

BRACHIANO. Nay, lower, you shall wear my
jewel lower. 251

FLAMINEO. That 's better ; she must wear his
jewel lower.

VITTORIA. To pass away the time, I'll tell your
grace

A dream I had last night.

BRACHIANO. Most wishedly.

VITTORIA. A foolish idle dream.

Methought I walked about the mid of night

Into a churchyard, where a goodly yew-tree

Spread her large root in ground. Under that yew,

As I sate sadly leaning on a grave 259

Chequered with cross sticks, there came stealing in

Your duchess and my husband : one of them

A pickaxe bore, the other a rusty spade ;

And in rough terms they gan to challenge me

About this yew.

BRACHIANO. That tree ?

VITTORIA. This harmless yew.

They told me my intent was to root up

That well-grown yew, and plant i' the stead of it

A withered blackthorn ; and for that they vowed

To bury me alive. My husband straight

With pickaxe gan to dig, and your fell duchess

With shovel, like a Fury, voided out 270

The earth, and scattered bones. Lord, how, methought,

I trembled ! and yet, for all this terror,

I could not pray.

FLAMINEO. No ; the devil was in your dream.

VITTORIA. When to my rescue there arose, methought,

A whirlwind, which let fall a massy arm

From that strong plant ;

And both were struck dead by that sacred yew,

In that base shallow grave that was their due.

FLAMINEO. Excellent devil ! she hath taught
him in a dream 279

To make away his duchess and her husband.

BRACHIANO. Sweetly shall I interpret this your
dream.
You are lodged within his arms who shall protect
you
From all the fevers of a jealous husband ;
From the poor envy of our phlegmatic duchess.
I'll seat you above law, and above scandal ;
Give to your thoughts the invention of delight,
And the fruition ; nor shall government
Divide me from you longer than a care
To keep you great : you shall to me at once   289
Be dukedom, health, wife, children, friends, and all.

CORNELIA. [Coming forward.] Woe to light
hearts, they still forerun our fall !

FLAMINEO. What Fury raised thee up ?—Away,
away !   [Exit ZANCHE.

CORNELIA. What make you here, my lord, this
dead of night ?
Never dropped mildew on a flower here
Till now.

FLAMINEO. I pray, will you go to bed, then,
Lest you be blasted ?

CORNELIA.   O, that this fair garden
Had with all poisoned herbs of Thessaly
At first been planted ; made a nursery
For witchcraft, rather than a burial plot   299
For both your honours !

VITTORIA.   Dearest mother, hear me.

CORNELIA. O, thou dost make my brow bend
to the earth,
Sooner than nature ! See, the curse of children !
In life they keep us frequently in tears ;
And in the cold grave leave us in pale fears.

BRACHIANO. Come, come, I will not hear you.

VITTORIA.   Dear, my lord—

CORNELIA. Where is thy duchess now, adul-
terous duke ?
Thou little dreamd'st this night she is come to
Rome.

FLAMINEO. How ! come to Rome !

VITTORIA.   The duchess !

BRACHIANO.   She had been better—

CORNELIA.   The lives of princes should like dials
    move,
Whose regular example is so strong,   310
They make the times by them go right or wrong.

FLAMINEO. So ; have you done ?

CORNELIA.   Unfortunate Camillo !

VITTORIA.   I do protest, if any chaste denial,
If anything but blood could have allayed
His long suit to me—

CORNELIA.   I will join with thee,
To the most woeful end e'er mother kneeled :
If thou dishonour thus thy husband's bed,
Be thy life short as are the funeral tears
In great men's.

BRACHIANO.   Fie, fie, the woman 's mad.

CORNELIA.   Be thy act, Judas-like—betray in
    kissing :   320
Mayst thou be envied during his short breath,
And pitied like a wretch after his death !

VITTORIA.   O me accurst !   [Exit.

FLAMINEO.   Are you out of your wits, my lord ?
I'll fetch her back again ?

BRACHIANO.   No, I'll to bed :
Send Doctor Julio to me presently.—
Uncharitable woman ! thy rash tongue
Hath raised a fearful and prodigious storm :
Be thou the cause of all ensuing harm.   [Exit.

FLAMINEO.   Now, you that stand so much upon
    your honour,
Is this a fitting time o' night, think you,   330
To send a duke home without e'er a man ?
I would fain know where lies the mass of wealth
Which you have hoarded for my maintenance,
That I may bear my beard out of the level
Of my lord's stirrup.

CORNELIA.   What ! because we are poor
Shall we be vicious ?

FLAMINEO.   Pray, what means have you
To keep me from the galleys or the gallows ?
My father proved himself a gentleman,
Sold all 's land, and, like a fortunate fellow,
Died ere the money was spent. You brought me
    up   340
At Padua, I confess, where, I protest,
For want of means (the university judge me)
I have been fain to heel my tutor's stockings,
At least seven years : conspiring with a beard,
Made me a graduate ; then to this duke's service.
I visited the court, whence I returned
More courteous, more lecherous by far,
But not a suit the richer : and shall I,
Having a path so open and so free
To my preferment, still retain your milk   350
In my pale forehead ? no, this face of mine
I'll arm, and fortify with lusty wine,
'Gainst shame and blushing.
    CORNELIA.   O, that I ne'er had borne thee !
    FLAMINEO.   So would I ;
I would the common'st courtezan in Rome
Had been my mother, rather than thyself.
Nature is very pitiful to whores,
To give them but few children, yet those children
Plurality of fathers : they are sure
They shall not want. Go, go,   360
Complain unto my great lord cardinal ;
Yet may be he will justify the act.
Lycurgus wondered much men would provide
Good stallions for their mares, and yet would
    suffer
Their fair wives to be barren.
    CORNELIA.   Misery of miseries !
                                            [Exit.
    FLAMINEO.   The duchess come to court ! I like
    not that.
We are engaged to mischief, and must on :
As rivers to find out the ocean   368
Flow with crook bendings beneath forcèd banks ;

Or as we see, to aspire some mountain's top,
The way ascends not straight, but imitates
The subtle foldings of a winter's snake ;
So who knows policy and her true aspèct,
Shall find her ways winding and indirect.   [Exit.

ACT THE SECOND

Scene I.—A Room in Francisco's Palace.

Enter Francisco de Medicis, Cardinal Monticelso,
   Marcello, Isabella, young Giovanni, with little
   Jaques the Moor.

FRANCISCO.   Have you not seen your husband
   since you arrived ?

ISABELLA.   Not yet, sir.

FRANCISCO.   Surely he is wondrous kind.
If I had such a dove-house as Camillo's,
I would set fire on 't, were 't but to destroy
The pole-cats that haunt to it.—My sweet cousin ! [1]

GIOVANNI.   Lord uncle, you did promise me a
   horse
And armour.

FRANCISCO.   That I did, my pretty cousin.—
Marcello, see it fitted.

MARCELLO.   My lord, the duke is here.

FRANCISCO.   Sister, away ! you must not yet be
   seen.

ISABELLA.   I do beseech you,   10
Entreat him mildly ; let not your rough tongue
Set us at louder variance : all my wrongs
Are freely pardoned ; and I do not doubt,
As men, to try the precious unicorn's horn,
Make of the powder a preservative circle,
And in it put a spider,[2] so these arms
Shall charm his poison, force it to obeying,

[1] Often used of nephews and nieces.
[2] The spider was supposed to be poisonous, and the
powder made of a unicorn's horn was a safeguard against
all poisons.

And keep him chaste from an infected straying.
   FRANCISCO. I wish it may. Be gone. Void [1] the
    chamber. [*Exeunt* ISABELLA, GIOVANNI, *and* JAQUES.

       Enter BRACHIANO *and* FLAMINEO.

You are welcome : will you sit ?—I pray, my lord,
Be you my orator, my heart 's too full ;   21
I'll second you anon.
   MONTICELSO.   Ere I begin,
Let me entreat your grace forgo all passion,
Which may be raisèd by my free discourse.
   BRACHIANO. As silent as i' the church : you
    may proceed.
   MONTICELSO. It is a wonder to your noble
    friends,
That you, [who] have, as 'twere, entered the world
With a free sceptre in your able hand,
And have to th' use of nature well applied
High gifts of learning, should in your prime age
Neglect your awful throne for the soft down   31
Of an insatiate bed. O, my lord,
The drunkard after all his lavish cups
Is dry, and then is sober ; so at length,
When you awake from this lascivious dream,
Repentance then will follow, like the sting
Placed in the adder's tail. Wretched are princes
When fortune blasteth but a petty flower
Of their unwieldy crowns, or ravisheth
But one pearl from their sceptres : but, alas,   40
When they to wilful shipwreck loose good fame,
All princely titles perish with their name !
   BRACHIANO. You have said, my lord.
   MONTICELSO.   Enough to give you taste
How far I am from flattering your greatness.
   BRACHIANO. Now you that are his second, what
    say you ?
Do not like young hawks fetch a course about :
Your game flies fair and for you.
   FRANCISCO.   Do not fear it :

        [1] Clear.

I'll answer you in your own hawking phrase.
Some eagles that should gaze upon the sun
Seldom soar high, but take their lustful ease ;   50
Since they from dunghill birds their prey can seize.
You know Vittoria ?

    BRACHIANO.   Yes.

    FRANCISCO.   You shift your shirt there,
When you retire from tennis ?

    BRACHIANO.   Happily.[1]

    FRANCISCO.   Her husband is lord of a poor
        fortune ;
Yet she wears cloth of tissue.

    BRACHIANO.   What of this ?—
Will you urge that, my good lord cardinal,
As part of her confession at next shrift,
And know from whence it sails ?

    FRANCISCO.   She is your strumpet.

    BRACHIANO.   Uncivil sir, there's hemlock in thy
        breath,
And that black slander. Were she a whore of
    mine,   60
All thy loud cannons, and thy borrowed Switzers,
Thy galleys, nor thy sworn confederates,
Durst not supplant her.

    FRANCISCO.   Let's not talk on thunder.
Thou hast a wife, our sister : would I had given
Both her white hands to death, bound and locked
    fast
In her last winding-sheet, when I gave thee
But one !

    BRACHIANO.   Thou hadst given a soul to God,
    then.

    FRANCISCO.   True :
Thy ghostly father, with all 's absolution,
Shall ne'er do so by thee.

    BRACHIANO.   Spit thy poison !

    FRANCISCO.   I shall not need ; lust carries her
      sharp whip   70

   [1] Often used from the fourteenth to the seventeenth
century in the sense of ' haply '.

At her own girdle. Look to 't, for our anger
Is making thunder-bolts.
    BRACHIANO.   Thunder ? in faith,
They are but crackers.
    FRANCISCO.   We'll end this with the cannon.
    BRACHIANO. Thou'lt get naught by it but iron
    in thy wounds,
And gunpowder in thy nostrils.
    FRANCISCO.   Better that,
Than change perfumes for plasters.
    BRACHIANO.   Pity on thee !
'Twere good you'd show your slaves or men con-
    demned
Your new-ploughed [1] forehead-defiance ! and I'll
    meet thee,
Even in a thicket of thy ablest men.
    MONTICELSO. My lords, you shall not word it
    any further   80
Without a milder limit.
    FRANCISCO.   Willingly.
    BRACHIANO. Have you proclaimed a triumph,
    that you bait
A lion thus ?
    MONTICELSO. My lord !
    BRACHIANO.   I am tame, I am tame, sir
    FRANCISCO. We send unto the duke for con-
    ference
'Bout levies 'gainst the pirates ; my lord duke
Is not at home : we come ourself in person ;
Still my lord duke is busied. But we fear,
When Tiber to each prowling passenger
Discovers flocks of wild ducks ; then, my lord,
'Bout moulting time I mean, we shall be certain
To find you sure enough, and speak with you.
    BRACHIANO.   Ha !
    FRANCISCO. A mere tale of a tub, my words are
    idle ;   92
But to express the sonnet by natural reason,—

[1] Referring to the frown on his brow ; there is no need
to adopt Dyce's suggestion of ' new-plumed '.

When stags grow melancholic, you'll find the
season.
MONTICELSO. No more, my lord : here comes
a champion
Shall end the difference between you both,—

Re-enter GIOVANNI.

Your son, the Prince Giovanni. See, my lords,
What hopes you store in him : this is a casket
For both your crowns, and should be held like dear.
Now is he apt for knowledge ; therefore know,
It is a more direct and even way   101
To train to virtue those of princely blood
By examples than by precepts : if by examples.
Whom should he rather strive to imitate
Than his own father ? be his pattern, then ;
Leave him a stock of virtue that may last,
Should fortune rend his sails and split his mast.
    BRACHIANO. Your hand, boy, growing to a
soldier ?
    GIOVANNI.   Give me a pike.
    FRANCISCO. What, practising your pike so
young, fair coz ?
    GIOVANNI. Suppose me one of Homer's frogs,
my lord,   110
Tossing my bullrush thus. Pray, sir, tell me,
Might not a child of good discretion
Be leader to an army ?
    FRANCISCO.   Yes, cousin, a young prince
Of good discretion might.
    GIOVANNI.   Say you so ?
Indeed, I have heard, 'tis fit a general
Should not endanger his own person oft ;
So that he make a noise when he 's o' horseback,
Like a Dansk [1] drummer, O, 'tis excellent !
He need not fight :—methinks his horse as well
Might lead an army for him. If I live,   120
I'll charge the French foe in the very front

    [1] Danish.

Of all my troops, the foremost man.

FRANCISCO.   What, what !

GIOVANNI.   And will not bid my soldiers up and
   follow,
But bid them follow me.

BRACHIANO.   Forward lapwing !
He flies with the shell on 's head.

FRANCISCO.   Pretty cousin !

GIOVANNI.   The first year, uncle, that I go to
   war,
All prisoners that I take I will set free
Without their ransom.

FRANCISCO.   Ha, without their ransom ?
How, then, will you reward your soldiers
That took those prisoners for you ?

GIOVANNI.   Thus, my lord ;
I'll marry them to all the wealthy widows   131
That fall that year.

FRANCISCO.   Why, then, the next year following,
You'll have no men to go with you to war.

GIOVANNI.   Why, then, I'll press the women to
   the war,
And then the men will follow.

MONTICELSO.   Witty prince !

FRANCISCO.   See, a good habit makes a child
   a man,
Whereas a bad one makes a man a beast.
Come, you and I are friends.

BRACHIANO.   Most wishedly ;
Like bones which, broke in sunder and well set,
Knit the more strongly.

FRANCISCO.   Call Camillo hither.
                        [Exit MARCELLO.
You have received the rumour, how Count Lodo-
   wick   141
Is turned a pirate ?

BRACHIANO.   Yes.

FRANCISCO.   We are now preparing
Some ships to fetch him in.   [Re-enter ISABELLA.]
                       Behold your duchess.

We now will leave you, and expect from you
Nothing but kind entreaty.
    BRACHIANO.   You have charmed me.
[Exeunt FRANCISCO, MONTICELSO, and GIOVANNI. FLAMINEO
                                    retires.
You are in health, we see,—
    ISABELLA.   And above health,
To see my lord well.
    BRACHIANO.   So I wonder much
What amorous whirlwind hurried you to Rome.
    ISABELLA.   Devotion, my lord.
    BRACHIANO.   Devotion ?
Is your soul charged with any grievous sin ?   150
    ISABELLA.   'Tis burdened with too many ; and
    I think,
The oftener that we cast our reckonings up,
Our sleeps will be the sounder.
    BRACHIANO.   Take your chamber !
    ISABELLA.   Nay, my dear lord, I will not have
    you angry :
Doth not my absence from you, now [1] two months,
Merit one kiss ?
    BRACHIANO.   I do not use to kiss.
If that will dispossess your jealousy,
I'll swear it to you.
    ISABELLA.   O my loved lord,
I do not come to chide. My jealousy ?
I am to learn what that Italian means.   160
You are as welcome to these longing arms
As I to you a virgin.
    BRACHIANO.   O, your breath !
Out upon sweetmeats and continued physic,—
The plague is in them !
    ISABELLA.   You have oft, for these two lips,
Neglected cassia or the natural sweets
Of the spring-violet : they are not yet much
    withered.
My lord, I should be merry : these your frowns
Show in a helmet lovely ; but on me,

             [1] From the quarto of 1665.

In such a peaceful interview, methinks 169
They are too-too roughly knit.

BRACHIANO. O, dissemblance !
Do you bandy factions 'gainst me ? have you learnt
The trick of impudent baseness, to complain
Unto your kindred ?

ISABELLA. Never, my dear lord.

BRACHIANO. Must I be hunted out ? or was't
  your trick
To meet some amorous gallant here in Rome,
That must supply our discontinuance ?

ISABELLA. I pray, sir, burst my heart ; and in
  my death
Turn to your ancient pity, though not love.

BRACHIANO. Because your brother is the cor-
  pulent duke, 179
That is, the great duke, 'sdeath, I shall not shortly
Racket away five hundred crowns at tennis,
But it shall rest upon record ! I scorn him
Like a shaved Polack ; [1] all his reverend wit
Lies in his wardrobe ; he's a discreet fellow
When he is made up in his robes of state.
Your brother, the great duke, because h' as galleys,
And now and then ransacks a Turkish fly-boat,
(Now all the hellish Furies take his soul !)
First made this match : accursèd be the priest
That sang the wedding mass, and even my issue !

ISABELLA. O, too-too far you have cursed !

BRACHIANO. Your hand I'll kiss :
This is the latest ceremony of my love. 192
Henceforth I'll never lie with thee ; by this,
This wedding-ring, I'll ne'er more lie with thee :
And this divorce shall be as truly kept
As if the judge had doomed it. Fare you well :
Our sleeps are severed.

ISABELLA. Forbid it, the sweet union
Of all things blessèd ! why, the saints in Heaven
Will knit their brows at that.

BRACHIANO. Let not thy love

_____
[1] Pole.

Make thee an unbeliever ; this my vow   200
Shall never, on my soul, be satisfied
With my repentance ; let thy brother rage
Beyond a horrid tempest or sea-fight,
My vow is fixed.
    ISABELLA.   O my winding-sheet !
Now shall I need thee shortly.—Dear my lord,
Let me hear once more what I would not hear :
Never ?
    BRACHIANO. Never.
    ISABELLA. O my unkind lord ! may your sins
      find mercy,
As I upon a woeful widowed bed
Shall pray for you, if not to turn your eyes   210
Upon your wretched wife and hopeful son,
Yet that in time you'll fix them upon Heaven !
    BRACHIANO. No more : go, go complain to the
      great duke.
    ISABELLA. No, my dear lord ; you shall have
      present witness
How I'll work peace between you. I will make
Myself the author of your cursèd vow ;
I have some cause to do it, you have none.
Conceal it, I beseech you, for the weal
Of both your dukedoms, that you wrought the
    means
Of such a separation : let the fault   220
Remain with my supposèd jealousy ;
And think with what a piteous and rent heart
I shall perform this sad ensuing part.

      Re-enter FRANCISCO and MONTICELSO.[1]

    BRACHIANO. Well,   take   your   course.—My
      honourable brother !
    FRANCISCO.   Sister !—This is not well, my lord.
      —Why, sister !—
She merits not this welcome.
    BRACHIANO.   Welcome, say ?

    [1] The 1672 quarto begins Scene ii here.

She hath given a sharp welcome.

FRANCISCO.   Are you foolish?
Come, dry your tears : is this a modest course
To better what is naught, to rail and weep ?
Grow to a reconcilement, or, by Heaven,   230
I'll ne'er more deal between you.

ISABELLA.   Sir, you shall not ;
No, though Vittoria, upon that condition,
Would become honest.

FRANCISCO.   Was your husband loud
Since we departed ?

ISABELLA.   By my life, sir, no ;
I swear by that I do not care to lose.
Are all these ruins of my former beauty
Laid out for a whore's triumph ?

FRANCISCO.   Do you hear ?
Look upon other women, with what patience
They suffer these slight wrongs ; with what
     justice   239
They study to requite them : take that course.

ISABELLA.   O, that I were a man, or that I had
     power
To execute my apprehended wishes !
I would whip some with scorpions.

FRANCISCO.   What ! turned Fury ?

ISABELLA.   To dig the strumpet's eyes out ; let
     her lie
Some twenty months a dying ; to cut off
Her nose and lips, pull out her rotten teeth ;
Preserve her flesh like mummia, for trophies
Of my just anger ! Hell to my affliction
Is mere snow-water. By your favour, sir ;—
Brother, draw near, and my lord cardinal ;—   250
Sir, let me borrow of you but one kiss :
Henceforth I'll never lie with you, by this,
This wedding-ring.

FRANCISCO.   How ? ne'er more lie with him ?

ISABELLA.   And this divorce shall be as truly
     kept
As if in throngèd court a thousand ears

Had heard it, and a thousand lawyers' hands
Sealed to the separation.

    BRACHIANO.   Ne'er lie with me ?

    ISABELLA.   Let not my former dotage
Make thee an unbeliever : this my vow
Shall never, on my soul, be satisfied   260
With my repentance; manet alta mente repostum.[1]

    FRANCISCO. Now, by my birth, you are a
       foolish, mad,
And jealous woman.

    BRACHIANO.   You see 'tis not my seeking.

    FRANCISCO. Was this your circle of pure
       unicorn's horn
You said should charm your lord ? now, horns
       upon thee,
For jealousy deserves them ! Keep your vow
And take your chamber.

    ISABELLA. No, sir ; I'll presently to Padua ;
I will not stay a minute.

    MONTICELSO.   O good madam !

    BRACHIANO. 'Twere best to let her have her
       humour :   270
Some half-day's journey will bring down her
       stomach,
And then she'll turn in post.

    FRANCISCO.   To see her come
To my lord cardinal for a dispensation
Of her rash vow, will beget excellent laughter.

    ISABELLA. [Aside.] Unkindness, do thy office ;
       poor heart, break :
Those are the killing griefs which dare not speak.
                             [Exit.

Re-enter MARCELLO with CAMILLO.

    MARCELLO. Camillo's come, my lord.

    FRANCISCO.   Where's the commission ?

    MARCELLO. 'Tis here.

    FRANCISCO.   Give me the signet. 278
[Exeunt FRANCISCO, MONTICELSO, CAMILLO, and MARCELLO.

              [1] Virgil, *Aeneid*, i. 26.

FLAMINEO.   My lord, do you mark their whispering ? I will compound a medicine, out of their two heads, stronger than garlic, deadlier than stibium : [1] the cantharides, which are scarce seen to stick upon the flesh when they work to the heart, shall not do it with more silence or invisible cunning.

BRACHIANO.   About the murder ?

FLAMINEO.   They are sending him to Naples, but I'll send him to Candy.

Enter DOCTOR JULIO.

Here's another property too.

BRACHIANO.   Oh, the doctor !   289

FLAMINEO.   A poor quack-salving knave, my lord ; one that should have been lashed for 's lechery, but that he confessed a judgement, had an execution laid upon him, and so put the whip to a non plus.

DOCTOR.   And was cozened, my lord, by an arranter knave than myself, and made pay all the colourable [2] execution.

FLAMINEO.   He will shoot pills into a man's guts shall make them have more ventages than a cornet or a lamprey ; he will poison a kiss ; and was once minded, for his master-piece, because Ireland breeds no poison, to have prepared a deadly vapour in a Spaniard's f—t, that should have poisoned all Dublin.   304

BRACHIANO.   O, Saint Anthony's fire !

DOCTOR.   Your secretary is merry, my lord.

FLAMINEO.   O thou cursed antipathy to nature ! —Look, his eye 's bloodshed, like a needle a chirurgeon stitcheth a wound with.—Let me embrace thee, toad, and love thee, O thou abominable loathsome gargarism, [3] that will fetch up lungs, lights, heart, and liver, by scruples !   312

BRACHIANO.   No more.—I must employ thee, honest doctor :

---

[1] Antimony.   [2] Fictitious.   [3] Gargle.

You must to Padua, and by the way,
Use some of your skill for us.
>DOCTOR.　　　　　　　　　　Sir, I shall.
>BRACHIANO.　But, for Camillo ?
>FLAMINEO.　He dies this night, by such a politic
>strain,
Men shall suppose him by 's own engine slain.
But for your duchess' death—
>DOCTOR.　　　　　　　　　I'll make her sure.
>BRACHIANO.　Small mischiefs are by greater
>made secure.　　　　　　　　　　　　　　320
>FLAMINEO.　Remember this, you slave ; when
knaves come to preferment, they rise as gallowses [1]
are raised i' the Low Countries, one upon another's
shoulders.　　　　　　　　　　[Exeunt Omnes.

SCENE II.[2]—The same.

Enter FRANCISCO, MONTICELSO, CAMILLO, and
MARCELLO.

>MONTICELSO.　Here is an emblem, nephew, pray
>peruse it :
'Twas thrown in at your window.
>CAMILLO.　　　　　　　　At my window ?
Here is a stag, my lord, hath shed his horns,
And for the loss of them the poor beast weeps :
The word,[3] Inopem me copia fecit.[4]
>MONTICELSO.　　　　　　　That is,
Plenty of horns hath made him poor of horns.
>CAMILLO.　What should this mean ?
>MONTICELSO.　　　　I'll tell you : 'tis given out
You are a cuckold.
>CAMILLO.　　　　　Is it given out so ?
I had rather such report as that, my lord,　　　9
Should keep within doors.

---

[1] Gallows—i.e. gallows birds, who were hanged from off
one another's shoulders.
[2] The 1672 quarto makes no break at this point.
[3] i.e. the motto under the picture.
[4] Ovid, *Metamorphoses* iii. 466.

FRANCISCO.   Have you any children ?
CAMILLO.   None, my lord.
FRANCISCO.   You are the happier.
I'll tell you a tale.
CAMILLO.   Pray, my lord.
FRANCISCO.   An old tale.
Upon a time Phoebus, the god of light,
Or him we call the Sun, would needs be married :
The gods gave their consent, and Mercury
Was sent to voice it to the general world.
But what a piteous cry there straight arose
Amongst smiths and felt-makers, brewers and
    cooks,
Reapers and butterwomen, amongst fishmongers,
And thousand other trades, which are annoyed
By his excessive heat ! 'twas lamentable.   21
They came to Jupiter all in a sweat,
And do forbid the banns. A great fat cook
Was made their speaker, who entreats of Jove
That Phoebus might be gelded ; for, if now,
When there was but one sun, so many men
Were like to perish by his violent heat,
What should they do if he were married,
And should beget more, and those children
Make fireworks like their father ? So say I ;   30
Only I will apply it to your wife :
Her issue, should not Providence prevent it,
Would make both nature, time, and man repent it.
    MONTICELSO.   Look you, cousin,
Go, change the air, for shame ; see if your absence
Will blast your cornucopia. Marcello
Is chosen with you joint commissioner
For the relieving our Italian coast   38
From pirates.
    MARCELLO.   I am much honoured in 't.
    CAMILLO.   But, sir,
Ere I return, the stag's horns may be sprouted
Greater than those are shed.
    MONTICELSO.   Do not fear it :
I'll be your ranger.

                                                E

CAMILLO.　　　　　　You must watch i' the nights;
Then 's the most danger.
FRANCISCO.　　　　　　Farewell, good Marcello:
All the best fortunes of a soldier's wish
Bring you a-ship-board !
CAMILLO.　Were I not best, now I am turn'd
　　soldier,
Ere that I leave my wife, sell all she hath,
And then take leave of her ?
MONTICELSO.　　　　　I expect good from you,
Your parting is so merry.
CAMILLO.　Merry, my lord ! o' the captain's
　　humour right ;　　　　　　　　　　　50
I am resolved to be drunk this night.
　　　　　　　　[Exeunt CAMILLO and MARCELLO.
FRANCISCO.　So, 'twas well fitted : now shall we
　　discern
How his wished absence will give violent way
To Duke Brachiano's lust.
MONTICELSO.　　　　　Why, that was it ;
To what scorned purpose else should we make
　　choice
Of him for a sea-captain ? and, besides,
Count Lodowick, which was rumoured for a pirate,
Is now in Padua.
FRANCISCO.　　　　Is 't true ?
MONTICELSO.　　　　　　Most certain.
I have letters from him, which are suppliant
To work his quick repeal from banishment :　　60
He means to address himself for pension
Unto our sister duchess.
FRANCISCO.　　　　　Oh, 'twas well :
We shall not want his absence past six days.
I fain would have the Duke Brachiano run
Into notorious scandal ; for there 's naught
In such cursed dotage to repair his name,
Only the deep sense of some deathless shame.
MONTICELSO.　It may be objected, I am dis-
　　honourable
To play thus with my kinsman ; but I answer,

For my revenge I'd stake a brother's life, 70
That, being wronged, durst not avenge himself.
    FRANCISCO.   Come, to observe this strumpet.
    MONTICELSO.   Curse of greatness !
Sure he'll not leave her ?
    FRANCISCO.   There's small pity in 't :
Like mistletoe on sear elms spent by weather,
Let him cleave to her, and both rot together.
                             [Exeunt.

      SCENE III.[1]—A Room in the House of CAMILLO.

Enter BRACHIANO, with one in the habit of a Conjurer.

    BRACHIANO.   Now, sir, I claim your promise :
    'tis dead midnight,
The time prefixed to show me, by your art,
How the intended murder of Camillo
And our loathed duchess grow to action.
    CONJURER.   You have won me by your bounty
    to a deed
I do not often practise. Some there are
Which by sophistic tricks aspire that name,
Which I would gladly lose, of nigromancer ; [2]
As some that use to juggle upon cards, 9
Seeming to conjure, when indeed they cheat ;
Others that raise up their confederate spirits
'Bout windmills, and endanger their own necks
For making of a squib ; and some there are
Will keep a curtal [3] to show juggling tricks,
And give out 'tis a spirit ; besides these,
Such a whole realm of almanac-makers, figure-
    flingers,[4]
—Fellows, indeed, that only live by stealth,
Since they do merely lie about stol'n goods,—
They'd make men think the devil were fast and
    loose, 19
With speaking fustian Latin. Pray, sit down :
Put on this night-cap sir, 'tis charmed ; and now

---

[1] Act III, Scene i, in the 1672 quarto.
[2] Necromancer.   [3] A little horse.
[4] Casters of horoscopes.

I'll show you, by my strong commanding art,
The circumstance that breaks your duchess' heart.

A DUMB SHOW.

Enter suspiciously JULIO and CHRISTOPHERO : they draw
  a curtain where BRACHIANO's picture is, they put on
  spectacles of glass, which cover their eyes and noses,
  and then burn perfumes afore the picture, and wash
  the lips of the picture ; that done, quenching the fire,
  and putting off their spectacles, they depart laughing.

Enter ISABELLA in her nightgown, as to bed-ward, with
  lights after her, COUNT LUDOVICO, GIOVANNI, GUID-
  ANTONIO,[1] and others waiting on her : she kneels down
  as to prayers, then draws the curtain of the picture,
  does three reverences to it, and kisses it thrice ; she
  faints, and will not suffer them to come near it ; dies :
  sorrow expressed in GIOVANNI and COUNT LODOVICO ;
  she is conveyed out solemnly.

BRACHIANO.   Excellent ! then she's dead ?
CONJURER.   She's poisoned
By the fumed picture. 'Twas her custom nightly,
Before she went to bed, to go and visit
Your picture, and to feed her eyes and lips
On the dead shadow. Doctor Julio,
Observing this, infects it with an oil
And other poisoned stuff, which presently   30
Did suffocate her spirits.
BRACHIANO.   Methought I saw
Count Lodowick there.
CONJURER.   He was : and by my art
I find he did most passionately dote
Upon your duchess. Now turn another way,
And view Camillo's far more politic fate.
Strike louder, music, from this charmèd ground,
To yield, as fits the act, a tragic sound !

The second DUMB SHOW.

Enter FLAMINEO, MARCELLO, CAMILLO, with four more, as
  Captains ; they drink healths, and dance : a vaulting-
  horse is brought into the room : MARCELLO and two

---

[1] Professor Sampson suggests this should be ' Gasparo,
Antonelli '.

more whispered out of the room, while FLAMINEO and
CAMILLO strip themselves into their shirts, as to vault ;
they compliment who shall begin : as CAMILLO is about
to vault, FLAMINEO pitcheth him upon his neck, and,
with the help of the rest, writhes his neck about ;
seems to see if it be broke, and lays him folded double,
as 't were, under the horse ; makes shows to call for
help : MARCELLO comes in, laments ; sends for the
Cardinal and Duke, who come forth with armed men ;
wonder at the act ; command the body to be carried
home ; apprehend FLAMINEO, MARCELLO, and the rest,
and go, as 't were, to apprehend VITTORIA.

BRACHIANO. 'Twas quaintly done ; but yet
    each circumstance
I taste not fully.

CONJURER.   O, 'twas most apparent :
You saw them enter, charged with their deep
    healths
To their boon voyage ; [1] and, to second that,   40
Flamineo calls to have a vaulting-horse
Maintain their sport ; the virtuous Marcello
Is innocently plotted forth the room ;
Whilst your eye saw the rest, and can inform you
The engine [2] of all.

BRACHIANO.   It seems Marcello and Flamineo
Are both committed.

CONJURER.   Yes, you saw them guarded ;
And now they are come with purpose to apprehend
Your mistress, fair Vittoria. We are now   50
Beneath her roof : 'twere fit we instantly
Make out by some back-postern.

BRACHIANO.   Noble friend,
You bind me ever to you : this shall stand
As the firm seal annexèd to my hand ;
It shall enforce a payment.

CONJURER.   Sir, I thank you.
                      [Exit BRACHIANO.
Both flowers and weeds spring when the sun is
    warm,
And great men do great good or else great harm.
                      [Exit.

---

[1] The French *bon voyage.*   [2] Ingenuity.

SCENE IV.[1]—Courtyard of the Mansion of MONTICELSO.

Enter FRANCISCO and MONTICELSO, their Chancellor and
Register.

FRANCISCO.   You have dealt discreetly, to obtain
the presence
Of all the grave lieger [2] ambassadors,
To hear Vittoria's trial.
MONTICELSO.   'Twas not ill ;
For, sir, you know we have naught but circum-
stances
To charge her with, about her husband's death :
Their approbation, therefore, to the proofs
Of her black lust shall make her infamous
To all our neighbouring kingdoms.   I wonder
If Brachiano will be here.
FRANCISCO.   O fie.   9
'Twere impudence too palpable.   [Exeunt.

Enter FLAMINEO and MARCELLO guarded, and a Lawyer.

LAWYER.   What, are you in by the week ? [3]   so,
I will try now whether thy wit be close prisoner.
Methinks none should sit upon thy sister but old
whore-masters.
FLAMINEO.   Or cuckolds ; for your cuckold is
your most terrible tickler of lechery.   Whore-
masters would serve ; for none are judges at tilting
but those that have been old tilters.
LAWYER.   My lord duke and she have been very
private.   20
FLAMINEO.   You are a dull ass ; 'tis threatened
they have been very public.
LAWYER.   If it can be proved they have but
kissed one another——
FLAMINEO.   What then ?
LAWYER.   My lord cardinal will ferret them.[4]

[1] Act III, Scene ii, in the 1672 quarto.
[2] Or ' ledger '—i.e. resident.
[3] Used in *Love's Labour's Lost* (v. ii. 66) for 'safely hooked',
of an admirer ; but no one has explained the phrase.
[4] Rout them out.

FLAMINEO. A cardinal, I hope, will not catch
conies.   28

LAWYER. For to sow kisses (mark what I say),
to sow kisses is to reap lechery ; and, I am sure,
a woman that will endure kissing is half won.

FLAMINEO. True, her upper part, by that rule :
if you will win her nether part too, you know what
follows.

LAWYER. Hark ; the ambassadors are lighted.

FLAMINEO. [Aside.] I do put on this feignèd garb
    of mirth
To gull suspicion.

MARCELLO.   O my unfortunate sister !
I would my dagger-point had cleft her heart
When she first saw Brachiano : you, 'tis said,
Were made his engine and his stalking-horse,   40
To undo my sister.

FLAMINEO.   I made a kind of path
To her and mine own preferment.

MARCELLO.   Your ruin.

FLAMINEO. Hum ! thou art a soldier,
Follow'st the great duke, feed'st his victories,
As witches do their serviceable spirits,
Even with thy prodigal blood : what hast got,
But, like the wealth of captains, a poor handful,
Which in thy palm thou bear'st as men hold water ?
Seeking to gripe it fast, the frail reward   49
Steals through thy fingers.

MARCELLO.   Sir !

FLAMINEO.   Thou hast scarce maintenance
To keep thee in fresh shamois.[1]

MARCELLO.   Brother !

FLAMINEO.   Hear me :—
And thus, when we have even poured ourselves
Into great fights, for their ambition
Or idle spleen, how shall we find reward ?
But as we seldom find the mistletoe
Sacred to physic, or the builder [2] oak,

---

[1] i.e. chamois leather, used for doublets.
[2] Used in building.

Without a mandrake by it ; so in our quest of
   gain,
Alas, the poorest of their forced dislikes
At a limb proffers, but at heart it strikes !
This is lamented doctrine.

MARCELLO.   Come, come.   60

FLAMINEO. When age shall turn thee
White as a blooming hawthorn—

  MARCELLO.   I'll interrupt you :—
For love of virtue bear an honest heart,
And stride o'er every politic respect,
Which, where they most advance, they most infect.
Were I your father, as I am your brother,
I should not be ambitious to leave you
A better patrimony.

FLAMINEO.   I'll think on 't.—
The lord ambassadors.

      [The Ambassadors pass over the stage severally.

LAWYER. O my sprightly Frenchman !—Do you
know him ? he's an admirable tilter.   71

FLAMINEO. I saw him at last tilting : he showed
like a pewter candlestick, fashioned like a man in
armour, holding a tilting-staff in his hand, little
bigger than a candle of twelve i' the pound.

LAWYER. O, but he's an excellent horseman.

FLAMINEO. A lame one in his lofty tricks : he
sleeps a-horseback, like a poulter.[1]

LAWYER. Lo you, my Spaniard !

FLAMINEO. He carries his face in 's ruff, as I have
seen a serving man carry glasses in a cypress
hatband, monstrous steady, for fear of breaking :
he looks like the claw of a blackbird, first salted,
and then broiled in a candle.   [Exeunt.

          [1] Poulterer.

ACT THE THIRD [1]

SCENE I.—A Hall in MONTICELSO's Mansion.

Enter FRANCISCO, MONTICELSO, the six lieger Ambassadors,
    BRACHIANO, VITTORIA, FLAMINEO, MARCELLO, Lawyer,
    a Guard, and Spectators.

MONTICELSO.   Forbear, my lord, here is no place
    assigned you :
This business by his holiness is left
To our examination.

BRACHIANO.   May it thrive with you !
          [Lays a rich gown under him.

FRANCISCO.   A chair there for his lordship !

BRACHIANO.   Forbear your kindness : an un-
    bidden guest
Should travel as Dutchwomen go to church,
Bear their stools with them.

MONTICELSO.   At your pleasure, sir.—
Stand to the table, gentlewoman.—Now, signior,
Fall to your plea.

LAWYER.   Domine judex, converte oculos in hanc
pestem, mulierum corruptissimam.   11

VITTORIA.   What's he ?

FRANCISCO.   A lawyer that pleads against you.

VITTORIA.   Pray, my lord, let him speak his
    usual tongue ;
I'll make no answer else.

FRANCISCO.   Why ? you understand Latin.

VITTORIA.   I do, sir ; but amongst this auditory
Which come to hear my cause, the half or more
May be ignorant in 't.

MONTICELSO.   Go on, sir.

VITTORIA.   By your favour,
I will not have my accusation clouded
In a strange tongue ; all this assembly   20

---

[1] The 1672 quarto makes no Scene-change here, but inserts
as heading ' the Arraignment of Vittoria ', as do all the
quartos.

Shall hear what you can charge me with.

FRANCISCO. Signior,
You need not stand on't much; pray, change
 your language.

MONTICELSO. O, for God's sake!—Gentlewoman, your credit
Shall be more famous by it.[1]

LAWYER. Well, then, have at you!

VITTORIA. I am at the mark, sir: I'll give aim [2]
 to you,
And tell you how near you shoot.

LAWYER. Most literated judges, please your
 lordships
So to connive your judgements to the view
Of this debauched and diversivolent [3] woman;
Who such a black concatenation   30
Of mischief hath effected, that to extirp
The memory of't, must be the consummation
Of her and her projections,—

VITTORIA. What's all this?

LAWYER. Hold your peace:
Exorbitant sins must have exulceration.

VITTORIA. Surely, my lords, this lawyer here
 hath swallowed
Some pothecaries' bills, or proclamations;
And now the hard and undigestible words
Come up, like stones we use give hawks for physic:
Why, this is Welsh to [4] Latin.

LAWYER. My lords, the woman
Knows not her tropes nor figures, nor is perfect
In the academic derivation   42
Of grammatical elocution.

FRANCISCO. Sir, your pains
Shall be well spared, and your deep eloquence
Be worthily applauded amongst those
Which understand you.

LAWYER. My good lord,—

---

[1] i.e. your reputation will become still more infamous.
[2] Act as marker.
[3] Desiring strife.   [4] Compared to.

FRANCISCO. Sir,
Put up your papers in your fustian bag,—
               [FRANCISCO speaks this as in scorn.
Cry mercy, sir, 'tis buckram—and accept
My notion of your learn'd verbosity.

    LAWYER. I most graduatically[1] thank your
      lordship :   50
I shall have use for them elsewhere.   [Exit.

    MONTICELSO. I shall be plainer with you, and
      paint out
Your follies in more natural red and white
Than that upon your cheek.

    VITTORIA.   O you mistake :
You raise a blood as noble in this cheek
As ever was your mother's.

    MONTICELSO. I must spare you, till proof cry
      ' whore ' to that.—
Observe this creature here, my honoured lords,
A woman of a most prodigious spirit,
In her effected.

    VITTORIA.   Honourable my lord,   60
It doth not suit a reverend cardinal
To play the lawyer thus.

    MONTICELSO.   O, your trade
Instructs your language.—
You see, my lords, what goodly fruit she seems ;
Yet, like those apples travellers report
To grow where Sodom and Gomorrah stood,
I will but touch her, and you straight shall see
She'll fall to soot and ashes.

    VITTORIA.   Your envenomed
Pothecary should do 't.

    MONTICELSO.   I am resolved.[2]
Were there a second Paradise to lose,   70
This devil would betray it.

    VITTORIA.   O poor charity !
Thou art seldom found in scarlet.

    MONTICELSO. Who knows not how, when
      several night by night

---

[1] In the manner of a graduate.   [2] Convinced.

Her gates were choked with coaches, and her rooms
Outbraved the stars with several kind of lights,
When she did counterfeit a prince's court
In music, banquets, and most riotous surfeits,
This whore, forsooth, was holy ?

    VITTORIA.   Ha ? whore ? what 's that ?

    MONTICELSO. Shall I expound whore to you ?
    sure, I shall ;   79
I'll give their perfect character. They are first,
Sweetmeats which rot the eater ; in man's nostril
Poisoned perfumes : they are cozening alchemy ;
Shipwrecks in calmest weather. What are whores ?
Cold Russian winters, that appear so barren
As if that nature had forgot the spring :
They are the true material fire of hell :
Worse than those tributes i' the Low Countries
    paid,
Exactions upon meat, drink, garments, sleep,
Ay, even on man's perdition, his sin :
They are those brittle evidences of law   90
Which forfeit all a wretched man's estate
For leaving out one syllable. What are whores ?
They are those flattering bells have all one tune,
At weddings and at funerals. Your rich whores
Are only treasuries by extortion filled,
And emptied by curs'd riot. They are worse,
Worse than dead bodies which are begged at
    gallows,
And wrought upon by surgeons, to teach man
Wherein he is imperfect. What 's a whore ?
She 's like the guilty counterfeited coin   100
Which, whosoe'er first stamps it, brings in trouble
All that receive it.

    VITTORIA.   This character scapes me.

    MONTICELSO. You, gentlewoman !
Take from all beasts and from all minerals
Their deadly poison—

    VITTORIA.   Well, what then ?

    MONTICELSO.   I'll tell thee ;
I'll find in thee a pothecary's shop,

To sample them all.

FRENCH AMBASSADOR.   She hath lived ill.

ENGLISH AMBASSADOR.   True ; but the cardinal's too bitter.

MONTICELSO.   You know what whore is. Next the devil adultery,
Enters the devil murder.

FRANCISCO.   Your unhappy   110
Husband is dead.

VITTORIA.   O, he's a happy husband :
Now he owes nature nothing.

FRANCISCO.   And by a vaulting-engine.

MONTICELSO.   An active plot ;
He jumped into his grave.

FRANCISCO.   What a prodigy was 't
That from some two yards' height a slender man
Should break his neck !

MONTICELSO.   I' the rushes ! [1]

FRANCISCO.   And what's more,
Upon the instant lose all use of speech,
All vital motion, like a man had lain
Wound up three days. Now mark each circumstance.

MONTICELSO.   And look upon this creature was his wife.   120
She comes not like a widow ; she comes armed
With scorn and impudence : is this a mourning-habit ?

VITTORIA.   Had I foreknown his death, as you suggest,
I would have bespoke my mourning.

MONTICELSO.   O, you are cunning.

VITTORIA.   You shame your wit and judgement,
To call it so. What ! is my just defence
By him that is my judge called impudence ?
Let me appeal, then, from this Christian court
To the uncivil Tartar.

MONTICELSO.   See, my lords,   129
She scandals our proceedings.

                [1] With which floors were strewed.

VITTORIA.   Humbly thus,
Thus low, to the most worthy and respected
Lieger ambassadors, my modesty
And womanhood I tender ; but withal,
So entangled in a cursèd accusation,
That my defence, of force, like Portia's,[1]
Must personate masculine virtue. To the point.
Find me but guilty, sever head from body,
We'll part good friends : I scorn to hold my life
At yours or any man's entreaty, sir.
      ENGLISH AMBASSADOR.   She hath a brave spirit.
      MONTICELSO.   Well, well,
      such counterfeit jewels   140
Make true ones oft suspected.
      VITTORIA.   You are deceived :
For know, that all your strict-combinèd heads,
Which strike against this mine of diamonds,
Shall prove but glassen hammers,—they shall
      break.
These are but feignèd shadows of my evils :
Terrify babes, my lord, with painted devils ;
I am past such needless palsy. For your names
Of whore and murderess, they proceed from you,
As if a man should spit against the wind ;
The filth returns in 's face.   150
      MONTICELSO. Pray you, mistress, satisfy me
      one question :
Who lodged beneath your roof that fatal night
Your husband brake his neck ?
      BRACHIANO.   [Rising from his seat.]   That question
Enforceth me break silence : I was there.
      MONTICELSO. Your business ?
      BRACHIANO.   Why, I came to comfort her,
And take some course for settling her estate,
Because I heard her husband was in debt
To you, my lord.
      MONTICELSO.   He was.

_____
[1] Dyce's conjecture for ' Perseus ' of the quartos. He
takes it to refer to the wife of Brutus ; but may it not be
the Portia of *The Merchant of Venice* (1594) ?

BRACHIANO.　　　　And 'twas strangely feared
That you would cozen her.

MONTICELSO.　　　　Who made you overseer ?

BRACHIANO. Why, my charity, my charity,
　　which should flow　　　　　　　　　160
From every generous and noble spirit
To orphans and to widows.

MONTICELSO.　　　　Your lust.

BRACHIANO. Cowardly dogs bark loudest :
　　sirrah priest,
I'll talk with you hereafter. Do you hear ?
The sword you frame of such an excellent temper
I'll sheathe in your own bowels.
There are a number of thy coat resemble
Your common post-boys.

MONTICELSO.　　　　Ha !

BRACHIANO.　　　　Your mercenary post-boys :
Your letters carry truth, but 'tis your guise　169
To fill your mouths with gross and impudent lies
　　　　　　　　　　　[Moves towards the door.

SERVANT. My lord, your gown.

BRACHIANO.　　　　Thou liest, 'twas my stool
Bestow 't upon thy master, that will challenge
The rest o' the household-stuff ; for Brachiano
Was ne'er so beggarly to take a stool
Out of another's lodging : let him make
Vallance for his bed on 't, or a demi-foot-cloth
For his most reverent moil.[1] Monticelso,
Nemo me impune lacessit.　　　　　　[Exit.

MONTICELSO. Your champion 's gone.

VITTORIA.　　　　The wolf may prey the better.

FRANCISCO. My lord, there 's great suspicion of
　　the murder,　　　　　　　　　　180
But no sound proof who did it. For my part,
I do not think she hath a soul so black
To act a deed so bloody : if she have,
As in cold countries husbandmen plant vines,
And with warm blood manure them, even so
One summer she will bear unsavoury fruit,

　　　　　　　[1] Mule.

And ere next spring wither both branch and root.
The act of blood let pass ; only descend
To matter of incontinence.

  VITTORIA. I discern poison under your gilded
   pills.   190
  MONTICELSO. Now the duke's gone, I will
   produce a letter,
Wherein 'twas plotted he and you should meet
At an apothecary's summer-house,
Down by the river Tiber,—view 't, my lords,—
Where, after wanton bathing and the heat
Of a lascivious banquet,—I pray read it,
I shame to speak the rest.

  VITTORIA.   Grant I was tempted ;
Temptation to lust proves not the act :
Casta est quam nemo rogavit.[1]
You read his hot love to me, but you want 200
My frosty answer.

  MONTICELSO. Frost i' the dog-days ? strange !
  VITTORIA. Condemn you me for that the duke
   did love me ?
So may you blame some fair and crystal river
For that some melancholic distracted man
Hath drown'd himself in 't.

  MONTICELSO.   Truly drown'd, indeed.
  VITTORIA. Sum up my faults, I pray, and you
   shall find,
That beauty and gay clothes, a merry heart,
And a good stomach to [a] feast, are all,
All the poor crimes that you can charge me with.
In faith, my lord, you might go pistol flies ; 210
The sport would be more noble.

  MONTICELSO.   Very good.
  VITTORIA. But take your course : it seems you
   have beggared me first,
And now would fain undo me. I have houses,
Jewels, and a poor remnant of crusadoes : [2]

---

[1] Ovid, *Amor*. i. 8.
[2] A Portuguese coin, called *Crusado* from the cross on one
side of it ; worth at the time about two or three shillings.

Would those would make you charitable !

MONTICELSO.   If the devil
Did ever take good shape, behold his picture.

VITTORIA.   You have one virtue left,—You will
not flatter me.

FRANCISCO.   Who brought this letter ?

VITTORIA.   I am not compelled to tell you.

MONTICELSO.   My lord duke sent to you a
thousand ducats   219
The twelfth of August.

VITTORIA.   'Twas to keep your cousin
From prison : I paid use for 't.

MONTICELSO.   I rather think
'Twas interest for his lust.

VITTORIA.   Who says so
But yourself ? if you be my accuser,
Pray, cease to be my judge : come from the
bench ;
Give in your evidence 'gainst me, and let these
Be moderators.[1] My lord cardinal,
Were your intelligencing ears as loving
As to [2] my thoughts, had you an honest tongue,
I would not care though you proclaimed them all.

MONTICELSO.   Go to, go to.   230
After your goodly and vainglorious banquet,
I'll give you a choke-pear.[3]

VITTORIA.   O' your own grafting ?

MONTICELSO.   You were born in Venice, honour-
ably descended
From the Vittelli : 'twas my cousin's fate,—
Ill may I name the hour,—to marry you :
He bought you of your father.

VITTORIA.   Ha !

MONTICELSO.   He spent there in six months
Twelve thousand ducats, and (to my acquaintance)
Received in dowry with you not one julio : [4]

---

[1] Judges.   [2] With regard to.
[3] Properly a rough kind of pear, so something hard to
swallow.
[4] A silver coin worth about sixpence.

'Twas a hard pennyworth, the ware being so light.
I yet but draw the curtain ; now to your picture :
You came from thence a most notorious strumpet,
And so you have continued.

VITTORIA.　　　　　　　My lord,—
MONTICELSO.　　　　　　　　　Nay, hear me ;
You shall have time to prate.　My Lord Bra-
　　chiano—　　　　　　　　　　　　　　243
Alas, I make but repetition
Of what is ordinary and Rialto talk,
And ballated,[1] and would be played o' the stage,
But that vice many times finds such loud friends
That preachers are charmed silent.—
You gentlemen, Flamineo and Marcello,
The court hath nothing now to charge you with,
Only you must remain upon your sureties　　251
For your appearance.

FRANCISCO.　　　　　I stand for Marcello.
FLAMINEO.　And my lord duke for me.
MONTICELSO.　For you, Vittoria, your public
　　fault,
Joined to the condition of the present time,
Takes from you all the fruits of noble pity.
Such a corrupted trial have you made
Both of your life and beauty, and been styled
No less an ominous fate than blazing stars
To princes : here's your sentence ; you are con-
　　fined　　　　　　　　　　　　　　260
Unto a house of convertites, and your bawd—
FLAMINEO. [Aside.] Who, I ?
MONTICELSO.　　　　　　The Moor.
FLAMINEO. [Aside.]　O, I am a sound man again.
VITTORIA.　A house of convertites ! what's
　　that ?
MONTICELSO.　　　　　　　　　A house
Of penitent whores.
VITTORIA.　　　　　Do the noblemen in Rome
Erect it for their wives, that I am sent
To lodge there ?

　　　　　[1] Made the subject of a ballad.

FRANCISCO.   You must have patience.

VITTORIA.   I must first have vengeance.
I fain would know if you have your salvation
By patent, that you proceed thus.

MONTICELSO.   Away with her !
Take her hence.   270

VITTORIA.   A rape ! a rape !

MONTICELSO.   How ?

VITTORIA.   Yes, you have ravished justice ;
Forced her to do your pleasure.

MONTICELSO.   Fie, she 's mad !

VITTORIA.   Die with those pills in your most
    cursèd maw
Should bring you health ! or while you sit o' the
    bench
Let your own spittle choke you !—

MONTICELSO.   She 's turned Fury.

VITTORIA.   That the last day of judgement may
    so find you,
And leave you the same devil you were before !
Instruct me, some good horse-leech, to speak
    treason ;
For since you cannot take my life for deeds,
Take it for words ! O woman's poor revenge,   280
Which dwells but in the tongue ! I will not
    weep ;
No, I do scorn to call up one poor tear
To fawn on your injustice ; bear me hence
Unto this house of—what 's your mitigating title ?

MONTICELSO.   Of convertites.

VITTORIA.   It shall not be a house of con-
    vertites ;
My mind shall make it honester to me
Than the Pope's palace, and more peaceable
Than thy soul, though thou art a cardinal.   289
Know this, and let it somewhat raise your spite,
Through darkness diamonds spread their richest
    light.

[Exit VITTORIA with Guards, followed by Spectators.

Re-enter BRACHIANO.[1]

BRACHIANO.   Now you and I are friends, sir,
  we'll shake hands
In a friend's grave together ; a fit place,
Being the emblem of soft peace, to atone [2] our
  hatred.
  FRANCISCO.   Sir, what 's the matter ?
  BRACHIANO.   I will not chase more blood from
    that loved cheek ;
You have lost too much already : fare you well.
                                                    [Exit.
  FRANCISCO.   How strange these words sound !
    what 's the interpretation ?   298
  FLAMINEO.   [Aside.]   Good ; this is a preface to
the discovery of the duchess' death : he carries it
well. Because now I cannot counterfeit a whining
passion for the death of my lady, I will feign a mad
humour for the disgrace of my sister ; and that
will keep off idle questions. Treason's tongue
hath a villainous palsy in 't : I will talk to any
man, hear no man, and for a time appear a politic
madman.   (Exit.

      Enter GIOVANNI and COUNT LODOVICO.

  FRANCISCO.   How now, my noble cousin ? what,
    in black ?
  GIOVANNI.   Yes, uncle, I was taught to imitate
    you
In virtue, and you [now] must imitate me   310
In colours of your garments. My sweet mother
Is——
  FRANCISCO.   How ! where ?
  GIOVANNI.   Is there ; no, yonder : indeed, sir,
    I'll not tell you,
For I shall make you weep.
  FRANCISCO.   Is dead ?
  GIOVANNI.   Do not blame me now ;
I did not tell you so.

───────────────

[1] Act III, Scene iii, in the 1672 quarto.   [2] Reconcile.

LODOVICO.   She's dead, my lord.

FRANCISCO.   Dead ?

MONTICELSO.   Blessed lady, thou art now above
    thy woes !—

Will't please your lordships to withdraw a little ?
                              [Exeunt Ambassadors.

GIOVANNI.   What do the dead do, uncle ? do
    they eat,

Hear music, go a-hunting, and be merry,   320
As we that live ?

FRANCISCO.   No, coz ; they sleep.

GIOVANNI.   Lord, Lord, that I were dead !
I have not slept these six nights.—When do they
    wake ?

FRANCISCO.   When God shall please.

GIOVANNI.   Good God, let her sleep ever !
For I have known her wake an hundred nights,
When all the pillow where she laid her head
Was brine-wet with her tears. I am to complain to
    you, sir ;

I'll tell you how they have used her now she's
    dead :

They wrapped her in a cruel fold of lead,
And would not let me kiss her.

FRANCISCO.   Thou didst love her.

GIOVANNI.   I have often heard her say she gave
    me suck,   331

And it should seem by that she dearly loved me,
Since princes seldom do it.

FRANCISCO.   O, all of my poor sister that
    remains !—

Take him away, for God's sake !
               [Exeunt GIOVANNI, LODOVICO, and MARCELLO.

MONTICELSO.   How now, my lord ?

FRANCISCO.   Believe me, I am nothing but her
    grave ;

And I shall keep her blessèd memory
Longer than thousand epitaphs.
               [Exeunt FRANCISCO and MONTICELSO.

SCENE II.[1]—The Courtyard of MONTICELSO'S Mansion.

Enter FLAMINEO as distracted.

FLAMINEO. We endure the strokes like anvils
or hard steel,
Till pain itself make us no pain to feel.
Who shall do me right now ? Is this the end of
service ? I'd rather go weed garlic ; travel
through France, and be mine own ostler ; wear
sheepskin linings, or shoes that stink of blacking ;
be entered into the list of the forty thousand pedlars
in Poland.

Enter Ambassadors of Savoy, France, and England,
followed by LODOVICO and MARCELLO.

Would I had rotted in some surgeon's house at
Venice, built upon the pox as well as on piles, ere
I had served Brachiano !   11

SAVOY AMBASSADOR. You must have comfort.

FLAMINEO. Your comfortable words are like
honey ; they relish well in your mouth that's
whole, but in mine that's wounded they go down
as if the sting of the bee were in them. Oh, they
have wrought their purpose cunningly, as if they
would not seem to do it of malice ! In this a politician imitates the devil, as the devil imitates a
cannon ; wheresoever he comes to do mischief, he
comes with his backside towards you.   21

FRENCH AMBASSADOR. The proofs are evident.

FLAMINEO. Proof ! 'twas corruption. O gold,
what a god art thou ! and O man, what a devil
art thou to be tempted by that cursed mineral !
Your diversivolent lawyer, mark him : knaves turn
informers, as maggots turn to flies ; you may catch
gudgeons with either. A cardinal ! I would he
would hear me : there's nothing so holy but
money will corrupt and putrify it, like victual
under the line. You are happy in England, my

---

[1] The 1672 quarto makes no break.

lord : here they sell justice with those weights they press men to death with. O horrible salary !

ENGLISH AMBASSADOR.   Fie, fie, Flamineo !   34

[Exeunt Ambassadors.

FLAMINEO.   Bells ne'er ring well, till they are at their full pitch ; and I hope yon cardinal shall never have the grace to pray well till he come to the scaffold.   If they were racked now to know the confederacy,—but your noblemen are privileged from the rack ; and well may, for a little thing would pull some of them a-pieces afore they came to their arraignment. Religion, oh, how it is commedled [1] with policy ! The first bloodshed in the world happened about religion. Would I were a Jew !   45

MARCELLO.   Oh, there are too many.

FLAMINEO.   You are deceived : there are not Jews enough, priests enough, nor gentlemen enough.

MARCELLO.   How ?   49

FLAMINEO.   I'll prove it ; for if there were Jews enough, so many Christians would not turn usurers; if priests enough, one should not have six benefices ; and if gentlemen enough, so many early mushrooms, whose best growth sprang from a dunghill, should not aspire to gentility. Farewell : let others live by begging ; be thou one of them practise the art of Wolner [2] in England, to swallow all 's given thee ; and yet let one purgation make thee as hungry again as fellows that work in a saw-pit. I'll go hear the screech-owl.   [Exit.

LODOVICO.   [Aside.] This was Brachiano's pander
      and 'tis strange   61
That, in such open and apparent guilt
Of his adulterous sister, he dare utter
So scandalous a passion. I must wind him.[3]

[1] Commingled.
[2] Of whom it is recorded that he was able to eat iron, glass, and oyster-shells.
[3] Track him by scent.

Re-enter FLAMINEO.

FLAMINEO. [Aside.] How dares this banished
  count return to Rome,
His pardon not yet purchased ? I have heard
The deceased duchess gave him pension,
And that he came along from Padua
I' the train of the young prince. There's some-
  what in 't :
Physicians, that cure poisons, still do work   70
With counter-poisons.

MARCELLO.   Mark this strange encounter.

FLAMINEO. [To LODOVICO.] The god of melan-
  choly turn thy gall to poison,
And let the stigmatic [1] wrinkles in thy face,
Like to the boisterous waves in a rough tide,
One still overtake another.

LODOVICO.   I do thank thee,
And I do wish ingeniously [2] for thy sake
The dog-days [3] all year long.

FLAMINEO.   How croaks the raven ?
Is our good duchess dead ?

LODOVICO.   Dead.

FLAMINEO.   O fate !
Misfortune comes, like the coroner's business,
Huddle upon huddle.   80

LODOVICO. Shalt thou and I join house-keeping?

FLAMINEO.   Yes, content :
Let 's be unsociably sociable,—

LODOVICO. Sit some three days together, and
  discourse—

FLAMINEO. Only with making faces : lie in our
  clothes,—

LODOVICO. With faggots for our pillows,—

FLAMINEO.   And be lousy—

LODOVICO. In taffata linings ; that 's genteel
  melancholy :
Sleep all day,—

---

[1] Disgraceful.   [2] Ingenuously.
[3] When malign influences were supposed to prevail.

FLAMINEO. Yes ; and, like your melancholic
   hare,
Feed after midnight.——
We are observed : see how yon couple grieve ! [1]
   LODOVICO. What a strange creature is a laugh-
   ing fool !
                                                            91
As if man were created to no use
But only to show his teeth.
   FLAMINEO.   I'll tell thee what,——
It would do well, instead of looking-glasses,
To set one's face each morning by a saucer
Of a witch's congealed blood.
   LODOVICO.   Precious gue ! [2]
We'll never part.
   FLAMINEO. Never, till the beggary of courtiers,
The discontent of churchmen, want of soldiers,
And all the creatures that hang manacled,
Worse than strappadoed, on the lowest felly   100
Of Fortune's wheel, be taught, in our two lives,
To scorn that world which life of means deprives.

                Enter ANTONELLI and GASPARO.

   ANTONELLI. My lord, I bring good news. The
   Pope, on 's death-bed,
At the earnest suit of the Great Duke of Florence,
Hath signed your pardon, and restored unto you——
   LODOVICO. I thank you for your news.——Look
   up again,
Flamineo ; see my pardon.
   FLAMINEO.   Why do you laugh ?
There was no such condition in our covenant.
   LODOVICO.   Why ?
   FLAMINEO. You shall not seem a happier man
   than I :
                                                            109

   [1] Presumably Antonelli and Gasparo are seen in the
distance laughing.
   [2] Rogue (Fr. *Gueux*). Both the B.M. copies of the
earliest quarto have ' grine rouge '. (May this = red groin,
the groin being elsewhere regarded as the seat of lust ?)
Other copies, according to Dyce, have ' gue '.

You know our vow, sir ; if you will be merry,
Do it i' the like posture as if some great man
Sate while his enemy were executed ;
Though it be very lechery [1] unto thee,
Do 't with a crabbèd politician's face.

LODOVICO. Your sister is a damnable whore.
FLAMINEO.   Ha !
LODOVICO. Look you, I spake that laughing.
FLAMINEO. Dost ever think to speak again ?
LODOVICO.   Do you hear ?
Wilt sell me forty ounces of her blood
To water a mandrake ?
FLAMINEO.   Poor lord, you did vow
To live a lousy creature.
LODOVICO.   Yes.
FLAMINEO.   Like one   120
That had for ever forfeited the daylight
By being in debt.
LODOVICO.   Ha, ha !
FLAMINEO. I do not greatly wonder you do
    break ;
Your lordship learned it long since. But I'll tell
    you——
LODOVICO. What ?
FLAMINEO.   And 't shall stick by you,—
LODOVICO.   I long for it.
FLAMINEO. This laughter scurvily becomes
    your face :
If you will not be melancholy, be angry.
                              [Strikes him.

See, now I laugh too.
MARCELLO. You are to blame : I'll force you
    hence.
LODOVICO.   Unhand me.
                    [Exeunt MARCELLO and FLAMINEO.
That e'er I should be forced to right myself   130
Upon a pander !
ANTONELLI.   My lord,—
LODOVICO.   H'ad been as good
            [1] Inordinate pleasure.

Met with his fist a thunderbolt.

GASPARO.   How this shows !

LODOVICO.   Ud's death, how did my sword miss
    him ?   These rogues
That are most weary of their lives still scape
The greatest dangers.
A pox upon him !   all his reputation,
Nay, all the goodness of his family,
Is not worth half this earthquake :
I learned it of no fencer to shake thus :   139
Come, I'll forget him, and go drink some wine.

                                   [Exeunt.

    SCENE III.[1]—A Room in the Palace of FRANCISCO.

      Enter FRANCISCO and MONTICELSO.

MONTICELSO.   Come, come, my lord, untie your
    folded thoughts,
And let them dangle loose as a bride's hair.
Your sister 's poisoned.

FRANCISCO.   Far be it from my thoughts
To seek revenge.

MONTICELSO.   What, are you turned all marble ?

FRANCISCO.   Shall I defy him, and impose a war
Most burdensome on my poor subjects' necks,
Which at my will I have not power to end ?
You know, for all the murders, rapes, and thefts,
Committed in the horrid lust of war,
He that unjustly caused it first proceed   10
Shall find it in his grave and in his seed.

MONTICELSO.   That 's not the course I'd wish
    you ;   pray, observe me.
We see that undermining more prevails
Than doth the cannon.   Bear your wrongs con-
    cealed,
And, patient as the tortoise, let this camel
Stalk o'er your back unbruised :   sleep with the
    lion,
And let this brood of secure foolish mice
Play with your nostrils, till the time be ripe

    [1] Scene iv in the 1672 quarto.

For the bloody audit and the fatal gripe :
Aim like a cunning fowler, close one eye,   20
That you the better may your game espy.

    FRANCISCO. Free me, my innocence, from
      treacherous acts !
I know there 's thunder yonder ; and I'll stand
Like a safe valley, which low bends the knee
To some aspiring mountain ; since I know
Treason, like spiders weaving nets for flies,
By her foul work is found, and in it dies.
To pass away these thoughts, my honoured lord,
It is reported you possess a book,
Wherein you have quoted,[1] by intelligence,   30
The names of all notorious offenders
Lurking about the city.

    MONTICELSO.   Sir, I do ;
And some there are which call it my black book :
Well may the title hold ; for though it teach not
The art of conjuring, yet in it lurk
The names of many devils.

    FRANCISCO.   Pray, let 's see it.
    MONTICELSO. I'll fetch it to your lordship.
                                [Exit.
    FRANCISCO.   Monticelso,
I will not trust thee ; but in all my plots
I'll rest as jealous as a town besieged.
Thou canst not reach what I intend to act :   40
Your flax soon kindles, soon is out again ;
But gold slow heats, and long will hot remain.

   Re-enter MONTICELSO, presents FRANCISCO with a book.

    MONTICELSO. 'Tis here, my lord.
    FRANCISCO. First, your intelligencers,[2] pray,
      let 's see.
    MONTICELSO. Their number rises strangely ;
      and some of them
You'd take for honest men. Next are panders,—
These are your pirates ; and these following leaves

     [1] Noted.   [2] Informers, spies.

For base rogues that undo young gentlemen
By taking up commodities,[1] for politic bankrupts ;
For fellows that are bawds to their own wives,
Only to put off [2] horses, and slight jewels,   51
Clocks, defaced plate, and such commodities,
At birth of their first children.
    FRANCISCO.   Are there such ?
    MONTICELSO.   These are for impudent bawds
That go in men's apparel ; for usurers
That share with scriveners for their good report-
    age ;
For lawyers that will antedate their writs :
And some divines you might find folded there,
But that I slip them o'er for conscience' sake.
Here is a general catalogue of knaves :   60
A man might study all the prisons o'er,
Yet never attain this knowledge.
    FRANCISCO.   Murderers !
Fold down the leaf, I pray.
Good my lord, let me borrow this strange doctrine.
    MONTICELSO.   Pray, use 't, my lord.
    FRANCISCO.   I do assure your lordship,
You are a worthy member of the state,
And have done infinite good in your discovery
Of these offenders.
    MONTICELSO.   Somewhat, sir.
    FRANCISCO.   O God !
Better than tribute of wolves paid in England : [3]
'Twill hang their skins o' the hedge.
    MONTICELSO.   I must make bold
To leave your lordship.
    FRANCISCO.   Dearly, sir, I thank you :
If any ask for me at court, report   72
You have left me in the company of knaves.
                 [Exit MONTICELSO.

[1] i.e. furnishing borrowers with goods, which the borrowers then sold to raise money. This was done to avoid
the laws against usury.
[2] Palm off on their wives' seducers.
[3] The Saxon king Edgar demanded a yearly tribute of
300 wolves from the Britons.

I gather now by this, some cunning fellow
That's my lord's officer, one that lately skipped
From a clerk's desk up to a justice' chair,
Hath made this knavish summons, and intends,
As the Irish rebels wont were to sell heads,
So to make prize of these. And thus it happens,
Your poor rogues pay for't which have not the
    means   80
To present bribe in fist : the rest o' the band
Are razed out of the knaves' record ; or else
My lord he winks at them with easy will ;
His man grows rich, the knaves are the knaves
    still.
But to the use I'll make of it ; it shall serve
To point me out a list of murderers,
Agents for any villainy. Did I want
Ten leash of courtezans, it would furnish me ;
Nay, laundress three armies. That in so little
    paper
Should lie the undoing of so many men !   90
'Tis not so big as twenty declarations.
See the corrupted use some make of books :
Divinity, wrested by some factious blood,
Draws swords, swells battles, and o'erthrows all
    good.
To fashion my revenge more seriously,
Let me remember my dead sister's face :
Call for her picture ? no, I'll close mine eyes,
And in a melancholic thought I'll frame

Enter ISABELLA's ghost.

Her figure 'fore me. Now I ha 't :—how strong
Imagination works ! how she can frame   100
Things which are not ! Methinks she stands afore
    me,
And by the quick idea of my mind,
Were my skill pregnant, I could draw her picture.
Thought, as a subtle juggler, makes us deem
Things supernatural, which yet have cause
Common as sickness. 'Tis my melancholy.—

How cam'st thou by thy death ?—How idle am I
To question mine own idleness !—Did ever
Man dream awake till now ?—Remove this object ;
Out of my brain with 't ! What have I to do　110
With tombs, or death-beds, funerals, or tears,
That have to meditate upon revenge ? [Exit Ghost.
So, now 'tis ended, like an old wives' story :
Statesmen think often they see stranger sights
Than madmen.　Come, to this weighty business :
My tragedy must have some idle mirth in't,
Else it will never pass.　I am in love,
In love with Corombona ;　and my suit
Thus halts to her in verse.—　　　　　　[Writes.
I have done it rarely :　O the fate of princes !
I am so used to frequent flattery,　　　　　121
That, being alone, I now flatter myself :
But it will serve ;　'tis sealed.

Enter Servant.[1]

　　　　　　　　　　　　　Bear this
To the house of convertites, and watch your leisure
To give it to the hands of Corombona,
Or to the matron, when some followers
Of Brachiano may be by.　Away !　[Exit Servant.
He that deals all by strength, his wit is shallow :
When a man's head goes through, each limb will
　　follow.
The engine for my business, bold Count Lodowick :
'Tis gold must such an instrument procure ;　131
With empty fist no man doth falcons lure.
Brachiano, I am now fit for thy encounter :
Like the wild Irish, I'll ne'er think thee dead
Till I can play at football with thy head.
Flectere si nequeo superos, Acheronta movebo.[2]
　　　　　　　　　　　　　　　　[Exit.

[1] ' Occasionally in old plays servants enter, as here,
without being summoned, just at the moment they happen
to be wanted.'—*Dyce.*
[2] Virgil, *Aeneid*, vii. 312.

ACT THE FOURTH

SCENE I.—A Room in the House of Convertites.

Enter the Matron and FLAMINEO.

MATRON. Should it be known the duke hath
    such recourse
To your imprisoned sister, I were like
To incur much damage by it.
FLAMINEO.   Not a scruple !
The Pope lies on his death-bed, and their heads
Are troubled now with other business
Than guarding of a lady.

Enter Servant.

SERVANT. Yonder's Flamineo in conference
With the matrona.—Let me speak with you ;
I would entreat you to deliver for me
This letter to the fair Vittoria——   10
MATRON. I shall, sir.
SERVANT.   With all care and secrecy.
Hereafter you shall know me, and receive
Thanks for this courtesy.   [Exit.
FLAMINEO.   How now ? what 's that ?
MATRON. A letter.
FLAMINEO. To my sister ? I'll see 't delivered.
                                        [Exit Matron.

Enter BRACHIANO.

BRACHIANO. What 's that you read, Flamineo ?
FLAMINEO.   Look.
BRACHIANO.   Ha !
[Reads.] 'To the most unfortunate, his best respected
Vittoria.'—
Who was the messenger ?
FLAMINEO.   I know not.
BRACHIANO.   No ?
Who sent it ?
FLAMINEO. Ud's foot, you speak as if a man

Should know what fowl is coffined in a baked meat
Afore you cut it up. 21
BRACHIANO. I'll open't, were't her heart.
What's here subscribed ?
' Florence ! ' this juggling is gross and palpable :
I have found out the conveyance.[1]—Read it, read
it !
FLAMINEO. [Reads.] ' Your tears I'll turn to
triumphs, be but mine :
Your prop is fall'n : I pity, that a vine,
Which princes heretofore have longed to gather,
Wanting supporters, now should fade and wither.'
Wine, i' faith, my lord, with lees would serve his
turn.— 30
' Your sad imprisonment I'll soon uncharm,
And with a princely uncontrollèd arm
Lead you to Florence, where my love and care
Shall hang your wishes in my silver hair.'—
A halter on his strange equivocation !—
' Nor for my years return me the sad willow :
Who prefer blossoms before fruit that's mellow ? '—
Rotten, on my knowledge, with lying too long i'
the bed-straw.—
' And all the lines of age this line convinces,[2] 40
The gods never wax old, no more do princes.'—
A pox on 't, tear it ; let 's have no more atheists,
for God's sake.
BRACHIANO. Ud's death, I'll cut her into
atomies,
And let th' irregular north wind sweep her up,
And blow her into his nostrils ! Where's this whore?
FLAMINEO. That—what do you call her ?
BRACHIANO. Oh, I could be mad,
Prevent [3] the cursed disease she'll bring me to,
And tear my hair off ! Where's this changeable
stuff ?
FLAMINEO. O'er head and ears in water, I
assure you : 50

[1] Ingenious device.
[2] i.e. this saying refutes all wrinkles. [3] Anticipate.

F

She is not for your wearing.

BRACHIANO.   In, you pander !

FLAMINEO.   What, me, my lord ? am I your dog ?

BRACHIANO.   A blood-hound !
Do you brave, do you stand me ?

FLAMINEO.   Stand you ! let those that have
    diseases run ;
I need no plasters.

BRACHIANO.   Would you be kicked ?

FLAMINEO.   Would you have your neck broke ?
I tell you, duke, I am not in Russia ;
My shins must be kept whole.

BRACHIANO.   Do you know me ?

FLAMINEO.   O, my lord, methodically :
As in this world there are degrees of evils,   60
So in this world there are degrees of devils.
You're a great duke, I your poor secretary.
I do look now for a Spanish fig, or an Italian salad,[1]
daily.

BRACHIANO.   Pander, ply your convoy,[2] and
leave your prating.

FLAMINEO.   All your kindness to me is like that
miserable courtesy of Polyphemus to Ulysses ; you
reserve me to be devoured last : you would dig
turfs out of my grave to feed your larks ; that
would be music to you.   Come, I'll lead you to her.

BRACHIANO.   Do you face me ?   72

FLAMINEO.   Oh, sir, I would not go before a politic
enemy with my back towards him, though there
were behind me a whirlpool.

SCENE II.[3]—VITTORIA'S Room in the House of Convertites.

Enter VITTORIA, BRACHIANO, and FLAMINEO.

BRACHIANO.   Can you read, mistress ? look upon
    that letter :
There are no characters nor hieroglyphics ;

---

[1] Two frequent vehicles for poison in Spain and Italy.
[2] i.e. escort me in.
[3] The 1672 quarto makes no change.

You need no comment : I am grown your receiver.[1]
God's precious ! you shall be a brave great lady,
A stately and advancèd whore.

VITTORIA.　　　　　　　　　Say, sir ?

BRACHIANO.　Come, come, let's see your cabinet,
　　discover
Your treasury of love-letters.　Death and Furies !
I'll see them all.

VITTORIA.　　　　Sir, upon my soul,
I have not any.　Whence was this directed ?

BRACHIANO.　Confusion on your politic ignor-
　　ance !　　　　　　　　　　　　　　　　10
You are reclaimed,[2] are you ?　I'll give you the
　　bells,
And let you fly to the devil.

FLAMINEO.　　　　　　　Ware hawk, my lord !

VITTORIA.　'Florence' !　this is some treache-
　　rous plot, my lord :
To me he ne'er was lovely, I protest,
So much as in my sleep.

BRACHIANO.　　　　　　　Right !　they are plots.
Your beauty ! Oh, ten thousand curses on't !
How long have I beheld the devil in crystal ?[3]
Thou hast led me, like an heathen sacrifice,
With music and with fatal yokes of flowers,
To my eternal ruin.　Woman to man　　　20
Is either a god or a wolf.

VITTORIA.　　　　　　My lord,—

BRACHIANO.　　　　　　　　Away !
We'll be as differing as two adamants ;
The one shall shun the other.　What, dost weep ?
Procure but ten of thy dissembling trade,
Ye'd furnish all the Irish funerals
With howling past wild Irish.

FLAMINEO.　　　　　　Fie, my lord !

BRACHIANO.　That hand, that cursèd hand,
　　which I have wearied
With doting kisses !—O my sweetest duchess,

----

[1] Procurer.　　　　[2] A play upon a term of hawking.
[3] A magic glass.

How lovely art thou now !—My loose thoughts
Scatter like quicksilver : I was bewitched ;   30
For all the world speaks ill of thee.
    VITTORIA.   No matter :
I'll live so now, I'll make that world recant,
And change her speeches. You did name your
    duchess.
    BRACHIANO. Whose death God pardon !
    VITTORIA.   Whose death God revenge
On thee, most godless duke !
    FLAMINEO. [Aside.] Now for two whirlwinds !
    VITTORIA. What have I gained by thee but
    infamy ?
Thou hast stained the spotless honour of my
    house,
And frighted thence noble society :
Like those, which, sick o' the palsy and retain[ing]
Ill-scenting foxes 'bout them, are still shunned
By those of choicer nostrils. What do you call
    this house ?   41
Is this your palace ? did not the judge style it
A house of penitent whores ? who sent me to it?
Who hath the honour to advance Vittoria
To this incontinent college ? is 't not you ?
Is 't not your high preferment ? Go, go, brag
How many ladies you have undone like me.
Fare you well, sir ; let me hear no more of you :
I had a limb corrupted to an ulcer,
But I have cut it off ; and now I'll go   5c
Weeping to Heaven on crutches. For your gifts,
I will return them all ; and I do wish
That I could make you full executor
To all my sins. Oh, that I could toss myself
Into a grave as quickly ! for all thou art worth
I'll not shed one tear more,—I'll burst first.
                    [She throws herself upon a bed.
    BRACHIANO. I have drunk Lethe.—Vittoria !
My dearest happiness ! Vittoria !
What do you ail, my love ? why do you weep ?
    VITTORIA. Yes, I now weep poniards, do you see ?

BRACHIANO.   Are not those matchless eyes mine?

VITTORIA.   I had rather
They were not matches ! [1]

BRACHIANO.   Is not this lip mine ?

VITTORIA.   Yes ; thus to bite it off, rather than
    give it thee.   63

FLAMINEO.   Turn to my lord, good sister.

VITTORIA.   Hence, you pander !

FLAMINEO.   Pander ! am I the author of your
    sin ?

VITTORIA.   Yes ; he's a base thief that a thief
    lets in.

FLAMINEO.   We're blown up, my lord.

BRACHIANO.   Wilt thou hear me ?
Once to be jealous of thee, is to express
That I will love thee everlastingly,
And never more be jealous.

VITTORIA.   O thou fool,   70
Whose greatness hath by much o'ergrown thy wit !
What dar'st thou do that I not dare to suffer,
Excepting to be still thy whore ? for that,
In the sea's bottom sooner thou shalt make
A bonfire.

FLAMINEO.   O, no oaths, for God's sake !

BRACHIANO.   Will you hear me !

VITTORIA.   Never.

FLAMINEO.   What a damned imposthume is a
    woman's will !
Can nothing break it ?—Fie, fie, my lord,
Women are caught as you take tortoises ;
She must be turned on her back.—Sister, by this
    hand,   80
I am on your side.—Come, come, you have
    wronged her :
What a strange credulous man were you, my lord,
To think the Duke of Florence would love her !
Will any mercer take another's ware
When once 'tis toused and sullied ?—And yet,
    sister,

[1] The three later quartos have ' matchless '.

How scurvily this frowardness becomes you !
Young leverets stand not long ; and women's
    anger
Should, like their flight, procure a little sport ;
A full cry for a quarter of an hour,   89
And then be put to the dead quat.[1]
    BRACHIANO.   Shall these eyes,
Which have so long time dwelt upon your face,
Be now put out ?
    FLAMINEO.   No cruel landlady i' th' world,
    which lends forth groats
To broom-men, and takes use for them, would
    do 't.—
Hand her, my lord, and kiss her : be not like
A ferret, to let go your hold with blowing.
    BRACHIANO.   Let us renew right hands.
    VITTORIA.   Hence !
    BRACHIANO.   Never shall rage
Or the forgetful wine make me commit
Like fault.
    FLAMINEO.   Now you are i' the way on 't,
    follow 't hard.
    BRACHIANO.   Be thou at peace with me, let all
    the world   100
Threaten the cannon.
    FLAMINEO.   Mark his penitence :
Best natures do commit the grossest faults,
When they're given o'er to jealousy, as best wine,
Dying, makes strongest vinegar. I'll tell you,—
The sea 's more rough and raging than calm rivers,
But not so sweet nor wholesome. A quiet woman
Is a still water under a great bridge ;
A man may shoot her safely.
    VITTORIA.   Oh, ye dissembling men !—
    FLAMINEO.   We sucked that, sister,
From women's breasts, in our first infancy.   110
    VITTORIA.   To add misery to misery !
    BRACHIANO.   Sweetest,—
    VITTORIA.   Am I not low enough ?

        [1] Squat.

Aye, aye, your good heart gathers like a snowball,
Now your affection's cold.

FLAMINEO.   Ud'sfoot, it shall melt
To a heart again, or all the wine in Rome
Shall run o' the lees for 't.

VITTORIA.   Your dog or hawk should be re-
    warded better
Than I have been.   I'll speak not one word more.

FLAMINEO.   Stop her mouth with a sweet kiss,
    my lord.   So,
Now the tide's turned, the vessel's come about.
He's a sweet armful.   Oh, we curled-haired men
Are still most kind to women!   This is well.   121

BRACHIANO.   That you should chide thus!

FLAMINEO.   O, sir, your little chimneys
Do ever cast most smoke!   I sweat for you.
Couple together with as deep a silence
As did the Grecians in their wooden horse.
My lord, supply your promises with deeds ;
You know that painted meat no hunger feeds.

BRACHIANO.   Stay! ingrateful Rome—

FLAMINEO.   Rome! it deserves
To be called Barbary for our villainous usage.

BRACHIANO.   Soft! the same project which the
    Duke of Florence   130
(Whether in love or gullery I know not)
Laid down for her escape, will I pursue.

FLAMINEO.   And no time fitter than this night,
    my lord :
The Pope being dead, and all the cardinals entered
The conclave for the electing a new Pope ;
The city in a great confusion ;
We may attire her in a page's suit,
Lay her [1] post horse[s], take shipping, and amain
For Padua.

BRACHIANO.   I'll instantly steal forth the Prince
    Giovanni,   140
And make for Padua.   You two with your old
    mother,

───────────

[1] Provide her with relays of.

And young Marcello that attends on Florence,
If you can work him to it, follow me :
I will advance you all :—for you, Vittoria,   144
Think of a duchess' title.

    FLAMINEO.   Lo you, sister !—
Stay, my lord ; I'll tell you a tale. The crocodile,
which lives in the river Nilus, hath a worm breeds
i' the teeth of 't, which puts it to extreme anguish :
a little bird, no bigger than a wren, is barber-
surgeon to this crocodile ; flies into the jaws of 't,
picks out the worm, and brings present remedy.
The fish, glad of ease, but ingrateful to her that
did it, that the bird may not talk largely of her
abroad for non-payment, closeth her chaps, intend-
ing to swallow her, and so put her to perpetual
silence. But nature, loathing such ingratitude,
hath armed this bird with a quill or prick on the
top o' th' head, which [1] wounds the crocodile i' the
mouth, forceth her open her bloody prison, and
away flies the pretty tooth-picker from her cruel
patient.[2]   161

    BRACHIANO. Your application is, I have not
      rewarded
The service you have done me.

    FLAMINEO.   No, my lord.—
You, sister, are the crocodile : you are blemished in
your fame, my lord cures it ; and though the com-
parison hold not in every particle, yet observe, re-
member what good the bird with the prick i' the
head hath done you, and scorn ingratitude.—
[Aside.] It may appear to some ridiculous
Thus to talk knave and madman, and sometimes
Come in with a dried sentence, stuft with sage :
But this allows my varying of shapes ;   172
Knaves do grow great by being great men's apes.
                        [Exeunt.

---

  [1] The two earlier quartos have, ' on the head, top o' th
which ' ; the two later omit ' o' th '.
  [2] This tale is an alteration of a fable told by Herodotus,
lib. ii, c. 68, about the trochilus.

SCENE III.—Before the Vatican.

Enter FRANCISCO, LODOVICO, GASPARO, and six
Ambassadors.

FRANCISCO. So, my lord, I commend your
diligence.
Guard well the conclave ; and, as the order is,
Let none have conference with the cardinals.
LODOVICO. I shall, my lord.—Room for the
ambassadors !
GASPARO. They're wondrous brave [1] to-day :
why do they wear
These several habits ?
LODOVICO.   Oh, sir, they 're knights
Of several orders : that lord i' the black cloak,
With the silver cross, is Knight of Rhodes ; the next,
Knight of St. Michael ; that, of the Golden Fleece ;
The Frenchman, there, Knight of the Holy Ghost ;
My lord of Savoy, Knight of the Annunciation ;
The Englishman is Knight of the honoured Garter,
Dedicated unto their saint, St. George. I could
Describe to you their several institutions,   14
With the laws annexed to their orders ; but that
time
Permits not such discovery.
FRANCISCO.   Where 's Count Lodowick ?
LODOVICO. Here, my lord.
FRANCISCO.   'Tis o' the point of dinner time :
Marshal the cardinals' service.
LODOVICO.   Sir, I shall.

Enter Servants, with several dishes covered.

Stand, let me search your dish : who 's this for ?
SERVANT. For my Lord Cardinal Monticelso.
LODOVICO. Whose this ?
SERVANT. For my Lord Cardinal of Bourbon.
FRENCH AMBASSADOR. Why doth he search the
dishes ? to observe   22
What meat is drest ?

[1] i.e. fine.

ENGLISH AMBASSADOR.   No, sir, but to prevent
Lest any letters should be conveyed in,
To bribe or to solicit the advancement
Of any cardinal.   When first they enter,
'Tis lawful for the ambassadors of princes
To enter with them, and to make their suit
For any man their prince affecteth best ;
But after, till a general election,   30
No man may speak with them.
    LODOVICO.   You that attend on the lord
      cardinals,
Open the window, and receive their viands !
    AN OFFICER.[1]   [At the window.] You must return
      the service : the lord cardinals
Are busied 'bout electing of the Pope ;
They have given o'er scrutiny, and are fall'n
To admiration.[2]
    LODOVICO.   Away, away !   [Exeunt Servants.
    FRANCISCO.   I'll lay a thousand ducats you hear
      news.
Of a Pope presently. Hark ! sure, he's elected :
Behold, my Lord of Arragon appears   40
On the church battlements.
    ARRAGON.   [On the church battlements.] Denuntio
vobis gaudium magnum.   Reverendissimus car-
dinalis Lorenzo de Monticelso electus est in sedem
apostolicam, et elegit sibi nomen Paulum Quartum.
    OMNES.   Vivat sanctus pater Paulus Quartus !

Enter Servant.

    SERVANT. Vittoria, my lord,—
    FRANCISCO.   Well, what of her ?
    SERVANT.   Is fled the city,—
    FRANCISCO.   Ha ?
    SERVANT.   With Duke Brachiano.
    FRANCISCO.   Fled ? Where's the Prince Giovanni ?
    SERVANT.   Gone with his father.

---

[1] In all the quartos ' A Cardinal.'
[2] The reading of all the quartos ; Professor Sampson
suggests ' adoration '.

FRANCISCO. Let the matrona of the convertites
Be apprehended.—Fled ! Oh, damnable ! 51

[Exit Servant.

[Aside.] How fortunate are my wishes ! why, 'twas
  this
I only laboured : I did send the letter
To instruct him what to do. Thy fame, fond duke,
I first have poisoned ; directed thee the way
To marry a whore : what can be worse ? This
  follows,—
The hand must act to drown the passionate tongue:
I scorn to wear a sword and prate of wrong.

Enter MONTICELSO in state.[1]

MONTICELSO. Concedimus vobis apostolicam
benedictionem et remissionem peccatorum.
My lord reports Vittoria Corombona 61
Is stol'n from forth the house of convertites
By Brachiano, and they're fled the city.
Now, though this be the first day of our state,
We cannot better please the divine power
Than to sequester from the holy Church
These cursed persons. Make it therefore known,
We do denounce excommunication
Against them both : all that are theirs in Rome
We likewise banish. Set on.

[Exeunt MONTICELSO, his train, Ambassadors, &c.

FRANCISCO. Come, dear Lodovico ;
You have ta'en the sacrament to prosecute 71
The intended murder. LODOVICO. With all constancy.
But, sir, I wonder you'll engage yourself
In person, being a great prince.
FRANCISCO. Divert me not.
Most of his court are of my faction,
And some are of my council. Noble friend,
Our danger shall be 'like in this design :
Give leave, part of the glory may be mine.

[Exeunt FRANCISCO and GASPARO.

[1] The 1672 quarto begins a new scene here.

Re-enter MONTICELSO.

MONTICELSO. Why did the Duke of Florence
   with such care
Labour [1] your pardon ? say.   80
   LODOVICO. Italian beggars will resolve you that,
Who, begging of an alms, bid those they beg of,
Do good for their own sakes ; or 't may be,
He spreads his bounty with a sowing hand,
Like kings, who many times give out of measure,
Not for desert so much, as for their pleasure.
   MONTICELSO. I know you 're cunning. Come,
   what devil was that
That you were raising ?
   LODOVICO.   Devil, my lord ?
   MONTICELSO.   I ask you
How doth the duke employ you, that his bonnet
Fell with such compliment unto his knee,   90
When he departed from you ?
   LODOVICO.   Why, my lord,
He told me of a resty Barbary horse
Which he would fain have brought to the career,
The sault, and the ring-galliard ; [2] now, my lord,
I have a rare French rider.
   MONTICELSO.   Take you heed
Lest the jade break your neck. Do you put me off
With your wild horse-tricks ? Sirrah, you do lie.
Oh, thou'rt a foul black cloud, and thou dost threat
A violent storm !
   LODOVICO.   Storms are i' the air, my lord :
I am too low to storm.
   MONTICELSO.   Wretched creature !
I know that thou art fashioned for all ill,   101
Like dogs that once get blood, they'll ever kill.
About some murder ? was 't not ?
   LODOVICO.   I'll not tell you :
And yet I care not greatly if I do ;
Marry, with this preparation. Holy father,
I come not to you as an intelligencer,

---

[1] Work for.   [2] Terms of horsemanship.

But as a penitent sinner : what I utter
Is in confession merely ; which you know
Must never be revealed.
    MONTICELSO.   You have o'erta'en me.
    LODOVICO. Sir, I did love Brachiano's duchess
      dearly,   110
Or rather I pursued her with hot lust,
Though she ne'er knew on 't. She was poisoned ;
Upon my soul, she was ; for which I have sworn
To avenge her murder.
    MONTICELSO.   To the Duke of Florence ?
    LODOVICO. To him I have.
    MONTICELSO.   Miserable creature !
If thou persist in this, 'tis damnable.
Dost thou imagine thou canst slide on blood,
And not be tainted with a shameful fall ?
Or, like the black and melancholic yew-tree,
Dost think to root thyself in dead men's graves,
And yet to prosper ? Instruction to thee   121
Comes like sweet showers to over-hardened
    ground ;
They wet, but pierce not deep. And so I leave thee,
With all the Furies hanging 'bout thy neck,
Till by thy penitence thou remove this evil,
In conjuring from thy breast that cruel devil.
                                       [Exit.
    LODOVICO. I'll give it o'er ; he says 'tis damnable,
Besides I did expect his suffrage,
By reason of Camillo's death.

      Re-enter FRANCISCO with a Servant.

    FRANCISCO. Do you know that count ?
    SERVANT.   Yes, my lord.
    FRANCISCO. Bear him these thousand ducats
    to his lodging ;   131
Tell him the Pope hath sent them. — [Aside.]
    Happily [1]
That will confirm [him] more than all the rest.
                                     [Exit.

         [1] Haply.

SERVANT.   Sir,—

LODOVICO.   To me, sir ?

SERVANT.   His Holiness hath sent you
A thousand crowns, and wills you, if you travel,
To make him your patron for intelligence.

LODOVICO.   His creature ever to be commanded.

                                      [Exit Servant.

Why, now 'tis come about.   He railed upon me ;
And yet these crowns were told out and laid ready
Before he knew my voyage.   O the art,   140
The modest form of greatness ! that do sit,
Like brides at wedding-dinners, with their looks
     turned
From the least wanton jest, their puling stomach
Sick of the modesty, when their thoughts are loose,
Even acting of those hot and lustful sports
Are to ensue about midnight : such his cunning :
He sounds my depth thus with a golden plummet.
I am doubly armed now.   Now to the act of blood.
There 's but three Furies found in spacious hell,
But in a great man's breast three thousand dwell.

                                          [Exit.

ACT THE FIFTH

SCENE I.[1]—A Room in BRACHIANO's Palace at Padua.

A passage over the stage of BRACHIANO, FLAMINEO, MAR-
    CELLO, HORTENSIO, VITTORIA, CORNELIA, ZANCHE, and
    others.

      Then re-enter FLAMINEO and HORTENSIO.

FLAMINEO.   In all the weary minutes of my life,
Day ne'er broke up till now.   This marriage
Confirms me happy.

HORTENSIO.   'Tis a good assurance.
Saw you not yet the Moor that 's come to court ?

FLAMINEO.   Yes, and conferred with him i' the
    duke's closet :
I have not seen a goodlier personage,

              [1] In the 1672 quarto, Act IV, Scene iv.

Nor ever talked with man better experienced
In state affairs or rudiments of war :
He hath, by report, served the Venetian
In Candy these twice seven years, and been chief
In many a bold design.

HORTENSIO. What are those two
That bear him company ? 12

FLAMINEO. Two noblemen of Hungary, that,
living in the emperor's service as commanders,
eight years since, contrary to the expectation of
all the court, entered into religion, into the strict
order of Capuchins : but, being not well settled
in their undertaking, they left their order, and
returned to court ; for which, being after troubled
in conscience, they vowed their service against the
enemies of Christ, went to Malta, were there
knighted, and in their return back, at this great
solemnity, they are resolved for ever to forsake
the world, and settle themselves here in a house of
Capuchins in Padua. 25

HORTENSIO. 'Tis strange.

FLAMINEO. One thing makes it so : they have
vowed for ever to wear, next their bare bodies,
those coats of mail they served in.

HORTENSIO. Hard penance ! Is the Moor a
Christian ? 30

FLAMINEO. He is.

HORTENSIO. Why proffers he his service to our
duke ?

FLAMINEO. Because he understands there 's like
to grow
Some wars between us and the Duke of Florence,
In which he hopes employment.
I never saw one in a stern bold look
Wear more command, nor in a lofty phrase
Express more knowing or more deep contempt
Of our slight airy courtiers. He talks
As if he had travelled all the princes' courts 40
Of Christendom : in all things strives to express,
That all that should dispute with him may know,

Glories, like glow-worms, afar off shine bright,
But looked to near, have neither heat nor light.—
The duke !

Re-enter BRACHIANO ; [1] with FRANCISCO disguised like
    MULINASSAR, LODOVICO disguised as CARLO, GASPARO
    disguised as PEDRO, bearing their swords and helmets ;
    and MARCELLO.

BRACHIANO.   You are nobly welcome.   We have
    heard at full
Your honourable service 'gainst the Turk.
To you, brave Mulinassar, we assign
A competent pension : and are inly sorry,
The vows of those two worthy gentlemen   50
Make them incapable of our proffered bounty.
Your wish is, you may leave your warlike swords
For monuments in our chapel : I accept it
As a great honour done me, and must crave
Your leave to furnish out our duchess' revels.
Only one thing, as the last vanity
You e'er shall view, deny me not to stay
To see a barriers prepared to-night :

[1] The earliest quarto has, ' Enter Brachiano, Florence
disguised like Mulinassar ; Lodovico, Antonelli, Gaspar,
Farnese bearing their swords and helmets.'   The three
later quartos have the same except that they omit the
word ' Farnese '.   The speech twenty lines down, ' Noble
my Lord . . . ' is assigned to ' Car.' in the first quarto, and
the speech following it, ' And all things . . . ' to ' Ped.'
Dyce accordingly inserted Carlo and Pedro in the stage
direction, and entered their names and that of Farnese
in the Dramatis Personae ; but evidently, as Professor
Sampson says, Carlo and Pedro are the names assumed by
Lodovico and Gasparo when disguised as Knights of Malta,
and the first quarto gives them sometimes their real, sometimes their assumed names.   Farnese may perhaps be
correct as the name of an attendant carrying the conspirators' weapons, but he is not mentioned again. Antonelli,
of whom no further mention is made in this scene, must have
been inserted by mistake ; he was not provided with any
disguise and took no further part in the play.   Marcello,
whose exit is given twenty lines lower, is not marked in the
quartos as entering.

You shall have private standings. It hath pleased
The great ambassadors of several princes,   60
In their return from Rome to their own countries,
To grace our marriage, and to honour me
With such a kind of sport.

    FRANCISCO.   I shall persuade them
To stay, my lord.

    [BRACHIANO.]   Set on there to the presence ! [1]
        [Exeunt BRACHIANO, FLAMINEO, MARCELLO, and
            HORTENSIO.

    LODOVICO. Noble my lord, most fortunately
      welcome !   [The Conspirators here embrace.
You have our vows, sealed with the sacrament,
To second your attempts.

    GASPARO.   And all things ready :
He could not have invented his own ruin
(Had he despaired) with more propriety.

    LODOVICO. You would not take my way.

    FRANCISCO.   'Tis better ordered.

    LODOVICO. T' have poisoned his prayer-book,
      or a pair [2] of beads,   71
The pummel of his saddle, his looking-glass,
Or th' handle of his racket,—Oh, that, that !
That while he had been bandying at tennis,
He might have sworn himself to hell, and strook
His soul into the hazard ! Oh, my lord,
I would have our plot be ingenious,
And have it hereafter recorded for example,
Rather than borrow example.

    FRANCISCO.   There's no way
More speeding than this thought on.

    LODOVICO.   On, then.

    FRANCISCO. And yet methinks that this revenge
      is poor,   81
Because it steals upon him like a thief.
To have ta'en him by the casque in a pitched field,
Led him to Florence !—

---

   [1] i.e. the presence chamber. This is given in all the
quartos to Francisco.
   [2] i.e. a string.

LODOVICO.   It had been rare : and there
Have crowned him with a wreath of stinking garlic,
T' have shown the sharpness of his government
And rankness of his lust.—Flamineo comes.

[Exeunt LODOVICO and GASPARO.

Re-enter FLAMINEO, with MARCELLO and ZANCHE.

MARCELLO.   Why doth this devil haunt you, say ?
FLAMINEO.   I know not ;
For, by this light, I do not conjure for her.
'Tis not so great a cunning as men think,   90
To raise the devil ; for here 's one up already :
The greatest cunning were to lay him down.
MARCELLO.   She is your shame.
FLAMINEO.   I prithee, pardon her.
In faith, you see, women are like to burs,
Where their affection throws them, there they'll
          stick.
ZANCHE.   That is my countryman, a goodly
          person :
When he 's at leisure, I'll discourse with him
In our own language.
FLAMINEO.   I beseech you do.   [Exit ZANCHE.
How is 't, brave soldier ? Oh, that I had seen
Some of your iron days ! I pray, relate   100
Some of your service to us.
FRANCISCO.   'Tis a ridiculous thing for a man
to be his own chronicle : I did never wash my
mouth with mine own praise for fear of getting
a stinking breath.
MARCELLO.   You're too stoical. The duke will
expect other discourse from you.   107
FRANCISCO.   I shall never flatter him : I have
studied man too much to do that. What difference
is between the duke and I ? no more than between
two bricks, all made of one clay ; only 't may be
one is placed on the top of a turret, the other in
the bottom of a well, by mere chance. If I were
placed as high as the duke, I should stick as fast,
make as fair a show, and bear out weather equally.

FLAMINEO. [Aside.] If this soldier had a patent to beg in churches, then he would tell them stories.

MARCELLO. I have been a soldier too.

FRANCISCO. How have you thrived ?

MARCELLO. Faith, poorly.   120

FRANCISCO. That's the misery of peace : only outsides are then respected. As ships seem very great upon the river, which show very little upon the seas, so some men i' the court seem colossuses in a chamber, who, if they came into the field, would appear pitiful pigmies.

FLAMINEO. Give me a fair room yet hung with arras, and some great cardinal to lug me by the ears as his endeared minion.

FRANCISCO. And thou mayst do the devil knows what villainy.   131

FLAMINEO. And safely.

FRANCISCO. Right : you shall see in the country, in harvest-time, pigeons, though they destroy never so much corn, the farmer dare not present the fowling-piece to them : why ? because they belong to the lord of the manor ; whilst your poor sparrows, that belong to the Lord of Heaven, they go to the pot for 't.   139

FLAMINEO. I will now give you some politic instructions. The duke says he will give you a pension : that's but bare promise ; get it under his hand. For I have known men that have come from serving against the Turk, for three or four months they have had pension to buy them new wooden legs and fresh plasters ; but, after, 'twas not to be had. And this miserable courtesy shows as if a tormentor should give hot cordial drinks to one three-quarters dead o' the rack, only to fetch the miserable soul again to endure more dog-days.

[Exit FRANCISCO.

Re-enter HORTENSIO and ZANCHE, with a Young Lord and two more.

How now, gallants ! what, are they ready for the barriers ?   152

YOUNG LORD. Yes ; the lords are putting on their armour.

HORTENSIO. What's he ?

FLAMINEO. A new upstart ; one that swears like a falconer, and will lie in the duke's ear day by day, like a maker of almanacs : and yet I knew him, since he came to the court, smell worse of sweat than an under tennis-court-keeper.   160

HORTENSIO. Look you, yonder's your sweet mistress.

FLAMINEO. Thou art my sworn brother : I'll tell thee, I do love that Moor, that witch, very constrainedly. She knows some of my villainy. I do love her just as a man holds a wolf by the ears : but for fear of turning upon me and pulling out my throat, I would let her go to the devil.

HORTENSIO. I hear she claims marriage of thee.

FLAMINEO. Faith, I made to her some such dark promise ; and, in seeking to fly from't, I run on, like a frighted dog with a bottle at's tail, that fain would bite it off, and yet dares not look behind him.—Now, my precious gipsy.   174

ZANCHE. Aye, your love to me rather cools than heats.

FLAMINEO. Marry, I am the sounder lover : we have many wenches about the town heat too fast.

HORTENSIO. What do you think of these perfumed gallants, then ?

FLAMINEO. Their satin cannot save them : I am confident   180
They have a certain spice of the disease ;
For they that sleep with dogs shall rise with fleas.

ZANCHE. Believe it ! A little painting and gay clothes
Make you loathe me.[1]

FLAMINEO. How ? love a lady for painting or

---

[1] i.e. attracted by the adornments of another lady, he began to hate Zanche. There is no need to follow the 1672 quarto, as Dyce, Symons, and Sampson do, and read 'love'.

gay apparel ? I'll unkennel one example more for thee. Aesop had a foolish dog that let go the flesh to catch the shadow : I would have courtiers be better divers.

ZANCHE.   You remember your oaths ?   190
FLAMINEO.   Lovers' oaths are like mariners' prayers, uttered in extremity ; but when the tempest is o'er, and that the vessel leaves tumbling, they fall from protesting to drinking. And yet, amongst gentlemen, protesting and drinking go together, and agree as well as shoemakers and Westphalia bacon. They are both drawers on ; for drink draws on protestation and protestation draws on more drink. Is not this discourse better now than the morality of your sunburnt gentleman ?   201

Re-enter CORNELIA.

CORNELIA.   Is this your perch, you haggard ? [1]
   fly to the stews.   [Striking ZANCHE.
FLAMINEO.   You should be clapt by the heels
   now : Strike i' the court !   [Exit CORNELIA.
ZANCHE.   She's good for nothing, but to make
   her maids
Catch cold a-nights : they dare not use a bed-staff [2]
For fear of her light fingers.
MARCELLO.   You're a strumpet,
An impudent one.   [Kicking ZANCHE.
FLAMINEO.   Why do you kick her ? say ;
Do you think that she's like a walnut-tree ?
Must she be cudgelled ere she bear good fruit ?
MARCELLO.   She brags that you shall marry her.
FLAMINEO.   What then ?
MARCELLO.   I had rather she were pitched upon
   a stake   · 211
In some new-seeded garden, to affright

---

[1] Wild hawk.
[2] According to Johnson, ' a wooden pin stuck anciently on sides of the bed-stead to hold the clothes from slipping ' ; it would be a handy weapon.

Her fellow crows thence.

FLAMINEO. You're a boy, a fool :
Be guardian to your hound ; I am of age.

MARCELLO. If I take her near you, I'll cut her
throat.

FLAMINEO. With a fan of feathers ?

MARCELLO. And, for you, I'll whip
This folly from you.

FLAMINEO. Are you choleric ?
I'll purge 't with rhubarb. [Threatens to strike him.

HORTENSIO. Oh ! your brother ?

FLAMINEO. Hang him !
He wrongs me most that ought to offend me least.—
I do suspect my mother played foul play 220
When she conceived thee.

MARCELLO. Now, by all my hopes,
Like the two slaughtered sons of Oedipus,
The very flames of our affection
Shall turn two ways. Those words I'll make thee
answer
With thy heart-blood.

FLAMINEO. Do, like the geese in the progress :[1]
You know where you shall find me.

MARCELLO. Very good. [Exit FLAMINEO.
An thou be'st a noble, friend, bear him my sword,
And bid him fit the length on't.

YOUNG LORD. Sir, I shall.
[Exeunt all but ZANCHE.

ZANCHE. He comes. Hence petty thought of
my disgrace !

Re-enter FRANCISCO.

I ne'er loved my complexion till now, 230
'Cause I may boldly say, without a blush,
I love you.

FRANCISCO. Your love is untimely sown ;
there 's a spring at Michaelmas, but 'tis but a faint

[1] Geese might object to a royal procession, but if they
tried to stop it they would probably get hurt. I suppose
there is an allusion to some fable.

one : I am sunk in years, and I have vowed never
to marry.   236
   ZANCHE. Alas ! poor maids get more lovers
than husbands. Yet you may mistake my wealth.
For, as when ambassadors are sent to congratulate
princes, there's commonly sent along with them
a rich present, so that, though the prince like not the
ambassador's person nor words, yet he likes well
of the presentment ; so I may come to you in the
same manner, and be better loved for my dowry
than my virtue.   245
   FRANCISCO. I'll think on the motion.
   ZANCHE.   Do : I'll now
Detain you no longer. At your better leisure
I'll tell you things shall startle your blood :
Nor blame me that this passion I reveal ;
Lovers die inward that their flames conceal. [Exit.
   FRANCISCO. Of all intelligence this may prove
     the best :   251
Sure, I shall draw strange fowl from this foul nest.
                         [Exit.

SCENE II.[1]—Another Room in the same.

Enter MARCELLO and CORNELIA.

   CORNELIA. I hear a whispering all about the
     court
You are to fight : who is your opposite ?
What is the quarrel ?
   MARCELLO.   'Tis an idle rumour.
   CORNELIA. Will you dissemble ? sure, you do
     not well
To fright me thus : you never look thus pale,
But when you are most angry. I do charge you
Upon my blessing,—nay, I'll call the duke,
And he shall school you.
   MARCELLO.   Publish not a fear
Which would convert to laughter : 'tis not so.
Was not this crucifix my father's ?

    [1] Act IV, Scene vi in the 1672 quarto.

CORNELIA.   Yes.   10
MARCELLO.   I have heard you say, giving my
    brother suck,
He took the crucifix between his hands,
And broke a limb off.
CORNELIA.   Yes ; but 'tis mended.

Enter FLAMINEO.

FLAMINEO.   I have brought your weapon back.
                        [Runs MARCELLO through.
CORNELIA.   Ha ! Oh, my horror !
MARCELLO.   You have brought it home, indeed.
CORNELIA.   Help ! Oh, he 's murdered !
FLAMINEO.   Do you turn your gall up ? I'll to
    sanctuary.
And send a surgeon to you.   [Exit.

Enter HORTENSIO.[1]

HORTENSIO.   How ? o' th' ground ?
MARCELLO.   O mother, now remember what I
    told
Of breaking of the crucifix ! Farewell.
There are some sins which Heaven doth duly
    punish   20
In a whole family. This it is to rise
By all dishonest means ! Let all men know,
That tree shall long time keep a steady foot
Whose branches spread no wider than the root.
                                          [Dies.
CORNELIA.   Oh !
My perpetual sorrow !
HORTENSIO.   Virtuous Marcello !
He 's dead.—Pray, leave him, lady : come, you
    shall.
CORNELIA.   Alas ! he is not dead ; he 's in a
trance. Why, here 's nobody shall get anything by
his death. Let me call him again, for God's sake !
HORTENSIO.[2]   I would you were deceived.   31

___
[1] The first two quartos add Carlo and Pedro.
[2] Assigned to Carlo in the first three quartos.

CORNELIA. Oh, you abuse me, you abuse me,
you abuse me ! How many have gone away thus,
for lack of tendance ! Rear up 's head, rear up 's
head : his bleeding inward will kill him.

HORTENSIO. You see he is departed.

CORNELIA. Let me come to him ; give me him
as he is : if he be turned to earth, let me but give
him one hearty kiss, and you shall put us both
into one coffin. Fetch a looking-glass : see if his
breath will not stain it : or pull out some feathers
from my pillow, and lay them to his lips. Will
you lose him for a little painstaking ? 43

HORTENSIO. Your kindest office is to pray for
him.

CORNELIA. Alas ! I would not pray for him yet.
He may live to lay me i' the ground, and pray for
me, if you'll let me come to him.

Enter BRACHIANO all armed save the beaver, with FLAMINEO,
FRANCISCO, LODOVICO, and Page carrying the beaver.

BRACHIANO. Was this your handiwork ?

FLAMINEO. It was my misfortune.

CORNELIA. He lies, he lies ; he did not kill him :
these have killed him that would not let him be
better looked to. 51

BRACHIANO. Have comfort, my grieved mother.

CORNELIA. Oh, you screech-owl !

HORTENSIO. Forbear, good madam.

CORNELIA. Let me go, let me go.

[She runs to FLAMINEO with her knife drawn, and,
coming to him, lets it fall.

The God of Heaven forgive thee ! Dost not wonder
I pray for thee ? I'll tell thee what 's the reason :
I have scarce breath to number twenty minutes ;
I'd not spend that in cursing. Fare thee well :
Half of thyself lies there ; and mayst thou live
To fill an hour-glass with his mouldered ashes,
To tell how thou shouldst spend the time to come
In blest repentance !

BRACHIANO. Mother, pray tell me 61

How came he by his death ? what was the quarrel ?
   CORNELIO. Indeed, my younger boy presumed
    too much
Upon his manhood, gave him bitter words,
Drew his sword first ; and so, I know not how,
For I was out of my wits, he fell with 's head
Just in my bosom.
   PAGE. This is not true, madam.
   CORNELIA.   I pray thee, peace.
One arrow 's grassed [1] already : it were vain
T" lose this for that will ne'er be found again.   70
   BRACHIANO. Go, bear the body to Cornelia's
    lodging :
And we command that none acquaint our duchess
With this sad accident. For you, Flamineo,
Hark you, I will not grant your pardon.
   FLAMINEO.   No ?
   BRACHIANO. Only a lease of your life ; and that
    shall last
But for one day : thou shalt be forced each evening
To renew it, or be hang'd.
   FLAMINEO.   At your pleasure.
      [LODOVICO sprinkles BRACHIANO's beaver with a
      poison.
Your will is law now, I'll not meddle with it.
   BRACHIANO. You once did brave me in your
    sister's lodging ;
I'll now keep you in awe for 't.—Where 's our
    beaver ?   80
   FRANCISCO. [Aside.] He calls for his destruction.
    —Noble youth,
I pity thy sad fate !—Now to the barriers.
This shall his passage to the black lake further ;
The last good deed he did, he pardoned murther.
                            [Exeunt.

---

[1] Lost in the grass

SCENE III.[1]—The Lists at Padua.

Charges and shouts. They fight at barriers ; first single
pairs, then three to three.

Enter BRACHIANO, FRANCISCO, and FLAMINEO, with others.

BRACHIANO. An armourer ! ud's death, an
armourer !
FLAMINEO. Armourer ! where 's the armourer ?
BRACHIANO. Tear off my beaver.
FLAMINEO.   Are you hurt, my lord ?

Enter ARMOURER.

BRACHIANO. Oh, my brain 's on fire ! the helmet
is poison'd.
ARMOURER.   My lord,
Upon my soul,—
BRACHIANO.   Away with him to torture !
There are some great ones that have hand in this,
And near about me.

Enter VITTORIA.

VITTORIA.   Oh, my loved lord ! poisoned ?
FLAMINEO. Remove the bar. Here's unfor-
tunate revels !
Call the physicians.

Enter two Physicians.

                    A plague upon you !   9
We have too much of your cunning here already :
I fear the ambassadors are likewise poisoned.
BRACHIANO. Oh, I am gone already ! the infec-
tion
Flies to the brain and heart. O thou strong heart !
There 's such a covenant 'tween the world and it,
They're loth to break.

Enter GIOVANNI.

GIOVANNI.   O my most loved father !
BRACHIANO. Remove the boy away.—

[1] Act v, Scene i, in the 1672 quarto.

Where 's this good woman ?—Had I infinite worlds,
They were too little for thee : must I leave thee ?—
What say you, screech-owls, is the venom mortal ?
   FIRST PHYSICIAN. Most deadly.
   BRACHIANO.   Most corrupted politic hangman,
You kill without book ; but your art to save   21
Fails you as oft as great men's needy friends.
I that have given life to offending slaves
And wretched murderers, have I not power
To lengthen mine own a twelvemonth ?—
Do not kiss me, for I shall poison thee.
This unction's sent from the great Duke of
   Florence.
   FRANCISCO. Sir, be of comfort.
   BRACHIANO. O thou soft natural death, that art
   joint-twin
To sweetest slumber ! no rough-bearded comet
Stares on thy mild departure ; the dull owl   31
Beats not against thy casement ; the hoarse wolf
Scents not thy carrion : pity winds thy corse,
Whilst horror waits on princes.
   VITTORIA.   I am lost for ever.
   BRACHIANO. How miserable a thing it is to die
'Mongst women howling !

     Enter LODOVICO and GASPARO, in the habit of
        Capuchins.
                  What are those ?
   FLAMINEO.   Franciscans :
They have brought the extreme unction.
   BRACHIANO. On pain of death, let no man name
   death to me :
It is a word infinitely terrible.
Withdraw into our cabinet.   40
   [Exeunt all but FRANCISCO and FLAMINEO, BRACHIANO
     being carried out.
   FLAMINEO. To see what solitariness is about
dying princes ! as heretofore they have unpeopled
towns, divorced friends, and made great houses
unhospitable, so now, O justice ! where are their

flatterers now ? Flatterers are but the shadows
of princes' bodies ; the least thick cloud makes
them invisible.

FRANCISCO.   There 's great moan made for him.

FLAMINEO.   Faith, for some few hours salt
water will run most plentifully in every office o'
the court : but, believe it, most of them do but
weep as over their stepmothers' graves.   52

FRANCISCO.   How mean you ?

FLAMINEO.   Why, they dissemble ; as some men
do that live within compass o' the verge.[1]

FRANCISCO.   Come, you have thrived well under
him.

FLAMINEO.   Faith, like a wolf[2] in a woman's
breast ; I have been fed with poultry : but, for
money, understand me, I had as good a will to
cozen him as e'er an officer of them all ; but I had
not cunning enough to do it.   62

FRANCISCO.   What didst thou think of him ?
faith, speak freely.

FLAMINEO.   He was a kind of statesman that
would sooner have reckoned how many cannon-
bullets he had discharged against a town, to count
his expense that way, than how many of his
valiant and deserving subjects he lost before it.

FRANCISCO.   Oh, speak well of the duke.   70

FLAMINEO.   I have done. Wilt hear some of my
court-wisdom ? To reprehend princes is dangerous ;
and to over-commend some of them is palpable
lying.

Re-enter LODOVICO.

FRANCISCO.   How is it with the duke ?

LODOVICO.   Most deadly ill.
He 's fall'n into a strange distraction :
He talks of battle and monopolies,
Levying of taxes ; and from that descends

---

[1] i. e. within the jurisdiction of the royal court.
[2] An ulcer. Raw meat was sometimes applied to ulcers to
draw them.

To the most brain-sick language.   His mind
    fastens
On twenty several objects, which confound   80
Deep sense with folly.   Such a fearful end
May teach some men that bear too lofty crest,
Though they live happiest, yet they die not best.
He hath conferred the whole state of the dukedom
Upon your sister, till the prince arrive
At mature age.

    FLAMINEO.   There's some good luck in that yet.

    FRANCISCO.   See, here he comes.

Enter BRACHIANO, presented in a bed,[1] VITTORIA, GASPARO,
        and others.

                    There's death in's face already.

    VITTORIA.   O my good lord !

    BRACHIANO.   Away ! you have abused me :
    [These speeches are several kinds of distractions, and
        in the action should appear so.
You have conveyed coin forth our territories,
Bought and sold offices, oppressed the poor,   90
And I ne'er dreamt on 't.   Make up your accounts :
I'll now be mine own steward.

    FLAMINEO.   Sir, have patience.

    BRACHIANO.   Indeed, I am to blame :
For did you ever hear the dusky raven
Chide blackness ? or was 't ever known the devil
Railed against cloven creatures ?

    VITTORIA.   O my lord !

    BRACHIANO.   Let me have some quails to supper.

    FLAMINEO.   Sir, you shall.

    BRACHIANO.   No, some fried dog-fish ; your
    quails feed on poison.
That old dog-fox, that politician, Florence !
I'll forswear hunting, and turn dog-killer :   100
Rare ! I'll be friends with him ; for, mark you, sir,
One dog still sets another a-barking.   Peace,
Peace ! yonder's a fine slave come in now.

    [1] The traverse, or curtain at the back of the stage, is
drawn disclosing Brachiano's bed-chamber.

FLAMINEO.   Where ?

BRACHIANO.   Why, there, in a blue bonnet, and
  a pair
Of breeches with a great cod-piece : ha, ha, ha !
Look you, his cod-piece is stuck full of pins,
With pearls o' the head of them.   Do not you know
  him ?

FLAMINEO.   No, my lord.

BRACHIANO.   Why, 'tis the devil ;
I know him by a great rose he wears on 's shoe
To hide his cloven foot.   I'll dispute with him ;
He 's a rare linguist.

VITTORIA.   My lord, here 's nothing.

BRACHIANO.   Nothing ? rare ! nothing ! when
  I want money,   112
Our treasury is empty, there is nothing :
I'll not be used thus.

VITTORIA.   Oh, lie still, my lord !

BRACHIANO.   See, see Flamineo, that killed his
  brother,
Is dancing on the ropes there, and he carries
A money-bag in each hand, to keep him even,
For fear of breaking 's neck.   And there 's a lawyer,
In a gown whipt with velvet, stares and gapes
When the money will fall.   How the rogue cuts
  capers !   120
It should have been in a halter.   'Tis there : what 's
  she ?

FLAMINEO.   Vittoria, my lord.

BRACHIANO.   Ha, ha, ha ! her hair
Is sprinkled with arras-powder,[1] that makes her
  look
As if she had sinned in the pastry.—What 's he ?

FLAMINEO.   A divine, my lord.

> [BRACHIANO seems here near his end : LODOVICO
> and GASPARO, in the habit of Capuchins, present
> him in his bed with a crucifix and hallowed
> candle.

BRACHIANO.   He will be drunk ; avoid him :

[1] Orris powder, which was the colour of flour.

Th' argument is fearful, when churchmen stagger
　in 't.
Look you, six grey rats, that have lost their tails,
Crawl up the pillow :　send for a rat-catcher :
I'll do a miracle, I'll free the court
From all foul vermin.　Where 's Flamineo ?　　　130
　　　FLAMINEO.　[Aside.]　I do not like that he names
　　　　me so often,
Especially on 's death-bed :　'tis a sign
I shall not live long.—See, he 's near his end.
　　　LODOVICO.　Pray, give us leave.—Attende, do-
　　　　mine Brachiane.
　　　FLAMINEO.　See, see how firmly he doth fix his
　　　　eye
Upon the crucifix.
　　　VITTORIA.　　　　　　Oh, hold it constant !
It settles his wild spirits ;　and so his eyes
Melt into tears.　　　　　　　　　　　　　138
　　　LODOVICO.　Domine Brachiane, solebas in bello
tutus esse tuo clypeo ;　nunc hunc clypeum hosti
tuo opponas infernali.　　　　　　[By the crucifix.
　　　GASPARO.　Olim hasta valuisti in bello ;　nunc
hanc sacram hastam vibrabis contra hostem
animarum.　　　　　　　　[By the hallowed taper.
　　　LODOVICO.　Attende, domine Brachiane ;　si
nunc quoque probas ea quae acta sunt inter nos,
flecte caput in dextrum.
　　　GASPARO.　Esto securus, domine Brachiane ;
cogita quantum habeas meritorum ;　denique
memineris meam animam pro tua oppignoratam
si quid esset periculi.　　　　　　　　　　151
　　　LODOVICO.　Si nunc quoque probas ea quae
acta sunt inter nos, flecte caput in laevum.—
He is departing :　pray, stand all apart,
And let us only whisper in his ears
Some private meditations, which our order
Permits you not to hear.
　　　　　　[Here, the rest being departed, LODOVICO and
　　　　　　　GASPARO discover themselves.
　　　GASPARO.　　　　　　　　Brachiano,—

LODOVICO.   Devil,
Brachiano, thou art damned.
   GASPARO.
                           Perpetually.
   LODOVICO.   A slave condemned and given up to
     the gallows
Is thy great lord and master.   159
   GASPARO.   True ; for thou
Art given up to the devil.
   LODOVICO.   O you slave !
You that were held the famous politician,
Whose art was poison—
   GASPARO.   And whose conscience, murder !
   LODOVICO.   That would have broke your wife's
     neck down the stairs,
Ere she was poisoned !
   GASPARO.   That had your villainous salads—
   LODOVICO.   And fine embroidered bottles and
     perfumes,
Equally mortal with a winter-plague !
   GASPARO.   Now there's mercury—
   LODOVICO.   And copperas—
   GASPARO.   And quicksilver—
   LODOVICO.   With other devilish pothecary stuff,
A-melting in your politic brains : dost hear ?   170
   GASPARO.   This is Count Lodovico.
   LODOVICO.   This, Gasparo :
And thou shalt die like a poor rogue.
   GASPARO.   And stink
Like a dead fly-blown dog.
   LODOVICO.   And be forgotten
Before thy funeral sermon.
   BRACHIANO.   Vittoria ! Vittoria !
   LODOVICO.   Oh, the cursèd devil
Comes to himself again ! we are undone,
   GASPARO.[1]   Strangle him in private.

       Enter VITTORIA and Attendants.

          What, will you call him again
To live in treble torments ? for charity,

   [1] The 1672 quarto begins Scene ii at this point.

                              G

For Christian charity, avoid the chamber.

                     [Exeunt VITTORIA and Attendants.

LODOVICO. You would prate, sir ? This is a
    true-love-knot   180
Sent from the Duke of Florence.

                           [BRACHIANO is strangled.

GASPARO.   What, is it done ?
LODOVICO. The snuff is out. No woman-
    keeper [1] i' th' world,
Though she had practised seven year at the pest-
    house,
Could have done 't quaintlier.

        Re-enter VITTORIA, FRANCISCO, FLAMINEO, and
                     Attendants.

                    My lords, he 's dead.

OMNES. Rest to his soul !
VITTORIA.   O me ! this place is hell.   [Exit.
FRANCISCO. How heavily she takes it !
FLAMINEO.   Oh, yes, yes ;
Had women navigable rivers in their eyes,
They would dispend them all : surely, I wonder
Why we should wish more rivers to the city,
When they sell water so good cheap. I'll tell thee,
These are but moonish shades of griefs or fears ;
There 's nothing sooner dry than women's tears.
Why, here 's an end of all my harvest ; he has given
    me nothing.   193
Court-promises ! let wise men count them cursed,
For while you live, he that scores best pays worst.
FRANCISCO. Sure, this was Florence' doing.
FLAMINEO.   Very likely.
Those are found weighty strokes which come from
    th' hand,
But those are killing strokes which come from th'
    head.
Oh, the rare tricks of a Machiavellian !   199
He doth not come, like a gross plodding slave,
And buffet you to death : no, my quaint knave,

             [1] Nurse.

He tickles you to death, makes you die laughing,
As if you had swallowed down a pound of saffron.
You see the feat, 'tis practised in a trice ;
To teach court-honesty, it jumps on ice.

    FRANCISCO. Now have the people liberty to
      talk,
And descant on his vices.

    FLAMINEO.   Misery of princes,
That must of force be censured by their slaves !
Not only blamed for doing things are ill,
But for not doing all that all men will :   210
One were better be a thresher.—Ud's death,
I would fain speak with this duke yet.

    FRANCISCO.   Now he's dead ?

    FLAMINEO. I cannot conjure ; but if prayers or
      oaths
Will get to the speech of him, though forty devils
Wait on him in his livery of flames,
I'll speak to him, and shake him by the hand,
Though I be blasted.   [Exit.

    FRANCISCO.   Excellent Lodovico !
What, did you terrify him at the last gasp ?

    LODOVICO. Yes, and so idly, that the duke had
      like
To have terrified us.

    FRANCISCO. How ?

    LODOVICO.   You shall hear that hereafter.

Enter ZANCHE.

See, yon's the infernal that would make up sport.
Now to the revelation of that secret   222
She promised when she fell in love with you.

    FRANCISCO. You're passionately met in this
      sad world.

    ZANCHE. I would have you look up, sir ; these
      court-tears
Claim not your tribute to them : let those weep
That guiltily partake in the sad cause.
I knew last night, by a sad dream I had,
Some mischief would ensue ; yet, to say truth,

My dream most concerned you.

    LODOVICO.   [Aside to FRANCISCO.]   Shall 's fall
    a-dreaming ?   230

    FRANCISCO.   Yes ; and for fashion sake I'll
    dream with her.

    ZANCHE.   Methought, sir, you came stealing to
    my bed.

    FRANCISCO.   Wilt thou believe me, sweeting ?
    by this light,

I was a-dreamt on thee too ; for methought
I saw thee naked.

    ZANCHE.   Fie, sir ! As I told you,
Methought you lay down by me.

    FRANCISCO.   So dreamt I ;
And lest thou shouldst take cold, I covered thee
With this Irish mantle.

    ZANCHE.   Verily, I did dream
You were somewhat bold with me : but to come
    to 't—

    LODOVICO. [Aside.]   How, how ! I hope you will
    not go to 't here.   240

    FRANCISCO.   Nay, you must hear my dream out.

    ZANCHE.   Well, sir, forth !

    FRANCISCO.   When I threw the mantle o'er thee,
    thou didst laugh
Exceedingly, methought.

    ZANCHE.   Laugh ?

    FRANCISCO.   And cried'st out,
The hair did tickle thee.

    ZANCHE.   There was a dream indeed !

    LODOVICO. [Aside.]   Mark her, I prithee ; she
    simpers like the suds
A collier hath been washed in.

    ZANCHE.   Come, sir, good fortune tends you.
    I did tell you
I would reveal a secret : Isabella,
The Duke of Florence' sister, was impoisoned
By a fumed picture ; and Camillo's neck   250
Was broke by damned Flamineo, the mischance
Laid on a vaulting-horse.

FRANCISCO.   Most strange !

ZANCHE.   Most true.

LODOVICO. [Aside.]   The bed of snakes is broke.

ZANCHE.   I sadly do confess I had a hand
In the black deed.

FRANCISCO.   Thou kept'st their counsel ?

ZANCHE.   Right ;
For which, urged with contrition, I intend
This night to rob Vittoria.

LODOVICO. [Aside.]   Excellent penitence !
Usurers dream on't while they sleep out sermons.

ZANCHE.   To further our escape, I have entreated
Leave to retire me, till the funeral,   260
Unto a friend i' the country : that excuse
Will further our escape. In coin and jewels
I shall at least make good unto your use
An hundred thousand crowns.

FRANCISCO.   O noble wench !

LODOVICO.   Those crowns we'll share.

ZANCHE.   It is a dowry,
Methinks, should make that sun-burnt proverb
    false,
And wash the Aethiop white.

FRANCISCO.   It shall. Away !

ZANCHE.   Be ready for our flight.

FRANCISCO.   An hour 'fore day. [Exit ZANCHE.
O strange discovery ! why, till now we knew not
The circumstance of either of their deaths.   270

Re-enter ZANCHE.

ZANCHE.   You'll wait about midnight in the
    chapel ?

FRANCISCO.   There. [Exit ZANCHE.

LODOVICO.   Why, now our action's justified.

FRANCISCO.   Tush for justice !
What harms it justice ? we now, like the partridge,
Purge the disease with laurel ; [1] for the fame
Shall crown the enterprise, and quit the shame.

                                        [Exeunt.

[1] ' Perdices lauri folio annuum fastidium purgant,' Pliny,
Nat. Hist., viii. 27.—*Reed.*

SCENE IV.[1]—A Room in the Palace at Padua.

Enter FLAMINEO and GASPARO, at one door; another way,
GIOVANNI, attended.

GASPARO. The young duke : did you e'er see
a sweeter prince ?

FLAMINEO. I have known a poor woman's
bastard better favoured ; this is behind him ; now,
to his face, all comparisons were hateful. Wise
was the courtly peacock that, being a great
minion, and being compared for beauty by some
dottrels [2] that stood by to the kingly eagle, said
the eagle was a far fairer bird than herself, not in
respect of her feathers, but in respect of her long
talons : his will grow out in time.—My gracious
lord !   12

GIOVANNI. I pray, leave me, sir.

FLAMINEO. Your grace must be merry : 'tis I
have cause to mourn ; for, wot you, what said the
little boy that rode behind his father on horse-
back ?

GIOVANNI. Why, what said he ?

FLAMINEO. ' When you are dead, father,' said
he, ' I hope then I shall ride in the saddle.' Oh,
'tis a brave thing for a man to sit by himself ! he
may stretch himself in the stirrups, look about,
and see the whole compass of the hemisphere.
You're now, my lord, i' th' saddle.   24

GIOVANNI. Study your prayers, sir, and be
     penitent :
'Twere fit you'd think on what hath former bin ;
I have heard grief named the eldest child of sin.

                                                  [Exit.

FLAMINEO. Study my prayers ! he threatens
     me divinely :
I am falling to pieces already. I care not, though,
like Anacharsis, I were pounded to death in a
mortar : and yet that death were fitter for usurers,

---

[1] Scene iii in the 1672 quarto.   [2] A species of plover.

gold and themselves to be beaten together, to
make a most cordial cullis [1] for the devil. 33
He hath his uncle's villainous look already,
In decimo sexto.

Enter Courtier.

Now, sir, what are you ?
COURTIER. It is the pleasure, sir, of the young
duke,
That you forbear the presence, and all rooms
That owe him reverence.
FLAMINEO. So, the wolf and the raven
Are very pretty fools when they are young.
Is it your office, sir, to keep me out ? 40
COURTIER. So the duke wills.
FLAMINEO. Verily, master courtier, extremity
is not to be used in all offices : say that a gentle-
woman were taken out of her bed about midnight,
and committed to Castle Angelo, [or] to the tower
yonder, with nothing about her but her smock,
would it not show a cruel part in the gentleman-
porter to lay claim to her upper garment, pull it
o'er her head and ears, and put her in naked ?
COURTIER. Very good : you are merry. [Exit.
FLAMINEO. Doth he make a court-ejectment of me ?
A flaming fire-brand casts more smoke without a
chimney than within 't. I'll smoor [2] some of them.

Enter FRANCISCO.

How now ! thou art sad. 54
FRANCISCO. I met even now with the most
piteous sight.
FLAMINEO. Thou meet'st another here, a pitiful
Degraded courtier.
FRANCISCO. Your reverend mother
Is grown a very old woman in two hours.
I found them winding of Marcello's corse ;
And there is such a solemn melody, 60

---

[1] Strong and savoury broth ; the old recipe books
recommend ' pieces of gold ' among its ingredients.—*Dyce.*
[2] Smother.

'Tween doleful songs, tears, and sad elegies,—
Such as old grandams watching by the dead
Were wont to outwear the nights with,—that,
        believe me,
I had no eyes to guide me forth the room,
They were so o'ercharged with water.
        FLAMINEO.   I will see them.
        FRANCISCO.   'Twere much uncharity in you ; for
        your sight
Will add unto their tears.
        FLAMINEO.   I will see them :
They are behind the traverse ; [1] I'll discover
Their superstitious howling.   [Draws the curtain.

CORNELIA,[2] ZANCHE, and three other Ladies discovered
        winding MARCELLO's corse. A Song.

        CORNELIA.   This rosemary is withered ; pray get
        fresh.   70
I would have these herbs grow up in his grave,
When I am dead and rotten. Reach the bays,
I'll tie a garland here about his head ;
'Twill keep my boy from lightning. This sheet
I have kept this twenty year, and every day
Hallowed it with my prayers : I did not think
He should have wore it.   77
        ZANCHE.   Look you who are yonder.
        CORNELIA.   Oh, reach me the flowers.
        ZANCHE.   Her ladyship 's foolish.
        LADY.   Alas ! her grief
Hath turned her child again !
        CORNELIA.   You're very welcome :
There 's rosemary for you ;—and rue for you ;—
                                        [TO FLAMINEO.
Heart's-ease for you ; I pray make much of it :
I have left more for myself.
        FRANCISCO.   Lady, who 's this ?
        CORNELIA.   You are, I take it, the grave-maker.
        FLAMINEO.   So.

————
    [1] A curtain on the stage.
    [2] Scene iv in the 1672 quarto begins here.

ZANCHE. 'Tis Flamineo.

CORNELIA. Will you make me such a fool ?
here's a white hand :
Can blood so soon be washed out ? let me see ;
When screech-owls croak upon the chimney-tops,
And the strange cricket i' the oven sings and hops,
When yellow spots do on your hands appear,　90
Be certain then you of a corse shall hear.
Out upon't, how 'tis speckled ! h'as handled a
toad, sure.　Cowslip-water is good for the memory :
pray, buy me three ounces of 't.

FLAMINEO. I would I were from hence.

CORNELIA. Do you hear, sir ? I'll give you
a saying which my grandmother was wont, when
she heard the bell toll, to sing o'er unto her lute.

FLAMINEO. Do, an you will, do.

CORNELIA. ' Call for the robin-red-breast and
the wren,　100
　　[CORNELIA doth this in several forms of distraction.
Since o'er shady groves they hover,
And with leaves and flowers do cover
The friendless bodies of unburied men.
Call unto his funeral dole
The ant, the field-mouse, and the mole,
To rear him hillocks that shall keep him warm,
And (when gay tombs are robbed) sustain no harm :
But keep the wolf far thence, that 's foe to men,
For with his nails he'll dig them up again.'
They would not bury him 'cause he died in a
quarrel ;　110
But I have an answer for them :
' Let holy Church receive him duly,
Since he paid the church-tithes truly.'
His wealth is summed, and this is all his store ;
This poor men get, and great men get no more.
Now the wares are gone, we may shut up shop.
Bless you all, good people.
　　　　　[Exeunt CORNELIA, ZANCHE, and Ladies.

FLAMINEO. I have a strange thing in me, to
the which

I cannot give a name, without it be
Compassion. I pray, leave me. [Exit FRANCISCO.
This night I'll know the utmost of my fate ; 121
I'll be resolved [1] what my rich sister means
To assign me for my service. I have lived
Riotously ill, like some that live in court,
And sometimes when my face was full of smiles,
Have felt the maze of conscience in my breast.
Oft gay and honoured robes those tortures try :
We think caged birds sing, when indeed they cry.

Enter BRACHIANO's ghost, in his leather cassock and breeches,
    boots and cowl ; in his hand a pot of lily-flowers, with
    a skull in it.

Ha ! I can stand thee : nearer, nearer yet !
What a mockery hath death made of thee ! thou
    look'st sad. 130
In what place art thou ? in yon starry gallery ?
Or in the cursèd dungeon ?—No ? not speak ?
Pray, sir, resolve me, what religion 's best
For a man to die in ? or is it in your knowledge
To answer me how long I have to live ?
That 's the most necessary question.
Not answer ? are you still like some great men
That only walk like shadows up and down,
And to no purpose ? say :—
            [The Ghost throws earth upon him, and shows
                him the skull.
What 's that ? Oh, fatal ! he throws earth upon me !
A dead man's skull beneath the roots of flowers !—
I pray, speak, sir : our Italian churchmen 142
Make us believe dead men hold conference
With their familiars, and many times
Will come to bed to them. and eat with them.
                            [Exit Ghost.
He 's gone ; and see, the skull and earth are
    vanished.
This is beyond melancholy. I do dare my fate
To do its worst. Now to my sister's lodging,

---

[1] Put out of doubt.

And sum up all these horrors : the disgrace
The prince threw on me ; next the piteous sight
Of my dead brother ; and my mother's dotage ;
And last this terrible vision : all these　　　152
Shall with Vittoria's bounty turn to good,
Or I will drown this weapon in her blood.　　[Exit.

SCENE V.—A Street in Padua.

Enter FRANCISCO and LODOVICO ; HORTENSIO watching
them.

LODOVICO.　My lord, upon my soul, you shall
　　no further ;
You have most ridiculously engaged yourself
Too far already.　For my part, I have paid
All my debts ; so, if I should chance to fall,
My creditors fall not with me ; and I vow
To quit all in this bold assembly
To the meanest follower.　My lord, leave the city,
Or I'll forswear the murder.　　　　　[Exit.
FRANCISCO.　Farewell, Lodovico :
If thou dost perish in this glorious act,　　10
I'll rear unto thy memory that fame
Shall in the ashes keep alive thy name.　　[Exit.
HORTENSIO.　There's some black deed on foot.
　　I'll presently
Down to the citadel, and raise some force.
These strong court-factions, that do brook no
　　checks,
In the career oft break the riders' necks.　　[Exit.

SCENE VI.[1]—A Room in the Palace.

Enter VITTORIA with a book in her hand, and ZANCHE ;
FLAMINEO following them.

FLAMINEO.　What, are you at your prayers ?
　　give o'er.
VITTORIA.　　　　　　　　　How, ruffian ?
FLAMINEO.　I come to you 'bout worldly business:

[1] This is still Scene v in the 1672 quarto.

Sit down, sit down :—nay, stay, blowze,[1] you may
    hear it :—
The doors are fast enough.

VITTORIA.   Ha ! are you drunk ?

FLAMINEO. Yes, yes, with wormwood-water :
    you shall taste
Some of it presently.

VITTORIA.   What intends the Fury ?

FLAMINEO. You are my lord's executrix ; and
    I claim
Reward for my long service.

VITTORIA.   For your service ?

FLAMINEO.   Come, therefore, here is pen and ink ;
    set down   9
What you will give me.

VITTORIA. [Writes.] There.

FLAMINEO.   Ha ! have you done already ?
'Tis a most short conveyance.

VITTORIA.   I will read it :
' I give that portion to thee, and no other,
Which Cain groaned under, having slain his brother.'

FLAMINEO. A most courtly patent to beg by !

VITTORIA.   You are a villain.

FLAMINEO. Is't come to this ? They say,
    affrights cure agues :
Thou hast a devil in thee ; I will try
If I can scare him from thee. Nay, sit still :
My lord hath left me yet two case of jewels   18
Shall make me scorn your bounty ; you shall see
    them.   [Exit.

VITTORIA. Sure, he's distracted.

ZANCHE.   Oh, he's desperate :
For your own safety give him gentle language.

Re-enter FLAMINEO with two case [2] of pistols.

FLAMINEO. Look, these are better far at a dead
    lift [3]
Than all your jewel-house.

---

[1] Beggar wench.   [2] i. e. two pairs.   [3] At an extremity.

VITTORIA.   And yet, methinks,
These stones have no fair lustre, they are ill set.

FLAMINEO.   I'll turn the right side towards you :
    you shall see
How they will sparkle.

VITTORIA.   Turn this horror from me !
What do you want ? what would you have me do ?
Is not all mine yours ? have I any children ?

FLAMINEO.   Pray thee, good woman, do not
    trouble me
With this vain worldly business ; say your
    prayers :   30
I made a vow to my deceasèd lord,
Neither yourself nor I should outlive him
The numbering of four hours.

VITTORIA.   Did he enjoin it ?

FLAMINEO.   He did ;   and 'twas a deadly
    jealousy,
Lest any should enjoy thee after him,
That urged him vow me to it. For my death,
I did propound it voluntarily, knowing,
If he could not be safe in his own court,
Being a great duke, what hope, then, for us ?

VITTORIA.   This is your melancholy and despair

FLAMINEO.   Away !   41
Fool [that] thou art to think that politicians
Do use to kill the effects of injuries
And let the cause live. Shall we groan in irons,
Or be a shameful and a weighty burden
To a public scaffold ? This is my resolve ;
I would not live at any man's entreaty,
Nor die at any's bidding.

VITTORIA.   Will you hear me ?

FLAMINEO.   My life hath done service to other
    men ;
My death shall serve mine own turn. Make you
    ready.   50

VITTORIA.   Do you mean to die indeed ?

FLAMINEO.   With as much pleasure
As e'er my father gat me.

VITTORIA.　　　　　　　Are the doors locked ?

ZANCHE.　Yes, madam.

VITTORIA.　Are you grown an atheist ?　will you
　　turn your body,
Which is the goodly palace of the soul,
To the soul's slaughter-house ?　Oh, the cursèd
　　devil,
—Which doth present us with all other sins
Thrice-candied o'er, despair with gall and stibium ;
Yet we carouse it off ;—　[Aside to ZANCHE.] Cry out
　　for help !—　　　　　　　　　　　　　　　59
Makes us forsake that which was made for man,
The world, to sink to that was made for devils,
Eternal darkness !

ZANCHE.　　　　　Help, help !

FLAMINEO.　　　　　　　　I'll stop your throat
With winter-plums.

VITTORIA.　　　I prithee, yet remember,
Millions are now in graves, which at last day
Like mandrakes shall rise shrieking.

FLAMINEO.　　　　　　　　Leave your prating,
For these are but grammatical laments,
Feminine arguments : and they move me,
As some in pulpits move their auditory,
More with their exclamation than sense
Of reason or sound doctrine.

ZANCHE.　[Aside to VITTORIA.]　Gentle madam,
Seem to consent, only persuade him teach　　71
The way to death ; let him die first.

VITTORIA.　　　　　　　　　'Tis good.
I apprehend it.
—To kill one's self is meat that we must take
Like pills, not chew 't, but quickly swallow it ;
The smart o' the wound, or weakness of the hand,
May else bring treble torments.

FLAMINEO.　　　　　　　I have held it
A wretched and most miserable life
Which is not able to die.

VITTORIA.　　　　　O, but frailty !
Yet I am now resolved : farewell, affliction !　　80

Behold, Brachiano, I that while you lived
Did make a flaming altar of my heart
To sacrifice unto you, now am ready
To sacrifice heart and all.—Farewell, Zanche !
  ZANCHE.   How, madam ! do you think that I'll
    outlive you ;
Especially when my best self, Flamineo,
Goes the same voyage ?
  FLAMINEO.   O, most loved Moor !
  ZANCHE.   Only by all my love let me entreat
    you,—
Since it is most necessary one of us
Do violence on ourselves,—let you or I   90
Be her sad taster, teach her how to die.
  FLAMINEO.   Thou dost instruct me nobly : take
    these pistols,
Because my hand is stained with blood already :
Two of these you shall level at my breast,
The other[1] 'gainst your own, and so we'll die
Most equally contented : but first swear
Not to outlive me.
  VITTORIA AND ZANCHE.   Most religiously.
  FLAMINEO.   Then here 's an end of me ; farewell,
    daylight !
And, O contemptible physic, that dost take
So long a study, only to preserve   100
So short a life, I take my leave of thee !—
These are two cupping-glasses that shall draw
                     [Showing the pistols.
All my infected blood out. Are you ready ?
  VITTORIA AND ZANCHE.   Ready.
  FLAMINEO.   Whither shall I go now ? O Lucian,
thy ridiculous purgatory ! to find Alexander the
Great cobbling shoes, Pompey tagging points, and
Julius Caesar making hair-buttons ! Hannibal
selling blacking, and Augustus crying garlic !
Charlemagne selling lists[2] by the dozen, and King
Pepin crying apples in a cart drawn with one horse !
Whether I resolve to fire, earth, water, air,   112

----

[1] i. e. others.   [2] Strips of cloth.

Or all the elements by scruples, I know not,
Nor greatly care.—Shoot, shoot :
Of all deaths the violent death is best ;
For from ourselves it steals ourselves so fast,
The pain, once apprehended, is quite past.

> [They shoot : he falls ; and they run to him, and tread
> upon him.

VITTORIA.   What, are you dropt ?

FLAMINEO.   I am mixed with earth already :
as you are noble,   119
Perform your vows, and bravely follow me.

VITTORIA.   Whither ? to hell ?

ZANCHE.   To most assured damnation ?

VITTORIA.   O thou most cursèd devil !

ZANCHE.   Thou art caught—

VITTORIA.   In thine own engine.   I tread the fire
out
That would have been my ruin.

FLAMINEO.   Will you be perjured ? what a
religious oath was Styx, that the gods never durst
swear by, and violate ! Oh, that we had such an
oath to minister, and to be so well kept in our
courts of justice !   129

VITTORIA.   Think whither thou art going.

ZANCHE.   And remember
What villainies thou hast acted.

VITTORIA.   This thy death
Shall make me like a blazing ominous star :
Look up and tremble.

FLAMINEO.   O, I am caught with a springe !

VITTORIA.   You see the fox comes many times
short home ;
'Tis here proved true.

FLAMINEO.   Killed with a couple of braches ! [1]

VITTORIA.   No fitter offering for the infernal Furies
Than one in whom they reigned while he was living.

FLAMINEO.   Oh, the way's dark and horrid ! I
cannot see :
Shall I have no company ?

[1] Bitch-hounds.

VITTORIA.   Oh, yes, thy sins
Do run before thee to fetch fire from hell,   140
To light thee thither.
    FLAMINEO.   Oh, I smell soot,
Most stinking soot ! the chimney is a-fire :
My liver's parboiled, like Scotch holly-bread ; [1]
There's a plumber laying pipes in my guts, it
    scalds.—
Wilt thou outlive me ?
    ZANCHE.   Yes, and drive a stake
Th[o]rough thy body ; for we'll give it out
Thou didst this violence upon thyself.
    FLAMINEO.   O cunning devils ! now I have tried
    your love,
And doubled all your reaches.—I am not wounded ;
                      [Rises.

The pistols held no bullets : 'twas a plot   150
To prove your kindness to me ; and I live
To punish your ingratitude. I knew,
One time or other, you would find a way
To give me a strong potion.—O men
That lie upon your death-beds, and are haunted
With howling wives, ne'er trust them ! they'll
    re-marry
Ere the worm pierce your winding-sheet, ere the
    spider
Make a thin curtain for your epitaphs.—   158
How cunning you were to discharge ! do you
practise at the Artillery-yard ?—Trust a woman ?
never, never ! Brachiano be my precedent. We
lay our souls to pawn to the devil for a little
pleasure, and a woman makes the bill of sale.
That ever man should marry ! For one Hyper-
mnestra that saved her lord and husband, forty-
nine of her sisters cut their husbands' throats all in
one night : there was a shoal of virtuous horse
leeches !—Here are two other instruments.
    VITTORIA.   Help, help !

   [1] i. e. holy-bread. Cotgrave (1650) gives '*Pain benist
d'Escosse.* A sodden sheep's liver.'—*Sampson*

Enter LODOVICO, GASPARO, and other Conspirators.[1]

FLAMINEO. What noise is that ? ha ! false
   keys i' the court !   170
LODOVICO. We have brought you a masque.
FLAMINEO. A matachin,[2] it seems by your
   drawn swords.
Churchmen turned revellers !
CONSPIRATORS.[3]   Isabella ! Isabella !
LODOVICO. Do you know us now ?
                    [They throw off their disguise.
FLAMINEO.   Lodovico ! and Gasparo !
LODOVICO. Yes ; and that Moor the duke gave
   pension to
Was the great Duke of Florence.
VITTORIA.   Oh, we are lost !
FLAMINEO. You shall not take justice from
   forth my hands,—
Oh, let me kill her !—I'll cut my safety
Through your coats of steel. Fate's a spaniel,
We cannot beat it from us. What remains now ?
Let all that do ill, take this precedent,—   181
Man may his fate foresee, but not prevent :
And of all axioms this shall win the prize,—
'Tis better to be fortunate than wise.
GASPARO. Bind him to the pillar.
VITTORIA.   Oh, your gentle pity !
I have seen a blackbird that would sooner fly
To a man's bosom, than to stay the gripe
Of the fierce sparrowhawk.
GASPARO.   Your hope deceives you.
VITTORIA. If Florence be i' the court, would he
   would kill me !

---

[1] The first two quartos have ' Enter Lod. Gasp. Pedro,
Carlo ' ; but see note on p. 164.
[2] A French and Italian sword-dance.
[3] The ' Con.' of the first two quartos seems to have been
unintelligible to all subsequent editors. The speech is given
to ' Gas.' in the two later quartos, to Carlo by Dyce, and to
Lodovico by Professor Sampson.

GASPARO. Fool ! princes give rewards with their
   own hands, 190
But death or punishment by the hands of others.

LODOVICO. Sirrah, you once did strike me : [now]
   I'll strike you
Into the centre.

FLAMINEO. Thou'lt do it like a hangman,
A base hangman, not like a noble fellow ;
For thou see'st I cannot strike again.

LODOVICO. Dost laugh ?

FLAMINEO. Would'st have me die, as I was
   born, in whining ?

GASPARO. Recommend yourself to Heaven.

FLAMINEO. No, I will carry
Mine own commendations thither.

LODOVICO. Oh, could I kill you forty times a day,
And use 't four year together, 'twere too little !
Naught grieves but that you are too few to feed
The famine of our vengeance. What dost think on ?

FLAMINEO. Nothing ; of nothing : leave thy
   idle questions. 203
I am i' th' way to study a long silence :
To prate were idle. I remember nothing.
There 's nothing of so infinite vexation
As man's own thoughts.

LODOVICO. O thou glorious strumpet !
Could I divide thy breath from this pure air
When 't leaves thy body, I would suck it up,
And breathe 't upon some dunghill.

VITTORIA. You, my death's-man !
Methinks thou dost not look horrid enough ; 211
Thou hast too good a face to be a hangman :
If thou be, do thy office in right form :
Fall down upon thy knees, and ask forgiveness.

LODOVICO. Oh, thou hast been a most prodigious
   comet,
But I'll cut off your train,—kill the Moor first.

VITTORIA. You shall not kill her first ; behold
   my breast :
I will be waited on in death ; my servant

Shall never go before me.

GASPARO.   Are you so brave ?

VITTORIA.   Yes, I shall welcome death
As princes do some great ambassadors ;   221
I'll meet thy weapon half way.

LODOVICO.   Thou dost tremble :
Methinks fear should dissolve thee into air.

VITTORIA.   Oh, thou art deceived, I am too true
    a woman :
Conceit can never kill me.   I'll tell thee what,
I will not in my death shed one base tear ;
Or if look pale, for want of blood, not fear.

GASPARO.[1]   Thou art my task, black Fury.

ZANCHE.   I have blood
As red as either of theirs : wilt drink some ?
'Tis good for the falling-sickness.   I am proud
Death cannot alter my complexion,   231
For I shall ne'er look pale.

LODOVICO.   Strike, strike,
With a joint motion !

     [They stab VITTORIA, ZANCHE, and FLAMINEO.

VITTORIA.   'Twas a manly blow !
The next thou giv'st, murder some sucking infant ;
And then thou wilt be famous.

FLAMINEO.   Oh, what blade is 't ?
[Is 't] a Toledo, or an English fox ?[2]
I ever thought a cutler should distinguish
The cause of my death, rather than a doctor.
Search my wound deeper ; tent it with the steel
That made it.

VITTORIA.   Oh, my greatest sin lay in my blood ;
Now my blood pays for 't.

FLAMINEO.   Thou 'rt a noble sister !
I love thee now : if woman do breed man,   242
She ought to teach him manhood : fare thee well.
Know, many glorious women that are famed
For masculine virtue have been vicious,
Only a happier silence did betide them :

  [1] Given to Carlo in the first quarto.
  [2] A slang term for a sword.

She hath no faults who hath the art to hide them.

VITTORIA.   My soul, like to a ship in a black
    storm,   248
Is driven, I know not whither.

FLAMINEO.   Then cast anchor.
Prosperity doth bewitch men, seeming clear ;
But seas do laugh, show white, when rocks are near.
We cease to grieve, cease to be fortune's slaves
Nay, cease to die, by dying. Art thou gone ?
And thou so near the bottom ? false report,
Which says that women vie with the nine Muses
For nine tough durable lives ! I do not look
Who went before, nor who shall follow me ;
No, at myself I will begin and end.   258
While we look up to Heaven, we confound
Knowledge with knowledge. Oh, I am in a mist !

VITTORIA.   Oh, happy they that never saw the
    court,
Nor ever knew great men but by report !   [Dies.

FLAMINEO. I recover like a spent taper, for a flash,
And instantly go out.
Let all that belong to great men remember th' old
wives' tradition, to be like the lions i' th' Tower on
Candlemas-day : to mourn if the sun shine, for
fear of the pitiful remainder of winter to come.
'Tis well yet there's some goodness in my death;
My life was a black charnel. I have caught   270
An everlasting cold ; I have lost my voice
Most irrecoverably. Farewell, glorious villains !
This busy trade of life appears most vain,
Since rest breeds rest, where all seek pain by pain.
Let no harsh flattering bells resound my knell ;
Strike, thunder, and strike loud, to my farewell !
                                    [Dies.

ENGLISH AMBASSADOR.   [Within.]   This way, this
    way ! break ope the doors ! this way !

LODOVICO.   Ha ! are we betrayed ?
Why, then let's constantly die all together ;
And having finished this most noble deed,   280
Defy the worst of fate, not fear to bleed.

Enter Ambassadors and GIOVANNI.

ENGLISH AMBASSADOR.   Keep back the prince :
    shoot, shoot.   [They shoot, and LODOVICO falls.
    LODOVICO.   Oh, I am wounded !
I fear I shall be ta'en.
    GIOVANNI.   You bloody villains,
By what authority have you committed
This massacre ?
    LODOVICO.   By thine.
    GIOVANNI.   Mine ?
    LODOVICO.   Yes ; thy uncle,
Which is a part of thee, enjoined us to 't :
Thou know'st me, I am sure ; I am Count Lodo-
    wick ;
And thy most noble uncle in disguise
Was last night in thy court.
    GIOVANNI.   Ha !
    GASPARO.[1]   Yes, that Moor
Thy father chose his pensioner.
    GIOVANNI.   He turned murderer ?—
Away with them to prison and to torture !   291
All that have hands in this shall taste our justice,
As I hope Heaven.
    LODOVICO.   I do glory yet
That I can call this act mine own. For my part,
The rack, the gallows, and the torturing wheel,
Shall be but sound sleeps to me : here 's my rest ;
I limned this night-piece, and it was my best.
    GIOVANNI.   Remove the bodies.—See, my hon-
    oured lord[s],
What use you ought make of their punishment :
Let guilty men remember, their black deeds   300
Do lean on crutches made of slender reeds.

                                  [Exeunt.

Instead of an EPILOGUE, only this of Martial
supplies me :

Haec fuerint nobis praemia, si placui.[2]

[1] Given to Carlo in the first Quarto.   [2] Martial ii. 91.

THE KNIGHT OF THE BURNING PESTLE

Francis Beaumont
(1584–1616)

AND

John Fletcher
(1579–1625)

The Knight of the Burning Pestle was perhaps acted in 1609, or at the latest 1611; in any case, on its first production it proved an entire failure. It was printed in quarto without the authors' names in 1613; of this edition Dr. Murch, in his edition of the play (New York, 1908), says that 'evidently it was not transcribed from the authors' MS., but from the prompters' books or the playhouse copies'. The play was revived in 1635 and was received with such favour that two new editions were printed in that year. The earlier of these corrects many of the obvious errors of spelling and punctuation in the 1613 edition, but it introduces several new readings which are evidently wrong. The later edition was perhaps produced in haste to satisfy the public demand; it is at all events less accurate than the earlier, its only improvement being in the punctuation.

The division of the Acts into Scenes and the insertion of most of the stage directions is the work of Weber, whose edition of Beaumont and Fletcher appeared in 1812. These essentials, together with a much needed revision of the text, were carried further by Dyce in his edition of 1843–6. His wide reading and power of patient research enabled him also to trace many references and allusions which had escaped previous editors. The play was edited by Mr. J. St. L. Strachey in the Mermaid Series (1887). The present text follows Dyce in the main, though I have restored a few readings from the early quartos which he had discarded. Beaumont's hand is said by most editors to be far more apparent in the play than Fletcher's; the *Cambridge History of English Literature* indeed assigns it entirely to Beaumont.

THE
KNIGHT OF
the Burning Pestle.

——————————— *Quod si*
Iudicium subtile, videndis artibus illud
Ad libros & ad hæc Musarum dona vocares:
Bœotum in crasso iurares aëre natos.
Horat. in Epist. ad Oct. Aug.

LONDON,
Printed for *Walter Burre*, and are to be sold at the
signe of the Crane in Paules Church-yard.
1 6 1 3.

DRAMATIS PERSONAE [1]

SPEAKER OF THE PROLOGUE.
A CITIZEN.
HIS WIFE.
RALPH, his Apprentice.
Boys.

VENTUREWELL, a Merchant. [2]
HUMPHREY.
MERRYTHOUGHT.
JASPER, } His Sons.
MICHAEL, }
TIM, } Apprentices.
GEORGE, }
Host.
Tapster.
Barber.
Three Men, supposed captives.
Sergeant.
WILLIAM HAMMERTON.
GEORGE GREENGOOSE.
Soldiers, and Attendants.

LUCE, Daughter of Venturewell.
Mistress MERRYTHOUGHT.
Woman, supposed a captive.
POMPIONA, Daughter of the King of Moldavia.

SCENE.—London and the neighbouring Country, excepting
        Act IV, sc. ii, where it is in Moldavia.

  [1] From Dyce.
  [2] In the quartos this is simply ' A rich Marchant '. Weber
inserted the name from Act III, sc. v.

THE KNIGHT OF THE
BURNING PESTLE

INDUCTION

Several Gentlemen sitting on Stools upon the Stage.[1] The Citizen, his Wife, and RALPH *sitting below among the Audience.*

Enter Speaker of the Prologue.

SPEAKER OF THE PROLOGUE. 'From all that's near the court, from all that's great,
Within the compass of the city-walls,
We now have brought our scene——'

Citizen leaps on the Stage.

CITIZEN. Hold your peace, goodman boy!

SPEAKER OF THE PROLOGUE. What do you mean, sir?

CITIZEN. That you have no good meaning: this seven years there hath been plays at this house, I have observed it, you have still girds at citizens; and now you call your play ' The London Merchant '.[2] Down with your title, boy! down with your title!   12

SPEAKER OF THE PROLOGUE. Are you a member of the noble city?

CITIZEN. I am.

SPEAKER OF THE PROLOGUE. And a freeman?

CITIZEN. Yea, and a grocer.

---

[1] The practice of accommodating gallants with seats on the stage is often alluded to in old plays.—*Weber.*

[2] There was a play of this name by Ford, which was never printed.—*Dyce.*

SPEAKER OF THE PROLOGUE. So, grocer, then, by your sweet favour, we intend no abuse to the city.   20

CITIZEN. No, sir ? yes, sir : if you were not resolved to play the Jacks,[1] what need you study for new subjects, purposely to abuse your betters ? why could not you be contented, as well as others, with ' The Legend of Whittington ', or ' The Life and Death of Sir Thomas Gresham, with the building of the Royal Exchange ', or ' The Story of Queen Eleanor, with the rearing of London Bridge upon Woolsacks ' ?   29

SPEAKER OF THE PROLOGUE. You seem to be an understanding man : what would you have us do, sir ?

CITIZEN. Why, present something notably in honour of the commons of the city.

SPEAKER OF THE PROLOGUE. Why, what do you say to ' The Life and Death of Fat Drake, or the Repairing of Fleet-privies ' ?

CITIZEN. I do not like that ; but I will have a citizen, and he shall be of my own trade.   39

SPEAKER OF THE PROLOGUE. Oh, you should have told us your mind a month since ; our play is ready to begin now.

CITIZEN. 'Tis all one for that ; I will have a grocer, and he shall do admirable things.

SPEAKER OF THE PROLOGUE. What will you have him do ?

CITIZEN. Marry, I will have him——

WIFE. [Below.] Husband, husband !

RALPH. [Below.] Peace, mistress.   49

WIFE. [Below.] Hold thy peace, Ralph ; I know what I do, I warrant ye.—Husband, husband !

CITIZEN. What sayst thou, cony ?

WIFE. [Below.] Let him kill a lion with a pestle, husband ! let him kill a lion with a pestle !

CITIZEN. So he shall.—I'll have him kill a lion with a pestle.

                    [1] Mockers.

WIFE. [Below.] Husband ! shall I come up, husband ?

CITIZEN. Aye, cony,—Ralph, help your mistress this way.—Pray, gentlemen, make her a little room.—I pray you, sir, lend me your hand to help up my wife : I thank you, sir.—So.

[Wife comes on the Stage.

WIFE. By your leave, gentlemen all ; I'm something troublesome : I'm a stranger here ; I was ne'er at one of these plays, as they say, before ; but I should have seen ' Jane Shore ' once ; and my husband hath promised me, any time this twelvemonth, to carry me to ' The Bold Beauchamps ', but in truth he did not. I pray you, bear with me.

CITIZEN. Boy, let my wife and I have a couple of stools, and then begin ; and let the grocer do rare things. [Stools are brought.

SPEAKER OF THE PROLOGUE. But, sir, we have never a boy to play him : every one hath a part already.

WIFE. Husband, husband, for God's sake, let Ralph play him ! beshrew me, if I do not think he will go beyond them all.

CITIZEN. Well remembered, wife.—Come up, Ralph.—I'll tell you, gentlemen ; let them but lend him a suit of reparel and necessaries, and, by gad, if any of them all blow wind in the tail on him, I'll be hanged. [RALPH comes on the Stage.

WIFE. I pray you, youth, let him have a suit of reparel.—I'll be sworn, gentlemen, my husband tells you true : he will act you sometimes at our house, that all the neighbours cry out on him ; he will fetch you up a couraging part so in the garret, that we are all as feared, I warrant you, that we quake again : we'll fear our children with him ; if they be never so unruly, do but cry, ' Ralph comes, Ralph comes ! ' to them, and they'll be as quiet as lambs.—Hold up thy head, Ralph ; show the gentlemen what thou canst do ;

speak a huffing part ; I warrant you, the gentlemen will accept of it.

CITIZEN. Do, Ralph, do.

RALPH. ' By Heavens, methinks, it were an
easy leap   99
To pluck bright honour from the pale-faced moon ;
Or dive into the bottom of the sea,
Where never fathom-line touched any ground,
And pluck up drowned honour from the lake of
hell.' [1]

CITIZEN. How say you, gentlemen, is it not as
I told you ?

WIFE. Nay, gentlemen, he hath played before [2],
my husband says, Mucedorus, before the wardens
of our company.

CITIZEN. Aye, and he should have played
Jeronimo with a shoemaker for a wager.   110

SPEAKER OF THE PROLOGUE. He shall have a
suit of apparel, if he will go in.

CITIZEN. In, Ralph, in, Ralph ; and set out
the grocery [3] in their kind, if thou lovest me.

[Exit RALPH.

WIFE. I warrant, our Ralph will look finely
when he 's dressed.

SPEAKER OF THE PROLOGUE. But what will you
have it called ?

CITIZEN. ' The Grocer's Honour.'   119

SPEAKER OF THE PROLOGUE. Methinks ' The
Knight of the Burning Pestle ' were better.

WIFE. I'll be sworn, husband, that 's as good
a name as can be.

CITIZEN. Let it be so.—Begin, begin ; my wife
and I will sit down.

SPEAKER OF THE PROLOGUE. I pray you, do.

CITIZEN. What stately music have you ? you
have shawms ?   128

---

[1] An inaccurate quotation from 1 *Henry IV*, I. iii.
[2] This word seems, as Dyce says, to have crept into the
text from the next line.
[3] The guild of grocers.

SPEAKER OF THE PROLOGUE. Shawms ! no.

CITIZEN. No ? I'm a thief, if my mind did not
give me so. Ralph plays a stately part, and he
must needs have shawms : I'll be at the charge
of them myself, rather than we'll be without
them.   134

SPEAKER OF THE PROLOGUE. So you are like
to be.

CITIZEN. Why, and so I will be : there's two
shillings ;—[Gives money.]—let's have the waits of
Southwark ; they are as rare fellows as any are
in England ; and that will fetch them all o'er the
water with a vengeance, as if they were mad.

SPEAKER OF THE PROLOGUE. You shall have
them. Will you sit down, then ?   143

CITIZEN. Aye.—Come, wife.

WIFE. Sit you merry all, gentlemen ; I'm bold
to sit amongst you for my ease.

       [Citizen and Wife sit down.

SPEAKER OF THE PROLOGUE. ' From all that's
  near the court, from all that's great
Within the compass of the city-walls,
We now have brought our scene. Fly far from
  hence
All private taxes,[1] immodest phrases,   150
Whatever may but show like vicious !
For wicked mirth never true pleasure brings,
But honest minds are pleased with honest things.'—
Thus much for that we do ; but for Ralph's part
you must answer for yourself.

CITIZEN. Take you no care for Ralph ; he'll
discharge himself, I warrant you.

       [Exit Speaker of Prologue.

WIFE. I' faith, gentlemen, I'll give my word for
Ralph.

    [1] Accusations.

ACT THE FIRST

Scene I.—A Room in the House of Venturewell.

Enter Venturewell and Jasper.

VENTUREWELL. Sirrah, I'll make you know you
    are my prentice,
And whom my charitable love redeemed
Even from the fall of fortune ; gave thee heat
And growth, to be what now thou art ; new-cast
    thee ;
Adding the trust of all I have, at home,
In foreign staples, or upon the sea,
To thy direction ; tied the good opinions
Both of myself and friends to thy endeavours ;
So fair were thy beginnings. But with these,
As I remember, you had never charge   10
To love your master's daughter, and even then
When I had found a wealthy husband for her ;
I take it, sir, you had not : but, however,
I'll break the neck of that commission,
And make you know you are but a merchant's
    factor.
    JASPER. Sir, I do liberally confess I am yours,
Bound both by love and duty to your service,
In which my labour hath been all my profit :
I have not lost in bargain, nor delighted
To wear your honest gains upon my back ;   20
Nor have I given a pension to my blood,
Or lavishly in play consumed your stock ;
These, and the miseries that do attend them,
I dare with innocence proclaim are strangers
To all my temperate actions. For your daughter,
If there be any love to my deservings
Borne by her virtuous self, I cannot stop it ;
Nor am I able to refrain her wishes.
She's private to herself, and best of knowledge
Whom she will make so happy as to sigh for : 30
Besides, I cannot think you mean to match her

Unto a fellow of so lame a presence,
One that hath little left of nature in him.
   VENTUREWELL. 'Tis very well, sir : I can tell
     your wisdom
How all this shall be cured.
   JASPER.   Your care becomes you.
   VENTUREWELL. And thus it shall [1] be, sir : I
     here discharge you
My house and service ; take your liberty ;
And when I want a son, I'll send for you.   [Exit.
   JASPER. These be the fair rewards of them that
     love !
Oh, you that live in freedom, never prove   40
The travail of a mind led by desire !

Enter LUCE.

   LUCE. Why, how now, friend ? struck with my
     father's thunder ?
   JASPER. Struck, and struck dead, unless the
     remedy
Be full of speed and virtue ; I am now,
What I expected long, no more your father's.
   LUCE. But mine.
   JASPER.   But yours, and only yours, I am ;
That 's all I have to keep me from the statute.
You dare be constant still ?
   LUCE.   Oh, fear me not !
In this I dare be better than a woman.
Nor shall his anger nor his offers move me,   50
Were they both equal to a prince's power.
   JASPER. You know my rival ?
   LUCE.   Yes, and love him dearly :
Even as I love an ague or foul weather :
I prithee, Jasper, fear him not.
   JASPER.   Oh, no !
I do not mean to do him so much kindness.
But to our own desires : you know the plot
We both agreed on ?

[1] In 1613 and 1635 (a) 'must '.

LUCE.   Yes, and will perform
My part exactly.
JASPER.   I desire no more.
Farewell, and keep my heart ; 'tis yours.
LUCE.   I take it ;
He must do miracles makes me forsake it.   60

[*Exeunt severally.*

[CITIZEN. Fie upon 'em, little infidels ! what
a matter's here now ! Well, I'll be hanged for a
halfpenny, if there be not some abomination
knavery in this play. Well ; let 'em look to't ;
Ralph must come, and if there be any tricks
a-brewing——

WIFE. Let 'em brew and bake too, husband,
a' God's name ; Ralph will find all out, I warrant
you, an they were older than they are.—[*Enter Boy.*]
—I pray, my pretty youth, is Ralph ready ?

BOY. He will be presently.   71

WIFE. Now, I pray you, make my commendations unto him, and withal carry him this stick of
liquorice : tell him his mistress sent it him ; and
bid him bite a piece ; 'twill open his pipes the
better, say.]   [*Exit Boy.*

SCENE II.—Another Room in the House of VENTUREWELL.

Enter VENTUREWELL and HUMPHREY.

VENTUREWELL. Come, sir, she's yours ; upon
    my faith, she's yours ;
You have my hand : for other idle lets[1]
Between your hopes and her, thus with a wind
They are scattered and no more. My wanton
    prentice,
That like a bladder blew himself with love,
I have let out, and sent him to discover
New masters yet unknown.
HUMPHREY.   I thank you, sir,
Indeed, I thank you, sir ; and, ere I stir,
It shall be known, however you do deem,

_____
[1] Hindrances.

I am of gentle blood, and gentle seem.   10
    VENTUREWELL.   Oh, sir, I know it certain.
    HUMPHREY.   Sir, my friend,
Although, as writers say, all things have end,
And that we call a pudding hath his two,
Oh, let it not seem strange, I pray, to you,
If in this bloody simile I put
My love, more endless than frail things or gut !
    [WIFE.   Husband, I prithee, sweet lamb, tell
me one thing; but tell me truly.—Stay, youths,
I beseech you, till I question my husband.
    CITIZEN.   What is it, mouse ?   20
    WIFE.   Sirrah, didst thou ever see a prettier
child ? how it behaves itself, I warrant ye, and
speaks and looks, and perts up the head !—I pray
you, brother, with your favour, were you never
none of Master Moncaster's [1] scholars ?
    CITIZEN.   Chicken, I prithee heartily, contain
thyself : the childer are pretty childer ; but when
Ralph comes, lamb——
    WIFE.   Aye, when Ralph comes, cony !—Well,
my youth, you may proceed.]   30
    VENTUREWELL.   Well, sir, you know my love,
        and rest, I hope,
Assured of my consent ; get but my daughter's,
And wed her when you please. You must be bold,
And clap in close unto her : come, I know
You have language good enough to win a wench.
    [WIFE.   A whoreson tyrant ! h'as been an old
stringer [2] in 's days, I warrant him.]
    HUMPHREY.   I take your gentle offer, and withal
Yield love again for love reciprocal.   39
    VENTUREWELL.   What, Luce ! within there !

                    Enter LUCE.

LUCE.   Called you, sir ?
VENTUREWELL.   I did :

    [1] Richard Mulcaster was head master of Merchant Taylors'
School (1561–86).
    [2] ' Similar to " striker ", denoting a wencher.'—*Weber.*

Give entertainment to this gentleman ;
And see you be not froward.—To her, sir :
My presence will but be an eye-sore to you.   [Exit.

> HUMPHREY.   Fair Mistress Luce, how do you ?
> are you well ?

Give me your hand, and then I pray you tell
How doth your little sister and your brother ;
And whether you love me or any other.

> LUCE.   Sir, these are quickly answered.
> HUMPHREY.   So they are,

Where women are not cruel. But how far
Is it now distant from the place we are in,   50
Unto that blessèd place, your father's warren ?

> LUCE.   What makes you think of that, sir ?
> HUMPHREY.   Even that face.

For, stealing rabbits whilom in that place,
God Cupid, or the keeper, I know not whether,
Unto my cost and charges brought you thither,
And there began——

> LUCE.   Your game, sir.
> HUMPHREY.   Let no game,

Or any thing that tendeth to the same,
Be ever more remembered, thou fair killer,
For whom I sate me down, and brake my tiller.[1]

> [WIFE.   There's a kind gentleman, I warrant
you : when will you do as much for me, George ?]

> LUCE.   Beshrew me, sir, I am sorry for your
> losses,   62

But, as the proverb says, I cannot cry :
I would you had not seen me !

> HUMPHREY.   So would I,

Unless you had more maw to do me good.

> LUCE.   Why, cannot this strange passion be
> withstood ?

Send for a constable, and raise the town.

> HUMPHREY.   Oh, no ! my valiant love will
> batter down

Millions of constables, and put to flight
Even that great watch of Midsummer-day at night.

---

[1] Steel bow, or crossbow.

LUCE. Beshrew me, sir, 'twere good I yielded,
    then ;   71
Weak women cannot hope, where valiant men
Have no resistance.
    HUMPHREY.   Yield, then ; I am full
Of pity, though I say it, and can pull
Out of my pocket thus a pair of gloves.
Look, Lucy, look ; the dog's tooth nor the dove's
Are not so white as these ; and sweet they be,
And whipt about with silk, as you may see.
If you desire the price, shoot from your eye
A beam to this place, and you shall espy   80
F S, which is to say, my sweetest honey,
They cost me three and twopence, or no money.
    LUCE. Well, sir, I take them kindly, and I
    thank you :
What would you more ?
    HUMPHREY.   Nothing.
    LUCE.   Why, then, farewell.
    HUMPHREY. Nor so, nor so ; for, lady, I must
    tell,
Before we part, for what we met together :
God grant me time and patience and fair weather !
    LUCE. Speak, and declare your mind in terms
    so brief.
    HUMPHREY. I shall : then, first and foremost,
    for relief
I call to you, if that you can afford it ;   90
I care not at what price, for, on my word, it
Shall be repaid again, although it cost me
More than I'll speak of now ; for love hath tost me
In furious blanket like a tennis-ball,
And now I rise aloft, and now I fall.
    LUCE. Alas, good gentleman, alas the day !
    HUMPHREY. I thank you heartily ; and, as I
    say,
Thus do I still continue without rest,
I' the morning like a man, at night a beast,
Roaring and bellowing mine own disquiet,   100
That much I fear, forsaking of my diet

Will bring me presently to that quandary,
I shall bid all adieu.
  LUCE.   Now, by St. Mary,
That were great pity !
  HUMPHREY.   So it were, beshrew me ;
Then, ease me, lusty Luce, and pity show me.
  LUCE. Why, sir, you know my will is nothing
   worth
Without my father's grant ; get his consent,
And then you may with [full] assurance try me.
  HUMPHREY. The worshipful your sire will not
   deny me ;
For I have asked him, and he hath replied, 110
' Sweet Master Humphrey, Luce shall be thy bride.'
  LUCE. Sweet Master Humphrey, then I am
   content.
  HUMPHREY. And so am I, in truth.
  LUCE.   Yet take me with you ; [1]
There is another clause must be annexed,
And this it is : I swore, and will perform it,
No man shall ever joy me as his wife
But he that stole me hence. If you dare venture,
I am yours (you need not fear ; my father loves
  you) ;
If not, farewell for ever !
  HUMPHREY.   Stay, nymph, stay :
I have a double gelding, coloured bay, 120
Sprung by his father from Barbarian kind ;
Another for myself, though somewhat blind,
Yet true as trusty tree.
  LUCE.   I am satisfied ;
And so I give my hand. Our course must lie
Through Waltham Forest, where I have a friend
Will entertain us. So, farewell, Sir Humphrey,
And think upon your business.   [Exit.
  HUMPHREY.   Though I die,
I am resolved to venture life and limb 128
For one so young, so fair, so kind, so trim.   [Exit.

 [1] Understand me ; the phrase usually means, make me
understand you.

[WIFE. By my faith and troth, George, and as I am virtuous, it is e'en the kindest young man that ever trod on shoe-leather.—Well, go thy ways ; if thou hast her not, 'tis not thy fault, 'faith.

CITIZEN. I prithee, mouse, be patient ; 'a shall have her, or I'll make some of 'em smoke for 't.

WIFE. That 's my good lamb, George.—Fie, this stinking tobacco kills me ! [1] would there were none in England !—Now, I pray, gentlemen, what good does this stinking tobacco do you ? nothing, I warrant you : make chimneys o' your faces !]

Scene III.—A Grocer's Shop.

Enter RALPH, as a Grocer, reading ' Palmerin of England ', with TIM and GEORGE.

[WIFE. Oh, husband, husband, now, now ! there 's Ralph, there 's Ralph.

CITIZEN. Peace, fool ! let Ralph alone.—Hark you, Ralph ; do not strain yourself too much at the first.—Peace !—Begin, Ralph.]   5

RALPH. [Reads.] ' Then [1] Palmerin and Trineus, snatching their lances from their dwarfs, and clasping their helmets, galloped amain after the giant ; and Palmerin, having gotten a sight of him, came posting amain, saying, " Stay, traitorous thief ! for thou mayst not so carry away her, that is worth the greatest lord in the world ; " and, with these words, gave him a blow on the shoulder, that he struck him besides his elephant. And Trineus, coming to the knight that had Agricola behind him, set him soon besides his horse, with his neck broken in the fall ; so that the princess, getting out of the throng, between joy and grief, said, " All happy knight, the mirror of all such as follow arms, now may I be well assured of the love thou bearest me." '—I wonder why the kings do not raise an army of fourteen or

[1] In the quartos ' men '.
[2] From *Palmerin D'Oliva, the Mirrour of Nobilitie* (1588).

fifteen hundred thousand men, as big as the army
that the Prince of Portigo brought against Rosicleer,
and destroy these giants ; they do much hurt to
wandering damsels, that go in quest of their
knights.

[WIFE.   Faith, husband, and Ralph says true ;
for they say the King of Portugal cannot sit at
his meat, but the giants and the ettins [1] will come
and snatch it from him.   31

CITIZEN.   Hold thy tongue.—On, Ralph !]

RALPH.   And certainly those knights are much
to be commended, who, neglecting their possessions,
wander with a squire and a dwarf through the
deserts to relieve poor ladies.

[WIFE.   Aye, by my faith,[2] are they, Ralph ;
let 'em say what they will, they are indeed. Our
knights neglect their possessions well enough, but
they do not the rest.]   40

RALPH.   There are no such courteous and fair
well-spoken knights in this age : they will call one
' the son of a whore ', that Palmerin of England
would have called ' fair sir ' ;   and one that
Rosicleer would have called ' right beauteous
damsel ', they will call ' damned bitch '.

[WIFE.   I'll be sworn will they, Ralph ; they
have called me so an hundred times about a
scurvy pipe of tobacco.]   49

RALPH.   But what brave spirit could be content
to sit in his shop, with a flappet of wood,[3] and a
blue apron before him, selling mithridatum and
dragon's-water to visited houses [4] that might
pursue feats of arms, and, through his noble
achievements, procure such a famous history to
be written of his heroic prowess ?

[CITIZEN.   Well said, Ralph ; some more of
those words, Ralph !

---

[1] Giants who were also cannibals.
[2] In the 1613 quarto ' by faith '.
[3] i. e. the counter.
[4] i. e. to houses visited by the plague.

WIFE. They go finely, by my troth.] 59

RALPH. Why should not I, then, pursue this course, both for the credit of myself and our company ? for amongst all the worthy books of achievements, I do not call to mind that I yet read of a grocer-errant : I will be the said knight.— Have you heard of any that hath wandered un-furnished of his squire and dwarf ? My elder prentice Tim shall be my trusty squire, and little George my dwarf. Hence, my blue apron ! Yet, in remembrance of my former trade, upon my shield shall be portrayed a Burning Pestle, and I will be called the Knight of the Burning Pestle.

[WIFE. Nay, I dare swear thou wilt not forget thy old trade ; thou wert ever meek.] 73

RALPH. Tim !

TIM. Anon.

RALPH. My beloved squire, and George my dwarf, I charge you that from henceforth you never call me by any other name but ' the right courteous and valiant Knight of the Burning Pestle ' ; and that you never call any female by the name of a woman or wench, but ' fair lady ', if she have her desires, if not, ' distressed damsel ' ; that you call all forests and heaths ' deserts ', and all horses ' palfreys '. 84

[WIFE. This is very fine, faith.—Do the gentle-men like Ralph, think you, husband ?

CITIZEN. Aye, I warrant thee ; the players would give all the shoes in their shop for him.]

RALPH. My beloved squire Tim, stand out. Admit this were a desert, and over it a knight-errant pricking,[1] and I should bid you inquire of his intents, what would you say ? 92

TIM. Sir, my master sent me to know whither you are riding ?

RALPH. No, thus : ' Fair sir, the right courteous and valiant Knight of the Burning Pestle com-manded me to inquire upon what adventure you

[1] Spurring, riding briskly.

are bound, whether to relieve some distressed
damsel, or otherwise.'

[CITIZEN.   Whoreson blockhead, cannot remem-
ber !   101

WIFE.   I' faith, and Ralph told him on 't before:
all the gentlemen heard him.—Did he not, gentlemen ? did not Ralph tell him on 't ?]

GEORGE.   Right courteous and valiant Knight of
the Burning Pestle, here is a distressed damsel to
have a halfpenny-worth of pepper.

[WIFE.   That 's a good boy ! see, the little boy
can hit it ; by my troth, it 's a fine child.]   109

RALPH.   Relieve her, with all courteous language.
Now shut up shop ; no more my prentice[s] but
my trusty squire and dwarf.   I must bespeak my
shield and arming pestle.   [Exeunt TIM and GEORGE.

[CITIZEN : Go thy ways, Ralph ! As I'm a true
man, thou art the best on 'em all.

WIFE.   Ralph, Ralph !

RALPH.   What say you, mistress ?

WIFE.   I prithee, come again quickly, sweet
Ralph.   119

RALPH.   By and by.]   [Exit.

SCENE IV.—A Room in MERRYTHOUGHT's House.

Enter Mistress MERRYTHOUGHT and JASPER.

MISTRESS MERRYTHOUGHT.   Give thee my blessing ! no, I'll ne'er give thee my blessing ; I'll see
thee hanged first ; it shall ne'er be said I gave thee
my blessing.   Thou art thy father's own son, of
the right blood of the Merrythoughts.   I may curse
the time that e'er I knew thy father ; he hath
spent all his own and mine too ; and when I tell
him of it, he laughs, and dances, and sings, and
cries, ' A merry heart lives long-a '.   And thou art
a wastethrift, and art run away from thy master
that loved thee well, and art come to me ; and
I have laid up a little for my younger son Michael,

and thou thinkest to bezzle[1] that, but thou shalt
never be able to do it.—Come hither, Michael !

Enter MICHAEL.

Come, Michael, down on thy knees ; thou shalt
have my blessing.   16
    MICHAEL. [*Kneels.*] I pray you, mother, pray to
God to bless me.
    MISTRESS MERRYTHOUGHT. God bless thee ! but
Jasper shall never have my blessing ; he shall be
hanged first : shall he not, Michael ? how sayst thou ?
    MICHAEL. Yes, forsooth, mother, and grace of
God.
    MISTRESS MERRYTHOUGHT. That's a good boy !
    [WIFE. I' faith, it's a fine-spoken child.]
    JASPER. Mother, though you forget a parent's
      love
I must preserve the duty of a child.
I ran not from my master, nor return
To have your stock maintain my idleness.   29
    [WIFE. Ungracious child, I warrant him ; hark,
how he chops logic with his mother !—Thou hadst
best tell her she lies ; do, tell her she lies.
    CITIZEN. If he were my son, I would hang him
up by the heels, and flay him, and salt him,
whoreson halter-sack ![2]]
    JASPER. My coming only is to beg your love,
Which I must ever, though I never gain it ;
And, howsoever you esteem of me,
There is no drop of blood hid in these veins
But, I remember well, belongs to you   40
That brought me forth, and would be glad for you
To rip them all again, and let it out
    MISTRESS MERRYTHOUGHT. I' faith, I had sorrow
enough for thee, God knows ; but I'll hamper thee
well enough. Get thee in, thou vagabond, get thee
in, and learn of thy brother Michael.
                [*Exeunt* JASPER *and* MICHAEL.

---

[1] Squander.   [2] Gallows-bird.

MERRYTHOUGHT.   [Singing within.]
>Nose, nose, jolly red nose,
>And who gave thee this jolly red nose?

MISTRESS MERRYTHOUGHT.   Hark, my husband !
he's singing and hoiting[1] ; and I'm fain to cark and
care, and all little enough.—Husband ! Charles !
Charles Merrythought !   52

Enter MERRYTHOUGHT.

MERRYTHOUGHT. [Sings.]
>Nutmegs and ginger, cinnamon and cloves ;
>And they gave me this jolly red nose.

MISTRESS MERRYTHOUGHT. If you would consider
your state, you would have little list to sing, i-wis.

MERRYTHOUGHT. It should never be considered,
while it were an estate, if I thought it would spoil
my singing.   59

MISTRESS MERRYTHOUGHT. But how wilt thou
do, Charles ? thou art an old man, and thou canst
not work, and thou hast not forty shillings left, and
thou eatest good meat, and drinkest good drink,
and laughest.

MERRYTHOUGHT. And will do.

MISTRESS MERRYTHOUGHT. But how wilt thou
come by it, Charles ?   67

MERRYTHOUGHT. How ! why, how have I done
hitherto this forty years ? I never came into my
dining room, but, at eleven and six o'clock, I found
excellent meat and drink o' the table ; my clothes
were never worn out, but next morning a tailor
brought me a new suit : and without question
it will be so ever ; use makes perfectness. If all
should fail, it is but a little straining myself
extraordinary, and laugh myself to death.

[WIFE. It's a foolish old man this ; is not he,
George ?

CITIZEN : Yes, cony.

WIFE. Give me a penny i' the purse while I live,
George.   81

---

[1] Indulging in riotous mirth.—*Nares.*

CITIZEN. Aye, by Lady, cony, hold thee there.]

MISTRESS MERRYTHOUGHT. Well, Charles; you promised to provide for Jasper, and I have laid up for Michael. I pray you, pay Jasper his portion : he's come home, and he shall not consume Michael's stock ; he says his master turned him away, but, I promise you truly, I think he ran away.

[WIFE. No, indeed, Mistress Merrythought ; though he be a notable gallows,[1] yet I'll assure you his master did turn him away, even in this place ; 'twas i' faith, within this half-hour, about his daughter ; my husband was by. 93

CITIZEN. Hang him, rogue ! he served him well enough : love his master's daughter ! By my troth, cony, if there were a thousand boys, thou wouldst spoil them all with taking their parts ; let his mother alone with him.

WIFE. Aye, George ; but yet truth is truth.]

MERRYTHOUGHT. Where is Jasper ? he's wel·come, however. Call him in ; he shall have his portion. Is he merry ? 102

MISTRESS MERRYTHOUGHT. Ah, foul chive [2] him, he is too merry !—Jasper ! Michael !

Re-enter JASPER and MICHAEL.

MERRYTHOUGHT. Welcome, Jasper ! though thou runnest away, welcome ! God bless thee ! 'Tis thy mother's mind thou shouldst receive thy portion ; thou hast been abroad, and I hope hast learned experience enough to govern it ; thou art of sufficient years ; hold thy hand—one, two, three, four, five, six, seven, eight, nine, there is ten shillings for thee. [Gives money.] Thrust thyself into the world with that, and take some settled course : if fortune cross thee, thou hast a retiring place ; come home to me ; I have twenty shillings left. Be a good husband ; that is, wear ordinary clothes, eat the best meat, and

---

[1] Gallows-bird.   [2] Evil befall him.

drink the best drink; be merry, and give to the
poor, and, believe me, thou hast no end of thy goods.

JASPER.   Long may you live free from all
thought of ill,   120
And long have cause to be thus merry still!
But, father——

MERRYTHOUGHT.   No more words, Jasper; get
thee gone. Thou hast my blessing; thy father's
spirit upon thee! Farewell, Jasper!   [Sings.]

But yet, or ere you part (oh, cruel!)
Kiss me, kiss me, sweeting, mine own dear jewel!
So, now begone; no words.   [Exit JASPER.

MISTRESS MERRYTHOUGHT.   So, Michael, now
get thee gone too.   130

MICHAEL.   Yes, forsooth, mother; but I'll have
my father's blessing first.

MISTRESS MERRYTHOUGHT.   No, Michael; 'tis
no matter for his blessing; thou hast my blessing; begone. I'll fetch my money and jewels,
and follow thee; I'll stay no longer with him,
I warrant thee. [Exit MICHAEL.]—Truly, Charles,
I'll be gone too.

MERRYTHOUGHT.   What! you will not?   139
MISTRESS MERRYTHOUGHT.   Yes, indeed will I.
MERRYTHOUGHT.   [Sings.]

Heigh-ho, farewell, Nan!
I'll never trust wench more again, if I can.

MISTRESS MERRYTHOUGHT.   You shall not think,
when all your own is gone, to spend that I have
been scraping up for Michael.

MERRYTHOUGHT.   Farewell, good wife; I expect
it not: all I have to do in this world, is to be
merry; which I shall, if the ground be not taken
from me; and if it be,   [Sings.]

When earth and seas from me are reft,   150
The skies aloft for me are left.

(Exeunt severally.

[WIFE.   I'll be sworn he's a merry old gentleman
for all that. [Music.] Hark, hark, husband, hark!
fiddles, fiddles! now surely they go finely. They

say 'tis present death for these fiddlers, to tune
their rebecks [1] before the great Turk's grace; is 't
not, George ?   [Enter a Boy and dances.]   But, look,
look ! here 's a youth dances !—Now, good youth,
do a turn o' the toe.—Sweetheart, i' faith, I'll have
Ralph come and do some of his gambols. He'll
ride the wild mare,[2] gentlemen, 'twould do your
hearts good to see him.—I thank you, kind youth ;
pray, bid Ralph come.   163
    CITIZEN.   Peace, cony !—Sirrah, you scurvy boy,
bid the players send Ralph ; or, by God's——an
they do not, I'll tear some of their periwigs beside
their heads : this is all riff-raff.]   [Exit Boy.

ACT THE SECOND

SCENE I.—A Room in the House of VENTUREWELL.

Enter VENTUREWELL and HUMPHREY.

VENTUREWELL.   And how, i' faith, how goes it
    now, son Humphrey ?
HUMPHREY.   Right worshipful, and my belovèd
    friend
And father dear, this matter 's at an end.
VENTUREWELL.   'Tis well : it should be so : I'm
    glad the girl
Is found so tractable.
HUMPHREY.   Nay, she must whirl
From hence (and you must wink ; for so, I say,
The story tells,) to-morrow before day.
    [WIFE.   George, dost thou think in thy con-
science now 'twill be a match ? tell me but what
thou think'st, sweet rogue. Thou seest the poor
gentleman, dear heart, how it labours and throbs,
I warrant you, to be at rest ! I'll go move the
father for 't.   13
    CITIZEN.   No, no ; I prithee, sit still, honey-
suckle ; thou'lt spoil all. If he deny him, I'll

---

[1] A sort of fiddle.   [2] Play at see-saw.

bring half a dozen good fellows myself, and in the
shutting of an evening, knock 't up, and there 's
an end.

    WIFE.   I'll buss thee for that, i' faith, boy. Well,
George, well, you have been a wag in your days,
I warrant you ; but God forgive you, and I do
with all my heart.]   22
    VENTUREWELL.   How was it, son ? you told
      me that to-morrow
Before daybreak, you must convey her hence.
    HUMPHREY.   I must, I must ; and thus it is
      agreed :
Your daughter rides upon a brown-bay steed,
I on a sorrel, which I bought of Brian,
The honest host of the Red roaring Lion,
In Waltham situate. Then, if you may,
Consent in seemly sort ; lest, by delay,   30
The Fatal Sisters come, and do the office,
And then you'll sing another song.
    VENTUREWELL.   Alas !
Why should you be thus full of grief to me,
That do as willing as yourself agree
To any thing, so it be good and fair ?
Then, steal her when you will, if such a pleasure
Content you both ; I'll sleep and never see it,
To make your joys more full. But tell me why
You may not here perform your marriage ?   39
    [WIFE.   God's blessing o' thy soul, old man !
i' faith, thou art loath to part true hearts. I see
'a has her, George ; and I'm as glad on 't !—Well,
go thy ways, Humphrey, for a fair-spoken man ;
I believe thou hast not thy fellow within the walls of
London ; an I should say the suburbs too, I should
not lie.—Why dost not rejoice with me, George ?
    CITIZEN.   If I could but see Ralph again, I were
as merry as mine host, i' faith.]
    HUMPHREY.   The cause you seem to ask, I thus
      declare—
Help me, O Muses nine ! Your daughter sware
A foolish oath, the more it was the pity ;   51

Yet no one but myself within this city
Shall dare to say so, but a bold defiance
Shall meet him, were he of the noble science ; [1]
And yet she sware, and yet why did she swear ?
Truly, I cannot tell, unless it were
For her own ease ; for, sure, sometimes an oath,
Being sworn thereafter, is like cordial broth ;
And this it was she swore, never to marry
But such a one whose mighty arm could carry
(As meaning me, for I am such a one)   61
Her bodily away, through stick and stone,
Till both of us arrive, at her request,
Some ten miles off, in the wild Waltham Forest.

    VENTUREWELL. If this be all, you shall not
      need to fear
Any denial in your love : proceed ;
I'll neither follow, nor repent the deed.

    HUMPHREY. Good night, twenty good nights,
      and twenty more,
And twenty more good nights,—that makes three
    score !   [Exeunt severally.

SCENE II.—Waltham Forest.

Enter Mistress MERRYTHOUGHT and MICHAEL.

    MISTRESS MERRYTHOUGHT. Come, Michael ; art
thou not weary, boy ?

    MICHAEL. No, forsooth, mother, not I.

    MISTRESS MERRYTHOUGHT. Where be we now,
child ?

    MICHAEL. Indeed, forsooth, mother, I cannot
tell, unless we be at Mile End. Is not all the
world Mile End, mother ?   8

    MISTRESS MERRYTHOUGHT. No, Michael, not all
the world, boy ; but I can assure thee, Michael,
Mile End is a goodly matter : there has been
a pitch-field, my child, between the naughty
Spaniels and the Englishmen ; [2] and the Spaniels

---

[1] i.e. a master of fencing.
[2] This must refer to a sham-fight.

ran away, Michael, and the Englishmen followed :
my neighbour Coxstone was there, boy, and killed
them all with a birding-piece.

MICHAEL. Mother, forsooth——

MISTRESS MERRYTHOUGHT. What says my white
boy ?   19

MICHAEL. Shall not my father go with us too ?

MISTRESS MERRYTHOUGHT. No, Michael, let thy
father go snick-up ; [1] he shall never come between
a pair of sheets with me again while he lives ; let
him stay at home, and sing for his supper, boy.
Come, child, sit down, and I'll show my boy fine
knacks, indeed. [They sit down : and she takes out a
casket.] Look here, Michael ; here's a ring, and
here's a brooch, and here's a bracelet, and here's
two rings more, and here's money and gold by
th' eye,[2] my boy.   30

MICHAEL. Shall I have all this, mother ?

MISTRESS MERRYTHOUGHT. Ay, Michael, thou
shalt have all, Michael.

[CITIZEN. How lik'st thou this, wench ?

WIFE. I cannot tell ; I would have Ralph,
George ; I'll see no more else, indeed, la ; and
I pray you, let the youths understand so much by
word of mouth ; for, I tell you truly, I'm afraid
o' my boy. Come, come, George, let's be merry
and wise : the child's a fatherless child ; and say
they should put him into a strait pair of gaskins,[3]
'twere worse than knot-grass ; [4] he would never
grow after it.]   43

Enter RALPH, TIM, and GEORGE.

[CITIZEN. Here's Ralph, here's Ralph !

WIFE. How do you, Ralph ? you are welcome,
Ralph, as I may say ; it's a good boy, hold up thy
head, and be not afraid ; we are thy friends,

---

[1] Go hang.
[2] '? in unlimited quantity —N.E.D.   [3] Breeches.
[4] Knot-grass was supposed, if taken in an infusion, to
prevent the growth of any animal.

Ralph ; the gentlemen will praise thee, Ralph, if
thou playest thy part with audacity. Begin, Ralph,
a' God's name !]

RALPH. My trusty squire, unlace my helm ; 50
give me my hat.
Where are we, or what desert may this be ?

GEORGE. Mirror of knighthood, this is, as I take
it, the perilous Waltham Down ; in whose bottom
stands the enchanted valley.

MISTRESS MERRYTHOUGHT. Oh, Michael, we are
betrayed, we are betrayed ! here be giants ! Fly,
boy ! fly, boy, fly !

[Exit with MICHAEL, leaving the casket.

RALPH. Lace on my helm again. What noise
is this ?
A gentle lady, flying the embrace 60
Of some uncourteous knight ! I will relieve her.
Go, squire, and say, the Knight, that wears this
Pestle
In honour of all ladies, swears revenge
Upon that recreant coward that pursues her ;
Go, comfort her, and that same gentle squire
That bears her company.

TIM. I go, brave knight. [Exit.

RALPH. My trusty dwarf and friend, reach me
my shield ;
And hold it while I swear. First, by my knight-
hood ;
Then by the soul of Amadis de Gaul,
My famous ancestor ; then by my sword 70
The beauteous Brionella girt about me ;
By this bright burning Pestle, of mine honour
The living trophy ; and by all respect
Due to distressèd damsels ; here I vow
Never to end the quest of this fair lady
And that forsaken squire till by my valour
I gain their liberty !

GEORGE. Heaven bless the knight
That thus relieves poor errant gentlewomen !

[Exeunt.

[WIFE. Aye, marry, Ralph, this has some savour
in 't ; I would see the proudest of them all offer to
carry his books after him. But, George, I will
not have him go away so soon ; I shall be sick
if he go away, that I shall : call Ralph again,
George, call Ralph again ; I prithee, sweetheart,
let him come fight before me, and let 's ha' some
drums and some trumpets, and let him kill all
that comes near him, an thou lov'st me, George !

CITIZEN. Peace a little, bird : he shall kill them
all, an they were twenty more on 'em than there
are.]   90

Enter JASPER.

JASPER. Now, Fortune, if thou be'st not only
ill,
Show me thy better face, and bring about
Thy desperate wheel, that I may climb at length,
And stand [secure].¹ This is our place of meeting,
If love have any constancy. Oh, age,
Where only wealthy men are counted happy !
How shall I please thee, how deserve thy smiles,
When I am only rich in misery ?
My father's blessing and this little coin
Is my inheritance ; a strong revénue !   100
From earth thou art, and to the earth I give thee :
[Throws away the money.
There grow and multiply, whilst fresher air
Breeds me a fresher fortune.—How ! illusion !
[Spies the casket.
What, hath the devil coined himself before me ?
'Tis metal good, it rings well ; I am waking,
And taking too, I hope. Now, God's dear blessing
Upon his heart that left it here ! 'tis mine ;
These pearls, I take it, were not left for swine.
[Exit with the casket.

[WIFE. I do not like that this unthrifty youth
should embezzle away the money ; the poor gentlewoman his mother will have a heavy heart for it,
God knows.   112

¹ A conjecture of Dyce's.

CITIZEN. And reason good, sweetheart.

WIFE. But let him go ; I'll tell Ralph a tale in 's ear shall fetch him again with a wanion,[1] I warrant him, if he be above ground ; and besides, George, here be a number of sufficient gentlemen can witness, and myself, and yourself, and the musicians, if we be called in question.   119

SCENE III.—Another part of the Forest.

Enter RALPH and GEORGE.

But here comes Ralph, George ; thou shalt hear him speak as he were an emperal.]

RALPH. Comes not sir squire again ?

GEORGE.   Right courteous knight,
Your squire doth come, and with him comes the
     lady,
For and [2] the Squire of Damsels, as I take it.

Enter TIM, Mistress MERRYTHOUGHT, and MICHAEL.

RALPH. Madam, if any service or devoir
Of a poor errant knight may right your wrongs,
Command it ; I am prest [3] to give you succour ;
For to that holy end I bear my armour.

MISTRESS MERRYTHOUGHT. Alas, sir ! I am a poor gentlewoman, and I have lost my money in this forest !   12

RALPH. Desert, you would say, lady ; and not lost
Whilst I have sword and lance. Dry up your tears,
Which ill befit the beauty of that face,
And tell the story, if I may request it,
Of your disastrous fortune.

MISTRESS MERRYTHOUGHT. Out, alas ! I left a thousand pound, a thousand pound, e'en all the money I had laid up for this youth, upon the sight of your mastership, you looked so grim, and, as

---

[1] Calamity ; the phrase is equivalent to 'with a vengeance'.

[2] And moreover.   [3] Ready.

I may say it, saving your presence, more like a
giant than a mortal man.

 RALPH. I am as you are, lady ; so are they ;
All mortal. But why weeps this gentle squire ?

 MISTRESS MERRYTHOUGHT. Has he not cause to
weep, do you think, when he hath lost his inheritance ?

 RALPH. Young hope of valour, weep not ; I am
  here
That will confound thy foe, and pay it dear 30
Upon his coward head, that dares deny
Distressèd squires and ladies equity.
I have but one horse, [up]on which shall ride
This fair lady behind me, and before
This courteous squire : fortune will give us more
Upon our next adventure. Fairly speed
Beside us, squire and dwarf, to do us need !
           [Exeunt.

 [CITIZEN. Did not I tell you, Nell, what your
man would do ? by the faith of my body, wench,
for clean action and good delivery, they may all
cast their caps at him.[1]   41

 WIFE. And so they may, i' faith ; for I dare
speak it boldly, the twelve companies of London
cannot match him, timber for timber. Well,
George, an he be not inveigled by some of these
paltry players, I ha' much marvel : but, George,
we ha' done our parts, if the boy have any grace
to be thankful.

 CITIZEN. Yes, I warrant you, duckling.]

   SCENE IV.—Another part of the Forest.

    Enter HUMPHREY and LUCE.

 HUMPHREY. Good Mistress Luce, however I in
  fault am
For your lame horse, you're welcome unto Waltham ;
But which way now to go, or what to say,

    [1] Own themselves beaten by him.

I know not truly, till it be broad day.

LUCE. Oh, fear not, Master Humphrey ; I am guide
For this place good enough.

HUMPHREY. Then, up and ride ;
Or, if it please you, walk for your repose ;
Or sit, or, if you will, go pluck a rose ; [1]
Either of which shall be indifferent
To your good friend and Humphrey, whose consent
Is so entangled ever to your will, 11
As the poor harmless horse is to the mill.

LUCE. Faith, an you say the word, we'll e'en sit down
And take a nap.

HUMPHREY. 'Tis better in the town,
Where we may nap together ; for, believe me,
To sleep without a snatch [2] would mickle grieve me.

LUCE. You're merry, Master Humphrey.

HUMPHREY. So I am,
And have been ever merry from my dam.

LUCE. Your nurse had the less labour.

HUMPHREY. Faith, it may be,
Unless it were by chance I did beray [3] me. 20

Enter JASPER.

JASPER. Luce ! dear friend Luce !

LUCE. Here, Jasper.

JASPER. You are mine.

HUMPHREY. If it be so, my friend, you use me fine :
What do you think I am ?

JASPER. An arrant noddy.

HUMPHREY. A word of obloquy ! Now, by God's body,
I'll tell thy master ; for I know thee well.

JASPER. Nay, an you be so forward for to tell,

---

[1] A euphemism for relieving nature.
[2] A snack, a hasty meal. [3] Befoul.

Take that, and that ; and tell him, sir, I gave it :
And say, I paid you well.   [Beats him.
   HUMPHREY.   Oh, sir, I have it
And do confess the payment ! Pray, be quiet.
   JASPER. Go, get you to your nightcap and the
    diet,   30
To cure your beaten bones.
   LUCE.   Alas, poor Humphrey ;
Get thee some wholesome broth, with sage and
    comfrey ;
A little oil of roses and a feather
To 'noint thy back withal.
   HUMPHREY.   When I came hither,
Would I had gone to Paris with John Dory ! [1]
   LUCE. Farewell, my pretty nump ; I am very
    sorry
I cannot bear thee company.
   HUMPHREY.   Farewell :
The devil's dam was ne'er so banged in hell.   38
         [Exeunt LUCE and JASPER.

[WIFE. This young Jasper will prove me another
thing, o' my conscience, an he may be suffered.
George, dost not see, George, how 'a swaggers, and
flies at the very heads o' folks, as he were a dragon ?
Well, if I do not do his lesson for wronging the
poor gentleman, I am no true woman. His friends
that brought him up might have been better occupied, i-wis, than have taught him these fegaries :
he 's e'en in the high way to the gallows, God
bless him !
   CITIZEN. You're too bitter, cony ; the young
man may do well enough for all this.   50
   WIFE. Come hither, Master Humphrey ; has
he hurt you ? now, beshrew his fingers for 't !
Here, sweetheart, here 's some green ginger for

---

[1] According to the old ballad, ' John Dory bought him an
ambling nag, To Paris for to ride-a '. When there he
promised ' good King John of France ' to bring to him
bound ' all the churls in merry England '. He was, however,
himself taken prisoner by Nichol, a Cornishman.

thee. Now, beshrew my heart, but 'a has peppernel [1]
in 's head, as big as a pullet's egg! Alas, sweet
lamb, how thy temples beat! Take the peace on
him, sweetheart, take the peace on him.

CITIZEN. No, no; you talk like a foolish
woman: I'll ha' Ralph fight with him, and swinge
him up well-favouredly.—Sirrah boy, come hither.
[Enter Boy.] Let Ralph come in and fight with
Jasper.

WIFE. Ay, and beat him well; he 's an unhappy
boy. 62

BOY. Sir, you must pardon us; the plot of our
play lies contrary; and 'twill hazard the spoiling
of our play.

CITIZEN. Plot me no plots! I'll ha' Ralph come
out; I'll make your house too hot for you else.

BOY. Why, sir, he shall; but if any thing fall
out of order, the gentlemen must pardon us. 71

CITIZEN. Go your ways, goodman boy! [Exit
Boy.] I'll hold him a penny, he shall have his
bellyful of fighting now. Ho, here comes Ralph!
no more!]

SCENE V.—Another part of the Forest.

Enter RALPH, Mistress MERRYTHOUGHT, MICHAEL, TIM,
and GEORGE.

RALPH. What knight is that, squire? ask him
if he keep
The passage, bound by love of lady fair,
Or else but prickant.[2]

HUMPHREY. Sir, I am no knight,
But a poor gentleman, that this same night
Had stolen from me, on yonder green,
My lovely wife, and suffered (to be seen
Yet extant on my shoulders) such a greeting,
That whilst I live I shall think of that meeting.

[WIFE. Ay, Ralph, he beat him unmercifully

---

[1] Apparently a lump or swelling.—*Nares.*
[2] Pricking or spurring along.

Ralph ; an thou sparest him, Ralph, I would thou
wert hanged.   11
    CITIZEN.   No more, wife, no more.]
    RALPH.   Where is the caitiff-wretch hath done
      this deed ?
Lady, your pardon ; that I may proceed
Upon the quest of this injurious knight.—
And thou, fair squire, repute me not the worse,
In leaving the great venture of the purse
And the rich casket, till some better leisure.
    HUMPHREY.   Here comes the broker hath pur-
      loined my treasure.

Enter JASPER and LUCE.

    RALPH.   Go, [trusty] squire, and tell him I am
      here,   20
An errant knight-at-arms, to crave delivery
Of that fair lady to her own knight's arms.
If he deny, bid him take choice of ground,
And so defy him.
    TIM.   From the Knight that bears
The Golden Pestle, I defy thee, knight,
Unless thou make fair restitution
Of that bright lady.
    JASPER.   Tell the knight that sent thee,
He is an ass ; and I will keep the wench,
And knock his head-piece.
    RALPH.   Knight, thou art but dead,
If thou recall not thy uncourteous terms.   30
    [WIFE.   Break 's pate, Ralph ; break 's pate,
Ralph, soundly !]
    JASPER.   Come, knight ; I am ready for you.
    Now your Pestle   [Snatches away his pestle.
Shall try what temper, sir, your mortar 's of.
With that he stood upright in his stirrups,
And gave the Knight of the calf-skin such
    a knock,   [Knocks RALPH down.
That he forsook his horse, and down he fell ;
And then he leaped upon him, and plucking off
His helmet——

HUMPHREY.   Nay, an my noble knight be down
    so soon,
                                                            40
Though I can scarcely go, I needs must run. [Exit.
[WIFE.   Run, Ralph, run, Ralph ; run for thy
life, boy ; Jasper comes, Jasper comes !]
                                    [Exit RALPH.
    JASPER.   Come Luce, we must have other arms
        for you :
Humphrey, and Golden Pestle, both adieu ! [Exeunt.
[WIFE.   Sure the devil (God bless us !) is in this
springald ! [1]   Why, George, didst ever see such
a fire-drake ? [2]   I am afraid my boy 's miscarried :
if he be, though he were Master Merrythought's
son a thousand times, if there be any law in
England, I'll make some of them smart for 't.   51
    CITIZEN.   No, no ; I have found out the matter,
sweetheart ; Jasper is enchanted ; as sure as we
are here, he is enchanted : he could no more have
stood in Ralph's hands than I can stand in my lord
mayor's.   I'll have a ring to discover all enchant-
ments, and Ralph shall beat him yet : be no more
vexed, for it shall be so.]

SCENE VI.—Before the Bell-Inn, Waltham.

Enter RALPH, Mistress MERRYTHOUGHT, MICHAEL, TIM,
            and GEORGE.

[WIFE.   Oh, husband, here 's Ralph again !—
Stay, Ralph, again, let me speak with thee.   How
dost thou, Ralph ? art thou not shrewdly hurt ?
the foul great lungies [3] laid unmercifully on thee :
there 's some sugar-candy for thee.   Proceed ; thou
shalt have another bout with him.
    CITIZEN.   If Ralph had him at the fencing-
school, if he did not make a puppy of him, and
drive him up and down the school, he should ne'er
come in my shop more.]   10

_____

[1] Youth.   [2] Fiery dragon.   [3] Lout.

MISTRESS MERRYTHOUGHT.   Truly Master Knight
of the Burning Pestle, I am weary.

MICHAEL.   Indeed, la, mother, and I am very
hungry.

RALPH.   Take comfort, gentle dame, and you,
        fair squire ;
For in this desert there must needs be placed
Many strong castles, held by courteous knights ;
And till I bring you safe to one of those,
I swear by this my order ne'er to leave you.

[WIFE.   Well said, Ralph !—George, Ralph was
ever comfortable, was he not ?   21

CITIZEN.   Yes, duck.

WIFE.   I shall ne'er forget him.   When he had
lost our child (you know it was strayed almost
alone to Puddle Wharf, and the criers were abroad
for it, and there it had drowned itself but for
a sculler), Ralph was the most comfortablest to
me : ' Peace, mistress,' says he, ' let it go ; I'll
get you another as good.'   Did he not, George,
did he not say so ?   30

CITIZEN.   Yes, indeed did he, mouse.]

GEORGE.   I would we had a mess of pottage and
a pot of drink, squire, and were going to bed !

TIM.   Why, we are at Waltham town's end, and
that's the Bell Inn.

GEORGE.   Take courage, valiant knight, damsel,
        and squire !
I have discovered, not a stone's cast off,
An ancient castle, held by the old knight
Of the most holy order of the Bell,
Who gives to all knights-errant entertain :   40
There plenty is of food, and all prepared
By the white hands of his own lady dear.
He hath three squires that welcome all his guests :
The first, hight Chamberlino, who will see
Our beds prepared, and bring us snowy sheets,
Where never footman stretched his buttered hams ;[1]

---

[1] Running footmen of the time used to have their legs
greased.

The second, hight Tapstero, who will see
Our pots full fillèd, and no froth therein ;
The third, a gentle squire, Ostlero hight,
Who will our palfreys slick with wisps of straw,
And in the manger put them oats enough,   51
And never grease their teeth with candle-snuff.[1]

[WIFE.   That same dwarf's a pretty boy, but
the squire's a groutnol.[2]]

    RALPH.   Knock at the gates, my squire, with
      stately lance.   [TIM knocks at the door.

Enter TAPSTER.

    TAPSTER.   Who's   there ?—You're   welcome,
gentlemen :   will you see a room ?

    GEORGE.   Right courteous and valiant Knight of
the Burning Pestle, this is the Squire Tapstero.

    RALPH.   Fair Squire Tapstero, I a wandering
      knight,   60
Hight of the Burning Pestle, in the quest
Of this fair lady's casket and wrought purse,
Losing myself in this vast wilderness,
Am to this castle well by fortune brought ;
Where, hearing of the goodly entertain
Your knight of holy order of the Bell
Gives to all damsels and all errant knights,
I thought to knock, and now am bold to enter.

    TAPSTER.   An't please you see a chamber, you
are very welcome.   [Exeunt.

[WIFE.   George, I would have something done,
and I cannot tell what it is.   72

    CITIZEN.   What is it, Nell ?

    WIFE.   Why, George, shall Ralph beat nobody
again ? prithee, sweetheart, let him.

    CITIZEN.   So he shall, Nell ; and if I join with
him, we'll knock them all.]

---

[1] A common trick of the ostlers at the time to prevent the
horses from eating the hay.—*Weber.*
[2] Thickhead, blockhead.

SCENE VII.—A Room in the House of VENTUREWELL.

Enter HUMPHREY and VENTUREWELL.

[WIFE.   Oh, George, here's Master Humphrey
again now that lost Mistress Luce, and Mistress
Luce's father.   Master Humphrey will do somebody's errand,[1] I warrant him.]

    HUMPHREY.   Father, it's true in arms I ne'er
      shall clasp her ;
For she is stoln away by your man Jasper.

    [WIFE.   I thought he would tell him.]

    VENTUREWELL.   Unhappy that I am, to lose
      my child !
Now I begin to think on Jasper's words,
Who oft hath urged to me thy foolishness :   10
Why didst thou let her go ? thou lov'st her not,
That wouldst bring home thy life, and not bring her.

    HUMPHREY.   Father, forgive me.   Shall I tell
      you true ?
Look on my shoulders, they are black and blue :
Whilst to and fro fair Luce and I were winding,
He came and basted me with a hedge-binding.

    VENTUREWELL.   Get men and horses straight :
      we will be there
Within this hour.   You know the place again ?

    HUMPHREY.   I know the place where he my
      loins did swaddle ;
I'll get six horses, and to each a saddle.   20

    VENTUREWELL.   Mean time I will go talk with
      Jasper's father.   [Exeunt severally.

[WIFE.   George, what wilt thou lay with me
now, that Master Humphrey has not Mistress
Luce yet ? speak, George, what wilt thou lay with
me ?

    CITIZEN.   No, Nell ; I warrant thee, Jasper is
at Puckeridge with her by this.

    WIFE.   Nay, George, you must consider Mistress
Luce's feet are tender ; and besides 'tis dark ; and,

---

[1] i.e. Play the knight-errant on somebody's behalf.

I promise you truly, I do not see how he should
get out of Waltham Forest with her yet.   31
    CITIZEN. Nay, cony, what wilt thou lay with
me, that Ralph has her not yet ?
    WIFE. I will not lay against Ralph, honey,
because I have not spoken with him.]

SCENE VIII.—A Room in MERRYTHOUGHT's House.
Enter MERRYTHOUGHT.

[WIFE. But look, George, peace ! here comes
the merry old gentleman again.]
    MERRYTHOUGHT.   [Sings.]

>   When it was grown to dark midnight,
>   And all were fast asleep,
>   In came Margaret's grimly ghost,
>   And stood at William's feet.

I have money, and meat, and drink beforehand,
till to-morrow at noon ; why should I be sad ?
methinks I have half a dozen jovial spirits within
me ! [Sings.]   10
    I am three merry men, and three merry men !

To what end should any man be sad in this world ?
give me a man that when he goes to hanging cries,

>   Troul¹ the black bowl to me !

and a woman that will sing a catch in her travail !
I have seen a man come by my door with a serious
face, in a black cloak, without a hat-band, carrying
his head as if he looked for pins in the street ;
I have looked out of my window half a year after,
and have spied that man's head upon London
Bridge. 'Tis vile : never trust a tailor that does
not sing at his work ; his mind is of nothing but
filching.   23
    [WIFE. Mark this, George ; 'tis worth noting ;
Godfrey my tailor, you know, never sings, and he
had fourteen yards to make this gown : and I'll

¹ Pass round.

be sworn, Mistress Penistone the draper's wife
had one made with twelve.]

MERRYTHOUGHT.   [Sings.]

> 'Tis mirth that fills the veins with blood,
> More than wine, or sleep, or food ;   30
> Let each man keep his heart at ease
> No man dies of that disease.
> He that would his body keep
> From diseases, must not weep ;
> But whoever laughs and sings,
> Never he his body brings
> Into fevers, gouts, or rheums,
> Or lingeringly his lungs consumes,
> Or meets with achès in the bone,
> Or catarrhs or griping stone ;   40
> But contented lives for ay ;
> The more he laughs, the more he may.

[WIFE.   Look, George ; how sayst thou by this,
George ? is 't not a fine old man ?—Now, God's
blessing o' thy sweet lips !—When wilt thou be so
merry, George ? faith, thou art the frowningest
little thing, when thou art angry, in a country.

CITIZEN.   Peace, cony ; thou shalt see him taken
down too, I warrant thee.

Enter VENTUREWELL.

Here 's Luce's father come now.]   50

MERRYTHOUGHT.   [Sings.]

> As you came from Walsingham,
>   From that holy land,
> There met you not with my true love
>   By the way as you came ?

VENTUREWELL.   Oh, Master Merrythought, my
    daughter 's gone !
This mirth becomes you not ; my daughter 's gone !

MERRYTHOUGHT.   [Sings.]

> Why, an if she be, what care I ?
> Or let her come, or go, or tarry.

VENTUREWELL.   Mock not my misery ; it is
  your son
(Whom I have made my own, when all forsook him)
Has stoln my only joy, my child, away.   61
MERRYTHOUGHT.   [Sings.]

> He set her on a milk-white steed,
>   And himself upon a grey ;
> He never turned his face again,
>   But he bore her quite away.

VENTUREWELL.   Unworthy of the kindness I
  have shown
To thee and thine ! too late I well perceive
Thou art consenting to my daughter's loss.
MERRYTHOUGHT.   Your daughter ! what a stir 's
here wi' your daughter ? Let her go, think no
more on her, but sing loud. If both my sons were
on the gallows, I would sing,   72
[Sings.]   Down, down, down they fall ;
>   Down, and arise they never shall.

VENTUREWELL.   Oh, might I behold her once
  again,
And she once more embrace her aged sire !
MERRYTHOUGHT.   Fie, how scurvily this goes !
' And she once more embrace her aged sire ' ?
You'll make a dog on her, will ye ? she cares
much for her aged sire, I warrant you.   80
[Sings.] She cares not for her daddy, nor
>   She cares not for her mammy,
> For she is, she is, she is, she is
>   My lord of Lowgave's lassy.

VENTUREWELL.   For this thy scorn I will pursue
  that son
Of thine to death.
MERRYTHOUGHT. Do ; and when you ha' killed him,
[Sings.] Give him flowers enow, palmer, give him
>   flowers enow ;
>   Give him red, and white, and blue, green,
>   and yellow.

VENTUREWELL. I'll fetch my daughter——
MERRYTHOUGHT. I'll hear no more o' your
daughter ; it spoils my mirth.   92
VENTUREWELL. I say, I'll fetch my daughter.
MERRYTHOUGHT. [Sings.]

> Was never man for lady's sake,
>   Down, down,
> Tormented as I poor Sir Guy,
>   De derry down,
> For Lucy's sake, that lady bright,
>   Down, down,
> As ever men beheld with eye,   100
>   De derry down.

VENTUREWELL. I'll be revenged, by Heaven !
                              [Exeunt severally.

[WIFE. How dost thou like this, George ?
CITIZEN. Why, this is well, cony ; but if Ralph
were hot once, thou shouldst see more.   [Music.
WIFE. The fiddlers go again, husband.
CITIZEN. Ay, Nell ; but this is scurvy music.
I gave the whoreson gallows money, and I think
he has not got me the waits of Southwark : if I
hear 'em not anon, I'll twinge him by the ears.—
You musicians, play Baloo !   111
WIFE. No, good George, let 's ha' Lachrymae !
CITIZEN. Why, this is it, cony.
WIFE. It 's all the better, George. Now, sweet
lamb, what story is that painted upon the cloth ?
the Confutation of St. Paul ?
CITIZEN. No, lamb ; that 's Ralph and Lucrece.
WIFE. Ralph and Lucrece ! which Ralph ? our
Ralph ?   119
CITIZEN. No, mouse ; that was a Tartarian.[1]
WIFE. A Tartarian ! Well, I would the fiddlers
had done, that we might see our Ralph again !]

---

[1] A cant word for a thief.—*Nares.*

ACT THE THIRD

SCENE I.—Waltham Forest.

Enter JASPER and LUCE.

JASPER.   Come, my dear dear ; though we have
    lost our way,
We have not lost ourselves.   Are you not weary
With this night's wandering, broken from your rest,
And frighted with the terror that attends
The darkness of this wild unpeopled place ?
    LUCE.   No, my best friend ; I cannot either fear,
Or entertain a weary thought, whilst you
(The end of all my full desires) stand by me :
Let them that lose their hopes, and live to languish
Amongst the number of forsaken lovers,   10
Tell the long weary steps, and number time,
Start at a shadow, and shrink up their blood,
Whilst I (possessed with all content and quiet)
Thus take my pretty love, and thus embrace him.
    JASPER.   You have caught me, Luce, so fast,
    that, whilst I live,
I shall become your faithful prisoner,
And wear these chains for ever.   Come, sit down,
And rest your body, too, too delicate
For these disturbances.—[They sit down.]   So : will
    you sleep ?
Come, do not be more able than you are ;   20
I know you are not skilful in these watches,
For women are no soldiers : be not nice,
But take it ; sleep, I say.
    LUCE.   I cannot sleep ;
Indeed, I cannot, friend.
    JASPER.   Why, then, we'll sing,
And try how that will work upon our senses.
    LUCE.   I'll sing, or say, or any thing but sleep.
    JASPER.   Come, little mermaid, rob me of my
    heart
With that enchanting voice.

LUCE.   You mock me, Jasper.   [They sing.
JASPER.   Tell me, dearest, what is love ?
LUCE.   'Tis a lightning from above ;   30
           'Tis an arrow, 'tis a fire,
           'Tis a boy they call Desire ;
               'Tis a smile
               Doth beguile
JASPER.   The poor hearts of men that prove.

           Tell me more, are women true ?
LUCE.   Some love change, and so do you.
JASPER.   Are they fair and never kind ?
LUCE.   Yes, when men turn with the wind.
JASPER.   Are they froward ?   40
LUCE.   Ever toward
           Those that love, to love anew.[1]

JASPER.   Dissemble it no more ; I see the god
Of heavy sleep lay on his heavy mace
Upon your eyelids.
LUCE.   I am very heavy.   [Sleeps.
JASPER.   Sleep, sleep ; and quiet rest crown thy
           sweet thoughts !
Keep from her fair blood distempers, startings,
Horrors, and fearful shapes ! let all her dreams
Be joys, and chaste delights, embraces, wishes,
And such new pleasures as the ravished soul   50
Gives to the senses !—So ; my charms have took.—
Keep her, you powers divine, whilst I contemplate
Upon the wealth and beauty of her mind !
She is only fair and constant, only kind,
And only to thee, Jasper. Oh, my joys !
Whither will you transport me ? let not fullness
Of my poor buried hopes come up together
And overcharge my spirits ! I am weak.
Some say (however ill) the sea and women   59
Are governed by the moon ; both ebb and flow,
Both full of changes ; yet to them that know,

---

[1] This song, with variations, and the addition of a third
stanza, occurs in Beaumont and Fletcher's play *The Captain*,
Act II, Scene ii.

And truly judge, these but opinions are,
And heresies, to bring on pleasing war
Between our tempers, that without these were
Both void of after-love and present fear ;
Which are the best of Cupid. Oh, thou child
Bred from despair, I dare not entertain thee,
Having a love without the faults of women,
And greater in her perfect goods than men !
Which to make good, and please myself the stronger,
Though certainly I am certain of her love,　　71
I'll try her, that the world and memory
May sing to after-times her constancy.—

　　　　　　　　　　　[Draws his sword.

Luce ! Luce ! awake !

LUCE.　　　　　　Why do you fright me, friend,
With those distempered looks ? what makes your
　sword
Drawn in your hand ? who hath offended you ?
I prithee, Jasper, sleep ; thou art wild with watch-
　ing.

JASPER.　Come, make your way to Heaven, and
　bid the world,
With all the villainies that stick upon it,
Farewell ; you're for another life.

LUCE.　　　　　　　　　　Oh, Jasper,
How have my tender years committed evil,　　81
Especially against the man I love,
Thus to be cropped untimely ?

JASPER.　　　　　　　Foolish girl,
Canst thou imagine I could love his daughter
That flung me from my fortune into nothing ?
Dischargèd me his service, shut the doors
Upon my poverty, and scorned my prayers,
Sending me, like a boat without a mast,
To sink or swim ? Come ; by this hand you die ;
I must have life and blood, to satisfy　　90
Your father's wrongs.

[WIFE.　Away, George, away ! raise the watch
at Ludgate, and bring a mittimus from the justice
for this desperate villain !—Now, I charge you,

gentlemen, see the king's peace kept !—Oh, my
heart, what a varlet 's this, to offer manslaughter
upon the harmless gentlewoman !

CITIZEN. I warrant thee, sweetheart, we'll have
him hampered.]

LUCE. Oh, Jasper, be not cruel ! 100
If thou wilt kill me, smile, and do it quickly,
And let not many deaths appear before me ;
I am a woman, made of fear and love,
A weak, weak woman ; kill not with thy eyes,
They shoot me through and through : strike, I am
ready ;
And, dying, still I love thee.

Enter VENTUREWELL, HUMPHREY, and Attendants.

VENTUREWELL. Whereabouts ?
JASPER. [Aside.] No more of this ; now to myself
again.
HUMPHREY. There, there he stands, with sword,
like martial knight, 108
Drawn in his hand ; therefore beware the fight,
You that be wise ; for, were I good Sir Bevis,
I would not stay his coming, by your leavès.
VENTUREWELL. Sirrah, restore my daughter !
JASPER. Sirrah, no.
VENTUREWELL. Upon him, then !
[They attack JASPER, and force LUCE from him.
[WIFE. So ; down with him, down with him,
down with him ! cut him i' the leg, boys, cut him
i' the leg !]
VENTUREWELL. Come your ways, minion : I'll
provide a cage
For you, you're grown so tame.—Horse her away.
HUMPHREY. Truly, I'm glad your forces have
the day. [Exeunt all except JASPER.
JASPER. They are gone, and I am hurt ; my
love is lost, 120
Never to get again. Oh, mé unhappy !
Bleed, bleed and die ! I cannot. Oh, my folly,
Thou hast betrayed me ! Hope, where art thou fled?

Tell me, if thou be'st anywhere remaining,
Shall I but see my love again ?   Oh, no !
She will not deign to look upon her butcher,
Nor is it fit she should ;   yet I must venture.
Oh, Chance, or Fortune, or whate'er thou art,
That men adore for powerful, hear my cry,
And let me loving live, or losing die !   [Exit.

  [WIFE.   Is 'a gone, George ?   131
  CITIZEN.   Ay, cony.

  WIFE.   Marry, and let him go, sweetheart.   By
the faith o' my body, 'a has put me into such
a fright, that I tremble (as they say) as 'twere an
aspen-leaf.   Look o' my little finger, George, how
it shakes.   Now, in truth, every member of my
body is the worse for 't.

  CITIZEN.   Come, hug in mine arms, sweet mouse ;
he shall not fright thee any more.   Alas, mine own
dear heart, how it quivers !]   141

    SCENE II.—A Room in the Bell Inn, Waltham.

Enter Mistress MERRYTHOUGHT, RALPH, MICHAEL, TIM,
    GEORGE, Host, and Tapster.

  [WIFE.   Oh, Ralph !   how dost thou, Ralph ?
How hast thou slept to-night ?   has the knight used
thee well ?

  CITIZEN.   Peace, Nell ;   let Ralph alone.]
  TAPSTER.   Master, the reckoning is not paid.
  RALPH.   Right courteous Knight, who, for the
   order's sake
Which thou hast ta'en, hang'st out the holy Bell,
As I this flaming Pestle bear about,
We render thanks to your puissant self,
Your beauteous lady, and your gentle squires,
For thus refreshing of our wearied limbs,   11
Stiffened with hard achievements in wild desert.

  TAPSTER.   Sir, there is twelve shillings to pay.
  RALPH.   Thou merry Squire Tapstero, thanks to
   thee

For comforting our souls with double jug : [1]
And, if adventurous fortune prick thee forth,
Thou jovial squire, to follow feats of arms,
Take heed thou tender every lady's cause,
Every true knight, and every damsel fair ;
But spill the blood of treacherous Saracens,   20
And false enchanters that with magic spells
Have done to death full many a noble knight.

HOST.   Thou valiant Knight of the Burning
Pestle, give ear to me ; there is twelve shillings to
pay, and, as I am a true knight, I will not bate
a penny.

[WIFE.   George, I prithee, tell me, must Ralph
pay twelve shillings now ?

CITIZEN.   No, Nell, no ; nothing but the old
knight is merry with Ralph.   30

WIFE.   Oh, is 't nothing else ? Ralph will be as
merry as he.]

RALPH.   Sir Knight, this mirth of yours becomes
    you well ;
But, to requite this liberal courtesy,
If any of your squires will follow arms,
He shall receive from my heroic hand
A knighthood, by the virtue of this Pestle.

HOST.   Fair Knight, I thank you for your noble
offer :   38
[But here's the reckoning,]therefore, gentle Knight,
Twelve shillings you must pay, or I must cap [2] you.

[WIFE.   Look, George ! did not I tell thee as
much ? the Knight of the Bell is in earnest.
Ralph shall not be beholding [3] to him : give him
his money, George, and let him go snick up.

CITIZEN.   Cap Ralph ! no !—Hold your hand,
Sir Knight of the Bell ; there 's your money [Gives
money] : have you any thing to say to Ralph now ?
Cap Ralph !   48

WIFE.   I would you should know it, Ralph has
friends that will not suffer him to be capt for ten

[1] Presumably ale of double strength.
[2] Arrest.   [3] For beholden.

times so much, and ten times to the end of that.—
Now take thy course, Ralph.]

MISTRESS MERRYTHOUGHT. Come, Michael ; thou
and I will go home to thy father ; he hath enough
left to keep us a day or two, and we'll set fellows abroad to cry our purse and casket :   shall
we, Michael ?

MICHAEL.   Aye, I pray, mother ; in truth my feet
are full of chilblains with travelling.   59

[WIFE.   Faith, and those chilblains are a foul
trouble. Mistress Merrythought, when your youth
comes home, let him rub all the soles of his feet,
and his heels, and his ankles, with a mouse-skin ;
or, if none of your people can catch a mouse, when
he goes to bed, let him roll his feet in the warm
embers, and, I warrant you, he shall be well ; and
you may make him put his fingers between his
toes, and smell to them ; it's very sovereign for
his head, if he be costive.]   69

MISTRESS MERRYTHOUGHT. Master Knight of
the Burning Pestle, my son Michael and I bid you
farewell : I thank your worship heartily for your
kindness.

RALPH.   Farewell, fair lady, and your tender
    squire.
If pricking through these deserts, I do hear
Of any traitorous knight, who through his guile
Hath light upon your casket and your purse,
I will despoil him of them, and restore them.

MISTRESS MERRYTHOUGHT.   I thank your worship.   [Exit with MICHAEL.

RALPH.   Dwarf, bear my shield ; squire, elevate
    my lance :—   81
And now farewell, you Knight of holy Bell.

[CITIZEN.   Aye, aye, Ralph, all is paid.]

RALPH.   But yet, before I go, speak, worthy
    knight,
If aught you do of sad adventures know,
Where errant knight may through his prowess win
Eternal fame, and free some gentle souls

From endless bonds of steel and lingering pain.

HOST. Sirrah, go to Nick the barber, and bid
him prepare himself, as I told you before, quickly.

TAPSTER. I am gone, sir.   [Exit. 91

HOST. Sir Knight, this wilderness affordeth none
But the great venture, where full many a knight
Hath tried his prowess, and come off with shame ;
And where I would not have you lose your life
Against no man, but furious fiend of hell.

RALPH. Speak on, Sir Knight ; tell what he is
    and where :
For here I vow, upon my blazing badge,
Never to blaze [1] a day in quietness,
But bread and water will I only eat,   100
And the green herb and rock shall be my couch,
Till I have quelled that man, or beast, or fiend,
That works such damage to all errant knights.

HOST. Not far from hence, near to a craggy cliff,
At the north end of this distressèd town,
. . . . there doth stand a lowly house,
Ruggedly builded, and in it a cave
In which an ugly giant now doth won, [2]
Yclepèd Barbaroso : in his hand
He shakes a naked lance of purest steel,   110
With sleeves turned up ; and him before he wears
A motley garment, to preserve his clothes
From blood of those knights which he massacres
And ladies gent : [3] without his door doth hang
A copper basin on a prickant spear ;
At which no sooner gentle knights can knock,
But the shrill sound fierce Barbaroso hears,
And rushing forth, brings in the errant knight,
And sets him down in an enchanted chair ;
Then with an engine, which he hath prepared,
With forty teeth, he claws his courtly crown ;
Next makes him wink, and underneath his chin
He plants a brazen piece of mighty bord, [4]   123

___

[1] Query, ' laze ' ; cf. Feltham (1627–77), ' So the bloudless
Tortoise . . . lazeth his life away.'
   [2] Dwell.   [3] Noble.   [4] Rim, circumference.

And knocks his bullets [1] round about his cheeks;
Whilst with his fingers, and an instrument
With which he snaps his hair off, he doth fill
The wretch's ears with a most hideous noise :
Thus every knight-adventurer he doth trim,
And now no creature dares encounter him.

RALPH. In God's name, I will fight with him.
    Kind sir,   130
Go but before me to this dismal cave,
Where this huge giant Barbaroso dwells,
And, by that virtue that brave Rosicleer
That damnèd brood of ugly giants slew,
And Palmerin Frannarco overthrew,
I doubt not but to curb this traitor foul,
And to the devil send his guilty soul.

HOST. Brave-sprighted Knight, thus far I will
    perform
This your request ; I'll bring you within sight
Of this most loathsome place, inhabited   140
By a more loathsome man ; but dare not stay,
For his main force swoops all he sees away.

RALPH. Saint George, set on before ! march
    squire and page !   [Exeunt.

[WIFE. George, dost think Ralph will confound
the giant ?

CITIZEN. I hold my cap to a farthing he does :
why, Nell, I saw him wrestle with the great Dutchman, and hurl him.   148

WIFE. Faith, and that Dutchman was a goodly
man, if all things were answerable to his bigness.
And yet they say there was a Scotchman higher
than he, and that they two and a knight [2] met, and
saw one another for nothing. But of all the sights
that ever were in London, since I was married,
methinks the little child that was so fair grown
about the members was the prettiest ; that and
the hermaphrodite.   157

---

[1] i.e. balls of soap.
[2] Dyce suggests that the words ' and a knight ' should
follow ' a Scotchman '.

CITIZEN. Nay, by your leave, Nell, Ninivie [1]
was better.

WIFE. Ninivie! oh, that was the story of Jone
and the wall, was it not, George?   161

CITIZEN. Yes, lamb.]

SCENE III.—The Street before MERRYTHOUGHT's House.

Enter Mistress MERRYTHOUGHT.

[WIFE. Look, George, here comes Mistress
Merrythought again! and I would have Ralph
come and fight with the giant; I tell you true,
I long to see 't.

CITIZEN. Good Mistress Merrythought, begone,
I pray you, for my sake; I pray you, forbear a
little; you shall have audience presently; I have
a little business.   8

WIFE. Mistress Merrythought, if it please you
to refrain your passion a little, till Ralph have
dispatched the giant out of the way, we shall think
ourselves much bound to you. [Exit Mistress MERRY-
THOUGHT.] I thank you, good Mistress Merrythought.

CITIZEN. Boy, come hither.   [Enter Boy.] Send
away Ralph and this whoreson giant quickly.

BOY. In good faith, sir, we cannot; you'll
utterly spoil our play, and make it to be hissed;
and it cost money; you will not suffer us to go
on with our plot.—I pray, gentlemen, rule him.

CITIZEN. Let him come now and dispatch this,
and I'll trouble you no more.   21

BOY. Will you give me your hand of that?

WIFE. Give him thy hand, George, do; and I'll
kiss him. I warrant thee, the youth means plainly.

BOY. I'll send him to you presently.

WIFE. [Kissing him.] I thank you, little youth.
[Exit Boy.] Faith, the child hath a sweet breath,
George; but I think it be troubled with the
worms; carduus benedictus and mare's milk were
the only thing in the world for 't.   30

_____
[1] i.e. the puppet-show of Nineveh.

SCENE IV.—Before a Barber's Shop, Waltham.

Enter RALPH, Host, TIM, and GEORGE.

WIFE. Oh, Ralph's here, George!—God send
thee good luck, Ralph!]

HOST. Puissant knight, yonder his mansion is.
Lo, where the spear and copper basin are!
Behold that string, on which hangs many a tooth,
Drawn from the gentle jaw of wandering knights!
I dare not stay to sound; he will appear.   [Exit.

RALPH. Oh, faint not, heart! Susan, my lady
   dear,
The cobbler's maid in Milk-street, for whose sake
I take these arms, oh, let the thought of thee   10
Carry thy knight through all adventurous deeds;
And, in the honour of thy beauteous self,
May I destroy this monster Barbaroso!—
Knock, squire, upon the basin, till it break
With the shrill strokes, or till the giant speak.

               [TIM knocks upon the basin.

Enter Barber.

[WIFE. Oh, George, the giant, the giant!—
Now, Ralph, for thy life!]

BARBER. What fond unknowing wight is this,
   that dares
So rudely knock at Barbaroso's cell,   19
Where no man comes but leaves his fleece behind?

RALPH. I, traitorous caitiff, who am sent by fate
To punish all the sad enormities
Thou hast committed against ladies gent
And errant knights. Traitor to God and men,
Prepare thyself; this is the dismal hour
Appointed for thee to give strict account
Of all thy beastly treacherous villainies.

BARBER. Foolhardy knight, full soon thou
   shalt aby
This fond reproach: thy body will I bang;   29
                  [Takes down his pole,
And, lo, upon that string thy teeth shall hang!

Prepare thyself, for dead soon shalt thou be.

                                    [They fight.

    RALPH.   Saint George for me !

    BARBER.   Gargantua for me !

    [WIFE.   To him, Ralph, to him ! hold up the
giant ; set out thy leg before, Ralph !

    CITIZEN.   Falsify a blow, Ralph, falsify a blow !
the giant lies open on the left side.

    WIFE.   Bear 't off, bear 't off still ! there, boy !—
Oh, Ralph's almost down, Ralph's almost down !]

    RALPH.   Susan, inspire me ! now have up again.

    [WIFE.   Up, up, up, up, up ! so, Ralph ! down
with him, down with him, Ralph !   41

    CITIZEN.   Fetch him o'er the hip, boy !

                          [RALPH knocks down the Barber.

    WIFE.   There, boy ! kill, kill, kill, kill, kill,
Ralph !

    CITIZEN.   No, Ralph ; get all out of him first.]

    RALPH.   Presumptuous man, see to what des-
            perate end
Thy treachery hath brought thee ! The just gods,
Who never prosper those that do despise them,
For all the villainies which thou hast done
To knights and ladies, now have paid thee home
By my stiff arm, a knight adventurous.   51
But say, vile wretch, before I send thy soul
To sad Avernus (whither it must go),
What captives holdst thou in thy sable cave ?

    BARBER.   Go in, and free them all ; thou hast
            the day.

    RALPH.   Go, squire and dwarf, search in this
            dreadful cave,
And free the wretched prisoners from their bonds.

                       [Exeunt TIM and GEORGE.

    BARBER.   I crave for mercy, as thou art a
            knight,
And scorn'st to spill the blood of those that beg.

    RALPH.   Thou show'd'st no mercy, nor shalt thou
            have any ;   60
Prepare thyself, for thou shalt surely die.

Re-enter TIM *leading a* Man *winking, with a Basin
under his Chin.*

TIM.   Behold, brave knight, here is one prisoner,
Whom this vile [1] man hath usèd as you see.

[WIFE.   This is the first wise word I heard the
squire speak.]

RALPH.   Speak what thou art, and how thou hast
    been used,
That I may give him condign punishment.

MAN.   I am a knight that took my journey post
Northward from London ; and in courteous wise
This giant trained me to his loathsome den,   70
Under pretence of killing of the itch ;
And all my body with a powder strewed,
That smarts and stings ; and cut away my beard,
And my curled locks wherein were ribands tied ;
And with a water washed my tender eyes,
(Whilst up and down about me still he skipt,)
Whose virtue is, that, till my eyes be wiped
With a dry cloth, for this my foul disgrace,
I shall not dare to look a dog i' the face.

[WIFE.   Alas, poor knight !—Relieve him, Ralph ;
relieve poor knights, whilst you live.]   81

RALPH.   My trusty squire, convey him to the
    town,
Where he may find relief.—Adieu, fair knight.

[*Exit* Man *with* TIM, *who presently re-enters.*

Re-enter GEORGE, *leading a second* Man, *with a patch over
his nose.*

GEORGE.   Puissant Knight, of the Burning
    Pestle hight,
See here another wretch, whom this foul beast
Hath scorched [2] and scored in this inhuman wise.

RALPH.   Speak me thy name, and eke thy place
    of birth,
And what hath been thy usage in this cave.

[1] The quartos have ' wild ', probably a misprint for ' vild ',
an early form of ' vile '.
[2] Slashed

SECOND MAN.   I am a knight, Sir Pockhole is my
  name,
And by my birth I am a Londoner,   90
Free by my copy, but my ancestors
Were Frenchmen all ; and riding hard this way
Upon a trotting horse, my bones did ache ;
And I, faint knight, to ease my weary limbs,
Light at this cave ; when straight this furious fiend,
With sharpest instrument of purest steel,
Did cut the gristle of my nose away,
And in the place this velvet plaster stands :
Relieve me, gentle knight, out of his hands !   99
  [WIFE.   Good Ralph, relieve Sir Pockhole, and
send him away ; for in truth his breath stinks.]
  RALPH.   Convey him straight after the other
    knight.—
Sir Pockhole, fare you well.
  SECOND MAN.   Kind sir, good night.
          [Exit with GEORGE, who presently re-enters.
  THIRD MAN. [Within.]   Deliver us !   [Cries within.
  WOMAN. [Within.]   Deliver us !
  [WIFE.   Hark, George, what a woeful cry there
is ! I think some woman lies-in there.]
  THIRD MAN. [Within.]   Deliver us !
  WOMAN. [Within.]   Deliver us !
  RALPH.   What ghastly noise is this ?   Speak,
    Barbaroso,   110
Or, by this blazing steel, thy head goes off !
  BARBER.   Prisoners of mine, whom I in diet
    keep.
Send lower down into the [inner] cave,
And in a tub that 's heated smoking hot,
There may they find them, and deliver them.
  RALPH.   Run, squire and dwarf ; deliver them
    with speed.   [Exeunt TIM and GEORGE.
  [WIFE.   But will not Ralph kill this giant ?
Surely I am afear'd, if he let him go, he will do as
much hurt as ever he did.
  CITIZEN.   Not so, mouse, neither, if he could
convert him.   121

WIFE. Aye, George, if he could convert him;
but a giant is not so soon converted as one of us
ordinary people. There's a pretty tale of a witch,
that had the devil's mark about her (God bless us !)
that had a giant to her son, that was called Lob-
lie-by-the-fire ; didst never hear it, George ?

CITIZEN. Peace, Nell, here comes the prisoners.]

Re-enter TIM, leading a third Man, with a glass of lotion
   in his hand, and GEORGE leading a Woman, with
   diet-bread and drink in her hand.

GEORGE. Here be these pinèd wretches, manful
          Knight,   129
That for this six weeks have not seen a wight.

RALPH. Deliver what you are, and how you came
To this sad cave, and what your usage was.

THIRD MAN. I am an errant knight that fol-
          lowed arms
With spear and shield ; and in my tender years
I stricken was with Cupid's fiery shaft,
And fell in love with this my lady dear,
And stole her from her friends in Turnbull-street,[1]
And bore her up and down from town to town,
Where we did eat and drink, and music hear ;
Till at the length at this unhappy town   140
We did arrive, and coming to this cave,
This beast us caught, and put us in a tub,[2]
Where we this two months sweat, and should have
          done
Another month, if you had not relieved us.

WOMAN. This bread and water hath our diet
          been,
Together with a rib cut from a neck
Of burnèd mutton ; hard hath been our fare :
Release us from this ugly giant's snare !

THIRD MAN. This hath been all the food we have
          received ;

---

[1] A street very notorious for its brothels at the time. Cf.
2 *Henry IV*, III. ii.

[2] A process of curing venereal disease by sweating.

But only twice a-day, for novelty,   150
He gave a spoonful of his [1] hearty broth
To each of us, through this same slender quill.

[Pulls out a syringe.

RALPH. From this infernal monster you shall go,
That useth knights and gentle ladies so !—
Convey them hence.

[Third Man and Woman are led off by TIM and GEORGE, who
presently re-enter.

[CITIZEN.   Cony, I can tell thee, the gentlemen
like Ralph.

WIFE.   Aye, George, I see it well enough.—
Gentlemen, I thank you all heartily for gracing
my man Ralph ; and I promise you, you shall see
him oftener.]   161

BARBER. Mercy, great knight ! I do recant my ill,
And henceforth never gentle blood will spill.

RALPH.   I give thee mercy ; but yet shalt thou
swear
Upon my Burning Pestle, to perform
Thy promise utterèd.

BARBER.   I swear and kiss.   [Kisses the pestle.

RALPH.   Depart, then, and amend.—

[Exit Barber.

Come, squire and dwarf ; the sun grows towards
his set,
And we have many more adventures yet. [Exeunt.

[CITIZEN.   Now Ralph is in this humour, I know
he would ha' beaten all the boys in the house, if
they had been set on him.   172

WIFE.   Aye, George, but it is well as it is : I
warrant you, the gentlemen do consider what it is
to overthrow a giant.]

SCENE V.—The Street before MERRYTHOUGHT's House.
Enter Mistress MERRYTHOUGHT and MICHAEL.

[WIFE.   But, look, George ; here comes Mistress
Merrythought, and her son Michael.—Now you are
welcome, Mistress Merrythought ; now Ralph has
done, you may go on.]

[1] 1613 has ' this.'.

MISTRESS MERRYTHOUGHT. Mick, my boy—
MICHAEL. Aye, forsooth, mother. 6
MISTRESS MERRYTHOUGHT. Be merry, Mick; we
are at home now ; where, I warrant you, you shall
find the house flung out of the windows. [Music
within.] Hark ! hey, dogs, hey ! this is the old
world, i' faith, with my husband. If I get in among
them, I'll play them such a lesson, that they shall
have little list to come scraping hither again—
Why, Master Merrythought ! husband ! Charles
Merrythought ! 15
MERRYTHOUGHT. [Appearing above, and singing.]

If you will sing, and dance, and laugh,
    And hollow, and laugh again,
And then cry, ' there, boy, there ! ' why, then,
    One, two, three, and four,
    We shall be merry within this hour. 20

MISTRESS MERRYTHOUGHT. Why, Charles, do you
not know your own natural wife ? I say, open the
door, and turn me out those mangy companions ;
'tis more than time that they were fellow and
fellow-like with you. You are a gentleman, Charles,
and an old man, and father of two children ; and
I myself (though I say it) by my mother's side
niece to a worshipful gentleman and a conductor ; [1]
he has been three times in his majesty's service at
Chester, and is now the fourth time, God bless him
and his charge, upon his journey. 31
MERRYTHOUGHT. [Sings.]

Go from my window, love, go ;
Go from my window, my dear !
    The wind and the rain
    Will drive you back again ;
You cannot be lodged here.

Hark you, Mistress Merrythought, you that walk
upon adventures, and forsake your husband,
because he sings with never a penny in his purse ;

---

[1] A carrier of goods.

what, shall I think myself the worse ? Faith, no,
I'll be merry. You come not here ; here's none
but lads of mettle, lives of a hundred years and
upwards ; care never drunk their bloods, nor want
made them warble ' Heigh-ho, my heart is heavy '.

MISTRESS MERRYTHOUGHT.   Why, Master Merrythought, what am I, that you should laugh me to
scorn thus abruptly ? am I not your fellow-feeler,
as we may say, in all our miseries ? your comforter
in health and sickness ? have I not brought you
children ? are they not like you, Charles ? look
upon thine own image, hard-hearted man ! and
yet for all this——   52

MERRYTHOUGHT.   [Sings.]

> Begone, begone, my juggy, my puggy,
> Begone, my love, my dear !
>   The weather is warm,
>   'Twill do thee no harm :
> Thou canst not be lodged here.——

Be merry, boys ! some light music, and more wine !
                                                  [Exit above.

[WIFE.   He's not in earnest, I hope, George, is
he ?   60

CITIZEN.   What if he be, sweetheart ?

WIFE.   Marry, if he be, George, I'll make bold
to tell him he's an ingrant[1] old man to use his
bed-fellow so scurvily.

CITIZEN.   What ! how does he use her, honey ?

WIFE.   Marry, come up, sir saucebox ! I think
you'll take his part, will you not ? Lord, how hot
you are grown ! you are a fine man, an' you had
a fine dog ; it becomes you sweetly !

CITIZEN.   Nay, prithee, Nell, chide not ; for,
as I am an honest man and a true Christian grocer,
I do not like his doings.   72

WIFE.   I cry you mercy, then, George ! you
know we are all frail and full of infirmities.—D'ye

---

[1] Ignorant.—*N.E.D.* ; but is it not more probably, as
the 1778 editor suggests, for ' ingrate ' ?

hear, Master Merrythought ? may I crave a word
with you ?]

MERRYTHOUGHT. [Appearing above.] Strike up
lively, lads !   78

[WIFE. I had not thought, in truth, Master
Merrythought, that a man of your age and discretion, as I may say, being a gentleman, and
therefore known by your gentle conditions,[1] could
have used so little respect to the weakness of his
wife ; for your wife is your own flesh, the staff of
your age, your yoke-fellow, with whose help you
draw through the mire of this transitory world ;
nay, she's your own rib : and again——]   87

MERRYTHOUGHT. [Sings.]

I come not hither for thee to teach,
I have no pulpit for thee to preach,
I would thou hadst kissed me under the breech,
     As thou art a lady gay.   91

[WIFE. Marry, with a vengeance ! I am heartily
sorry for the poor gentlewoman : but if I were thy
wife, i' faith, greybeard, i' faith——

CITIZEN. I prithee, sweet honeysuckle, be content.

WIFE. Give me such words, that am a gentlewoman born ! hang him, hoary rascal ! Get me
some drink, George ; I am almost molten with
fretting : now, beshrew his knave's heart for it !]
                                        [Exit Citizen.

MERRYTHOUGHT. Play me a light lavolta.[2]
Come, be frolic.   100
Fill the good fellows wine.

MISTRESS MERRYTHOUGHT. Why, Master Merrythought, are you disposed to make me wait here ?
You'll open, I hope ; I'll fetch them that shall
open else.

MERRYTHOUGHT. Good woman, if you will sing,
I'll give you something ; if not—   [Sings.]
     You are no love for me, Margaret,
     I am no love for you.—   109

     [1] Qualities.
     [2] A lively dance for two persons.

Come aloft, boys, aloft !   [Exit above.

MISTRESS MERRYTHOUGHT. Now a churl's f—t
in your teeth, sir !—Come, Mick, we'll not trouble
him ; 'a shall not ding us i' the teeth with his
bread and his broth, that he shall not. Come,
boy ; I'll provide for thee, I warrant thee. We'll
go to Master Venturewell's, the merchant : I'll
get his letter to mine host of the Bell in Waltham ;
there I'll place thee with the tapster : will not
that do well for thee, Mick ? and let me alone for
that old cuckoldly knave your father ; I'll use
him in his kind, I warrant ye.   [Exeunt.

Re-enter Citizen with Beer.

[WIFE. Come, George, where 's the beer ?   122
CITIZEN. Here, love.

WIFE. This old fornicating fellow will not out
of my mind yet.—Gentlemen, I'll begin to you all ;
and I desire more of your acquaintance with all
my heart. [Drinks.] Fill the gentlemen some beer,
George.[1] [Enter Boy.] Look, George, the little boy 's
come again : methinks he looks something like
the Prince of Orange in his long stocking, if he had
a little harness about his neck. George, I will have
him dance Fading. Fading is a fine jig,[2] I'll
assure you, gentlemen.—Begin, brother. [Boy dances.]
Now 'a capers, sweetheart !—Now a turn o' the
toe, and then tumble ! cannot you tumble, youth ?
BOY. No, indeed forsooth.   136
WIFE. Nor eat fire ?
BOY. Neither.
WIFE. Why, then, I thank you heartily ; there 's
twopence to buy you points [3] withal.]

[1] In the quartos the scene ends at this point, what follows
being given under Act IV, Scene i. Colman made the change
in his edition of 1778.
[2] The dance took its name from the burden of an Irish
song, and both seem to have been of a licentious description.
—*Dyce.*
[3] Tagged laces used to attach the hose or breeches to the
doublet, &c.

ACT THE FOURTH

SCENE I.—A Street.

Enter JASPER and Boy.

JASPER.   There, boy, deliver this; [Gives a letter.]
but do it well.
Hast thou provided me four lusty fellows,
Able to carry me ? and art thou perfect
In all thy business ?

BOY.   Sir, you need not fear ;
I have my lesson here, and cannot miss it :
The men are ready for you, and what else
Pertains to this employment.

JASPER.   There, my boy ;   [Gives money.]
Take it, but buy no land.

BOY.   Faith, sir, 'twere rare
To see so young a purchaser. I fly,
And on my wings carry your destiny.   10

JASPER.   Go, and be happy ! [Exit Boy.] Now,
my latest hope,
Forsake me not, but fling thy anchor out,
And let it hold ! Stand fixed, thou rolling stone,
Till I enjoy my dearest ! Hear me, all
You powers, that rule in men, celestial !   [Exit.

[WIFE. Go thy ways ; thou art as crooked a
sprig as ever grew in London. I warrant him,
he'll come to some naughty end or other ; for
his looks say no less : besides, his father (you
know, George) is none of the best ; you heard
him take me up like a flirt-gill,[1] and sing bawdy
songs upon me ; but, i' faith, if I live, George——

CITIZEN. Let me alone, sweetheart : I have a
trick in my head shall lodge him in the Arches [2]
for one year, and make him sing peccavi ere I
leave him ; and yet he shall never know who hurt
him neither.   27

[1] A woman of light or loose behaviour.
[2] The prison belonging to the Court of Arches, the
ecclesiastical court of appeal for the province of Canterbury.

WIFE.   Do, my good George, do !

CITIZEN.   What shall we have Ralph do now, boy ?   30

BOY.   You shall have what you will, sir.

CITIZEN.   Why, so, sir ; go and fetch me him, then, and let the Sophy of Persia come and christen him a child.[1]

BOY.   Believe me, sir, that will not do so well ; 'tis stale ; it has been had before at the Red Bull.[2]

WIFE.   George, let Ralph travel over great hills, and let him be very weary, and come to the King of Cracovia's house, covered with [black] velvet ; and there let the king's daughter stand in her window, all in beaten gold, combing her golden locks with a comb of ivory ; and let her spy Ralph, and fall in love with him, and come down to him, and carry him into her father's house; and then let Ralph talk with her.   45

CITIZEN.   Well said, Nell ; it shall be so.—Boy, let's ha't done quickly.

BOY.   Sir, if you will imagine all this to be done already, you shall hear them talk together ; but we cannot present a house covered with black velvet, and a lady in beaten gold.   51

CITIZEN.   Sir boy, let's ha't as you can, then.

BOY.   Besides, it will show ill-favouredly to have a grocer's prentice to court a king's daughter.

CITIZEN.   Will it so sir ? you are well read in histories ! I pray you, what was Sir Dagonet ? was not he prentice to a grocer in London ?[3] Read the play of ' The Four Prentices of London ',[4] where they toss their pikes so. I pray you, fetch him in, sir, fetch him in.   60

---

[1] An allusion to an incident in *The Travailes of the Three English Brothers*, a play by Day, Rowley, and Wilkins, printed in 1607.—*Dyce*.

[2] A playhouse in St. John's Street, Clerkenwell.

[3] He was not a grocer's apprentice, but a knight in *Morte d'Arthur*.

[4] By Heywood, first printed in 1615, but acted several years earlier.

BOY. It shall be done.—It is not our fault, gentlemen. [Exit.

WIFE. Now we shall see fine doings, I warrant thee, George.]

SCENE II.—A Hall in the King of Moldavia's Court.

Enter POMPIONA, RALPH, TIM, and GEORGE.

[WIFE. Oh, here they come ! how prettily the King of Cracovia's daughter is dressed !

CITIZEN. Aye, Nell, it is the fashion of that country, I warrant thee.]

POMPIONA. Welcome, Sir Knight, unto my
    father's court,
King of Moldavia ; unto me Pompiona,
His daughter dear ! But, sure, you do not like
Your entertainment, that will stay with us
No longer but a night.

RALPH. Damsel right fair,
I am on many sad adventures bound, 10
That call me forth into the wilderness ;
Besides, my horse's back is something galled,
Which will enforce me ride a sober pace.
But many thanks, fair lady, be to you
For using errant knight with courtesy !

POMPIONA. But say, brave knight, what is your
    name and birth ?

RALPH. My name is Ralph ; I am an English
    man,
(As true as steel, a hearty Englishman,)
And prentice to a grocer in the Strand
By deed indent, of which I have one part : 20
But fortune calling me to follow arms,
On me this holy order I did take
Of Burning Pestle, which in all men's eyes
I bear, confounding ladies' enemies.

POMPIONA. Oft have I heard of your brave
    countrymen,
And fertile soil and store of wholesome food ;
My father oft will tell me of a drink

In England found, and nipitato [1] called,
Which driveth all the sorrow from your hearts.

    RALPH.   Lady, 'tis true ; you need not lay your
      lips   30
To better nipitato than there is.

    POMPIONA.   And of a wild fowl he will often speak,
Which powdered [2]-beef-and-mustard callèd is :
For there have been great wars 'twixt us and you ;
But truly, Ralph, it was not 'long of me.
Tell me then, Ralph, could you contented be
To wear a lady's favour in your shield ?

    RALPH.   I am a knight of [a] religious order,
And will not wear a favour of a lady
That trusts in Antichrist and false traditions.   40

    [CITIZEN.   Well said, Ralph ! convert her, if
thou canst.]

    RALPH.   Besides, I have a lady of my own
In merry England, for whose virtuous sake
I took these arms ; and Susan is her name,
A cobbler's maid in Milk Street ; whom I vow
Ne'er to forsake whilst life and Pestle last.

    POMPIONA.   Happy that cobbling dame, whoe'er
      she be,
That for her own, dear Ralph, hath gotten thee !
Unhappy I, that ne'er shall see the day   50
To see thee more, that bear'st my heart away !

    RALPH.   Lady, farewell ; I needs must take my
      leave.

    POMPIONA.   Hard-hearted Ralph, that ladies
      dost deceive !

    [CITIZEN.   Hark thee, Ralph : there's money
for thee [Gives money]; give something in the King
of Cracovia's house ; be not beholding to him.]

    RALPH.   Lady, before I go, I must remember
Your father's officers, who truth to tell,
Have been about me very diligent :   59
Hold up thy snowy hand, thou princely maid !
There's twelve-pence for your father's chamberlain;
And [there's] another shilling for his cook,

       [1] Nippitate, strong ale.   [2] Salted.

For, by my troth, the goose was roasted well ;
And twelve-pence for your father's horse-keeper,
For 'nointing my horse-back, and for his butter [1]
There is another shilling ; to the maid
That washed my boot-hose there's an English groat
And two-pence to the boy that wiped my boots ;
And last, fair lady, there is for yourself
Three-pence, to buy you pins at Bumbo Fair. 70
   POMPIONA. Full many thanks ; and I will keep
    them safe
Till all the heads be off, for thy sake, Ralph.
   RALPH. Advance, my squire and dwarf ! I
    cannot stay.
   POMPIONA. Thou kill'st my heart in parting
    thus away. [Exeunt.
[WIFE. I commend Ralph yet, that he will not
stoop to a Cracovian ; there's properer women in
London than any are there, I-wis.

  SCENE III.—A Room in the House of VENTUREWELL.

  Enter VENTUREWELL, HUMPHREY, LUCE, and Boy.

   WIFE. But here comes Master Humphrey and
his love again now, George.
   CITIZEN. Aye, cony ; peace.]
   VENTUREWELL. Go, get you up ; I will not be
    entreated ;
And, gossip mine, I'll keep you sure hereafter
From gadding out again with boys and unthrifts :
Come, they are women's tears ; I know your
    fashion.—
Go, sirrah, lock her in, and keep the key
Safe as you love your life. [Exeunt LUCE and Boy.
              Now, my son Humphrey,
You may both rest assurèd of my love 10
In this, and reap your own desire.
   HUMPHREY. I see this love you speak of,
    through your daughter,
Although the hole be little ; and hereafter

      [1] Used for the horse's back.

Will yield the like in all I may or can,
Fitting a Christian and a gentleman.

 VENTUREWELL. I do believe you, my good son,
  and thank you ;
For 'twere an impudence to think you flattered.

 HUMPHREY. It were, indeed ; but shall I tell
  you why ?
I have been beaten twice about the lie.

 VENTUREWELL. Well, son, no more of compli-
  ment. My daughter   20
Is yours again : appoint the time and take her ;
We'll have no stealing for it ; I myself
And some few of our friends will see you married.

 HUMPHREY. I would you would, i' faith ! for, be
  it known,
I ever was afraid to lie alone.

 VENTUREWELL. Some three days hence, then.

 HUMPHREY.   Three days ! let me see :
'Tis somewhat of the most ; yet I agree,
Because I mean against the appointed day
To visit all my friends in new array.

Enter Servant.

 SERVANT. Sir, there's a gentlewoman without
would speak with your worship.   31

 VENTUREWELL. What is she ?

 SERVANT. Sir, I asked her not.

 VENTUREWELL. Bid her come in. [Exit Servant.

Enter Mistress MERRYTHOUGHT and MICHAEL.

 MISTRESS MERRYTHOUGHT. Peace be to your
worship ! I come as a poor suitor to you, sir, in
the behalf of this child.

 VENTUREWELL. Are you not wife to Merrythought ?   39

 MISTRESS MERRYTHOUGHT. Yes, truly. Would
I had ne'er seen his eyes ! he has undone me and
himself and his children ; and there he lives at
home, and sings and hoits [1] and revels among his

---

[1] Indulges in riotous mirth.

drunken companions ! but, I warrant you, where
to get a penny to put bread in his mouth he
knows not : and therefore, if it like your worship,
I would entreat your letter to the honest host of
the Bell in Waltham, that I may place my child
under the protection of his tapster, in some settled
course of life.   50

VENTUREWELL.   I'm glad the heavens have
          heard my prayers. Thy husband,
When I was ripe in sorrows, laughed at me ;
Thy son, like an unthankful wretch, I having
Redeemed him from his fall, and made him mine,
To show his love again, first stole my daughter,
Then wronged this gentleman, and, last of all,
Gave me that grief had almost brought me down
Unto my grave, had not a stronger hand
Relieved my sorrows. Go, and weep as I did,
And be unpitied ; for I here profess   60
An everlasting hate to all thy name.

MISTRESS MERRYTHOUGHT.   Will you so, sir ?
how say you by that ?—Come, Mick ; let him
keep his wind to cool his porridge.[1] We'll go to
thy nurse's, Mick : she knits silk stockings, boy ;
and we'll knit too, boy, and be beholding to none
of them all.   [Exit with Michael.

Enter Boy.

BOY.   Sir, I take it you are the master of this
          house.

VENTUREWELL.   How then, boy ?

BOY.   Then to yourself, sir, comes this letter.
                                              [Gives letter.

VENTUREWELL.   From whom, my pretty boy ?

BOY.   From him that was your servant ; but no
          more   7[2]
Shall that name ever be, for he is dead :
Grief of your purchased [2] anger broke his heart.

---

[1] 1613 and 1635 (a) have 'porrage'; 1635 (b) has
'pottage'.
[2] Incurred by his own act.

I saw him die, and from his hand received
This paper, with a charge to bring it hither :
Read it, and satisfy yourself in all.

VENTUREWELL. [Reads.] Sir, that I have wronged
your love I must confess ; in which I have purchased to myself, besides mine own undoing, the
ill opinion of my friends. Let not your anger,
good sir, outlive me, but suffer me to rest in
peace with your forgiveness : let my body (if
a dying man may so much prevail with you) be
brought to your daughter, that she may truly
know my hot flames are now buried, and withal
receive a testimony of the zeal I bore her virtue.
Farewell for ever, and be ever happy !

JASPER.

God's hand is great in this : I do forgive him ;
Yet I am glad he 's quiet, where I hope   90
He will not bite again.—Boy, bring the body,
And let him have his will, if that be all.

BOY. 'Tis here without, sir.

VENTUREWELL.   So, sir ; if you please,
You may conduct it in ; I do not fear it.

HUMPHREY. I'll be your usher, boy ; for,
    though I say it,
He owed me something once, and well did pay it.

[Exeunt.

SCENE IV.—Another Room in the House of
VENTUREWELL.

Enter LUCE.

LUCE. If there be any punishment inflicted
Upon the miserable, more than yet I feel,
Let it together seize me, and at once
Press down my soul ! I cannot bear the pain
Of these delaying tortures.—Thou that art
The end of all, and the sweet rest of all,
Come, come, O Death ! bring me to thy peace ;
And blot out all the memory I nourish
Both of my father and my cruel friend !—
Oh, wretched maid, still living to be wretched,

To be a say [1] to Fortune in her changes,   11
And grow to number times and woes together !
How happy had I been, if, being born,
My grave had been my cradle !

Enter Servant.

SERVANT.   By your leave,
Young mistress, here 's a boy hath brought a coffin :
What 'a would say, I know not ; but your father
Charged me to give you notice. Here they come.
                                            [Exit.

Enter Boy, and two Men bearing a Coffin.

LUCE.   For me I hope 'tis come, and 'tis most
    welcome.

BOY.   Fair mistress, let me not add greater grief
To that great store you have already. Jasper   20
(That whilst he lived was yours, [but] now [is] dead
And here enclosed) commanded me to bring
His body hither, and to crave a tear
From those fair eyes (though he deserved not pity),
To deck his funeral ; for so he bid me
Tell her for whom he died.

LUCE.   He shall have many.—
Good friends, depart a little, whilst I take
My leave of this dead man, that once I loved. —
                                  [Exeunt Boy and Men.
Hold yet a little, life ! and then I give thee
To thy first heavenly being. Oh, my friend !   30
Hast thou deceived me thus, and got before me ?
I shall not long be after. But, believe me,
Thou wert too cruel, Jasper, 'gainst thyself,
In punishing the fault I could have pardoned,
With so untimely death : thou didst not wrong
    me,
But ever wert most kind, most true, most loving ;
And I the most unkind, most false, most cruel !
Didst thou but ask a tear ? I'll give thee all,
Even all my eyes can pour down, all my sighs,
And all myself, before thou goest from me.   40

[1] Subject for experiment.

These [1] are but sparing rites ; but if thy soul
Be yet about this place, and can behold
And see what I prepare to deck-thee with,
It shall go up, borne on the wings of peace,
And satisfied. First will I sing thy dirge,
Then kiss thy pale lips, and then die myself,
And fill one coffin and one grave together.

[Sings.] Come, you whose loves are dead,
   And, whiles I sing,
   Weep, and wring   50
  Every hand, and every head
  Bind with cypress and sad yew ,
  Ribands black and candles blue
  For him that was of men most true !

  Come with heavy moaning,[2]
   And on his grave
   Let him have
  Sacrifice of sighs and groaning ;
  Let him have fair flowers enow,
  White and purple, green and yellow, 60
  For him that was of men most true !

Thou sable cloth, sad cover of my joys,
I lift thee up, and thus I meet with death.
  [Removes the Cloth, and JASPER rises out of the Coffin.
 JASPER. And thus you meet the living.
 LUCE.   Save me, Heaven !
 JASPER. Nay, do not fly me, fair ; I am no
  spirit :
Look better on me ; do you know me yet ?
 LUCE. Oh, thou dear shadow of my friend !
 JASPER.   Dear substance !
I swear I am no shadow ; feel my hand,
It is the same it was ; I am your Jasper,
Your Jasper that 's yet living, and yet loving. 70
Pardon my rash attempt, my foolish proof
I put in practice of your constancy ;
For sooner should my sword have drunk my blood,
And set my soul at liberty, than drawn

  [1] 'There' in the quartos. [2] 'Mourning' in the quartos.

The least drop from that body : for which boldness
Doom me to any thing ; if death, I take it,
And willingly.

LUCE.   This death I'll give you for it ;

[Kisses him.

So ; now I am satisfied you are no spirit,
But my own truest, truest, truest friend,   79
Why do you come thus to me ?

JASPER.   First, to see you ;
Then to convey you hence.

LUCE.   It cannot be ;
For I am locked up here, and watched at all hours,
That 'tis impossible for me to 'scape.

JASPER. Nothing more possible. Within this
    coffin
Do you convey yourself : let me alone
I have the wits of twenty men about me ;
Only I crave the shelter of your closet
A little, and then fear me not.[1] Creep in,
That they may presently convey you hence.   89
Fear nothing, dearest love ; I'll be your second ;

*[LUCE lies down in the Coffin and JASPER covers her with
the cloth.*

Lie close : so ; all goes well yet.—Boy !

Re-enter Boy and Men.

BOY.   At hand, sir.

JASPER. Convey away the coffin, and be wary.

BOY. 'Tis done already.

[Exeunt Men with the Coffin.

JASPER.   Now must I go conjure

[Exit into a Closet.

Enter VENTUREWELL.

VENTUREWELL. Boy, boy !

BOY.   Your servant, sir.

VENTUREWELL. Do me this kindness, boy (hold,
    here's a crown) ;
Before thou bury the body of this fellow,
Carry it to his old merry father, and salute him

        [1] i. e. fear not for me.

                K

From me, and bid him sing ; he hath cause.

BOY.   I will, sir.

VENTUREWELL.   And then bring me word what
tune he is in,   100
And have another crown ; but do it truly.
I have fitted him a bargain now will vex him.

BOY.   God bless your worship's health, sir !

VENTUREWELL.   Farewell, boy !   [Exeunt severally.

SCENE V.—A Street before MERRYTHOUGHT's House.

Enter MERRYTHOUGHT.

[WIFE.   Ah, old Merrythought, art thou there
again ? let 's hear some of thy songs.]

MERRYTHOUGHT.   [Sings.]

Who can sing a merrier note
Than he that cannot change a groat ?

Not a denier [1] left, and yet my heart leaps : I do
wonder yet, as old as I am, that any man will
follow a trade, or serve, that may sing and laugh,
and walk the streets. My wife and both my
sons are I know not where ; I have nothing
left, nor know I how to come by meat to supper ;
yet am I merry still, for I know I shall find
it upon the table at six o'clock ; therefore, hang
thought !   13

[Sings.]   I would not be a serving-man
To carry the cloak-bag still,
Nor would I be a falconer
The greedy hawks to fill ;
But I would be in a good house,
And have a good master too ;
But I would eat and drink of the best,
And no work would I do.   21

This is it that keeps life and soul together, mirth ;
this is the philosopher's stone that they write so
much on, that keeps a man ever young.

[1] A small copper coin.

Enter Boy.

BOY.   Sir, they say they know all your money is gone, and they will trust you for no more drink.

MERRYTHOUGHT.   Will they not ? let 'em choose! The best is, I have mirth at home, and need not send abroad for that ; let them keep their drink to themselves.   30

[*Sings.*]

For Jillian of Berry, she dwells on a hill,
And she hath good beer and ale to sell,
And of good fellows she thinks no ill ;
    And thither will we go now, now, now,
    And thither will we go now.

And when you have made a little stay,
You need not ask what is to pay,
But kiss your hostess, and go your way ;
    And thither will we go now, now, now,
    And thither will we go now.   40

Enter another Boy.

SECOND BOY.   Sir, I can get no bread for supper.

MERRYTHOUGHT.   Hang bread and supper ! let 's preserve our mirth, and we shall never feel hunger, I'll warrant you.   Let 's have a catch, boys ; follow me, come.

[*They sing.*]   Ho, ho, nobody at home !
    Meat, nor drink, nor money ha' we none.
        Fill the pot, Eedy,
        Never more need I.   49

MERRYTHOUGHT.   So, boys ; enough.   Follow me.   Let 's change our place, and we shall laugh afresh.   [*Exeunt.*

[WIFE.   Let him go, George ; 'a shall not have any countenance from us, nor a good word from any i' the company, if I may strike stroke in 't.

CITIZEN.   No more 'a sha' not, love.   But, Nell, I will have Ralph do a very notable matter now, to the eternal honour and glory of all grocers.— Sirrah ! you there, boy ! Can none of you hear ?

Enter Boy.

BOY. Sir, your pleasure ?   60

CITIZEN. Let Ralph come out on May-day in
the morning, and speak upon a conduit, with all
his scarfs about him, and his feathers, and his
rings, and his knacks.

BOY. Why, sir, you do not think of our plot;
what will become of that, then ?

CITIZEN. Why, sir, I care not what become
on 't : I'll have him come out, or I'll fetch him out
myself ; I'll have something done in honour of the
city : besides, he hath been long enough upon
adventures. Bring him out quickly ; or, if I come
in amongst you——   72

BOY. Well, sir, he shall come out ; but if our
play miscarry, sir, you are like to pay for 't.

CITIZEN. Bring him away, then !   [Exit Boy.]

WIFE. This will be brave, i' faith ! George,
shall not he dance the morris too, for the credit of
the Strand ?

CITIZEN. No, sweetheart, it will be too much for
the boy.   80

Enter RALPH, dressed as a May-lord.

Oh, there he is, Nell ! he 's reasonable well in
reparel : but he has not rings enough.]

RALPH. London, to thee I do present the merry
month of May ;
Let each true subject be content to hear me what
I say :
For from the top of conduit-head, as plainly may
appear,
I will both tell my name to you, and wherefore I
came here.
My name is Ralph, by due descent, though not
ignoble I,
Yet far inferior to the flock [1] of gracious grocery ;
And by the common counsel of my fellows in the
Strand,

---

[1] Dyce suggests ' stock '; for ' grocery ', see note on p. 210.

With gilded staff and crossèd scarf, the May-lord
    here I stand.   90
Rejoice, O English hearts, rejoice ! rejoice, O
    lovers dear !
Rejoice, O city, town, and country ! rejoice, eke
    every shire !
For now the fragrant flowers do spring and sprout
    in seemly sort,
The little birds do sit and sing, the lambs do make
    fine sport ;
And now the birchen-tree doth bud, that makes
    the schoolboy cry ;
The morris rings, while hobby-horse doth foot it
    feateously ;
The lords and ladies now abroad, for their disport
    and play,
Do kiss sometimes upon the grass, and sometimes
    in the hay ;
Now butter with a leaf of sage is good to purge
    the blood ;   99
Fly Venus and phlebotomy, for they are neither good ;
Now little fish on tender stone begin to cast their
    bellies,
And sluggish snails, that erst were mewed,[1] do
    creep out of their shellies ;
The rumbling rivers now do warm, for little boys
    to paddle ;
The sturdy steed now goes to grass, and up they
    hang his saddle ;
The heavy hart, the bellowing buck, the rascal,[2]
    and the pricket,[3]
Are now among the yeoman's peas, and leave the
    fearful thicket :
And be like them, O you, I say, of this same
    noble town,
And lift aloft your velvet heads, and slipping off
    your gown,

[1] Shut up, confined; the quartos have 'mute'
[2] A young lean, or inferior deer.
[3] A buck in his second year.

With bells on legs, and napkins clean unto your
    shoulders tied,[1]
With scarfs and garters as you please, and ' Hey
    for our town ! ' cried,   110
March out, and show your willing minds, by
    twenty and by twenty,
To Hogsdon[2] or to Newington, where ale and
    cakes are plenty ;
And let it ne'er be said for shame, that we the
    youths of London
Lay thrumming of our caps[3] at home, and left our
    custom undone.
Up, then, I say, both young and old, both man
    and maid a-maying,
With drums, and guns that bounce aloud, and merry
    tabor playing !
Which to prolong, God save our king, and send his
    country peace,
And root out treason from the land ! and so, my
    friends, I cease.   [Exit.

ACT THE FIFTH

SCENE I.—A Room in the House of VENTUREWELL.

Enter VENTUREWELL.

VENTUREWELL. I will have no great store of
company at the wedding ; a couple of neighbours
and their wives ; and we will have a capon in
stewed broth, with marrow, and a good piece of
beef stuck with rosemary.

Enter JASPER, with his Face mealed.

JASPER. Forbear thy pains, fond man ! it is
too late.
VENTUREWELL. Heaven bless me ! Jasper !
JASPER.   Aye, I am his ghost,

---

[1] Accoutrements of the morris-dancers.   [2] Hoxton.
[3] A proverbial phrase for useless, trifling work ; literally,
fastening threads on our caps.

Whom thou hast injured for his constant love ;
Fond worldly wretch ! who dost not understand
In death that true hearts cannot parted be.　　10
First know, thy daughter is quite borne away
On wings of angels, through the liquid air,
To far out of thy reach, and never more
Shalt thou behold her face : but she and I
Will in another world enjoy our loves ;
Where neither father's anger, poverty,
Nor any cross that troubles earthly men,
Shall make us sever our united hearts.
And never shalt thou sit or be alone
In any place, but I will visit thee　　20
With ghastly looks, and put into thy mind
The great offences which thou didst to me.
When thou art at thy table with thy friends,
Merry in heart, and filled with swelling wine,
I'll come in midst of all thy pride and mirth,
Invisible to all men but thyself,
And whisper such a sad tale in thine ear
Shall make thee let the cup fall from thy hand,
And stand as mute and pale as death itself.

VENTUREWELL.. Forgive me, Jasper ! Oh, what
　　might I do,
　　　　　　　　　　　　　　　　　30
Tell me, to satisfy thy troubled ghost ?

JASPER. There is no means ; too late thou
　　think'st on this.

VENTUREWELL. But tell me what were best for
　　me to do ?

JASPER. Repent thy deed, and satisfy my father,
And beat fond Humphrey out of thy doors. [Exit.
[WIFE. Look, George ; his very ghost would
have folks beaten.]

Enter HUMPHREY.

HUMPHREY. Father, my bride is gone, fair
　　Mistress Luce :
My soul's the fount of vengeance, mischief's sluice.

VENTUREWELL. Hence, fool, out of my sight
　　with thy fond passion !
　　　　　　　　　　　　　　　　40

Thou hast undone me.   [Beats him.

HUMPHREY.   Hold, my father dear,
For Luce thy daughter's sake, that had no peer !

VENTUREWELL.   Thy father, fool ? there's some
    blows more ; begone.—   [Beats him.
Jasper, I hope thy ghost be well appeased
To see thy will performed. Now will I go
To satisfy thy father for thy wrongs.   [Aside and exit.

HUMPHREY. What shall I do ? I have been
    beaten twice,
And Mistress Luce is gone. Help me, device !
Since my true love is gone, I never more,
Whilst I do live, upon the sky will pore ;   50
But in the dark will wear out my shoe-soles
In passion in Saint Faith's church under Paul's.[1]
                                              [Exit.

[WIFE. George, call Ralph hither ; if you love
me, call Ralph hither : I have the bravest thing
for him to do, George ; prithee, call him quickly.

CITIZEN.   Ralph ! why, Ralph, boy !

Enter RALPH.

RALPH.   Here, sir.

CITIZEN. Come hither, Ralph ; come to thy
mistress, boy.   59

WIFE.   Ralph, I would have thee call all the
youths together in battle-ray, with drums, and
guns, and flags, and march to Mile End in pompous
fashion, and there exhort your soldiers to be merry
and wise, and to keep their beards from burning,
Ralph ; and then skirmish, and let your flags fly,
and cry, ' Kill, kill, kill ! ' My husband shall lend
you his jerkin, Ralph, and there's a scarf ; for the
rest, the house shall furnish you, and we'll pay
for 't.   Do it bravely, Ralph ; and think before
whom you perform, and what person you represent.

RALPH.   I warrant you, mistress ; if I do it not,
for the honour of the city and the credit of my
master, let me never hope for freedom !   73

[1] See above, note on p. 56.

WIFE. 'Tis well spoken, i' faith. Go thy ways ; thou art a spark indeed.

CITIZEN. Ralph, Ralph, double your files bravely, Ralph !
                                                        77
RALPH. I warrant you, sir.   [Exit.

CITIZEN. Let him look narrowly to his service ; I shall take him else. I was there myself a pikeman once, in the hottest of the day, wench ; had my feather shot sheer away, the fringe of my pike burnt off with powder, my pate broken with a scouring-stick,[1] and yet, I thank God, I am here.
                                          [Drums within.
WIFE. Hark, George, the drums !   85

CITIZEN. Ran, tan, tan, tan ; ran, tan ! Oh, wench, an thou hadst but seen little Ned of Aldgate, Drum-Ned, how he made it roar again, and laid on like a tyrant, and then struck softly till the ward came up, and then thundered again, and together we go ! ' Sa, sa, sa, bounce ! ' quoth the guns ; ' Courage, my hearts ! ' quoth the captains ; ' Saint George ! ' quoth the pikemen ; and withal, here they lay, and there they lay : and yet for all this I am here, wench.

WIFE. Be thankful for it, George ; for indeed 'tis wonderful.]
                                                     97

SCENE II.—A Street (and afterwards Mile End).

Enter RALPH and Company of Soldiers (among whom are WILLIAM HAMMERTON and GEORGE GREENGOOSE), with drums and colours.

RALPH. March fair, my hearts ! Lieutenant, beat the rear up.—Ancient,[2] let your colours fly ; but have a great care of the butchers' hooks at Whitechapel ; they have been the death of many a fair ancient.—Open your files, that I may take a view both of your persons and munition.—Sergeant, call a muster.

SERGEANT. A stand !—William Hammerton, pewterer !

---

¹ The cleaning-rod of a gun.   ² Ensign.

HAMMERTON. Here, captain !   10

RALPH. A corselet and a Spanish pike ; 'tis well : can you shake it with a terror ?

HAMMERTON. I hope so, captain.

RALPH. Charge upon me. [He charges on Ralph.]— 'Tis with the weakest : put more strength, William Hammerton, more strength. As you were again !— Proceed, Sergeant.

SERGEANT. George Greengoose, poulterer !

GREENGOOSE. Here !

RALPH. Let me see your piece, neighbour Green-goose : when was she shot in ?   21

GREENGOOSE. An 't like you, master captain, I made a shot even now, partly to scour her, and partly for audacity.

RALPH. It should seem so certainly, for her breath is yet inflamed ; besides, there is a main fault in the touchhole, it runs and stinketh ; and I tell you moreover, and believe it, ten such touch-holes would breed the pox in the army. Get you a feather, neighbour, get you a feather, sweet oil, and paper, and your piece may do well enough yet. Where 's your powder ?   32

GREENGOOSE. Here.

RALPH. What, in a paper ! as I am a soldier and a gentleman, it craves a martial court ! you ought to die for 't. Where 's your horn ? answer me to that.

GREENGOOSE. An 't like you, sir, I was oblivious.

RALPH. It likes me not you should be so ; 'tis a shame for you, and a scandal to all our neigh-bours, being a man of worth and estimation, to leave your horn behind you : I am afraid 'twill breed example. But let me tell you no more on 't.— Stand, till I view you all.—What 's become o' the nose of your flask ?   45

FIRST SOLDIER. Indeed, la, captain, 'twas blown away with powder.

RALPH. Put on a new one at the city's charge.— Where 's the stone of this piece ?

SECOND SOLDIER. The drummer took it out to
light tobacco.   51

RALPH. 'Tis a fault, my friend ; put it in again.
—You want a nose,—and you a stone.—Sergeant,
take a note on 't, for I mean to stop it in the pay.—
Remove, and march ! [They march.] Soft and fair,
gentlemen, soft and fair ! double your files ! as
you were ! faces about ! Now, you with the
sodden face, keep in there ! Look to your match,
sirrah, it will be in your fellow's flask anon. So ;
make a crescent now ; advance your pikes ; stand
and give ear ! [1]—Gentlemen, countrymen, friends,
and my fellow-soldiers, I have brought you this
day, from the shops of security and the counters
of content, to measure out in these furious fields
honour by the ell, and prowess by the pound. Let
it not, oh, let it not, I say, be told hereafter,
the noble issue of this city fainted ; but bear
yourselves in this fair action like men, valiant
men, and free men ! Fear not the face of the
enemy, nor the noise of the guns, for, believe me,
brethren, the rude rumbling of a brewer's car[t] is
far more terrible, of which you have a daily experience ; neither let the stink of powder offend
you, since a more valiant stink is nightly with you.
To a resolved mind his home is everywhere :   75
I speak not this to take away
The hope of your return ; for you shall see
(I do not doubt it) and that very shortly
Your loving wives again and your sweet children,
Whose care [2] doth bear you company in baskets.
Remember, then, whose cause you have in hand,
And, like a sort [3] of true-born scavengers,   82
Scour me this famous realm of enemies.
I have no more to say but this :
Stand to your tacklings, lads, and show to the
      world

  [1] They are supposed to have now arrived at Mile End.—
Dyce.
         [2] i. e. the provisions.   [3] Company, band.

You can as well brandish a sword as shake an
    apron.
Saint George, and on, my hearts !

  ALL.   Saint George, Saint George ! [Exeunt.

 [WIFE. 'Twas well done, Ralph ! I'll send thee
a cold capon a-field and a bottle of March beer ;
and, it may be, come myself to see thee.   90

 CITIZEN. Nell, the boy hath deceived me much ;
I did not think it had been in him. He has performed such a matter, wench, that, if I live, next
year I'll have him captain of the galley-foist,[1] or
I'll want my will.]

  SCENE III.—A Room in MERRYTHOUGHT'S House.

    Enter MERRYTHOUGHT.

 MERRYTHOUGHT. Yet, I thank God, I break not
a wrinkle more than I had. Not a stoop,[1] boys?
Care, live with cats : I defy thee ! My heart is as
sound as an oak ; and though I want drink to wet
my whistle, I can sing ;

[Sings.] Come no more there, boys, come no more
    there ;
For we shall never whilst we live come any more
    there.

   Enter Boy, and two Men bearing a Coffin.

 BOY. God save you, sir !

 MERRYTHOUGHT. It 's a brave boy. Canst thou
sing ?   10

 BOY. Yes, sir, I can sing ; but 'tis not so
necessary at this time.

 MERRYTHOUGHT. [Sings.]

    Sing we, and chant it ;
    Whilst love doth grant it.

 BOY. Sir, sir, if you knew what I have brought
you, you would have little list to sing.

  [1] The Lord Mayor's barge. [2] A drinking vessel.

MERRYTHOUGHT. [Sings.]
> Oh, the Mimon [1] round,
> Full long I have thee sought,
> And now I have thee found,
> And what hast thou here brought ?   20

BOY. A coffin, sir, and your dead son Jasper
in it.   [Exit with Men.

MERRYTHOUGHT. Dead ! [Sings.]
> Why, farewell he !
> Thou wast a bonny boy,
> And I did love thee.

Enter JASPER.

JASPER. Then, I pray you, sir, do so still.

MERRYTHOUGHT. Jasper's ghost ! [Sings.]
> Thou art welcome from Stygian lake so soon ;
> Declare to me what wondrous things in Pluto's
>   court are done.   30

JASPER. By my troth, sir, I ne'er came there ;
'tis too hot for me, sir.

MERRYTHOUGHT. A merry ghost, a very merry
ghost !   [Sings.]
> And where is your true love ? Oh, where is yours ?

JASPER. Marry, look you, sir !
[*Removes the cloth, and* LUCE *rises up out of the Coffin.*

MERRYTHOUGHT. Ah, ha ! art thou good at
that, i' faith ?

[Sings.] With hey, trixy, terlery-whiskin,
>   The world it runs on wheels :   40
>   When the young man's . . . ,
>   Up goes the maiden's heels.

Mistress MERRYTHOUGHT *and* MICHAEL *within.*

MISTRESS MERRYTHOUGHT. [Within.] What,
Master Merrythought ! will you not let's in ?
what do you think shall become of us ?

---

[1] I cannot find any explanation of this word, which apparently means 'the world'. It is ignored by all the editors !

MERRYTHOUGHT.   [Sings.]
>   What voice is that that calleth at our door ?

MISTRESS MERRYTHOUGHT.   [Within.] You know
me well enough ; I am sure I have not been such
a stranger to you.

MERRYTHOUGHT.   [Sings.]
>   And some they whistled, and some they sung,
>   Hey, down, down !   51
>   And some did loudly say,
>   Ever as the Lord Barnet's horn blew,
>   ' Away, Musgrave, away ! '

MISTRESS MERRYTHOUGHT. [Within.] You will not
have us starve here, will you, Master Merrythought ?

JASPER.   Nay, good sir, be persuaded ; she is
>   my mother :
If her offences have been great against you,
Let your own love remember she is yours,
And so forgive her.

LUCE.   Good Master Merrythought,
Let me entreat you ; I will not be denied.   61

MISTRESS MERRYTHOUGHT. [Within.] Why, Master
Merrythought, will you be a vexed thing still ?

MERRYTHOUGHT.   Woman, I take you to my
love again ; but you shall sing before you enter ;
therefore dispatch your song and so come in.

MISTRESS MERRYTHOUGHT.   [Within.] Well, you
must have your will, when all 's done.—Mick, what
song canst thou sing, boy ?

MICHAEL.   [Within.]   I can sing none, forsooth, but
' A Lady's Daughter, of Paris properly ',   71
[Sings within.]   It was a lady's daughter, &c.

>   MERRYTHOUGHT opens the Door ; enter Mistress
>   MERRYTHOUGHT and MICHAEL.

MERRYTHOUGHT.   Come, you 're welcome home
again.
[Sings.]   If such danger be in playing,
>   And jest must to earnest turn,
>   You shall go no more a-maying——

VENTUREWELL. [Within.] Are you within, sir?
Master Merrythought!

    JASPER. It is my master's voice : good sir, go
      hold him   80
In talk, whilst we convey ourselves into
Some inward room.   [Exit with LUCE.

    MERRYTHOUGHT. What are you? are you merry?
You must be very merry, if you enter.

    VENTUREWELL. [Within.] I am, sir.

    MERRYTHOUGHT. Sing, then.

    VENTUREWELL. [Within.] Nay, good sir, open
      to me.

    MERRYTHOUGHT.   Sing, I say,
Or, by the merry heart, you come not in!

    VENTUREWELL. [Within.] Well, sir, I'll sing.

      [Sings.] Fortune, my foe, &c.   89

MERRYTHOUGHT opens the Door : Enter VENTUREWELL.

    MERRYTHOUGHT. You are welcome, sir, you are
welcome : you see your entertainment ; pray you,
be merry.

    VENTUREWELL. Oh, Master Merrythought, I
      am come to ask you
Forgiveness for the wrongs I offered you,
And your most virtuous son ! they're infinite ;
Yet my contrition shall be more than they :
I do confess my hardness broke his heart,
For which just Heaven hath given me punishment
More than my age can carry ; his wandering spirit,
Not yet at rest, pursues me everywhere,   100
Crying, ' I'll haunt thee for thy cruelty '.
My daughter, she is gone, I know not how,
Taken invisible, and whether living
Or in [the] grave, 'tis yet uncertain to me.
Oh, Master Merrythought, these are the weights
Will sink me to my grave ! forgive me, sir.

    MERRYTHOUGHT. Why, sir, I do forgive you ;
      and be merry :
And if the wag in 's lifetime played the knave,

Can you forgive him too ?

VENTUREWELL.   With all my heart, sir.

MERRYTHOUGHT.   Speak it again, and heartily.

VENTUREWELL.   I do, sir ;
Now, by my soul, I do.   111

Re-enter LUCE and JASPER.

MERRYTHOUGHT. [Sings.]

> With that came out his paramour ;
> She was as white as the lily flower :
>   Hey, troul, troly, loly !
> With that came out her own dear knight ;
> He was as true as ever did fight, &c.

Sir, if you will forgive 'em, clap their hands
together ; there 's no more to be said i' the matter.

VENTUREWELL. I do, I do.

[CITIZEN. I do not like this. Peace, boys !
Hear me, one of you : everybody's part is come
to an end but Ralph's, and he 's left out.   122

BOY. 'Tis 'long of yourself, sir ; we have
nothing to do with his part.

CITIZEN. Ralph, come away !—Make [an end]
on him, as you have done of the rest, boys ; come.

WIFE. Now, good husband, let him come out
and die.

CITIZEN. He shall, Nell.—Ralph, come away
quickly, and die, boy !   130

BOY. 'Twill be very unfit he should die, sir,
upon no occasion—and in a comedy, too.

CITIZEN. Take you no care of that, sir boy ; is
not his part at an end, think you, when he 's
dead ?—Come away, Ralph !]

Enter RALPH, with a forked Arrow through his Head.

RALPH. When I was mortal,[1] this my costive
        corps
Did lap up figs and raisins in the Strand ;
Where sitting, I espied a lovely dame,

---

[1] A parody on the speech of Andrea's ghost in Kyd's
Spanish Tragedy.

Whose master wrought with lingel [1] and with awl,
And underground he vampèd many a boot.   140
Straight did her love prick forth me, tender sprig,
To follow feats of arms in warlike wise
Through Waltham Desert ; where I did perform
Many achievements, and did lay on ground
Huge Barbaroso, that insulting giant,
And all his captives set [2] at liberty.
Then honour pricked me from my native soil
Into Moldavia, where I gained the love
Of Pompiana,[3] his belovèd daughter ;
But yet proved constant to the black-thumbed
    maid   150
Susan, and scornèd Pompiana's love ;
Yet liberal I was, and gave her pins,
And money for her father's officers.
I then returnèd home, and thrust myself
In action, and by all men chosen was
Lord of the May, where I did flourish it,
With scarfs and rings, and posy in my hand.
After this action I preferrèd was,
And chosen city-captain at Mile End,
With hat and feather, and with leading-staff,
And trained my men, and brought them all off
    clear,   161
Save one man that berayed him [4] with the noise.
But all these things I Ralph did undertake
Only for my belovèd Susan's sake.
Then coming home, and sitting in my shop
With apron blue, Death came into my stall
To cheapen aquavitae ; but ere I
Could take the bottle down and fill a taste,
Death caught a pound of pepper in his hand,
And sprinkled all my face and body o'er,   170
And in an instant vanishèd away.
    [CITIZEN. 'Tis a pretty fiction, i' faith.]

[1] Shoemaker's thread.
[2] The quartos have ' soon set '.
[3] Called ' Pompiona ' above, Act IV, Scene ii.
[4] Befouled himself.

RALPH. Then took I up my bow and shaft in hand,
And walked into Moorfields to cool myself :
But there grim cruel Death met me again,
And shot this forkèd arrow through my head ;
And now I faint ; therefore be warned by me,
My fellows every one, of forkèd heads !
Farewell, all you good boys in merry London !
Ne'er shall we more upon Shrove Tuesday meet,
And pluck down houses of iniquity ;—[1]   181
My pain increaseth ;—I shall never more
Hold open, whilst another pumps, both legs,
Nor daub a satin gown with rotten eggs ;
Set up a stake, oh, never more I shall !
I die ! fly, fly, my soul, to Grocers' Hall !
Oh, oh, oh, &c.   [Dies.

[WIFE. Well said, Ralph ! do your obeisance to
the gentlemen, and go your ways : well said,
Ralph !]   190
        [RALPH rises, make obeisance, and exit.
MERRYTHOUGHT. Methinks all we, thus kindly
and unexpectedly reconciled, should not depart
without a song.
VENTUREWELL. A good motion.
MERRYTHOUGHT. Strike up, then !

Song.

Better music ne'er was known
Than a quire of hearts in one.
Let each other, that hath been
Troubled with the gall or spleen,
Learn of us to keep his brow   200
Smooth and plain, as ours are now !
Sing ! though before the hour of dying,
He shall rise, and then be crying,
' Hey, ho, 'tis nought but mirth
That keeps the body from the earth ! '
                                            [Exeunt.

---

[1] One of the favourite amusements of the London prentices
on Shrove Tuesday consisted in attacking houses of ill-fame.

CITIZEN. Come, Nell, shall we go ? the play's
done. 207

WIFE. Nay, by my faith, George, I have more
manners than so ; I'll speak to these gentlemen
first.—I thank you all, gentlemen, for your patience
and countenance to Ralph, a poor fatherless child ;
and if I might see you at my house, it should go
hard but I would have a pottle [1] of wine and a
pipe of tobacco for you : for, truly, I hope you
do like the youth, but I would be glad to know the
truth ; I refer it to your own discretions, whether
you will applaud him or no ; for I will wink, and
whilst you shall do what you will, I thank you
with all my heart. God give you good night !—
Come, George. [Exeunt.

[1] A measure holding two quarts.

PHILASTER
OR
LOVE LIES A-BLEEDING

Francis Beaumont
(1584–1616)
AND
John Fletcher
(1579–1625)

Philaster was, according to Dryden, the first play which brought Beaumont and Fletcher into esteem, 'for before that they had written two or three very unsuccessfully'. It was probably produced in 1610, or, as some think, two years earlier, and first printed in 1620. In this edition about the first hundred lines of the play and the whole of the last two scenes are almost entirely different from any subsequent edition, but the rest of the play gives some readings, apparently correct, which are found in no other edition. In a prefatory note by the publisher in the second impression—i.e. edition (1622), mention is made of 'some dangerous and gaping wounds which [Philaster and Arethusa] received in the first Impression'; these he says he has 'adventured to bind up'. As this edition was issued three years before Fletcher's death, it has a special value in determining the text. Five other quarto editions appeared from 1628 to 1661, and in 1679 the play appeared in the Second Folio edition of the *Works*.

The division of the Acts into Scenes and the insertion of the stage directions are, as was said in the prefatory note to *The Knight of the Burning Pestle*, mainly due to Weber and Dyce. The play was included by Mr. J. St. L. Strachey in his Mermaid selection (1887), and has been edited with some useful notes by Dr. F. S. Boas in the Temple Classics (1898).

PHYLASTER.

Or, Loue lyes a Bleeding.

Acted at the Globe by his Maiesties Seruants.

Written by ⎰ *Francis Baymont* ⎱ *Gent.*
⎱ and ⎰
⎰ *Iohn Fletcher.* ⎱

Printed at *London* for *Thomas Walkley*, and are to be sold at his

DRAMATIS PERSONAE

KING [of Sicily and Calabria, a Usurper.]
PHILASTER, Heir to the Crown of Sicily.
PHARAMOND, Prince of Spain.
DION, a Lord.
CLEREMONT, } Noble Gentlemen, his Associates.
THRASILINE, }
An old Captain.
Citizens.
A Country Fellow.
Two Woodmen.
Guards, Attendants.

ARETHUSA, Daughter of the King.
EUPHRASIA, Daughter of Dion, disguised as a Page under
    the name of Bellario.
MEGRA, a Court Lady.
GALATEA, a Lady attending the Princess.
Two other Ladies.

SCENE.—Messina and its neighbourhood.

PHILASTER

ACT THE FIRST

SCENE I.—The Presence Chamber in the Palace.

Enter DION, CLEREMONT, and THRASILINE.

CLEREMONT. Here's nor lords nor ladies.

DION. Credit me, gentlemen, I wonder at it. They received strict charge from the King to attend here : besides, it was boldly published, that no officer should forbid any gentleman that desired to attend and hear.

CLEREMONT. Can you guess the cause ?

DION. Sir, it is plain, about the Spanish Prince, that's come to marry our kingdom's heir and be our sovereign. 10

THRASILINE. Many, that will seem to know much, say she looks not on him like a maid in love.

DION. Oh, sir, the multitude, that seldom know anything but their own opinions, speak that they would have ; but the prince, before his own approach, received so many confident messages from the state, that I think she's resolved to be ruled. 19

CLEREMONT. Sir, it is thought, with her he shall enjoy both these kingdoms of Sicily and Calabria.

DION. Sir, it is without controversy so meant. But 'twill be a troublesome labour for him to enjoy both these kingdoms with safety, the right heir to one of them living, and living so virtuously ; especially, the people admiring the bravery of his mind and lamenting his injuries.

CLEREMONT. Who ? Philaster ? 28

DION. Yes ; whose father, we all know, was by our late King of Calabria unrighteously deposed from his fruitful Sicily. Myself drew some blood in those wars, which I would give my hand to be washed from.

CLEREMONT. Sir, my ignorance in state-policy will not let me know why, Philaster being heir to one of these kingdoms, the King should suffer him to walk abroad with such free liberty.   37

DION. Sir, it seems your nature is more constant than to inquire after state-news. But the King, of late, made a hazard of both the kingdoms, of Sicily and his own, with offering but to imprison Philaster ; at which the city was in arms, not to be charmed down by any state-order or proclamation, till they saw Philaster ride through the streets pleased [1] and without a guard ; at which they threw their hats and their arms from them ; some to make bonfires, some to drink, all for his deliverance : which wise men say is the cause the King labours to bring in the power of a foreign nation to awe his own with.   50

Enter GALATEA, a Lady, and MEGRA.[2]

THRASILINE. See, the ladies ! What 's the first ?

DION. A wise and modest gentlewoman that attends the princess.

CLEREMONT. The second ?

DION. She is one that may stand still discreetly enough, and ill-favouredly dance her measure ; simper when she is courted by her friend, and slight her husband.

CLEREMONT. The last ?   59

DION. Marry, I think she is one whom the state keeps for the agents of our confederate princes ; she'll cog [3] and lie with a whole army, before the league shall break. Her name is common through

---

[1] Query ' released '.—*Dyce.*

[2] All early editions have ' Megra and a Lady ', but their ensuing characters given by Dion make it certain that this order should be reversed.

[3] Cheat, cajole.

the kingdom, and the trophies of her dishonour
advanced beyond Hercules' Pillars.   She loves to
try the several constitutions of men's bodies ; and,
indeed, has destroyed the worth of her own body
by making experiment upon it for the good of the
commonwealth.

CLEREMONT.   She's a profitable member.   70
[They talk apart.

MEGRA.   Peace, if you love me : you shall see
these gentlemen stand their ground and not court us.

GALATEA.   What if they should ?

LADY.   What if they should !

MEGRA.   Nay, let her alone.—What if they
should ? Why, if they should, I say they were
never abroad : what foreigner would do so ? it
writes them directly untravelled.

GALATEA.   Why, what if they be ?

LADY.   What if they be !   80

MEGRA.   Good madam, let her go on.—What if
they be ? why, if they be, I will justify, they
cannot maintain discourse with a judicious lady,
nor make a leg [1] nor say ' excuse me '.

GALATEA.   Ha, ha, ha !

MEGRA.   Do you laugh, madam ?

DION.   [Comes forward.] Your desires upon you,
ladies !

MEGRA.   Then you must sit beside us.

DION.   I shall sit near you then, lady.   90

MEGRA.   Near me, perhaps : but there 's a lady
endures no stranger ; and to me you appear
a very strange fellow.

LADY.   Methinks he's not so strange ; he would
quickly be acquainted.

THRASILINE.   Peace, the King !

Enter KING, PHARAMOND, ARETHUSA, and Attendants.

KING.   To give a stronger testimony of love
Than sickly promises (which commonly
In princes find both birth and burial
    99

[1] Bow.

In one breath) we have drawn you, worthy sir,
To make your fair endearments to our daughter,
And worthy services known to our subjects,
Now loved and wondered at ; next, our intent
To plant you deeply our immediate heir
Both to our blood and kingdoms. For this lady
(The best part of your life, as you confirm me,
And I believe), though her few years and sex
Yet teach her nothing but her fears and blushes,
Desires without desire, discourse ¹ and knowledge
Only of what herself is to herself,   110
Make her feel moderate health ; and when she
      sleeps,
In making no ill day, knows no ill dreams :
Think not, dear sir, these undivided parts,
That must mould up a virgin, are put on
To show her so, as borrowed ornaments,
To speak her perfect love to you, or add
An artificial shadow to her nature—
No, sir ;
I boldly dare proclaim her yet no woman.
But woo her still, and think her modesty   120
A sweeter mistress than the offered language
Of any dame, were she a queen, whose eye
Speaks common loves and comforts to her servants.²
Last, noble son (for so I now must call you),
What I have done thus public, is not only
To add a comfort in particular
To you or me, but all ; and to confirm
The nobles and the gentry of these kingdoms
By oath to your succession, which shall be
Within this month at most.   130
      THRASILINE.   [Aside to CLEREMONT and DION.] This
will be hardly done.
      CLEREMONT.   It must be ill done, if it be done.
      DION.   When 'tis at best, 'twill be but half done,
      whilst
So brave a gentleman is wronged and flung off.

----

¹ Reason.   ² Suitors.

THRASILINE.   I fear.

CLEREMONT.   Who does not ?

DION.   I fear not for myself, and yet I fear too :
Well, we shall see, we shall see. No more.

PHARAMOND.   Kissing your white hand, mistress,
   I take-leave
To thank your royal father ; and thus far   140
To be my own free trumpet. Understand,
Great King, and these your subjects, mine that
   must be
(For so deserving you have spoke me, sir,
And so deserving I dare speak myself),
To what a person, of what eminence,
Ripe expectation, of what faculties,
Manners and virtues, you would wed your king-
   doms ;
You in me have your wishes. Oh, this country !
By more than all the gods, I hold it happy ;   149
Happy in their dear memories that have been
Kings great and good ; happy in yours that is ;
And from you (as a chronicle to keep
Your noble name from eating age) do I
Opine [it in] [1] myself most happy. Gentlemen,
Believe me in a word, a prince's word,
There shall be nothing to make up a kingdom
Mighty and flourishing, defencèd, feared,
Equal to be commanded and obeyed,
But through the travails of my life I'll find it,
And tie it to this country. And I vow   160
My reign shall be so easy to the subject,
That every man shall be his prince himself
And his own law—yet I his prince and law.
And, dearest lady, to your dearest self
(Dear in the choice of him whose name and lustre
Must make you more and mightier) let me say,
You are the blessed'st living ; for, sweet princess,
You shall enjoy a man of men to be
Your servant ; you shall make him yours, for
   whom   169

[1] A conjecture of Seward's, adopted by Theobald.

Great queens must die.

    THRASILINE.   [Aside as before.] Miraculous !

    CLEREMONT.   This speech

Calls him Spaniard, being nothing but a large

Inventory of his own commendations.

    DION. I wonder what's his price ; for certainly

He'll sell himself, he has so praised his shape.

But here comes one more worthy those large

    speeches,

Enter PHILASTER.

Than the large speaker of them.

Let me be swallowed quick, if I can find,

In all the anatomy of yon man's virtues,

One sinew sound enough to promise for him,

He shall be constable. By this sun, he'll ne'er

    make king   180

Unless it be of trifles, in my poor judgement.

    PHILASTER. [Kneeling.] Right noble sir, as low

    as my obedience,

And with a heart as loyal as my knee,

I beg your favour.

    KING.   Rise ; you have it, sir.

                             [PHILASTER rises.

    DION. Mark but the King, how pale he looks,

    he fears !

Oh, this same whorson conscience, how it jades us !

    KING. Speak your intents, sir.

    PHILASTER.   Shall I speak 'em freely ?

Be still my royal sovereign.

    KING.   As a subject,

We give you freedom.

    DION. [Aside.]   Now it heats.

    PHILASTER.   Then thus I turn

My language to you, prince ; you, foreign man !

Ne'er stare nor put on wonder, for you must 191

Endure me, and you shall. This earth you tread

    upon

(A dowry, as you hope, with this fair princess),

By my dead father (oh, I had a father,

Whose memory I bow to !) was not left
To your inheritance, and I up and living—
Having myself about me and my sword,
The souls of all my name and memories,
These arms and some few friends beside the gods—
To part so calmly with it, and sit still   200
And say, ' I might have been '.   I tell thee, Phara-
        mond,
When thou art king, look I be dead and rotten,
And my name ashes : for, hear me, Pharamond !
This very ground thou goest on, this fat earth
My father's friends made fertile with their faiths,
Before that day of shame shall gape and swallow
Thee and thy nation, like a hungry grave,
Into her hidden bowels ; prince, it shall ;
By the just gods, it shall !

PHARAMOND.   He 's mad ; beyond cure, mad.

DION.   [Aside.]   Here is a fellow has some fire
        in 's veins :   211
The outlandish prince looks like a tooth-drawer.

PHILASTER.   Sir prince of popinjays,[1] I'll make
        it well
Appear to you I am not mad.

KING.   You displease us :
You are too bold.

PHILASTER.   No, sir, I am too tame,
Too much a turtle, a thing born without passion,
A faint shadow, that every drunken cloud
Sails over, and makes nothing.

KING.   I do not fancy this.
Call our physicians : sure, he 's somewhat tainted.

THRASILINE.   [Aside to DION and CLEREMONT.]   I do
        not think 'twill prove so.   220

DION.   H'as given him a general purge already,
For all the right he has ; and now he means
To let him blood.   Be constant, gentlemen :
By heaven, I'll run his hazard,
Although I run my name out of the kingdom !

CLEREMONT.   Peace, we are all one soul.

----
[1] Parrots.

PHARAMOND.   What you have seen in me to stir
  offence,
I cannot find, unless it be this lady,
Offered into mine arms with the succession ;
Which I must keep (though it hath pleased your
    fury   230
To mutiny within you), without disputing
Your genealogies, or taking knowledge
Whose branch you are : the King will leave it me,
And I dare make it mine. You have your answer.
  PHILASTER.   If thou wert sole inheritor to him
That made the world his, and couldst see no sun
Shine upon anything but thine ; were Pharamond
As truly valiant as I feel him cold,
And ringed among the choicest of his friends
(Such as would blush to talk such serious follies,
Or back such bellied commendations),   241
And from this presence, spite of all these bugs,[1]
You should hear further from me.
  KING.   Sir,
You wrong the prince ; I gave you not this freedom
To brave our best friends : you deserve our frown.
Go to ; be better tempered.
  PHILASTER.   It must be, sir,
When I am nobler used.
  GALATEA.   Ladies,
This would have been a pattern of succession,
Had he ne'er met this mischief. By my life,
He is the worthiest the true name of man   250
This day within my knowledge.
  MEGRA.   I cannot tell what you may call your
    knowledge ;
But the other is the man set in my eye :
Oh, 'tis a prince of wax ![2]
  GALATEA.   A dog it is.
  KING.   Philaster, tell me
The injuries you aim at in your riddles.
  PHILASTER.   If you had my eyes, sir, and suffer
    ance,

_____

    [1] Bugbears.   [2] i. e. well moulded.

My griefs upon you and my broken fortunes,
My wants great, and now naught but hopes and
        fears
                                                    259
My wrongs would make ill riddles to be laughed at.
Dare you be still my king, and right me not ?
    KING.   Give me your wrongs in private.
    PHILASTER.   Take them,
And ease me of a load would bow strong Atlas.
                            [They talk apart.
    CLEREMONT.   He dares not stand the shock.
    DION.   I cannot blame him ; there's danger in 't.
Every man in this age has not a soul of crystal, for
all men to read their actions through : men's
hearts and faces are so far asunder, that they hold
no intelligence. Do but view yon stranger well,
and you shall see a fever through all his bravery,
and feel him shake like a true tenant : [1] if he give
not back his crown again upon the report of an
elder-gun,[2] I have no augury.   273
    KING.   Go to ;
Be more yourself, as you respect our favour ;
You'll stir us else. Sir, I must have you know,
That you are, and shall be, at our pleasure, what
Fashion we will put upon you. Smooth your brow,
Or by the gods——
    PHILASTER.   I am dead, sir ; you're my fate.
        It was not I   280
Said, I was wronged : I carry all about me
My weak stars lead me to, all my weak fortunes.
Who dares in all this presence speak (that is
But man of flesh, and may be mortal), tell me,
I do not most entirely love this prince,
And honour his full virtues !
    KING.   Sure, he's possessed.
    PHILASTER.   Yes, with my father's spirit. It's
        here, O King,
A dangerous spirit ! now he tells me, King,

---

[1] i.e. not like a lord.   The 1620 quarto has 'truant' ·
Theobald suggests 'recreant', and Mitford 'tyrant'.
[2] Pop-gun.

L

I was a king's heir, bids me be a king,   289
And whispers to me, these are all my subjects.
'Tis strange he will not let me sleep, but dives
Into my fancy, and there gives me shapes
That kneel and do me service, cry me king :
But I'll suppress him ; he's a factious spirit,
And will undo me. Noble sir, your hand ;
I am your servant.
   KING.   Away ! I do not like this :
I'll make you tamer, or I'll dispossess you
Both of your life and spirit. For this time
I pardon your wild speech, without so much
As your imprisonment.   300
  [Exeunt KING, PHARAMOND, ARETHUSA, and Attendants.
  DION.   I thank you, sir ! you dare not for the
   people.
  GALATEA.   Ladies, what think you now of this
   brave fellow ?
  MEGRA.   A pretty talking fellow, hot at hand.
But eye yon stranger : is he not a fine complete
gentleman ? Oh, these strangers, I do affect them
strangely ! they do the rarest home-things, and
please the fullest ! As I live, I could love all the
nation over and over for his sake.   308
  GALATEA.   Gods comfort your poor head-piece,
lady ! 'tis a weak one, and had need of a night-cap.
      [Exeunt GALATEA, MEGRA, and Lady.
  DION.   See, how his fancy labours ! Has he not
Spoke home and bravely ? what a dangerous train
Did he give fire to ! how he shook the King,
Made his soul melt within him, and his blood
Run into whey ! it stood upon his brow
Like a cold winter-dew.
  PHILASTER.   Gentlemen,
You have no suit to me ? I am no minion :
You stand, methinks, like men that would be
   courtiers,
If I could well be flattered at a price,   319
Not to undo your children. You're all honest:
Go, get you home again, and make your country

A virtuous court, to which your great ones may,
In their diseased age, retire and live recluse.

CLEREMONT. How do you, worthy sir ?

PHILASTER.   Well, very well ;
And so well that, if the King please, I find
I may live many years.

DION.   The King must please,
Whilst we know what you are and who you are,
Your wrongs and virtues. Shrink not, worthy sir,
But add your father to you ; in whose name
We'll waken all the gods, and conjure up   330
The rods of vengeance, the abusèd people,
Who, like to raging torrents, shall swell high,
And so begirt [1] the dens of these male-dragons,
That, through the strongest safety, they shall beg
For mercy at your sword's point.

PHILASTER.   Friends, no more ;
Our ears may be corrupted ; 'tis an age
We dare not trust our wills to. Do you love me ?

THRASILINE. Do we love Heaven and honour ?

PHILASTER.   My Lord Dion, you had
A virtuous gentlewoman called you father ;
Is she yet alive ?

DION.   Most honoured sir, she is ;   340
And, for the penance but of an idle dream,
Has undertook a tedious pilgrimage.

Enter a Lady.

PHILASTER. Is it to me,
Or any of these gentlemen, you come ?

LADY. To you, brave lord ; the princess would
    entreat
Your present company.

PHILASTER. The princess send for me ! you are
    mistaken.

LADY. If you be called Philaster, 'tis to you.

PHILASTER. Kiss her fair hand, and say I will
    attend her.   [Exit Lady.

DION. Do you know what you do ?

[1] The same word as ' begird ', but never used literally.

PHILASTER.   Yes; go to see a woman.
CLEREMONT.   But do you weigh the danger you
   are in ?   351
PHILASTER.   Danger in a sweet face !
By Jupiter, I must not fear a woman !
   THRASILINE.   But are you sure it was the
   princess sent ?
It may be some foul train to catch your life.
   PHILASTER.   I do not think it, gentlemen ; she 's
   noble.
Her eye may shoot me dead, or those true red
And white friends in her cheeks may steal my soul
   out ;
There 's all the danger in 't : but, be what may,
Her single name hath armèd me.   [Exit.
   DION.   Go on,   360
And be as truly happy as thou 'rt fearless !
Come, gentlemen, let 's make our friends acquainted,
Lest the King prove false.   [Exeunt.

SCENE II.—ARETHUSA's Room in the Palace.

Enter ARETHUSA and a Lady.

ARETHUSA.   Comes he not ?
   LADY.   Madam ?
ARETHUSA.   Will Philaster come ?
   LADY.   Dear madam, you were wont to credit me
At first.
   ARETHUSA.   But didst thou tell me so ?
I am forgetful, and my woman's strength
Is so o'ercharged with dangers like to grow
About my marriage, that these under-things
Dare not abide in such a troubled sea.
How looked he when he told thee he would come ?
   LADY.   Why, well.
ARETHUSA.   And not a little fearful ?
   LADY.   Fear, madam ? sure, he knows not what
   it is.   10
ARETHUSA.   You all are of his faction ; the
   whole court

Is bold in praise of him ; whilst I
May live neglected, and do noble things,
As fools in strife throw gold into the sea,
Drowned in the doing. But, I know he fears.

LADY.　Fear, madam ?　methought, his looks
　　hid more
Of love than fear.

ARETHUSA.　　　　　Of love ?　to whom ?　to you ?
Did you deliver those plain words I sent,
With such a winning gesture and quick look　　19
That you have caught him ?

LADY.　　　　　　　　Madam, I mean to you.

ARETHUSA.　Of love to me ?　alas, thy ignorance
Lets thee not see the crosses of our births !
Nature, that loves not to be questionèd
Why she did this or that, but has her ends,
And knows she does well, never gave the world
Two things so opposite, so contrary,
As he and I am : if a bowl of blood,
Drawn from this arm of mine, would poison thee,
A draught of his would cure thee. Of love to me !

LADY.　Madam, I think I hear him.

ARETHUSA.　　　　　　　Bring him in.　[Exit Lady.
You gods, that would not have your dooms with-
　　stood,
　　　　　　　　　　　　　　　　　　31
Whose holy wisdoms at this time it is,
To make the passions of a feeble maid
The way unto your justice, I obey.

　　　　　Re-enter Lady with PHILASTER.

LADY.　Here is my Lord Philaster.

ARETHUSA.　　　　　　　　Oh, 'tis well.
Withdraw yourself.　　　　　　　　[Exit Lady.

PHILASTER.　　　　Madam, your messenger
Made me believe you wished to speak with me.

ARETHUSA.　'Tis true, Philaster ; but the words
　　are such
I have to say, and do so ill beseem
The mouth of woman, that I wish them said,　40
And yet am loath to speak them. Have you known

That I have aught detracted from your worth ?
Have I in person wronged you ? or have set
My baser instruments to throw disgrace
Upon your virtues ?
  PHILASTER.   Never, madam, you.
  ARETHUSA. Why, then, should you, in such
   a public place,
Injure a princess, and a scandal lay
Upon my fortunes, famed to be so great,
Calling a great part of my dowry in question ?
  PHILASTER. Madam, this truth which I shall
   speak will be   50
Foolish : but, for your fair and virtuous self,
I could afford myself to have no right
To anything you wished.
  ARETHUSA.   Philaster, know,
I must enjoy these kingdoms
  PHILASTER.   Madam, both ?
  ARETHUSA. Both, or I die : by heaven, I die,
   Philaster,
If I not calmly may enjoy them both.
  PHILASTER. I would do much to save that noble
   life :
Yet would be loath to have posterity
Find in our stories, that Philaster gave
His right unto a sceptre and a crown   60
To save a lady's longing.
  ARETHUSA.   Nay, then, hear :
I must and will have them, and more——
  PHILASTER.   What more ?
  ARETHUSA. Or lose that little life the gods
   prepared
To trouble this poor piece of earth withal.
  PHILASTER. Madam, what more ?
  ARETHUSA.   Turn, then, away thy face.
  PHILASTER. No.
  ARETHUSA. Do.
  PHILASTER. I can endure it. Turn away my
   face !
I never yet saw enemy that looked

So dreadfully, but that I thought myself   70
As great a basilisk as he ; or spake
So horribly, but that I thought my tongue
Bore thunder underneath, as much as his ;
Nor beast that I could turn from : shall I then
Begin to fear sweet sounds ? a lady's voice,
Whom I do love ? Say, you would have my life ;
Why, I will give it you ; for 'tis to me
A thing so loathed, and unto you that ask
Of so poor use, that I shall make no price :
If you entreat, I will unmovedly hear.   80

    ARETHUSA.   Yet, for my sake, a little bend thy
      looks.

    PHILASTER.   I do.

    ARETHUSA.   Then know, I must have
      them and thee.

    PHILASTER.   And me ?

    ARETHUSA.   Thy love ; without
      which, all the land
Discovered yet will serve me for no use
But to be buried in.

    PHILASTER.   Is 't possible ?

    ARETHUSA.   With it, it were too little to bestow
On thee. Now, though thy breath do strike me
      dead
(Which, know, it may), I have unript my breast.

    PHILASTER.   Madam, you are too full of noble
      thoughts,
To lay a train for this contemnèd life,   90
Which you may have for asking : to suspect
Were base, where I deserve no ill. Love you !
By all my hopes, I do, above my life !
But how this passion should proceed from you
So violently, would amaze a man
That would be jealous.

    ARETHUSA.   Another soul into my body shot
Could not have filled me with more strength and
      spirit
Than this thy breath. But spend not hasty time
In seeking how I came thus : 'tis the gods,   100

The gods, that make me so ; and, sure, our love
Will be the nobler and the better blest,
In that the secret justice of the gods
Is mingled with it.   Let us leave, and kiss ;
Lest some unwelcome guest should fall betwixt us.
And we should part without it.
                                    'Twill be ill

      PHILASTER.

I should abide here long.
      ARETHUSA.   'Tis true ; and worse
You should come often.   How shall we devise
To hold intelligence, that our true loves,
On any new occasion, may agree   110
What path is best to tread ?
      PHILASTER.   I have a boy,
Sent by the gods, I hope, to this intent,
Not yet seen in the court.   Hunting the buck,
I found him sitting by a fountain's side,
Of which he borrowed some to quench his thirst,
And paid the nymph again as much in tears.
A garland lay him by, made by himself
Of many several flowers bred in the vale,
Stuck in that mystic order that the rareness
Delighted me : but ever when he turned   120
His tender eyes upon 'em, he would weep,
As if he meant to make 'em grow again.
Seeing such pretty helpless innocence
Dwell in his face, I asked him all his story :
He told me that his parents gentle died,
Leaving him to the mercy of the fields,
Which gave him roots ; and of the crystal springs,
Which did not stop their courses ; and the sun,
Which still, he thanked him, yielded him his light.
Then took he up his garland, and did show   130
What every flower, as country-people hold,
Did signify, and how all, ordered thus,
Expressed his grief ; and, to my thoughts, did read
    read
The prettiest lecture of his country-art
That could be wished : so that methought I could
Have studied it.   I gladly entertained

Him, who was glad to follow ; and have got
The trustiest, loving'st, and the gentlest boy
That ever master kept. Him will I send
To wait on you, and bear our hidden love. 140

Re-enter Lady.

ARETHUSA. 'Tis well ; no more.

LADY. Madam, the prince is come to do his
service.

ARETHUSA. What will you do, Philaster, with
yourself ?

PHILASTER. Why, that which all the gods have
pointed out
For me.

ARETHUSA. Dear, hide thyself.—Bring in the
prince. [Exit Lady.

PHILASTER. Hide me from Pharamond !
When thunder speaks, which is the voice of God,
Though I do reverence, yet I hide me not ;
And shall a stranger-prince have leave to brag
Unto a foreign nation, that he made 150
Philaster hide himself ?

ARETHUSA. He cannot know it.

PHILASTER. Though it should sleep for ever to
the world,
It is a simple sin to hide myself,
Which will for ever on my conscience lie.

ARETHUSA. Then, good Philaster, give him
scope and way
In what he says ; for he is apt to speak
What you are loath to hear : for my sake, do.

PHILASTER. I will.

Re-enter Lady with PHARAMOND.

PHARAMOND. My princely mistress, as true
lovers ought,
I come to kiss these fair hands, and to show,
[Exit Lady.
In outward ceremonies, the dear love 161
Writ in my heart.

PHILASTER.   If I shall have an answer
No directlier, I am gone.

PHARAMOND.   To what would he
Have answer?

ARETHUSA.   To his claim unto the kingdom.

PHARAMOND.   Sirrah, I forbare you before the
King——

PHILASTER.   Good sir, do so still: I would not
talk with you.

PHARAMOND.   But now the time is fitter: do
but offer
To make mention of right to any kingdom,
Though it be scarce habitable——

PHILASTER.   Good sir,   169
Let me go.

PHARAMOND.   And by the gods—

PHILASTER.   Peace, Pharamond!
If thou——

ARETHUSA.   Leave us, Philaster.

PHILASTER.   I have done.   [Going.

PHARAMOND.   You are gone! by Heaven I'll
fetch you back.

PHILASTER.   You shall not need.   [Returning.

PHARAMOND.   What now?

PHILASTER.   Know, Pharamond,
I loathe to brawl with such a blast as thou,
Who art naught but a valiant voice; but if
Thou shalt provoke me further, men shall say,
' Thou wert ', and not lament it.

PHARAMOND.   Do you slight
My greatness so, and in the chamber of
The princess?

PHILASTER.   It is a place to which I must confess
I owe a reverence; but were 't the church,   180
Aye, at the altar, there 's no place so safe,
Where thou dar'st injure me, but I dare kill thee:
And for your greatness, know, sir, I can grasp
You and your greatness thus, thus into nothing.
Give not a word, not a word back! Farewell.
[Exit.

PHARAMOND. 'Tis an odd fellow, madam ; we
   must stop
His mouth with some office when we are married.
   ARETHUSA. You were best make him your con-
      troller.
   PHARAMOND. I think he would discharge it well.
      But, madam,
I hope our hearts are knit ; and yet so slow   190
The ceremonies of state are, that 'twill be long
Before our hands be so. If then you please,
Being agreed in heart, let us not wait
For dreaming form, but take a little stolen
Delights, and so prevent [1] our joys to come.
   ARETHUSA. If you dare speak such thoughts,
I must withdraw in honour.   [Exit.
   PHARAMOND. The constitution of my body will
never hold out till the wedding ; I must seek
elsewhere.   [Exit.

ACT THE SECOND

SCENE I.—A Room in the Palace.

Enter PHILASTER and BELLARIO.

   PHILASTER. And thou shalt find her honourable,
      boy ;
Full of regard unto thy tender youth,
For thine own modesty ; and, for my sake,
Apter to give than thou wilt be to ask,
Aye, or deserve.
   BELLARIO.   Sir, you did take me up
When I was nothing ; and only yet am something
By being yours. You trusted me unknown ;
And that which you were apt to conster [as]
A simple innocence in me, perhaps
Might have been craft, the cunning of a boy   10
Hardened in lies and theft : yet ventured you
To part my miseries and me ; for which,

[1] Anticipate.

I never can expect to serve a lady
That bears more honour in her breast than you.
   PHILASTER. But, boy, it will prefer thee. Thou
     art young,
And bear'st a childish overflowing love
To them that clap thy cheeks and speak thee fair
     yet ;
But when thy judgement comes to rule those
     passions,
Thou wilt remember best those careful friends
That placed thee in the noblest way of life.   20
She is a princess I prefer [1] thee to.
   BELLARIO. In that small time that I have seen
     the world,
I never knew a man hasty to part with
A servant he thought trusty : I remember,
My father would prefer the boys he kept
To greater men than he ; but did it not
Till they were grown too saucy for himself.
   PHILASTER. Why, gentle boy, I find no fault at
     all
In thy behaviour.
   BELLARIO.   Sir, if I have made
A fault of ignorance, instruct my youth :   30
I shall be willing, if not apt, to learn ;
Age and experience will adorn my mind
With larger knowledge ; and if I have done
A wilful fault, think me not past all hope
For once. What master holds so strict a hand
Over his boy, that he will part with him
Without one warning ? Let me be corrected,
To break my stubbornness, if it be so,
Rather than turn me off ; and I shall mend.
   PHILASTER. Thy love doth plead so prettily to
     stay,   40
That, trust me, I could weep to part with thee.
Alas, I do not turn thee off ! thou know'st
It is my business that doth call thee hence ;
And when thou art with her, thou dwell'st with me.

           [1] Recommend.

Think so, and 'tis so : and when time is full,
That thou hast well discharged this heavy trust,
Laid on so weak a one, I will again
With joy receive thee ; as I live, I will !
Nay, weep not, gentle boy. 'Tis more than time
Thou didst attend the princess.

    BELLARIO.   I am gone.   50
But since I am to part with you, my lord,
And none knows whether I shall live to do
More service for you, take this little prayer :
Heaven bless your loves, your fights, all your
    designs !
May sick men, if they have your wish, be well ;
And Heaven hate those you curse, though I be
    one !   [Exit.
    PHILASTER.   The love of boys unto their lords is
    strange ;
I have read wonders of it : yet this boy
For my sake (if a man may judge by looks
And speech) would out-do story. I may see   60
A day to pay him for his loyalty.   [Exit.

SCENE II.—A Gallery in the Palace.

Enter PHARAMOND.

    PHARAMOND. Why should these ladies stay so
long ? They must come this way : I know the
queen employs 'em not ; for the reverend mother
sent me word, they would all be for the garden.
If they should all prove honest [1] now, I were in
a fair taking ; I was never so long without sport
in my life, and, in my conscience, 'tis not my fault.
Oh, for our country ladies !

Enter GALATEA.

Here's one bolted ; I'll hound at her.—   9
Madam !
    GALATEA. Your grace !
    PHARAMOND.   Shall I not be a trouble ?

    [1] Chaste.

GALATEA. Not to me, sir.

PHARAMOND.   Nay, nay, you are too quick.
By this sweet hand——

GALATEA. You'll be forsworn, sir ; 'tis but an
old glove.
If you will talk at distance, I am for you :
But, good prince, be not bawdy, nor do not brag ;
These two I bar ;
And then, I think, I shall have sense enough
To answer all the weighty apophthegms
Your royal blood shall manage.

PHARAMOND. Dear lady, can you love ?   20

GALATEA. Dear, prince! how dear? I ne'er cost
you a coach yet, nor put you to the dear repentance
of a banquet. Here's no scarlet, sir, to blush the
sin out it was given for. This wire mine own hair
covers ; and this face has been so far from being
dear to any, that it ne'er cost a penny painting ;
and, for the rest of my poor wardrobe, such as
you see, it leaves no hand behind it, to make
the jealous mercer's wife curse our good doings.

PHARAMOND. You mistake me, lady.   30

GALATEA. Lord, I do so : would you or I could
help it !

PHARAMOND. You 're very dangerous bitter,
like a potion.

GALATEA. No, sir, I do not mean to purge you,
though
I mean to purge a little time on you.

PHARAMOND. Do ladies of this country use to
give
No more respect to men of my full being ?   36

GALATEA. Full being ! I understand you not,
unless your grace means growing to fatness ; and
then your only remedy (upon my knowledge, prince)
is, in a morning, a cup of neat white wine brewed
with carduus, then fast till supper ; about eight
you may eat ; use exercise, and keep a sparrowhawk ; you can shoot in a tiller : [1] but, of all, your

———
[1] Shoot with a cross-bow.

grace must fly phlebotomy, fresh pork, conger,
and clarified whey; they are all dullers of the
vital spirits.
46

PHARAMOND. Lady, you talk of nothing all this
while.

GALATEA. 'Tis very true, sir; I talk of you.

PHARAMOND. [Aside.] This is a crafty wench; I
like her wit well; 'twill be rare to stir up a leaden
appetite: she's a Danaë, and must be courted in
a shower of gold.—Madam, look here; all these,
and more than——
53

GALATEA. What have you there, my lord?
gold? now, as I live, 'tis fair gold! You would
have silver for it, to play with the pages: you
could not have taken me in a worse time; but,
if you have present use, my lord, I'll send my
man with silver and keep your gold for you.

[Takes gold.

PHARAMOND. Lady, lady!
60

GALATEA. She's coming, sir, behind, will take
white money.— [Aside.] Yet for all this I'll match
ye.
[Exit behind the hangings.

PHARAMOND. If there be but two such more in
this kingdom, and near the court, we may even
hang up our harps. Ten such camphire [1] constitutions as this would call the golden age again
in question, and teach the old way for every ill-
faced husband to get his own children; and what
a mischief that would breed, let all consider!
70

Enter MEGRA.

Here's another: if she be of the same last, the
devil shall pluck her on.—Many fair mornings,
lady.

MEGRA. As many mornings bring as many days,
Fair, sweet and hopeful to your grace!

PHARAMOND. [Aside.] She gives good words yet;
sure this wench is free.—
If your more serious business do not call you,

[1] Camphor was believed to be an antaphrodisiac.

Let me hold quarter with you ; we will talk
An hour out quickly.

    MEGRA.   What would your grace talk of ?

    PHARAMOND.   Of some such pretty subject as
        yourself :   80
I'll go no further than your eye, or lip ;
There 's theme enough for one man for an age.

    MEGRA. Sir, they stand right, and my lips are
        yet even, smooth,
Young enough, ripe enough, and red enough,
Or my glass wrongs me.

    PHARAMOND. Oh, they are two twinned cherries
        dyed in blushes
Which those fair suns above with their bright beams
Reflect upon and ripen. Sweetest beauty,   83
Bow down those branches, that the longing taste
Of the faint looker-on may meet those blessings,
And taste and live.

    MEGRA. [Aside.] Oh, delicate sweet prince !
She that hath snow enough about her heart
To take the wanton spring of ten such lines off,
May be a nun without probation.—Sir,
You have in such neat poetry gathered a kiss,
That if I had but five lines of that number,
Such pretty begging blanks,[1] I should commend
Your forehead or your cheeks, and kiss you too.

    PHARAMOND. Do it in prose ; you cannot miss
        it, madam.   99

    MEGRA. I shall, I shall.

    PHARAMOND.   By my life, but you shall not ;
I'll prompt you first. [Kisses her.] Can you do it now ?

    MEGRA. Methinks 'tis easy, now you ha' done 't
        before me ;
But yet I should stick at it.

    PHARAMOND.   Stick till to-morrow ;
I'll never part you, sweetest. But we lose time :
Can you love me ?

    MEGRA. Love you, my lord ! how would you
        have me love you ?

               [1] Blank verses.

PHARAMOND.   I'll teach you in a short sentence,
'cause I will not load your memory : this is all ;
love me, and lie with me.

MEGRA.   Was it lie with you, you said ? 'tis
impossible.
                                                        110
PHARAMOND.   Not to a willing mind, that will
endeavour : if I do not teach you to do it as easily
in one night as you'll go to bed, I'll lose my royal
blood for 't.

MEGRA.   Why, prince, you have a lady of your
own
That yet wants teaching.

PHARAMOND.   I'll sooner teach a mare the old
measures,[1] than teach her anything belonging to
the function.   She's afraid to lie with herself, if
she have but any masculine imaginations about
her.   I know, when we are married, I must ravish
her.
                                                        122
MEGRA.   By my honour, that's a foul fault,
indeed ;
But time and your good help will wear it out, sir.

PHARAMOND.   And for any other I see, excepting your dear self, dearest lady, I had rather be
Sir Tim the schoolmaster, and leap a dairymaid,
madam.

MEGRA.   Has your grace seen the court-star,
Galatea ?

PHARAMOND.   Out upon her ! she's as cold of
her favour as an apoplex : she sailed by but
now.
                                                        132
MEGRA.   And how do you hold her wit, sir ?

PHARAMOND.   I hold her wit ?   The strength of
all the guard cannot hold it, if they were tied to
it ; she would blow 'em out of the kingdom.   They
talk of Jupiter ; he's but a squib-cracker to her :
look well about you, and you may find a tongue-
bolt.[2]   But speak, sweet lady, shall I be freely
welcome ?
                                                        140

[1] Stately dances.
[2] i.e. an arrow from her tongue sticking in you.

MEGRA.   Whither ?

PHARAMOND.   To your bed. If you mistrust my
faith, you do me the unnoblest wrong.

MEGRA.   I dare not, prince, I dare not.

PHARAMOND.   Make your own conditions, my
purse shall seal 'em ; and what you dare imagine
you can want, I'll furnish you withal : give two
hours to your thoughts every morning about it.
Come, I know you are bashful ;
Speak in my ear, will you be mine ? Keep this,
And with it me : soon I will visit you.   151
                              [Gives her a ring.

MEGRA.   My lord,
My chamber 's most unsafe ; but when 'tis night,
I'll find some means to slip into your lodging ;
Till when——

PHARAMOND.   Till when, this and my heart go
    with thee !   [Exeunt severally.

Re-enter GALATEA.

GALATEA.   Oh, thou pernicious petticoat prince !
are these your virtues ? Well, if I do not lay
a train to blow your sport up, I am no woman :
and, Lady Towsabel,[1] I'll fit you for 't.   [Exit.

SCENE III.—ARETHUSA'S Room in the Palace.
Enter ARETHUSA and a Lady.

ARETHUSA.   Where 's the boy ?

LADY.   Within, madam.

ARETHUSA.   Gave you him gold to buy him
    clothes ?

LADY.   I did.

ARETHUSA.   And has he done 't ?

LADY.   Yes, madam.

ARETHUSA.   'Tis a pretty
Sad-talking boy, is it not ? Asked you his
    name ?

LADY.   No, madam.

_____
[1] Or Dowsabel—i.e. Douce et belle.

Enter GALATEA.

ARETHUSA.   Oh, you are welcome. What
good news ?

GALATEA. As good as any one can tell your
grace,
That says, she has done that you would have
wished.

ARETHUSA. Hast thou discovered ?

GALATEA.   I have strained a point
Of modesty for you.

ARETHUSA.   I prithee, how ?

GALATEA. In listening after bawdry. I see, let
a lady   10
Live never so modestly, she shall be sure to find
A lawful time to hearken after bawdry.
Your prince, brave Pharamond, was so hot on 't !

ARETHUSA. With whom ?

GALATEA.   Why, with the lady I suspected :
I can tell the time and place.

ARETHUSA.   Oh, when, and where ?

GALATEA. To-night, his lodging.

ARETHUSA.   Run thyself
Into the presence ; mingle there again
With other ladies ; leave the rest to me.

[Exit GALATEA.

[Aside.] If destiny (to whom we dare not say,
Why thou didst [1] this) have not decreed it so,   20
In lasting leaves (whose smallest characters
Were never altered yet), this match shall break.
—Where 's the boy ?

LADY.   Here, madam.

Enter BELLARIO, richly dressed.

ARETHUSA.   Sir,
You are sad to change your service ; is 't not so ?

BELLARIO. Madam, I have not changed ; I wait
on you,
To do him service.

                [1] Theobald suggests, ' didst thou.'

ARETHUSA.   Thou disclaim'st in me.
Tell me thy name.

   BELLARIO.   Bellario.

   ARETHUSA.   Thou canst sing and play ?

   BELLARIO.   If grief will give me leave, madam,
   I can.

   ARETHUSA.   Alas, what kind of grief can thy
   years know ?
Hadst thou a curst[1] master when thou went'st to
   school ?   30
Thou art not capable of other grief ;
Thy brows and cheeks are smooth as waters be
When no breath troubles them : believe me, boy,
Care seeks out wrinkled brows and hollow eyes,
And builds himself caves, to abide in them.
Come, sir, tell me truly, doth your lord love me ?

   BELLARIO.   Love, madam ?   I know not what
   it is.

   ARETHUSA.   Canst thou know grief, and never
   yet knew'st love ?
Thou art deceived, boy.   Does he speak of me
As if he wished me well ?

   BELLARIO.   If it be love   40
To forget all respect to his own friends
With thinking of your face ; if it be love
To sit cross-armed and sigh away the day,
Mingled with starts, crying your name as loud
And hastily as men i' the streets do fire ;
If it be love to weep himself away
When he but hears of any lady dead
Or killed, because it might have been your chance ;
If, when he goes to rest (which will not be),   49
'Twixt every prayer he says, to name you once,
As others drop a bead, be to be in love,
Then, madam, I dare swear he loves you.

   ARETHUSA.   Oh, you're a cunning boy, and
   taught to lie
For your lord's credit ! but thou know'st a lie
That bears this sound is welcomer to me

                [1] Cross.

Than any truth that says he loves me not.
Lead the way, boy.—Do you attend me too.—
'Tis thy lord's business hastes me thus. Away !
[Exeunt.

SCENE IV.—Before PHARAMOND'S Lodging in the Court
of the Palace.

Enter DION, CLEREMONT, THRASILINE, MEGRA, and
GALATEA.

DION.   Come, ladies, shall we talk a round ? As
men
Do walk a mile, women should talk an hour
After supper : 'tis their exercise.
GALATEA.   'Tis late.
MEGRA.   'Tis all
My eyes will do to lead me to my bed.
GALATEA. I fear, they are so heavy, you'll
scarce find
The way to your own lodging with 'em to-night.

Enter PHARAMOND.

THRASILINE.   The prince !
PHARAMOND.   Not a-bed, ladies ? you 're good
sitters-up :
What think you of a pleasant dream, to last   10
Till morning ?
MEGRA.   I should choose, my lord, a pleasing
wake before it.

Enter ARETHUSA and BELLARIO.

ARETHUSA.   'Tis well, my lord ; you 're courting
of these ladies.—
Is 't not late, gentlemen ?
CLEREMONT.   Yes, madam.
ARETHUSA.   Wait you there. [Exit.
MEGRA. [Aside.]   She 's jealous, as I live.—Look
you, my lord,
The princess has a Hylas, an Adonis.
PHARAMOND.   His form is angel-like.

MEGRA.   Why, this is he
That must, when you are wed, sit by your pillow
Like young Apollo, with his hand and voice
Binding your thoughts in sleep ; the princess
Does provide him for you and for herself.   21
    PHARAMOND.   I find no music in these boys.
    MEGRA.   Nor I :
They can do little, and that small they do,
They have not wit to hide.
    DION.   Serves he the princess ?
    THRASILINE.   Yes.
    DION.   'Tis a sweet boy : how brave she keeps
      him !
    PHARAMOND.   Ladies all, good rest ; I mean to
      kill a buck
To-morrow morning ere you've done your dreams.
    MEGRA.   All happiness attend your grace !   [Exit
PHARAMOND.]   Gentlemen, good rest.—Come, shall
we to bed ?   30
    GALATEA.   Yes.—All good night.
    DION.   May your dreams be true to you !—
                 [Exeunt GALATEA and MEGRA.
What shall we do, gallants ? 'tis late. The King
Is up still : see, he comes ; a guard along
With him.

Enter KING with ARETHUSA, Guards, and Attendants.

    KING.   Look your intelligence be true.
    ARETHUSA.   Upon my life, it is : and I do hope
Your highness will not tie me to a man
That in the heat of wooing throws me off,
And takes another.
    DION.   What should this mean ?
    KING.   If it be true,
That lady had been better [to] have embraced
Cureless diseases. Get you to your rest :   41
You shall be righted.
             [Exeunt ARETHUSA and BELLARIO.]
           —Gentlemen, draw near ;
We shall employ you. Is young Pharamond

Come to his lodging ?

DION.   I saw him enter there.

KING. Haste, some of you, and cunningly discover
If Megra be in her lodging.   [Exit DION.

CLEREMONT.   Sir,
She parted hence but now, with other ladies.

KING. [Aside.] If she be there, we shall not need
    to make
A vain discovery of our suspicion.   50
You gods, I see that who unrighteously
Holds wealth or state from others shall be cursed
In that which meaner men are blest withal :
Ages to come shall know no male of him
Left to inherit, and his name shall be
Blotted from earth ; if he have any child,
It shall be crossly matched ; the gods themselves
Shall sow wild strife betwixt her lord and her.
Yet, if it be your wills, forgive the sin
I have committed ; let it not fall   60
Upon this understanding [1] child of mine !
She has not broke your laws. But how can I
Look to be heard of gods that must be just,
Praying upon the ground I hold by wrong ?

Re-enter DION.

DION. Sir, I have asked, and her women swear
she is within ; but they, I think, are bawds. I told
'em, I must speak with her ; they laughed, and
said, their lady lay speechless. I said, my business
was important ; they said, their lady was about
it. I grew hot, and cried, my business was a matter
that concerned life and death ; they answered, so
was sleeping, at which their lady was. I urged
again, she had scarce time to be so since last I saw
her : they smiled again, and seemed to instruct
me that sleeping was nothing but lying down and
winking. Answers more direct I could not get :
in short, sir, I think she is not there.   77

_____

[1] i. e. standing under, and so exposed to injury. The
1620 quarto has ' undeserving '.

KING. 'Tis then no time to dally.—You o' the
   guard,
Wait at the back door of the prince's lodging,
And see that none pass thence, upon your lives.—
                    [Exeunt Guards.
Knock, gentlemen ; knock loud ; louder yet.   81
    [DION, CLEREMONT, &c. knock at the door of
              PHARAMOND's Lodging.
What, has their pleasure taken off their hearing ?
I'll break your meditations.—Knock again.—
Not yet ? I do not think he sleeps, having this
   Larum   by   him.—Once   more.—Pharamond !
   prince !   [PHARAMOND appears at a window.
   PHARAMOND. What saucy groom knocks at
   this dead of night ?
Where be our waiters ? By my vexèd soul,
He meets his death that meets me, for this boldness.
   KING. Prince, prince, you wrong your thoughts ;
   we are your friends :
Come down.
   PHARAMOND. The King ?
   KING.   The same, sir. Come down, sir :
We have cause of present counsel with you.   91

Enter PHARAMOND below.

   PHARAMOND. If your grace please to use me,
   I'll attend you
To your chamber.
   KING. No, 'tis too late, prince; I'll make bold
   with yours.
   PHARAMOND. I have some private reasons to
   myself
Make me unmannerly, and say you cannot.—
Nay, press not forward, gentlemen ; he must
Come through my life that comes here.
   KING. Sir, be resolved [1] I must and will come.—
   Enter.
   PHARAMOND. I will not be dishonoured :   100
He that enters, enters upon his death.
                [1] Assured.

Sir, 'tis a sign you make no stranger of me,
To bring these renegadoes to my chamber
At these unseasoned hours.

KING.   Why do you
Chafe yourself so ? you are not wronged nor shall
    be ;
Only I'll search your lodging, for some cause
To ourself known.—Enter, I say.

PHARAMOND.   I say, no.

[MEGRA appears at a window.

MEGRA.   Let 'em enter, prince, let 'em enter ;
I am up and ready : I know their business ;
'Tis the poor breaking of a lady's honour   110
They hunt so hotly after ; let 'em enjoy it.—
You have your business, gentlemen ; I lay here.
Oh, my lord the King, this is not noble in you
To make public the weakness of a woman !

KING.   Come down.

MEGRA.   I dare, my lord. Your hootings and
    your clamours,
Your private whispers and your broad fleerings,
Can no more vex my soul than this base carriage :
But I have vengeance yet in store for some   119
Shall, in the most contempt you can have of me,
Be joy and nourishment.

KING.   Will you come down ?

MEGRA.   Yes, to laugh at your worst ; but I
    shall wring you,
If my skill fail me not.   [Exit above.

KING.   Sir, I must dearly chide you for this
    looseness ;
You have wronged a worthy lady : but, no more.—
Conduct him to my lodging and to bed.

[Exeunt PHARAMOND and Attendants.

CLEREMONT.   [Aside to DION.]   Get him another
wench, and you bring him to bed indeed.   128

DION.   'Tis strange a man cannot ride a stage
or two, to breathe himself, without a warrant.
If this gear hold, that lodgings be searched
thus, pray God we may lie with our own wives in

safety, that they be not by some trick of state
mistaken !

Enter MEGRA below.

KING. Now, lady of honour, where's your
    honour now ?
No man can fit your palate but the prince :
Thou most ill-shrouded rottenness, thou piece
Made by a painter and a 'pothecary,
Thou troubled sea of lust, thou wilderness
Inhabited by wild thoughts, thou swoln cloud
Of infection, thou ripe mine of all diseases,   141
Thou all-sin, all-hell, and last all-devils, tell me,
Had you none to pull on with your courtesies
But he that must be mine, and wrong my
    daughter ?
By all the gods, all these, and all the pages,
And all the court, shall hoot thee through the
    court,
Fling rotten oranges, make ribald rhymes,
And sear thy name with candles upon walls !
Do you laugh, Lady Venus ?
    MEGRA.   Faith, sir, you must pardon me ;
I cannot choose but laugh to see you merry.   150
If you do this, O King ! nay, if you dare do it,
By all those gods you swore by, and as many
More of my own, I will have fellows, and such
Fellows in it, as shall make noble mirth !
The princess, your dear daughter, shall stand by
    me
On walls, and sung in ballads, any thing :
Urge me no more ; I know her and her haunts,
Her lays, leaps, and outlays, and will discover all ;
Nay, will dishonour her. I know the boy   159
She keeps ; a handsome boy, about eighteen ;
Know what she does with him, where, and when.
Come, sir, you put me to a woman's madness,
The glory of a fury ; and if I do not
Do't to the height——
    KING.   What boy is this she raves at ?

MEGRA. Alas! good-minded prince, you know
not these things!
I am loth to reveal 'em. Keep this fault,
As you would keep your health from the hot air
Of the corrupted people, or, by Heaven,
I will not fall alone. What I have known
Shall be as public as a print; all tongues   170
Shall speak it as they do the language they
Are born in, as free and commonly; I'll set it,
Like a prodigious star, for all to gaze at,
So high and glowing, that kingdoms¹ far and
    foreign
Shall read it there, nay, travel with it, till they find
No tongue to make it more, nor no more people;
And then behold the fall of your fair princess!
    KING. Has she a boy?
    CLEREMONT. So please your grace, I have seen
    a boy wait on her,
A fair boy.
    KING.   Go, get you to your quarter: 180
For this time I will study to forget you.
    MEGRA. Do you study to forget me, and I'll
    study
To forget you.   [Exeunt KING and MEGRA, severally.
    CLEREMONT. Why, here's a male spirit fit for
Hercules. If ever there be Nine Worthies of women,
this wench shall ride astride and be their captain.
    DION. Sure, she has a garrison of devils in her
tongue, she uttered such balls of wild-fire: she
has so nettled the King, that all the doctors in the
country will scarce cure him. That boy was
a strange-found-out antidote to cure her infections;
that boy, that princess' boy; that brave, chaste,
virtuous lady's boy; and a fair boy, a well-spoken
boy! All these considered can make nothing else—
but there I leave you, gentlemen.   195
    THRASILINE. Nay, we'll go wander with you.
                                        [Exeunt.

¹ Theobald's correction for the quarto reading, 'And so
high and glowing that other kingdoms', &c.

ACT THE THIRD

SCENE I.—The Court of the Palace.

Enter DION, CLEREMONT, and THRASILINE.

CLEREMONT. Nay, doubtless, 'tis true.

DION.   Aye ; and 'tis the gods
That raised this punishment, to scourge the King
With his own issue. Is it not a shame
For us that should write noble in the land,
For us that should be freemen, to behold
A man that is the bravery of his age,
Philaster, pressed down from his royal right
By this regardless [1] King ? and only look
And see the sceptre ready to be cast
Into the hands of that lascivious lady   10
That lives in lust with a smooth boy, now to be
    married
To yon strange prince, who, but that people please
To let him be a prince, is born a slave
In that which should be his most noble part,
His mind ?

THRASILINE.   That man that would not
    stir with you
To aid Philaster, let the gods forget
That such a creature walks upon the earth !

CLEREMONT. Philaster is too backward in 't
    himself.
The gentry do await it, and the people,
Against their nature, are all bent for him,   20
And like a field of standing corn, that 's moved
With a stiff gale, their heads bow all one way.

DION.   The only cause that draws Philaster back
From this attempt is the fair princess' love,
Which [2] he admires, and we can now confute.

THRASILINE. Perhaps he'll not believe it.

DION.   Why, gentlemen,
'Tis without question so.

----

[1] Unworthy.   [2] i. e. Whom.

CLEREMONT. Aye, 'tis past speech,
She lives dishonestly : but how shall we,
If he be curious,[1] work upon his faith ?
    THRASILINE. We all are satisfied within our-
selves.   30
    DION. Since it is true, and tends to his own
good,
I'll make this new report to be my knowledge ;
I'll say I know it ; nay, I'll swear I saw it.
    CLEREMONT. It will be best.
    THRASILINE.   'Twill move him.
    DION.   Here he comes.

Enter PHILASTER.

Good morrow to your honour : we have spent
Some time in seeking you.
    PHILASTER.   My worthy friends,
You that can keep your memories to know
Your friend in miseries, and cannot frown
On men disgraced for virtue, a good day
Attend you all ! What service may I do   40
Worthy your acceptation ?
    DION.   My good lord,
We come to urge that virtue, which we know
Lives in your breast, forth. Rise, and make a
head :
The nobles and the people are all dulled
With this usurping King ; and not a man,
That ever heard the word, or knew such a thing
As virtue, but will second your attempts.
    PHILASTER. How honourable is this love in you
To me that have deserved none ! Know, my
friends
(You, that were born to shame your poor Philaster
With too much courtesy), I could afford   51
To melt myself in thanks : but my designs
Are not yet ripe : suffice it, that ere long
I shall employ your loves ; but yet the time
Is short of what I would.

[1] Particular.

DION.   The time is fuller, sir, than you expect ;
That which hereafter will not, perhaps, be reached
By violence may now be caught.   As for the King,
You know the people have long hated him ;
But now the princess, whom they loved——   60
    PHILASTER.   Why, what of her ?
    DION.   Is loathed as much as he.
    PHILASTER.   By what strange means ?
    DION.   She's known a whore.
    PHILASTER.   Thou liest.
    DION.   My lord——
    PHILASTER.   Thou liest,
        [Offers to draw his sword : they hold him.
And thou shalt feel it ! I had thought thy mind
Had been of honour.   Thus to rob a lady
Of her good name, is an infectious sin
Not to be pardoned : be it false as hell,
'Twill never be redeemed, if it be sown
Amongst the people, fruitful to increase
All evil they shall hear.   Let me alone   70
That I may cut off falsehood whilst it springs !
Set hills on hills betwixt me and the man
That utters this, and I will scale them all,
And from the utmost top fall on his neck,
Like thunder from a cloud.
    DION.   This is most strange :
Sure, he does love her.
    PHILASTER.   I do love fair truth :
She is my mistress, and who injures her
Draws vengeance from me.   Sirs, let go my arms.
    THRASILINE.   Nay, good my lord, be patient.
    CLEREMONT.   Sir,
Remember this is your honoured friend, that comes
To do his service, and will show you why
He uttered this.
    PHILASTER.   I ask you pardon, sir ;
My zeal to truth made me unmannerly :
Should I have heard dishonour spoke of you,
Behind your back, untruly, I had been
As much distempered and enraged as now.

DION. But this, my lord, is truth.

PHILASTER. Oh, say not so!
Good sir, forbear to say so ; 'tis then truth,
That womankind is false : urge it no more ;
It is impossible. Why should you think   90
The princess light ?

DION. Why, she was taken at it.

PHILASTER. 'Tis false ! by Heaven, 'tis false !
it cannot be !
Can it ? Speak, gentlemen ; for God's love, speak !
Is 't possible ? Can women all be damned ?

DION. Why, no, my lord.

PHILASTER. Why, then, it cannot be.

DION. And she was taken with her boy.

PHILASTER. What boy ?

DION. A page, a boy that serves her.

PHILASTER. Oh, good gods !
A little boy ?

DION. Aye ; know you him, my lord ?

PHILASTER. [Aside.] Hell and sin know him !
Sir, you are deceived ;
I'll reason it a little coldly with you :   100
If she were lustful, would she take a boy,
That knows not yet desire ? she would have one
Should meet her thoughts and know the sin he
acts,
Which is the great delight of wickedness.
You are abused, and so is she, and I.

DION. How you, my lord ?

PHILASTER. Why, all the world's abused
In an unjust report.

DION. Oh, noble sir, your virtues cannot look
Into the subtle thoughts of woman !
In short, my lord, I took them ; I myself.   110

PHILASTER. Now, all the devils, thou didst !
Fly from my rage !
Would thou hadst ta'en devils engendering plagues,
When thou didst take them ! Hide thee from my
eyes !
Would thou hadst taken thunder on thy breast,

When thou didst take them ; or been strucken
     dumb
For ever ; that this foul deed might have slept
In silence !

    THRASILINE.   Have you known him so ill-
          tempered ?

    CLEREMONT.   Never before.

    PHILASTER.   The winds, that are let loose
From the four several corners of the earth,
And spread themselves all over sea and land,   120
Kiss not a chaste one. What friend bears a sword
To run me thorough ?

    DION.   Why, my lord, are you
So moved at this ?

    PHILASTER.   When any fall from virtue,
I am distract ; I have an interest in 't.

    DION.   But, good my lord, recall yourself, and
          think
What 's best to be done.

    PHILASTER.   I thank you ; I will do it :
Please you to leave me ; I'll consider of it.
To-morrow I will find your lodging forth,   128
And give you answer.

    DION.   All the gods direct you
The readiest way !

    THRASILINE.   He was extreme impatient.

    CLEREMONT.   It was his virtue and his noble
          mind.   [Exeunt DION, CLEREMONT, and THRASILINE.

    PHILASTER.   I had forgot to ask him where he
          took them ;
I'll follow him. Oh, that I had a sea
Within my breast, to quench the fire I feel !
More circumstances will but fan this fire :
It more afflicts me now, to know by whom
This deed is done, than simply that 'tis done ;
And he that tells me this is honourable,
As far from lies as she is far from truth.   139
Oh, that, like beasts. we could not grieve ourselves
With that we see not ! Bulls and rams will fight
To keep their females, standing in their sight ;

But take 'em from them, and you take at once
Their spleens away ; and they will fall again
Unto their pastures, growing fresh and fat ;
And taste the waters of the springs as sweet
As 'twas before, finding no start in sleep :
But miserable man——

Enter BELLARIO.

           See, see, you gods,
He walks still ; and the face you let him wear
When he was innocent is still the same,   150
Not blasted ! Is this justice ? do you mean
To entrap mortality, that you allow
Treason so smooth a brow ? I cannot now
Think he is guilty.

    BELLARIO.   Health to you, my lord !
The princess doth commend her love, her life,
And this, unto you.   [Gives a letter.
    PHILASTER.   Oh, Bellario,
Now I perceive she loves me ! she does show it
In loving thee, my boy : she has made thee brave.
    BELLARIO. My lord, she has attired me past my
    wish,
Past my desert ; more fit for her attendant, 160
Though far unfit for me who do attend.
    PHILASTER. Thou art grown courtly, boy. [Aside.]
    —Oh, let all women,
That love black deeds, learn to dissemble here !
Here, by this paper, she does write to me
As if her heart were mines of adamant
To all the world besides ; but, unto me,
A maiden-snow that melted with my looks.—
Tell me, my boy, how doth the princess use thee ?
For I shall guess her love to me by that.
    BELLARIO. Scarce like her servant, but as if
    I were   170
Something allied to her, or had preserved
Her life three times by my fidelity ;
As mothers fond do use their only sons,
As I'd use one that's left unto my trust,

M

For whom my life should pay if he met harm,
So she does use me.

PHILASTER. Why, 'tis wondrous well :
But what kind language does she feed thee with ?

BELLARIO. Why, she does tell me she will trust
my youth
With all her loving secrets, and does call me
Her pretty servant ; bids me weep no more   180
For leaving you ; she'll see my services
Regarded :[1] and such words of that soft strain,
That I am nearer weeping when she ends
Than ere she spake.

PHILASTER. This is much better still.

BELLARIO. Are you not ill, my lord ?

PHILASTER. Ill ? no, Bellario.

BELLARIO. Methinks your words fall not from
off your tongue
So evenly, nor is there in your looks
That quietness that I was wont to see.

PHILASTER. Thou art deceived, boy : and she
strokes thy head ?

BELLARIO. Yes.   190

PHILASTER. And she does clap thy cheeks ?

BELLARIO. She does, my lord.

PHILASTER. And she does kiss thee, boy ? ha !

BELLARIO. How, my lord ?

PHILASTER. She kisses thee ?

BELLARIO. Never, my lord, by heaven.

PHILASTER. That's strange, I know she does.

BELLARIO. No, by my life.

PHILASTER. Why then she does not love me.
Come, she does:
I bade her do it ; I charged her, by all charms
Of love between us, by the hope of peace
We should enjoy, to yield thee all delights
Naked as to her bed ; I took her oath   199
Thou should'st enjoy her. Tell me, gentle boy,
Is she not paralleless ? is not her breath
Sweet as Arabian winds when fruits are ripe ?

    [1] 'Rewarded,' in the 1620 quarto.

Are not her breasts two liquid ivory balls ?
Is she not all a lasting mine of joy ?

    BELLARIO.   Aye, now I see why my disturbèd
      thoughts
Were so perplexed : when first I went to her,
My heart held augury. You are abused ;
Some villain has abused you : I do see
Whereto you tend. Fall rocks upon his head
That put this to you ! 'tis some subtle train   210
To bring that noble frame of yours to naught.

    PHILASTER.   Thou think'st I will be angry with
      thee. Come,
Thou shalt know all my drift : I hate her more
Than I love happiness, and placed thee there
To pry with narrow eyes into her deeds.
Hast thou discovered ? is she fallen to lust,
As I would wish her ? Speak some comfort to me.

    BELLARIO.   My lord, you did mistake the boy
      you sent :
Had she the lust of sparrows or of goats,
Had she a sin that way, hid from the world,   220
Beyond the name of lust, I would not aid
Her base desires : but what I came to know
As servant to her, I would not reveal,
To make my life last ages.

    PHILASTER.   Oh, my heart !
This is a salve worse than the main disease.
Tell me thy thoughts ; for I will know the least
                 [Draws his sword.
That dwells within thee, or will rip thy heart
To know it : I will see thy thoughts as plain
As I do now thy face.

    BELLARIO.   Why, so you do.   229
She is (for aught I know) by all the gods,   [Kneels.
As chaste as ice ! but were she foul as hell,
And I did know it thus, the breath of kings,
The points of swords, tortures, nor bulls of brass,
Should draw it from me.

    PHILASTER.   Then it is no time
To dally with thee : I will take thy life,

For I do hate thee : I could curse thee now.

BELLARIO. If you do hate, you could not curse
me worse ;
The gods have not a punishment in store
Greater for me than is your hate.

PHILASTER. Fie, fie, 239
So young and so dissembling ! Tell me when
And where thou didst enjoy her, or let plagues
Fall upon me, if I destroy thee not !

BELLARIO. By Heaven I never did ; and when
I lie
To save my life, may I live long and loathed !
Hew me asunder, and, whilst I can think,
I'll love those pieces you have cut away
Better than those that grow, and kiss those limbs
Because you made 'em so.

PHILASTER. Fear'st thou not death ?
Can boys contemn that ?

BELLARIO. Oh, what boy is he
Can be content to live to be a man, 250
That sees the best of men thus passionate,
Thus without reason ?

PHILASTER. Oh, but thou dost not know
What 'tis to die.

BELLARIO. Yes, I do know, my lord :
'Tis less than to be born ; a lasting sleep ;
A quiet resting from all jealousy,
A thing we all pursue ; I know, besides,
It is but giving over of a game
That must be lost.

PHILASTER. But there are pains, false boy,
For perjured souls : think but on those, and then
Thy heart will melt, and thou wilt utter all. 260

BELLARIO. May they fall all upon me whilst I live,
If I be perjured, or have ever thought
Of that you charge me with ! If I be false,
Send me to suffer in those punishments
You speak of ; kill me !

PHILASTER. Oh, what should I do ?
Why, who can but believe him ? he does swear

So earnestly, that if it were not true,
The gods would not endure him.   [Sheaths his sword.]
　　　　　　　　Rise, Bellario :   [BELLARIO rises.
Thy protestations are so deep, and thou
Dost look so truly when thou utter'st them,   270
That, though I know 'em false as were my hopes,
I cannot urge thee further.   But thou wert
To blame to injure me, for I must love
Thy honest looks, and take no revenge upon
Thy tender youth :   a love from me to thee
Is firm, whate'er thou dost :   it troubles me
That I have called the blood out of thy cheeks,
That did so well become thee.   But, good boy,
Let me not see thee more :   something is done
That will distract me, that will make me mad,
If I behold thee.   If thou tender'st me,[1]   281
Let me not see thee.

　　BELLARIO.　　　　　　I will fly as far
As there is morning, ere I give distaste
To that most honoured mind.   But through these
　　tears,
Shed at my hopeless parting, I can see
A world of treason practised upon you,
And her, and me.   Farewell for evermore
If you shall hear that sorrow struck me dead,
And after find me loyal, let there be
A tear shed from you in my memory,   290
And I shall rest at peace.   　　　　　　[Exit.
　　PHILASTER.　　　　　Blessing be with thee,
Whatever thou deserv'st !—Oh, where shall I
Go bathe this body ?   Nature too unkind ;
That made no medicine for a troubled mind !
　　　　　　　　　　　　　　　　　[Exit.

SCENE II.—ARETHUSA'S Room in the Palace.
Enter ARETHUSA.

　　ARETHUSA.   I marvel my boy comes not back
　　again :
But that I know my love will question him
　　　　　　　　[1] Hast regard for me.

Over and over,—how I slept, waked, talked ;
How I remembered him when his dear name
Was last spoke ; and how when I sighed, wept,
  sung,
And ten thousand such ;—I should be angry at his
  stay.

Enter KING.

KING. What, at your meditations ! Who attends
  you ?
ARETHUSA. None but my single self : I need no
  guard ;
I do no wrong, nor fear none.
KING.   Tell me, have   9
You not a boy ?
ARETHUSA.   Yes, sir.
KING.   What kind of boy ?
ARETHUSA. A page, a waiting-boy.
KING.   A handsome boy?
ARETHUSA. I think he be not ugly : well qualified
And dutiful I know him ; I took him not
For beauty.
KING.   He speaks and sings and plays ?
ARETHUSA.   Yes, sir.
KING. About eighteen ?
ARETHUSA.   I never asked his age.
KING. Is he full of service ?
ARETHUSA. By your pardon, why do you ask ?
KING. Put him away.
ARETHUSA.   Sir !
KING.   Put him away, I say.
H'as done you that good service shames me to
  speak of.
ARETHUSA. Good sir, let me understand you.
KING.   If you fear me,
Show it in duty ; put away that boy.   20
ARETHUSA. Let me have reason for it, sir, and
  then
Your will is my command.
KING. Do not you blush to ask it ? Cast him
  off,

Or I shall do the same to you. You 're one
Shame with me, and so near unto myself,
That, by my life, I dare not tell myself
What you, myself, have done.

ARETHUSA. What have I done, my lord ?

KING. 'Tis a new language, that all love to
learn :
The common people speak it well already ; 30
They need no grammar. Understand me well ;
There be foul whispers stirring. Cast him off,
And suddenly : do it ! Farewell. [Exit.

ARETHUSA. Where may a maiden live securely
free,
Keeping her honour fair ? Not with the living ;
They feed upon opinions, errors, dreams,
And make 'em truths ; they draw a nourishment
Out of defamings, grow upon disgraces ;
And, when they see a virtue fortified
Strongly above the battery of their tongues, 40
Oh, how they cast to sink it ! and, defeated,
(Soul-sick with poison) strike the monuments
Where noble names lie sleeping, till they sweat,
And the cold marble melt.

Enter PHILASTER.

PHILASTER. Peace to your fairest thoughts,
dearest mistress !

ARETHUSA. Oh, my dearest servant,[1] I have
a war within me !

PHILASTER. He must be more than man that
makes these crystals
Run into rivers. Sweetest fair, the cause ?
And, as I am your slave, tied to your goodness,
Your creature, made again from what I was 50
And newly-spirited, I'll right your honour.

ARETHUSA. Oh, my best love, that boy !

PHILASTER. What boy ?

ARETHUSA. The pretty boy you gave me——

PHILASTER. What of him ?

---

[1] Lover.

ARETHUSA.   Must be no more mine.
PHILASTER.   Why ?
ARETHUSA.   They are jealous of him.
PHILASTER.   Jealous ! who ?
ARETHUSA.   The King.
PHILASTER.   [Aside.]   Oh, my misfortune !
Then 'tis no idle jealousy.—Let him go.
    ARETHUSA.   Oh, cruel !
Are you hard-hearted too ? who shall now tell you
How much I loved you ? who shall swear it to you,
And weep the tears I send ? who shall now bring
    you   60
Letters, rings, bracelets ? lose his health in
    service ?
Wake tedious nights in stories of your praise ?
Who shall now sing your crying elegies,
And strike a sad soul into senseless pictures,
And make them mourn ? who shall take up his
    lute,
And touch it till he crown a silent sleep
Upon my eyelids, making me dream, and cry,
' Oh, my dear, dear Philaster ! '
    PHILASTER.   [Aside.]   Oh, my heart !
Would he had broken thee, that made thee know
This lady was not loyal !—Mistress,   70
Forget the boy ; I'll get thee a far better.
    ARETHUSA.   Oh, never, never such a boy again
As my Bellario !
    PHILASTER.   'Tis but your fond affection.
    ARETHUSA.   With thee, my boy, farewell for ever
All secrecy in servants ! Farewell faith,
And all desire to do well for itself !
Let all that shall succeed thee for thy wrongs
Sell and betray chaste love !
    PHILASTER.   And all this passion for a boy ?
    ARETHUSA.   He was your boy, and you put him
    to me,   80
And the loss of such must have a mourning for['t.]
    PHILASTER.   Oh, thou forgetful woman !
    ARETHUSA.   How, my lord ?

PHILASTER. False Arethusa !
Hast thou a medicine to restore my wits,
When I have lost 'em ? If not, leave to talk,
And [to] do thus.
ARETHUSA. Do what, sir ? would you sleep ?
PHILASTER. For ever, Arethusa. Oh, you gods,
Give me a worthy patience ! Have I stood
Naked, alone, the shock of many fortunes ?
Have I seen mischiefs numberless and mighty
Grow like a sea upon me ? Have I taken 91
Danger as stern as death into my bosom,
And laughed upon it, made it but a mirth,
And flung it by ? Do I live now like him,
Under this tyrant King, that languishing
Hears his sad bell and sees his mourners ? Do I
Bear all this bravely, and must sink at length
Under a woman's falsehood ? Oh, that boy,
That cursèd boy ! None but a villain boy
To ease your lust ?
ARETHUSA. Nay, then, I am betrayed :
I feel the plot cast for my overthrow. 101
Oh, I am wretched !
PHILASTER. Now you may take that little right
    I have
To this poor kingdom : give it to your joy ;
For I have no joy in it. Some far place,
Where never womankind durst set her foot
For [1] bursting with her poisons, must I seek,
And live to curse you :
There dig a cave, and preach to birds and beasts
What woman is, and help to save them from you ;
How heaven is in your eyes, but in your hearts
More hell than hell has ; how your tongues, like
    scorpions, 112
Both heal and poison ; how your thoughts are
    woven
With thousand changes in one subtle web,
And worn so by you ; how that foolish man,

---

[1] i.e. For fear of. It was supposed that venomous creatures
could not live in certain places.

That reads the story of a woman's face
And dies believing it, is lost for ever ;   117
How all the good you have is but a shadow,
I' the morning with you, and at night behind you,
Past and forgotten ; how your vows are frosts,
Fast for a night, and with the next sun gone ;
How you are, being taken all together,
A mere confusion, and so dead a chaos,
That love cannot distinguish. These sad texts,
Till my last hour, I am bound to utter of you.
So, farewell all my woe, all my delight !   [Exit.
    ARETHUSA.   Be merciful, ye gods, and strike me
    dead !
What way have I deserved this ? Make my breast
Transparent as pure crystal, that the world,
Jealous of me, may see the foulest thought
My heart holds. Where shall a woman turn her
    eyes,   131
To find out constancy ?

Enter BELLARIO.

                    Save me, how black
And guiltily, methinks, that boy looks now !
—Oh, thou dissembler, that, before thou spak'st,
Wert in thy cradle false, sent to make lies
And betray innocents ! Thy lord and thou
May glory in the ashes of a maid
Fooled by her passion ; but the conquest is
Nothing so great as wicked. Fly away !
Let my command force thee to that which shame
Would do without it. If thou understood'st
The loathèd office thou hast undergone,   142
Why, thou wouldst hide thee under heaps of hills,
Lest men should dig and find thee.
    BELLARIO.   Oh, what god,
Angry with men, hath sent this strange disease
Into the noblest minds ? Madam, this grief
You add unto me is no more than drops
To seas, for which they are not seen to swell ;
My lord hath struck his anger through my heart

And let out all the hope of future joys.   150
You need not bid me fly ; I came to part,
To take my latest leave.   Farewell for ever !
I durst not run away in honesty
From such a lady, like a boy that stole
Or made some grievous fault.   The power of gods
Assist you in your sufferings !   Hasty time
Reveal the truth to your abusèd lord
And mine, that he may know your worth ; whilst I
Go seek out some forgotten place to die !   [Exit.
   ARETHUSA.   Peace guide thee ! Thou hast over-
     thrown me once ;   160
Yet, if I had another Troy to lose,
Thou, or another villain with thy looks,
Might talk me out of it, and send me naked,
My hair dishevelled, through the fiery streets.

Enter a Lady.

   LADY.   Madam, the King would hunt, and calls
     for you
With earnestness.
   ARETHUSA.   I am in tune to hunt !
—Diana, if thou canst rage with a maid
As with a man, let me discover thee
Bathing, and turn me to a fearful hind,
That I may die pursued by cruel hounds,   170
And have my story written in my wounds !
                           [Exeunt.

ACT THE FOURTH

SCENE I.—Before the Palace.

Enter KING, PHARAMOND, ARETHUSA, GALATEA, MEGRA,
   DION, CLEREMONT, THRASILINE, and Attendants.
   KING.   What, are the hounds before and all the
     woodmen,
Our horses ready and our bows bent ?
   DION.   All, sir.
   KING.   [To PHARAMOND.] You are cloudy, sir :
     come, we have forgotten

Your venial trespass ; let not that sit heavy
Upon your spirit ; here's none dare utter it.

DION. [Aside to THRASILINE.] He looks like an old
surfeited stallion after his leaping, dull as a dormouse. See how he sinks ! The wench has shot
him between wind and water, and, I hope, sprung
a leak.   10

THRASILINE. He needs no teaching, he strikes
sure enough : his greatest fault is, he hunts too
much in the purlieus ; [1] would he would leave off
poaching !

DION. And for his horn, h'as left it at the
lodge where he lay late. Oh, he's a precious
lymehound ! [2] turn him loose upon the pursuit
of a lady, and if he lose her, hang him up i' the
slip. When my fox-bitch Beauty grows proud,[3]
I'll borrow him.   20

KING. Is your boy turned away ?

ARETHUSA.   You did command, sir,
And I obeyed you.

KING.   'Tis well done. Hark ye further.
                                          [They talk apart.

CLEREMONT. Is't possible this fellow should
repent ? methinks, that were not noble in him ;
and yet he looks like a mortified member, as if
he had a sick man's salve [4] in 's mouth. If a worse
man had done this fault now, some physical justice
or other would presently (without the help of an
almanack) have opened the obstructions of his liver,
and let him blood with a dog-whip.   30

DION. See, see how modestly yon lady looks,
as if she came from churching with her neighbours !
Why, what a devil can a man see in her face but
that she's honest ?

---

[1] Common haunts.
[2] A bloodhound ; a lyam is a leash.   [3] In heat.
[4] An allusion to a work by Thomas Becon, or Beacon,
entitled *The Sicke Man's Salve*, 1561, which was several
times reprinted.

THRASILINE. Faith, no great matter to speak of ; a foolish twinkling with the eye, that spoils her coat ;[1] but he must be a cunning herald that finds it.   38

DION. See how they muster one another ! Oh, there's a rank regiment where the devil carries the colours and his dam [is] drum-major ! now the world and the flesh come behind with the carriage.[2]   43

CLEREMONT. Sure this lady has a good turn done her against her will ; before she was common talk, now none dare say cantharides can stir her. Her face looks like a warrant, willing and commanding all tongues, as they will answer it, to be tied up and bolted when this lady means to let herself loose. As I live, she has got her a goodly protection and a gracious ; and may use her body discreetly for her health's sake, once a week, excepting Lent and dog-days. Oh, if they were to be got for money, what a large sum would come out of the city for these licences !   55

KING. To horse, to horse ! we lose the morning, gentlemen.   [Exeunt.

SCENE II.—A Forest.
Enter two Woodmen.

FIRST WOODMAN. What, have you lodged the deer ?

SECOND WOODMAN. Yes, they are ready for the bow.

FIRST WOODMAN. Who shoots ?

SECOND WOODMAN. The princess.

FIRST WOODMAN. No, she'll hunt.

SECOND WOODMAN. She'll take a stand, I say.

FIRST WOODMAN. Who else ?

SECOND WOODMAN. Why, the young stranger-prince.   11

---

[1] Alluding to mullets, or stars, introduced into coats-of-arms to distinguish the younger branches of a family.—*Mason.*   [2] Baggage.

FIRST WOODMAN.   He shall shoot in a stone-bow [1]
for me.   I never loved his beyond-sea-ship since
he forsook the say,[2] for paying ten shillings.   He
was there at the fall of a deer, and would needs
(out of his mightiness) give ten groats for the
dowcets ;   marry,   his steward would have the
velvet-head [3] into the bargain, to turf [4] his hat
withal.   I think he should love venery [5] ;   he is an
old Sir Tristram ;   for, if you be remembered, he
forsook the stag once to strike a rascal milking in
a meadow, and her he killed in the eye.   Who
shoots else ?   23
SECOND WOODMAN.   The Lady Galatea.
FIRST WOODMAN.   That's a good wench, an she
would not chide us for tumbling of her women in
the brakes.   She's liberal, and, by the gods, they
say she's honest ;   and whether that be a fault,
I have nothing to do.   There's all ?   29
SECOND WOODMAN.   No, one more ;   Megra.
FIRST WOODMAN.   That's a firker [6] i' faith, boy ;
there's a wench will ride her haunches as hard after
a kennel of hounds as a hunting saddle, and when
she comes home, get 'em clapt, and all is well
again.   I have known her lose herself three times
in one afternoon (if the woods have been answerable), and it has been work enough for one man
to find her, and he has sweat for it.   She rides
well and she pays well.   Hark ! let's go.   [Exeunt.

Enter PHILASTER.

PHILASTER.   Oh, that I had been nourished in
            these woods   40
With milk of goats and acorns, and not known
The right of crowns nor the dissembling trains

---

[1] A cross-bow for shooting stones.   Such sport would be
contemptible to a forester.
[2] Cutting open the deer to see how fat he was.   For = for
fear of.
[3] The pile on a hart's horns when they first shoot forth.
[4] Re-cover.   [5] With a play on the word.   [6] Frisker.

Of women's looks ; but digged myself a cave,
Where I, my fire, my cattle, and my bed,
Might have been shut together in one shed ;
And then had taken me some mountain-girl,
Beaten with winds, chaste as the hardened rocks
Whereon she dwelt, that might have strewed my
    bed   48
With leaves and reeds, and with the skins of beasts,
Our neighbours, and have borne at her big breasts
My large coarse issue ! This had been a life
Free from vexation.   [Steps aside.

Enter BELLARIO.

BELLARIO.   Oh, wicked men !
An innocent may walk safe among beasts ;
Nothing assaults me here. See, my grieved lord
Sits as his soul were searching out a way
To leave his body !—Pardon me, that must
Break thy last commandment ; for I must speak :
You that are grieved can pity ; hear, my lord !
    PHILASTER.   Is there a creature yet so miserable,
That I can pity ?
    BELLARIO.   Oh, my noble lord,   60
View my strange fortune, and bestow on me,
According to your bounty (if my service
Can merit nothing), so much as may serve
To keep that little piece I hold of life
From cold and hunger !
    PHILASTER.   Is it thou ? be gone !
Go, sell those misbeseeming clothes thou wear'st,
And feed thyself with them.
    BELLARIO.   Alas, my lord, I can get nothing for
    them !
The silly country-people think 'tis treason
To touch such gay things.
    PHILASTER.   Now, by the gods, this is
Unkindly done, to vex me with thy sight.   71
Thou'rt fallen again to thy dissembling trade :
How shouldst thou think to cozen me again ?
Remains there yet a plague untried for me ?

Even so thou wept'st, and looked'st, and spok'st
When first I took thee up :
Curse on the time ! If thy commanding tears
Can work on any other, use thy art ;
I'll not betray it. Which way wilt thou take,
That I may shun thee ? for thine eyes are poison
To mine, and I am loath to grow in rage :   81
This way, or that way ?

    BELLARIO. Any will serve ; but I will choose
to have
That path in chase that leads unto my grave.

                          [Exeunt severally.

Enter on one side DION, and on the other the two
        Woodmen.

    DION. This is the strangest sudden chance !
You, woodman !

    FIRST WOODMAN. My Lord Dion ?

    DION. Saw you a lady come this way on a
sable horse studded with stars of white ?

    SECOND WOODMAN. Was she not young and tall ?

    DION. Yes. Rode she to the wood or to the
plain ?   91

    SECOND WOODMAN. Faith, my lord, we saw
none.   [Exeunt Woodmen.

    DION. Pox of your questions then !

Enter CLEREMONT.

What, is she found ?

    CLEREMONT. Nor will be, I think.

    DION. Let him seek his daughter himself. She
cannot stray about a little necessary natural
business, but the whole court must be in arms :
when she has done, we shall have peace.   100

    CLEREMONT. There's already a thousand father-
less tales amongst us. Some say, her horse ran
away with her ; some, a wolf pursued her ; others,
it was a plot to kill her, and that armed men were
seen in the wood : but questionless she rode away
willingly.

Enter KING, THRASILINE, and Attendants.

KING.   Where is she ?

CLEREMONT.   Sir, I cannot tell.

KING.   How's that ?
Answer me so again !

CLEREMONT.   Sir, shall I lie ?

KING.   Yes, lie and damn, rather than tell me
    that.
I say again, where is she ? Mutter not !—   110
Sir, speak you ; where is she ?

DION.   Sir, I do not know.

KING.   Speak that again so boldly, and, by
    Heaven,
It is thy last !—You, fellows, answer me ;
Where is she ? Mark me, all ; I am your King :
I wish to see my daughter ; show her me ;
I do command you all, as you are subjects,
To show her me ! What ! am I not your King ?
If aye, then am I not to be obeyed ?

DION.   Yes, if you command things possible and
    honest.

KING.   Things possible and honest ! Hear me,
    thou,
                               120
Thou traitor, that dar'st confine thy King to things
Possible and honest ! show her me,
Or, let me perish, if I cover not
All Sicily with blood !

DION.   Faith, I cannot,
Unless you tell me where she is.

KING.   You have betrayed me ; you have let
    me lose
The jewel of my life. Go, bring her me,
And set her here before me : 'tis the King
Will have it so ; whose breath can still the winds,
Uncloud the sun, charm down the swelling sea,
And stop the floods of heaven. Speak, can it not ?

DION. No.

KING.   No ? cannot the breath of kings do
    this ?
                               132

DION. No ; nor smell sweet itself, if once the lungs
Be but corrupted.

KING.   Is it so ? Take heed !

DION. Sir, take you heed how you dare the powers
That must be just.

KING.   Alas ! what are we kings ?
Why do you gods place us above the rest,
To be served, flattered, and adored, till we
Believe we hold within our hands your thunder,
And when we come to try the power we have,
There 's not a leaf shakes at our threatenings ?
I have sinned, 'tis true, and here stand to be
        punished ;   142
Yet would not thus be punished : let me choose
My way, and lay it on !

DION. [Aside.] He articles with the gods. Would
somebody would draw bonds for the performance
of covenants betwixt them !

Enter PHARAMOND, GALATEA, and MEGRA.

KING. What, is she found ?

PHARAMOND.   No ; we have ta'en her horse ;
He galloped empty by. There 's some treason.
You, Galatea, rode with her into the wood ;   150
Why left you her ?

GALATEA.   She did command me.

KING. Command ! you should not.

GALATEA. 'Twould ill become my fortunes and
        my birth
To disobey the daughter of my King.

KING. You 're all cunning to obey us for our
        hurt ;
But I will have her.

PHARAMOND.   If I have her not,
By this hand, there shall be no more Sicily.

DION. [Aside.] What, will he carry it to Spain
        in 's pocket ?

PHARAMOND. I will not leave one man alive,
        but the King,
A cook, and a tailor.   160

DION. [Aside.] Yet you may do well to spare
your lady-bedfellow ; and her you may keep for
a spawner.

KING. [Aside.] I see
The injuries I have done must be revenged.

DION. Sir, this is not the way to find her out.

KING. Run all, disperse yourselves. The man
　　that finds her,
Or (if she be killed), the traitor, I'll make him great.

DION. [Aside.] I know some would give five
thousand pounds to find her. 　　　　　　　170

PHARAMOND. Come, let us seek.

KING. 　　　　　　　Each man a several way ;
Here I myself.

DION. 　　　　　Come, gentlemen, we here.

CLEREMONT. Lady, you must go search too.

MEGRA. I had rather be searched myself.

　　　　　　　　　　　　　　[Exeunt severally.

SCENE III.—Another part of the Forest.
　　　　　Enter ARETHUSA.

ARETHUSA. Where am I now ? Feet, find me
　　out a way,
Without the counsel of my troubled head :
I'll follow you boldly about these woods,
O'er mountains, thorough brambles, pits, and
　　floods.
Heaven, I hope, will ease me : I am sick.

　　　　　　　　　　　　　　　[Sits down.

　　　　　　Enter BELLARIO.

BELLARIO. Yonder's my lady. Heaven knows
　　I want
Nothing, because I do not wish to live ;
Yet I will try her charity.—Oh hear, 　　　　8
You that have plenty ! from that flowing store
Drop some on dry ground.—See, the lively red
Is gone to guard her heart ! I fear she faints.—
Madam ! look up !—She breathes not.—Open
　　once more

Those rosy twins, and send unto my lord
Your latest farewell !—Oh, she stirs.—How is it,
Madam ? speak comfort.

ARETHUSA. 'Tis not gently done,
To put me in a miserable life,
And hold me there : I prithee, let me go ;
I shall do best without thee ; I am well.

Enter PHILASTER.

PHILASTER. I am to blame to be so much in
     rage :
I'll tell her coolly when and where I heard   20
This killing truth. I will be temperate
In speaking, and as just in hearing.——
Oh, monstrous ! Tempt me not, ye gods ! good
     gods,
Tempt not a frail man ! What 's he, that has
     a heart,
But he must ease it here !

BELLARIO. My lord, help, help !
The princess !

ARETHUSA. I am well : forbear.

PHILASTER. [Aside.] Let me love lightning, let
     me be embraced
And kissed by scorpions, or adore the eyes
Of basilisks, rather than trust the tongues   29
Of hell-bred women ! Some good god look down,
And shrink these veins up ; stick me here a stone,
Lasting to ages in the memory
Of this damned act !—Hear me, you wicked ones !
You have put hills of fire into this breast,
Not to be quenched with tears ; for which may
     guilt
Sit on your bosoms ! at your meals and beds
Despair await you ! What, before my face ?
Poison of asps between your lips ! diseases
Be your best issues ! Nature make a curse,   39
And throw it on you !

ARETHUSA. Dear Philaster, leave
To be enraged, and hear me.

PHILASTER.　　　　　　　　　　I have done ;
Forgive my passion.　Not the calmèd sea,
When Aeolus locks up his windy brood,
Is less disturbed than I :　I'll make you know it.
Dear Arethusa, do but take this sword,
　　　　　　　　　　[Offers his drawn sword.
And search how temperate a heart I have ;
Then you and this your boy may live and reign
In lust without control.　Wilt thou, Bellario ?
I prithee kill me ;　thou art poor, and may'st
Nourish ambitious thoughts ;　when I am dead,
Thy way were freer.　Am I raging now ?　　　51
If I were mad, I should desire to live.
Sirs,[1] feel my pulse, whether you have known
A man in a more equal tune to die.
　　BELLARIO.　Alas, my lord, your pulse keeps
　　　madman's time !
So does your tongue.
　　PHILASTER.　　　　　You will not kill me, then ?
　　ARETHUSA.　Kill you !
　　BELLARIO.　　　　　Not for the world !
　　PHILASTER.　　　　　　　　I blame not thee,
Bellario :　thou hast done but that which gods
Would have transformed themselves to do.　Be
　　gone,
Leave me without reply ;　this is the last　　　60
Of all our meetings—[Exit BELLARIO.]　Kill me with
　　this sword ;
Be wise, or worse will follow :　we are two
Earth cannot bear at once.　Resolve to do,
Or suffer.
　　ARETHUSA.　If my fortune be so good to let me
　　　fall
Upon thy hand, I shall have peace in death.
Yet tell me this, will there be no slanders,
No jealousy in the other world ?　no ill there ?
　　PHILASTER.　　　　　　　　　　　　No.
　　ARETHUSA.　Show me, then, the way.
　　　[1] ' Sir ' was a term of address to females as well as to men.—
Weber.

PHILASTER. Then guide my feeble hand,
You that have power to do it, for I must 70
Perform a piece of justice !—If your youth
Have any way offended Heaven, let prayers
Short and effectual reconcile you to it.

ARETHUSA. I am prepared.

Enter a Country Fellow.

COUNTRY FELLOW. I'll see the King, if he be in
the forest ; I have hunted him these two hours ;
if I should come home and not see him, my sisters
would laugh at me. I can see nothing but people
better horsed than myself, that out-ride me ; I can
hear nothing but shouting. These kings had need
of good brains ; this whooping is able to put a
mean man out of his wits. There's a courtier with
his sword drawn ; by this hand, upon a woman,
I think ! 84

PHILASTER. Are you at peace ?

ARETHUSA. With heaven and earth.

PHILASTER. May they
Divide thy soul and body ! [Wounds her.

COUNTRY FELLOW. Hold, dastard ! strike a
woman ! Thou 'rt a craven, I warrant thee : thou
wouldst be loth to play half a dozen venies [1] at
wasters [2] with a good fellow for a broken head.

PHILASTER. Leave us, good friend. 91

ARETHUSA. What ill-bred man art thou, to
intrude thyself
Upon our private sports, our recreations ?

COUNTRY FELLOW. God 'uds me, I understand
you not ; but I know the rogue has hurt you.

PHILASTER. Pursue thy own affairs : it will be ill
To multiply blood upon my head ; which thou
Wilt force me to.

COUNTRY FELLOW. I know not your rhetoric ;
but I can lay it on, if you touch the woman. 100

PHILASTER. Slave, take what thou deservest !
[They fight.

---

[1] Venues—i.e. bouts. [2] Wooden swords.

ARETHUSA.   Heaven guard my lord !
COUNTRY FELLOW.   Oh, do you breathe ?
PHILASTER.   [Aside.]   I hear the tread of people.
    I am hurt :
The gods take part against me : could this boor
Have held me thus else ? I must shift for life,
Though I do loathe it. I would find a course
To lose it rather by my will than force.   [Exit.
COUNTRY FELLOW.   I cannot follow the rogue.
I pray thee, wench, come and kiss me now.   109

Enter PHARAMOND, DION, CLEREMONT, THRASILINE,
            and Woodmen.

PHARAMOND.   What art thou ?
COUNTRY FELLOW.   Almost killed I am for a
foolish woman ; a knave has hurt her.
PHARAMOND.   The   princess,   gentlemen !—
    Where 's the wound, madam !
Is it dangerous ?
ARETHUSA.   He has not hurt me.
COUNTRY FELLOW.   By God, she lies ; h'as hurt
her in the breast ; look else.
PHARAMOND.   O, sacred spring of innocent
    blood !
DION.   'Tis above wonder ! who should dare
this ?
ARETHUSA.   I felt it not.   120
PHARAMOND.   Speak, villain, who has hurt the
    princess ?
COUNTRY FELLOW.   Is it the princess ?
DION.   Aye.
COUNTRY FELLOW.   Then I have seen something
yet.
PHARAMOND.   But who has hurt her ?
COUNTRY FELLOW.   I told you, a rogue ; I ne'er
saw him before, I.
PHARAMOND.   Madam, who did it ?
ARETHUSA.   Some dishonest wretch ;
Alas, I know him not, and do forgive him !   130
COUNTRY FELLOW.   He's hurt too ; he cannot

go far ; I made my father's old fox [1] fly about his
ears.

PHARAMOND. How will you have me kill him ?

ARETHUSA. Not at all ;
'Tis some distracted fellow.

PHARAMOND. By this hand,
I'll leave ne'er a piece of him bigger than a nut,
And bring him all to you in my hat.

ARETHUSA. Nay, good sir,
If you do take him, bring him quick [2] to me,
And I will study for a punishment
Great as his fault. 140

PHARAMOND. I will.

ARETHUSA. But swear.

PHARAMOND. By all my love, I will.—
Woodmen, conduct the princess to the King,
And bear that wounded fellow to [his] dressing.—
Come, gentlemen, we'll follow the chase close.

[Exeunt on one side PHARAMOND, DION, CLEREMONT,
and THRASILINE ; exit on the other ARETHUSA
attended by the First Woodman.

COUNTRY FELLOW. I pray you, friend, let me
see the King.

SECOND WOODMAN. That you shall, and receive
thanks.

COUNTRY FELLOW. If I get clear of this, I'll go
see no more gay sights. [Exeunt.

SCENE IV.—Another part of the Forest.

Enter BELLARIO.

BELLARIO. A heaviness near death sits on my
brow,
And I must sleep. Bear me, thou gentle bank,
For ever, if thou wilt. You sweet ones all,

[Lies down.
Let me unworthy press you : I could wish
I rather were a corse strewed o'er with you
Than quick above you. Dullness shuts mine eyes

---

[1] Broadsword.   [2] Alive.

And I am giddy : oh, that I could take
So sound a sleep that I might never wake !

[Sleeps.

Enter PHILASTER.

PHILASTER.   I have done ill ; my conscience calls
    me false,
To strike at her that would not strike at me.   10
When I did fight, methought I heard her pray
The gods to guard me. She may be abused,
And I a loathèd villain : if she be,
She will conceal who hurt her. He has wounds
And cannot follow ; neither knows he me.
Who 's this ? Bellario sleeping ! If thou be'st
Guilty, there is no justice that thy sleep
Should be so sound, and mine, whom thou hast
    wronged,   [Cry within.
So broken. Hark ! I am pursued. You gods
I'll take this offered means of my escape :   20
They have no mark to know me but my blood,
If she be true ; if false, let mischief light
On all the world at once ! Sword, print my wounds
Upon this sleeping boy ! I have none, I think,
Are mortal, nor would I lay greater on thee.

[Wounds BELLARIO.

BELLARIO.   Oh, death, I hope, is come ! Blest
    be that hand !
It meant me well. Again, for pity's sake !
PHILASTER.   I have caught myself ;   [Falls.
The loss of blood hath stayed my flight. Here,
    here,   29
Is he that struck thee : take thy full revenge ;
Use me, as I did mean thee, worse than death ;
I'll teach thee to revenge. This luckless hand
Wounded the princess ; tell my followers [1]
Thou didst receive these hurts in staying me,
And I will second thee ; get a reward.
BELLARIO.   Fly, fly, my lord, and save yourself !
PHILASTER.   How 's this ?
Wouldst thou I should be safe ?

       [1] Pursuers.

BELLARIO.   Else were it vain
For me to live. These little wounds I have
Have not bled much : reach me that noble hand ;
I'll help to cover you.

PHILASTER.   Art thou true to me ?

BELLARIO. Or let me perish loathed ! Come,
    my good lord,   41
Creep in amongst those bushes : who does know
But that the gods may save your much-loved
    breath ?

PHILASTER.   Then I shall die for grief, if not for
    this,
That I have wounded thee. What wilt thou do ?

BELLARIO. Shift for myself well. Peace ! I
    hear 'em come.   [PHILASTER creeps into a bush.

[Voices within.] Follow, follow, follow ! that way
    they went.

BELLARIO. With my own wounds I'll bloody
    my own sword.
I need not counterfeit to fall ; Heaven knows
That I can stand no longer.   [Falls.

Enter PHARAMOND, DION, CLEREMONT, and
                THRASILINE.

PHARAMOND. To this place we have tracked
    him by his blood.   51

CLEREMONT. Yonder, my lord, creeps one away.

DION. Stay, sir ! what are you ?

BELLARIO. A wretched creature, wounded in
    these woods
By beasts : relieve me, if your names be men,
Or I shall perish.

DION.   This is he, my lord,
Upon my soul, that hurt her ; 'tis the boy,
That wicked boy, that served her.

PHARAMOND.   Oh, thou damned
In thy creation ! what cause couldst thou shape
To hurt the princess ?

BELLARIO.   Then I am betrayed.   60

DION. Betrayed ! no, apprehended.

BELLARIO.   I confess,
(Urge it no more) that, big with evil thoughts,
I set upon her, and did make my aim
Her death. For charity let fall at once
The punishment you mean, and do not load
This weary flesh with tortures.

PHARAMOND.   I will know
Who hired thee to this deed.

BELLARIO.   Mine own revenge.

PHARAMOND.   Revenge ! for what ?

BELLARIO.   It pleased her to receive
Me as her page, and, when my fortunes ebbed,
That men strid o'er them careless, she did shower
Her welcome graces on me, and did swell   71
My fortunes till they overflowed their banks,
Threatening the men that crossed 'em ; when, as so
        swift
As storms arise at sea, she turned her eyes
To burning suns upon me, and did dry
The streams she had bestowed, leaving me worse
And more contemned than other little brooks,
Because I had been great. In short, I knew
I could not live, and therefore did desire
To die revenged.

PHARAMOND.   If tortures can be found   80
Long as thy natural life, resolve to feel
The utmost rigour.

CLEREMONT.   Help to lead him hence.

[PHILASTER creeps out of the bush.

PHILASTER.   Turn back, you ravishers of inno-
        cence !
Know ye the price of that you bear away
So rudely ?

PHARAMOND.   Who 's that ?

DION.   'Tis the Lord Philaster.

PHILASTER.   'Tis not the treasure of all kings in
        one,
The wealth of Tagus, nor the rocks of pearl
That pave the court of Neptune, can weigh down
That virtue. It was I that hurt the princess.

Place me, some god, upon a pyramis   90
Higher than hills of earth, and lend a voice
Loud as your thunder to me, that from thence
I may discourse to all the under-world
The worth that dwells in him !

> PHARAMOND.   How 's this ?

> BELLARIO.   My lord, some man weary of life,
That would be glad to die.

> PHILASTER.   Leave these untimely courtesies,
> Bellario.

> BELLARIO.   Alas, he 's mad ! Come, will you
> lead me on ?

> PHILASTER.   By all the oaths that men ought
> most to keep,

And gods do punish most when men do break,
He touched her not.—Take heed, Bellario,   101
How thou dost drown the virtues thou hast shown
With perjury.—By all the gods, 'twas I !
You know she stood betwixt me and my right.

> PHARAMOND.   Thy own tongue be thy judge !

> CLEREMONT.   It was Philaster.

> DION.   Is 't not a brave boy ?

Well, sirs, I fear me we were all deceived.

> PHILASTER.   Have I no friend here ?

> DION.   Yes.

> PHILASTER.   Then show it : some
Good body lend a hand to draw us nearer.
Would you have tears shed for you when you
die ?   110
Then lay me gently on his neck, that there
I may weep floods and breathe forth my spirit.
'Tis not the wealth of Plutus, nor the gold

> [Embraces BELLARIO.

Locked in the heart of earth, can buy away
This armful from me : this had been a ransom
To have redeemed the great Augustus Caesar.
Had he been taken. You hard-hearted men,
More stony than these mountains, can you see
Such clear pure blood drop, and not cut your flesh
To stop his life ? to bind whose bitter wounds,

Queens ought to tear their hair, and with their
 tears   121
Bathe 'em.—Forgive me, thou that art the wealth
Of poor Philaster !

Enter KING, ARETHUSA, and Guard.

KING.   Is the villain ta'en ?

PHARAMOND.   Sir, here be two confess the deed,
 but say
It was Philaster.

PHILASTER.   Question it no more ;
It was.

KING.   The fellow that did fight with him,
Will tell us that.

ARETHUSA.   Ay me ! I know he will.

KING.   Did not you know him ?

ARETHUSA.   Sir, if it was he,
He was disguised.

PHILASTER.   [Aside.]   I was so. Oh, my stars,
That I should live still.

KING.   Thou ambitious fool,
Thou that hast laid a train for thy own life !—
Now I do mean to do, I'll leave to talk.   132
Bear them to prison.

ARETHUSA.   Sir, they did plot together to take
 hence
This harmless life ; should it pass unrevenged,
I should to earth go weeping : grant me, then,
By all the love a father bears his child,
Their custodies, and that I may appoint
Their tortures and their deaths.

DION.   Death ! Soft ; our law
Will not reach that for this fault.   140

KING.   'Tis granted ; take 'em to you with a
 guard.—
Come, princely Pharamond, this business past,
We may with more security go on
To your intended match.

[Exeunt all except DION, CLEREMONT,
and THRASILINE.

CLEREMONT. I pray that this action lose not
Philaster the hearts of the people.

DION. Fear it not ; their over-wise heads will
think it but a trick. [Exeunt.

ACT THE FIFTH

SCENE I.—Before the Palace.

Enter DION, CLEREMONT, and THRASILINE.

THRASILINE. Has the King sent for him to death ?

DION. Yes ; but the King must know 'tis not
in his power to war with Heaven.

CLEREMONT. We linger time ; the King sent
for Philaster and the headsman an hour ago.

THRASILINE. Are all his wounds well ?

DION. All ; they were but scratches ; but the
loss of blood made him faint.

CLEREMONT. We dally, gentlemen.

THRASILINE. Away !   10

DION. We'll scuffle hard before he perish.
[Exeunt.

SCENE II.—A Prison.

Enter PHILASTER, ARETHUSA, and BELLARIO.

ARETHUSA. Nay, faith, Philaster, grieve not ;
we are well.

BELLARIO. Nay, good my lord, forbear ; we are
wondrous well.

PHILASTER. Oh, Arethusa, oh, Bellario,
Leave to be kind !
I shall be shut [1] from Heaven, as now from earth,
If you continue so. I am a man
False to a pair of the most trusty ones
That ever earth bore : can it bear us all ?
Forgive, and leave me. But the King hath sent
To call me to my death : oh, show it me,   10
And then forget me ! and for thee, my boy,

[1] So the 1620 quarto ; the others have ' shot '.

I shall deliver words will mollify
The hearts of beasts to spare thy innocence.
    BELLARIO.   Alas, my lord, my life is not a thing
Worthy your noble thoughts ! 'tis not a life,
'Tis but a piece of childhood thrown away.
Should I outlive you, I should then outlive
Virtue and honour ; and when that day comes,
If ever I shall close these eyes but once,
May I live spotted for my perjury,   20
And waste by limbs to nothing !
    ARETHUSA.   And I (the woeful'st maid that ever
      was,
Forced with my hands to bring my lord to death)
Do by the honour of a virgin swear
To tell no hours beyond it !
    PHILASTER.   Make me not hated so.
    ARETHUSA.   Come from this prison all joyful to
      our deaths !
    PHILASTER.   People will tear me, when they find
      you true
To such a wretch as I ; I shall die loathed.
Enjoy your kingdoms peaceably, whilst I   30
For ever sleep forgotten with my faults :
Every just servant,[1] every maid in love,
Will have a piece of me, if you be true.
    ARETHUSA.   My dear lord, say not so.
    BELLARIO.   A piece of you !
He was not born of woman that can cut
It and look on.
    PHILASTER.   Take me in tears betwixt you, for
      my heart
Will break with shame and sorrow.
    ARETHUSA.   Why, 'tis well.
    BELLARIO.   Lament no more.
    PHILASTER.   Why, what would you have done
If you had wronged me basely, and had found
Your life no price compared to mine ? for love, sirs,
Deal with me truly.
    BELLARIO.   'Twas mistaken, sir.   42
        [1] Wooer.

PHILASTER.   Why, if it were ?
BELLARIO.   Then, sir, we would have asked
You pardon.
PHILASTER.   And have hope to enjoy it ?
ARETHUSA.   Enjoy it ! aye.
PHILASTER.   Would you indeed ? be plain.
BELLARIO.   We would, my lord.
PHILASTER.   Forgive me, then.
ARETHUSA.   So, so.
BELLARIO.   'Tis as it should be now.
PHILASTER.   Lead to my death.   [Exeunt.

SCENE III.—A State-room in the Palace.

Enter KING, DION, CLEREMONT, THRASILINE, and
Attendants.

KING.   Gentlemen, who saw the prince ?
CLEREMONT.   So please you, sir, he 's gone to
    see the city
And the new platform,[1] with some gentlemen
Attending on him.
KING.   Is the princess ready
To bring her prisoner out ?
THRASILINE.   She waits your grace.
KING.   Tell her we stay.   [Exit THRASILINE.
DION.   [Aside.] King, you may be deceived yet :
The head you aim at cost more setting on
Than to be lost so lightly.   If it must off ;
Like a wild overflow, that swoops before him   9
A golden stack, and with it shakes down bridges,
Cracks the strong hearts of pines, whose cable-roots
Held out a thousand storms, a thousand thunders;
And, so made mightier, takes whole villages
Upon his back, and in that heat of pride
Charges strong towns, towers, castles, palaces,
And lays them desolate ; so shall thy head,
Thy noble head, bury the lives of thousands,
That must bleed with thee like a sacrifice,
In thy red ruins.

----

[1] A terrace on a wall or building.

Enter ARETHUSA, PHILASTER, BELLARIO in a robe and
garland, and THRASILINE.

KING.   How now ? what masque is this ?
BELLARIO.   Right royal sir, I should   20
Sing you an epithalamium of these lovers,
But having lost my best airs with my fortunes,
And wanting a celestial harp to strike
This blessèd union on, thus in glad story
I give you all. These two fair cedar-branches
The noblest of the mountain where they grew,
Straightest and tallest, under whose still shades
The worthier beasts have made their lairs, and
    slept
Free from the fervour of the Sirian star   29
And the fell thunder-stroke, free from the clouds,
When they were big with humour, and delivered
In thousand spouts their issues to the earth ;
Oh, there was none but silent quiet there !
Till never-pleasèd Fortune shot up shrubs,
Base under-brambles, to divorce these branches ;
And for a while they did so, and did reign
Over the mountain, and choke up his beauty
With brakes, rude thorns and thistles, till the sun
Scorched them even to the roots and dried them
    there :
And now a gentle gale hath blown again,   40
That made these branches meet and twine together,
Never to be unarm'd.[1] The god that sings
His holy numbers over marriage-beds
Hath knit their noble hearts ; and here they stand
Your children, mighty King : and I have done.
KING. How, how ?
ARETHUSA.   Sir, if you love it in plain truth
(For now there is no masquing in 't), this gentle-
    man,
The prisoner that you gave me, is become
My keeper, and through all the bitter throes

---

[1] So the 1620 quarto ; the others have ' divided ', with
the same sense.

Your jealousies and his ill fate have wrought him,
Thus nobly hath he struggled, and at length   51
Arrived here my dear husband.

  KING.   Your dear husband !—
Call in the Captain of the Citadel.—
There you shall keep your wedding. I'll provide
A masque shall make your Hymen turn his saffron
Into a sullen coat, and sing sad requiems
To your departing souls ;
Blood shall put out your torches ; and, instead
Of gaudy flowers about your wanton necks,
An axe shall hang like a prodigious meteor,   60
Ready to crop your loves' sweets. Hear, you gods !
From this time do I shake all title off
Of father to this woman, this base woman ;
And what there is of vengeance in a lion
Chafed ¹ among dogs or robbed of his dear young,
The same, enforced more terrible, more mighty,
Expect from me !

  ARETHUSA. Sir, by that little life I have left to
  swear by,
There's nothing that can stir me from myself.
What I have done, I have done without repentance,
For death can be no bugbear unto me,   71
So long as Pharamond is not my headsman.

  DION. [Aside.] Sweet peace upon thy soul, thou
  worthy maid,
Whene'er thou diest ! For this time I'll excuse
 thee,
Or be thy prologue.

  PHILASTER.   Sir, let me speak next ;
And let my dying words be better with you
Than my dull living actions. If you aim
At the dear life of this sweet innocent,
You are a tyrant and a savage monster,
That feeds upon the blood you gave a life to ;   80
Your memory shall be as foul behind you,
As you are living ; all your better deeds

  ¹ So the first quarto ; the others have ' Chast ' ; the
1679 folio has ' Cast '

Shall be in water writ, but this in marble ;
No chronicle shall speak you, though your own,
But for the shame of men.　No monument,
Though high and big as Pelion, shall be able
To cover this base murder ? make it rich
With brass, with purest gold and shining jasper,
Like the Pyramids ; lay on epitaphs
Such as make great men gods ; my little marble
That only clothes my ashes, not my faults,　　91
Shall far outshine it.　And for after-issues,
Think not so madly of the heavenly wisdoms,
That they will give you more for your mad rage
To cut off, unless it be some snake, or something
Like yourself, that in his birth shall strangle you.
Remember my father, King ! there was a fault,
But I forgive it : let that sin persuade you
To love this lady ; if you have a soul,
Think, save her, and be savèd.　For myself,　　100
I have so long expected this glad hour,
So languished under you, and daily withered,
That, by the gods, it is a joy to die ;
I find a recreation in 't.

Enter a Gentleman.

GENTLEMAN.　Where is the King ?
KING.　　　　　　　Here.
GENTLEMAN.　　　　　Get you to your strength,
And rescue the Prince Pharamond from danger ;
He 's taken prisoner by the citizens,
Fearing [1] the Lord Philaster.
DION.　　　　　　[Aside.]　Oh, brave fellows [2] !
Mutiny, my fine dear countrymen, mutiny !　　109
Now, my brave valiant foremen, show your weapons
In honour of your mistresses !

Enter a Second Gentleman.

SECOND GENTLEMAN.　Arm, arm, arm, arm !
KING.　　　　　　　A thousand devils take 'em !

---

[1] i.e. Fearing for.
[2] So the first quarto ; the others have ' followers '.

DION. [Aside.]   A thousand blessings on 'em !

SECOND GENTLEMAN.   Arm, O King ! The city
    is in mutiny,
Led by an old grey ruffian, who comes on
In rescue of the Lord Philaster.

KING.   Away to the citadel ! I'll see them safe,
And then cope with these burghers. Let the guard
And all the gentlemen give strong attendance.
    [Exeunt all except DION, CLEREMONT, and THRASILINE.

CLEREMONT.   The city up ! this was above our
    wishes.   120

DION.   Aye, and the marriage too. By my life,
This noble lady has deceived us all.
A plague upon myself, a thousand plagues,
For having such unworthy thoughts of her dear
    honour !
Oh, I could beat myself ! or do you beat me,
And I'll beat you ; for we had all one thought.

CLEREMONT.   No, no, 'twill but lose time.

DION.   You say true. Are your swords sharp ?
—Well, my dear countrymen What-[d']-ye-lacks,[1] if
you continue, and fall not back upon the first
broken shin, I'll have you chronicled and chronicled,
and cut [2] and chronicled, and all-to bepraised and
sung in sonnets, and bawled in new brave ballads,
that all tongues shall troul you in saecula saecu-
lorum, my kind can-carriers.   135

THRASILINE.   What, if a toy [3] take 'em i' the
heels now, and they run all away, and cry, ' the
devil take the hindmost ' ?

DION.   Then the same devil take the foremost
too, and souse him for his breakfast ! If they all
prove cowards, my curses fly amongst them, and
be speeding ! May they have murrains reign to
keep the gentlemen at home unbound in easy
frieze ! may the moths branch [4] their velvets, and
their silks only be worn before sore eyes ! may

---

[1] i. e. shopkeepers ; from their usual address to the
passers-by.

[2] Engraved.   [3] Whim.   [4] Embroider.

their false lights undo 'em, and discover presses,[1] holes, stains, and oldness in their stuffs, and make them shop-rid [2] ! may they keep whores and horses, and break [3] ; and live mewed up with necks of beef and turnips ! may they have many children, and none like the father ! may they know no language but that gibberish they prattle to their parcels, unless it be the goatish Latin they write in their bonds—and may they write that false, and lose their debts !   155

Re-enter KING.

KING.   Now the vengeance of all the gods confound them ! How they swarm together ! what a hum they raise !—Devils choke your wild throats ! If a man had need to use their valours, he must pay a brokage for it, and then bring 'em on, and they will fight like sheep. 'Tis Philaster, none but Philaster, must allay this heat : they will not hear me speak, but fling dirt at me and call me tyrant. Oh, run, dear friend, and bring the Lord Philaster ! speak him fair ; call him prince ; do him all the courtesy you can ; commend me to him. Oh, my wits, my wits !   [*Exit* CLEREMONT.

DION.   [*Aside.*]   Oh, my brave countrymen ! as I live, I will not buy a pin out of your walls[4] for this ; nay, you shall cozen me, and I'll thank you, and send you brawn and bacon, and soil you every long vacation a brace of foremen,[5] that at Michaelmas shall come up fat and kicking.   173

KING.   What they will do with this poor prince, the gods know, and I fear.

DION.   Why, sir, they'll flay him, and make church-buckets on 's skin, to quench rebellion ; then clap a rivet in 's sconce, and hang him up for a sign.

---

[1] Creases.   [2] Shop-soiled.   [3] Become bankrupt.
[4] i.e. anywhere else than in your shops.
[5] i.e. fatten a couple of geese on green food.

Enter PHILASTER and CLEREMONT.

KING.   Oh, worthy sir, forgive me ! do not make
Your miseries and my faults meet together,   181
To bring a greater danger. Be yourself,
Still sound amongst diseases. I have wronged you ;
And though I find it last, and beaten to it,
Let first your goodness know it. Calm the people,
And be what you were born to : take your love,
And with her my repentance, all my wishes
And all my prayers. By the gods, my heart speaks
    this ;
And if the least fall from me not performed,
May I be struck with thunder !

PHILASTER.   Mighty sir,   190
I will not do your greatness so much wrong,
As not to make your word truth. Free the
    princess
And the poor boy, and let me stand the shock
Of this mad sea-breach, which I'll either turn,
Or perish with it.

KING.   Let your own word free them.

PHILASTER.   Then thus I take my leave, kissing
    your hand,
And hanging on your royal word. Be kingly,
And be not moved, sir : I shall bring you peace
Or never bring myself back.

KING.   All the gods   199
Go with thee.   [Exeunt.

SCENE IV.—A Street.

Enter an old Captain and Citizens with PHARAMOND
prisoner.

CAPTAIN.   Come, my brave myrmidons, let us
    fall on !
Let your caps swarm, my boys, and your nimble
    tongues
Forget your mother-gibberish of ' What do you
    lack,'
And set your mouths ope, children, till your palates

Fall frighted half a fathom past the cure
Of bay-salt and gross pepper, and then cry
' Philaster, brave Philaster ! ' Let Philaster
Be deeper in request, my ding-a-dings,
My pairs of dear indentures, kings of clubs,[1]   9
Than your cold water-camlets,[2] or your paintings
Spitted with copper. Let not your hasty silks,
Or your branched cloth of bodkin, or your tissues,
Dearly belovèd of spiced cake and custard,
Your Robin Hoods, Scarlets, and Johns, tie your
     affections
In durance[3] to your shops. No, dainty duckers,[4]
Up with your three-piled[5] spirits, your wrought
     valours[6] ;
And let your uncut cholers make the King feel
The measure of your mightiness. Philaster !
Cry, my rose-nobles, cry !

   ALL.   Philaster ! Philaster !   20

   CAPTAIN.   How do you like this, my lord-
     prisoner[7] ?

These are mad boys, I tell you ; these are things
That will not strike their top-sails to a foist,[8]
And let a man-of-war, an argosy,
Hull and cry cockles.[9]

   PHARAMOND.   Why, you rude slave, do you
     know what you do ?

   CAPTAIN.   My pretty prince of puppets, we do
     know ;

And give your greatness warning that you talk
No more such bug's-words,[10] or that soldered
     crown

---

[1] Clubs were formerly the favourite weapons of the London
shopkeepers and apprentices.
  [2] A fabric with a watered surface.
  [3] So the first quarto ; the others have ' darkness '.
  [4] Cringers, bowers.
  [5] ' Three-pile ' was velvet of the finest quality.
  [6] Velures, velvet.
  [7] So only in the first quarto ; the others have ' Prince '.
  [8] A barge.   [9] Float idly and be hanged.
 [10] Swaggering words.

Shall be scratched with a musket. Dear prince
    Pippin,   30
Down with your noble blood, or, as I live,
I'll have you coddled.[1]—Let him loose, my spirits :
Make us a round ring with your bills,[2] my Hectors,
And let us see what this trim man dares do.
Now, sir, have at you ! here I lie ;
And with this swashing blow (do you see, sweet
    prince ?)
I could hock your grace, and hang you up cross-
    legged,
Like a hare at a poulter's, and do this with this
    wiper.[3]

    PHARAMOND. You will not see me murdered,
    wicked villains ?

    FIRST CITIZEN. Yes, indeed, will we, sir ; we
    have not seen one   40
For a great while.

    CAPTAIN.   He would have weapons, would he ?
Give him a broadside, my brave boys, with your
    pikes ;
Branch me his skin in flowers like a satin,
And between every flower a mortal cut.—
Your royalty shall ravel !—Jag him, gentlemen ;
I'll have him cut to the kell,[4] then down the seams.
Oh, for a whip to make him galloon-laces !
I'll have a coach-whip.

    PHARAMOND.   Oh, spare me, gentlemen !
    CAPTAIN. Hold, hold ;
The man begins to fear and know himself ;   50
He shall for this time only be seeled up,[5]
With a feather through his nose, that he may only
See heaven, and think whither he is going.
Nay, my beyond-sea sir, we will proclaim you :
You would be king !
Thou tender heir-apparent to a church-ale,[6]

---

    [1] Boiled.   [2] Pikes or halberds.   [3] Cloth.
    [4] Or caul, the membrane enclosing the intestines.
    [5] Have his eyes stitched up, as was done with a hawk to
tame it.   [6] A parochial merry-making.

Thou slight prince of single sarcenet,
Thou royal ring-tail, fit to fly at nothing
But poor men's poultry, and have every boy
Beat thee from that too with his bread and butter !

PHARAMOND. Gods keep me from these hell-
hounds !   61

FIRST CITIZEN. Shall 's geld him, captain ?

CAPTAIN. No, you shall spare his dowcets, my
dear donsels [1];

As you respect the ladies, let them flourish :
The curses of a longing woman kill
As speedy as a plague, boys.

FIRST CITIZEN. I'll have a leg, that 's certain.

SECOND CITIZEN.   I'll have an arm.

THIRD CITIZEN. I'll have his nose, and at mine
own charge build

A college and clap 't upon the gate.[2]

FOURTH CITIZEN. I'll have his little gut to
string a kit [3] with :   70

For certainly a royal gut will sound like silver.

PHARAMOND. Would they were in thy belly, and
I past

My pain once !

FIFTH CITIZEN. Good captain, let me have his
liver to feed ferrets.

CAPTAIN. Who will have parcels else ? speak.

PHARAMOND. Good gods, consider me ! I shall
be tortured.

FIRST CITIZEN. Captain, I'll give you the trim-
ming of your two-hand sword,   77

And let me have his skin to make false scabbards.

SECOND CITIZEN. He had no horns, sir, had he ?

CAPTAIN.   No, sir, he 's a pollard :

What wouldst thou do with horns ?

SECOND CITIZEN.   Oh, if he had had,
I would have made rare hafts and whistles of 'em ;
But his shin-bones, if they be sound, shall serve me.

[1] Youths.
[2] In allusion to Brazenose College, Oxford, founded 1509.
[3] A small fiddle.

Enter PHILASTER.

ALL. Long live Philaster, the brave Prince
  Philaster !

PHILASTER. I thank you, gentlemen. But why
  are these
Rude weapons brought abroad, to teach your
  hands
Uncivil trades ?

CAPTAIN.   My royal Rosicleer,[1]
We are thy myrmidons, thy guard, thy roarers ;
And when thy noble body is in durance,
Thus do we clap our musty murrions [2] on,
And trace the streets in terror. Is it peace,   90
Thou Mars of men ? is the King sociable,
And bids thee live ? art thou above thy foemen,
And free as Phoebus ? speak. If not, this stand
Of royal blood shall be abroach, a-tilt,
And run even to the lees of honour.

PHILASTER. Hold, and be satisfied : I am
  myself
Free as my thoughts are : by the gods, I am !

CAPTAIN. Art thou the dainty darling of the
  King ?
Art thou the Hylas to our Hercules ?
Do the lords bow, and the regarded scarlets [3]   100
Kiss their gummed golls,[4] and cry ' We are your
  servants ' ?
Is the court navigable, and the presence stuck
With flags of friendship ? If not, we are thy castle,
And this man sleeps.

PHILASTER. I am what I desire to be, your
  friend ;
I am what I was born to be, your prince.

PHARAMOND. Sir, there is some humanity in you ;
You have a noble soul : forget my name,

---

[1] The hero of a Spanish romance, translated into English
as *The Mirrour of Knighthood.*
[2] Morions.
[3] The men in uniform whom you notice.
[4] Scented hands.

And know my misery : set me safe aboard
From these wild cannibals, and, as I live,　　　110
I'll quit this land for ever.　There is nothing,—
Perpetual prisonment, cold, hunger, sickness
Of all sorts, of all dangers, and all together,
The worst company of the worst men, madness, age,
To be as many creatures as a woman,
And do as all they do, nay, to despair,—
But I would rather make it a new nature,
And live with all those, than endure one hour
Amongst these wild dogs.

 PHILASTER.　I do pity you.—Friends, discharge
  your fears ;
Deliver me the prince : I'll warrant you　　　120
I shall be old enough to find my safety.

 THIRD CITIZEN.　Good sir, take heed he does not
  hurt you ;
He is a fierce man, I can tell you, sir.

 CAPTAIN.　Prince, by your leave, I'll have a
  surcingle,
And make [1] you like a hawk.

 PHILASTER.　Away, away, there is no danger in
  him :
Alas, he had rather sleep to shake his fit off !
Look you, friends, how gently he leads ! Upon my
  word,
He's tame enough, he needs no further watching.
Good my friends, go to your houses,　　　131
And by me have your pardons and my love ;
And know there shall be nothing in my power
You may deserve, but you shall have your wishes :
To give you more thanks, were to flatter you.
Continue still your love ; and, for an earnest,
Drink this.　　　　　　　　　　　[Gives money.

 ALL.　Long mayst thou live, brave prince, brave
  prince, brave prince !

     [Exeunt PHILASTER and PHARAMOND.

 CAPTAIN.　Go thy ways, thou art the king of
  courtesy !

     [1] Train.

Fall off again, my sweet youths. Come,   140
And every man trace to his house again,
And hang his pewter up ; then to the tavern,
And bring your wives in muffs. We will have
    music ;
And the red grape shall make us dance and rise,
    boys.   [Exeunt.

Scene V.—A Room in the Palace.

Enter King, Arethusa, Galatea, Megra, Dion, Cleremont, Thrasiline, Bellario, *and Attendants.*

KING.   Is it appeased ?
DION.   Sir, all is quiet as this dead of night,
As peaceable as sleep. My lord Philaster
Brings on the prince himself.
KING.   Kind gentleman !
I will not break the least word I have given
In promise to him : I have heaped a world
Of grief upon his head, which yet I hope
To wash away.

Enter Philaster *and* Pharamond.

CLEREMONT.   My lord is come.
KING.   My son !
Blest be the time that I have leave to call
Such virtue mine ! Now thou art in mine arms,
Methinks I have a salve unto my breast   11
For all the stings that dwell there. Streams of
    grief
That I have wronged [1] thee, and as much of joy
That I repent it, issue from mine eyes :
Let them appease thee. Take thy right ; take her ;
She is thy right too ; and forget to urge
My vexèd soul with that I did before.
PHILASTER.   Sir, it is blotted from my memory,
Past and forgotten.—For you, prince of Spain,
Whom I have thus redeemed, you have full leave
To make an honourable voyage home.   21

    [1] All the quartos have ' wrought '.

And if you would go furnished to your realm
With fair provision, I do see a lady,
Methinks, would gladly bear you company :
How like you this piece ?

MEGRA.   Sir, he likes it well,
For he hath tried it, and hath found it worth
His princely liking. We were ta'en a-bed ;
I know your meaning. I am not the first
That nature taught to seek a fellow forth ;
Can shame remain perpetually in me,   30
And not in others ? or have princes salves
To cure ill names, that meaner people want ?

PHILASTER. What mean you ?

MEGRA.   You must get another ship,
To bear the princess and her boy together.

DION. How now !

MEGRA. Others took me, and I took her and
him
At that all women may be ta'en some time :
Ship us all four, my lord ; we can endure
Weather and wind alike.

KING. Clear thou thyself, or know not me for
father.   40

ARETHUSA. This earth, how false it is ! What
means is left for me
To clear myself ? It lies in your belief :
My lords, believe me ; and let all things else
Struggle together to dishonour me.

BELLARIO. Oh, stop your ears, great King, that
I may speak
As freedom would ! then I will call this lady
As base as are her actions : hear me, sir ;
Believe your heated blood when it rebels
Against your reason, sooner than this lady.

MEGRA. By this good light, he bears it hand-
somely.   50

PHILASTER. This lady ! I will sooner trust the
wind
With feathers, or the troubled sea with pearl,
Than her with any thing. Believe her not.

Why, think you, if I did believe her words,
I would outlive 'em ?   Honour cannot take
Revenge on you ;   then what were to be known
But death ?
    KING.   Forget her, sir, since all is knit
Between us.   But I must request of you
One favour, and will sadly be denied.   59
    PHILASTER.   Command, whate'er it be.
    KING.   Swear to be true
To what you promise.
    PHILASTER.   By the powers above,
Let it not be the death of her or him,
And it is granted !
    KING.   Bear away that boy
To torture :   I will have her cleared or buried.
    PHILASTER.   Oh, let me call my word back,
        worthy sir !
Ask something else :   bury my life and right
In one poor grave ;   but do not take away
My life and fame at once.
    KING.   Away with him !   It stands irrevocable.
    PHILASTER.   Turn all your eyes on me :   here
        stands a man,   70
The falsest and the basest of this world.
Set swords against this breast, some honest man,
For I have lived till I am pitied !
My former deeds were hateful ;   but this last
Is pitiful, for I unwillingly
Have given the dear preserver of my life
Unto his torture.   Is it in the power
Of flesh and blood to carry this, and live ?
                 [Offers to stab himself.
    ARETHUSA.   Dear sir, be patient yet !   Oh, stay
        that hand !   79
    KING.   Sirs, strip that boy.
    DION.   Come, sir ;   your tender flesh
Will try your constancy.
    BELLARIO.   Oh, kill me, gentlemen !
    DION.   No.—Help, sirs.
    BELLARIO.   Will you torture me ?

KING.   Haste there ;
Why stay you ?
BELLARIO.   Then I shall not break my vow,
You know, just gods, though I discover all.
KING.   How's that ? will he confess ?
DION.   Sir, so he says.
KING.   Speak then.
BELLARIO.   Great King, if you command
This lord to talk with me alone, my tongue,
Urged by my heart, shall utter all the thoughts
My youth hath known ; and stranger things than
      these
You hear not often.
KING.   Walk aside with him.   90
                [DION and BELLARIO walk apart.
DION.   Why speak'st thou not ?
BELLARIO.   Know you this face, my lord ?
DION.   No.
BELLARIO.   Have you not seen it, nor the like ?
DION.   Yes, I have seen the like, but readily
I know not where.
BELLARIO.   I have been often told
In court of one Euphrasia, a lady,
And daughter to you ; betwixt whom and me
They that would flatter my bad face would swear
There was such strange resemblance, that we two
Could not be known asunder, drest alike.   99
DION.   By Heaven, and so there is !
BELLARIO.   For her fair sake,
Who now doth spend the spring-time of her life
In holy pilgrimage, move to the King,
That I may scape this torture.
DION.   But thou speak'st
As like Euphrasia as thou dost look.
How came it to thy knowledge that she lives
In pilgrimage ?
BELLARIO.   I know it not, my lord ;
But I have heard it, and do scarce believe it.
DION.   Oh, my shame ! is it possible ? Draw
      near,

That I may gaze upon thee. Art thou she,   109
Or else her murderer ? [1] where wert thou born ?

BELLARIO.   In Syracusa.

DION.   What's thy name ?

BELLARIO.   Euphrasia.

DION.   Oh, 'tis just, 'tis she !
Now I do know thee. Oh, that thou hadst died,
And I had never seen thee nor my shame !
How shall I own thee ? shall this tongue of mine
E'er call thee daughter more ?

BELLARIO.   Would I had died indeed ! I wish it
    too :
And so I must have done by vow, ere published
What I have told, but that there was no means
To hide it longer. Yet I joy in this,   120
The princess is all clear.

KING.   What, have you done ?

DION.   All is discovered.

PHILASTER.   Why then hold you me ?
                          [Offers to stab himself.
All is discovered ! Pray you, let me go.

KING.   Stay him.

ARETHUSA.   What is discovered ?

DION.   Why, my shame.
It is a woman : let her speak the rest.

PHILASTER.   How ? that again !

DION.   It is a woman.

PHILASTER.   Blessed be you powers that favour
    innocence !

KING.   Lay hold upon that lady.   [MEGRA is seized.

PHILASTER.   It is a woman, sir !—Hark, gentle-
    men,
It is a woman !—Arethusa, take   130
My soul into thy breast, that would be gone
With joy. It is a woman ! Thou art fair,
And virtuous still to ages, in despite
Of malice.

[1] It was the received opinion in some barbarous countries
that the murderer inherited the qualities and shape of his
victim.—*Mason*.

KING. Speak you, where lies his shame ?

BELLARIO. I am his daughter.

PHILASTER. The gods are just.

DION. I dare accuse none ; but, before you two,
The virtue of our age, I bend my knee
For mercy. [Kneels.

PHILASTER. [Raising him.] Take it freely ; for
    I know,
Though what thou didst were undiscreetly done,
'Twas meant well.

ARETHUSA. And for me, I have a power
To pardon sins, as oft as any man   141
Has power to wrong me.

CLEREMONT. Noble and worthy !

PHILASTER. But, Bellario
(For I must call thee still so), tell me why
Thou didst conceal thy sex. It was a fault,
A fault, Bellario, though thy other deeds
Of truth outweighed it : all these jealousies
Had flown to nothing, if thou hadst discovered
What now we know.

BELLARIO. My father oft would speak
Your worth and virtue ; and, as I did grow   150
More and more apprehensive,[1] I did thirst
To see the man so raised.[2] But yet all this
Was but a maiden-longing, to be lost
As soon as found ; till, sitting in my window,
Printing my thoughts in lawn, I saw a god,
I thought (but it was you), enter our gates :
My blood flew out and back again, as fast
As I had puffed it forth and sucked it in
Like breath : then was I called away in haste
To entertain you. Never was a man,   160
Heaved from a sheep-cote to a sceptre, raised
So high in thoughts as I : you left a kiss
Upon these lips then, which I mean to keep
From you for ever : I did hear you talk,
Far above singing. After you were gone,

  [1] Capable of understanding.
  [2] Extolled ; but Dyce suggests that a ' p ' has dropped out.

I grew acquainted with my heart, and searched
What stirred it so : alas, I found it love !
Yet far from lust ; for, could I but have lived
In presence of you, I had had my end.
For this I did delude my noble father   170
With a feigned pilgrimage, and dressed myself
In habit of a boy ; and, for I knew
My birth no match for you, I was past hope
Of having you ; and, understanding well
That when I made discovery of my sex
I could not stay with you, I made a vow,
By all the most religious things a maid
Could call together, never to be known,
Whilst there was hope to hide me from men's eyes,
For other than I seemed, that I might ever   180
Abide with you. Then sat I by the fount,
Where first you took me up.
    KING.   Search out a match
Within our kingdom, where and when thou wilt,
And I will pay thy dowry ; and thyself
Wilt well deserve him.
    BELLARIO.   Never, sir, will I
Marry ; it is a thing within my vow :
But, if I may have leave to serve the princess,
To see the virtues of her lord and her,
I shall have hope to live.
    ARETHUSA.   I, Philaster,
Cannot be jealous, though you had a lady   190
Drest like a page to serve you ; nor will I
Suspect her living here.—Come, live with me ,
Live free as I do. She that loves my lord,
Cursed be the wife that hates her !
    PHILASTER.   I grieve such virtue should be laid
      in earth
Without an heir.—Hear me, my royal father :
Wrong not the freedom of our souls so much,
To think to take revenge of that base woman ;
Her malice cannot hurt us. Set her free   199
As she was born, saving from shame and sin.
    KING.   Set her at liberty. But leave the court :

This is no place for such.—You, Pharamond,
Shall have free passage, and a conduct home
Worthy so great a prince.　When you come there,
Remember 'twas your faults that lost you her,
And not my purposed will.

PHARAMOND.　　　　　I do confess,
Renownèd sir.

KING.　Last, join your hands in one.　Enjoy,
　Philaster,
This kingdom, which is yours, and, after me,
Whatever I call mine.　My blessing on you !　　210
All happy hours be at your marriage-joys,
That you may grow yourselves over all lands,
And live to see your plenteous branches spring
Wherever there is sun !　Let princes learn
By this to rule the passions of their blood ;
For what Heaven wills can never be withstood.

　　　　　　　　　　　　　　[Exeunt,

THE DUCHESS OF MALFI

John Webster
(?1580–1625)

The Duchess of Malfi was certainly put on the stage before 1614, but it was not printed till 1623. This edition, says Dyce, 'is by far the most correct of the quartos', but many of its mistakes are corrected in the second quarto of 1640. The library at Harvard, according to Professor Sampson, possesses a quarto edition which he assigns to 1660. Later quartos appeared in 1678 and 1708, the latter adding considerably to the stage directions, which in earlier editions were very scanty. Dyce in his admirable edition of Webster (1830; second edition, 1857) first assigned localities to the various scenes. The play was edited by J. A. Symonds in the Mermaid series (1888), by Professor Vaughan in the Temple Classics (1896), and by Professor M. W. Sampson in 1904; the last edition is the fullest and most valuable, the editor having collated all the early quartos with the exception of the one at Harvard.

The chief difficulty in editing the play arises from the irregularity of a good deal of Webster's verse and his occasional use of metric prose. It is as true as ever it was that 'tout ce qui n'est point prose est vers; et tout ce qui n'est point vers est prose'; but the reader of *The Duchess of Malfi* has no easy task to determine which is which. By judicious stressing and slurring and the admission of fragmentary lines almost any of the prose in the play can be read as verse. The early quartos afford no help, as the prose passages are cut up in lengths and each line begins with a capital letter as though it were verse. After much hesitation I have

decided to treat as prose any lines which did not seem
to scan of themselves, rather than to torture them into
a metric guise. This can easily be done by any one on
a second or third reading, but the result can never be
musical, and unless the stresses are marked by accents—
a hideous confession of metric inefficiency—the reader
is sure not to get the beat of the line right at the first
attempt, and in straining to find the metre he is apt to
lose the meaning. In the matter of line-division I have
in places been compelled to differ from previous editors ;
but the question is one of such nicety of ear and depends
so much on the intonation of the voice, that I should
not be surprised if subsequent editors found themselves
compelled to differ from me. The early quartos are in
this respect hopelessly inaccurate.

THE
TRAGEDY
OF THE DVTCHESSE
Of Malfy.

*As it was Presented priuatly, at the Black-
Friers; and publiquely at the Globe, By the*
Kings Maiesties Seruants.

The perfect and exact Coppy, with diuerse
things Printed, that the length of the Play would
not beare in the Presentment.

VVritten by *John Webster.*

Hora.——— *Si quid*----
———*Candidus Imperti si non his vtere mecum.*

LONDON:

Printed by NICHOLAS OKES, for IOHN
WATERSON, and are to be sold at the
signe of the Crowne, in *Paules*
Church-yard, 1623.

DRAMATIS PERSONAE

FERDINAND, Duke of Calabria.
THE CARDINAL, his Brother.
ANTONIO BOLOGNA, Steward of the household to the Duchess.
DELIO, his Friend.
DANIEL DE BOSOLA, Gentleman of the horse to the Duchess.
CASTRUCHIO.[1]
MARQUIS OF PESCARA.
COUNT MALATESTE.
SILVIO, a Lord, of Milan } Gentlemen attending on the
RODERIGO. } Duchess.
GRISOLAN.
Doctor.
Several Madmen, Pilgrims, Executioners, Officers, Attendants, &c.

DUCHESS OF MALFI, sister of Ferdinand and the Cardinal.
CARIOLA, her Woman.
JULIA, Castruchio's Wife, and the Cardinal's Mistress.
Old Lady, Ladies and Children.

SCENE.—AMALFI, ROME, and MILAN.

[1] In Italian, Castruccio ; see note on p. 88.

ugly, gross images
up to classics p 420

THE DUCHESS OF MALFI

ACT THE FIRST

SCENE I.—Amalfi. The Presence-chamber in the Duchess's
Palace.

Enter ANTONIO *and* DELIO.

DELIO.   You are welcome to your country, dear
    Antonio ;
You have been long in France, and you return
A very formal Frenchman in your habit :
How do you like the French court ?
    ANTONIO.   I admire it :
In seeking to reduce both state and people
To a fix'd order, their judicious king
Begins at home ; quits [1] first his royal palace
Of flattering sycophants, of dissolute
And infamous persons,—which [2] he sweetly terms
His master's masterpiece, the work of Heaven ;
Considering duly that a prince's court   11
Is like a common fountain, whence should flow
Pure silver drops in general, but if 't chance
Some curs'd example poison 't near the head,
Death and diseases through the whole land spread.
And what is 't makes this blessed government
But a most provident council, who dare freely
Inform him the corruption of the times ?
Though some o' th' court hold it presumption
To instruct princes what they ought to do,   20
It is a noble duty to inform them
What they ought to foresee.—Here comes Bosola,

[1] Frees.
[2] i.e. which action ; but Professor Vaughan takes the
antecedent to be ' palace ', and Professor Sampson ' persons '.

The only court-gall ; yet I observe his railing
Is not for simple love of piety :
Indeed, he rails at those things which he wants ;
Would be as lecherous, covetous, or proud,
Bloody, or envious, as any man,
If he had means to be so.—Here's the Cardinal.

Enter the CARDINAL and BOSOLA.

BOSOLA. I do haunt you still.

CARDINAL. So. 30

BOSOLA. I have done you better service than to
be slighted thus. Miserable age, where only the
reward of doing well is the doing of it !

CARDINAL. You enforce your merit too much.

BOSOLA. I fell into the galleys in your service ;
where, for two years together, I wore two towels
instead of a shirt, with a knot on the shoulder,
after the fashion of a Roman mantle. Slighted
thus ? I will thrive some way : blackbirds fatten
best in hard weather ; why not I in these dog-
days ? [1] 41

CARDINAL. Would you could become honest !

BOSOLA. With all your divinity do but direct
me the way to it. I have known many travel far
for it, and yet return as arrant knaves as they
went forth, because they carried themselves always
along with them. [Exit Cardinal.] Are you gone ?
Some fellows, they say, are possessed with the
devil, but this great fellow were able to possess the
greatest devil, and make him worse. 50

ANTONIO. He hath denied thee some suit ?

BOSOLA. He and his brother are like plum-trees
that grow crooked over standing-pools ; they are
rich and o'er-laden with fruit, but none but crows,
pies, and caterpillars feed on them. Could I be one
of their flattering panders, I would hang on their
ears like a horseleech, till I were full, and then
drop off. I pray, leave me. Who would rely upon
these miserable dependencies, in expectation to be

[1] See note 3 on p. 140.

advanc'd to-morrow ?   what   creature ever fed
worse than hoping Tantalus ?   nor ever died any
man more fearfully than he that hop'd for a
pardon.   There are rewards for hawks and dogs
when they have done us service ; but for a soldier
that hazards his limbs in a battle, nothing but a
kind of geometry is his last supportation.   66

   DELIO.   Geometry ?

   BOSOLA.   Aye, to hang in a fair pair of slings,
take his latter swing in the world upon an honourable pair of crutches, from hospital to hospital.
Fare ye well, sir : and yet do not you scorn us ;
for places in the court are but like beds in the
hospital, where this man's head lies at that man's
foot, and so lower and lower.   [Exit.

   DELIO.   I knew this fellow seven years in the
      galleys
                                          75
For a notorious murder ; and 'twas thought
The Cardinal suborn'd it : he was releas'd
By the French general, Gaston de Foix,
When he recover'd Naples.

   ANTONIO.   'Tis great pity
He should be thus neglected : I have heard   80
He 's very valiant.   This foul melancholy
Will poison all his goodness ; for, I'll tell you,
If too immoderate sleep be truly said
To be an inward rust unto the soul,
It then doth follow want of action
Breeds all black malcontents ; and their close
      rearing,
Like moths in cloth, do hurt for want of wearing.

   DELIO.[1]   The presence 'gins to fill : you pro-
      mis'd me
To make me the partaker of the natures   89
Of some of your great courtiers.

   ANTONIO.   The lord Cardinal's,
And other strangers' that are now in court ?
I shall.—Here comes the great Calabrian duke.

   [1] The early quartos mark Scene ii as beginning here.

Enter FERDINAND, CASTRUCHIO, SILVIO, RODERIGO,
GRISOLAN, and Attendants.

FERDINAND. Who took the ring oftenest ? [1]

SILVIO. Antonio Bologna, my lord.

FERDINAND. Our sister duchess's great-master of
her household ? give him the jewel.—When shall
we leave this sportive action, and fall to action
indeed ?

CASTRUCHIO. Methinks, my lord, you should
not desire to go to war in person.   100

FERDINAND. Now for some gravity :—why, my
lord ?

CASTRUCHIO. It is fitting a soldier arise to be
a prince, but not necessary a prince descend to
be a captain.

FERDINAND. No ?

CASTRUCHIO. No, my lord ; he were far better
do it by a deputy.

FERDINAND. Why should he not as well sleep
or eat by a deputy ? this might take idle, offensive,
and base office from him, whereas the other
deprives him of honour.   112

CASTRUCHIO. Believe my experience, that realm
is never long in quiet where the ruler is a soldier.

FERDINAND. Thou told'st me thy wife could not
endure fighting.

CASTRUCHIO. True, my lord.

FERDINAND. And of a jest she broke of a captain
she met full of wounds : I have forgot it.

CASTRUCHIO. She told him, my lord, he was
a pitiful fellow, to lie, like the children of Ismael,
all in tents.[2]   122

FERDINAND. Why, there's a wit were able to
undo all the chirurgeons o' the city ; for although
gallants should quarrel, and had drawn their
weapons, and were ready to go to it, yet her
persuasions would make them put up.

[1] In tilting at the ring.

[2] In surgery, *tent* is a roll of lint or other material placed
in a wound.

CASTRUCHIO.   That she would, my lord.

FERDINAND.[1]   How do you like my Spanish gennet ?   130

RODERIGO.   He is all fire.

FERDINAND.   I am of Pliny's opinion, I think he was begot by the wind ; he runs as if he were ballass'd [2] with quicksilver.

SILVIO.   True, my lord, he reels from the tilt often.

RODERIGO AND GRISOLAN.   Ha, ha, ha !   137

FERDINAND.   Why do you laugh ? methinks you that are courtiers should be my touchwood, take fire when I give fire ; that is, laugh [but] when I laugh, were the subject never so witty.

CASTRUCHIO.   True, my lord : I myself have heard a very good jest, and have scorn'd to seem to have so silly a wit as to understand it.

FERDINAND.   But I can laugh at your fool, my lord.

CASTRUCHIO.   He cannot speak, you know, but he makes faces : my lady cannot abide him.

FERDINAND.   No ?   149

CASTRUCHIO.   Nor endure to be in merry company ; for she says too much laughing, and too much company, fills her too full of the wrinkle.

FERDINAND.   I would, then, have a mathematical instrument made for her face, that she might not laugh out of compass.—I shall shortly visit you at Milan, Lord Silvio.

SILVIO.   Your grace shall arrive most welcome.

FERDINAND.   You are a good horseman, Antonio : you have excellent riders in France : what do you think of good horsemanship ?   160

ANTONIO.   Nobly, my lord : as out of the Grecian horse issued many famous princes, so out of brave horsemanship arise the first sparks of growing resolution, that raise the mind to noble action.

[1] An emendation of Professor Sampson's ; all previous editions give the speech to Castruchio.

[2] Ballasted or freighted.

FERDINAND. You have bespoke it worthily.

SILVIO. Your brother, the lord Cardinal, and sister duchess.

Re-enter CARDINAL, with DUCHESS, CARIOLA, and JULIA.

CARDINAL. Are the galleys come about ?

GRISOLAN.   They are, my lord.

FERDINAND. Here 's the Lord Silvio is come to take his leave.

DELIO. [Aside to ANTONIO.] Now, sir, your promise ; what 's that Cardinal ?   170
I mean his temper ? they say he 's a brave fellow,
Will play his five thousand crowns at tennis, dance,
Court ladies, and one that hath fought single combats.

ANTONIO. Some such flashes superficially hang on him for form ; but observe his inward character : he is a melancholy churchman ; the spring in his face is nothing but the engendering of toads ; where he is jealous of any man, he lays worse plots for them than ever was impos'd on Hercules, for he strews in his way flatter[er]s, panders, intelligencers,[1] atheists, and a thousand such political monsters. He should have been Pope ; but instead of coming to it by the primitive decency of the Church, he did bestow bribes so largely and so impudently as if he would have carried it away without Heaven's knowledge. Some good he hath done——

DELIO. You have given too much of him. What 's his brother ?

ANTONIO. The duke there ? a most perverse and turbulent nature :
What appears in him mirth is merely outside ;
If he laughs heartily, it is to laugh   191
All honesty out of fashion.

DELIO.   Twins ?

ANTONIO.   In quality.
He speaks with others' tongues, and hears men's suits

───────────
[1] Informers.

With others' ears ; will seem to sleep o' th' bench
Only to entrap offenders in their answers ;
Dooms men to death by information ;
Rewards by hearsay.

DELIO.   Then the law to him
Is like a foul black cobweb to a spider,—
He makes [of] it his dwelling and a prison
To entangle those shall feed him.

ANTONIO.   Most true : 200
He never pays debts unless they be shrewd turns,
And those he will confess that he doth owe.
Last, for his brother there, the Cardinal,
They that do flatter him most say oracles
Hang at his lips ; and verily I believe them,
For the devil speaks in them.
But for their sister, the right noble duchess,
You never fixed your eye on three fair medals
Cast in one figure, of so different temper.
For her discourse, it is so full of rapture,   210
You only will begin then to be sorry
When she doth end her speech, and wish, in wonder,
She held it less vain-glory to talk much,
Than your penance to hear her : whilst she speaks,
She throws upon a man so sweet a look,
That it were able [to] [1] raise one to a galliard [2]
That lay in a dead palsy, and to dote
On that sweet countenance ; but in that look
There speaketh so divine a continence
As cuts off all lascivious and vain hope.   220
Her days are practis'd in such noble virtue,
That sure her nights, nay, more, her very sleeps,
Are more in heaven than other ladies' shrifts.
Let all sweet ladies break their flattering glasses,
And dress themselves in her.

DELIO.   Fie, Antonio,
You play the wire-drawer [3] with her commenda-
    tions.

----

[1] From the 1678 quarto.
[2] A lively dance in triple time.
[3] i.e. spin out at tedious length.

ANTONIO.   I'll case the picture up : only thus
 much ;
All her particular worth grows to this sum,—
She stains the time past, lights the time to come.
 CARIOLA. You must attend my lady in the gallery,
Some half an hour hence.
 ANTONIO.   I shall.   231
                    [Exeunt ANTONIO and DELIO.
 FERDINAND.   Sister, I have a suit to you.
 DUCHESS.   To me, sir ?
 FERDINAND.   A gentleman here, Daniel de
 Bosola,
One that was in the galleys—
 DUCHESS.   Yes, I know him.
 FERDINAND.   A worthy fellow he is : pray, let
 me entreat for
The provisorship of your horse.
 DUCHESS.   Your knowledge of him
Commends him and prefers him.
 FERDINAND.   Call him hither.
                         [Exit Attendant.
We [are] now upon parting. Good Lord Silvio,
Do us commend to all our noble friends   239
At the leaguer.
 SILVIO.   Sir, I shall.
 DUCHESS.[1]   You are for Milan ?
 SILVIO.   I am.
 DUCHESS.   Bring the caroches.[2] We'll bring
 you down
To the haven.   [Exeunt all but FERDINAND and the
                                        CARDINAL.
 CARDINAL.   Be sure you entertain [3] that Bosola
For your intelligence : I would not be seen in 't ;
And therefore many times I have slighted him
When he did court our furtherance, as this morning.
 FERDINAND.   Antonio, the great-master of her
 household,

 [1] Professor Sampson's correction for the ' Ferd.' of the
quartos.
 [2] Coaches.   [3] Make use of.

Had been far fitter.

CARDINAL.   You are deceiv'd in him :
His nature is too honest for such business.—
He comes : I'll leave you.   [Exit.

                Re-enter BOSOLA.

BOSOLA.   I was lur'd to you.
FERDINAND. My brother, here, the Cardinal
    could never   250
Abide you.
BOSOLA.   Never since he was in my debt.
FERDINAND. Maybe some oblique character in
    your face
Made him suspect you.
BOSOLA.   Doth he study physiognomy ?
There 's no more credit to be given to th' face
Than to a sick man's urine, which some call
The physician's whore because she cozens him.
He did suspect me wrongfully.
FERDINAND.   For that
You must give great men leave to take their times.
Distrust doth cause us seldom be deceiv'd :
You see the oft shaking of the cedar-tree   260
Fastens it more at root.
BOSOLA.   Yet, take heed ;
For to suspect a friend unworthily
Instructs him the next way to suspect you,
And prompts him to deceive you.
FERDINAND. [Giving him money.] There 's gold.
BOSOLA.   So :
What follows ? never rained such showers as these
Without thunderbolts i' th' tail of them : whose
    throat must I cut ?
FERDINAND. Your inclination to shed blood
    rides post
Before my occasion to use you. I give you that
To live i' th' court here, and observe the duchess ;
To note all the particulars of her haviour,   270
What suitors do solicit her for marriage,
And whom she best affects. She 's a young widow :

                                          o

I would not have her marry again.

    BOSOLA.   No, sir ?

    FERDINAND. Do not you ask the reason ; but
    be satisfied

I say I would not.

    BOSOLA.   It seems you would create me

One of your familiars.

    FERDINAND.   Familiar ? what 's that ?

    BOSOLA. Why, a very quaint invisible devil in
    flesh,

An intelligencer.

    FERDINAND.   Such a kind of thriving thing

I would wish thee ; and ere long thou may'st arrive

At a higher place by 't.

    BOSOLA.   Take your devils,   280

Which hell calls angels ; these curs'd gifts would
    make

You a corrupter, me an impudent traitor ;

And should I take these, they'd take me [to] hell.

    FERDINAND. Sir, I'll take nothing from you
    that I have given :

There is a place that I procur'd for you

This morning, the provisorship o' th' horse ;

Have you heard on 't ?

    BOSOLA.   No.

    FERDINAND. 'Tis yours : is 't not worth thanks ?

    BOSOLA. I would have you curse yourself now,
    that your bounty,

Which makes men truly noble, e'er should make
    me

A villain. Oh, that to avoid ingratitude   290

For the good deed you have done me, I must do

All the ill man can invent ! Thus the devil

Candies all sins o'er ; and what heaven terms vile,

That names he complimental.[1]

    FERDINAND.   Be yourself ;

Keep your old garb of melancholy ; 'twill express

You envy those that stand above your reach,

Yet strive not to come near 'em : this will gain

            [1] Required by courtesy.

Access to private lodgings, where yourself
May, like a politic dormouse—
 BOSOLA.   As I have seen some
Feed in a lord's dish, half asleep, not seeming 300
To listen to any talk ; and yet these rogues
Have cut his throat in a dream. What 's my place ?
The provisorship o' th' horse ? say, then, my
  corruption
Grew out of horse-dung : I am your creature.
 FERDINAND.   Away ! [Exit.
 BOSOLA. Let good men, for good deeds, covet
  good fame,
Since place and riches oft are bribes of shame :
Sometimes the devil doth preach.   [Exit.

   SCENE II.—A Gallery in the Duchess's Palace.

 Enter FERDINAND, DUCHESS, CARDINAL, and CARIOLA.

 CARDINAL. We are to part from you ; and your
  own discretion
Must now be your director.
 FERDINAND.   You are a widow :
You know already what man is ; and therefore
Let not youth, high promotion, eloquence—
 CARDINAL.   No,
Nor any thing without the addition, honour,
Sway your high blood.
 FERDINAND. Marry ! they are most luxurious [1]
Will wed twice.
 CARDINAL. Oh, fie !
 FERDINAND.   Their livers are more spotted
Than Laban's sheep.
 DUCHESS.   Diamonds are of most value,
They say, that have passed through most jewellers'
  hands.   9
 FERDINAND. Whores by that rule are precious.
 DUCHESS.   Will you hear me ?
I'll never marry.

     [1] Lascivious.

CARDINAL.   So most widows say ;
But commonly that motion lasts no longer
Than the turning of an hour-glass : the funeral
    sermon
And it end both together.
    FERDINAND.   Now hear me :
You live in a rank pasture, here, i' th' court ;
There is a kind of honey-dew that 's deadly ;
'Twill poison your fame ;   look to 't :   be not
    cunning ;
For they whose faces do belie their hearts
Are witches ere they arrive at twenty years,   19
Aye, and give the devil suck.
    DUCHESS.   This is terrible good counsel.
    FERDINAND.   Hypocrisy is woven of a fine small
        thread,
Subtler than Vulcan's engine : [1] yet, believe 't,
Your darkest actions, nay, your privat'st thoughts,
Will come to light.
    CARDINAL.   You may flatter yourself,
And take your own choice ;   privately be married
Under the eaves of night—
    FERDINAND.   Think 't the best voyage
That e'er you made ;   like the irregular crab,
Which, though 't goes backward, thinks that it
        goes right
Because it goes its own way ;   but observe,
Such weddings may more properly be said   30
To be executed than celebrated.
    CARDINAL.   The marriage night
Is the entrance into some prison.
    FERDINAND.   And those joys,
Those lustful pleasures, are like heavy sleeps
Which do forerun man's mischief.
    CARDINAL.   Fare you well.
Wisdom begins at the end : remember it.   [Exit.
    DUCHESS.   I think this speech between you both
        was studied,
It came so roundly off.

        [1] The net in which he caught Mars and Venus.

FERDINAND.   You are my sister;
This was my father's poniard, do you see?
I'd be loth to see 't look rusty, 'cause 'twas his.
I would have you to give o'er these chargeable
     revels:
A visor and a mask are whispering-rooms   41
That were never built for goodness;—fare ye
     well;—
And women like that part which, like the lamprey,
Hath never a bone in 't.
    DUCHESS.   Fie, sir!
    FERDINAND.   Nay,
I mean the tongue; variety of courtship:
What cannot a neat knave with a smooth tale
Make a woman believe? Farewell, lusty widow.
                                        [Exit.
    DUCHESS.   Shall this move me? If all my royal
          kindred
Lay in my way unto this marriage,   49
I'd make them my low footsteps: and even now,
Even in this hate, as men in some great battles,
By apprehending danger, have achiev'd
Almost impossible actions (I have heard soldiers
     say so),
So I through frights and threatenings will assay
This dangerous venture. Let old wives report
I wink'd and chose a husband.—Cariola,
To thy known secrecy I have given up
More than my life—my fame.
    CARIOLA.   Both shall be safe;
For I'll conceal this secret from the world
As warily as those that trade in poison   60
Keep poison from their children.
    DUCHESS.   Thy protestation
Is ingenious [1] and hearty: I believe it.
Is Antonio come?
    CARIOLA.   He attends you.
    DUCHESS.   Good dear soul.
Leave me; but place thyself behind the arras,
                    [1] Ingenuous.

Where thou mayst overhear us. Wish me good
          speed ;
For I am going into a wilderness
Where I shall find nor path nor friendly clue
To be my guide.   [CARIOLA goes behind the arras.

Enter ANTONIO.
                    I sent for you : sit down ;
Take pen and ink, and write : are you ready ?
          ANTONIO.   Yes.
          DUCHESS.   What did I say ?   70
          ANTONIO.   That I should write somewhat.
          DUCHESS.   Oh, I remember.
After these triumphs and this large expense,
It 's fit, like thrifty husbands, we inquire
What 's laid up for to-morrow.
          ANTONIO.   So please your beauteous excellence.
          DUCHESS.   Beauteous ?
Indeed, I thank you : I look young for your
          sake ;
You have ta'en my cares upon you.
          ANTONIO.   I'll fetch your grace
The particulars of your revenue and expense.
          DUCHESS.   Oh, you are an upright treasurer :
          but you mistook ;
For when I said I meant to make inquiry   80
What 's laid up for to-morrow, I did mean
What 's laid up yonder for me.
          ANTONIO.   Where ?
          DUCHESS.   In heaven.
I am making my will (as 'tis fit princes should,
In perfect memory), and, I pray, sir, tell me,
Were not one better make it smiling, thus,
Than in deep groans and terrible ghastly looks,
As if the gifts we parted with procur'd
That violent distraction ? [1]
          ANTONIO.   Oh, much better.
          DUCHESS.   If I had a husband now, this care
          were quit :

          [1] Destruction, in the first two quartos.

But I intend to make you overseer.   90
What good deed shall we first remember ? say.

ANTONIO.   Begin with that first good deed began
    i' th' world
After man's creation, the sacrament of marriage :
I'd have you first provide for a good husband ;
Give him all.

DUCHESS.   All ?

ANTONIO.   Yes, your excellent self.

DUCHESS.   In a winding-sheet ?

ANTONIO.   In a couple.

DUCHESS.   Saint Winfred,
That were a strange will !

ANTONIO.   'Twere strange[r] if there were no
    will in you
To marry again.

DUCHESS.   What do you think of marriage ?

ANTONIO. I take 't, as those that deny purgatory ;
It locally contains or Heaven or hell ;   101
There 's no third place in 't.

DUCHESS.   How do you affect it ?

ANTONIO.   My banishment, feeding my melan-
    choly,
Would often reason thus.

DUCHESS.   Pray, let 's hear it.

ANTONIO.   Say a man never marry, nor have
    children,
What takes that from him ? only the bare name
Of being a father, or the weak delight
To see the little wanton ride a-cock-horse
Upon a painted stick, or hear him chatter   109
Like a taught starling.

DUCHESS.   Fie, fie, what 's all this ?
One of your eyes is blood-shot ; use my ring to 't,
They say 'tis very sovereign : 'twas my wedding-
    ring,
And I did vow never to part with it
But to my second husband.

ANTONIO.   You have parted with it now.

DUCHESS.   Yes, to help your eyesight.

ANTONIO.   You have made me stark blind.
DUCHESS.   How?
ANTONIO.   There is a saucy and ambitious devil
Is dancing in this circle.
DUCHESS.   Remove him.
ANTONIO.   How?
DUCHESS.   There needs small conjuration, when
    your finger
May do it : thus ; is it fit ?
            [She puts the ring upon his finger : he kneels.
ANTONIO.   What said you ?
DUCHESS.   Sir,
This goodly roof of yours is too low built ;   120
I cannot stand upright in 't nor discourse,
Without I raise it higher : raise yourself ;
Or, if you please, my hand to help you : so.
                        [Raises him.
ANTONIO.   Ambition, madam, is a great man's
    madness,
That is not kept in chains and close-pent rooms,
But in fair lightsome lodgings, and is girt
With the wild noise of prattling visitants,
Which makes it lunatic beyond all cure.
Conceive not I am so stupid but I aim [1]   129
Whereto your favours tend : but he 's a fool
That, being a-cold, would thrust his hands i' th'
    fire
To warm them.
DUCHESS.   So, now the ground's broke,
You may discover what a wealthy mine
I make you lord of.
ANTONIO.   O my unworthiness !
DUCHESS.   You were ill to sell yourself :
This darkening of your worth is not like that
Which tradesmen use i' th' city ; their false lights
Are to rid bad wares off : and I must tell you,
If you will know where breathes a complete man
(I speak it without flattery), turn your eyes,   140
And progress through yourself.
                    [1] Guess

ANTONIO.   Were there nor heaven
Nor hell, I should be honest : I have long serv'd
    virtue,
And ne'er ta'en wages of her.
DUCHESS.   Now she pays it.
The misery of us that are born great !
We are forc'd to woo, because none dare woo us ;
And as a tyrant doubles with his words,
And fearfully equivocates, so we
Are forc'd to express our violent passions
In riddles and in dreams, and leave the path
Of simple virtue, which was never made   150
To seem the thing it is not. Go, go brag
You have left me heartless ; mine is in your
    bosom :
I hope 'twill multiply love there. You do tremble :
Make not your heart so dead a piece of flesh,
To fear more than to love me. Sir, be confident :
What is 't distracts you ? This is flesh and blood,
    sir ;
'Tis not the figure cut in alabaster
Kneels at my husband's tomb. Awake, awake,
    man !
I do here put off all vain ceremony,
And only do appear to you a young widow   160
That claims you for her husband, and, like a
    widow,
I use but half a blush in 't.
ANTONIO.   Truth speak for me ;
I will remain the constant sanctuary
Of your good name.
DUCHESS.   I thank you, gentle love :
And 'cause you shall not come to me in debt,
Being now my steward, here upon your lips
I sign your Quietus est.[1] This you should have
    begg'd now :
I have seen children oft eat sweetmeats thus,
As fearful to devour them too soon.   169
    ANTONIO. But for your brothers ?
                ¹ Acquittance.

DUCHESS. Do not think of them :
All discord without this circumference
Is only to be pitied, and not fear'd :
Yet, should they know it, time will easily
Scatter the tempest.

ANTONIO. These words should be mine,
And all the parts you have spoke, if some part of it
Would not have savour'd flattery.

DUCHESS. Kneel.

[CARIOLA comes from behind the arras.

ANTONIO. Ha !

DUCHESS. Be not amazed ; this woman 's of my
counsel :
I have heard lawyers say, a contract in a chamber
Per verba [de] presenti is absolute marriage.

[She and ANTONIO kneel.

Bless, heaven, this sacred gordian, which let
violence [1]   180
Never untwine !

ANTONIO. And may our sweet affections, like
the spheres,
Be still in motion !

DUCHESS. Quickening, and make
The like soft music !

ANTONIO. That we may imitate the loving palms,
Best emblem of a peaceful marriage, that ne'er
Bore fruit, divided !

DUCHESS. What can the Church force more ?

ANTONIO. That fortune may not know an
accident,
Either of joy or sorrow, to divide   189
Our fixèd wishes !

DUCHESS. How can the Church build faster ?
We now are man and wife, and 'tis the Church
That must but echo this.—Maid, stand apart :
I now am blind.

ANTONIO. What 's your conceit in this ?

DUCHESS. I would have you lead your fortune
by the hand

[1] The arrangement of these lines is very questionable.

Unto your marriage bed :
(You speak in me this, for we now are one :)
We'll only lie, and talk together, and plot
To appease my humorous kindred ; and if you
please,
Like the old tale in ' Alexander and Lodowick ',[1]
Lay a naked sword between us, keep us chaste.
Oh, let me shroud my blushes in your bosom,   201
Since 'tis the treasury of all my secrets !

      [*Exeunt* DUCHESS and ANTONIO.

 CARIOLA.   Whether the spirit of greatness or of
  woman
Reign most in her, I know not ; but it shows
A fearful madness : I owe her much of pity. [*Exit.*

ACT THE SECOND

SCENE I.—A Room in the Palace of the DUCHESS.

Enter BOSOLA and CASTRUCHIO.

 BOSOLA.   You say you would fain be taken for
an eminent courtier ?

 CASTRUCHIO.   'Tis the very main of my ambition.

 BOSOLA.   Let me see : you have a reasonable
good face for 't already, and your nightcap ex-
presses your ears sufficient largely. I would have
you learn to twirl the strings of your band with
a good grace, and in a set speech, at th' end of
every sentence, to hum three or four times, or blow
your nose till it smart again, to recover your
memory. When you come to be a president in
criminal causes, if you smile upon a prisoner, hang
him, but if you frown upon him and threaten
him, let him be sure to scape the gallows.   15

 CASTRUCHIO.   I would be a very merry president.

[1] *The Two Faithful Friends, the pleasant History of
Alexander and Lodwicke,* is reprinted from the Pepys collection
in Evans's *Old Ballads.—Dyce*

BOSOLA.   Do not sup o' nights ; 'twill beget you an admirable wit.

CASTRUCHIO.   Rather it would make me have a good stomach to quarrel ; for they say, your roaring boys eat meat seldom, and that makes them so valiant.   But how shall I know whether the people take me for an eminent fellow ?   23

BOSOLA.   I will teach a trick to know it : give out you lie a-dying, and if you hear the common people curse you, be sure you are taken for one of the prime nightcaps.[1]

Enter an Old Lady.

You come from painting now.

OLD LADY.   From what ?   29

BOSOLA.   Why, from your scurvy face-physic. To behold thee not painted inclines somewhat near a miracle ; these in thy face here were deep ruts and foul sloughs the last progress.[2]   There was a lady in France that, having had the small-pox, flayed the skin off her face to make it more level ; and whereas before she look'd like a nutmeg-grater, after she resembled an abortive hedgehog.

OLD LADY.   Do you call this painting ?

BOSOLA.   No, no, but you call [it] careening of an old morphewed[3] lady, to make her disembogue[4] again : there's rough-cast phrase to your plastic.[5]

OLD LADY.   It seems you are well acquainted with my closet.   43

BOSOLA.   One would suspect it for a shop of witchcraft, to find in it the fat of serpents, spawn of snakes, Jews' spittle, and their young children's ordure ; and all these for the face.   I would sooner eat a dead pigeon taken from the soles of the feet of one sick of the plague than kiss one of you fasting.   Here are two of you, whose sin of your youth is the very patrimony of the physician ; makes him renew his foot-cloth with the spring, and

---

[1] A cant name for the Mohocks of the time.
[2] State procession.   [3] Leprous.   [4] Discharge herself.
[5] i. e. plain language instead of your fine phrases.

change his high-priced courtezan with the fall of
the leaf.   I do wonder you do not loathe your-
selves.   Observe my meditation now.
What thing is in this outward form of man
To be belov'd ?   We account it ominous,
If nature do produce a colt, or lamb,
A fawn, or goat, in any limb resembling
A man, and fly from 't as a prodigy :   60
Man stands amaz'd to see his deformity
In any other creature but himself.
But in our own flesh, though we bear diseases
Which have their true names only ta'en from
        beasts,—
As the most ulcerous wolf and swinish measle,[1]—
Though we are eaten up of lice and worms,
And though continually we bear about us
A rotten and dead body, we delight
To hide it in rich tissue : all our fear,   70
Nay, all our terror, is lest our physician
Should put us in the ground to be made sweet.—
Your wife 's gone to Rome : you two couple, and
        get you
To the wells at Lucca to recover your aches.
I have other work on foot.
                        [Exeunt CASTRUCHIO and Old Lady.
                    I observe our duchess
Is sick a-days, she pukes, her stomach seethes,
The fins of her eye-lids look most teeming blue,
She wanes i' th' cheek, and waxes fat i' th' flank,
And, contrary to our Italian fashion,
Wears a loose-bodied gown : there 's somewhat in 't.
I have a trick may chance discover it,   81
A pretty one ; I have brought some apricocks,
The first our spring yields.

    Enter ANTONIO and DELIO, talking together apart.

    DELIO.   And so long since married ?
You amaze me.

    [1] A disease to which swine are subject, not the same as
the human ailment.

ANTONIO.   Let me seal your lips for ever :
For, did I think that anything but th' air
Could carry these words from you, I should wish
You had no breath at all.—Now, sir, in your con-
        templation ?
You are studying to become a great wise fellow ?

BOSOLA.   Oh, sir, the opinion of wisdom is a foul
tetter [1] that runs all over a man's body : if
simplicity direct us to have no evil, it directs us to
a happy being ; for the subtlest folly proceeds from
the subtlest wisdom : let me be simply honest.

ANTONIO.   I do understand your inside.

BOSOLA.   Do you so ?

ANTONIO.   Because you would not seem to
        appear to th' world   95
Puff'd up with your preferment, you continue
This out-of-fashion melancholy : leave it, leave it.

BOSOLA.   Give me leave to be honest in any
phrase, in any compliment whatsoever.   Shall I
confess myself to you ?   I look no higher than I
can reach : they are the gods that must ride on
winged horses.   A lawyer's mule of a slow pace
will both suit my disposition and business ; for,
mark me, when a man's mind rides faster than his
horse can gallop, they quickly both tire.

ANTONIO.   You would look up to heaven, but
        I think   106
The devil, that rules i' th' air, stands in your light.

BOSOLA.   Oh, sir, you are lord of the ascendant,
chief man with the duchess ; a duke was your
cousin-german remov'd.   Say you were lineally
descended from King Pepin, or he himself, what
of this ? search the heads of the greatest rivers in
the world, you shall find them but bubbles of water.
Some would think the souls of princes were brought
forth by some more weighty cause than those of
meaner persons : they are deceiv'd, there 's the
same hand to them ; the like passions sway them ;
the same reason that makes a vicar go to law **for**

---

[1] Skin disease.

a tithe-pig, and undo his neighbours, makes them
spoil a whole province, and batter down goodly
cities with the cannon.   121

Enter DUCHESS and Ladies.

DUCHESS.   Your arm, Antonio : do I not grow
    fat ?
I am exceeding short-winded.—Bosola,
I would have you, sir, provide for me a litter ;
Such a one as the Duchess of Florence rode in.

BOSOLA.   The duchess used one when she was
    great with child.

DUCHESS.   I think she did.—Come hither, mend
    my ruff ;
Here, when ? ¹
Thou art such a tedious lady ; and thy breath smells
Of lemon-peels ; would thou hadst done !   Shall
    I swoon   130
Under thy fingers !   I am so troubled
With the mother ! ²

BOSOLA. [Aside.]   I fear too much.

DUCHESS.   I have heard you say
That the French courtiers wear their hats on 'fore
The king.

ANTONIO.   I have seen it.

DUCHESS.   In the presence ?

ANTONIO.   Yes.

DUCHESS.   Why should not we bring up that
    fashion ?   'Tis
Ceremony more than duty that consists
In the removing of a piece of felt :
Be you the example to the rest o' th' court ;
Put on your hat first.

ANTONIO.   You must pardon me :
I have seen, in colder countries than in France,
Nobles stand bare to th' prince ; and the dis-
    tinction   141
Methought show'd reverently.

BOSOLA.   I have a present for your grace.

¹ A common exclamation of impatience.   ² Hysteria.

DUCHESS. For me, sir ?

BOSOLA. Apricocks, madam.

DUCHESS. O, sir, where are they ?
I have heard of none to-year.

BOSOLA. [Aside.] Good ; her colour rises.

DUCHESS. Indeed, I thank you : they are
wondrous fair ones.
What an unskilful fellow is our gardener !
We shall have none this month.

BOSOLA. Will not your grace pare them ?

DUCHESS. No : they taste of musk, methinks ;
indeed they do.

BOSOLA. I know not : yet I wish your grace
had pared 'em.   150

DUCHESS. Why ?

BOSOLA. I forgot to tell you, the knave
gardener,
Only to raise his profit by them the sooner,
Did ripen them in horse-dung.

DUCHESS. O, you jest.—
You shall judge : pray taste one.

ANTONIO. Indeed, madam,
I do not love the fruit.

DUCHESS. Sir, you are loath
To rob us of our dainties : 'tis a delicate fruit ;
They say they are restorative.

BOSOLA. 'Tis a pretty art,
This grafting.

DUCHESS. 'Tis so ; a bettering of nature.

BOSOLA. To make a pippin grow upon a crab,
A damson on a blackthorn.—[Aside.] How greedily
she eats them !   160
A whirlwind strike off these bawd farthingales !
For, but for that and the loose-bodied gown,
I should have discovered apparently
The young springal[1] cutting a caper in her belly.

DUCHESS. I thank you, Bosola : they were
right good ones,
If they do not make me sick.

---

[1] Stripling.

ANTONIO.   How now, madam ?

DUCHESS.   This green fruit and my stomach are
   not friends :
How they swell me !

BOSOLA. [Aside.] Nay, you are too much swelled
   already.

DUCHESS.   Oh, I am in an extreme cold sweat !

BOSOLA.   I am very sorry.

DUCHESS.   Lights to my chamber !—O good
   Antonio,   170
I fear I am undone !

DELIO.   Lights there, lights !

   [Exeunt DUCHESS and Ladies.—Exit, on the other
       side, BOSOLA.]

ANTONIO.   O my most trusty Delio, we are lost !
I fear she 's fall'n in labour ; and there 's left
No time for her remove.

DELIO.   Have you prepar'd
Those ladies to attend her ? and procur'd
That politic safe conveyance for the midwife
Your duchess plotted ?

ANTONIO.   I have.

DELIO.   Make use, then, of this forc'd occasion :
Give out that Bosola hath poison'd her   179
With these apricocks ; that will give some colour
For her keeping close.

ANTONIO.   Fie, fie, the physicians
Will then flock to her.

DELIO.   For that you may pretend
She'll use some prepar'd antidote of her own,
Lest the physicians should re-poison her.

ANTONIO.   I am lost in amazement : I know not
   what to think on 't.   [Exeunt.

SCENE II.—A Hall in the same Palace.

Enter BOSOLA.

BOSOLA.   So, so, there 's no question but her
tetchiness and most vulturous eating of the
apricocks are apparent signs of breeding.

Enter an Old Lady.

Now ?

OLD LADY.   I am in haste, sir.

BOSOLA.   There was a young waiting-woman had a monstrous desire to see the glass-house——

OLD LADY.   Nay, pray let me go.

BOSOLA.   And it was only to know what strange instrument it was should swell up a glass to the fashion of a woman's belly.   11

OLD LADY.   I will hear no more of the glass-house. You are still abusing women ?

BOSOLA.   Who, I ? no ; only, by the way now and then, mention your frailties. The orange-tree bear[s] ripe and green fruit and blossoms all together ; and some of you give entertainment for pure love, but more for more precious reward. The lusty spring smells well ; but drooping autumn tastes well. If we have the same golden showers that rained in the time of Jupiter the thunderer, you have the same Danaës still, to hold up their laps to receive them. Didst thou never study the mathematics ?   24

OLD LADY.   What's that, sir ?

BOSOLA.   Why, to know the trick how to make a many lines meet in one centre. Go, go, give your foster-daughters good counsel : tell them, that the devil takes delight to hang at a woman's girdle, like a false rusty watch, that she cannot discern how the time passes.   [Exit Old Lady.

Enter ANTONIO, DELIO, RODERIGO, and GRISOLAN.

ANTONIO.   Shut up the court-gates.

RODERIGO.   Why, sir ? what's the danger ?

ANTONIO.   Shut up the posterns presently, and call   33
All the officers o' th' court.

GRISOLAN.   I shall instantly.
                                                                  [Exit.

ANTONIO.   Who keeps the key o' th' park gate ?

RODERIGO. Forobosco.[1]
ANTONIO. Let him bring 't presently.

Re-enter GRISOLAN *with Servants.*

FIRST SERVANT. O, gentlemen o' the court, the
foulest treason !

BOSOLA. [Aside.] If that these apricocks should be
poison'd now,
Without my knowledge !

FIRST SERVANT. There was taken even now
A Switzer in the duchess' bed chamber—

SECOND SERVANT. A Switzer ?

FIRST SERVANT. With a pistol in his great cod-
piece.

BOSOLA. Ha, ha, ha ! 41

FIRST SERVANT. The cod-piece was the case for 't.

SECOND SERVANT. There was
A cunning traitor : who would have search'd his
cod-piece ?

FIRST SERVANT. True, if he had kept out of the
ladies' chambers :
And all the moulds of his buttons were leaden bullets.

SECOND SERVANT. O wicked cannibal !
A fire-lock in 's cod-piece !

FIRST SERVANT. 'Twas a French plot,
Upon my life.

SECOND SERVANT. To see what the devil can do !

ANTONIO. [Are] all the officers here ?

SERVANTS. We are.

ANTONIO. Gentlemen,
We have lost much plate you know ; and but this
evening 50
Jewels, to the value of four thousand ducats,
Are missing in the duchess' cabinet.
Are the gates shut ?

SERVANT. Yes.

ANTONIO. 'Tis the duchess' pleasure

---

[1] This character is included in the quarto dramatis
personae and assigned to an actor, but he is not mentioned
elsewhere in the play.

Each officer be lock'd into his chamber
Till the sun-rising ; and to send the keys
Of all their chests and of their outward doors
Into her bed-chamber. She is very sick.

RODERIGO. At her pleasure.

ANTONIO.   She entreats you take 't not ill :
The innocent shall be the more approv'd by it.

BOSOLA.   Gentleman o' th' wood-yard, where's
    your Switzer now ?   60

FIRST SERVANT.   By this hand, 'twas credibly
reported by one o' th' black guard.[1]

              [Exeunt all except ANTONIO and DELIO.

DELIO.   How fares it with the duchess ?

ANTONIO.   She's expos'd
Unto the worst of torture, pain and fear.

DELIO.   Speak to her all happy comfort.

ANTONIO.   How I do play the fool with mine own
    danger !
You are this night, dear friend, to post to
    Rome :
My life lies in your service.

DELIO.   Do not doubt me.

ANTONIO.   Oh, 'tis far from me : and yet fear
    presents me
Somewhat that looks like danger.

DELIO.   Believe it,   70
'Tis but the shadow of your fear, no more ;
How superstitiously we mind our evils !
The throwing down salt, or crossing of a hare,
Bleeding at nose, the stumbling of a horse,
Or singing of a cricket, are of power
To daunt whole man in us. Sir, fare you well :
I wish you all the joys of a bless'd father :
And, for my faith, lay this unto your breast,—
Old friends, like old swords, still are trusted best.
                                          [Exit.

              Enter CARIOLA.

CARIOLA.   Sir, you are the happy father of a
    son :   80

              [1] See note on p. 96.

Your wife commends him to you.

ANTONIO.   Blessèd comfort !—
For Heaven' sake tend her well : I'll presently
Go set a figure for 's nativity.   [Exeunt.

SCENE III.—The Courtyard of the same Palace.

Enter BOSOLA, with a dark lantern.

BOSOLA.   Sure I did hear a woman shriek : list, ha !
And the sound came, if I receiv'd it right,
From   the   duchess'   lodgings.   There 's   some
    stratagem
In the confining all our courtiers
To their several wards : I must have part of it ;
My intelligence will freeze else.   List, again !
It may be 'twas the melancholy bird,
Best friend of silence and of solitariness,
The owl, that scream'd so.—Ha ! Antonio ?

Enter ANTONIO with a Candle, his Sword drawn.

ANTONIO.   I heard some noise.—Who 's there ?
    what art thou ? speak.   10
BOSOLA.   Antonio ? put not your face nor body
To such a forc'd expression of fear :
I am Bosola, your friend.
ANTONIO.   Bosola !—
[Aside.] This mole does undermine me.—Heard you
    not
A noise even now ?
BOSOLA.   From whence ?
ANTONIO.   From the duchess' lodging.
BOSOLA.   Not I : did you ?
ANTONIO.   I did, or else I dream'd.
BOSOLA.   Let 's walk towards it.
ANTONIO.   No : it may be 'twas
But the rising of the wind.
BOSOLA.   Very likely.
Methinks 'tis very cold, and yet you sweat :
You look wildly.
ANTONIO.   I have been setting a figure   20

For the duchess' jewels.

BOSOLA.   Ah, and how falls your question ?
Do you find it radical ? [1]

ANTONIO.   What 's that to you ?
'Tis rather to be questioned what design,
When all men were commanded to their lodgings,
Makes you a night-walker.

BOSOLA.   In sooth, I'll tell you :
Now all the court 's asleep, I thought the devil
Had least to do here ; I came to say my prayers ;
And if it do offend you I do so,
You are a fine courtier.

ANTONIO. [Aside.]   This fellow will undo me.—
You gave the duchess apricocks to-day :   30
Pray Heaven they were not poison'd !

BOSOLA.   Poison'd ? [2] A Spanish fig
For the imputation !

ANTONIO.   Traitors are ever confident
Till they are discover'd. There were jewels stol'n
    too :
In my conceit, none are to be suspected
More than yourself.

BOSOLA.   You are a false steward.

ANTONIO.   Saucy slave, I'll pull thee up by the
    roots.

BOSOLA.   Maybe the ruin will crush you to
    pieces.

ANTONIO.   You are an impudent snake indeed,
    sir :
Are you scarce warm, and do you show your sting ?
You libel well, sir.

BOSOLA.   No, sir : copy it out,   40
And I will set my hand to 't.

ANTONIO. [Aside.]   My nose bleeds.
One that were superstitious would count
This ominous, when it merely comes by chance :
Two letters, that are wrought here for my name,
Are drown'd in blood !
Mere accident.—For you, sir, I'll take order

---

[1] i. e. capable of solution.   [2] Query, omit this word.

I' th' morn you shall be safe :—[Aside.] 'tis that
  must colour
Her lying-in : —sir, this door you pass not :
I do not hold it fit that you come near
The duchess' lodgings, till you have quit your-
  self.—   50
[Aside.] The great are like the base, nay, they are
  the same,
When they seek shameful ways to avoid shame.
                                                      [Exit.
  BOSOLA. Antonio hereabout did drop a paper :—
Some of your help, false friend : [Opening his lantern.]
  —Oh, here it is.
What 's here ? a child's nativity calculated ?
                                                    [Reads.
  ' The duchess was deliver'd of a son, 'tween the
hours twelve and one in the night, Anno Dom.
1504,'—that 's this year—' decimo nono Decembris,'
—that 's this night,—' taken according to the
meridian of Malfi,'—that 's our duchess : happy
discovery !—' The lord of the first house being
combust in the ascendant, signifies short life ; and
Mars being in a human sign, join'd to the tail of
the Dragon, in the eighth house, doth threaten
a violent death. Caetera non scrutantur.'   65
Why, now 'tis most apparent : this precise fellow
Is the duchess' bawd :—I have it to my wish !
This is a parcel of intelligency
Our courtiers were cas'd up for : it needs must
  follow
That I must be committed on pretence   70
Of poisoning her ; which I'll endure, and laugh at.
If one could find the father now ! but that
Time will discover. Old Castruchio
I' th' morning posts to Rome : by him I'll send
A letter that shall make her brothers' galls
O'erflow their livers. This was a thrifty way.
Though lust do mask in ne'er so strange disguise,
She 's oft found witty, but is never wise.   [Exit.

SCENE IV.—A Room in the Palace of the CARDINAL
at Rome.

Enter CARDINAL and JULIA.

CARDINAL.   Sit : thou art my best of wishes.
Prithee, tell me
What trick didst thou invent to come to Rome
Without thy husband.   Why, my lord, I told him
JULIA.
I came to visit an old anchorite
Here for devotion.
CARDINAL.   Thou art a witty false one,—
I mean, to him.
JULIA.   You have prevailed with me
Beyond my strongest thoughts ! I would not now
Find you inconstant.
CARDINAL.   Do not put thyself
To such a voluntary torture, which proceeds
Out of your own guilt.
JULIA.   How, my lord ?
CARDINAL.   You fear
My constancy, because you have approved   11
Those giddy and wild turning[s] in yourself.
JULIA.   Did you e'er find them ?
CARDINAL.   Sooth, generally for women ;
A man might strive to make glass malleable,
Ere he should make them fixed.
JULIA.   So, my lord.
CARDINAL. We had need go borrow that
fantastic glass
Invented by Galileo the Florentine
To view another spacious world i' th' moon,
And look to find a constant woman there.
JULIA.   This is very well, my lord.
CARDINAL.   Why do you weep ?
Are tears your justification ? the self-same tears
Will fall into your husband's bosom, lady,   22
With a loud protestation that you love him
Above the world. Come, I'll love you wisely,
That 's jealously ; since I am very certain

You cannot make me cuckold.

JULIA.   I'll go home
To my husband.

CARDINAL.   You may thank me, lady,
I have taken you off your melancholy perch,
Bore you upon my fist, and show'd you game,
And let you fly at it.—I pray thee, kiss me.—
When thou wast with thy husband, thou wast
    watch'd   31
Like a tame elephant :—still you are to thank
    me :—
Thou hadst only kisses from him and high feeding ;
But what delight was that ? 'twas just like one
That hath a little fingering on the lute,
Yet cannot tune it :—still you are to thank me.

JULIA.   You told me of a piteous wound i' th'
    heart
And a sick liver, when you wooed me first,
And spake like one in physic.

CARDINAL.   Who's that ?—

Enter Servant.

Rest firm, for my affection to thee,   40
Lightning moves slow to 't.

SERVANT.   Madam, a gentleman,
That's come post from Malfi, desires to see you.

CARDINAL.   Let him enter : I'll withdraw.

                                           [*Exit.*
SERVANT.   He says
Your husband, old Castruchio, is come to Rome,
Most pitifully tir'd with riding post.   [*Exit.*

Enter DELIO.

JULIA.   Signior Delio ! [*Aside.*] 'tis one of my
    old suitors.

DELIO.   I was bold to come and see you.

JULIA.   Sir, you are welcome.

DELIO.   Do you lie here ?

JULIA.   Sure, your own experience
Will satisfy you no : our Roman prelates

Do not keep lodging for ladies.

DELIO.　　　　　　　Very well :　　50
I have brought you no commendations from your
　　husband,
For I know none by him.

JULIA.　　　　　　I hear he 's come to Rome.

DELIO.　I never knew man and beast, of a horse
　　and a knight,
So weary of each other : if he had had a good back,
He would have undertook to have borne his horse,
His breech was so pitifully sore.

JULIA.　　　　　　　　Your laughter
Is my pity.

DELIO.　　　Lady, I know not whether
You want money, but I have brought you some.

JULIA.　From my husband ?

DELIO.　　　　　No, from mine own allowance.

JULIA.　I must hear the condition, ere I be bound
　　to take it.　　　　　　　　　60

DELIO.　Look on 't, 'tis gold : hath it not a fine
　　colour ?

JULIA.　I have a bird more beautiful.

DELIO.　Try the sound on 't.

JULIA.　　　　　　A lute-string far exceeds it :
It hath no smell, like cassia or civet ;
Nor is it physical, though some fond doctors
Persuade us seethe 't in cullises.[1]　I'll tell you,
This is a creature bred by——

Re-enter Servant.

SERVANT.　　　　　　Your husband 's come,
Hath deliver'd a letter to the Duke of Calabria
That, to my thinking, hath put him out of his wits.
　　　　　　　　　　　　　　　　　[Exit.

JULIA.　Sir, you hear :　　　　　　70
Pray, let me know your business and your suit
As briefly as can be.

DELIO.　With good speed : I would wish you,
At such time as you are non-resident

———————
[1] See note 1 on p. 187.

With your husband, my mistress.

    JULIA.   Sir, I'll go ask my husband if I shall,
And straight return your answer.   [Exit.

    DELIO.   Very fine !
Is this her wit, or honesty, that speaks thus ?
I heard one say the duke was highly mov'd
With a letter sent from Malfi. I do fear
Antonio is betray'd : how fearfully   80
Shows his ambition now ! unfortunate fortune !
They pass through whirlpools, and deep woes do
    shun,
Who the event weigh ere the action's done. [Exit.

    SCENE V.—Another Room in the same Palace.

    Enter CARDINAL, and FERDINAND with a letter.

    FERDINAND.   I have this night digged up a
    mandrake.

    CARDINAL.   Say you ?

    FERDINAND.   And I am grown mad with 't.

    CARDINAL.   What 's the prodigy ?

    FERDINAND.   Read there,—a sister damn'd :
    she 's loose i' th' hilts ;
Grown a notorious strumpet.

    CARDINAL.   Speak lower.

    FERDINAND.   Lower ?
Rogues do not whisper 't now, but seek to publish 't
(As servants do the bounty of their lords)
Aloud ; and with a covetous searching eye,
To mark who note them. O, confusion seize her !
She hath had most cunning bawds to serve her
    turn,
And more secure conveyances for lust   10
Than towns of garrison for service.

    CARDINAL.   Is 't possible ?
Can this be certain ?

    FERDINAND.   Rhubarb, oh, for rhubarb
To purge this choler ! here 's the cursèd day
To prompt my memory ; and here 't shall stick
Till of her bleeding heart I make a sponge

To wipe it out.

CARDINAL.   Why do you make yourself
So wild a tempest ?

FERDINAND.   Would I could be one,
That I might toss her palace 'bout her ears,
Root up her goodly forests, blast her meads,
And lay her general territory as waste   20
As she hath done her honours.

CARDINAL.   Shall our blood,
The royal blood of Arragon and Castile,
Be thus attainted ?

FERDINAND.   Apply desperate physic :
We must not now use balsamum, but fire,
The smarting cupping-glass, for that 's the mean
To purge infected blood, such blood as hers.
There is a kind of pity in mine eye,—
I'll give it to my handkercher ; and now 'tis here,
I'll bequeath this to her bastard.

CARDINAL.   What to do ?

FERDINAND. Why, to make soft lint for his
     mother's wounds,   30
When I have hewed her to pieces.

CARDINAL.   Curs'd creature !
Unequal nature, to place women's hearts
So far upon the left side !

FERDINAND.   Foolish men,
That e'er will trust their honour in a bark
Made of so slight weak bulrush as is woman,
Apt every minute to sink it !

CARDINAL. Thus ignorance, when it hath pur-
     chas'd honour,
It cannot wield it.

FERDINAND.   Methinks I see her laughing—
Excellent hyena ! Talk to me somewhat, quickly,
Or my imagination will carry me   40
To see her in the shameful act of sin.

CARDINAL. With whom ?

FERDINAND.   Happily [1] with some strong-
     thigh'd bargeman,

     [1] Often used for ' haply '.

Or one [o'] the woodyard that can quoit the
    sledge [1]
Or toss the bar, or else some lovely squire
That carries coals up to her privy lodgings.
    CARDINAL. You fly beyond your reason.
    FERDINAND.   Go to, mistress!
'Tis not your whore's milk that shall quench my
    wild fire,
But your whore's blood.
    CARDINAL. How idly shows this rage, which
    carries you,
As men convey'd by witches through the air,   50
On violent whirlwinds! this intemperate noise
Fitly resembles deaf men's shrill discourse,
Who talk aloud, thinking all other men
To have their imperfection.
    FERDINAND.   Have not you
My palsy?
    CARDINAL. Yes, I can be angry, [but]
Without this rupture:[2] there is not in nature
A thing that makes man so deform'd, so beastly,
As doth intemperate anger. Chide yourself.
You have divers men who never yet express'd
Their strong desire of rest but by unrest,   60
By vexing of themselves. Come, put yourself
In tune.
    FERDINAND.   So; I will only study to seem
The thing I am not. I could kill her now,
In you, or in myself; for I do think
It is some sin in us heaven doth revenge
By her.
    CARDINAL. Are you stark mad?
    FERDINAND.   I would have their bodies
Burnt in a coal-pit with the ventage stopp'd,
That their curs'd smoke might not ascend to
    heaven;
Or dip the sheets they lie in in pitch or sulphur,
Wrap them in 't, and then light them like a match;
Or else to boil their bastard to a cullis,   71

    [1] Throw the hammer.   [2] Outburst.

And give't his lecherous father to renew
The sin of his back.

    CARDINAL.   I'll leave you.

    FERDINAND.   Nay, I have done.
I am confident, had I been damn'd in hell,
And should have heard of this, it would have put me
Into a cold sweat. In, in; I'll go sleep.
Till I know who leaps my sister, I'll not stir:
That known, I'll find scorpions to string my whips,
And fix her in a general eclipse.   [Exeunt.

ACT THE THIRD

SCENE I.—A Room in the Palace of the DUCHESS.

Enter ANTONIO and DELIO.

    ANTONIO.   Our noble friend, my most beloved Delio!
Oh, you have been a stranger long at court;
Came you along with the Lord Ferdinand?

    DELIO.   I did, sir: and how fares your noble duchess?

    ANTONIO.   Right fortunately well: she's an excellent
Feeder of pedigrees; since you last saw her,
She hath had two children more, a son and daughter.

    DELIO.   Methinks 'twas yesterday: let me but wink,
And not behold your face, which to mine eye
Is somewhat leaner, verily I should dream   10
It were within this half-hour.

    ANTONIO.   You have not been in law, friend Delio,
Nor in prison, nor a suitor at the court,
Nor begged the reversion of some great man's place,
Nor troubled with an old wife, which doth make
Your time so insensibly hasten.

DELIO. Pray, sir, tell me,
Hath not this news arriv'd yet to the ear
Of the lord cardinal'?

ANTONIO. I fear it hath :
The Lord Ferdinand, that's newly come to court,
Doth bear himself right dangerously.

DELIO. Pray, why?

ANTONIO. He is so quiet that he seems to sleep
The tempest out, as dormice do in winter : 22
Those houses that are haunted are most still
Till the devil be up.

DELIO. What say the common people?

ANTONIO. The common rabble do directly say
She is a strumpet.

DELIO. And your graver heads
Which would be politic, what censure [1] they ?

ANTONIO. They do observe I grow to infinite
purchase,[2]
The left hand way, and all suppose the duchess
Would amend it, if she could ; for, say they, 30
Great princes, though they grudge their officers
Should have such large and unconfinèd means
To get wealth under them, will not complain,
Lest thereby they should make them odious
Unto the people ; for other obligation
Of love or marriage between her and me
They never dream of.

DELIO. The Lord Ferdinand
Is going to bed.

Enter DUCHESS, FERDINAND, and BOSOLA.

FERDINAND. I'll instantly to bed,
For I am weary.—I am to bespeak 39
A husband for you.

DUCHESS. For me, sir ? pray, who is 't ?

FERDINAND. The great Count Malateste.

DUCHESS. Fie upon him !
A count ? he's a mere stick of sugar-candy ;
You may look quite thorough him. When I choose

---

[1] Think. [2] Acquired property, wealth.

A husband, I will marry for your honour.

FERDINAND.   You shall do well in 't.—How is 't,
    worthy Antonio ?

DUCHESS.   But, sir, I am to have private con-
    ference with you

About a scandalous report is spread

Touching mine honour.

FERDINAND.   Let me be ever deaf to 't :

One of Pasquil's [1] paper bullets, court-calumny,

A pestilent air, which princes' palaces   50

Are seldom purged of.   Yet, say that it were
    true,

I pour it in your bosom, my fix'd love

Would strongly excuse, extenuate, nay, deny

Faults, were they apparent in you.   Go, be safe

In your own innocency.

DUCHESS. [Aside.]   O bless'd comfort !

This deadly air is purg'd.

            [Exeunt DUCHESS, ANTONIO, and DELIO.

FERDINAND.   Her guilt treads on

Hot-burning coulters.—Now, Bosola,

How thrives our intelligence ?

BOSOLA.   Sir, uncertainly

'Tis rumour'd she hath had three bastards, but

By whom we may go read i' th' stars.

FERDINAND.   Why, some

Hold opinion all things are written there.   61

BOSOLA.   Yes, if we could find spectacles to read
    them.

I do suspect there hath been some sorcery

Us'd on the duchess.

FERDINAND.   Sorcery ? to what purpose ?

BOSOLA.   To make her dote on some desertless
    fellow

She shames to acknowledge.

FERDINAND.   Can your faith give way

To think there 's power in potions or in charms,

To make us love whether we will or no ?

BOSOLA.   Most certainly.

             [1] Or Pasquin's.

FERDINAND.   Away ! these are mere gulleries,
    horrid things,   70
Invented by some cheating mountebanks
To abuse us. Do you think that herbs or charms
Can force the will ? Some trials have been made
In this foolish practice, but the ingredients
Were lenitive poisons, such as are of force
To make the patient mad ; and straight the witch
Swears by equivocation they are in love.   77
The witchcraft lies in her rank blood. This night
I will force confession from her. You told me
You had got, within these two days, a false key
Into her bed-chamber.

    BOSOLA.   I have.
    FERDINAND.   As I would wish.
    BOSOLA.   What do you intend to do ?
    FERDINAND.   Can you guess ?
    BOSOLA.   No.
    FERDINAND.   Do not ask, then :
He that can compass me, and know my drifts,
May say he hath put a girdle 'bout the world,
And sounded all her quicksands.

    BOSOLA.   I do not
Think so.
    FERDINAND.   What do you think, then, pray ?
    BOSOLA.   That you
Are your own chronicle too much, and grossly
Flatter yourself.
    FERDINAND.   Give me thy hand ; I thank thee :
I never gave pension but to flatterers,   90
Till I entertained thee. Farewell.
That friend a great man's ruin strongly checks,
Who rails into his belief all his defects.   [Exeunt.

SCENE II.—The Bedchamber of the DUCHESS.

Enter DUCHESS, ANTONIO, and CARIOLA.

DUCHESS.   Bring me the casket hither, and the
    glass.—
You get no lodging here to-night, my lord.

                                   P

ANTONIO. Indeed, I must persuade one.

DUCHESS. Very good:
I hope in time 'twill grow into a custom,
That noblemen shall come with cap and knee
To purchase a night's lodging of their wives.

ANTONIO. I must lie here.

DUCHESS. Must! you are a lord of misrule.

ANTONIO. Indeed, my rule is only in the night.

DUCHESS. To what use will you put me?

ANTONIO. We'll sleep together.

DUCHESS. Alas, 10
What pleasure can two lovers find in sleep!

CARIOLA. My lord, I lie with her often; and I know
She'll much disquiet you.

ANTONIO. See, you are complain'd of.

CARIOLA. For she's the sprawling'st bedfellow.

ANTONIO. I shall like her
The better for that.

CARIOLA. Sir, shall I ask you a question?

ANTONIO. Oh, I pray thee, Cariola.

CARIOLA. Wherefore still, when you lie
With my lady, do you rise so early?

ANTONIO. Labouring men
Count the clock oftenest, Cariola, are glad
When their task's ended.

DUCHESS. I'll stop your mouth.
[Kisses him.

ANTONIO. Nay, that's but one; Venus had two soft doves 20
To draw her chariot; I must have another—
[She kisses him again.
When wilt thou marry, Cariola?

CARIOLA. Never, my lord.

ANTONIO. Oh, fie upon this single life! forgo it.
We read how Daphne, for her peevish [1] flight,
Became a fruitless bay-tree; Syrinx turn'd
To the pale empty reed; Anaxarete
Was frozen into marble: whereas those

---

[1] Foolish.

Which married, or prov'd kind unto their friends,
Were by a gracious influence transhap'd
Into the olive, pomegranate, mulberry,   30
Became flowers, precious stones, or eminent stars.
    CARIOLA.   This is a vain poetry : but I pray you
    tell me,
If there were propos'd me, wisdom, riches, and
    beauty,
In three several young men, which should I
    choose ?
    ANTONIO.   'Tis a hard question : this was Paris'
    case,
And he was blind in 't, and there was great cause ;
For how was 't possible he could judge right,
Having three amorous goddesses in view,
And they stark naked ? 'twas a motion
Were able to benight the apprehension   40
Of the severest counsellor of Europe.
Now I look on both your faces so well form'd,
It puts me in mind of a question I would ask.
    CARIOLA.   What is 't ?
    ANTONIO.   I do wonder why hard-favour'd
    ladies,
For the most part, keep worse-favour'd waiting-
    women
To attend them, and cannot endure fair ones.
    DUCHESS.   Oh, that's soon answer 'd.
Did you ever in your life know an ill painter
Desire to have his dwelling next door to the shop
Of an excellent picture-maker ? 'twould disgrace
His face-making, and undo him. I prithee,   51
When were we so merry ?—My hair tangles.
    ANTONIO.   Pray thee, Cariola, let 's steal forth
    the room,
And let her talk to herself : I have divers times
Serv'd her the like, when she hath chaf'd extremely.
I love to see her angry. Softly, Cariola.
                [Exeunt ANTONIO and CARIOLA.
    DUCHESS.   Doth not the colour of my hair 'gin to
    change ?

When I wax grey, I shall have all the court
Powder their hair with arras,[1] to be like me.
You have cause to love me ; I enter'd you into my
    heart   60
Before you would vouchsafe to call for the keys.

          Enter FERDINAND *behind.*

We shall one day have my brothers take you
    napping ;
Methinks his presence, being now in court,
Should make you keep your own bed ; but you'll
    say
Love mix'd with fear is sweetest. I'll assure you,
You shall get no more children till my brothers
Consent to be your gossips. Have you lost your
    tongue ?
'Tis welcome :   68
For know, whether I am doom'd to live or die,
I can do both like a prince.
    FERDINAND.   Die, then, quickly !
            [*Giving her a poniard.*
Virtue, where art thou hid ? what hideous thing
Is it that doth eclipse thee ?
    DUCHESS.   Pray, sir, hear me.
    FERDINAND. Or is it true thou art but a bare
    name,
And no essential thing ?
    DUCHESS.   Sir,—
    FERDINAND.   Do not speak.
    DUCHESS. No, sir : I will plant my soul in
    mine ears, to hear you,
    FERDINAND. O most imperfect light of human
    reason,
That mak'st [us] so unhappy to foresee
What we can least prevent ! Pursue thy wishes,
And glory in them : there 's in shame no comfort
But to be past all bounds and sense of shame. 80
    DUCHESS. I pray, sir, hear me : I am married.
    FERDINAND.   So !

    [1] Orris powder, which was the colour of flour.

DUCHESS.   Happily, not to your liking : but for
    that,
Alas, your shears do come untimely now
To clip the bird's wings that 's already flown !
Will you see my husband ?

FERDINAND.   Yes, if I could change
Eyes with a basilisk.

DUCHESS.   Sure, you came hither
By his confederacy.

FERDINAND.   The howling of a wolf   87
Is music to thee, screech-owl : prithee, peace.—
Whate'er thou art that hast enjoy'd my sister,
For I am sure thou hear'st me, for thine own sake
Let me not know thee. I came hither prepar'd
To work thy discovery ; yet am now persuaded
It would beget such violent effects
As would damn us both. I would not for ten
    millions
I had beheld thee : therefore use all means
I never may have knowledge of thy name ;
Enjoy thy lust still, and a wretched life,
On that condition.—And for thee, vile woman,
If thou do wish thy lecher may grow old   99
In thy embracements, I would have thee build
Such a room for him as our anchorites
To holier use inhabit. Let not the sun
Shine on him till he 's dead ; let dogs and monkeys
Only converse with him, and such dumb things
To whom nature denies use to sound his name ;
Do not keep a paraquito, lest she learn it ;
If thou do love him, cut out thine own tongue,
Lest it bewray him.

DUCHESS.   Why might not I marry ?
I have not gone about in this to create   109
Any new world or custom.

FERDINAND.   Thou art undone ;
And thou hast ta'en that massy sheet of lead
That hid thy husband's bones, and folded it
About my heart.

DUCHESS.   Mine bleeds for 't.

FERDINAND.   Thine ? thy heart ?
What should I name 't unless a hollow bullet
Fill'd with unquenchable wild-fire ?

DUCHESS.   You are in this
Too strict ; and were you not my princely brother,
I would say, too wilful : my reputation
Is safe.

FERDINAND.   Dost thou know what reputation
    is ?
I'll tell thee,—to small purpose, since the instruc-
    tion
Comes now too late.   120
Upon a time Reputation, Love, and Death,
Would travel o'er the world ; and it was concluded
That they should part, and take three several ways.
Death told them, they should find him in great
    battles,
Or cities plagu'd with plagues : Love gives them
    counsel
To inquire for him 'mongst unambitious shepherds,
Where dowries were not talk'd of, and sometimes
'Mongst quiet kindred that had nothing left
By their dead parents : ' Stay,' quoth Reputation,
' Do not forsake me ; for it is my nature,   130
If once I part from any man I meet,
I am never found again.'   And so for you :
You have shook hands with Reputation,
And made him invisible.   So, fare you well :
I will never see you more.

DUCHESS.   Why should only I,
Of all the other princes of the world,   136
Be cas'd up, like a holy relic ? I have youth
And a little beauty.

FERDINAND.   So you have some virgins
That are witches.   I will never see thee more.

[Exit.

Re-enter ANTONIO with a pistol, and CARIOLA.

DUCHESS.   You saw this apparition ?
ANTONIO.   Yes : we are

Betray'd. How came he hither ?—I should turn
This to thee, for that.   [Pointing the pistol at CARIOLA.
   CARIOLA.   Pray, sir, do ; and when
That you have cleft my heart, you shall read there
Mine innocence.
   DUCHESS.   That gallery gave him entrance.
   ANTONIO. I would this terrible thing would
    come again,
That, standing on my guard, I might relate
My warrantable love.—   [She shows the poniard.
               Ha ! what means this ?
   DUCHESS. He left this with me.
   ANTONIO.   And it seems did wish
You would use it on yourself.
   DUCHESS.   His action seem'd
To intend so much.
   ANTONIO.   This hath a handle to 't.
As well as a point : turn it towards him, and
So fasten the keen edge in his rank gall.   152
               [Knocking within.
How now ! who knocks ? more earthquakes ?
   DUCHESS.   I stand
As if a mine beneath my feet were ready
To be blown up.
   CARIOLA.   'Tis Bosola.
   DUCHESS.   Away !
O misery ! methinks unjust actions
Should wear these masks and curtains, and not we.
You must instantly part hence : I have fashion'd it
Already.   [Exit ANTONIO.

Enter BOSOLA.

   BOSOLA. The duke your brother is ta'en up in
    a whirlwind,   160
Hath took horse, and 's rid post to Rome.
   DUCHESS.   So late ?
   BOSOLA. He told me, as he mounted into th'
    saddle,
You were undone.
   DUCHESS. Indeed, I am very near it.

BOSOLA.   What's the matter ?

DUCHESS. Antonio, the master of our house-
   hold,
Hath dealt so falsely with me in's accounts :
My brother stood engag'd with me for money
Ta'en up of certain Neapolitan Jews,
And Antonio lets the bonds be forfeit.   169

BOSOLA. Strange !—[Aside.] This is cunning.

DUCHESS.   And hereupon
My brother's bills at Naples are protested
Against.—Call up our officers.

BOSOLA.   I shall.   [Exit.

                  Re-enter ANTONIO.

DUCHESS. The place that you must fly to is
   Ancona :
Hire a house there ; I'll send after you
My treasure and my jewels. Our weak safety
Runs upon enginous wheels :[1] short syllables
Must stand for periods. I must now accuse you
Of such a feignèd crime as Tasso calls
Magnanima menzogna, a noble lie,
'Cause it must shield our honours.—Hark ! they
   are coming.   180

              Re-enter BOSOLA and Officers.

ANTONIO. Will your grace hear me ?

DUCHESS. I have got well by you ; you have
   yielded me
A million of loss : I am like to inherit
The people's curses for your stewardship.
You had the trick in audit-time to be sick,
Till I had sign'd your quietus ; and that cur'd you
Without help of a doctor.—Gentlemen,
I would have this man be an example to you all ;
So shall you hold my favour ; I pray, let him ;
For h'as done that, alas, you would not think of,
And, because I intend to be rid of him,   191
I mean not to publish.—Use your fortune elsewhere.

         [1] i.e. is rapidly leaving us.

ANTONIO.   I am strongly arm'd to brook my
    overthrow ;
As commonly men bear with a hard year,
I will not blame the cause on 't ; but do think
The necessity of my malevolent star
Procures this, not her humour.   Oh, the inconstant
And rotten ground of service ! you may see,
'Tis even like him, that in a winter night,
Takes a long slumber o'er a dying fire,   200
A-loth to part from 't ; yet parts thence as cold
As when he first sat down.
    DUCHESS.   We do confiscate,
Towards the satisfying of your accounts,
All that you have.
    ANTONIO.   I am all yours ; and 'tis very fit
All mine should be so.
    DUCHESS.   So, sir, you have your pass.
    ANTONIO.   You may see, gentlemen, what 'tis to
    serve
A prince with body and soul.   [Exit.
    BOSOLA.   [1]Here's an example for extortion :
what moisture is drawn out of the sea, when foul
weather comes, pours down, and runs into the sea
again.   211
    DUCHESS.   I would know what are your opinions
of this Antonio.
    SECOND OFFICER.   He could not abide to see
a pig's head gaping : I thought your grace would
find him a Jew.
    THIRD OFFICER.   I would you had been his
officer, for your own sake.
    FOURTH OFFICER.   You would have had more
money.   220
    FIRST OFFICER.   He stopped his ears with black
wool, and to those came to him for money said he
was thick of hearing.
    SECOND OFFICER.   Some said he was an herma-
phrodite, for he could not abide a woman.

---

[1] The next sixty or seventy lines may be read as a kind of
galloping blank verse, but they read more easily as prose.

FOURTH OFFICER. How scurvy proud he would look when the treasury was full! Well, let him go!

FIRST OFFICER. Yes, and the chippings of the buttery fly after him, to scour his gold chain!

DUCHESS. Leave us. [Exeunt officers.] What do you think of these?   231

BOSOLA. That these are rogues that in 's prosperity, but to have waited on his fortune, could have wish'd his dirty stirrup riveted through their noses, and follow'd after 's mule, like a bear in a ring; would have prostituted their daughters to his lust; made their first-born intelligencers; thought none happy but such as were born under his blest planet, and wore his livery: and do these lice drop off now? Well, never look to have the like again: he hath left a sort of flattering rogues behind him; their doom must follow. Princes pay flatterers in their own money: flatterers dissemble their vices, and they dissemble their lies;[1] that 's justice. Alas, poor gentleman!   245

DUCHESS. Poor? he hath amply fill'd his coffers.

BOSOLA. Sure, he was too honest. Pluto,[2] the god of riches, when he 's sent by Jupiter to any man, he goes limping, to signify that wealth that comes on God's name comes slowly; but when he 's sent on the devil's errand, he rides post and comes in by scuttles.[3] Let me show you what a most unvalued jewel you have in a wanton humour thrown away, to bless the man shall find him. He was an excellent courtier and most faithful; a soldier that thought it as beastly to know his own value too little as devilish to acknowledge it too much. Both his virtue and form deserv'd a far better fortune: his discourse rather delighted to judge itself than show itself: his breast was fill'd with all perfection, and yet it seem'd a private whispering-room, it made so little noise of 't.   262

[1] i. e. Flatterers pretend that kings have no vices, and kings pretend that flatterers tell no lies.
[2] Put for Plutus.   [3] Short, hurried runs.

DUCHESS.   But he was basely descended.

BOSOLA.   Will you make yourself a mercenary
herald, rather to examine men's pedigrees than
virtues ?   You shall want him :   for know, an
honest statesman to a prince is like a cedar planted
by a spring ;   the spring bathes the tree's root, the
grateful tree rewards it with his shadow :   you
have not done so.   I would sooner swim to the
Bermoothes on two politicians' rotten bladders,
tied together with an intelligencer's heart-string,
than depend on so changeable a prince's favour.
Fare thee well, Antonio !   since the malice of the
world would needs down with thee, it cannot be
said yet that any ill happened unto thee, considering thy fall was accompanied with virtue.   277

DUCHESS.   Oh, you render me excellent music !

BOSOLA.   Say you ?

DUCHESS.   This good one that you speak of is
    my husband.

BOSOLA.   Do I not dream ?   can this ambitious
    age   280
Have so much goodness in 't as to prefer
A man merely for worth, without these shadows
Of wealth and painted honours ?   possible ?

DUCHESS.   I have had three children by him.

BOSOLA.   Fortunate lady !
For you have made your private nuptial bed
The humble and fair seminary of peace.
No question but many an unbeneficed scholar
Shall pray for you for this deed, and rejoice
That some preferment in the world can yet
Arise from merit.   The virgins of your land   290
That have no dowries shall hope your example
Will raise them to rich husbands.   Should you want
Soldiers, 'twould make the very Turks and Moors
Turn Christians, and serve you for this act.
Last, the neglected poets of your time,
In honour of this trophy of a man,
Raised by that curious engine, your white hand,
Shall thank you, in your grave, for 't ; and make that

More reverend than all the cabinets
Of living princes. For Antonio,   300
His fame shall likewise flow from many a pen,
When heralds shall want coats to sell to men.

 DUCHESS. As I taste comfort in this friendly
  speech,
So would I find concealment.

 BOSOLA. Oh, the secret of my prince,
Which I will wear on th' inside of my heart !

 DUCHESS. You shall take charge of all my coin
  and jewels,
And follow him ; for he retires himself
To Ancona.

 BOSOLA. So.

 DUCHESS.   Whither, within few days,
I mean to follow thee.

 BOSOLA.   Let me think :   310
I would wish your grace to feign a pilgrimage
To our Lady of Loretto, scarce seven leagues
From fair Ancona ; so may you depart
Your country with more honour, and your flight
Will seem a princely progress, retaining
Your usual train about you.

 DUCHESS.   Sir, your direction
Shall lead me by the hand.

 CARIOLA.   In my opinion,
She were better progress to the baths at Lucca,
Or go visit the Spa in Germany ;
For, if you will believe me, I do not like   320
This jesting with religion, this feigned
Pilgrimage.

 DUCHESS. Thou art a superstitious fool :
Prepare us instantly for our departure.
Past sorrows, let us moderately lament them ;
For those to come, seek wisely to prevent them.

       [Exeunt DUCHESS and CARIOLA.

 BOSOLA. A politician is the devil's quilted [1]
  anvil ;
He fashions all sins on him, and the blows

     [1] i.e. muffled.

Are never heard : he may work in a lady's chamber,
As here for proof. What rests but I reveal
All to my lord ? Oh, this base quality   330
Of intelligencer ! why, every quality i' th' world
Prefers [1] but gain or commendation :
Now for this act I am certain to be rais'd,
And men that paint weeds to the life are prais'd.

             [Exit.

SCENE III.—A Room in the CARDINAL'S Palace at Rome.

Enter CARDINAL, FERDINAND, MALATESTE, PESCARA,
    SILVIO, and DELIO.

CARDINAL. Must we turn soldier, then ?
MALATESTE.   The emperor,
Hearing your worth that way, ere you attain'd
This reverend garment, joins you in commission
With the right fortunate soldier the Marquis of
   Pescara,
And the famous Lannoy.
CARDINAL.   He that had the honour
Of taking the French king prisoner ?
MALATESTE.   The same.
Here 's a plot [2] drawn for a new fortification
At Naples.   [They talk apart.
FERDINAND. This great Count Malateste, I
   perceive,   9
Hath got employment ?
DELIO.   No employment, my lord ;
A marginal note in the muster-book, that he is
A voluntary lord.
FERDINAND. He 's no soldier ?
DELIO. He has worn gunpowder in 's hollow
  tooth for the toothache.
SILVIO. He comes to the leaguer [3] with a full
  intent
To eat fresh beef and garlic, means to stay
Till the scent be gone, and straight return to
  court.

 [1] Produces.   [2] Plan.   [3] Camp.

DELIO. He hath read all the late service as the city chronicle relates it ; and keeps two pewterers going, only to express battles in model.

SILVIO. Then he'll fight by the book. 20

DELIO. By the almanac, I think, to choose good days and shun the critical ; that's his mistress's scarf.

SILVIO. Yes, he protests he would do much for that taffeta.

DELIO. I think he would run away from a battle, to save it from taking [1] prisoner.

SILVIO. He is horribly afraid gunpowder will spoil the perfume on 't. 29

DELIO. I saw a Dutchman break his pate once for calling him pot-gun ; he made his head have a bore in 't like a musket.

SILVIO. I would he had made a touchhole to 't. He is indeed a guarded sumpter-cloth,[2] only for the remove of the court.

Enter BOSOLA and speaks to FERDINAND and the
CARDINAL.

PESCARA. Bosola arriv'd ? what should be the business ?
Some falling-out amongst the cardinals.
These factions amongst great men, they are like
Foxes ; when their heads are divided, 39
They carry fire in their tails, and all the country
About them goes to wrack for 't.

SILVIO. What 's that Bosola ?

DELIO. I knew him in Padua—a fantastical scholar, like such who study to know how many knots was in Hercules' club, of what colour Achilles' beard was, or whether Hector were not troubled with the toothache. He hath studied himself half blear-ey'd to know the true symmetry of Caesar's nose by a shoeing-horn ; and this he did to gain the name of a speculative man.[3]

[1] i. e. being taken.   [2] An ornamented horse-cloth.
[3] i. e. a student.

PESCARA.   Mark Prince Ferdinand :   50
A very salamander lives in 's eye,
To mock the eager violence of fire.

SILVIO. That Cardinal hath made more bad
faces with his oppression than ever Michael Angelo
made good ones : he lifts up 's nose, like a foul
porpoise before a storm.

PESCARA.   The Lord Ferdinand laughs.

DELIO.   Like a deadly cannon that lightens
Ere it smokes.

PESCARA.   These are your true pangs of death,
The pangs of life, that struggle with great states-
      men.

DELIO. In such a deformed silence witches
      whisper   60
Their charms.

CARDINAL.   Doth she make religion her riding-
      hood
To keep her from the sun and tempest ?

FERDINAND.   That,
That damns her. Methinks her fault and beauty,
Blended together, show like leprosy,
The whiter, the fouler. I make it a question
Whether her beggarly brats were ever christened.

CARDINAL.   I will instantly solicit the state of
      Ancona   67
To have them banish'd.

FERDINAND.   You are for Loretto ?
I shall not be at your ceremony ; fare you well.—
Write to the Duke of Malfi, my young nephew
She had by her first husband, and acquaint him
With 's mother's honesty.

BOSOLA.   I will.

FERDINAND.   Antonio !
A slave that only smell'd of ink and counters,
And never in 's life look'd like a gentleman,
But in the audit-time.—Go, go presently,
Draw me out an hundred and fifty of our horse,
And meet me at the fort-bridge.   [Exeunt

SCENE IV.—The Shrine of Our Lady of Loretto.

Enter Two Pilgrims.

FIRST PILGRIM.   I have not seen a goodlier shrine
  than this ;
Yet I have visited many.

SECOND PILGRIM.   The Cardinal of Arragon
Is this day to resign his cardinal's hat :
His sister duchess likewise is arriv'd
To pay her vow of pilgrimage.   I expect
A noble ceremony.

FIRST PILGRIM.   No question.
—They come.

Here the ceremony of the CARDINAL'S instalment, in the
  habit of a soldier, [is] performed in delivering up his
  cross, hat, robes, and ring, at the shrine, and investing
  him with sword, helmet, shield, and spurs ; then ANTONIO,
  the DUCHESS, and their children, having presented
  themselves at the shrine, are, by a form of banishment
  in dumb-show expressed towards them by the CARDINAL
  and the state of Ancona, banished : during all which
  ceremony, this ditty is sung, to very solemn music, by
  divers churchmen.

Arms and honours deck thy story,
To thy fame's eternal glory !
Adverse fortune ever fly thee ;   10
No disastrous fate come nigh thee !

I alone will sing thy praises,
Whom to honour virtue raises ;
And thy study, that divine is,
Bent to martial discipline is.
Lay aside all those robes lie by thee ;
Crown thy arts with arms, they'll beautify thee.

O worthy of worthiest name, adorn'd in this
  manner,
Lead bravely thy forces on under war's warlike
  banner !
Oh, mayst thou prove fortunate in all martial
  courses !   20

Guide thou still by skill in arts and forces !
Victory attend thee nigh, whilst fame sings loud
    thy powers ;
Triumphant conquest crown thy head, and bless-
    ings pour down showers ! [1]

                    [Exeunt all except the Two Pilgrims.

  FIRST PILGRIM.   Here's a strange turn of state !
    who would have thought
So great a lady would have match'd herself
Unto so mean a person ? yet the Cardinal
Bears himself much too cruel.

  SECOND PILGRIM.   They are banish'd.

  FIRST PILGRIM.   But I would ask what power
    hath this state
Of Ancona to determine of a free prince ?

  SECOND PILGRIM.   They are a free state, sir, and
    her brother show'd   30
How that the Pope, fore-hearing of her looseness,
Hath seiz'd into th' protection of the Church
The dukedom which she held as dowager.

  FIRST PILGRIM.   But by what justice ?

  SECOND PILGRIM.   Sure, I think by none,
Only her brother's instigation.

  FIRST PILGRIM.   What was it with such violence
    he took
Off from her finger ?

  SECOND PILGRIM.   'Twas her wedding-ring ;
Which he vow'd shortly he would sacrifice
To his revenge.

  FIRST PILGRIM.   Alas, Antonio !
If that a man be thrust into a well,   40
No matter who sets hand to 't, his own weight
Will bring him sooner to th' bottom. Come, let's
    hence.
Fortune makes this conclusion general,
All things do help th' unhappy man to fall.

                           [Exeunt.

   [1] ' The Author disclaims this Ditty to be his.'—(Note in
the 1623 quarto.)

SCENE V.—Near Loretto.

Enter DUCHESS, ANTONIO, Children, CARIOLA, *and*
Servants.

DUCHESS. Banish'd Ancona ?

ANTONIO.   Yes, you see what power
Lightens in great men's breath.

DUCHESS.   Is all our train
Shrunk to this poor remainder ?

ANTONIO.   These poor men,
Which have got little in your service, vow
To take your fortune : but your wiser buntings,
Now they are fledg'd, are gone.

DUCHESS.   They have done wisely.
This puts me in mind of death : physicians thus,
With their hands full of money, use to give o'er
Their patients.

ANTONIO.   Right the fashion of the world :
From decayed fortunes every flatterer shrinks ;
Men cease to build where the foundation sinks.

DUCHESS. I had a very strange dream to-night.

ANTONIO.   What was't ?

DUCHESS. Methought I wore my coronet of
      state,   13
And on a sudden all the diamonds
Were chang'd to pearls.

ANTONIO.   My interpretation
Is, you'll weep shortly ; for to me the pearls
Do signify your tears.

DUCHESS.   The birds that live
I' th' field on the wild benefit of nature
Live happier than we ; for they may choose their
      mates,
And carol their sweet pleasures to the spring.

Enter BOSOLA *with a letter.*

BOSOLA. You are happily o'erta'en.

DUCHESS.   From my brother ?

BOSOLA. Yes, from the Lord Ferdinand your
      brother   22

All love and safety.

DUCHESS.   Thou dost blanch mischief,
Wouldst make it white. See, see, like to calm
   weather
At sea before a tempest, false hearts speak fair
To those they intend most mischief.   [Reads.
   ' Send Antonio to me ; I want his head in a
business.'
A politic equivocation !
He doth not want your counsel, but your head ;
That is, he cannot sleep till you be dead.   31
And here 's another pitfall that 's strew'd o'er
With roses : mark it, 'tis a cunning one :   [Reads.
   ' I stand engaged for your husband for several
debts at Naples : let not that trouble him ; I had
rather have his heart than his money : '—
And I believe so too.

BOSOLA.   What do you believe ?

DUCHESS.   That he so much distrusts my hus-
   band's love,
He will by no means believe his heart is with him
Until he see it : the devil is not cunning   40
Enough to circumvent us in riddles.

BOSOLA.   Will you reject that noble and free
   league
Of amity and love which I present you ?

DUCHESS.   Their league is like that of some
   politic kings,
Only to make themselves of strength and power
To be our after-ruin : tell them so.

BOSOLA.   And what from you ?

ANTONIO.   Thus tell him ; I will not come.

BOSOLA.   And what of this ?   [Pointing to the letter.

ANTONIO.   My brothers have dispers'd
Blood-hounds abroad ; which till I hear are
   muzzl'd,
No truce, though hatch'd with ne'er such politic skill,
Is safe, that hangs upon our enemies' will.   51
I'll not come at them.

BOSOLA.   This proclaims your breeding :

Every small thing draws a base mind to fear,
As the adamant draws iron. Fare you well, sir
You shall shortly hear from 's.   [Exit.
    DUCHESS.   I suspect some ambush :
Therefore by all my love I do conjure you
To take your eldest son, and fly towards Milan.
Let us not venture all this poor remainder
In one unlucky bottom.
    ANTONIO.   You counsel safely.
Best of my life, farewell. Since we must part,   60
Heaven hath a hand in 't ; but no otherwise
Than as some curious artist takes in sunder
A clock or watch, when it is out of frame,
To bring 't in better order.
    DUCHESS.   I know not
Which is best, to see you dead, or part with you.
—Farewell, boy :
Thou art happy that thou hast not understanding
To know thy misery ; for all our wit
And reading brings us to a truer sense
Of sorrow.—In the eternal church, sir,   70
I do hope we shall not part thus.
    ANTONIO.   Oh, be of comfort !
Make patience a noble fortitude,
And think not how unkindly we are used :
Man, like to cassia, is prov'd best being bruised.
    DUCHESS. Must I, like to a slave-born Russian,
Account it praise to suffer tyranny ?
And yet, O heaven, thy heavy hand is in 't !
I have seen my little boy oft scourge his top,   78
And compar'd myself to 't : naught made me e'er
Go right but heaven's scourge-stick.
    ANTONIO.   Do not weep :
Heaven fashion'd us of nothing, and we strive
To bring ourselves to nothing.—Farewell, Cariola,
And thy sweet armful.—If I do never see thee more,
Be a good mother to your little ones,
And save them from the tiger : fare you well.
    DUCHESS : Let me look upon you once more ;
      for that speech

Came from a dying father.—Your kiss is colder
Than that I have seen an holy anchorite
Give to a dead man's skull.

ANTONIO. My heart is turn'd to a heavy lump
of lead, 90
With which I sound my danger : fare you well.

[Exeunt ANTONIO and his Son.

DUCHESS. My laurel is all withered.

CARIOLA. Look, madam, what a troop of armèd
men
Make toward us.

DUCHESS. Oh, they are very welcome :
When Fortune's wheel is over-charg'd with princes,
The weight makes it move swift : I would have my
ruin
Be sudden.

Re-enter BOSOLA visarded, with a Guard.

I am your adventure, am I not ?

BOSOLA. You are : you must see your husband
no more.

DUCHESS. What devil art thou that counterfeits heaven's thunder ?

BOSOLA. Is that terrible ? I would have you
tell me whether 100
Is that note worse that frights the silly birds
Out of the corn, or that which doth allure them
To the nets ? you have hearkened to the last too
much.

DUCHESS. Oh, misery ! like to a rusty o'er-
charg'd cannon,
Shall I never fly in pieces ?—Come, to what prison ?

BOSOLA. To none.

DUCHESS. Whither, then ?

BOSOLA. To your palace.

DUCHESS. I have heard
That Charon's boat serves to convey all o'er
The dismal lake, but brings none back again.

BOSOLA. Your brothers mean you safety and
pity.

DUCHESS.   Pity !
With such a pity men preserve alive   110
Pheasants and quails, when they are not fat
    enough
To be eaten.
    BOSOLA.   These are your children ?
    DUCHESS.   Yes.
    BOSOLA.   Can they prattle ?
    DUCHESS.   No ;
But I intend, since they were born accurs'd,
Curses shall be their first language.
    BOSOLA.   Fie, madam !
Forget this base, low fellow,—
    DUCHESS.   Were I a man,
I'd beat that counterfeit face into thy other.
    BOSOLA.   One of no birth.
    DUCHESS.   Say that he was born mean,
Man is most happy when 's own actions
Be arguments and examples of his virtue.   120
    BOSOLA.   A barren, beggarly virtue !
    DUCHESS.   I prithee, who is greatest ? can you
        tell ?
Sad tales befit my woe : I'll tell you one.
A salmon, as she swam unto the sea,
Met with a dog-fish, who encounters her
With this rough language : ' Why art thou so
    bold
To mix thyself with our high state of floods,
Being no eminent courtier, but one
That for the calmest and fresh time o' the year
Dost live in shallow rivers, rank'st thyself   130
With silly smelts and shrimps ? and darest thou
Pass by our dog-ship without reverence ? '
' Oh ! ' quoth the salmon, ' sister, be at peace :
Thank Jupiter we both have pass'd the net !
Our value never can be truly known,
Till in the fisher's basket we be shown :
I' th' market then my price may be the higher,
Even when I am nearest to the cook and fire.'
So to great men the moral may be stretchèd ;

Men oft are valued high, when they 're most
    wretched.——   140
But come, whither you please. I am arm'd 'gainst
    misery ;
Bent to all sways of the oppressor's will :
There 's no deep valley but near some great hill.
                          [Exeunt.

ACT THE FOURTH

SCENE I.—A Room in the DUCHESS's Palace at Malfi.

Enter FERDINAND *and* BOSOLA.

FERDINAND.   How doth our sister duchess bear
    herself
In her imprisonment ?
  BOSOLA.   Nobly : I'll describe her.
She 's sad as one long used to 't, and she seems
Rather to welcome the end of misery
Than shun it ; a behaviour so noble
As gives a majesty to adversity :
You may discern the shape of loveliness
More perfect in her tears than in her smiles :
She will muse four hours together ; and her
    silence,
Methinks, expresseth more than if she spake.   10
  FERDINAND. Her melancholy seems to be
    fortified
With a strange disdain.
  BOSOLA.   'Tis so ; and this restraint,
Like English mastiffs that grow fierce with tying,
Makes her too passionately apprehend
Those pleasures she 's kept from.
  FERDINAND.   Curse upon her !
I will no longer study in the book
Of another's heart. Inform her what I told you.
                          [Exit.

Enter DUCHESS.

BOSOLA.   All comfort to your grace !
DUCHESS.   I will have none.

Pray thee, why dost thou wrap thy poison'd pills
In gold and sugar ?   20
 BOSOLA. Your elder brother, the Lord Ferdinand,
Is come to visit you, and sends you word,
'Cause once he rashly made a solemn vow
Never to see you more, he comes i' th' night ;
And prays you gently neither torch nor taper
Shine in your chamber : he will kiss your hand,
And reconcile himself ; but for his vow
He dares not see you.
 DUCHESS.   At his pleasure.—Take hence
  the lights.—
He's come.   29

     Enter FERDINAND.

 FERDINAND. Where are you ?
 DUCHESS.   Here sir.
 FERDINAND.   This darkness suits you well.
 DUCHESS. I would ask you pardon.
 FERDINAND.   You have it ; for I account it
The honorabl'st revenge, where I may kill,
To pardon.—Where are your cubs ?
 DUCHESS.   Whom ?
 FERDINAND.   Call them your children ;
For though our national law distinguish bastards
From true legitimate issue, compassionate nature
Makes them all equal.
 DUCHESS.   Do you visit me for this ?
You violate a sacrament o' th' Church
Shall make you howl in hell for't.
 FERDINAND.   It had been well
Could you have liv'd thus always ; for, indeed,
You were too much i' th' light :—but no more ;
I come to seal my peace with you. Here's a hand
     [Gives her a dead man's hand.
To which you have vow'd much love ; the ring
  upon 't   42
You gave
 DUCHESS. 1 affectionately kiss it.
 FERDINAND. Pray, do, and bury the print of it
  in your heart.

I will leave this ring with you for a love-token ;
And the hand as sure as the ring ; and do not doubt
But you shall have the heart too : when you need
    a friend,
Send it to him that owned it ; you shall see
Whether he can aid you.
DUCHESS.   You are very cold :
I fear you are not well after your travel.—   50
Ha ! lights !——Oh, horrible !
FERDINAND.   Let her have lights enough.
                                                [Exit.
DUCHESS. What witchcraft doth he practise,
    that he hath left
A dead man's hand here ?
    [Here is discovered, behind a traverse,[1] the artificial
        figures of ANTONIO and his Children, appearing
        as if they were dead.
BOSOLA.   Look you, here's the piece from which
    'twas ta'en.
He doth present you this sad spectacle,
That, now you know directly they are dead,
Hereafter you may wisely cease to grieve
For that which cannot be recovered.
DUCHESS. There is not between heaven and
    earth one wish
I stay for after this : it wastes me more   60
Than were't my picture, fashion'd out of wax,
Stuck with a magical needle, and then buried
In some foul dunghill ; and yond's an excellent
    property
For a tyrant, which I would account mercy.
BOSOLA.   What's that ?
DUCHESS. If they would bind me to that life-
    less trunk,
And let me freeze to death.
BOSOLA.   Come, you must live.
DUCHESS. That's the greatest torture souls feel
    in hell,
In hell, that they must live, and cannot die.
                    [1] Curtain.

Portia, I'll new kindle thy coals again,   69
And revive the rare and almost dead example
Of a loving wife.
    BOSOLA.   Oh, fie ! despair ? remember
You are a Christian.
    DUCHESS.   The Church enjoins fasting :
I'll starve myself to death.
    BOSOLA.   Leave this vain sorrow.
Things being at the worst begin to mend : the bee
When he hath shot his sting into your hand, may then
Play with your eyelid.
    DUCHESS.   Good comfortable fellow,
Persuade a wretch that 's broke upon the wheel
To have all his bones new set ; entreat him live
To be executed again. Who must dispatch me ?
I account this world a tedious theatre,   80
For I do play a part in 't 'gainst my will.
    BOSOLA. Come, be of comfort ; I will save your
    life.
    DUCHESS.   Indeed,
I have not leisure to tend so small a business.
    BOSOLA. Now, by my life, I pity you.
    DUCHESS.   Thou art a fool, then,
To waste thy pity on a thing so wretched
As cannot pity it[self]. I am full of daggers.
Puff, let me blow these vipers from me.

Enter Servant.

What are you ?
    SERVANT.   One that wishes you long life.
    DUCHESS. I would thou wert hang'd for the
    horrible curse
Thou hast given me : I shall shortly grow one
Of the miracles of pity. I'll go pray ;—   91
No, I'll go curse.
    BOSOLA.   Oh, fie !
    DUCHESS.   I could curse the stars—
    BOSOLA. Oh, fearful !
    DUCHESS. And those three smiling seasons of
    the year

Into a Russian winter : nay, the world
To its first chaos.

BOSOLA.   Look you, the stars shine still.

DUCHESS.   Oh, but you must
Remember, my curse hath a great way to go.—
Plagues, that make lanes through largest families
Consume them !—

BOSOLA.   Fie, lady !

DUCHESS.   Let them, like tyrants,
Never be remembered but for the ill they have
    done ;   101
Let all the zealous prayers of mortified
Churchmen forget them !—

BOSOLA.   Oh, uncharitable !

DUCHESS.   Let Heaven a little while cease crown-
    ing martyrs,
To punish them !—
Go, howl them this, and say, I long to bleed :
It is some mercy when men kill with speed.

               [Exeunt DUCHESS and Servant.

         Re-enter FERDINAND.

FERDINAND.   Excellent, as I would wish ; she 's
    plagued in art :
These presentations are but fram'd in wax
By the curious master in that quality,   110
Vincentio Lauriola, and she takes them
For true substantial bodies.

BOSOLA.   Why do you do this ?

FERDINAND.   To bring her to despair.

BOSOLA.   'Faith, end here,
And go no farther in your cruelty :
Send her a penitential garment to put on
Next to her delicate skin, and furnish her
With beads and prayer-books.

FERDINAND.   Damn her ! that body of hers,
While that my blood ran pure in 't, was more worth
Than that which thou wouldst comfort, called a
    soul.   119
I will send her masks of common courtezans,

Have her meat serv'd up by bawds and ruffians,
And, 'cause she'll needs be mad, I am resolv'd
To remove forth the common hospital
All the mad-folk, and place them near her lodging ;
There let them practise together, sing and dance,
And act their gambols to the full o' th' moon :
If she can sleep the better for it, let her.
Your work is almost ended.

BOSOLA.   Must I see her again?
FERDINAND.   Yes.
BOSOLA.   Never.
FERDINAND.   You must.
BOSOLA.   Never in mine own shape ;
That's forfeited by my intelligence   130
And this last cruel lie : when you send me next,
The business shall be comfort.
FERDINAND.   Very likely ;
Thy pity is nothing of kin to thee. Antonio
Lurks about Milan : thou shalt shortly thither
To feed a fire as great as my revenge,
Which ne'er will slack till it have spent his fuel :
Intemperate agues make physicians cruel.
                                        [Exeunt.

SCENE II.—Another Room in the DUCHESS's Lodging.

Enter DUCHESS and CARIOLA.

DUCHESS.   What hideous noise was that ?
CARIOLA.   'Tis the wild consort [1]
Of madmen, lady, which your tyrant brother
Hath plac'd about your lodging : this tyranny,
I think, was never practis'd till this hour.
DUCHESS.   Indeed, I thank him : nothing but
    noise and folly
Can keep me in my right wits ; whereas reason
And silence make me stark mad. Sit down ;
Discourse to me some dismal tragedy.
CARIOLA.   Oh, 'twill increase your melancholy.
DUCHESS.   Thou art deceived :

[1] Band.

To hear of greater grief would lessen mine.   10
This is a prison ?
   CARIOLA.   Yes, but you shall live
To shake this durance off.
   DUCHESS.   Thou art a fool :
The robin-redbreast and the nightingale
Never live long in cages.
   CARIOLA.   Pray, dry your eyes.
What think you of, madam ?
   DUCHESS.   Of nothing ; when I muse thus,
I sleep.
   CARIOLA.   Like a madman, with your eyes open ?
   DUCHESS.   Dost thou think we shall know one
      another in th' other world ?
   CARIOLA.   Yes, out of question.
   DUCHESS.   Oh, that it were possible
We might but hold some two days' conference
With the dead ! From them I should learn some-
      what, I am sure,   20
I never shall know here.   I'll tell thee a miracle ;
I am not mad yet, to my cause of sorrow :
Th' heaven o'er my head seems made of molten brass,
The earth of flaming sulphur, yet I am not mad.
I am acquainted with sad misery
As the tann'd galley-slave is with his oar ;
Necessity makes me suffer constantly,
And custom makes it easy.   Who do I look like
      now ?
   CARIOLA.   Like to your picture in the gallery,
A deal of life in show, but none in practice ;   30
Or rather like some reverend monument
Whose ruins are even pitied.
   DUCHESS.   Very proper ;
And Fortune seems only to have her eyesight
To behold my tragedy.—
How now ! what noise is that ?

                  Enter Servant.

   SERVANT.   I am come to tell you
Your brother hath intended you some sport.

A great physician, when the Pope was sick
Of a deep melancholy, presented him   38
With several sorts of madmen, which wild object
Being full of change and sport, forc'd him to laugh,
And so the imposthume broke : the self-same cure
The duke intends on you.

> DUCHESS.   Let them come in.

> SERVANT.   There 's a mad lawyer ; and a secular
> priest ;

A doctor that hath forfeited his wits
By jealousy ; an astrologian
That in his works said such a day o' th' month
Should be the day of doom, and, failing of 't,
Ran mad ; an English tailor crazed i' th' brain
With the study of new fashions ; a gentleman-
usher
Quite beside himself with care to keep in mind
The number of his lady's salutations   51
Or ' How do you['s] ' she employ'd him in each
morning ;
A farmer, too, an excellent knave in grain,
Mad 'cause he was hindered transportation :
And let one broker that 's mad loose to these,
You'd think the devil were among them.

> DUCHESS. Sit, Cariola.—Let them loose when
> you please,

For I am chain'd to endure all your tyranny.

Enter Madmen.

Here this Song is sung by a Madman to a dismal kind of
music.

> Oh, let us howl some heavy note,
>   Some deadly dogged howl,   60
> Sounding as from the threatening throat
>   Of beasts and fatal fowl !
> As ravens, screech-owls, bulls, and bears,
>   We'll bell,[1] and bawl our parts,
> Till irksome noise have cloy'd your ears
>   And còrrosived your hearts.

[1] Bellow.

At last, whenas our quire wants breath,
  Our bodies being blest,
We'll sing, like swans, to welcome death,
  And die in love and rest.   70

FIRST MADMAN. Doom's-day not come yet? I'll draw it nearer by a perspective, or make a glass that shall set all the world on fire upon an instant. I cannot sleep ; my pillow is stuffed with a litter of porcupines.

SECOND MADMAN. Hell is a mere glass-house, where the devils are continually blowing up women's souls on hollow irons, and the fire never goes out.

THIRD MADMAN. I will lie with every woman in my parish the tenth night ; I will tithe them over like haycocks.   81

FOURTH MADMAN. Shall my pothecary out-go me because I am a cuckold ? I have found out his roguery ; he makes alum of his wife's urine, and sells it to Puritans that have sore throats with overstraining.

FIRST MADMAN. I have skill in heraldry.

SECOND MADMAN. Hast ?

FIRST MADMAN. You do give for your crest a woodcock's head with the brains picked out on 't ; you are a very ancient gentleman.   91

THIRD MADMAN. Greek is turn'd Turk : we are only to be sav'd by the Helvetian translation.[1]

FIRST MADMAN. Come on, sir, I will lay the law to you.

SECOND MADMAN. Oh, rather lay a corrosive : the law will eat to the bone.

THIRD MADMAN. He that drinks but to satisfy nature is damned.   99

FOURTH MADMAN. If I had my glass here, I would show a sight should make all the women here call me mad doctor.

FIRST MADMAN. What 's he ? a rope-maker ?

---

[1] Sc. of the Bible, made by English refugees at Geneva and published in 1560.

SECOND MADMAN.   No, no, no, a snuffling knave that, while he shows the tombs, will have his hand in a wench's placket.

THIRD MADMAN.   Woe to the caroche[1] that brought home my wife from the masque at three o'clock in the morning ! it had a large feather-bed in it.   110

FOURTH MADMAN.   I have pared the devil's nails forty times, roasted them in raven's eggs, and cur'd agues with them.

THIRD MADMAN.   Get me three hundred milch-bats, to make possets to procure sleep.

FOURTH MADMAN.   All the college may throw their caps at me :[2] I have made a soap-boiler costive ; it was my masterpiece.   118

[Here the dance, consisting of Eight Madmen, with music
     answerable thereunto ; after which, BOSOLA, like
     an Old Man, enters.

DUCHESS.   Is he mad too ?
SERVANT.   Pray, question him. I'll leave you.
                              [Exeunt Servant and Madmen.
BOSOLA.   I am come to make thy tomb.
DUCHESS.   Ha ! my tomb ?
Thou speak'st as if I lay upon my deathbed,
Gasping for breath : dost thou perceive me sick ?
BOSOLA.   Yes, and the more dangerously, since
     thy sickness
Is insensible.
DUCHESS.   Thou art not mad, sure : dost know
     me ?
BOSOLA.   Yes.
DUCHESS.   Who am I ?   125
BOSOLA.   Thou art a box of worm-seed, at best but a salvatory[3] of green mummy. What 's this flesh ? a little crudded[4] milk, fantastical puff-paste. Our bodies are weaker than those paper-prisons boys use to keep flies in ; more con-temptible, since ours is to preserve earthworms.

¹ Coach.   ² See note on p. 234.   ³ Ointment-box.   ⁴ Curded.

Didst thou ever see a lark in a cage ? Such is the
soul in the body : this world is like her little turf
of grass, and the heaven o'er our heads, like her
looking-glass, only gives us a miserable knowledge
of the small compass of our prison.

DUCHESS. Am not I thy duchess ? 137

BOSOLA. Thou art some great woman, sure, for
riot begins to sit on thy forehead (clad in grey
hairs) twenty years sooner than on a merry milk-
maid's. Thou sleep'st worse than if a mouse should
be forc'd to take up her lodging in a cat's ear :
a little infant that breeds its teeth, should it lie
with thee, would cry out, as if thou wert the more
unquiet bedfellow.

DUCHESS. I am Duchess of Malfi still.

BOSOLA. That makes thy sleeps so broken :
Glories, like glow-worms, afar off shine bright,
But looked to near, have neither heat nor light.

DUCHESS. Thou art very plain. 150

BOSOLA. My trade is to flatter the dead, not
the living ; I am a tomb-maker.

DUCHESS. And thou com'st to make my tomb ?

BOSOLA. Yes.

DUCHESS. Let me be a little merry :—of what
stuff wilt thou make it ? 156

BOSOLA. Nay, resolve me first, of what fashion ?

DUCHESS. Why, do we grow fantastical in our
death-bed ? do we affect fashion in the grave ?

BOSOLA. Most ambitiously. Princes' images on
their tombs do not lie, as they were wont, seeming
to pray up to heaven ; but with their hands under
their cheeks, as if they died of the toothache : they
are not carved with their eyes fix'd upon the stars ;
but as their minds were wholly bent upon the
world, the self-same way they seem to turn their
faces.

DUCHESS. Let me know fully therefore the effect
Of this thy dismal preparation,
This talk fit for a charnel.

BOSOLA. Now I shall :— 170

Q

Enter Executioners, with a coffin, cords, and a bell.

Here is a present from your princely brothers ;
And may it arrive welcome, for it brings
Last benefit, last sorrow.
    DUCHESS.   Let me see it :
I have so much obedience in my blood,
I wish it in their veins to do them good.
    BOSOLA.   This is your last presence-chamber.
    CARIOLA.   O my sweet lady !
    DUCHESS.   Peace ; it affrights not me.
    BOSOLA.   I am the common bellman,
That usually is sent to condemn'd persons
The night before they suffer.
    DUCHESS.   Even now
Thou said'st thou wast a tomb-maker.
    BOSOLA.   'Twas to bring you
By degrees to mortification. Listen.   181

    Hark, now every thing is still
    The screech-owl and the whistler shrill
    Call upon our dame aloud,
    And bid her quickly don her shroud !
    Much you had of land and rent ;
    Your length in clay 's now competent : [1]
    A long war disturb'd your mind ;
    Here your perfect peace is sign'd.   189
    Of what is 't fools make such vain keeping ?
    Sin their conception, their birth weeping,
    Their life a general mist of error,
    Their death a hideous storm of terror.
    Strew your hair with powders sweet,
    Don clean linen, bathe your feet,
    And (the foul fiend more to check)
    A crucifix let bless your neck :
    'Tis now full tide 'tween night and day ;
    End your groan, and come away.

    CARIOLA.   Hence, villains, tyrants, murderers !
    alas !   200

        [1] i.e. all you require.

What will you do with my lady ?—Call for help.

DUCHESS.   To whom ? to our next neighbours ?
    they are mad-folks.

BOSOLA.   Remove that noise.

DUCHESS.   Farewell, Cariola.
In my last will I have not much to give :
A many hungry guests have fed upon me ;
Thine will be a poor reversion.

CARIOLA.   I will die with her.

DUCHESS.   I pray thee, look thou giv'st my little
    boy
Some syrup for his cold, and let the girl
Say her prayers ere she sleep.

            [CARIOLA is forced out by the Executioners.
                     Now what you please :
What death ?

BOSOLA.   Strangling ;   210
Here are your executioners.

DUCHESS.   I forgive them :
The apoplexy, catarrh, or cough o' th' lungs,
Would do as much as they do.

BOSOLA.   Doth not death fright you ?

DUCHESS.   Who would be afraid on 't,
Knowing to meet such excellent company
In th' other world ?

BOSOLA.   Yet, methinks,
The manner of your death should much afflict you :
This cord should terrify you.

DUCHESS.   Not a whit :
What would it pleasure me to have my throat cut
With diamonds ? or to be smothered   220
With cassia ? or to be shot to death with pearls ?
I know death hath ten thousand several doors
For men to take their exits ; and 'tis found
They go on such strange geometrical hinges,
You may open them both ways.—Any way, for
    heaven sake,
So I were out of your whispering. Tell my
    brothers
That I perceive death, now I am well awake,

Best gift is they can give or I can take.
I would fain put off my last woman's fault,
I'd not be tedious to you.

    FIRST EXECUTIONER.   We are ready.   230
    DUCHESS. Dispose my breath how please you ;
      but my body
Bestow upon my women, will you ?

    FIRST EXECUTIONER.   Yes.
    DUCHESS. Pull, and pull strongly, for your able
      strength
Must pull down heaven upon me :—
Yet stay ; heaven-gates are not so highly arch'd
As princes' palaces ; they that enter there
Must go upon their knees [Kneels].—Come, violent
    death,
Serve for mandragora to make me sleep !—
Go tell my brothers, when I am laid out,
They then may feed in quiet.   240
                    [They strangle her.
    BOSOLA. Where's the waiting woman ? Fetch
      her : some other
Strangle the children.
             [Exeunt Executioners, some of whom return with
                 CARIOLA.
Look you, there sleeps your mistress.
    CARIOLA.   Oh, you are damn'd
Perpetually for this ! My turn is next,
Is 't not so order'd ?
    BOSOLA.   Yes, and I am glad
You are so well prepar'd for 't.
    CARIOLA.   You are deceiv'd, sir,
I am not prepar'd for 't, I will not die ;
I will first come to my answer, and know
How I have offended.
    BOSOLA.   Come, dispatch her.—
You kept her counsel ; now you shall keep ours.
    CARIOLA. I will not die, I must not ; I am
      contracted   251
To a young gentleman.
    FIRST EXECUTIONER. Here's your wedding-ring.

CARIOLA. Let me but speak with the duke ; I'll
discover
Treason to his person.

BOSOLA.   Delays :—throttle her.

FIRST EXECUTIONER. She bites and scratches.

CARIOLA.   If you kill me now,
I am damn'd ; I have not been at confession
This two years.

BOSOLA. [To Executioners.] When ? [1]

CARIOLA.   I am quick with child.

BOSOLA.   Why, then,
Your credit's sav'd.

            [They strangle CARIOLA..
                 Bear her into th' next room ;
Let this lie still.

      [Exeunt the Executioners with the body of CARIOLA.

            Enter FERDINAND.

FERDINAND.   Is she dead ?

BOSOLA.   She is what
You'd have her. But here begin your pity :   260
                    [Shows the Children strangled.[2]
Alas, how have these offended ?

FERDINAND.   The death
Of young wolves is never to be pitied.

BOSOLA.   Fix
Your eye here.

FERDINAND.   Constantly.

BOSOLA.   Do you not weep ?
Other sins only speak ; murder shrieks out :
The element of water moistens the earth,
But blood flies upwards and bedews the heavens.

FERDINAND. Cover her face ; mine eyes dazzle :
      she died young.

BOSOLA. I think not so ; her infelicity
Seem'd to have years too many.

FERDINAND.   She and I were twins ;
And should I die this instant, I had liv'd   270

[1] A common exclamation of impatience.
[2] Probably by drawing a curtain, as on pp. 178, 461.

Her time to a minute.

BOSOLA.   It seems she was born first :
You have bloodily approv'd the ancient truth,
That kindred commonly do worse agree
Than remote strangers.

FERDINAND.   Let me see her face
Again. Why didst not thou pity her ? what
An excellent honest man mightst thou have been,
If thou hadst borne her to some sanctuary !
Or, bold in a good cause, oppos'd thyself,
With thy advancèd sword above thy head,
Between her innocence and my revenge !   280
I bade thee, when I was distracted of my wits,
Go kill my dearest friend, and thou hast done 't.
For let me but examine well the cause :
What was the meanness of her match to me ?
Only I must confess I had a hope,
Had she continu'd widow, to have gain'd
An infinite mass of treasure by her death :
And that was the main cause ; her marriage,
That drew a stream of gall quite through my
     heart.
For thee, as we observe in tragedies   290
That a good actor many times is curs'd
For playing a villain's part, I hate thee for 't,
And, for my sake, say, thou hast done much ill
     well

BOSOLA. Let me quicken your memory, for I
     perceive
You are falling into ingratitude : I challenge
The reward due to my service.

FERDINAND.   I'll tell thee
What I'll give thee.

BOSOLA.   Do.

FERDINAND.   I'll give thee a pardon
For this murder.

BOSOLA.   Ha !

FERDINAND.   Yes, and 'tis
The largest bounty I can study to do thee.
By what authority didst thou execute   300

This bloody sentence ?

BOSOLA.   By yours.

FERDINAND.   Mine ? was I her judge ?
Did any ceremonial form of law
Doom her to not-being ? did a complete jury
Deliver her conviction up i' th' court ?
Where shalt thou find this judgement register'd,
Unless in hell ? See, like a bloody fool,
Thou'st forfeited thy life, and thou shalt die for 't.

BOSOLA.   The office of justice is perverted quite
When one thief hangs another. Who shall dare
To reveal this ?

FERDINAND.   Oh, I'll tell thee ;   310
The wolf shall find her grave, and scrape it up,
Not to devour the corpse, but to discover
The horrid murder.

BOSOLA.   You, not I, shall quake for 't.

FERDINAND.   Leave me.

BOSOLA.   I will first receive my pension.

FERDINAND.   You are a villain.

BOSOLA.   When your ingratitude
Is judge, I am so.

FERDINAND.   Oh, horror, that not the fear
Of him which binds the devils can prescribe man
Obedience !—Never look upon me more.

BOSOLA.   Why, fare thee well.   319
Your brother and yourself are worthy men :
You have a pair of hearts are hollow graves,
Rotten, and rotting others ; and your vengeance,
Like two chain'd bullets, still goes arm in arm :
You may be brothers ; for treason, like the plague,
Doth take much in a blood. I stand like one
That long hath ta'en a sweet and golden dream :
I am angry with myself, now that I wake.

FERDINAND.   Get thee into some unknown part
    o' th' world,
That I may never see thee.

BOSOLA.   Let me know
Wherefore I should be thus neglected. Sir,   330
I serv'd your tyranny, and rather strove

To satisfy yourself than all the world :
And though I loath'd the evil, yet I lov'd
You that did counsel it ; and rather sought
To appear a true servant than an honest man.
    FERDINAND. I'll go hunt the badger by owl-
      light :
'Tis a deed of darkness.   [Exit.
    BOSOLA. He's   much   distracted.   Off, my
      painted honour !
While with vain hopes our faculties we tire,
We seem to sweat in ice and freeze in fire.   340
What would I do, were this to do again ?
I would not change my peace of conscience
For all the wealth of Europe.—She stirs ; here's
    life :—
Return, fair soul, from darkness, and lead mine
Out of this sensible hell :—she's warm, she
    breathes :—
Upon thy pale lips I will melt my heart,
To store them with fresh colour.—Who's there !
Some cordial drink !—Alas ! I dare not call :
So pity would destroy pity.—Her eye opes,
And heaven in it seems to ope, that late was shut,
To take me up to mercy.   351
    DUCHESS. Antonio !
    BOSOLA.   Yes, madam, he is living ;
The dead bodies you saw were but feign'd statues :
He's reconcil'd to your brothers : the Pope hath
    wrought
The atonement.
    DUCHESS.   Mercy !   [Dies.
    BOSOLA. Oh, she's gone again! there the cords of
    life broke.
Oh, sacred innocence, that sweetly sleeps
On turtles' feathers, whilst a guilty conscience
Is a black register wherein is writ
All our good deeds and bad, a perspective   360
That shows us hell ! That we cannot be suffer'd
To do good when we have a mind to it !
This is manly sorrow ; these tears, I am very certain,

Never grew in my mother's milk : my estate
Is sunk below the degree of fear : where were
These penitent fountains while she was living ?
Oh, they were frozen up ! Here is a sight
As direful to my soul as is the sword
Unto a wretch hath slain his father. Come, I'll
    bear thee   369
Hence, and execute thy last will ; that's deliver
Thy body to the reverend dispose
Of some good women : that the cruel tyrant
Shall not deny me. Then I'll post to Milan,
Where somewhat I will speedily enact
Worth my dejection.   [Exit with the body.

ACT THE FIFTH

SCENE I.—A Public Place in Milan.

Enter ANTONIO and DELIO.

ANTONIO. What think you of my hope of
    reconcilement
To the Arragonian brethren ?
DELIO.   I misdoubt it ;
For though they have sent their letters of safe-
    conduct
For your repair to Milan, they appear
But nets to entrap you. The Marquis of Pescara,
Under whom you hold certain land in cheat,[1]
Much 'gainst his noble nature hath been mov'd
To seize those lands ; and some of his dependants
Are at this instant making it their suit
To be invested in your revenues.   10
I cannot think they mean well to your life
That do deprive you of your means of life
Your living.
ANTONIO. You are still an heretic
To any safety I can shape myself.

---

[1] Escheat, subject to forfeiture on the outlawry of the
tenant.

DELIO. Here comes the marquis : I will make myself
Petitioner for some part of your land,
To know whither it is flying.

ANTONIO. I pray do.

[Withdraws to back.

Enter PESCARA.

DELIO. Sir, I have a suit to you.

PESCARA. To me ?

DELIO. An easy one :
There is the citadel of Saint Bennet,
With some demesnes, of late in the possession
Of Antonio Bologna,—please you bestow them on me. 21

PESCARA. You are my friend ; but this is such a suit,
Nor fit for me to give, nor you to take.

DELIO. No, sir ?

PESCARA. I will give you ample reason for 't
Soon in private :—here 's the Cardinal's mistress.

Enter JULIA.

JULIA. My lord, I am grown your poor petitioner,
And should be an ill beggar, had I not
A great man's letter here, the Cardinal's,
To court you in my favour. [Gives a letter.

PESCARA. He entreats for you
The citadel of Saint Bennet, that belong'd 30
To the banish'd Bologna.

JULIA. Yes.

PESCARA I could not
Have thought of a friend I could rather pleasure with it :
'Tis yours.

JULIA. Sir, I thank you ; and he shall know
How doubly I am engag'd both in your gift,
And speediness of giving, which makes your grant
The greater. [Exit.

ANTONIO. [Aside.] How they fortify themselves

With my ruin !

DELIO.   Sir, I am little bound to you.

PESCARA.   Why?

DELIO.   Because you denied this suit to me, and gave 't
To such a creature.

PESCARA.   Do you know what it was ?
It was Antonio's land ; not forfeited   40
By course of law, but ravish'd from his throat
By the Cardinal's entreaty : it were not fit
I should bestow so main a piece of wrong
Upon my friend ; 'tis a gratification
Only due to a strumpet, for it is injustice.
Shall I sprinkle the pure blood of innocents
To make those followers I call my friends
Look ruddier upon me ? I am glad
This land, ta'en from the owner by such wrong,
Returns again unto so foul an use   50
As salary for his lust. Learn, good Delio,
To ask noble things of me, and you shall find
I'll be a noble giver.

DELIO.   You instruct me well.

ANTONIO. [Aside.] Why, here 's a man now would fright impudence
From sauciest beggars.

PESCARA.   Prince Ferdinand 's come to Milan,
Sick, as they give out, of an apoplexy ;
But some say 'tis a frenzy : I am going
To visit him.   [Exit

ANTONIO.   'Tis a noble old fellow.

DELIO. What course do you mean to take, Antonio ?

ANTONIO.   This night I mean to venture all my fortune,   60
Which is no more than a poor lingering life,
To the Cardinal's worst of malice : I have got
Private access to his chamber ; and intend
To visit him about the mid of night,
As once his brother did our noble duchess.
It may be that the sudden apprehension

Of danger,—for I'll go in mine own shape,—
When he shall see it fraight [1] with love and duty,
May draw the poison out of him, and work
A friendly reconcilement : if it fail,   70
Yet it shall rid me of this infamous calling ;
For better fall once than be ever falling.

  DELIO. I'll second you in all danger ; and, howe'er,
My life keeps rank with yours.

  ANTONIO.   You are still my lov'd
And best friend.   [Exeunt.

  SCENE II.—A Gallery in the CARDINAL'S Palace at
        Milan.

    Enter PESCARA and Doctor.

  PESCARA. Now, doctor, may I visit your patient ?

  DOCTOR. If 't please your lordship : but he 's instantly
To take the air here in the gallery
By my direction.

  PESCARA. Pray thee, what 's his disease ?

  DOCTOR. A very pestilent disease, my lord,
They call [it] lycanthropia.

  PESCARA.   What 's that ?
I need a dictionary to 't.

  DOCTOR.   I'll tell you.
In those that are possess'd with 't there o'erflows
Such melancholy humour they imagine
Themselves to be transformed into wolves ;   10
Steal forth to churchyards in the dead of night,
And dig dead bodies up : as two nights since
One met the duke 'bout midnight in a lane
Behind Saint Mark's Church, with the leg of a man
Upon his shoulder ; and he howl'd fearfully ;
Said he was a wolf, only the difference
Was, a wolf's skin was hairy on the outside,
His on the inside ; bade them take their swords,

       [1] Fraught.

Rip up his flesh, and try : straight I was sent for,
And, having minister'd to him, found his grace
Very well recovered.   21

    PESCARA.   I am glad on 't.

    DOCTOR.   Yet not without some fear
Of a relapse. If he grow to his fit again,
I'll go a nearer way to work with him
Than ever Paracelsus dream'd of ; if
They'll give me leave, I'll buffet his madness
Out of him. Stand aside ; he comes.

Enter FERDINAND, CARDINAL, MALATESTE, *and* BOSOLA.

    FERDINAND.   Leave me.

    MALATESTE.   Why doth your lordship love this
    solitariness ?

    FERDINAND.   Eagles commonly fly alone : they
are crows, daws, and starlings that flock together.
Look, what 's that follows me ?   31

    MALATESTE.   Nothing, my lord.

    FERDINAND.   Yes.

    MALATESTE.   'Tis your shadow.

    FERDINAND.   Stay it ; let it not haunt me.

    MALATESTE.   Impossible, if you move, and the
    sun shine.

    FERDINAND.   I will throttle it.

                      [*Throws himself on the ground.*

    MALATESTE.   O, my lord, you are angry with
    nothing.

    FERDINAND.   You are a fool : how is 't possible
I should catch my shadow, unless I fall upon 't ?
When I go to hell, I mean to carry a bribe ; for,
look you, good gifts evermore make way for the
worst persons.   43

    PESCARA.   Rise, good my lord.

    FERDINAND.   I am studying the art of patience.

    PESCARA.   'Tis a noble virtue.

    FERDINAND.   To drive six snails before me from
this town to Moscow ; neither use goad nor whip
to them, but let them take their own time ;—
the patient'st man i' th' world match me for an

experiment ;—and I'll crawl after like a sheep-
biter.

CARDINAL.   Force him up.   [They raise him.

FERDINAND.   Use me well, you were best.
What I have done, I have done : I'll confess
nothing.

DOCTOR.   Now let me come to him.—Are you
mad, my lord ? are you out of your princely
wits ?

FERDINAND.   What 's he ?   60

PESCARA.   Your doctor.

FERDINAND.   Let me have his beard saw'd off,
and his eyebrows fil'd more civil.

DOCTOR.   I must do mad tricks with him, for
that 's the only way on 't.—I have brought your
grace a salamander's skin to keep you from sun-
burning.

FERDINAND.   I have cruel sore eyes.

DOCTOR.   The white of a cockatrix's egg is
present remedy.   70

FERDINAND.   Let it be a new laid one, you were
best.—Hide me from him : physicians are like
kings,—they brook no contradiction.

DOCTOR.   Now he begins to fear me : now let
me alone with him.

CARDINAL.   How now ? put off your gown ?

DOCTOR.   Let me have some forty urinals fill'd
with rose-water : he and I'll go pelt one another
with them.—Now he begins to fear me.—Can you
fetch a frisk,[1] sir ?—Let him go, let him go, upon
my peril : I find by his eye he stands in awe of
me ; I'll make him as tame as a dormouse.   82

FERDINAND.   Can you fetch your frisks, sir ?—
I will stamp him into a cullis, flay off his skin, to
cover one of the anatomies [2] this rogue hath set
i' th' cold yonder in Barber-Chirurgeon's-hall.—
Hence, hence ! you are all of you like beasts for
sacrifice : there 's nothing left of you but tongue
and belly, flattery and lechery.   [Exit.

[1] Cut a caper.   [2] Skeletons.

PESCARA.   Doctor, he did not fear you throughly.
DOCTOR.   True ;
I was somewhat too forward.
BOSOLA.   Mercy upon me,
What a fatal judgement hath fall'n upon this
    Ferdinand !   92
PESCARA.   Knows your grace what accident hath
    brought
Unto the prince this strange distraction ?
CARDINAL. [Aside.] I must feign somewhat.—
Thus they say it grew.
You have heard it rumour'd, for these many years
None of our family dies but there is seen
The shape of an old woman, which is given
By tradition to us to have been murder'd
By her nephews for her riches. Such a figure   100
One night, as the prince sat up late at 's book,
Appear'd to him ; when crying out for help,
The gentlemen of 's chamber found his grace
All on a cold sweat, alter'd much in face
And language : since which apparition,
He hath grown worse and worse, and I much fear
He cannot live.
BOSOLA.   Sir, I would speak with you.
PESCARA.   We'll leave your grace,
Wishing to the sick prince, our noble lord,
All health of mind and body.
CARDINAL.   You are most welcome.
        [Exeunt PESCARA, MALATESTE, and Doctor.
Are you come ? so.—[Aside.] This fellow must not
    know   111
By any means I had intelligence
In our duchess' death ; for, though I counsell'd it,
The full of all th' engagement seem'd to grow
From Ferdinand.—Now, sir, how fares our sister ?
I do not think but sorrow makes her look
Like to an oft-dyed garment : she shall now
Taste comfort from me. Why do you look so
    wildly ?
Oh, the fortune of your master here the prince

Dejects you ; but be you of happy comfort : 120
If you'll do one thing for me I'll entreat,
Though he had a cold tombstone o'er his bones,
I'd make you what you would be.
    BOSOLA.   Anything ;
Give it me in a breath, and let me fly to 't :
They that think long small expedition win,
For musing much o' th' end cannot begin.

Enter JULIA.

    JULIA.   Sir, will you come in to supper ?
    CARDINAL.   I am busy ;
Leave me.
    JULIA. [Aside.] What an excellent shape hath
      that fellow !   [Exit.
    CARDINAL. 'Tis thus. Antonio lurks here in
      Milan :   129
Inquire him out, and kill him. While he lives,
Our sister cannot marry ; and I have thought
Of an excellent match for her. Do this, and style
    me
Thy advancement.
    BOSOLA.   But by what means shall I find
    him out ?
    CARDINAL.   There is a gentleman called Delio
Here in the camp, that hath been long approv'd
His loyal friend. Set eye upon that fellow ;
Follow him to mass ; maybe Antonio,
Although he do account religion
But a school-name, for fashion of the world
May accompany him ; or else go inquire out
Delio's confessor, and see if you can bribe   141
Him to reveal it. There are a thousand ways
A man might find to trace him ; as to know
What fellows haunt the Jews for taking up
Great sums of money, for sure he 's in want ;
Or else to go to th' picture-makers, and learn
Who bought [1] her picture lately : some of these
Happily may take.

         [1] ' Brought ', in the early editions.

BOSOLA.   Well, I'll not freeze i' th' business :
I would see that wretched thing, Antonio,
Above all sights i' th' world.

CARDINAL.   Do, and be happy.   [Exit.

BOSOLA. This fellow doth breed basilisks in 's
    eyes,   151
He 's nothing else but murder ; yet he seems
Not to have notice of the duchess' death.
'Tis his cunning : I must follow his example ;
There cannot be a surer way to trace
Than that of an old fox.

Re-enter JULIA, *with a pistol.*

JULIA.   So, sir, you are well met.

BOSOLA. How now ?

JULIA.   Nay, the doors are fast
    enough : Now, sir,
I will make you confess your treachery.

BOSOLA.   Treachery ?

JULIA.   Yes,
Confess to me which of my women 'twas
You hired to put love-powder into my drink ?   160

BOSOLA. Love-powder ?

JULIA.   Yes, when I was at Malfi.
Why should I fall in love with such a face else ?
I have already suffer'd for thee so much pain,
The only remedy to do me good
Is to kill my longing.

BOSOLA.   Sure, your pistol holds
Nothing but perfumes or kissing-comfits.[1]
Excellent lady ! You have a pretty way on 't
To discover your longing. Come, come, I'll disarm
    you,
And arm you thus : yet this is wondrous strange.

JULIA. Compare thy form and my eyes to-
    gether, you'll find   170
My love no such great miracle. Now you'll say
I am wanton : this nice modesty in ladies
Is but a troublesome familiar that haunts them.

     [1] Perfumed sugar-plums, to sweeten the breath.

BOSOLA.   Know you me, I am a blunt soldier.
JULIA.   The better:
Sure, there wants fire where there are no lively
    sparks
Of roughness.
        BOSOLA.   And I want compliment.
        JULIA.   Why, ignorance
In courtship cannot make you do amiss,
If you have a heart to do well.
        BOSOLA.   You are very fair.
        JULIA.   Nay, if you lay beauty to my charge,
I must plead unguilty.
        BOSOLA.   Your bright eyes carry
A quiver of darts in them sharper than sunbeams.
        JULIA.   You will mar me with commendation,
Put yourself to the charge of courting me,   183
Whereas now I woo you.
        BOSOLA. [Aside.] I have it, I will work upon this
            creature.—
Let us grow most amorously familiar :
If the great Cardinal now should see me thus,
Would he not count me a villain ?
        JULIA.   No ; he might
Count me a wanton, not lay a scruple
Of offence on you ; for if I see and steal   190
A diamond, the fault is not i' th' stone,
But in me the thief that purloins it. I am sudden
With you : we that are great women of pleasure
Use to cut off these uncertain wishes
And unquiet longings, and in an instant join
The sweet delight and the pretty excuse together.
Had you been i' th' street, under my chamber-
        window,
Even there I should have courted you.
        BOSOLA.   Oh, you are
An excellent lady !
        JULIA.   Bid me do somewhat for you
Presently to express I love you.
        BOSOLA.   I will ;   200
And if you love me, fail not to effect it.

The Cardinal is grown wondrous melancholy ;
Demand the cause, let him not put you off
With feign'd excuse ; discover the main ground
  on 't.
   JULIA.   Why would you know this ?
   BOSOLA.   I have depended on him,
And I hear that he is fall'n in some disgrace
With the emperor : if he be, like the mice
That forsake falling houses, I would shift
To other dependence.
   JULIA.   You shall not need
Follow the wars : I'll be your maintenance.   210
   BOSOLA.   And I your loyal servant : but I
  cannot
Leave my calling.
   JULIA.   Not leave an ungrateful
General for the love of a sweet lady ?
You are like some cannot sleep in feather-beds,
But must have blocks for their pillows.
   BOSOLA.   Will you do this ?
   JULIA.   Cunningly.
   BOSOLA.   To-morrow I'll expect th' intelligence.
   JULIA.   To-morrow ? get you into my cabinet ;
You shall have it with you. Do not delay me,
No more than I do you : I am like one   220
That is condemn'd ; I have my pardon promis'd,
But I would see it seal'd. Go, get you in :
You shall see me wind my tongue about his heart
Like a skein of silk.   [Exit BOSOLA.

Re-enter CARDINAL

   CARDINAL.   Where are you ?

Enter Servants.

   SERVANTS.   Here.
   CARDINAL.   Let none, upon your lives, have
  conference
With the Prince Ferdinand, unless I know it.—
[Aside.] In this distraction he may reveal
The murder.   [Exeunt Servants.

         Yond 's my lingering consumption :
I am weary of her, and by any means   229
Would be quit of.
    JULIA.   How now, my lord ? what ails you ?
    CARDINAL. Nothing.
    JULIA.   Oh, you are much alter'd :
    come, I must be
Your secretary, and remove this lead
From off your bosom : what 's the matter ?
    CARDINAL.   I may not
Tell you.
    JULIA.   Are you so far in love with sorrow
You cannot part with part of it ? or think you
I cannot love your grace when you are sad
As well as merry ? or do you suspect
I, that have been a secret to your heart
These many winters, cannot be the same   239
Unto your tongue ?
    CARDINAL.   Satisfy thy longing,—
The only way to make thee keep my counsel
Is, not to tell thee.
    JULIA.   Tell your echo this,
Or flatterers, that like echoes still report
What they hear though most imperfect, and not
    me ;
For if that you be true unto yourself,
I'll know.
    CARDINAL. Will you rack me ?
    JULIA.   No, judgement shall
Draw it from you : it is an equal fault,
To tell one's secrets unto all or none.
    CARDINAL. The first argues folly.
    JULIA.   But the last tyranny.
    CARDINAL. Very well : why, imagine I have
    committed   250
Some secret deed which I desire the world
May never hear of.
    JULIA.   Therefore may not I know it ?
You have conceal'd for me as great a sin
As adultery. Sir, never was occasion

For perfect trial of my constancy
Till now : sir, I beseech you————
    CARDINAL.   You'll repent it.
    JULIA. Never.
    CARDINAL. It hurries thee to ruin : I'll not tell
    thee.
Be well advis'd, and think what danger 'tis
To receive a prince's secrets : they that do,   260
Had need have their breasts hoop'd with adamant
To contain them. I pray thee, yet be satisfi'd ;
Examine thine own frailty ; 'tis more easy
To tie knots than unloose them : 'tis a secret
That, like a lingering poison, may chance lie
Spread in thy veins, and kill thee seven year hence.
    JULIA. Now you dally with me.
    CARDINAL.   No more ; thou shalt know it.
By my appointment the great Duchess of Malfi
And two of her young children, four nights since,
Were strangled.
    JULIA.   O Heaven ! sir, what have you done !
    CARDINAL. How now ? how settles this ?
    think you your bosom   271
Will be a grave dark and obscure enough
For such a secret ?
    JULIA.   You have undone yourself, sir.
    CARDINAL. Why ?
    JULIA.   It lies not in me to conceal it.
    CARDINAL.   No ?
Come, I will swear you to 't upon this book.
    JULIA. Most religiously.
    CARDINAL.   Kiss it. [She kisses the book.
    Now you shall
Never utter it ; thy curiosity
Hath undone thee : thou 'rt poison'd with that book ;
Because I knew thou couldst not keep my counsel,
I have bound thee to 't by death.

Re-enter BOSOLA.

    BOSOLA.   For pity sake
Hold !

CARDINAL.   Ha ! Bosola ?

JULIA.   I forgive you   282
This equal piece of justice you have done ;
For I betray'd your counsel to that fellow :
He overheard it ; that was the cause I said
It lay not in me to conceal it.

BOSOLA.   O foolish woman,
Couldst not thou have poison'd him ?

JULIA.   'Tis weakness,
Too much to think what should have been done.
   I go,
I know not whither.   [Dies.

CARDINAL.   Wherefore com'st thou hither ?

BOSOLA.   That I might find a great man like
   yourself,   290
Not out of his wits as the Lord Ferdinand,
To remember my service.

CARDINAL.   I'll have thee hew'd in pieces.

BOSOLA.   Make not yourself such a promise of
   that life
Which is not yours to dispose of.

CARDINAL.   Who plac'd thee here ?

BOSOLA.   Her lust, as she intended.

CARDINAL.   Very well :
Now you know me for your fellow-murderer.

BOSOLA.   And wherefore should you lay fair
   marble colours
Upon your rotten purposes to me ?
Unless you imitate some that do plot great treasons,
And when they have done, go hide themselves i' th'
   graves   300
Of those were actors in 't ?

CARDINAL.   No more ; there is
A fortune attends thee.

BOSOLA.   Shall I go sue
To Fortune any longer ? 'Tis the fool's
Pilgrimage.

CARDINAL.   I have honours in store for thee.

BOSOLA.   There are a many ways that conduct to
   seeming

Honour, and some of them very dirty ones.

CARDINAL.   Throw
To the devil thy melancholy. The fire burns well ;
What need we keep a stirring of 't, and make
A greater smother ? Thou wilt kill Antonio ?

BOSOLA. Yes.

CARDINAL.   Take up that body.

BOSOLA.   I think I shall
Shortly grow the common beare[r] for church-
    yards.   311

CARDINAL. I will allow thee some dozen of
    attendants
To aid thee in the murder.

BOSOLA. Oh, by no means. Physicians that
apply horse-leeches to any rank swelling use to
cut off their tails, that the blood may run through
them the faster : let me have no train when I go
to shed blood, lest it make me have a greater when
I ride to the gallows.

CARDINAL.   Come to me after midnight, to help
    to remove   320
That body to her own lodging : I'll give out
She died o' th' plague ; 'twill breed the less inquiry
After her death.

BOSOLA.   Where 's Castruchio her husband ?

CARDINAL.   He 's rode to Naples, to take posses-
    sion
Of Antonio's citadel.

BOSOLA.   Believe me, you have done
A very happy turn.

CARDINAL.   Fail not to come :
There is the master-key of our lodgings ; and by
    that
You may conceive what trust I plant in you.

BOSOLA.   You shall find me ready. [Exit CARDINAL.
                                    O poor Antonio,
Though nothing be so needful to thy estate
As pity, yet I find nothing so dangerous ;   331
I must look to my footing :
In such slippery ice-pavements men had need

To be frost-nailed well, they may break their
    necks else ;
The precedent's here afore me. How this man
Bears up in blood ! seems fearless ! Why, 'tis well :
Security some men call the suburbs of hell,
Only a dead wall between. Well, good Antonio,
I'll seek thee out ; and all my care shall be
To put thee into safety from the reach   **340**
Of these most cruel biters that have got
Some of thy blood already. It may be,
I'll join with thee in a most just revenge :
The weakest arm is strong enough that strikes
With the sword of justice. Still methinks the
    duchess
Haunts me.—There, there, 'tis nothing but my
    melancholy.
O Penitence, let me truly taste thy cup,
That throws men down only to raise them up ! [Exit.

    SCENE III.—A Fortification at Milan.

    Enter ANTONIO and DELIO.

  DELIO. Yond's the Cardinal's window. This
    fortification
Grew from the ruins of an ancient abbey ;
And to yond side o' th' river lies a wall,
Piece of a cloister, which in my opinion
Gives the best echo that you ever heard,
So hollow and so dismal, and withal
So plain in the distinction of our words,
That many have suppos'd it is a spirit
That answers.

    ANTONIO.   I do love these ancient ruins.
We never tread upon them but we set   **10**
Our foot upon some reverend history :
And, questionless, here in this open court,
Which now lies naked to the injuries
Of stormy weather, some men lie interr'd
Lov'd the church so well, and gave so largely to 't,
They thought it should have canopied their bones
Till doomsday ; but all things have their end :

Churches and cities, which have diseases
Like to men, must have like death that we have.
    ECHO. ' Like death that we have.' 20
    DELIO. Now the echo hath caught you.
    ANTONIO.   It groaned, methought, and gave
A very deadly accent.
    ECHO.   ' Deadly accent.'
    DELIO. I told you 'twas a pretty one : you may
    make it
A huntsman, or a falconer, a musician,
Or a thing of sorrow.
    ECHO.   ' A thing of sorrow.'
    ANTONIO. Aye, sure, that suits it best.
    ECHO.   ' That suits it best.'
    ANTONIO. 'Tis very like my wife's voice.
    ECHO.   ' Aye, wife's voice.'
    DELIO. Come, let 's walk further from 't. I
    would not have you
Go to th' Cardinal's to-night : do not.
    ECHO.   ' Do not.'
    DELIO. Wisdom doth not more moderate wast-
    ing sorrow 30
Than time : take time for 't ; be mindful of thy
    safety.
    ECHO. ' Be mindful of thy safety.'
    ANTONIO.   Necessity compels me :
Make scrutiny throughout the passes of
Your own life, you'll find it impossible
To fly your fate.
    ECHO.   ' Oh, fly your fate.'
    DELIO.   Hark !
The dead stones seem to have pity on you, and
    give you
Good counsel.
    ANTONIO.   Echo, I will not talk with thee,
For thou art a dead thing.
    ECHO.   ' Thou art a dead thing.'
    ANTONIO. My duchess is asleep now, 39
And her little ones, I hope sweetly : O Heaven,
Shall I never see her more ?

ECHO.   ' Never see her more.'

ANTONIO. I mark'd not one repetition of the echo
But that ; and on the sudden a clear light
Presented me a face folded in sorrow.

DELIO. Your fancy merely.

ANTONIO.   Come, I'll be out of this ague,
For to live thus is not indeed to live ;
It is a mockery and abuse of life :
I will not henceforth save myself by halves ;
Lose all, or nothing.

DELIO.   Your own virtue save you !
I'll fetch your eldest son, and second you :   50
It may be that the sight of his own blood
Spread in so sweet a figure may beget
The more compassion. However, fare you well.
Though in our miseries Fortune have a part,
Yet in our noble sufferings she hath none :
Contempt of pain, that we may call our own.

                            [Exeunt.

SCENE IV.—A Room in the CARDINAL'S Palace.

Enter CARDINAL, PESCARA, MALATESTE, RODERIGO, and
GRISOLAN.

CARDINAL. You shall not watch to-night by the sick prince ;
His grace is very well recover'd.

MALATESTE. Good my lord, suffer us.

CARDINAL.   Oh, by no means ;
The noise, and change of object in his eye,
Doth more distract him : I pray, all to bed ;
And though you hear him in his violent fit,
Do not rise, I entreat you.

PESCARA.   So, sir ; we shall not.

CARDINAL. Nay, I must have you promise upon your honours,
For I was enjoin'd to 't by himself ; and he seem'd
To urge it sensibly.

PESCARA.   Let our honours bind   10

This trifle.

CARDINAL. Nor any of your followers.

MALATESTE.   Neither.

CARDINAL. It may be, to make trial of your
promise,
When he's asleep, myself will rise and feign
Some of his mad tricks, and cry out for help,
And feign myself in danger.

MALATESTE.   If your throat were cutting,
I'd not come at you, now I have protested against it.

CARDINAL. Why, I thank you.

GRISOLAN.   'Twas a foul storm to-night.

RODERIGO. The Lord Ferdinand's chamber
shook like an osier.

MALATESTE. 'Twas nothing but pure kindness
in the devil,
To rock his own child.   20

          [Exeunt all except the CARDINAL.

CARDINAL. The reason why I would not suffer
these
About my brother, is, because at midnight
I may with better privacy convey
Julia's body to her own lodging. Oh, my con-
science !
I would pray now ; but the devil takes away my
heart
For having any confidence in prayer.
About this hour I appointed Bosola
To fetch the body : when he hath serv'd my turn,
He dies.   [Exit.

          Enter BOSOLA.

BOSOLA. Ha ! 'twas the Cardinal's voice ; I
heard him name   30
Bosola and my death. Listen ; I hear
One's footing.

          Enter FERDINAND.

FERDINAND. Strangling is a very quiet death.

BOSOLA. [Aside.] Nay, then, I see I must stand
upon my guard.

FERDINAND. What say to that? whisper
softly; do you agree to 't? So; it must be done
i' th' dark : the Cardinal would not for a thousand
pounds the doctor should see it.   [Exit.

     BOSOLA. My death is plotted; here's the con-
     sequence of murder.
We value not desert nor Christian breath,   40
When we know black deeds must be cur'd with
     death.

     Enter ANTONIO and Servant.

     SERVANT. Here stay, sir, and be confident,
     I pray :
I'll fetch you a dark lantern.   [Exit.
     ANTONIO.   Could I take him
At his prayers, there were hope of pardon.
     BOSOLA.   Fall right, my sword!—[Stabs him.
I'll not give thee so much leisure as to pray.
     ANTONIO. Oh, I am gone! Thou hast ended a
     long suit
In a minute.
     BOSOLA.   What art thou?
     ANTONIO.   A most wretched thing,
That only have thy benefit in death,
To appear myself.

     Re-enter Servant with a lantern.

     SERVANT.   Where are you, sir?
     ANTONIO. Very near my home.—Bosola?
     SERVANT.   Oh, misfortune!
     BOSOLA. Smother thy pity, thou art dead else.—
     Antonio?   51
The man I would have saved 'bove mine own life!
We are merely the stars' tennis-balls, struck and
     bandied
Which way please them.—O good Antonio,
I'll whisper one thing in thy dying ear
Shall make thy heart break quickly! thy fair
     duchess
And two sweet children——
     ANTONIO.   Their very names

Kindle a little life in me.

BOSOLA.   Are murder'd.

ANTONIO.   Some men have wish'd to die
At the hearing of sad tidings ; I am glad   60
That I shall do 't in sadness : [1] I would not now
Wish my wounds balm'd nor heal'd, for I have no use
To put my life to.   In all our quest of greatness,
Like wanton boys, whose pastime is their care,
We follow after bubbles blown in th' air,
Pleasure of life, what is 't ? only the good
Hours of an ague ; merely a preparative
To rest, to endure vexation.   I do not ask
The process of my death ; only commend me
To Delio.

BOSOLA.   Break, heart !

ANTONIO.   And let my son   70
Fly the courts of princes.   [Dies.

BOSOLA.   Thou seem'st
To have lov'd Antonio ?

SERVANT.   I brought him hither,
To have reconcil'd him to the Cardinal.

BOSOLA.   I do not ask thee that.
Take him up, if thou tender thine own life,
And bear him where the lady Julia
Was wont to lodge.—Oh, my fate moves swift ;
I have this Cardinal in the forge already ;
Now I'll bring him to th' hammer. O direful mis-
     prision ! [2]
I will not imitate things glorious,   80
No more than base ; I'll be mine own example.—
On, on, and look thou represent, for silence,
The thing thou bear'st.   [Exeunt.

SCENE V.—Another Room in the same.

Enter CARDINAL, with a book.

CARDINAL.   I am puzzled in a question about
     hell :
He says, in hell there 's one material fire,

------

[1] i. e. in earnest.   [2] Mistake.

And yet it shall not burn all men alike.
Lay him by. How tedious is a guilty conscience !
When I look into the fish-ponds in my garden,
Methinks I see a thing arm'd with a rake,
That seems to strike at me.

Enter BOSOLA, *and Servant bearing Antonio's body.*

Now, art thou come?
Thou look'st ghastly :   8
There sits in thy face some great determination
Mix'd with some fear.

BOSOLA.   Thus it lightens into action :
I am come to kill thee.

CARDINAL.   Ha !—Help ! our guard !

BOSOLA. Thou art deceived ; they are out of
thy howling.

CARDINAL. Hold ; and I will faithfully divide
Revenues with thee.

BOSOLA.   Thy prayers and proffers
Are both unseasonable.

CARDINAL.   Raise the watch !
We are betrayed !

BOSOLA.   I have confin'd your flight :
I'll suffer your retreat to Julia's chamber,
But no further.

CARDINAL.   Help ! we are betrayed !

Enter, above, PESCARA, MALATESTE, RODERIGO, *and*
GRISOLAN.

MALATESTE. Listen.

CARDINAL.   My dukedom for rescue !

RODERIGO.   Fie upon
His counterfeiting [1]

MALATESTE.   Why, 'tis not the Cardinal.

RODERIGO. Yes, yes, 'tis he : but I'll see him
hang'd   21
Ere I'll go down to him.

CARDINAL.   Here 's a plot upon me ;
I am assaulted ! I am lost, unless some rescue.

GRISOLAN. He doth this pretty well ; but it
will not serve

To laugh me out of mine honour.

CARDINAL.   The sword 's at my throat !

RODERIGO.   You would not bawl so loud then.

MALATESTE.   Come, come,
Let 's go to bed : he told us thus much aforehand.

PESCARA.   He wish'd you should not come at
  him ; but, believe 't,
The accent of the voice sounds not in jest :   29
I'll down to him, howsoever, and with engines
Force ope the doors.   [Exit above.

RODERIGO.   Let 's follow him aloof,
And note how the Cardinal will laugh at him.
        [Exeunt, above, MALATESTE, RODERIGO, and GRISOLAN.

BOSOLA.   There 's for you first, [Kills the Servant.
'Cause you shall not unbarricade the door
To let in rescue.

CARDINAL.   What cause hast thou to pursue my
  life ?

BOSOLA.   Look there.

CARDINAL.   Antonio ?

BOSOLA.   Slain by my hand unwittingly.
Pray, and be sudden : when thou killed'st thy
  sister,
Thou took'st from Justice her most equal balance,
And left her naught but her sword.

CARDINAL.   Oh, mercy !

BOSOLA.   Now it seems thy greatness was only
  outward ;   41
For thou fall'st faster of thyself than calamity
Can drive thee. I'll not waste longer time ; there !
                                [Stabs him.

CARDINAL.   Thou hast hurt me.

BOSOLA.   Again !   [Stabs him again.

CARDINAL.   Shall I die like a leveret,
Without any resistance ?—Help, help, help !
I am slain !

          Enter FERDINAND.

FERDINAND. Th' alarum ? give me a fresh horse ;
Rally the vaunt-guard, or the day is lost.

Yield, yield ! I give you the honour of arms,
Shake my sword over you ; will you yield ?
    CARDINAL.   Help me ;
I am your brother !
    FERDINAND.   The devil ! My brother fight
Upon the adverse party ?
        [He wounds the Cardinal, and, in the scuffle,
        gives BOSOLA his death-wound.
              There flies your ransom.
    CARDINAL.   O justice !   52
I suffer now for what hath former bin :
Sorrow is held the eldest child of sin.
    FERDINAND. Now you 're brave fellows. Caesar's
fortune was harder than Pompey's ; Caesar died
in the arms of prosperity, Pompey at the feet of
disgrace. You both died in the field. The pain 's
nothing : pain many times is taken away with the
apprehension of greater, as the toothache with the
sight of a barber that comes to pull it out : there 's
philosophy for you.   62
    BOSOLA. Now my revenge is perfect.—Sink,
    thou main cause   [Kills FERDINAND.
Of my undoing !—The last part of my life
Hath done me best service.
    FERDINAND. Give me some wet hay ; I am
broken-winded. I do account this world but a dog-
kennel : I will vault credit [1] and affect high
pleasures beyond death.
    BOSOLA.   He seems to come to himself, now he 's
    so near   70
The bottom.
    FERDINAND. My sister, O my sister ! there 's
    the cause on 't.
Whether we fall by ambition, blood, or lust,
Like diamonds we are cut with our own dust.
                      [Dies.
    CARDINAL. Thou hast thy payment too.
    BOSOLA. Yes, I hold my weary soul in my
    teeth ·
          [1] Do incredible deeds.

'Tis ready to part from me. I do glory
That thou, which stood'st like a huge pyramid
Begun upon a large and ample base,
Shalt end in a little point, a kind of nothing.   80

Enter, below, PESCARA, MALATESTE, RODERIGO,
and GRISOLAN.

PESCARA.   How now, my lord ?
MALATESTE.   O sad disaster !
RODERIGO.   How
Comes this ?
BOSOLA.   Revenge for the Duchess of Malfi
    murdered
By th' Arragonian brethren ; for Antonio
Slain by [t]his hand ; for lustful Julia
Poison'd by this man ; and lastly for myself,
That was an actor in the main of all,
Much 'gainst mine own good nature, yet i' th' end
Neglected.
PESCARA.   How now, my lord ?
CARDINAL.   Look to my brother : he gave us
    these large wounds,   89
As we were struggling here i' the rushes. And now,
I pray, let me be laid by and never thought of.
                                        [Dies.
PESCARA.   How fatally, it seems, he did with-
    stand
His own rescue !
MALATESTE.   Thou wretched thing of blood,
How came Antonio by his death ?
BOSOLA.   In a mist :
I know not how : such a mistake as I
Have often seen in a play. Oh, I am gone !
We are only like dead walls or vaulted graves,
That, ruin'd, yield no echo. Fare you well.
It may be pain, but no harm, to me to die   99
In so good a quarrel. Oh, this gloomy world !
In what a shadow, or deep pit of darkness,
Doth, womanish and fearful, mankind live !
Let worthy minds ne'er stagger in distrust

                                        R

To suffer death or shame for what is just :
Mine is another voyage.   [Dies.
   PESCARA.   The noble Delio, as I came to the
     palace,
Told me of Antonio's being here, and show'd me
A pretty gentleman, his son and heir.

Enter DELIO and ANTONIO's Son.

   MALATESTE.   O sir,
You come too late !
   DELIO.   I heard so, and was arm'd for 't,
Ere I came. Let us make noble use   111
Of this great ruin ; and join all our force
To establish this young hopeful gentleman
In 's mother's right.   These wretched eminent
     things
Leave no more fame behind 'em, than should one
Fall in a frost, and leave his print in snow ;
As soon as the sun shines, it ever melts,
Both form and matter.   I have ever thought
Nature doth nothing so great for great men
As when she 's pleas'd to make them lords of
     truth :   120
Integrity of life is fame's best friend,
Which nobly, beyond death, shall crown the end.
                        [Exeunt.

A NEW WAY TO PAY OLD DEBTS

Philip Massinger

(1583–1639)

A New Way to Pay Old Debts was acted some time before
1626 and was first printed in 1633. After that it does
not appear to have been reprinted, except in Dodsley's
Collection (1744), till Massinger's *Works* were edited in
four volumes by T. Coxeter in 1759, with a second
edition in 1761. T. M. Mason edited the *Works* in 1779
and W. Gifford in 1805 (third edition 1840). The play
was included in Mr. Arthur Symons's selection from
Massinger in the Mermaid series (1887), and was edited
by Mr. K. Deighton (1893) and in the Temple Dramatists by Mr. G. Stronach (1904). It has been often reprinted in selections of plays. The few variations from
the original text which appear in the present edition
are the corrections of early editors; they are for the
most part pointed out in footnotes.

A NEW WAY TO PAY

OLD DEBTS
A COMOEDIE

As it hath beene often acted at the Phœnix in Drury-Lane, by the Queenes Maiesties seruants.

The Author.

PHILIP MASSINGER.

LONDON,
Printed by *E. P.* for *Henry Seyle*, dwelling in S. *Pauls* Church-yard, at the signe of the Tygers head. Anno. M. DC. XXXIII.

DRAMATIS PERSONAE

LORD LOVELL.
SIR GILES OVERREACH, a cruel extortioner.
FRANK WELLBORN, a Prodigal.
TOM ALLWORTH, a young Gentleman, [Stepson to Lady
    Allworth and] Page to Lord Lovell.
GREEDY, a hungry Justice of Peace.
MARRALL, a Term-Driver;[1] a creature of Sir Giles Over-
    reach.
ORDER, Steward ⎫
AMBLE, Usher   ⎬ to Lady Allworth.
FURNACE, Cook ⎭
WATCHALL, Porter
WILLDO, a Parson.
TAPWELL, an Alehouse Keeper.
Creditors, Servants, &c.

LADY ALLWORTH, a rich Widow.
MARGARET, Daughter of Sir Giles Overreach.
FROTH, Wife of Tapwell.
Chambermaid.
Waiting Woman.

SCENE.—The Country near Nottingham.

[1] According to *N. E. D.*, one who comes up to the Law
Courts for the Term ; but does it not rather mean, one who
insists on hard terms in a lease or other contract ?

A NEW WAY TO PAY OLD DEBTS

ACT THE FIRST

SCENE I.—Before TAPWELL'S House.

Enter WELLBORN in tattered apparel, TAPWELL, and
FROTH.

WELLBORN.   No bouse ? nor no tobacco ?

TAPWELL.   Not a suck, sir ;
Nor the remainder of a single can
Left by a drunken porter, all night palled too.

FROTH.   Not the dropping of the tap for your
   morning's draught, sir :
'Tis verity, I assure you.

WELLBORN.   Verity, you brache ! [1]
The devil turned precisian ! Rogue, what am I ?

TAPWELL.   Troth, durst I trust you with a
   looking-glass,
To let you see your trim shape, you would quit me,
And take the name yourself.

WELLBORN.   How, dog !

TAPWELL.   Even so, sir.
And I must tell you, if you but advance   10
Your Plymouth cloak [2], you shall be soon instructed
There dwells, and within call, if it please your
   worship,
A potent monarch called the constable,
That does command a citadel called the stocks ;
Whose guards are certain files of rusty billmen,
Such as with great dexterity will hale
Your tattered, lousy——

[1] Bitch.
[2] A cudgel, the only form of cloak which many poor
sailors landed at Plymouth could afford.

WELLBORN.   Rascal ! slave !
FROTH.   No rage, sir.
TAPWELL.   At his own peril : Do not put your-
   self
In too much heat, there being no water near   19
To quench your thirst ; and sure, for other liquor,
As mighty ale, or beer, they are things, I take it,
You must no more remember ; not in a dream, sir.
   WELLBORN. Why, thou unthankful villain,
   dar'st thou talk thus ?
Is not thy house, and all thou hast, my gift ?
   TAPWELL.   I find it not in chalk ; and Timothy
   Tapwell
Does keep no other register.
   WELLBORN.   Am not I he
Whose riots fed and clothed thee ? wert thou not
Born on my father's land, and proud to be
A drudge in his house ?
   TAPWELL.   What I was, sir, it skills [1] not ;
What you are, is apparent : now, for a farewell,
Since you talk of father, in my hope it will torment
   you,   31
I'll briefly tell your story. Your dead father,
My quondam master, was a man of worship,
Old Sir John Wellborn, justice of peace and
   quorum,
And stood fair to be custos rotulorum ;
Bare the whole sway of the shire, kept a great
   house,   36
Relieved the poor, and so forth ; but he dying,
And the twelve hundred a year coming to you,
Late Master Francis, but now forlorn Wellborn——
   WELLBORN. Slave, stop ! or I shall lose myself.
   FROTH.   Very hardly ;
You cannot out of your way.
   TAPWELL.   But to my story :
You were then a lord of acres, the prime gallant,
And I your under-butler ; note the change now :
You had a merry time of 't ; hawks and hounds,

              [1] Matters.

With choice of running horses ; mistresses
Of all sorts and all sizes, yet so hot,
As their embraces made your lordship melt ;
Which your uncle, Sir Giles Overreach, observing
(Resolving not to lose a drop of them),
On foolish mortgages, statutes, and bonds,   50
For a while supplied your looseness, and then left
    you.
    WELLBORN. Some curate hath penned this
    invective, mongrel,
And you have studied it.
    TAPWELL.   I have not done yet :
Your land gone, and your credit not worth a
    token,[1]
You grew the common borrower ; no man 'scaped
Your paper-pellets, from the gentleman
To the beggars on highways, that sold you switches
In your gallantry.
    WELLBORN.   I shall switch your brains out.
    TAPWELL. Where poor Tim Tapwell, with a
    little stock,   59
Some forty pounds or so, bought a small cottage ;
Humbled myself to marriage with my Froth here,
Gave entertainment——
    WELLBORN.   Yes, to whores and canters,[2]
Clubbers by night.
    TAPWELL.   True, but they brought in profit,
And had a gift to pay for what they called for,
And stuck not like your mastership. The poor
    income
I gleaned from them hath made me in my parish
Thought worthy to be scavenger, and in time
I may rise to be overseer of the poor ;
Which if I do, on your petition, Wellborn,
I may allow you thirteen-pence a quarter,   70
And you shall thank my worship.

---

[1] From the time of Elizabeth till 1813 tradesmen and others
were allowed to issue tokens of various values which they
were bound to accept as payment.
   [2] Vagabonds.

WELLBORN. Thus, you dog-bolt,[1]
And thus—— [Beats and kicks him.
TAPWELL. [To his wife.] Cry out for help !
WELLBORN. Stir, and thou diest :
Your potent prince, the constable, shall not save
    you.
Hear me, ungrateful hell-hound ! did not I
Make purses for you ? then you licked my boots,
And thought your holiday cloak too coarse to clean
    them.
'Twas I that, when I heard thee swear if ever
Thou couldst arrive at forty pounds thou wouldst
Live like an emperor, 'twas I that gave it
In ready gold. Deny this, wretch !
    TAPWELL. I must, sir ;
For, from the tavern to the taphouse, all,   81
On forfeiture of their licences, stand bound
Never to remember who their best guests were,
If they grew poor like you.
    WELLBORN. They are well rewarded
That beggar themselves to make such cuckolds
    rich.
Thou viper, thankless viper ! impudent bawd !—
But since you are grown forgetful, I will help
Your memory, and tread you into mortar,
Nor leave one bone unbroken. [Beats him again.
    TAPWELL. Oh !
    FROTH. Ask mercy.

Enter ALLWORTH.

    WELLBORN. 'Twill not be granted.
    ALLWORTH. Hold—for my sake, hold.
Deny me, Frank ! they are not worth your anger.
    WELLBORN. For once thou hast redeemed them
    from this sceptre ; [Showing his cudgel.
But let them vanish, creeping on their knees,
And, if they grumble, I revoke my pardon.   94
    FROTH. This comes of your prating, husband ;
    you presumed

    [1] Mean rascal, a word of unknown origin.

On your ambling wit, and must use your glib
　　tongue,
Though you are beaten lame for 't.
　　TAPWELL.　　　　　　　　　Patience, Froth ;
There 's law to cure our bruises.
　　　　　　　　　[They go off on their hands and knees.
　　WELLBORN.　　　　　　　Sent to your mother ?
　　ALLWORTH.　My lady, Frank, my patroness, my
　　all !
She 's such a mourner for my father's death,
And, in her love to him, so favours me,　　　　101
That I cannot pay too much observance to her ;
There are few such stepdames.
　　WELLBORN.　　　　　　　　'Tis a noble widow,
And keeps her reputation pure, and clear
From the least taint of infamy ;　her life,
With the splendour of her actions, leaves no tongue
To envy or detraction.　Prithee tell me,
Has she no suitors ?
　　ALLWORTH.　　Even the best of the shire, Frank,
My lord excepted ;　such as sue and send,　　109
And send and sue again, but to no purpose :
Their frequent visits have not gained her presence.
Yet she 's so far from sullenness and pride,
That I dare undertake you shall meet from her
A liberal entertainment :　I can give you
A catalogue of her suitors' names.
　　WELLBORN.　　　　　　　　　Forbear it,
While I give you good counsel :　I am bound to it.
Thy father was my friend, and that affection
I bore to him, in right descends to thee ;
Thou art a handsome and a hopeful youth,
Nor will I have the least affront stick on thee,
If I with any danger can prevent it.　　　　121
　　ALLWORTH.　I thank your noble care ;　but, pray
　　you, in what
Do I run the hazard ?
　　WELLBORN.　　　　　　Art thou not in love ?
Put it not off with wonder.
　　ALLWORTH.　　　　　　　In love, at my years ?

WELLBORN.   You think you walk in clouds, but
   are transparent.
I have heard all, and the choice that you have
   made,
And with my finger can point out the north star
By which the loadstone of your folly 's guided ;
And., to confirm this true, what think you of
Fair Margaret, the only child and heir   130
Of Cormorant Overreach ?   Does it blush and
   start,
To hear her only named ?   blush at your want
Of wit and reason.
   ALLWORTH.   You are too bitter, sir.
   WELLBORN.   Wounds of this nature are not to
   be cured
With balms, but corrosives.   I must be plain :
Art thou scarce manumised from the porter's
   lodge [1]
And yet sworn servant to the pantofle,[2]
And dar'st thou dream of marriage ?   I fear
'Twill be concluded for impossible
That there is now, or [3] e'er shall be hereafter,   140
A handsome page or player's boy of fourteen
But either loves a wench or drabs love him ;
Court-waiters not exempted.
   ALLWORTH.   This is madness.
Howe'er you have discovered my intents,
You know my aims are lawful ;   and if ever
The queen of flowers, the glory of the spring,
The sweetest comfort to our smell, the rose,
Sprang from an envious briar, I may infer
There 's such disparity in their conditions
Between the goddess of my soul, the daughter,
And the base churl her father.
   WELLBORN.   Grant this true,
As I believe it, canst thou ever hope   153
To enjoy a quiet bed with her whose father

_____
[1] Where servants and dependants were punished.
[2] Slipper. Fr. _pantoufle_.
[3] ' Nor', 1633.

Ruined thy state ?
    ALLWORTH.   And yours too.
    WELLBORN.   I confess it ;
True ; I must tell you as a friend, and freely,
That, where impossibilities are apparent,
'Tis indiscretion to nourish hopes.
Canst thou imagine (let not self-love blind thee)
That Sir Giles Overreach, that, to make her great
In swelling titles, without touch of conscience
Will cut his neighbour's throat, and I hope his own
    too,   161
Will e'er consent to make her thine ? Give o'er,
And think of some course suitable to thy rank,
And prosper in it.
    ALLWORTH.   You have well advised me.
But in the meantime you that are so studious
Of my affairs wholly neglect your own :
Remember yourself, and in what plight you are.
    WELLBORN.   No matter, no matter.
    ALLWORTH.   Yes, 'tis much material :
You know my fortune and my means ; yet some-
    thing
I can spare from myself to help your wants.
                        [Giving him money.
    WELLBORN.   How 's this ?
    ALLWORTH.   Nay, be not angry ; there's
    eight pieces   171
To put you in better fashion.
    WELLBORN.   Money from thee !
From a boy ! a stipendiary ! one that lives
At the devotion of a stepmother
And the uncertain favour of a lord !
I'll eat my arms first. Howsoe'er blind Fortune
Hath spent the utmost of her malice on me—
Though I am vomited out of an alehouse,
And thus accoutred—know not where to eat,
Or drink, or sleep, but underneath this canopy—
Although I thank thee, I despise thy offer :   181
And as I in my madness broke my state
Without the assistance of another's brain,

In my right wits I'll piece it ; at the worst,
Die thus and be forgotten.

ALLWORTH.   A strange humour !

[Exeunt.

SCENE II.—A Room in Lady ALLWORTH'S House.

Enter ORDER, AMBLE, FURNACE, and WATCHALL.

ORDER.   Set all things right, or, as my name is
    Order,
And by this staff of office that commands you,
This chain and double ruff, symbols of power,
Whoever misses in his function,
For one whole week makes forfeiture of his break-
    fast,
And privilege in the wine-cellar.

AMBLE.   You are merry,
Good master steward.

FURNACE.   Let him ; I'll be angry.

AMBLE.   Why, fellow Furnace, 'tis not twelve
    o'clock yet,
Nor dinner taking up ; then, 'tis allowed,
Cooks, by their places, may be choleric.   10

FURNACE.   You think you have spoke wisely,
    goodman Amble,
My lady's go-before !

ORDER.   Nay, nay, no wrangling.

FURNACE.   Twit me with the authority of the
    kitchen !
At all hours, and all places, I'll be angry ;
And thus provoked, when I am at my prayers
I will be angry.

AMBLE.   There was no hurt meant.

FURNACE.   I am friends with thee ; and yet I
    will be angry.

ORDER.   With whom ?

FURNACE.   No matter whom : yet, now
    I think on it,
I am angry with my lady.

WATCHALL.   Heaven forbid, man !

ORDER.   What cause has she given thee ?

FURNACE.   Cause enough, master steward.
I was entertained by her to please her palate,   21
And, till she forswore eating, I performed it.
Now, since our master, noble Allworth, died,
Though I crack my brains to find out tempting
    sauces,
And raise fortifications in the pastry
Such as might serve for models in the Low
    Countries ;
Which, if they had been practis'd at Breda,[1]
Spinola might have thrown his cap at it,[2] and ne'er
    took it.

AMBLE.   But you had wanted matter there to
    work on.

FURNACE.   Matter ! with six eggs, and a strike
    of rye meal,   30
I had kept the town till doomsday, perhaps longer.

ORDER.   But what's this to your pet against my
    lady ?

FURNACE.   What's this ? marry this ; when I
    am three parts roasted
And the fourth part parboiled, to prepare her viands,
She keeps her chamber, dines with a panada [3]
Or water-gruel, my sweat never thought on.

ORDER.   But your art is seen in the dining-room.

FURNACE.   By whom ?
By such as pretend love to her, but come
To feed upon her. Yet, of all the harpies
That do devour her, I am out of charity   40
With none so much as the thin-gutted squire
That's stolen into commission.

ORDER.   Justice Greedy ?

FURNACE.   The same, the same : meat's cast
    away upon him,
It never thrives. He holds this paradox,

---

[1] Taken by the Spaniards under Spinola in 1625 after
a ten months' siege.

[2] Own himself beaten by it. Cf. above, p. 234.

[3] A sort of bread-and-butter pudding.

Who eats not well, can ne'er do justice well :
His stomach's as insatiate as the grave,
Or strumpets' ravenous appetites. [Knocking within.
WATCHALL.   One knocks. [Exit.
ORDER.   Our late young master !

Re-enter WATCHALL and ALLWORTH.

AMBLE.   Welcome, sir.
FURNACE.   Your hand ;
If you have a stomach, a cold bake-meat's ready.
ORDER.   His father's picture in little.
FURNACE.   We are all your servants.   50
AMBLE.   In you he lives.
ALLWORTH.   At once, my thanks to all ;
This is yet some comfort. Is my lady stirring ?

Enter Lady ALLWORTH, Waiting Woman, and
                 Chambermaid.

ORDER.   Her presence answers for us.
LADY ALLWORTH.   Sort those silks well.
I'll take the air alone.
            [Exeunt Waiting Woman and Chambermaid.
FURNACE.   You air and air ;
But will you never taste but spoon-meat more ?
To what use serve I ?
LADY ALLWORTH.   Prithee, be not angry ;
I shall ere long ; i' the meantime, there is gold
To buy thee aprons, and a summer suit.
FURNACE.   I am appeased, and Furnace now
      grows cool.[1]
LADY ALLWORTH.   And, as I gave directions, if
      this morning   60
I am visited by any, entertain them
As heretofore ; but say, in my excuse,
I am indisposed.
ORDER.   I shall, madam.
LADY ALLWORTH.   Do, and leave me ;
Nay, stay you, Allworth.
            [Exeunt ORDER, AMBLE, FURNACE, and WATCHALL.

_____

[1] The original has ' Cooke ', which may possibly be right.

ALLWORTH.   I shall gladly grow here,
To wait on your commands.
    LADY ALLWORTH.   So soon turned courtier ?
    ALLWORTH. Style not that courtship, madam,
      which is duty
Purchased on your part.
    LADY ALLWORTH.   Well, you shall o'ercome ;
I'll not contend in words. How is it with
Your noble master ?
    ALLWORTH.   Ever like himself,   6ç
No scruple lessened in the full weight of honour.
He did command me, pardon my presumption,
As his unworthy deputy, to kiss
Your ladyship's fair hands.
    LADY ALLWORTH.   I am honoured in
His favour to me. Does he hold his purpose
For the Low Countries ?
    ALLWORTH.   Constantly, good madam ;
But he will in person first present his service.
    LADY ALLWORTH. And how approve you of his
      course ? you are yet
Like virgin parchment, capable of any
Inscription, vicious or honourable.
I will not force your will, but leave you free   8o
To your own election.
    ALLWORTH.   Any form you please
I will put on ; but, might I make my choice,
With humble emulation I would follow
The path my lord marks to me.
    LADY ALLWORTH.   'Tis well answered,
And I commend your spirit : you had a father,
Blessed be his memory ! that some few hours
Before the will of Heaven took him from me,
Who [1] did commend you, by the dearest ties
Of perfect love between us, to my charge ;
And, therefore, what I speak, you are bound to hear
With such respect as if he lived in me.   91
He was my husband, and howe'er you are not
Son of my womb, you may be of my love,

    [1] The repetition of the relative suggests a corrupt text.

Provided you deserve it.

ALLWORTH.　　　　　　I have found you,
Most honoured madam, the best mother to me ;
And, with my utmost strengths of care and service,
Will labour that you never may repent
Your bounties showered upon me.

　　LADY ALLWORTH.　　　　　　I much hope it.
These were your father's words : ' If e'er my son
Follow the war, tell him it is a school　　　100
Where all the principles tending to honour
Are taught, if truly followed : but for such
As repair thither, as a place in which
They do presume they may with licence practise
Their lusts and riots, they shall never merit
The noble name of soldiers. To dare boldly,
In a fair cause, and for the[ir] country's safety,
To run upon the cannon's mouth undaunted ;
To obey their leaders, and shun mutinies ;
To bear with patience the winter's cold　　　110
And summer's scorching heat, and not to faint,
When plenty of provision fails, with hunger ;
Are the essential parts make up a soldier,
Not swearing, dice, or drinking.'

　　ALLWORTH.　　　　　　There 's no syllable
You speak, but is to me an oracle,
Which but to doubt were impious.　　　To conclude :

　　LADY ALLWORTH.
Beware ill company, for often men
Are like to those with whom they do converse ;
And, from one man I warn[1] you, and that 's
　　　Wellborn :
Not 'cause he 's poor, that rather claims your pity ;
But that he 's in his manners so debauched,　　　121
And hath to vicious courses sold himself.
'Tis true, your father loved him, while he was
Worthy the loving ; but if he had lived
To have seen him as he is, he had cast him off,
As you must do.

　　ALLWORTH.　　　I shall obey in all things.

　　　　　　　[1] ' warn'd ', 1633.

LADY ALLWORTH. Follow [1] me to my chamber,
you shall have gold
To furnish you like my son, and still supplied,
As I hear from you.

ALLWORTH. I am still your creature.

[Exeunt.

SCENE III.—A Hall in the same.

Enter OVERREACH, GREEDY, ORDER, AMBLE, FURNACE,
WATCHALL, and MARRALL.

GREEDY. Not to be seen ?

OVERREACH. Still cloistered up ? Her reason,
I hope, assures her, though she make herself
Close prisoner ever for her husband's loss,
'Twill not recover him.

ORDER. Sir, it is her will,
Which we, that are her servants, ought to serve, [2]
And not dispute. Howe'er, you are nobly welcome ;
And, if you please to stay, that you may think so,
There came, not six days since, from Hull, a pipe
Of rich Canary, which shall spend itself   9
For my lady's honour.

GREEDY. Is it of the right race ?

ORDER. Yes, Master Greedy.

AMBLE. [Aside to FURNACE.] How his mouth
runs o'er !

FURNACE. I'll make it run, and run.—Save
your good worship !

GREEDY. Honest Master Cook, thy hand ; again :
how I love thee !
Are the good dishes still in being ? speak, boy.

FURNACE. If you have a mind to feed, there is
a chine
Of beef, well seasoned.

GREEDY. Good !

FURNACE. A pheasant, larded.

GREEDY. That I might now give thanks for 't !

FURNACE. Other kickshaws.

1 ' You follow ', 1633.   2 ' serve it ', 1033.

Besides, there came last night, from the forest of
　　Sherwood,
The fattest stag I ever cooked.

　　GREEDY.　　　　　　　　　A stag, man?

　　FURNACE.　A stag, sir; part of it['s] prepared for
　　dinner,　　　　　　　　　　　　　　　　20
And baked in puff-paste.

　　GREEDY.　　　　　　　　Puff-paste too! Sir Giles,
A ponderous chine of beef! a pheasant larded!
And red deer too, Sir Giles, and baked in puff-
　　paste!
All business set aside, let us give thanks here.

　　FURNACE. [Aside.]　How the lean skeleton's rapt!

　　OVERREACH.　　　　　　　You know we cannot.

　　MARRALL.　Your worships are to sit on a com-
　　mission,
And if you fail to come, you lose the cause.

　　GREEDY.　Cause me no causes. I'll prove't, for
　　such a dinner,
We may put off a commission : you shall find it
Henrici decimo quarto.

　　OVERREACH.　　　　　Fie, Master Greedy!　30
Will you lose me a thousand pounds for a dinner?
No more, for shame! we must forget the belly
When we think of profit.

　　GREEDY.　　　　　　Well, you shall o'er-rule me;
I could e'en cry now.—Do you hear, Master Cook,
Send but a corner of that immortal pasty,
And I, in thankfulness, will, by your boy,
Send you—a brace of three-pences.

　　FURNACE. [Aside.]　　　Will you be so prodigal?

Enter WELLBORN.

　　OVERREACH.　Remember me to your lady.—
Who have we here?

　　WELLBORN.　You know me.

　　OVERREACH.　　　　　I did once, but now I will not;
Thou art no blood of mine. Avaunt, thou beggar!
If ever thou presume to own me more,　　41
I'll have thee caged and whipped.

GREEDY.   I'll grant the warrant.—
Think of pie-corner, Furnace !
                    [Exeunt OVERREACH, GREEDY, and MARRALL.
WATCHALL.   Will you out, sir ?
I wonder how you durst creep in.
ORDER.   This is rudeness,
And saucy impudence.
AMBLE.   Cannot you stay
To be served, among your fellows, from the
    basket,[1]
But you must press into the hall ?
FURNACE.   Prithee, vanish
Into some outhouse, though it be the pigsty ;
My scullion shall come to thee.

Enter ALLWORTH.

WELLBORN.   This is rare !
Oh, here 's Tom Allworth. Tom !
ALLWORTH.   We must be strangers ;
Nor would I have you seen here for a million.
                                        [Exit.
WELLBORN. Better and better ! He contemns
    me too !
                                        52

Enter Waiting Woman and Chambermaid.

WOMAN. Foh, what a smell 's here ! what
    thing 's this ?
CHAMBERMAID.   A creature
Made out of the privy ; let us hence, for love's
    sake,
Or I shall swoon.
WOMAN.   I begin to faint already.
                    [Exeunt Waiting Woman and Chambermaid
WATCHALL. Will [you] know your way ? ·
AMBLE.   Or shall we teach it you,
By the head and shoulders ?
WELLBORN.   No ; I will not stir ;
Do you mark, I will not : let me see the wretch
That dares attempt to force me. Why, you slaves,

                    [1] For the broken victuals.

Created only to make legs, and cringe ;   60
To carry in a dish, and shift a trencher ;
That have not souls only to hope a blessing
Beyond black-jacks or flagons ; you, that were
    born
Only to consume meat and drink, and batten
Upon reversions !—who advances ? who
Shows me the way ?
　ORDER.　　　　　　　My lady !

Enter Lady ALLWORTH, Waiting Woman, and
            Chambermaid.

CHAMBERMAID.　　　　　　Here's the monster.
WOMAN. Sweet madam, keep your glove to
    your nose.
CHAMBERMAID.　　　　　　　　Or let me
Fetch some perfumes may be predominant ;
You wrong yourself else.
　WELLBORN.　　　　　Madam, my designs
Bear me to you.
　LADY ALLWORTH. To me !
　WELLBORN.　　　And though I have met with
But ragged entertainment from your grooms here,
I hope from you to receive that noble usage   72
As may become the true friend of your husband,
And then I shall forget these.
　LADY ALLWORTH.　　　　I am amazed
To see and hear this rudeness. Dar'st thou think,
Though sworn, that it can ever find belief,
That I, who to the best men of this country
Denied my presence since my husband's death,
Can fall so low as to change words with thee ?
Thou son of infamy ! forbear my house,   80
And know and keep the distance that's between us ;
Or, though it be against my gentler temper,
I shall take order you no more shall be
An eyesore to me.
　WELLBORN.　　　Scorn me not, good lady ;
But, as in form you are angelical,
Imitate the heavenly natures, and vouchsafe

At the least awhile to hear me. You will grant
The blood that runs in this arm is as noble
As that which fills your veins ; those costly jewels,
And those rich clothes you wear, your men's
    observance, 90
And women's flattery, are in you no virtues,
Nor these rags, with my poverty, in me vices.
You have a fair fame, and, I know, deserve it ;
Yet, lady, I must say, in nothing more
Than in the pious sorrow you have shown
For your late noble husband.

    ORDER. [Aside to FURNACE.] How she starts !
    FURNACE. And hardly can keep finger from the
      eye,
To hear him named.

    LADY ALLWORTH. Have you aught else to say ?
    WELLBORN. That husband, madam, was once
      in his fortune 99
Almost as low as I ; want, debts, and quarrels
Lay heavy on him : let it not be thought
A boast in me, though I say, I relieved him.
'Twas I that gave him fashion ; mine the sword,
That did on all occasions second his ;
I brought him on and off with honour, lady ;
And when in all men's judgements he was sunk,
And, in his own hopes, not to be buoyed [1] up,
I stepped unto him, took him by the hand,
And set him upright.

    FURNACE. [Aside.] Are not we base rogues, 109
That could forget this ?

    WELLBORN. I confess, you made him
Master of your estate ; nor could your friends,
Though he brought no wealth with him, blame you
    for it ;
For he had a shape, and to that shape a mind
Made up of all parts, either great or noble ;
So winning a behaviour, not to be
Resisted, madam.

    LADY ALLWORTH. 'Tis most true, he had.

            [1] 'bung'd', 1633.

WELLBORN.   For his sake, then, in that I was
    his friend,
Do not contemn me.
    LADY ALLWORTH.   For what's past excuse me,
I will redeem it. Order, give the gentleman   119
A hundred pounds.
    WELLBORN.   No, madam, on no terms :
I will nor beg nor borrow sixpence of you,
But be supplied elsewhere, or want thus ever.
Only one suit I make, which you deny not
To strangers ; and 'tis this.   [Whispers to her.
    LADY ALLWORTH.   Fie ! nothing else ?
    WELLBORN. Nothing, unless you please to
    charge your servants
To throw away a little respect upon me.
    LADY ALLWORTH.   What you demand is yours.
    WELLBORN.   I thank you, lady.
[Aside.]   Now what can be wrought out of such a
    suit
Is yet in supposition.—I have said all ;   129
When you please, you may retire.
                                [Exit Lady ALLWORTH.
            [To the Servants.]   Nay, all's forgotten ;
And, for a lucky omen to my project,
Shake hands, and end all quarrels in the cellar.
    ORDER.   Agreed, agreed.
    FURNACE.   Still merry Master Wellborn.
                                        [Exeunt.

ACT THE SECOND

SCENE I.—A Room in OVERREACH's House.

Enter OVERREACH and MARRALL.

OVERREACH.   He's gone, I warrant thee ; this
    commission crushed him.
    MARRALL.   Your worships have the way on't,
    and ne'er miss
To squeeze these unthrifts into air : and yet,
The chapfallen justice did his part, returning

For your advantage the certificate,
Against his conscience, and his knowledge too.
With your good favour, to the utter ruin
Of the poor farmer.
    OVERREACH.   'Twas for these good ends
I made him a justice : he that bribes his belly,
Is certain to command his soul.
    MARRALL.   I wonder,   10
Still with your licence, why, your worship having
The power to put this thin-gut in commission,
You are not in 't yourself ?
    OVERREACH.   Thou art a fool ;
In being out of office I am out of danger ;
Where, if I were a justice, besides the trouble,
I might or out of wilfulness or error
Run myself finely into a premunire,
And so become a prey to the informer.
No, I'll have none of 't ; 'tis enough I keep
Greedy at my devotion : so he serve   20
My purposes, let him hang or damn, I care not ;
Friendship is but a word.
    MARRALL.   You are all wisdom.
    OVERREACH. I would be wordly wise ; for the
    other wisdom,
That does prescribe us a well governed life,
And to do right to others as ourselves,
I value not an atom.
    MARRALL.   What course take you,
With your good patience, to hedge in the manor
Of your neighbour, Master Frugal ? as 'tis said
He will nor sell, nor borrow, nor exchange ;
And his land, lying in the midst of your many lord-
    ships,   30
Is a foul blemish.
    OVERREACH.   I have thought on 't, Marrall,
And it shall take. I must have all men sellers,
And I the only purchaser.
    MARRALL.   'Tis most fit, sir.
    OVERREACH. I'll therefore buy some cottage
    near his manor,

Which done, I'll make my men break ope his
        fences,
Ride o'er his standing corn, and in the night
Set fire on his barns, or break his cattle's legs :
These trespasses draw on suits, and suits expenses,
Which I can spare, but will soon beggar him.
When I have harried him thus two or three year,
Though he sue in forma pauperis, in spite   41
Of all his thrift and care, he'll grow behindhand.

 MARRALL.   The best I ever heard ! I could adore
  you.

 OVERREACH.   Then, with the favour of my man
  of law,
I will pretend some title : want will force him
To put it to arbitrament ; then, if he sell
For half the value, he shall have ready money,
And I possess his land.

 MARRALL.   'Tis above wonder !
Wellborn was apt to sell, and needed not   49
These fine arts, sir, to hook him in.

 OVERREACH.   Well thought on.
This varlet, Marrall, lives too long, to upbraid me
With my close cheat put upon him. Will nor cold
Nor hunger kill him ?

 MARRALL.   I know not what to think on't.
I have used all means ; and the last night I caused
His host, the tapster, to turn him out of doors ;
And have been since with all your friends and
        tenants,
And, on the forfeit of your favour, charged them,
Though a crust of mouldy bread would keep him
        from starving,
Yet they should not relieve him. This is done, sir.

 OVERREACH.   That was something, Marrall ; but
  thou must go further,   60
And suddenly, Marrall.

 MARRALL.   Where, and when you please, sir.

 OVERREACH.   I would have thee seek him out,
  and, if thou canst,
Persuade him that 'tis better steal than beg ;

Then, if I prove he has but robbed a henroost,
Not all the world shall save him from the gallows.
Do anything to work him to despair ;
And 'tis thy masterpiece.

MARRALL.   I will do my best, sir.

OVERREACH.   I am now on my main work with
   the Lord Lovell,
The gallant-minded, popular Lord Lovell,
The minion of the people's love.   I hear   70
He's come into the country, and my aims are
To insinuate myself into his knowledge,
And then invite him to my house.

MARRALL.   I have you ;
This points at my young mistress.

OVERREACH.   She must part with
That humble title, and write honourable,
Right honourable, Marrall, my right honourable
   daughter,
If all I have, or e'er shall get, will do it.
I will have her well attended ; there are ladies
Of errant [1] knights decayed and brought so low,
That for cast clothes and meat will gladly serve her.
And 'tis my glory, though I come from the city,
To have their issue whom I have undone,   82
To kneel to mine as bondslaves.

MARRALL.   'Tis fit state, sir.

OVERREACH.   And therefore, I'll not have a
   chambermaid
That ties her shoes, or any meaner office,
But such whose fathers were right worshipful
'Tis a rich man's pride ! there having ever been
More than a feud, a strange antipathy,
Between us and true gentry.

Enter WELLBORN.

MARRALL.   See who's here, sir.

OVERREACH.   Hence, monster ! prodigy !

WELLBORN.   Sir, your wife's nephew ;
She and my father tumbled in one belly.   91

[1] For arrant, undoubted.

OVERREACH. Avoid my sight ! thy breath's
   infectious, rogue !
I shun thee as a leprosy, or the plague.
Come hither, Marrall—[Aside.] this is the time to
   work him.   [Exit.
MARRALL. I warrant you, sir.
WELLBORN.   By this light I think he's mad.
MARRALL. Mad ! had you took compassion on
   yourself,
You long since had been mad.
   WELLBORN.   You have took a course,
Between you and my venerable uncle,
To make me so.
   MARRALL.   The more pale-spirited you, 99
That would not be instructed. I swear deeply——
   WELLBORN. By what ?
   MARRALL.   By my religion.
   WELLBORN.   Thy religion !
The devil's creed :—but what would you have
   done ?
   MARRALL. Had there been but one tree in all
   the shire,
Nor any hope to compass a penny halter,
Before, like you, I had outlived my fortunes,
A withe had served my turn to hang myself.
I am zealous in your cause ; pray you hang yourself,
And presently, as you love your credit.
   WELLBORN.   I thank you.
   MARRALL. Will you stay till you die in a ditch,
   or lice devour you ?——
Or, if you dare not do the feat yourself,   110
But that you'll put the state to charge and trouble,
Is there no purse to be cut, house to be broken,
Or market-woman with eggs, that you may murder,
And so dispatch the business ?   Here's variety,
   WELLBORN.
I must confess ; but I'll accept of none
Of all your gentle offers, I assure you.
   MARRALL. Why, have you hope ever to eat
   again,

Or drink ? or be the master of three farthings ?
If you like not hanging, drown yourself! take
    some course   119
For your reputation.
    WELLBORN.   'Twill not do, dear tempter,
With all the rhetoric the fiend hath taught you.
I am as far as thou art from despair ;
Nay, I have confidence, which is more than hope,
To live, and suddenly, better than ever.
    MARRALL. Ha ! ha ! these castles you build in
    the air
Will not persuade me or to give or lend
A token to you.
    WELLBORN.   I'll be more kind to thee :
Come, thou shalt dine with me.
    MARRALL.   With you !
    WELLBORN.   Nay more, dine gratis.
    MARRALL. Under what hedge, I pray you ? or
    at whose cost ?
Are they padders [1] or abram-men [2] that are your
    consorts ?   130
    WELLBORN. Thou art incredulous ; but thou
    shalt dine,
Not alone at her house, but with a gallant lady ;
With me, and with a lady.
    MARRALL.   Lady ! what lady ?
With the Lady of the Lake,[3] or Queen of Fairies ?
For I know it must be an enchanted dinner.
    WELLBORN. With the Lady Allworth, knave.
    MARRALL.   Nay, now there 's hope
Thy brain is cracked.
    WELLBORN.   Mark there, with what respect
I am entertained.
    MARRALL. With choice, no doubt, of dog-whips.
Why, dost thou ever hope to pass her porter ?
    WELLBORN. 'Tis not far off, go with me ; trust
    thine own eyes.   140

    [1] Footpads.
    [2] Vagabonds who pretended to be mad.
    [3] The enchantress in the *Morte d'Arthur*.

MARRALL.   Troth, in my hope, or my assurance rather,
To see thee curvet, and mount like a dog in a blanket,
If ever thou presume to pass her threshold,
I will endure thy company.
    WELLBORN.   Come along then.
            •   [Exeunt.

SCENE II.—A Room in Lady ALLWORTH's House.

Enter ALLWORTH, Waiting Woman, Chambermaid, ORDER, AMBLE, FURNACE, and WATCHALL.

    WOMAN.   Could you not command your leisure one hour longer ?
    CHAMBERMAID.   Or half an hour ?
    ALLWORTH.   I have told you what my haste is :
Besides, being now another's, not mine own,
Howe'er I much desire to enjoy you longer,
My duty suffers, if, to please myself,
I should neglect my lord.
    WOMAN.   Pray you do me the favour
To put these few quince-cakes into your pocket ;
They are of mine own preserving.
    CHAMBERMAID.   And this marmalade ;
'Tis comfortable for your stomach.
    WOMAN.   And, at parting,
Excuse me if I beg a farewell from you.   10
    CHAMBERMAID.   You are still before me. I move the same suit, sir.
              [ALLWORTH kisses them severally.
    FURNACE. [Aside.] How greedy these chamberers are of a beardless chin !
I think the tits will ravish him.
    ALLWORTH.   My service
To both.
    WOMAN.   Ours waits on you.
    CHAMBERMAID.   And shall do ever.
    ORDER.   You are my lady's charge, be therefore careful

That you sustain your parts.

WOMAN. We can bear, I warrant you
            [Exeunt Waiting Woman and Chambermaid.

FURNACE. Here, drink it off ; the ingredients are
    cordial,
And this the true elixir ; it hath boiled
Since midnight for you. 'Tis the quintessence
Of five cocks of the game, ten dozen of sparrows,
Knuckles of veal, potatoe-roots and marrow,   21
Coral and ambergris : were you two years older,
And I had a wife, or gamesome mistress,
I durst trust you with neither : you need not bait
After this, I warrant you, though your journey's
    long ;
You may ride on the strength of this till to-morrow
    morning.

ALLWORTH. Your courtesies overwhelm me : I
    much grieve
To part from such true friends, and yet find
    comfort ;
My attendance on my honourable lord,
Whose resolution holds to visit my lady,   30
Will speedily bring me back.
                    [Knocking within. Exit WATCHALL.

MARRALL. [Within.] Dar'st thou venture further?

WELLBORN. [Within.] Yes, yes, and knock again.

ORDER.   'Tis he ; disperse !

AMBLE. Perform it bravely.

FURNACE.   I know my cue, ne'er doubt me.
                    [Exeunt all but ALLWORTH.

Re-enter WATCHALL, ceremoniously introducing WELLBORN
            and MARRALL.

WATCHALL. Beast that I was, to make you
    stay ! most welcome ;
You were long since expected.

WELLBORN.   Say so much
To my friend, I pray you.

WATCHALL.   For your sake, I will, sir.

MARRALL. [Aside.] For his sake !

WELLBORN.   Mum ; this is nothing.

MARRALL.   More than ever
I would have believed, though I had found it in my
    primer.

ALLWORTH.   When I have given you reasons for
    my late harshness,
You'll pardon and excuse me ; for, believe me,
Though now I part abruptly, in my service   41
I will deserve it.

MARRALL. [Aside.] Service ! with a vengeance !

WELLBORN.   I am satisfied : farewell, Tom.

ALLWORTH.   All joy stay with you ! [Exit.

Re-enter AMBLE.

AMBLE.   You are happily encountered ; I yet
    never
Presented one so welcome as I know
You will be to my lady.

MARRALL.   [Aside.]   This is some vision,
Or, sure, these men are mad, to worship a dung-
    hill ;
It cannot be a truth.

WELLBORN.   Be still a pagan,
An unbelieving infidel ; be so, miscreant,
And meditate on ' blankets,' and on ' dog-whips ' !

Re-enter FURNACE.

FURNACE.   I am glad you are come ; until I
    know your pleasure   51
I knew not how to serve up my lady's dinner.

MARRALL. [Aside.] His pleasure ! is it possible ?

WELLBORN.   What 's thy will ?

FURNACE.   Marry, sir, I have some grouse, and
    turkey chicken,
Some rails and quails, and my lady willed me ask
    you,
What kind of sauces best affect your palate,
That I may use my utmost skill to please it.

MARRALL. [Aside.] The devil 's entered this cook :
    sauce for his palate !

That, on my knowledge, for almost this twelve-
    month,
Durst wish but cheese-parings and brown bread on
    Sundays.   60
  WELLBORN.   That way I like them best.
  FURNACE.   It shall be done, sir. [Exit.
  WELLBORN.   What think you of ' the hedge we
    shall dine under ' ?
Shall we feed gratis ?
  MARRALL.   I know not what to think
Pray you make me not mad.

Re-enter ORDER.

  ORDER.   This place becomes you not ;
Pray you walk, sir, to the dining-room.
  WELLBORN.   I am well here,
Till her ladyship quits her chamber.
  MARRALL.   [Aside.]   Well here, say you ?
'Tis a rare change ! but yesterday you thought
Yourself well in a barn, wrapped up in peas-straw.

Re-enter Waiting Woman and Chambermaid.

  WOMAN.   Oh ! sir, you are wished for.
  CHAMBERMAID.   My lady dreamt, sir, of you.
  WOMAN.   And the first command she gave, after
    she rose,   70
Was (her devotions done) to give her notice
When you approached here.
  CHAMBERMAID.   Which is done, on my virtue.
  MARRALL. [Aside.] I shall be converted ; I begin
    to grow
Into a new belief, which saints nor angels
Could have won me to have faith in.
  WOMAN.   Sir, my lady !

Enter Lady ALLWORTH.

  LADY ALLWORTH.   I come to meet you, and
    languished till I saw you.
This first kiss is for form ; I allow a second
To such a friend.   [Kisses WELLBORN.

S

MARRALL. [Aside.] To such a friend ! Heaven
 bless me !
WELLBORN. I am wholly yours ; yet, madam,
 if you please
To grace this gentleman with a salute——   80
MARRALL. [Aside.] Salute me at his bidding !
WELLBORN.   I shall receive it
As a most high favour.
LADY ALLWORTH. Sir, you may command me.
                    [Advances to kiss MARRALL, who retires.
WELLBORN. Run backward from a lady ! and
 such a lady !
MARRALL. To kiss her foot is, to poor me, a
 favour
I am unworthy of.   [Offers to kiss her foot.
LADY ALLWORTH. Nay, pray you rise ;
And since you are so humble, I'll exalt you :
You shall dine with me to-day, at mine own table.
MARRALL. Your ladyship's table ! I am not
 good enough
To sit at your steward's board.
LADY ALLWORTH.   You are too modest :
I will not be denied.

                    Re-enter FURNACE.

FURNACE.   Will you still be babbling
Till your meat freeze on the table ? the old trick
 still ;   91
My art ne'er thought on !
LADY ALLWORTH.   Your arm, Master Well-
 born :——
[To MARRALL.] Nay, keep us company.
MARRALL.   I was ne'er so graced.
        [Exeunt WELLBORN, Lady ALLWORTH, AMBLE,
          MARRALL, Waiting Woman, and Chambermaid.
ORDER. So ! we have played our parts, and are
 come off well ;
But if I know the mystery, why my lady
Consented to it, or why Master Wellborn
Desired it, may I perish !

FURNACE.   Would I had
The roasting of his heart that cheated him,
And forces the poor gentleman to these shifts !
By fire !—for cooks are Persians, and swear by it,—
Of all the griping and extorting tyrants   101
I ever heard or read of, I ne'er met
A match to Sir Giles Overreach.
   WATCHALL.   What will you take
To tell him so, fellow Furnace ?
   FURNACE.   Just as much
As my throat is worth, for that would be the price
   on 't.
To have a usurer that starves himself,
And wears a cloak of one and twenty years
On a suit of fourteen groats, bought of the hang-
   man,
To grow rich, and then purchase, is too common :
But this Sir Giles feeds high, keeps many servants,
Who must at his command do any outrage ;   111
Rich in his habit, vast in his expenses ;
Yet he to admiration still increases
In wealth and lordships.
   ORDER.   He frights men out of their estates,
And breaks through all law-nets, made to curb ill
   men,
As they were cobwebs. No man dares reprove him.
Such a spirit to dare and power to do were never
Lodged so unluckily.

Re-enter AMBLE.

   AMBLE.   Ha ! ha ! I shall burst.
   ORDER.   Contain thyself, man.
   FURNACE.   Or make us partakers
Of your sudden mirth.
   AMBLE.   Ha ! ha ! my lady has got
Such a guest at her table !—this term-driver,[1]
   Marrall,   121
This snip of an attorney——
   FURNACE.   What of him, man ?

     [1] See note on p. 506.

AMBLE.   The knave thinks still he's at the cook's
   shop in Ram Alley,[1]
Where the clerks divide, and the elder is to choose ;
And feeds so slovenly !
   FURNACE.   Is this all ?
   AMBLE.   My lady
Drank to him for fashion sake, or to please Master
   Wellborn ;
As I live, he rises, and takes up a dish
In which there were some remnants of a boiled
   capon,
And pledges her in white broth !
   FURNACE.   Nay, 'tis like
The rest of his tribe.
   AMBLE.   And when I brought him wine,
He leaves his stool, and, after a leg or two,   131
Most humbly thanks my worship.
   ORDER.   [Looking off.] Rose already ?
   AMBLE.   I shall be chid.

Re-enter Lady ALLWORTH, WELLBORN, and MARRALL.

   FURNACE.   My lady frowns.
   LADY ALLWORTH.   [To AMBLE.] You wait well !
Let me have no more of this ; I observed your
   jeering :
Sirrah, I'll have you know, whom I think worthy
To sit at my table, be he ne'er so mean,
When I am present, is not your companion.
   ORDER.   Nay, she'll preserve what's due to her.
   FURNACE.   This refreshing
Follows your flux of laughter.
   LADY ALLWORTH. [To WELLBORN.] You are master
Of your own will. I know so much of manners,
As not to inquire your purposes ; in a word,   141
To me you are ever welcome, as to a house
That is your own.
   WELLBORN.   [Aside to MARRALL.]   Mark that.
   MARRALL.   With reverence, sir,

---

[1] One of the avenues into the Temple from Fleet Street.—
Gifford.

An it like your worship.

WELLBORN.   Trouble yourself no further,
Dear madam ; my heart's full of zeal and service,
However in my language I am sparing.
Come, Master Marrall.

MARRALL.   I attend your worship.
                              [Exeunt WELLBORN and MARRALL.

LADY ALLWORTH.   I see in your looks you are
    sorry, and you know me
An easy mistress : be merry ; I have forgot all.
Order and Furnace, come with me ; I must give
    you   150
Further directions.

ORDER.   What you please.

FURNACE.   We are ready.
                                        [Exeunt.

SCENE III.—The Country near Lady ALLWORTH'S
                        House.

Enter WELLBORN, and MARRALL bare-headed.

WELLBORN.   I think I am in a good way.

MARRALL.   Good, sir ? the best way,
The certain best way.

WELLBORN.   There are casualties
That men are subject to.

MARRALL.   You are above them ;
And as you are already worshipful,
I hope ere long you will increase in worship,
And be right worshipful.

WELLBORN.   Prithee do not flout me :
What I shall be, I shall be. Is 't for your ease,
You keep your hat off ?

MARRALL.   Ease ? an it like your worship,
I hope Jack Marrall shall not live so long,
To prove himself such an unmannerly beast,   10
Though it hail hazel-nuts, as to be covered
When your worship's present.

WELLBORN.   [Aside.] Is not this a true rogue,
That, out of mere hope of a future cozenage,
Can turn thus suddenly ? 'tis rank already.

MARRALL. I know your worship 's wise, and needs
  no counsel,
Yet if, in my desire to do you service,
I humbly offer my advice (but still
Under correction), I hope I shall not
Incur your high displeasure.
    WELLBORN.   No ; speak freely.
    MARRALL. Then, in my judgement, sir, my
  simple judgement   21
(Still with your worship's favour), I could wish
  you
A better habit, for this cannot be
But much distasteful to the noble lady
(I say no more) that loves you : for, this morning,
To me, and I am but a swine to her,
Before the assurance of her wealth perfumed you,
You savoured not of amber.
    WELLBORN.   I do now, then ?
    MARRALL. This your batoon hath got a touch
  of it.——   [Kisses the end of his cudgel.
Yet, if you please, for change, I have twenty
  pounds here,   30
Which, out of my true love, I['ll] presently
Lay down at your worship's feet ; 'twill serve to
  buy you
A riding suit.
    WELLBORN. But where 's the horse ?
    MARRALL.   My gelding
Is at your service : nay, you shall ride me,
Before your worship shall be put to the trouble
To walk afoot. Alas ! when you are lord
Of this lady's manor, as I know you will be,
You may with the lease of glebe land, called
  Knave's-acre,
A place I would manure,[1] requite your vassal.
    WELLBORN. I thank thy love, but must make
  no use of it ;   40
What 's twenty pounds ?
    MARRALL.   'Tis all that I can make, sir.

──────────
[1] Occupy.

WELLBORN.   Dost thou think, though I want clothes, I could not have them,
For one word to my lady ?

MARRALL.   As I know not that !

WELLBORN.   Come, I'll tell thee a secret, and so leave thee.
I'll not give her the advantage, though she be
A gallant-minded lady, after we are married
(There being no woman but is sometimes froward),
To hit me in the teeth, and say, she was forced
To buy my wedding-clothes, and took me on
With a plain riding-suit, and an ambling nag.   50
No, I'll be furnished something like myself,
And so farewell : for thy suit touching Knave's-acre,
When it is mine, 'tis thine.   [Exit.

MARRALL.   I thank your worship.
How was [I] cozened in the calculation
Of this man's fortune ! my master cozened too,
Whose pupil I am in the art of undoing men ;
For that is our profession ! Well, well, Master Wellborn,
You are of a sweet nature, and fit again to be cheated :   58
Which, if the Fates please, when you are possessed
Of the land and lady, you, sans question, shall be.
I'll presently think of the means.
                    [Walks by, musing.

Enter OVERREACH, speaking to a Servant within.

OVERREACH.   Sirrah, take my horse.
I'll walk to get me an appetite ; 'tis but a mile,
And exercise will keep me from being pursy.
Ha ! Marrall ! is he conjuring ? perhaps
The knave has wrought the prodigal to do
Some outrage on himself, and now he feels
Compunction in his conscience for 't : no matter,
So it be done. Marrall !

MARRALL.   Sir.

OVERREACH.   How succeed we

In our plot on Wellborn ?

MARRALL. Never better, sir.

OVERREACH. Has he hanged or drowned himself ?

MARRALL. No, sir, he lives ; 70
Lives once more to be made a prey to you,
A greater prey than ever.

OVERREACH. Art thou in thy wits ?
If thou art, reveal this miracle, and briefly.

MARRALL. A lady, sir, is fallen in love with him.

OVERREACH. With him ? what lady ?

MARRALL. The rich Lady Allworth.

OVERREACH. Thou dolt ! how dar'st thou speak this ?

MARRALL. I speak truth.
And I do so but once a year, unless
It be to you, sir : we dined with her ladyship,
I thank his worship.

OVERREACH. His worship !

MARRALL. As I live, sir,
I dined with him, at the great lady's table, 80
Simple as I stand here ; and saw when she kissed
him,
And would, at his request, have kissed me too ;
But I was not so audacious as some youths are,
That [1] dare do anything, be it ne'er so absurd
And sad after performance.

OVERREACH. Why, thou rascal !
To tell me these impossibilities !
Dine at her table ? and kiss him ? or thee ?——
Impudent varlet, have not I myself,
To whom great countesses' doors have oft flew
open, 89
Ten times attempted, since her husband's death,
In vain, to see her, though I came—a suitor ?
And yet your good solicitorship, and rogue Wellborn,
Were brought into her presence, feasted with
her !——

[1] 'And' 1633.

But that I know thee a dog that cannot blush,
This most incredible lie would call up one
On thy buttermilk cheeks.

    MARRALL.   Shall I not trust my eyes, sir,
Or taste ? I feel her good cheer in my belly.

    OVERREACH.   You shall feel me, if you give not
      over, sirrah :
Recover your brains again, and be no more gulled
With a beggar's plot, assisted by the aids   100
Of serving-men and chambermaids, for beyond
    these
Thou never saw'st a woman, or I'll quit you
From my employments.

    MARRALL.   Will you credit this yet ?
On my confidence of their marriage, I offered
    Wellborn——
[Aside.]   I would give a crown now I durst say his
    worship——
My nag, and twenty pounds.

    OVERREACH.   Did you so, idiot ?
                      [Strikes him down.
Was this the way to work him to despair,
Or rather to cross me ?

    MARRALL.   Will your worship kill me ?

    OVERREACH.   No, no ; but drive the lying spirit
    out of you.   109

    MARRALL.   He's gone.

    OVERREACH.   I have done then : now, forgetting
Your late imaginary feast and lady,
Know, my Lord Lovell dines with me to-morrow.
Be careful naught be wanting to receive him ;
And bid my daughter's women trim her up,
Though they paint her, so she catch the lord, I'll
    thank them :
There's a piece for my late blows.

    MARRALL.   [Aside.]   I must yet suffer :
But there may be a time——

    OVERREACH.   Do you grumble ?

    MARRALL.   No, sir.
                      [Exeunt.

ACT THE THIRD

Scene I.—The Country near Overreach's House.

Enter Lord Lovell, Allworth, and Servants.

LOVELL.   Walk the horses down the hill : some-
thing in private
I must impart to Allworth.   [Exeunt Servants.
ALLWORTH.   Oh, my lord,
What sacrifice of reverence, duty, watching,
Although I could put off the use of sleep,
And ever wait on your commands [to] serve them ;
What dangers, though in ne'er so horrid shapes,
Nay death itself, though I should run to meet it,
Can I, and with a thankful willingness suffer !
But still the retribution will fall short
Of your bounties showered upon me.
LOVELL.   Loving youth,
Till what I purpose be put into act,   11
Do not o'erprize it ; since you have trusted me
With your soul's nearest, nay, her dearest secret,
Rest confident 'tis in a cabinet locked
Treachery shall never open.   I have found you
(For so much to your face I must profess,
Howe'er you guard your modesty with a blush
     for 't)
More zealous in your love and service to me
Than I have been in my rewards.
ALLWORTH.   Still great ones,
Above my merit.
LOVELL.   Such your gratitude calls them :
Nor am I of that harsh and rugged temper   21
As some great men are taxed with, who imagine
They part from the respect due to their honours
If they use not all such as follow them,
Without distinction of their births, like slaves.
I am not so conditioned : I can make
A fitting difference between my footboy
And a gentleman by want compelled to serve me.

ALLWORTH.   'Tis thankfully acknowledged ; you
    have been
More like a father to me than a master :   30
Pray you, pardon the comparison.
    LOVELL.   I allow it ;
And, to give you assurance I am pleased in 't,
My carriage and demeanour to your mistress,
Fair Margaret, shall truly witness for me
I can command my passions.
    ALLWORTH.   'Tis a conquest
Few lords can boast of when they are tempted—
    Oh !
    LOVELL.   Why do you sigh ? can you be doubt-
    ful of me ?
By that fair name I in the wars have purchased,
And all my actions, hitherto untainted,
I will not be more true to mine own honour   40
Than to my Allworth !
    ALLWORTH.   As you are the brave Lord Lovell,
Your bare word only given is an assurance
Of more validity and weight to me
Than all the oaths, bound up with imprecations.
Which, when they would deceive, most courtiers
    practise ;
Yet being a man (for, sure, to style you more
Would relish of gross flattery), I am forced,
Against my confidence of your worth and virtues,
To doubt, nay more, to fear.
    LOVELL.   So young, and jealous !
    ALLWORTH.   Were you to encounter with a
    single foe,   50
The victory were certain ; but to stand
The charge of two such potent enemies,
At once assaulting you, as wealth and beauty,
And those too seconded with power, is odds
Too great for Hercules.
    LOVELL.   Speak your doubts and fears,
Since you will nourish them, in plainer language,
That I may understand them.
    ALLWORTH.   What 's your will,

Though I lend arms against myself (provided
They may advantage you), must be obeyed.
My much-loved lord, were Margaret only fair,
The cannon of her more than earthly form,   61
Though mounted high, commanding all beneath it,
And rammed with bullets of her sparkling eyes,
Of all the bulwarks that defend your senses
Could batter none [1] but that which guards your
　　sight.
But when the well-tuned accents of her tongue
Make music to you, and with numerous sounds
Assault your hearing (such as Ulysses, if he [2]
Now lived again, howe'er he stood the Sirens,
Could not resist), the combat must grow doubtful
Between your reason and rebellious passions.   71
Add this too ; when you feel her touch, and breath
Like a soft western wind when it glides o'er
Arabia, creating gums and spices,
And, in the van, the nectar of her lips,
Which you must taste, bring[s] the battalia on,
Well armed, and strongly lined with her discourse,
And knowing manners, to give entertainment ;—
Hippolytus himself would leave Diana,   79
To follow such a Venus.
　　LOVELL.   Love hath made you
Poetical, Allworth.
　　ALLWORTH.   Grant all these beat off,
Which if it be in man to do, you'll do it,
Mammon, in Sir Giles Overreach, steps in
With heaps of ill-got gold, and so much land,
To make her more remarkable, as would tire
A falcon's wings in one day to fly over.
O my good lord ! these powerful aids, which
　　would
Make a misshapen negro beautiful
(Yet are but ornaments to give her lustre,
That in herself is all perfection), must   90
Prevail for her : I here release your trust ;

----

[1] 'more,' 1633.
[2] 'if Ulysses,' 1633 ; corrected by Gifford.

'Tis happiness enough for me to serve you
And sometimes, with chaste eyes, to look upon her.
    LOVELL.   Why, shall I swear ?
    ALLWORTH.   Oh, by no means, my lord ;
And wrong not so your judgement to the world
As from your fond indulgence to a boy,
Your page, your servant, to refuse a blessing
Divers great men are rivals for.
    LOVELL.   Suspend
Your judgement till the trial. How far is it
To Overreach' house ?
    ALLWORTH.   At the most, some half-hour's
    riding ;   100
You'll soon be there.
    LOVELL.   And you the sooner freed
From your jealous fears.
    ALLWORTH.   O that I durst but hope it !
                             [Exeunt.

SCENE II.—A Room in OVERREACH'S House.

Enter OVERREACH, GREEDY, and MARRALL.

    OVERREACH.   Spare for no cost ; let my dressers
    crack with the weight
Of curious viands.
    GREEDY.   ' Store indeed 's no sore,' sir.
    OVERREACH.   That proverb fits your stomach,
    Master Greedy.—
And let no plate be seen but what 's pure gold,
Or such whose workmanship exceeds the matter
That it is made of ; let my choicest linen
Perfume the room, and, when we wash, the water,
With precious powders mixed, so please my lord,
That he may with envy wish to bathe so ever.
    MARRALL.   'Twill be very chargeable.
    OVERREACH.   Avaunt, you drudge !
Now all my laboured ends are at the stake,   11
Is 't a time to think of thrift ? Call in my daughter.
                          [Exit MARRALL.
And, Master Justice, since you love choice dishes,

And plenty of them——
    GREEDY.   As I do, indeed, sir,
Almost as much as to give thanks for them.
    OVERREACH.   I do confer that providence,[1] with
      my power
Of absolute command to have abundance,
To your best care.
    GREEDY.   I'll punctually discharge it,
And give the best directions. Now am I,   19
In mine own conceit, a monarch ; at the least,
Arch-president of the boiled, the roast, the baked ;
For which I will eat often, and give thanks
When my belly 's braced up like a drum, and that 's
      pure justice.   [Exit.
    OVERREACH.   I[t] must be so : should the foolish
      girl prove modest,
She may spoil all ; she had it not from me,
But from her mother ; I was ever forward,
As she must be, and therefore I'll prepare her.

Enter MARGARET.

Alone—and let your women wait without.   28
    MARGARET.   Your pleasure, sir ?
    OVERREACH.   Ha ! this is a neat dressing !
These orient pearls and diamonds well placed too !
The gown affects me not, it should have been
Embroidered o'er and o'er with flowers of gold ;
But these rich jewels and quaint fashion help it.
And how below ? since oft the wanton eye,
The face observed, descends unto the foot,
Which being well proportioned, as yours is,
Invites as much as perfect white and red,
Though without art. How like you your new
      woman,
The Lady Downfallen ?
    MARGARET.   Well, for a companion ;
Not as a servant.
    OVERREACH.   Is she humble, Meg,   40
And careful too, her ladyship forgotten ?

<hr>

[1] Management.

MARGARET.   I pity her fortune.

OVERREACH.   Pity her ? trample on her !
I took her up in an old tamin [1] gown
(Even starved for want of twopenny chops), to
    serve thee,
And if I understand she but repines
To do thee any duty, though ne'er so servile,
I'll pack her to her knight, where I have lodged
    him,
Into the counter, [2] and there let them howl
    together.

MARGARET.   You know your own ways ; but
    for me, I blush   49
When I command her, that was once attended
With persons not inferior to myself
In birth.

OVERREACH.   In birth ! why, art thou not my
    daughter,
The blest child of my industry and wealth ?
Why, foolish girl, was't not to make thee great
That I have run, and still pursue, those ways
That hale down curses on me, which I mind not ?
Part with these humble thoughts, and apt thyself
To the noble state I labour to advance thee ;
Or, by my hopes to see thee honourable,
I will adopt a stranger to my heir,   60
And throw thee from my care : do not provoke me.

MARGARET.   I will not, sir ; mould me which
    way you please.

Re-enter GREEDY.

OVERREACH.   How ! interrupted !

GREEDY.   'Tis matter of importance.
The cook, sir, is self-willed, and will not learn
From my experience : there's a fawn brought in,
    sir,
And, for my life, I cannot make him roast it
With a Norfolk dumpling in the belly of it ;
And, sir, we wise men know, without the dumpling

    A thin woollen stuff. Fr. *étamine.*   [2] Prison.

'Tis not worth threepence.

OVERREACH.   Would it were whole in thy belly,
To stuff it out ! cook it any way ; prithee, leave
    me.   70

GREEDY.   Without order for the dumpling ?

OVERREACH.   Let it be dumpled
Which way thou wilt ; or tell him, I will scald him
In his own cauldron.

GREEDY.   I had lost my stomach
Had I lost my mistress dumpling ; I'll give thanks
    for 't.   [Exit.

OVERREACH.   But to our business, Meg ; you
    have heard who dines here ?

MARGARET.   I have, sir.

OVERREACH.   'Tis an honourable man ;
A lord, Meg, and commands a regiment
Of soldiers, and, what 's rare, is one himself,
A bold and understanding one : and to be
A lord, and a good leader, in one volume,   80
Is granted unto few but such as rise up
The kingdom's glory

Re-enter GREEDY.

GREEDY.   I'll resign my office,
If I be not better obeyed.

OVERREACH.   'Slight, art thou frantic ?

GREEDY.   Frantic ! 'twould make me a frantic,
    and stark mad,
Were I not a justice of peace and quorum too,
Which this rebellious cook cares not a straw for.
There are a dozen of woodcocks——

OVERREACH.   Make thyself
Thirteen, the baker's dozen.

GREEDY.   I am contented,
So they may be dressed to my mind ; he has found
    out   89
A new device for sauce, and will not dish them
With toasts and butter ; my father was a tailor,
And my name, though a justice, Greedy Wood-
    cock ;

And, ere I'll see my lineage so abused,
I'll give up my commission.

    OVERREACH. [Calling off.]   Cook !—Rogue, obey
      him !
—I have given the word, pray you now remove
    yourself
To a collar of brawn, and trouble me no further.

    GREEDY.   I will, and meditate what to eat at
      dinner.   [Exit.

    OVERREACH.   And as I said, Meg, when this gull
      disturbed us,
This honourable lord, this colonel,   99
I would have thy husband.

    MARGARET.   There 's too much disparity
Between his quality and mine, to hope it.

    OVERREACH.   I more than hope 't, and doubt not
      to effect it.
Be thou no enemy to thyself ; my wealth
Shall weigh his titles down, and make you equals.
Now for the means to assure him thine, observe
    me ;
Remember he 's a courtier, and a soldier,
And not to be trifled with ; and, therefore, when
He comes to woo you, see you do not coy it :
This mincing modesty has spoiled many a match
By a first refusal, in vain after hoped for.   110

    MARGARET. You'll have me, sir, preserve the
      distance that
Confines a virgin ?

    OVERREACH.   Virgin me no virgins !
I must have you lose that name, or you lose me.
I will have you private—start not—I say, private ;
If thou art my true daughter, not a bastard,
Thou wilt venture alone with one man, though he
    came
Like Jupiter to Semele, and come off, too ;
And therefore, when he kisses you, kiss close.

    MARGARET.   I have heard this is the strumpet's
      fashion, sir,
Which I must never learn.

OVERREACH.   Learn any thing,   120
And from any creature that may make thee great ;
From the devil himself.

MARGARET. [Aside.] This is but devilish doctrine !

OVERREACH.   Or, if his blood grow hot, suppose
    he offer
Beyond this, do not you stay till it cool,
But meet his ardour ; if a couch be near,
Sit down on 't, and invite him.

MARGARET.   In your house,
Your own house, sir ? for heaven's sake, what are
    you then ?
Or what shall I be, sir ?

OVERREACH.   Stand not on form ;
Words are no substances.

MARGARET.   Though you could dispense
With your own honour, cast aside religion,   130
The hopes of heaven, or fear of hell, excuse me,
In worldly policy, this is not the way
To make me his wife ; his whore, I grant it may do.
My maiden honour so soon yielded up,
Nay, prostituted, cannot but assure him
I, that am light to him, will not hold weight
Whene'er [1] tempted by others ; so, in judgement,
When to his lust I have given up my honour,
He must and will forsake me.

OVERREACH.   How ! forsake thee ?
Do I wear a sword for fashion ? or is this arm
Shrunk up or withered ? does there live a man
Of that large list I have encountered with   142
Can truly say I e'er gave inch of ground
Not purchased with his blood that did oppose me ?
Forsake thee when the thing is done ? he dares not.
Give me but proof he has enjoyed thy person,
Though all his captains, echoes to his will,
Stood armed by his side to justify the wrong,
And he himself in the head of his bold troop,
Spite of his lordship, and his colonelship,   150
Or the judge's favour, I will make him render

    [1] Gifford's conjecture for ' When he is ', in the original.

A bloody and a strict account, and force him,
By marrying thee, to cure thy wounded honour !
I have said it.

Re-enter MARRALL.

MARRALL.   Sir, the man of honour's come
Newly alighted.
OVERREACH.   In, without reply ;
And do as I command, or thou art lost.
                                    [Exit MARGARET.
Is the loud music I gave order for
Ready to receive him ?
MARRALL.   'Tis, sir.
OVERREACH.   Let them sound
A princely welcome. [Exit MARRALL.] Roughness
      awhile leave me ;
For fawning now, a stranger to my nature,   160
Must make way for me.

Loud music. Enter Lord LOVELL, GREEDY, ALLWORTH,
                    and MARRALL.

LOVELL.   Sir, you meet your trouble.
OVERREACH. What you are pleased to style so
      is an honour
Above my worth and fortunes.
ALLWORTH. [Aside.]   Strange, so humble !
OVERREACH. A justice of peace, my lord.
                        [Presents GREEDY to him.
LOVELL.   Your hand, good sir.
GREEDY. [Aside.] This is a lord, and some think
      this a favour ;
But I had rather have my hand in my dumpling.
OVERREACH. Room for my lord.
LOVELL.   I miss, sir, your fair daughter
To crown my welcome.
OVERREACH.   May it please my lord
To taste a glass of Greek wine first, and suddenly
She shall attend my lord.
LOVELL.   You'll be obeyed, sir.
                    [Exeunt all but OVERREACH.

OVERREACH.   'Tis to my wish : as soon as come,
   ask for her !   171
Why, Meg ! Meg Overreach.—

Re-enter MARGARET.

                       How ! tears in your eyes !
Hah ! dry them quickly, or I'll dig them out.
Is this a time to whimper ? meet that greatness
That flies into thy bosom, think what 'tis
For me to say, My honourable daughter ;
And thou, when I stand bare, to say, Put on ;
Or, Father, you forget yourself. No more :
But be instructed, or expect——he comes.   179

Re-enter Lord LOVELL, GREEDY, ALLWORTH, and
MARRALL.

A black-browed girl, my lord.
                       [Lord LOVELL kisses MARGARET.
   LOVELL.   As I live, a rare one.
   ALLWORTH. [Aside.] He's ta'en already : I am lost.
   OVERREACH. [Aside.]   That kiss
Came twanging off, I like it.—Quit the room.
       [Exeunt all but OVERREACH, LOVELL, and MARGARET.
A little bashful, my good lord, but you,
I hope, will teach her boldness.
   LOVELL.   I am happy
In such a scholar : but——
   OVERREACH.   I am past learning,
And therefore leave you to yourselves.
           [Aside to MARGARET.] Remember.   [Exit.
   LOVELL.   You see, fair lady, your father is
      solicitous
To have you change the barren name of virgin
Into a hopeful wife.
   MARGARET.   His haste, my lord,   189
Holds no power o'er my will.
   LOVELL.   But o'er your duty.
   MARGARET.   Which forced too much, may break.
   LOVELL.   Bend rather, sweetest :
Think of your years.

MARGARET.   Too few to match with yours :
And choicest fruits too soon plucked, rot and
    wither.

LOVELL.   Do you think I am old ?

MARGARET.   I am sure I am too young.

LOVELL.   I can advance you.

MARGARET.   To a hill of sorrow ;
Where every hour I may expect to fall,
But never hope firm footing. You are noble,
I of a low descent, however rich ;   198
And tissues matched with scarlet suit but ill.
Oh, my good lord, I could say more, but that
I dare not trust these walls.

LOVELL.   Pray you, trust my ear then.

Re-enter OVERREACH *behind, listening.*

OVERREACH.   Close at it ! whispering ! this is
    excellent !
And, by their postures, a consent on both parts.

Re-enter GREEDY *behind.*

GREEDY.   Sir Giles, Sir Giles !

OVERREACH.   The great fiend stop that clapper !

GREEDY.   It must ring out, sir, when my belly
    rings noon.
The baked-meats are run out, the roast turned
    powder.

OVERREACH.   I shall powder you,

GREEDY.   Beat me to dust, l care not ;
In such a cause as this, I'll die a martyr.

OVERREACH.   Marry, and shall, you barathrum [1]
    of the shambles !   [*Strikes him.*

GREEDY.   How ! strike a justice of peace ! 'tis
    petty treason,   200
Edwardi quinto : but that you are my friend,
I would [2] commit you without bail or mainprize.[3]

OVERREACH.   Leave your bawling, sir, or I shall
    commit you

---

[1] Abyss. Cf. Hor. *Epis.* I. xv. 31, 'barathrumque macelli'.
[2] 'could,' 1633.   [3] Surety.

Where you shall not dine to-day : disturb my lord,
When he is in discourse ?
    GREEDY.   Is 't a time to talk
When we should be munching ?
    LOVELL.   Hah ! I heard some noise.
    OVERREACH. Mum, villain ; vanish ! shall we
      break a bargain
Almost made up ?   [Thrusts GREEDY off.
    LOVELL.   Lady, I understand you,
And rest most happy in your choice, believe it ;
I'll be a careful pilot to direct   210
Your yet uncertain bark to a port of safety.
    MARGARET.   So shall your honour save two lives,
      and bind us
Your slaves for ever.
    LOVELL.   I am in the act rewarded,
Since it is good ; howe'er, you must put on
An amorous carriage towards me to delude
Your subtle father.
    MARGARET.   I am prone to[1] that.
    LOVELL. Now break we off our conference.—
    Sir Giles !
Where is Sir Giles ?   [OVERREACH comes forward.

    Re-enter ALLWORTH, MARRALL, and GREEDY.

    OVERREACH.   My noble lord ; and how
Does your lordship find her ?
    LOVELL.   Apt, Sir Giles, and coming ;[2]
And I like her the better.
    OVERREACH.   So do I too.   220
    LOVELL. Yet should we take forts at the first
    assault,
'Twere poor in the defendant ; I must confirm her
With a love-letter or two, which I must have
Delivered by my page, and you give way to 't.
    OVERREACH. With all my soul :—a towardly
    gentleman !
Your hand, good Master Allworth ; know my
    house

---

    [1] Ready for.   [2] Complaisant.

Is ever open to you.

    ALLWORTH. [Aside.] 'Twas shut till now.

    OVERREACH. Well done, well done, my honour-
    able daughter !

Thou'rt so already : know this gentle youth,

And cherish him, my honourable daughter.   230

    MARGARET. I shall, with my best care.

                         [Noise within, as of a coach.

    OVERREACH.   A coach !

    GREEDY.   More stops

Before we go to dinner ! Oh, my guts !

Enter Lady ALLWORTH and WELLBORN.

    LADY ALLWORTH. If I find welcome,

You share in it ; if not, I'll back again,

Now I know your ends ; for I come armed for all

Can be objected.

    LOVELL.   How ! the Lady Allworth ?

    OVERREACH. And thus attended ?

        [LOVELL kisses Lady ALLWORTH, Lady ALLWORTH
           kisses MARGARET.

    MARRALL.   No, I am a dolt !

The spirit of lies hath entered me !'

    OVERREACH.   Peace, Patch ; [1]

'Tis more than wonder ! an astonishment

That does possess me wholly !

    LOVELL.   Noble lady,   240

This is a favour, to prevent [2] my visit,

The service of my life can never equal.

    LADY ALLWORTH. My lord, I laid wait for you,
    and much hoped

You would have made my poor house your first
inn :

And therefore doubting that you might forget me,

Or too long dwell here, having such ample cause,

In this unequalled beauty, for your stay,

And fearing to trust any but myself

With the relation of my service to you,

---

[1] Fool, from the nickname of Cardinal Wolsey's jester.

[2] Anticipate.

I borrowed so much from my long restraint 250
And took the air in person to invite you.

    LOVELL. Your bounties are so great, they rob
      me, madam,
Of words to give you thanks.

    LADY ALLWORTH. Good Sir Giles Overreach.
                          [Kisses him.
--How dost thou, Marrall ? liked you my meat so
      ill,
You'll dine no more with me ?

    GREEDY. I will, when you please,
An it like your ladyship.

    LADY ALLWORTH. When you please, Master
      Greedy ;
If meat can do it, you shall be satisfied.
And now, my lord, pray take into your knowledge
This gentleman ; [Presents WELLBORN.] howe'er his
      outside 's coarse,
His inward linings are as fine and fair 260
As any man's ; wonder not I speak at large :
And howsoe'er his humour carries him
To be thus accoutred, or what taint soever,
For his wild life, hath stuck upon his fame,
He may, ere long, with boldness, rank himself
With some that have contemned him. Sir Giles
      Overreach,
If I am welcome, bid him so.

    OVERREACH. My nephew !
He has been too long a stranger : faith you have,
Pray let it be mended.
               [LOVELL confers aside with WELLBORN.

    MARRALL. [Aside to OVERREACH.] Why, sir, what
      do you mean ?
This is ' rogue Wellborn, monster, prodigy, 270
That should hang or drown himself ' ; no man of
      worship,
Much less your nephew

    OVERREACH. Well, sirrah, we shall reckon
For this hereafter.

    MARRALL. I'll not lose my jeer,

Though I be beaten dead for't.

WELLBORN.   Let my silence plead
In my excuse, my lord, till better leisure
Offer itself to hear a full relation
Of my poor fortunes.

LOVELL.   I would hear, and help them.

OVERREACH.   Your dinner waits you.

LOVELL.   Pray you lead, we follow.

LADY ALLWORTH.   Nay, you are my guest ; come,
    dear Master Wellborn.   [Exeunt all but GREEDY.

GREEDY.   ' Dear Master Wellborn ' !   So she
    said : Heaven ! Heaven !   280
If my belly would give me leave, I could ruminate
All day on this : I have granted twenty warrants
To have him committed, from all prisons in the
    shire,
To Nottingham gaol ; and now, ' Dear Master
    Wellborn ' !
And, ' My good nephew ' !—but I play the fool
To stand here prating, and forget my dinner.

Re-enter MARRALL.

Are they set, Marrall ?

MARRALL.   Long since ; pray you a word, sir.

GREEDY.   No wording now.

MARRALL.   In troth, I must ; my master,
Knowing you are his good friend, makes bold with
    you,   289
And does entreat you, more guests being come in
Than he expected, especially his nephew,
The table being full too, you would excuse him,
And sup with him on the cold meat.

GREEDY.   How ! no dinner,
After all my care ?

MARRALL.   'Tis but a penance for
A meal ; besides, you broke your fast.

GREEDY.   That was
But a bit to stay my stomach : a man in com-
    mission
Give place to a tatterdemalion !

MARRALL.   No bug [1] words, sir ;
Should his worship hear you——
    GREEDY.   Lose my dumpling too,
And buttered toasts, and woodcocks !
    MARRALL.   Come, have patience.
If you will dispense a little with your worship,
And sit with the waiting women, you'll have
        dumpling,   301
Woodcock, and buttered toasts too.
    GREEDY.   This revives me :
I will gorge there sufficiently.
    MARRALL.   This is the way, sir.
                                    [Exeunt.

SCENE III.—Another Room in OVERREACH'S House.

Enter OVERREACH, as from dinner.

    OVERREACH.   She's caught !   O women !—she
        neglects my lord,
And all her compliments applies [2] to Wellborn !
The garments of her widowhood laid by,
She now appears as glorious as the spring ;
Her eyes fixed on him, in the wine she drinks,
He being her pledge, she sends him burning kisses,
And sits on thorns, till she be private with him.
She leaves my meat to feed upon his looks,
And if in our discourse he be but named,   9
From her a deep sigh follows.   But why grieve I
At this ? it makes for me ; if she prove his,
All that is hers is mine, as I will work him.

Enter MARRALL.

    MARRALL.   Sir, the whole board is troubled at
        your rising.
    OVERREACH.   No matter, I'll excuse it : prithee,
        Marrall,
Watch an occasion to invite my nephew
To speak with me in private.
    MARRALL.   Who ? ' the rogue

            [1] Big.   [2] 'applied ', 1633.

The lady scorned to look on ' ?

OVERREACH. You are a wag.

Enter Lady ALLWORTH *and* WELLBORN.

MARRALL. See, sir, she's come, and cannot be
  without him.

LADY ALLWORTH. With your favour, sir, after
  a plenteous dinner,
I shall make bold to walk a turn or two,   20
In your rare garden.

OVERREACH. There's an arbour too,
If your ladyship please to use it.

LADY ALLWORTH. Come, Master Wellborn.
        [*Exeunt Lady* ALLWORTH *and* WELLBORN.

OVERREACH. Grosser and grosser! now I
  believe the poet
Feigned not, but was historical, when he wrote
Pasiphaë was enamoured of a bull :
This lady's lust's more monstrous.

Enter Lord LOVELL, MARGARET, *and the rest.*

                        My good lord,
Excuse my manners.

LOVELL. There needs none, Sir Giles,
I may ere long say father, when it pleases
My dearest mistress to give warrant to it.

OVERREACH. She shall seal to it, my lord, and
  make me happy.   30

Re-enter WELLBORN *and Lady* ALLWORTH.

MARGARET. My lady is returned.

LADY ALLWORTH. Provide my coach,
I'll instantly away ; my thanks, Sir Giles,
For my entertainment.

OVERREACH, 'Tis your nobleness
To think it such.

LADY ALLWORTH. I must do you a further wrong
In taking away your honourable guest.

LOVELL. I wait on you, madam ; farewell
  good Sir Giles.

LADY ALLWORTH. Good Mistress Margaret !
nay, come, Master Wellborn,
I must not leave you behind ; in sooth, I must
not.
OVERREACH.   Rob me not, madam, of all joys
at once ;
Let my nephew stay behind : he shall have my
coach,   40
And, after some small conference between us,
Soon overtake your ladyship.
LADY ALLWORTH.   Stay not long, sir.
LOVELL.   This parting kiss : [Kisses MARGARET.]
you shall every day hear from me,
By my faithful page.
ALLWORTH.   'Tis a service I am proud of.
    [Exeunt Lord LOVELL, Lady ALLWORTH, ALLWORTH,
        and MARRALL.
OVERREACH.   Daughter, to your chamber.—
[Exit MARGARET.]—   You may wonder, nephew,
After so long an enmity between us,
I should desire your friendship.
WELLBORN.   So I do, sir ;
'Tis strange to me.
OVERREACH.   But I'll make it no wonder ;
And what is more, unfold my nature to you.   49
We worldly men, when we see friends and kinsmen
Past hope sunk in their fortunes, lend no hand
To lift them up, but rather set our feet
Upon their heads, to press them to the bottom ;
As, I must yield, with you I practised it :
But, now I see you in a way to rise,
I can and will assist you ; this rich lady
(And I am glad of 't) is enamoured of you ;
'Tis too apparent, nephew.
WELLBORN.   No such thing :
Compassion rather, sir.
OVERREACH.   Well, in a word,
Because your stay is short, I'll have you seen   60
No more in this base shape ; nor shall she say,
She married you like a beggar, or in debt.

WELLBORN. [Aside.] He'll run into the noose,
and save my labour.

OVERREACH. You have a trunk of rich clothes,
not far hence,
In pawn ; I will redeem them ; and that no
clamour
May taint your credit for your petty debts,
You shall have a thousand pounds to cut them off,
And go a free man to the wealthy lady.

WELLBORN. This done, sir, out of love, and no
ends else——

OVERREACH. As it is, nephew.

WELLBORN. Binds me still your servant.

OVERREACH. No compliments, you are stayed
for : ere you have supped   71
You shall hear from me.—My coach, knaves, for
my nephew.—
To-morrow I will visit you.

WELLBORN. Here 's an uncle
In a man's extremes ! how much they do belie you,
That say you are hard-hearted !

OVERREACH. My deeds, nephew,
Shall speak my love ; what men report I weigh
not.   [Exeunt.

ACT THE FOURTH

SCENE I.—A Room in Lady ALLWORTH's House.

Enter Lord LOVELL and ALLWORTH.

LOVELL. 'Tis well ; give me my cloak ; I now
discharge you
From further service : mind your own affairs,
I hope they will prove successful.

ALLWORTH. What is blest
With your good wish, my lord, cannot but prosper.
Let aftertimes report, and to your honour,
How much I stand engaged, for I want language
To speak my debt ; yet if a tear or two
Of joy, for your much goodness, can supply

My tongue's defects, I could——
 LOVELL.   Nay, do not melt`:
This ceremonial thanks to me's superfluous. 10
 OVERREACH. [Within.] Is my lord stirring?
 LOVELL. 'Tis he! oh, here's your letter: let
  him in.

   Enter OVERREACH, GREEDY, and MARRALL.

 OVERREACH. A good day to my lord!
 LOVELL.   You are an early riser,
Sir Giles.
 OVERREACH. And reason, to attend your lord-
  ship.
 LOVELL. And you, too, Master Greedy, up so
  soon!
 GREEDY. In troth, my lord, after the sun is up,
I cannot sleep, for I have a foolish stomach
That croaks for breakfast. With your lordship's
  favour,
I have a serious question to demand
Of my worthy friend Sir Giles.
 LOVELL.   Pray you use your pleasure.
 GREEDY. How far, Sir Giles, and pray you
  answer me   . 21
Upon your credit, hold you it to be
From your manor-house, to this of my Lady
  Allworth's?
 OVERREACH. Why, some four mile.
 GREEDY.   How! four mile, good Sir Giles?
Upon your reputation, think better;
For if you do abate but one half-quarter
Of five, you do yourself the greatest wrong
That can be in the world; for four miles riding
Could not have raised so huge an appetite
As I feel gnawing on me.
 MARRALL.   Whether you ride, 30
Or go afoot, you are that way still provided,
An it please your worship.
 OVERREACH.   How now, sirrah? prating
Before my lord? no deference? Go to my nephew,

See all his debts discharged, and help his worship
To fit on his rich suit.

 MARRALL. [Aside.] I may fit you too.
Tossed like a dog still !   [Exit.

 LOVELL.   I have writ this morning
A few lines to my mistress, your fair daughter.

 OVERREACH. 'Twill fire her, for she's wholly
  yours already :—
Sweet Master Allworth, take my ring ; 'twill carry
 you
To her presence, I dare warrant you ; and there
 plead   40
For my good lord, if you shall find occasion.
That done, pray ride to Nottingham, get a licence,
Still by this token. I'll have it dispatched,
And suddenly, my lord, that I may say,
My honourable, nay, right honourable daughter.

 GREEDY. Take my advice, young gentleman,
  get your breakfast ;
'Tis unwholesome to ride fasting : I'll eat with you.
And eat to purpose.

 OVERREACH.   Some Fury's in that gut !
Hungry again ? did you not devour, this morning,
A shield of brawn, and a barrel of Colchester
 oysters ?   50

 GREEDY. Why, that was, sir, only to scour my
  stomach,
A kind of a preparative. Come, gentleman,
I will not have you feed like the hangman of
 Flushing,
Alone, while I am here.

 LOVELL.   Haste your return

 ALLWORTH. I will not fail, my lord.

 GREEDY.   Nor I, to line
My Christmas coffer. [Exeunt GREEDY and ALLWORTH.

 OVERREACH.   To my wish : we are private.
I come not to make offer with my daughter
A certain portion, that were poor and trivial :
In one word, I pronounce all that is mine,
In lands or leases, ready coin or goods, 60

With her, my lord, comes to you ; nor shall you
    have
One motive to induce you to believe
I live too long, since every year I'll add
Something unto the heap, which shall be yours too.
    LOVELL.   You are a right kind father.
    OVERREACH.   You shall have reason
To think me such. How do you like this seat ?
It is well wooded, and well watered, the acres
Fertile and rich ; would it not serve for change,
To entertain your friends in a summer progress ?
What thinks my noble lord ?
    LOVELL.   'Tis a wholesome air,
And well-built pile ; and she that 's mistress of it,
Worthy the large revenue.
    OVERREACH.   She the mistress !   72
It may be so for a time : but let my lord
Say only that he likes it, and would have it,
I say, ere long 'tis his.
    LOVELL.   Impossible ,
    OVERREACH. You do conclude too fast, not
    knowing me,
Nor the engines that I work by. 'Tis not alone
The Lady Allworth's lands, for those, once Well-
    born's
(As by her dotage on him I know they will be),
Shall soon be mine ; but point out any man's 80
In all the shire, and say they lie convenient,
And useful for your lordship, and once more
I say aloud, they are yours.
    LOVELL.   I dare not own
What 's by unjust and cruel means extorted ;
My fame and credit are more dear to me,
Than so to expose them to be censured by
The public voice.
    OVERREACH.   You run, my lord, no hazard.
Your reputation shall stand as fair,
In all good men's opinions, as now ;
Nor can my actions, though condemned for ill,
Cast any foul aspersion upon yours.   91

For, though I do contemn report myself
As a mere sound, I still will be so tender
Of what concerns you, in all points of honour,
That the immaculate whiteness of your fame,
Nor your unquestionèd integrity,
Shall e'er be sullied with one taint or spot
That may take from your innocence and candour.
All my ambition is to have my daughter   99
Right honourable, which my lord can make her ;
And might I live to dance upon my knee
A young Lord Lovell, born by her unto you,
I write nil ultra to my proudest hopes.
As for possessions and annual rents,
Equivalent to maintain you in the port
Your noble birth and present state requires,
I do remove that burthen from your shoulders,
And take it on mine own : for, though I ruin
The country to supply your riotous waste,
The scourge of prodigals, want, shall never find
    you.   110
    LOVELL.   Are you not frighted with the impre-
        cations
And curses of whole families, made wretched
By your sinister practices ?
    OVERREACH.   Yes, as rocks are,
When foamy billows split themselves against
Their flinty ribs ; or as the moon is moved,
When wolves, with hunger pined, howl at her
    brightness.
I am of a solid temper, and, like these,
Steer on a constant course : with mine own sword,
If called into the field, I can make that right,
Which fearful enemies murmured at as wrong.
Now, for these other piddling complaints   121
Breathed out in bitterness ; as when they call me
Extortioner, tyrant, cormorant, or intruder
On my poor neighbour's right, or grand incloser
Of what was common, to my private use ;
Nay, when my ears are pierced with widows'
    cries,

                                            T

And undone orphans wash with tears my threshold,
I only think what 'tis to have my daughter
Right honourable ; and 'tis a powerful charm
Makes me insensible of remorse, or pity,   130
Or the least sting of conscience.

LOVELL.   I admire [1]
The toughness of your nature.

OVERREACH.   'Tis for you,
My lord, and for my daughter, I am marble ;
Nay more, if you will have my character
In little, I enjoy more true delight
In my arrival to my wealth these dark
And crooked ways than you shall e'er take pleasure
In spending what my industry hath compassed.
My haste commands me hence ; in one word,
        therefore,
Is it a match ?

LOVELL.   I hope, that is past doubt now.

OVERREACH.   Then rest secure ; not the hate of
        all mankind here,   141
Nor fear of what can fall on me hereafter,
Shall make me study aught but your advancement
One story higher : an earl ! if gold can do it.
Dispute not my religion, nor my faith ;
Though I am borne thus headlong by my will,
You may make choice of what belief you please,
To me they are equal ; so, my lord, good morrow.
                                            [Exit.

LOVELL.   He's gone—I wonder how the earth
        can bear
Such a portent ! I, that have lived a soldier,   150
And stood the enemy's violent charge undaunted,
To hear this blasphemous beast am bathed all
        over
In a cold sweat : yet, like a mountain, he
(Confirmed in atheistical assertions)
Is no more shaken than Olympus [2] is

    [1] Wonder at.
    [2] It is Parnassus, not Olympus, that has two peaks ; see
Ovid, *Met.* i. 316.

When angry Boreas loads his double head
With sudden drifts of snow.

Enter Lady ALLWORTH, Waiting Woman, and AMBLE

LADY ALLWORTH.   Save you, my lord !
Disturb I not your privacy ?
        LOVELL.   No, good madam ;
For your own sake I am glad you came no sooner,
Since this bold bad man, Sir Giles Overreach,
Made such a plain discovery of himself,   161
And read this morning such a devilish matins,
That I should think it a sin next to his
But to repeat it.
        LADY ALLWORTH.   I ne'er pressed, my lord,
On others' privacies ; yet, against my will,
Walking, for health' sake, in the gallery
Adjoining to your lodgings, I was made
(So vehement and loud he was) partaker
Of his tempting offers.
        LOVELL.   Please you to command
Your servants hence, and I shall gladly hear
Your wiser counsel.
        LADY ALLWORTH.   'Tis, my lord, a woman's,
But true and hearty ; [To the Servants.]—wait in the
        next room,   172
But be within call ; yet not so near to force me
To whisper my intents.
        AMBLE.   We are taught better
By you, good madam.
        WAITING WOMAN.   And well know our distance.
        LADY ALLWORTH.   Do so, and talk not : 'twill
        become your breeding.
                              [Exeunt AMBLE and Woman.
Now, my good lord : if I may use my freedom,
As to an honoured friend——
        LOVELL.   You lessen else
Your favour to me.
        LADY ALLWORTH.   I dare then say thus ;
As you are noble (howe'er common men   180
Make sordid wealth the object and sole end

Of their industrious aims) 'twill not agree
With those of eminent blood, who are engaged
More to prefer [1] their honours than to increase
The state left to them by their ancestors,   ❧
To study large additions to their fortunes,
And quite neglect their births :—though I must
        grant,
Riches, well got, to be a useful servant,
But a bad master.

LOVELL.   Madam, 'tis confessed ;   189
But what infer you from it ?

LADY ALLWORTH.   This, my lord ;
That as all wrongs, though thrust into one scale,
Slide of themselves off when right fills the other,
And cannot bide the trial ; so all wealth,
I mean if ill-acquired, cemented to honour
By virtuous ways achieved and bravely purchased,
Is but as rubbish poured into a river
(Howe'er intended to make good the bank),
Rendering the water, that was pure before,
Polluted and unwholesome. I allow
The heir of Sir Giles Overreach, Margaret,   200
A maid well qualified and the richest match
Our north part can make boast of ; yet she cannot,
With all that she brings with her, fill their mouths,
That never will forget who was her father ;
Or that my husband Allworth's lands, and Well-
        born's
(How wrung from both needs now no repetition),
Were real motives that more worked your lordship
To join your families, than her form and virtues :
You may conceive the rest.

LOVELL.   I do, sweet madam,
And long since have considered it. I know,   210
The sum of all that makes a just man happy
Consists in the well choosing of his wife :
And there, well to discharge it, does require
Equality of years, of birth, of fortune ;
For beauty being poor, and not cried up

                    [1] Advance.

By birth or wealth, can truly mix with neither.
And wealth, where there's such difference in years,
And fair descent, must make the yoke uneasy :—
But I come nearer.

    LADY ALLWORTH. Pray you do, my lord.

    LOVELL. Were Overreach' states thrice cen-
       tupled, his daughter   220
Millions of degrees much fairer than she is,
Howe'er I might urge precedents to excuse me,
I would not so adulterate my blood
By marrying Margaret, and so leave my issue
Made up of several pieces, one part scarlet,
And the other London blue. In my own tomb
I will inter my name first.

    LADY ALLWORTH. [Aside.] I am glad to hear
      this.——
Why then, my lord, pretend you marriage to
    her ?
Dissimulation but ties false knots
On that straight line by which you, hitherto,   230
Have measured all your actions.

    LOVELL.   I make answer,
And aptly, with a question. Wherefore have you,
That, since your husband's death, have lived a
    strict
And chaste nun's life, on the sudden given your-
    self
To visits and entertainments ? think you, madam,
'Tis not grown public conference ? or the favours
Which you too prodigally have thrown on Wellborn,
Being too reserved before, incur not censure ?

    LADY ALLWORTH. I am innocent here ; and, on
    my life, I swear
My ends are good.

    LOVELL.   On my soul, so are mine   240
To Margaret ; but leave both to the event :
And since this friendly privacy does serve
But as an offered means unto ourselves,
To search each other farther, you having shown
Your care of me, I my respect to you,

Deny me not, but still in chaste words, madam,
An afternoon's discourse.

LADY ALLWORTH.   So ; I shall hear you.

[Exeunt.

SCENE II.—Before TAPWELL'S House.

Enter TAPWELL and FROTH.

TAPWELL. Undone, undone ! this was your
counsel, Froth.

FROTH. Mine ? I defy thee : did not Master
Marrall

(He has marred all, I am sure) strictly command
us,

On pain of Sir Giles Overreach' displeasure,
To turn the gentleman out of doors ?

TAPWELL.   'Tis true ;
But now he 's his uncle's darling, and has got
Master Justice Greedy, since he filled his belly,
At his commandment, to do anything ;
Woe, woe to us !

FROTH.   He may prove merciful.

TAPWELL. Troth, we do not deserve it at his
hands.   10
Though he knew all the passages of our house,
As the receiving of stolen goods, and bawdry,
When he was rogue Wellborn no man would believe
him,
And then his information could not hurt us ;
But now he is right worshipful again,
Who dares but doubt his testimony ? methinks,
I see thee, Froth, already in a cart,
For a close [1] bawd, thine eyes even pelted out
With dirt and rotten eggs ; and my hand hissing,
If I scape the halter, with the letter R [2]   20
Printed upon it.

FROTH.   Would that were the worst !
That were but nine days' wonder : as for credit,
We have none to lose ; but we shall lose the money

---

[1] Secret.   [2] For Rogue.

He owes us, and his custom; there's the hell on 't.

TAPWELL. He has summoned all his creditors
    by the drum,
And they swarm about him like so many soldiers
On the pay day : and has found out such a new
    way
To pay his old debts, as 'tis very likely
He shall be chronicled for it !

FROTH.   He deserves it
More than ten pageants. But are you sure his
    worship   30
Comes this way to my lady's ?

            [A cry within : Brave master Wellborn !

TAPWELL.   Yes :—I hear him.

FROTH. Be ready with your petition, and pre-
    sent it
To his good grace.

Enter WELLBORN in a rich habit, followed by MARRALL,
    GREEDY, ORDER, FURNACE, and Creditors ; TAPWELL
    kneeling, delivers his bill of debt.

WELLBORN.   How 's this ! petitioned too ?—
But note what miracles the payment of
A little trash, and a rich suit of clothes,
Can work upon these rascals ! I shall be,
I think, Prince Wellborn.

MARRALL.   When your worship 's married,
You may be—I know what I hope to see you.

WELLBORN. Then look thou for advancement.

MARRALL.   To be known
Your worship's bailiff, is the mark I shoot at.   40

WELLBORN. And thou shalt hit it.

MARRALL.   Pray you, sir, dispatch
These needy followers, and for my admittance,
Provided you'll defend me from Sir Giles,
Whose service I am weary of, I'll say something
You shall give thanks for.

WELLBORN.   Fear me not Sir Giles.

GREEDY. Who, Tapwell ? I remember thy wife
    brought me,

Last new-year's tide, a couple of fat turkeys.

    TAPWELL. And shall do every Christmas, let
      your worship
But stand my friend now.

    GREEDY.   How ! with Master Wellborn ?
I can do anything with him on such terms.—— 50
See you this honest couple, they are good souls
As ever drew out fosset :[1] have they not
A pair of honest faces ?

    WELLBORN.   I o'erheard you,
And the bribe he promised. You are cozened in
    them ;
For, of all the scum that grew rich by my riots,
This, for a most unthankful knave, and this,
For a base bawd and whore, have worst deserved
    me,
And therefore speak not for them : by your place
You are rather to do me justice ; lend me your ear :
——Forget his turkeys, and call in his licence 60
And, at the next fair, I'll give you a yoke of oxen
Worth all his poultry.

    GREEDY.   I am changed on the sudden
In my opinion ! come near ; nearer, rascal.
And, now I view him better, did you e'er see
One look so like an archknave ? his very counte-
    nance,
Should an understanding judge but look upon him,
Would hang him, though he were innocent.

    TAPWELL AND FROTH.   Worshipful sir.——
    GREEDY. No, though the Great Turk came,
    instead of turkeys,
To beg my favour, I am inexorable. 69
Thou hast an ill name : besides thy musty ale,
That hath destroyed many of the king's liege
    people,
Thou never hadst in thy house, to stay men's
    stomachs,
A piece of Suffolk cheese or gammon of bacon,
Or any esculent, as the learned call it,

              [1] Faucet, vent-peg.

For their emolument, but sheer drink only.
For which gross fault I here do damn thy licence,
Forbidding thee ever to tap or draw ;
For, instantly, I will, in mine own person,   78
Command the constable to pull down thy sign,
And do it before I eat.

    FROTH.   No mercy ?

    GREEDY.   Vanish !
If I show any, may my promised oxen gore me !

    TAPWELL.   Unthankful   knaves   are   ever   so
        rewarded.   [Exeunt GREEDY, TAPWELL, and FROTH.

    WELLBORN.   Speak ; what are you ?

    FIRST CREDITOR.   A decayed vintner, sir,
That might have thrived, but that your worship
        broke me
With trusting you with muskadine [1] and eggs,
And five pound suppers, with your after drinkings,
When you lodged upon the Bankside.

    WELLBORN.   I remember.

    FIRST CREDITOR.   I have not been hasty, nor e'er
        laid [2] to arrest you ;
And therefore, sir——

    WELLBORN.   Thou art an honest fellow,
I'll set thee up again ; see his bill paid.——   90
What are you ?

    SECOND CREDITOR.   A tailor once, but now mere
        botcher.
I gave you credit for a suit of clothes,
Which was all my stock, but you failing in pay-
        ment,
I was removed from the shopboard, and confined
Under a stall.

    WELLBORN.   See him paid ; and botch no more.

    SECOND CREDITOR.   I ask no interest, sir.

    WELLBORN.   Such tailors need not ;
If their bills are paid in one and twenty year,

---

[1] Muscatel wine and eggs were taken as a pick-me-up.
See Dekker, *Northward Ho*, IV. i. '*Bell.* How took he this
drench down ? *May.* Like eggs and muscadine, at a gulp.'
[2] Intended.

They are seldom losers.   [To Third Creditor.]   Oh, I
    know thy face,   98
Thou wert my surgeon : you must tell no tales ;
Those days are done.   I will pay you in private.
    ORDER.   A royal gentleman !
    FURNACE.   Royal as an emperor !
He'll prove a brave master ; my good lady knew
To choose a man.
    WELLBORN.   See all men else discharged ;
And since old debts are cleared by a new way,
A little bounty will not misbecome me ;
There's something, honest cook, for thy good
    breakfasts ;
And this, [To ORDER.] for your respect : take't, 'tis
    good gold,
And I able to spare it.
    ORDER.   You are too munificent.
    FURNACE.   He was ever so.
    WELLBORN.   Pray you, on before.
    THIRD CREDITOR.   Heaven bless you !
    MARRALL.   At four o'clock ; the rest know
    where to meet me.   110
            [Exeunt ORDER, FURNACE, and Creditors.
    WELLBORN.   Now, Master Marrall, what's the
    weighty secret
You promised to impart ?
    MARRALL.   Sir, time nor place
Allow me to relate each circumstance,
This only, in a word ; I know Sir Giles
Will come upon you for security
For his thousand pounds, which you must not
    consent to.
As he grows in heat, as I am sure he will,
Be you but rough, and say he's in your debt
Ten times the sum, upon sale of your land ;
I had a hand in't (I speak it to my shame)   120
When you were defeated of it.
    WELLBORN.   That's forgiven.
    MARRALL.   I shall deserve it : then urge him to
    produce

The deed in which you passed it over to him,
Which I know he'll have about him, to deliver
To the Lord Lovell, with many other writings,
And present monies : I'll instruct you further,
As I wait on your worship : if I play not my prize
To your full content, and your uncle's much
    vexation,
Hang up Jack Marrall.

   WELLBORN.   I rely upon thee.

                                 [Exeunt.

      SCENE III.—A Room in OVERREACH'S House.

        Enter ALLWORTH and MARGARET.

   ALLWORTH.   Whether to yield the first praise to
    my lord's
Unequalled temperance or your constant sweetness,
That I yet live, my weak hands fastened on
Hope's anchor, spite of all storms of despair,
I yet rest doubtful.

   MARGARET.   Give it to Lord Lovell ;
For what in him was bounty, in me 's duty.
I make but payment of a debt to which
My vows, in that high office registered,
Are faithful witnesses.

   ALLWORTH.   'Tis true, my dearest :
Yet, when I call to mind how many fair ones   10
Make wilful shipwreck of their faiths and oaths
To God and man, to fill the arms of greatness,
And you rise up [no] less [1] than a glorious star,
To the amazement of the world,—hold out
Against the stern authority of a father,
And spurn at honour, when it comes to court you ;
I am so tender of your good, that faintly,
With your wrong, I can wish myself that right
You yet are pleased to do me.

   MARGARET.   Yet, and ever.
To me what 's title, when content is wanting ?
Or wealth, raked up together with much care,

    [1] ' rise up less than,' 1633. Corrected by Dodsley.

And to be kept with more, when the heart pines
In being dispossessed of what it longs for   23
Beyond the Indian mines ? or the smooth brow
Of a pleased sire, that slaves me to his will,
And, so his ravenous humour may be feasted
By my obedience, and he see me great,
Leaves to my soul nor faculties nor power
To make her own election ?

    ALLWORTH.   But the dangers
That follow the repulse——

    MARGARET.   To me they are nothing ;
Let Allworth love, I cannot be unhappy.   31
Suppose the worst, that, in his rage, he kill me ;
A tear or two, by you dropt on my hearse,
In sorrow for my fate, will call back life
So far as but to say, that I die yours ;
I then shall rest in peace : or should he prove
So cruel, as one death would not suffice
His thirst of vengeance, but with lingering torments
In mind and body I must waste to air,   39
In poverty joined with banishment ; so you share
In my afflictions, which I dare not wish you,
So high I prize you, I could undergo them
With such a patience as should look down
With scorn on his worst malice.

    ALLWORTH.   Heaven avert
Such trials of your true affection to me !
Nor will it unto you, that are all mercy,
Show so much rigour : but since we must run
Such desperate hazards, let us do our best
To steer between them.

    MARGARET.   Your lord 's ours, and sure ;
And, though but a young actor, second me   50
In doing to the life what he has plotted,

        Enter OVERREACH behind.

The end may yet prove happy. Now, my All-
    worth——

    ALLWORTH. [Seeing her father.] To your letter,
    and put on a seeming anger.

MARGARET. I'll pay my lord all debts due to
 his title ;
And when with terms, not taking from his honour,
He does solicit me, I shall gladly hear him.
But in this peremptory, nay, commanding way,
To appoint a meeting, and, without my know-
 ledge,
A priest to tie the knot can ne'er be undone
Till death unloose it, is a confidence   60
In his lordship will deceive him.

 ALLWORTH.   I hope better,
Good lady.

 MARGARET. Hope, sir, what you please : for me
I must take a safe and secure course ; I have
A father, and without his full consent,
Though all lords of the land kneeled for my favour,
I can grant nothing.

 OVERREACH. [Coming forward.] I like this obedience:
But whatsoe'er my lord writes, must and shall be
Accepted and embraced. Sweet Master Allworth,
You show yourself a true and faithful servant
To your good lord ; he has a jewel of you. 70
How ! frowning, Meg ? are these looks to receive
A messenger from my lord ? what 's this ? give me
 it.

 MARGARET. A piece of arrogant paper, like the
 inscriptions.

 OVERREACH. [Reads.] ' Fair mistress, from your
 servant learn, all joys
That we can hope for, if deferred, prove toys ;
Therefore this instant, and in private, meet
A husband, that will gladly at your feet
Lay down his honours, tendering them to you
With all content, the church being paid her due.'
—Is this the arrogant piece of paper ? fool ! 80
Will you still be one ? in the name of madness
 what
Could his good honour write more to content you ?
Is there aught else to be wished, after these two,
That are already offered ; marriage first.

And lawful pleasure after ?   what would you more ?
   MARGARET.   Why, sir, I would be married like
     your daughter ;
Not hurried away i' the night I know not whither,
Without all ceremony ;   no friends invited
To honour the solemnity.
   ALLWORTH.   An 't please your honour
For so before to-morrow I must style you,   90
My lord desires this privacy, in respect
His honourable kinsmen are afar off,
And his desires to have it done brook not
So long delay as to expect their coming ;
And yet he stands resolved, with all due pomp,
As running at the ring, plays, masks, and tilting,
To have his marriage at court celebrated,
When he has brought your honour up to London.
   OVERREACH.   He tells you true ;   'tis the
     fashion, on my knowledge :
Yet the good lord, to please your peevishness,
Must put it off, forsooth ! and lose a night,   101
In which perhaps he might get two boys on thee.
Tempt me no further ; if you do, this goad
                       [Points to his sword.
Shall prick you to him.
   MARGARET.   I could be contented,
Were you but by, to do a father's part,
And give me in the church.
   OVERREACH.   So my lord have you,
What do I care who gives you ? since my lord
Does purpose to be private, I'll not cross him.
I know not, Master Allworth, how my lord
May be provided, and therefore there 's a purse
Of gold, 'twill serve this night's expense ; to-
     morrow   111
I'll furnish him with any sums : in the mean-
     time,
Use my ring to my chaplain ; he is beneficed
At my manor of Got'em, and called Parson Willdo :
'Tis no matter for a licence, I'll bear him out
     in 't.

MARGARET. With your favour, sir, what warrant
is your ring ?
He may suppose I got that twenty ways,
Without your knowledge ; and then to be refused
Were such a stain upon me !—if you pleased, sir,
Your presence would do better.
    OVERREACH.   Still perverse !
I say again, I will not cross my lord ;   121
Yet I'll prevent [1] you too.—Paper and ink,
there !
    ALLWORTH.   I can furnish you.
    OVERREACH.   I thank you, I can write then.
                                         [Writes.

    ALLWORTH.   You may, if you please, put out the
name of my lord,
In respect he comes disguised, and only write,
' Marry her to this gentleman.'
    OVERREACH.   Well advised.
'Tis done ; away ;—[MARGARET kneels.] My bless-
ing, girl ? thou hast it.
Nay, no reply, be gone :—good Master Allworth,
This shall be the best night's work you ever made.
    ALLWORTH.   I hope so, sir.
                    [Exeunt ALLWORTH and MARGARET.
    OVERREACH.   Farewell !—Now all's cocksure :
Methinks I hear already knights and ladies   131
Say, ' Sir Giles Overreach, how is it with
Your honourable daughter ? has her honour
Slept well to-night ? ' or, ' Will her honour please
To accept this monkey, dog, or paroquito '
(This is state in ladies), ' or my eldest son
To be her page, and wait upon her trencher ? '
My ends, my ends are compassed—then for Well-
born
And the lands ; were he once married to the
widow—   139
I have him here—I can scarce contain myself,
I am so full of joy, nay, joy all over.   [Exit.

                 [1] Anticipate.

ACT THE FIFTH

SCENE I.—A Room in Lady ALLWORTH's House.

Enter Lord LOVELL, Lady ALLWORTH, and AMBLE.

LADY ALLWORTH.   By this you know how strong
    the motives were
That did, my lord, induce me to dispense
A little with my gravity, to advance,
In personating [1] some few favours to him,
The plots and projects of the down-trod Wellborn.
Nor shall I e'er repent, although I suffer
In some few men's opinions for 't, the action ;
For he that ventured all for my dear husband
Might justly claim an obligation from me
To pay him such a courtesy ; which had I   10
Coyly or over-curiously denied,
It might have argued me of little love
To the deceased.   What you intended, madam,
    LOVELL.
For the poor gentleman hath found good success ;
For, as I understand, his debts are paid,
And he once more furnished for fair employment :
But all the arts that I have used to raise
The fortunes of your joy and mine, young All-
    worth,
Stand yet in supposition, though I hope well :
For the young lovers are in wit more pregnant
Than their years can promise ; and for their
    desires,   21
On my knowledge, they are equal.
    LADY ALLWORTH.   As my wishes
Are with yours, my lord. Yet give me leave to
    fear
The building, though well grounded : to deceive
Sir Giles, that 's both a lion and a fox
In his proceedings, were a work beyond
The strongest undertakers ; not the trial

[1] Counterfeiting.

Of two weak innocents.

LOVELL.   Despair not, madam :
Hard things are compassed oft by easy means ;
And judgement, being a gift derived from Heaven,
Though sometimes lodged in the hearts of worldly
    men,   31
That ne'er consider from whom they receive it,
Forsakes such as abuse the giver of it.
Which is the reason that the politic
And cunning statesman, that believes he fathoms
The counsels of all kingdoms on the earth,
Is by simplicity oft over-reached.
    LADY ALLWORTH.   May he be so ! yet, in his
      name to express it
Is a good omen.
    LOVELL.   May it to myself
Prove so, good lady, in my suit to you !   40
What think you of the motion ?
    LADY ALLWORTH.   Troth, my lord,
My own unworthiness may answer for me ;
For had you, when that I was in my prime
(My virgin flower uncropped) presented me
With this great favour ; looking on my lowness
Not in a glass of self-love, but of truth,
I could not but have thought it as a blessing
Far, far beyond my merit.
    LOVELL.   You are too modest,
And undervalue that which is above
My title, or whatever I call mine.   50
I grant, were I a Spaniard, to marry
A widow might disparage me ; but being
A true-born Englishman, I cannot find
How it can taint my honour : nay, what 's more,
That which you think a blemish is to me
The fairest lustre.   You already, madam,
Have given sure proofs how dearly you can cherish
A husband that deserves you ; which confirms me,
That, if I am not wanting in my care
To do you service, you'll be still the same   60
That you were to your Allworth : in a word.

Our years, our states, our births are not unequal,
You being descended nobly, and allied so ;
If then you may be won to make me happy,
But join your lips to mine, and that shall be
A solemn contract.
   LADY ALLWORTH.   I were blind to my own good,
Should I refuse it ; [Kisses him.]   yet, my lord,
      receive me
As such a one, the study of whose whole life
Shall know no other object but to please you.
   LOVELL.   If I return not, with all tenderness,
Equal respect to you, may I die wretched !   71
   LADY ALLWORTH.   There needs no protestation,
      my lord,
To her that cannot doubt.—

          Enter WELLBORN, handsomely apparelled.

                              You are welcome, sir.
Now you look like yourself.
   WELLBORN.   And will continue
Such in my free acknowledgement, that I am
Your creature, madam, and will never hold
My life mine own, when you please to command it.
   LOVELL.   It is a thankfulness that well becomes
      you ;
You could not make choice of a better shape
To dress your mind in.
   LADY ALLWORTH.   For me, I am happy   80
That my endeavours prospered. Saw you of late
Sir Giles, your uncle ?
   WELLBORN.   I heard of him, madam,
By his minister, Marrall ; he 's grown into strange
      passions
About his daughter : this last night he looked for
Your lordship at his house, but missing you,
And she not yet appearing, his wise head
Is much perplexed and troubled.
   LOVELL.   It may be,
Sweetheart, my project took.
   LADY ALLWORTH.   I strongly hope.

OVERREACH. [Within.] Ha ! find her, booby,
thou huge lump of nothing, 89
I'll bore thine eyes out else.
WELLBORN. May it please your lordship
For some ends of mine own, but to withdraw
A little out of sight, though not of hearing,
You may, perhaps, have sport.
LOVELL. You shall direct me. [Steps aside.

Enter OVERREACH, with distracted looks, driving in
MARRALL before him, with a box.

OVERREACH. I shall sol fa you,[1] rogue !
MARRALL. Sir, for what cause
Do you use me thus ?
OVERREACH. Cause, slave ? why, I am angry,
And thou a subject only fit for beating,
And so to cool my choler. Look to the writing ;
Let but the seal be broke upon the box
That has slept in my cabinet these three years,
I'll rack thy soul for 't.
MARRALL. [Aside.] I may yet cry quittance,
Though now I suffer, and dare not resist. 101
OVERREACH. Lady, by your leave, did you see
my daughter, lady ?
And the lord her husband ? are they in your house ?
If they are, discover, that I may bid them joy ;
And, as an entrance to her place of honour,
See your ladyship on her left hand, and make
curtsies
When she nods on you ; which you must receive
As a special favour.
LADY ALLWORTH. When I know, Sir Giles,
Her state requires such ceremony, I shall pay it ;
But, in the meantime, as I am myself, 110
I give you to understand, I neither know
Nor care where her honour is.
OVERREACH. When you once see her
Supported, and led by the lord her husband,
You'll be taught better.—Nephew.

---

[1] Presumably, make you sing out.

WELLBORN. Sir.

OVERREACH. No more ?

WELLBORN. 'Tis all I owe you.

OVERREACH. Have your redeemed rags
Made you thus insolent ?

WELLBORN. Insolent to you ?
Why, what are you, sir, unless in your years,
At the best, more than myself ?

OVERREACH. [Aside.] His fortune swells him :
'Tis rank,[1] he 's married.

LADY ALLWORTH. This is excellent !

OVERREACH. Sir, in calm language, though I
    seldom use it, 120
I am familiar with the cause that makes you
Bear up thus bravely ; there 's a certain buzz
Of a stolen marriage, do you hear ? of a stolen
    marriage,
In which, 'tis said, there 's somebody hath been
    cozened ;
I name no parties.

WELLBORN. Well, sir, and what follows ?

OVERREACH. Marry, this ; since you are per-
    emptory. Remember,
Upon mere hope of your great match, I lent you
A thousand pounds : put me in good security,
And suddenly, by mortgage or by statute,
Of some of your new possessions, or I'll have you
Dragged in your lavender robes [2] to the jail : you
    know me, 531
And therefore do not trifle.

WELLBORN. Can you be
So cruel to your nephew, now he 's in
The way to rise ? was this the courtesy
You did me ' in pure love, and no ends else ' ?

OVERREACH. End me no ends ! engage the
    whole estate,
And force your spouse to sign it, you shall have

---

[1] Obvious.

[2] To 'lay a thing in lavender' was a cant phrase for
pawning it.—*Gifford.*

Three or four thousand more, to roar and swagger
And revel in bawdy taverns.

WELLBORN.   And beg after ; 139
Mean you not so ?

OVERREACH.   My thoughts are mine, and free.
Shall I have security ?

WELLBORN.   No, indeed you shall not,
Nor bond, nor bill, nor bare acknowledgement
Your great looks fright not me.

OVERREACH.   But my deeds shall.
Outbraved !   [Both draw.

LADY ALLWORTH.   Help, murder ! murder !

Enter Servants and separate them.

WELLBORN.   Let him come on,
With all his wrongs and injuries about him,
Armed with his cut-throat practices to guard him ;
The right that I bring with me will defend me,
And punish his extortion.

OVERREACH.   That I had thee   148
But single in the field !

LADY ALLWORTH.   You may ; but make not
My house your quarrelling scene.

OVERREACH.   Were't in a church,
By Heaven and Hell, I'll do't !

MARRALL.   [Aside to WELLBORN.] Now put him to
The showing of the deed.

WELLBORN.   This rage is vain, sir ;
For fighting, fear not, you shall have your hands
    full,
Upon the least incitement ; and whereas
You charge me with a debt of a thousand pounds,
If there be law (howe'er you have no conscience),
Either restore my land, or I'll recover
A debt, that's truly due to me from you,
In value ten times more than what you challenge.

OVERREACH.   I in thy debt ?   O impudence !
    did I not purchase   160
The land left by thy father, that rich land,
That had continuèd in Wellborn's name

Twenty descents ; which, like a riotous fool,
Thou didst make sale of ? Is not here, inclosed,
The deed that does confirm it mine ?

    MARRALL.   [Aside to WELLBORN.]   Now, now !

    WELLBORN.   I do acknowledge none ; I ne'er
      passed over
Any such land : I grant, for a year or two
You had it in trust ; which if you do discharge,
Surrendering the possession, you shall ease
Yourself and me of chargeable suits in law,   170
Which, if you prove not honest, as I doubt it,
Must of necessity follow.

    LADY ALLWORTH.   In my judgement,
He does advise you well.

    OVERREACH.   Good ! good ! conspire
With your new husband, lady ; second him
In his dishonest practices ; but when
This manor is extended [1] to my use,
You'll speak in an humbler key, and sue for favour.

    LADY ALLWORTH.   Never : do not hope it.

    WELLBORN.   Let despair first seize me.

    OVERREACH.   Yet, to shut up thy mouth, and
      make thee give
Thyself the lie, the loud lie, I draw out   180
The precious evidence ; if thou canst forswear
Thy hand and seal, and make a forfeit of
Thy ears to the pillory, see ! here's that will make
My interest clear— Ha !

          [Opens the box, and displays the bond.

    LADY ALLWORTH.   A fair skin of parchment.

    WELLBORN.   Indented, I confess, and labels too ;
But neither wax nor words. How ! thunder-
    struck ?
Not a syllable to insult with ? My wise uncle,
Is this your precious evidence, this that makes
Your interest clear ?

    OVERREACH.   I am o'erwhelmed with wonder !
What prodigy is this ? what subtle devil   190
Hath razed out the inscription ? the wax

    [1] Seized under a writ.

Turned into dust !—the rest of my deeds whole
As when they were delivered, and this only
Made nothing ! do you deal with witches, rascal ?
There is a statute [1] for you, which will bring
Your neck in an hempen circle ; yes, there is ;
And now 'tis better thought for, cheater, know
This juggling shall not save you.

WELLBORN.   To save thee,
Would beggar the stock of mercy.

OVERREACH.   Marrall !

MARRALL.   Sir.

OVERREACH.   [Aside to MARRALL.]   Though the
     witnesses are dead, your testimony   200
Help with an oath or two : and for thy master,
Thy liberal master, my good honest servant,
I know thou wilt swear anything, to dash
This cunning sleight : besides, I know thou art
A public notary, and such stand in law
For a dozen witnesses : the deed being drawn too
By thee, my careful Marrall, and delivered
When thou wert present, will make good my title.
Wilt thou not swear this ?

MARRALL.   I ? no, I assure you :
I have a conscience not seared up like yours ;   210
I know no deeds.

OVERREACH.   Wilt thou betray me ?

MARRALL.   [To WELLBORN.]   Keep him
From using of his hands, I'll use my tongue,
To his no little torment.

OVERREACH.   Mine own varlet
Rebel against me ?

MARRALL.   Yes, and uncase you too.
' The idiot, the patch, the slave, the booby,
The property fit only to be beaten
For your morning exercise ', your ' football ', or
' The unprofitable lump of flesh ', your ' drudge ',
Can now anatomize you, and lay open
All your black plots, and level with the earth   220

[1] By 1 James I, c. 12, the use of witchcraft was made
felony without benefit of clergy

Your hill of pride, and, with these gabions[1]
   guarded,
Unload my great artillery, and shake,
Nay pulverize, the walls you think defend you.
   LADY ALLWORTH.   How he foams at the mouth
      with rage !
   WELLBORN.   To him again.
   OVERREACH.   Oh, that I had thee in my gripe, I
      would tear thee
Joint after joint !
   MARRALL.   I know you are a tearer,
But I'll have first your fangs pared off, and then
Come nearer to you ; when I have discovered,
And made it good before the judge, what ways
And devilish practices you used, to cozen[2]   230
An army of whole families, who, yet live[3]
And but enrolled for soldiers, were able
To take in[4] Dunkirk.
   WELLBORN.   All will come out.
   LADY ALLWORTH.   The better.
   OVERREACH. But that I will live, rogue, to torture
      thee,
And make thee wish, and kneel in vain, to die,
These swords that keep thee from me should fix
      here,
Although they made my body but one wound,
But I would reach thee.
   LOVELL.   [Aside.]   Heaven's hand is in this ;
One bandog[5] worry the other !
   OVERREACH.   I play the fool,
And make my anger but ridiculous :   240
There will be a time and place, there will be,
      cowards,
When you shall feel what I dare do.
   WELLBORN.   I think so :
You dare do any ill, yet want true valour

---

[1] Baskets filled with earth and used in fortifications.
[2] ' to cozen with ', 1633.
[3] Needlessly altered to ' alive ' by Gifford.
[4] Capture.   [5] A dog kept tied up.

To be honest, and repent.

OVERREACH.   They are words I know not,
Nor e'er will learn.   Patience, the beggar's virtue,

Enter GREEDY *and* PARSON WILLDO.

Shall find no harbour here :—after these storms
At length a calm appears.   Welcome, most wel-
      come !
There's comfort in thy looks ; is the deed done ?
Is my daughter married ? say but so, my chaplain,
And I am tame.

WILLDO.   Married ? yes, I assure you.

OVERREACH.   Then vanish all sad thoughts !
      there's more gold for thee.   251
My doubts and fears are in the titles drowned
Of my honourable, my right honourable daughter.

GREEDY.   Here will be feasting ! at least for a
      month
I am provided : empty guts, croak no more.
You shall be stuffed like bagpipes, not with wind,
But bearing dishes.[1]

OVERREACH. [To WILLDO.]   Instantly be here ?
To my wish ! to my wish !—Now you that plot
      against me,
And hoped to trip my heels up, that contemned me,
Think on't and tremble :— [Loud music.]— they
      come ! I hear the music.   260
A lane there for my lord !

WELLBORN.   This sudden heat
May yet be cooled, sir.

OVERREACH.   Make way there for my lord !

Enter ALLWORTH *and* MARGARET.

MARGARET.   Sir, first your pardon, then your
      blessing, with
Your full allowance of the choice I have made.
As ever you could make use of your reason,
                                            [Kneeling.
Grow not in passion ; since you may as well
      ¹ Substantial dishes.

Call back the day that's past, as untie the knot
Which is too strongly fastened : not to dwell
Too long on words, this is my husband.

    OVERREACH.   How ?

    ALLWORTH.   So I assure you ; all the rites of
       marriage,   270
With every circumstance, are past. Alas ! sir,
Although I am no lord, but a lord's page,
Your daughter and my loved wife mourns not for it ;
And, for right honourable son-in-law, you may say,
Your dutiful daughter.

    OVERREACH. [To WILLDO.]   Devil ! are they
       married ?

    WILLDO.   Do a father's part, and say, Heaven
       give them joy !

    OVERREACH. Confusion and ruin ! speak, and
       speak quickly,
Or thou art dead.

    WIILDO.   They are married.

    OVERREACH.   Thou hadst better
Have made a contract with the king of fiends,   279
Than these :—my brain turns !

    WILLDO.   Why this rage to me ?
Is not this your letter, sir, and these the words ?
' Marry her to this gentleman '.

    OVERREACH.   It cannot—
Nor will I e'er believe it, 'sdeath ! I will not ;
That I, that in all passages I touched
At wordly profit have not left a print
Where I have trod for the most curious search
To trace my footsteps, should be gulled by children,
Baffled and fooled, and all my hopes and labours
Defeated and made void !

    WELLBORN.   As it appears,   289
You are so, my grave uncle.

    OVERREACH.   Village nurses
Revenge their wrongs with curses ; I'll not waste
A syllable, but thus I take the life
Which, wretched, I gave to thee.

                              [Offers to kill MARGARET.]

LOVELL.   [Coming forward.]   Hold, for your own
  sake !
Though charity to your daughter hath quite left
  you,
Will you do an act, though in your hopes lost here,
Can leave no hope for peace or rest hereafter ?
Consider ; at the best you are but a man,
And cannot so create your aims, but that
They may be crossed.
          OVERREACH.   Lord ! thus I spit at thee,
And at thy counsel ; and again desire thee,   300
And as thou art a soldier, if thy valour
Dares show itself where multitude and example
Lead not the way, let 's quit the house, and change
Six words in private.   I am ready.
          LOVELL.
          LADY ALLWORTH.   Stay, sir !
Contest with one distracted ?
          WELLBORN.   You'll grow like him,
Should you answer his vain challenge.
          OVERREACH.   Are you pale ?
Borrow his help : though Hercules call it odds,
I'll stand against both as I am, hemmed in thus !
Since, like a Libyan lion in the toil,
My fury cannot reach the coward hunters,   310
And only spends itself, I'll quit the place :
Alone I can do nothing ; but I have servants
And friends to second me ; and if I make not
This house a heap of ashes (by my wrongs,
What I have spoke I will make good !), or leave
One throat uncut—if it be possible,
Hell, add to my afflictions !   [Exit.
          MARRALL.   Is 't not brave sport ?
          GREEDY.   Brave sport ! I am sure it has ta'en
  away my stomach ;   318
I do not like the sauce.
          ALLWORTH.   Nay, weep not, dearest,
Though it express your pity ; what 's decreed
Above, we cannot alter.   His threats move me
          LADY ALLWORTH.

No scruple, madam.

    MARRALL.   Was it not a rare trick,
An it please your worship, to make the deed
    nothing ?
I can do twenty neater, if you please
To purchase and grow rich ; for I will be
Such a solicitor and steward for you,
As never worshipful had.

    WELLBORN.   I do believe thee ;
But first discover the quaint means you used
To raze out the conveyance.

    MARRALL.   They are mysteries
Not to be spoke in public : certain minerals   330
Incorporated in the ink and wax—
Besides, he gave me nothing, but still fed me
With hopes and blows ; and that was the induce-
    ment
To this conundrum. If it please your worship
To call to memory, this mad beast once caused me
To urge you or to drown or hang yourself ;
I'll do the like to him, if you command me.

    WELLBORN.   You are a rascal ! he that dares be
    false
To a master, though unjust, will ne'er be true
To any other. Look not for reward   340
Or favour from me ; I will shun thy sight
As I would do a basilisk's ; thank my pity,
If thou keep thy ears ; howe'er, I will take order
Your practice shall be silenced.

    GREEDY.   I'll commit him,
If you'll have me, sir.

    WELLBORN.   That were to little purpose ;
His conscience be his prison. Not a word,
But instantly be gone.

    ORDER.   Take this kick with you.
    AMBLE. And this.

    FURNACE.   If that I had my cleaver here,
I would divide your knave's head.

    MARRALL.   This is the haven
False servants still arrive at.   [Exit.

Re-enter OVERREACH.

LADY ALLWORTH.   Come again !   350
LOVELL.   Fear not, I am your guard.
WELLBORN.   His looks are ghastly.
WILLDO.   Some little time I have spent, under
   your favours,
In physical studies, and if my judgement err not,
He 's mad beyond recovery : but observe him,
And look to yourselves.
   OVERREACH.   Why, is not the whole world
Included in myself ? to what use then
Are friends and servants ? Say there were a
   squadron
Of pikes, lined through with shot, when I am
   mounted
Upon my injuries, shall I fear to charge them ?
No : I'll through the battalia, and that routed,
          [Flourishing his sword sheathed.[1]
I'll fall to execution.—Ha ! I am feeble :   361
Some undone widow sits upon mine arm,
And takes away the use of 't ; and my sword,
Glued to my scabbard with wronged orphans'
   tears,
Will not be drawn. Ha ! what are these ? sure,
   hangmen,
That come to bind my hands, and then to drag me
Before the judgement-seat : now they are new
   shapes,
And do appear like Furies, with steel whips
To scourge my ulcerous soul. Shall I then fall
Ingloriously, and yield ? no ; spite of Fate,
I will be forced to hell like to myself.   371
Though you were legions of accursed spirits,
Thus would I fly among you.
          [Rushes forward, and flings himself on the ground.
   WELLBORN.   There 's no help ;
Disarm him first, then bind him.
   GREEDY.   Take a mittimus,

          [1] 'unsheathed,' 1633.

And carry him to Bedlam.

LOVELL. How he foams !

WELLBORN. And bites the earth !

WILLDO. Carry him to some dark room,
There try what art can do for his recovery.

MARGARET. Oh, my dear father !

[They force OVERREACH off.

ALLWORTH. You must be patient, mistress.

LOVELL. Here is a precedent to teach wicked
men, 379
That when they leave religion, and turn atheists,
Their own abilities leave them. Pray you take
comfort,
I will endeavour you shall be his guardians
In his distractions : and for your land, Master
Wellborn,
Be it good or ill in law, I'll be an umpire
Between you, and this, the undoubted heir
Of Sir Giles Overreach : for me, here's the anchor
That I must fix on.

ALLWORTH. What you shall determine,
My lord, I will allow of.

WELLBORN. 'Tis the language
That I speak too ; but there is something else
Beside the repossession of my land, 390
And payment of my debts, that I must practise.
I had a reputation, but 'twas lost
In my loose course ; and [un]til I redeem it
Some noble way, I am but half made up.
It is a time of action ; if your lordship
Will please to confer a company upon me
In your command, I doubt not in my service
To my king and country but I shall do something
That may make me right again.

LOVELL. Your suit is granted,
And you loved for the motion.

WELLBORN. [Coming forward.] Nothing wants
then 400
But your allowance—and in that our all
Is comprehended ; it being known, nor we,

Nor he that wrote the comedy, can be free,
Without your manumission ; which if you
Grant willingly, as a fair favour due
To the poet's and our labours (as you may,
For we despair not, gentlemen, of the play),
We jointly shall profess your grace hath might
To teach us action, and him how to write.

[Exeunt.